## Advance Praise for
## Drama: A Pocket Anthology, *Third Edition*

"A collection of plays that represents a variety of time periods and approaches to theater. It is inexpensive for students, covers a good range of material, and includes some work from female playwrights."

Maryam Barrie
*Washtenaw Community College*

"My favorite part of Gwynn's book is the introduction. I . . . appreciate all the material that a professor could use to enhance the course. It is also good for students because they could refresh their memory and keep dramatic conventions straight in their heads."

Paul Graham
*West Virginia University*

"A set of well-chosen plays that represent some of the best in the Western tradition presented with useful support apparatus."

James Stick
*Des Moines Area Community College*

". . . offers an excellent selection of plays without the costly frills . . . a real find."

Charles Trainor
*Sierra College*

**R. S. Gwynn** has edited several other books, including *Poetry: A Pocket Anthology, Fiction: A Pocket Anthology, Drama: A Pocket Anthology; The Longman Anthology of Short Fiction* (with Dana Gioia); and *Contemporary American Poetry: A Pocket Anthology* (with April Lindner). He has also authored five collections of poetry, including *No Word of Farewell: Selected Poems, 1970–2000*. In 2004, Gwynn received the Michael Braude Award for light verse from the American Academy of Arts and Letters.

Professor Gwynn teaches at Lamar University in Beaumont, Texas.

# Drama

# Drama

## A Pocket Anthology

**THIRD EDITION**

*Edited by*

## R. S. Gwynn
*Lamar University*

PENGUIN ACADEMICS

PEARSON
Longman

New York  San Francisco  Boston
London  Toronto  Sydney  Tokyo  Singapore  Madrid
Mexico City  Munich  Paris  Cape Town  Hong Kong  Montreal

Managing Editor: Erika Berg
Executive Marketing Manager: Ann Stypuloski
Project Coordination and Electronic Page Makeup: Pre-Press Company, Inc.
Senior Cover Designer/Manager: Nancy Danahy
Cover Photo: © Getty Images, Inc.
Manufacturing Manager: Mary Fischer
Printer and Binder: Courier Corp.
Cover Printer: Phoenix Color Corp.

For permission to use copyrighted material, grateful acknowledgment is made to the copyright holders on p. 615, which are hereby made part of this copyright page.

Library of Congress Cataloging-in-Publication Data

Drama : a pocket anthology / edited by R.S. Gwynn.— 3rd ed.
    p. cm. — (Penguin academics)
    Subtitle on earlier ed.: A Longman pocket anthology.
    Includes index.
    ISBN 0-321-27722-8
    1. Drama—Collection.    I. Gwynn, R. S. II. Series.

PN6112.D68    2005
808.82—dc22                                                    2005047640

Please visit us at http://www.ablongman.com/gwynn

For more information about the Penguin Academics series, please contact us by mail at Longman Publishers, attn. Marketing Department, 1185 Avenue of the Americas, 25th Floor, New York, NY 10036, or by e-mail at www.ablongman.com

ISBN 0-321-27722-8

5 6 7 8 9 10—CRW—08 07

# *Contents*

# *Preface*

When the Pocket Anthology series first appeared over a decade ago, our chief aim was to offer a clear alternative to the anthologies of fiction, poetry, and drama that were available at the time. *Drama: A Pocket Anthology,* now in the Penguin Academics Series, is in its third edition. *Drama* is designed to be used in a wide range of courses. This brief anthology can be bundled with one or more of a rich selection of the most popular Penguin titles, which Longman offers at significantly reduced prices. Also, *Drama* has been published with two companion volumes, *Fiction* and *Poetry,* and in a combined edition, *Literature.* Your Longman representative can supply full details about these books and available Penguin titles.

*Drama* addresses the four wishes and concerns most commonly expressed by both instructors and students. First, of course, is the variety of selections it contains. The contents of *Drama* have been shaped by the advice of experienced instructors who have cited authors and plays that are most often taught and which possess proven appeal to students. Admittedly, a pocket anthology has to be very selective in its contents, so we are especially proud that the twelve plays in this book include both established canonical writers and also contemporary playwrights like August Wilson, David Ives, and Paula Vogel, who reflect the diversity that is essential to any study of contemporary theatre. The range of dramatic genres in *Drama* includes a Greek tragedy, a Shakespearean tragedy, an example of a problem play by Ibsen, and nine plays from the twentieth century, ranging from one-act comedy and drama to modern tragedy to poetic realism to contemporary social drama. We have also included a list of other Penguin titles that may be bundled with this book (see p. 619). We strongly believe that the plays in *Drama* will provide a reading experience that is not only educational but thought-provoking and enjoyable as well.

Our second aim was flexibility. We wanted a book that could be used as both a primary and supplemental text in a wide range of courses, ranging from introduction to drama to advanced courses in theatre or playwriting. When combined with one of its companion volumes, *Fiction* or *Poetry,* or with novels, collections of short stories or poems by individual authors, or plays available from Penguin, *Drama* may also be used in introductory literature courses. *Drama* contains, in addition to its generous selection of plays, biographical headnotes for authors, an introduction that covers the techniques and terminology of the genre, and a concise section on writing about drama and research procedures. As a further aid to instructors and students, MyLiteratureLab (http://www.myliteraturelab.com), a password-protected website, offers students a rich source of guidance in the key areas of reading, interpretation, writing, and research. Of special note are the distinctive Longman Lectures. These audio lectures, given by many of Longman's prestigious authors, provide students with insights and support about reading and interpreting the most popular works of literature, including the plays *Oedipus the King* and *A Doll House.*

Third, we wanted an affordable book. Full-sized introductory drama books now cost upwards of fifty dollars. Longman is committed to keeping the price of the Pocket Anthology series reasonable without compromising on design or typeface. We believe that readers will find that the attractive layout of *Drama* is preferable to the cramped margins and minuscule fonts found in many literature textbooks. Because of its low cost, *Drama* may be easily supplemented in individual courses with texts on the history of the theatre, guides to playwriting, handbooks of grammar and usage, or with manuals of style. The price of *Drama* remains low, and we believe that the earlier editions' claim that the book represents "a new standard of value" remains accurate.

Finally, we stressed portability. Many instructors expressed concern for students who must carry large literature books, many of which now approach 2000 pages, across large campuses in backpacks already laden with books and materials for other courses. A semester is a short time, and few courses can cover more than a fraction of the material that many full-sized collections contain. Because most instructors focus on a single genre at a time, *Drama* and its companion volumes, *Fiction* and *Poetry,* remain compact yet self-contained editions that, if a snug fit in most pockets, are still easy to handle and carry. We trust that sympathetic instructors and their students will be grateful for a book that does not add a physical burden to the already heavy intellectual one required by college courses.

In closing, we would like to express our gratitude to the instructors who reviewed the current edition and offered invaluable recommendations for improvements. They are: Francis G. Babcock, Louisiana State University; Maryam Barrie, Washtenaw Community College; Paul D. Bawek, Florida Southern College; Paul Castagno, Ohio University; Marla K. Dean, University of Montevallo; Verna Foster, Loyola University of Chicago; Paul Graham, West Virginia University; Bethany Larson, Buena Vista University; Donna Long, Fairmont State University;

James F. Scott, Saint Louis University; and Jeffrey P. Stephens, Oklahoma State University.

We are also grateful to the instructors who commented on the second edition: Melanie Abrams, California State University, San Bernadino; Jeff Cofer, Bellevue Community College; Verna Foster, Loyola University, Chicago; Janet Gardner, University of Massachusetts, Dartmouth; Christine Gilmore, University of Toledo; Dennis G. Jerz, University of Wisconsin–Eau Claire; Kevin Kerrane, University of Delaware; James Stick, Des Moines Area Community College; and Karin Westman, Kansas State University.

The editor also wishes to thank Beverly Williams for her assistance in preparing this edition.

R. S. Gwynn
*Lamar University*

# *Introduction*

## The Play's the Thing

The theater, located in the heart of a rejuvenated downtown business district, is a relic of the silent movie era that has been restored to something approaching its former glory. While only a few members of tonight's audience can actually remember it in its heyday, the expertise of the organist seated at the antique Wurlitzer instills a sense of false nostalgia in the crowd, now settling by twos and threes into red, plush-covered seats and looking around in search of familiar faces. Just as the setting is somewhat out of the ordinary, so is this group. Unlike movie audiences, they are for the most part older and less casually dressed. There are few small children present, and even the teenagers seem to be on their best behavior. Oddly, no one is eating popcorn or noisily drawing on a soda straw. A mood of seriousness and anticipation hovers over the theater, and those who have lived in the town long enough can spot the spouse or companion of one of the principal actors nervously folding a program or checking a watch.

As the organ magically descends into the recesses of the orchestra pit, the lights dim, a hush falls over the crowd, and the curtain creakily rises. There is a general murmur of approval at the ingenuity and many hours of hard work that have transformed empty space into a remarkable semblance of an upper-class drawing room in the early 1900s. Dressed as a domestic servant, a young woman, known to the audience from her frequent appearances in local television commercials, enters and begins to dust a table. She hums softly to herself. A tall young man, in everyday life a junior partner in a local law firm, wanders in carrying a tennis racket. The maid turns, sees him, and catches her breath, startled. "Why Mr. Fenton!" she exclaims. . . .

And the world begins.

The full experience of drama—whether at an amateur production like the little theater performance described here or at a huge Broadway playhouse—is much more complex than that of any other form of literature. The word **drama** itself comes from a Greek word meaning "a thing that is done," and the roots of both **theater** and **audience** call to mind the acts of seeing and hearing, respectively. Like other communal public activities—religious services, sporting events, meetings of political or fraternal organizations—drama has evolved over many centuries its own set of customs, rituals, and rules. The exact shape of these characteristics—**dramatic conventions**—may differ from country to country or from period to period, but they all have one aim in common, namely to define and govern an art form whose essence is to be found in public performances of written texts. No other form of literature shares this primary goal. Before we can discuss drama purely as literature, we should first ponder some aspects of its unique status as "a thing that is done."

It is worth noting that dramatists are also called playwrights. Note the spelling; a "wright" is a maker, as old family names like Cartwright or Boatwright attest. If a play is in fact *made* rather than written, then a playwright is similar to an architect who has designed a unique building. The concept may be his or hers, but the construction project requires the contributions of many other hands before the sparkling steel and glass tower alters the city's skyline. In the case of a new play, money will have to be raised by a producer, a director chosen, a cast found, a crew assembled, a set designed and built, and many hours of rehearsal completed before the curtain can be raised for the first time. Along the way, modifications to the original play may become necessary, and it is possible that the author will listen to advice from the actors, director, or stage manager and incorporate their opinions into any revisions. Professional theater is, after all, a branch of show business, and no play will survive its premiere for long if it does not attract paying crowds. The dramatists we read and study so reverently today managed to reach large popular audiences in their time. Even ancient Greek playwrights like Sophocles and Euripides must have stood by surreptitiously "counting the house" as the open-air seats slowly filled, and Shakespeare prospered as part-owner of the Globe theater to the extent that he was able to retire to his hometown at the ripe old age of forty-seven.

Beside this rich communal experience, the solitary act of reading a play seems a poor substitute, contrary to the play's very nature (only a small category known as **closet drama** comprises plays intended to be read instead of acted). Yet dramatists like Shakespeare and Ibsen are counted among the giants of world literature, and their works are annually read by far more people than actually see these plays performed. In reading a play, we are forced to pay close attention to such matters as **set description**, particularly with a playwright like Ibsen, who lavishes great attention on the design of his set; references to **properties** or "props" that will figure in the action of the play; physical description of characters and costumes; **stage directions** indicating the movements and gestures made by actors in scenes; and any other **stage business**, that is, action without dialogue. Many modern dramatists are very scrupulous in detailing these matters; writers of earlier periods, however, provided little or no instruction. Reading Sophocles or Shakespeare, we are forced to concentrate on the characters' words to envision how actions and other characters were originally conceived. Reading aloud, alone or in a group, or following along in the text while listening to a recorded performance is particularly recommended for verse plays like *Oedipus the King* or *Othello*. Also, versions of many of the plays contained in this book are currently available on videotape. While viewing a film is an experience of a different kind from seeing a live performance, film versions obviously provide a convenient insight into the ways in which great actors have interpreted their roles. Seeing the joy in the face of Anthony Hopkins when, as Othello, he lands triumphantly in Cyprus and rejoins his bride makes his tragic fall even more poignant.

## Origins of Drama

No consensus exists about the exact date of the birth of drama, but according to most authorities, it originated in Greece over 2500 years ago, an outgrowth of rites of worship of the god Dionysus, who was associated with male fertility, agriculture (especially the cultivation of vineyards), and seasonal renewal. In these Dionysian festivals a group of fifty citizens of Athens, known as a **chorus**, outfitted and trained by a leader, or *choragos,* would perform hymns of praise to the god, known as **dithyrambic poetry**. The celebration concluded with the ritual sacrifice of a goat, or *tragos*. The two main genres of drama originally took their names from these rituals; comedy comes from *kômos,* the Greek word for a festivity. These primitive revels were invariably accompanied with a union of the sexes (*gamos* in Greek, a word that survives in English words like "monogamy") celebrating fertility and continuance of the race, an ancient custom still symbolically observed in the "fade-out kiss" that concludes most comedies. Tragedy, on the other hand, literally means "song of the goat," taking its name from the animal that was killed on the altar *(thymele)*, cooked, and shared by the celebrants with their god.

Around 600 B.C. certain refinements took place. In the middle of the sixth century B.C. an official springtime festival, known as the Greater or City Dionysia, was established in Athens, and prizes for the best dithyrambic poems were first awarded. At about the same time a special ***orchestra,*** or "dancing place," was constructed, a circular area surrounding the altar, and permanent seats, or a *theatron* ("seeing place"), arranged in a semicircle around the orchestra were added. At the back of the orchestra the façade of a temple (the *skene*) and a raised "porch" in front of it (the *proskenion,* in later theaters the **proscenium**) served as a backdrop, usually representing the palace of the ruler; walls extending to either side of the *skene,* the *parodoi,* served to conceal backstage activity from the audience. A wheeled platform, or *eccyclema,* could be pushed through the door of the *skene* to reveal the tragic consequences of a play's climax (there was no onstage "action" in Greek tragedy). Behind the *skene* a crane-like device called a *mechane* (or ***deus ex machina***) could be used to lower a god from the heavens or represent a spectacular effect like the flying chariot drawn by dragons at the conclusion of Euripides's *Medea.*

In 535 B.C. a writer named Thespis won the annual competition with a startling innovation. Thespis separated one member of the chorus (called a *hypocrites,* or "actor") and had him engage in **dialogue,** spoken lines representing conversation, with the remaining members. If we define drama primarily as a story related through live action and recited dialogue, then Thespis may rightly be called the father of drama, and his name endures in "thespian," a synonym for actor.

The century after Thespis, from 500–400 B.C., saw many refinements in the way tragedies were performed and is considered the golden age of Greek drama. In this century, the careers of the three great tragic playwrights—Aeschylus (525–456 B.C.), Sophocles (496?–406 B.C.), and Euripides (c. 480–406 B.C.)—and the greatest comic playwright, Aristophanes (450?–385? B.C.) overlapped. It is no coincidence that in this remarkable period Athens, under the leadership of the general Pericles (495–429 B.C.), reached the height of its wealth, influence, and cultural development and was home to the philosophers Socrates (470–399 B.C.) and Plato (c. 427–347 B.C.). Aristotle (384–322 B.C.), the third of the great Athenian philosophers, was also a literary critic who wrote the first extended analysis of drama.

# Aristotle on Tragedy

The earliest work of literary criticism in western civilization is Aristotle's *Poetics*, an attempt to define and classify the different literary genres that use rhythm, language, and harmony. Aristotle identifies four genres—epic poetry, dithyrambic poetry, comedy, and tragedy—which have in common their attempts at imitation, or *mimesis*, of various types of human activity.

Aristotle comments most fully on tragedy, and his definition of the genre demands close examination:

> *A tragedy, then, is the imitation of an action that is serious and also, as having magnitude, complete in itself; in language with pleasurable accessories, each kind brought in separately in the parts of the work; in a dramatic, not in a narrative form; with incidents arousing pity and fear, wherewith to accomplish its catharsis of such emotions.*

First we should note that the imitation here is of *action*. Later in the passage, when Aristotle differentiates between narrative and dramatic forms of literature, it is clear that he is referring to tragedy as a type of literature written primarily for public performance. Furthermore, tragedy must be serious and must have magnitude. By this, Aristotle implies that issues of life and death must be involved and that these issues must be of public import. In many Greek tragedies, the fate of the *polis*, or city, of which the chorus is the voice, is bound up with the actions taken by the main character in the play. Despite their rudimentary form of democracy, the people of Athens would have been perplexed by a tragedy with an ordinary citizen at its center; magnitude in tragedy demands that only the affairs of persons of high rank are of sufficient importance for tragedy. Aristotle further requires that this imitated action possess a sense of completeness. At no point does he say that a tragedy has to end with a death or even in a state of unhappiness; he does require, however, that the audience sense that after the last words are spoken no further story cries out to be told.

The next part of the passage may confuse the modern reader. By "language with pleasurable accessories" Aristotle means the poetic devices of rhythm and, in the choral parts of the tragedy, music and dance as well. Reading the choral passages in a Greek tragedy, we are likely to forget that these passages were intended to be chanted or sung ("chorus" and "choir" share the same root) and danced as well ("choreography" comes from this root as well).

The rest of Aristotle's definition dwells on the emotional effects of tragedy on the audience. Pity and fear are to be evoked—pity because we must care for the characters and to some extent empathize with them, fear because we come to realize that the fate they endure involves acts—of which murder and incest are only two—that civilized men and women most abhor. Finally, Aristotle's word *catharsis* has proved controversial over the centuries. The word literally means "a purging," but readers have debated whether Aristotle is referring to a release of harmful emotions or a transformation of them. In either case, the implication is that viewing a tragedy has a beneficial effect on an audience, perhaps because the viewers' deepest fears are brought to light in a make-believe setting. How many of us, at the end of some particularly wrenching film, have turned to a companion and said, "Thank god, it was only a movie"? The sacrificial animal from whom tragedy took its name was, after all, only a stand-in whose blood was offered to the gods as a substitute for a human subject. The protagonist of a tragedy remains, in many ways, a "scapegoat" on whose head we project our own unconscious terrors.

Aristotle identifies six elements of a tragedy, and these elements are still useful in analyzing not only tragedies but other types of plays as well. In order of importance they are **plot, characterization, theme, diction, melody,** and **spectacle**. Despite the fact that the *Poetics* is over two thousand years old, Aristotle's elements still provide a useful way of understanding how plays work.

## Plot

Aristotle considers plot the chief element of a play, and it is easy to see this when we consider that in discussing a film with a friend we usually give a brief summary, or **synopsis,** of the plot, stopping just short of "giving it away" by telling how the story concludes. Aristotle defines plot as "the combination of incidents, or things done in the story," and goes on to give the famous formulation that a plot "is that which has a beginning, middle, and end." Aristotle notes that the best plots are selective in their use of material and have an internal coherence and logic. Two opposite terms that Aristotle introduced are still in use, although with slightly different meanings. By a **unified plot** we generally mean one that takes place in roughly a twenty-four hour period; in a short play with a unified plot like Susan Glaspell's *Trifles,* the action is continuous. By **episodic plot** we mean one that spreads its action out over a longer period of time. A play which has a unified plot, a single setting, and no subplots is said to observe the **three unities,** which critics in some eras have virtually insisted on as ironclad rules. Although most plots are chronological, playwrights in the last half-century have experimented, sometimes radically, with such straightforward progression through time. Arthur Miller's *Death of a Salesman* effectively blends **flashbacks** to past events with his action, and David Ives's *Sure Thing* plays havoc with chronology, allowing his protagonist to "replay" his previous scenes until he has learned the way to the "sure thing" of the title.

Two other important elements of most successful plots that Aristotle mentions are **reversal** (*peripeteia* in Greek, also known as **peripety**), and **recognition** (*anagnorisis* in Greek, also known as **discovery**). By reversal he means a change "from one state of things within the play to its opposite." Aristotle cites one example from *Oedipus the King:* "the Messenger, who, coming to gladden Oedipus and to remove his fears as to his mother, reveals the secret of his birth"; but an earlier reversal in the same play occurs when Jocasta (Iocastê in the translation used here), attempting to alleviate Oedipus's fears of prophecies, inadvertently mentions the "place where three roads meet" where Oedipus killed a man he took to be a stranger. Most plays have more than a single reversal; each episode or act builds on the main character's hopes that his or her problems will be solved, only to dash those expectations as the play proceeds. Recognition, the second term, is perhaps more properly an element of characterization because it involves a character's "change from ignorance to knowledge." If the events of the plot have not served to illuminate the character about his or her failings, then the audience is likely to feel that the story has lacked depth. The kind of self-knowledge that tragedies provides is invariably accompanied by suffering and won at great emotional cost. In comedy, on the other hand, reversals may bring relief to the characters, and recognition may bring about the happy conclusion of the play.

A typical plot may be broken down into several components. First comes the **exposition,** which provides the audience with essential information—who, what, when, where—that it needs to know before the play can continue. A novelist or short story writer can present information directly with some sort of variation on the "Once upon a time" opening. But dramatists have particular problems with exposition because facts must be presented in the form of dialogue and action. Greek dramatists used the first two parts of a tragedy, relying on the audience's familiarity with the myths being retold, to set up the initial situation of the play. Other types of drama use a single character to provide expository material. Medieval morality plays often use a "heavenly messenger" to deliver the opening speech, and some of Shakespeare's plays employ a single character named "Chorus" who speaks an introductory prologue and "sets the scene" for later portions of the plays as well. In *The Glass Menagerie,* Tom Wingfield fulfills this role in an unusual manner, telling the audience at the beginning, "I am the narrator of the play, and also a character in it." Occasionally, we even encounter the least elegant solution to the problem of dramatic exposition, employing minor characters whose sole function is to provide background information in the play's opening scene. Countless drawing-room comedies have raised the curtain on a pair of servants in the midst of a gossipy conversation which catches the audience up on the doings of the family members who comprise the rest of the cast.

The second part of a plot is called the **complication,** the interjection of some circumstance or event that shakes up the stable situation that has existed before the play's opening and begins the **rising action** of the play, during which the audience's tension and expectations become tightly intertwined and involved with the characters and the events they experience. Complication in a play may be both external and internal. A plague, a threatened invasion, or a conclusion of a war are typical examples of external complication, outside events which affect the characters' lives. Many other plays rely primarily on an internal complication, a single character's failure in business or love that comes from a weakness in his or her personality. Often the complication is heightened by **conflict** between two characters whom events have forced into collision with each other. Whatever the case, the complication of the plot usually introduces a problem that the characters cannot avoid. The rising action, which constitutes the body of the play, usually contains a number of moments of **crisis,** when solutions crop up momentarily but quickly disappear. These critical moments in the scenes may take the form of the kinds of reversals discussed above, and the audience's emotional involvement in the plot generally hinges on the characters' rising and falling hopes.

The central moment of crisis in the play is the **climax,** or the moment of greatest tension, which initiates the **falling action** of the plot. Perhaps "moments" of greatest tension would be a more exact phrase, for skillful playwrights know how to wring as much tension as possible from the audience. In the best plots, everything in earlier parts of the play has pointed to this scene. In tragedy, the climax is traditionally accompanied with physical action and violence—a duel, a suicide, a murder—and the play's highest pitch of emotion.

The final part of a plot is the **dénouement, or resolution.** The French word literally refers to the untying of a knot, and we might compare the emotional effects of climax and dénouement to a piece of cloth twisted tighter and tighter as the play progresses and then untwisted as the action winds down. The dénouement returns the play and its characters to a stable situation, although not the same one that existed at the beginning of the play, and gives some indication of what the future holds for them. A dénouement may be either closed or open. A **closed dénouement** ties up everything neatly and explains all unanswered questions the audience might have; an **open dénouement** leaves a few tantalizing loose ends.

Several other plot terms should also be noted. Aristotle mentions, not altogether favorably, plots with "double issues." The most common word for this is **subplot,** a less important story involving minor characters that may mirror the main plot of the play. Some plays may even have more than one subplot. Occasionally a playwright finds it necessary to drop hints about coming events in the plot, perhaps to keep the audience from complaining that certain incidents have happened "out of the blue." This is called **foreshadowing.** If a climactic incident that helps to resolve the plot has not been adequately prepared for, the playwright may be accused of having resorted to a *deus ex machina* ending, which takes its name from the *mechane* that once literally lowered a god or goddess into the midst of the dramatic proceedings. An ending of this sort, like that of an old western movie in which the cavalry arrives out of nowhere just as the wagon train is about to be annihilated, is rarely satisfactory.

Finally, the difference between **suspense** and **dramatic irony** should be addressed. Both of these devices generate tension in the audience, although through opposite means—suspense when the audience does not know what is about to happen; dramatic irony, paradoxically, when it does. Much of our pleasure in reading a new play lies in speculating about what will happen next, but in Greek tragedy the original audience would be fully familiar with the basic outlines of the mythic story before the action even began. Thus, dramatic irony occurs at moments when the audience is more knowledgeable about events than the on-stage characters are. In some plays, our foreknowledge of certain events is so strong that we may want to cry out a warning to the characters.

## Characterization

The Greek word *agon* means "debate" and refers to the central issue or conflict of a play. From *agon* we derive two words commonly used to denote the chief characters in a play: **protagonist,** literally the "first speaker," and **antagonist,** one who speaks against him. Often the word "hero" is used as a synonym for protagonist, but we should be careful in its application; indeed, in many modern plays it may be more appropriate to speak of the protagonist as an **anti-hero** because he or she may possess few, if any, of the traditional attributes of a hero. Similarly, the word "villain" brings to mind a black-mustached, sneering character in a top hat and opera cloak from an old-fashioned **melodrama** (a play whose complications are solved happily at the last minute by the "triumph of good over evil"), and usually has little application to the complex characters one encounters in a serious play.

Aristotle, in his discussion of characterization, stresses the complexity that marks the personages in the greatest plays. Nothing grows tiresome more quickly than a perfectly virtuous man or woman at the center of a play, and nothing is more offensive to the audience than seeing absolute innocence despoiled. Although Aristotle stresses that a successful protagonist must be better than ordinary men and women, he also insists that the protagonist be somewhat less than perfect:

> *There remains, then, the intermediate kind of personage, a man not preeminently virtuous and just, whose misfortune, however, is brought upon him not by vice and depravity but by some error of judgment . . . .*

Aristotle's word for this error is *hamartia,* which is commonly translated as "tragic flaw" but might more properly be termed a "great error." Whether he means some innate flaw, like a psychological defect, or simply a great mistake is open to question, but writers of tragedies have traditionally created deeply flawed protagonists. In ordinary circumstances, the protagonist's strength of character may allow him to prosper, but under the pressure of events he may crack when one small chink in his armor widens and leaves him vulnerable. A typical flaw in tragedies is *hubris,* arrogance or excessive pride, which leads the protagonist into errors that might have been avoided if he or she had listened to the advice of others. Although he does not use the term himself, Aristotle touches on the concept of **poetic justice,** the audience's sense that virtue and vice have been fairly dealt with in the play and that the protagonist's punishment is to some degree deserved.

We should bear in mind that the greatest burden of characterization in drama falls on the actor or actress who undertakes a role. No matter how well-written a part is, in the hands of an incompetent or inappropriate performer the character will not be credible. Vocal inflection, gesture, and even the strategic use of silence are the stock in trade of actors, for it is up to them to convince us that we are involved in the sufferings and joys of real human beings. No two actors will play the same part in the same manner. We are lucky to have two excellent film versions of Shakespeare's *Henry the Fifth* available. Comparing the cool elegance of Laurence Olivier with the rough and ready exuberance of Kenneth Branagh is a wonderful short course in the equal validity of two radically different approaches to the same role.

In reading, there are several points to keep in mind about main characters. Physical description, while it may be minimal at best, is worth paying close attention to. To cite one example from the plays contained in this edition, Shakespeare identifies Othello simply as a "Moor," a native of North Africa. Race and color are important causes of conflict in the play, to be sure, but through the years the part has been played with equal success by both black and white actors. The important issue in *Othello* is that the tragic hero is a cultural misfit in the Venetian society from which he takes a wife; he is a widely respected military leader but an outsider all the same. Shakespeare provides us with few other details of his appearance, but we can probably assume that he is a large and powerful warrior, capable of commanding men by his mere presence. Sometimes an author will give a character a name that is an indicator of his or her personality and appearance. Oedipus's name, in Greek, refers to his scarred feet. Willy Loman, the failed protagonist of Arthur Miller's *Death of a Salesman,* bears a surname ("low man") which may contain a pun on his character, a device called a **characternym.**

**Character motivation** is another point of characterization to ponder. Why do characters act in a certain manner? What do they hope to gain from their actions? In some cases these motives are clear enough and may be discussed openly by the characters. In other plays, motivation is more elusive, as the playwright deliberately mystifies the audience by presenting characters who perhaps are not fully aware of the reasons for their compulsions. Modern dramatists, influenced by advances in psychology, have often refused to reduce characters' actions to simple equations of cause and effect.

Two conventions that the playwright may employ in revealing motivation are **soliloquy** and **aside.** A soliloquy is a speech made by a single character on stage alone. Hamlet's soliloquies, among them some of the most famous passages in all drama, show us the process of his mind as he toys with various plans of revenge but delays putting them into action. The aside is a brief remark (traditionally delivered to the side of a raised hand) that an actor makes directly to the audience and that the other characters on stage cannot hear. Occasionally an aside reveals a reason for a character's behavior in a scene. Neither of these devices is as widely used in today's theater as in earlier periods, but they remain part of the dramatist's collection of techniques.

Minor characters are also of great importance in a successful play, and there are several different traditional types. A **foil,** a minor character with whom a major character sharply contrasts, is used primarily as a sounding board for ideas. A **confidant** is a trusted friend or servant to whom a major character speaks frankly and openly; confidants fulfill in some respects one role that the chorus plays in Greek tragedy. **Stock characters** are stereotypes that are useful for advancing the plot and fleshing out the scenes, particularly in comedies. Hundreds of plays have employed pair of innocent young lovers, sharp-tongued servants, and meddling mothers-in-law as part of their casts. **Allegorical characters** in morality plays like *Everyman* are clearly labeled by their names and, for the most part, are personifications of human attributes (Beauty, Good Deeds) or of theological concepts (Confession). **Comic relief** in a tragedy may be provided by minor characters like Shakespeare's fools or clowns.

## Theme

Aristotle has relatively little to say about the theme of a play, simply noting that "Thought of the personages is shown in everything to be effected by their language." Because he focuses to such a large degree on the emotional side of tragedy—its stimulation of pity and fear—he seems to give less importance to the role of drama as a serious forum for the discussion of ideas, referring his readers to another of his works, *The Art of Rhetoric,* where these matters have greater prominence. Nevertheless, **theme,** the central idea or ideas that a play discusses, is important in Greek tragedy and in the subsequent history of the theater. The trilogies of early playwrights were thematically unified around an *aition,* a Greek word for the origin of a custom, just as a typical elementary school Thanksgiving pageant portrays how the holiday traditions were first established in the Plymouth Colony.

Some dramas are explicitly **didactic** in their intent, existing with the specific aim of instructing the audience in ethical, religious, or political areas. A **morality play,** a popular type of drama in the late Middle Ages, is essentially a sermon on sin and redemption rendered in dramatic terms. More subtle in its didacticism is the **problem play** of the late nineteenth century, popularized by Ibsen, which uses the theater as a forum for the serious debate of social issues like industrial pollution or women's rights. The **drama of ideas** of playwrights like George Bernard Shaw does not merely present social problems; it goes further, actually advancing programs of reform. In the United States during the Great Depression of the 1930s, Broadway theaters featured a great deal of **social drama,** in which radical social and political programs were openly propagandized. In the ensuing decades, the theater has remained a popular site for examining issues of race, class, and gender, as successes like *Fences* or *How I Learned to Drive* will attest.

Keep in mind, however, that plays are not primarily religious or political forums. If we are not entertained and moved by a play's language, action, and plot, then it is unlikely that we will respond to its message. The author who has to resort to long sermons from a *raisonneur,* the French word for a character (like Cléante in Molière's *Tartuffe*) who serves primarily as the voice of reason (i.e., the mouthpiece for the playwright's opinions), is not likely to hold the audience's sympathy or attention for long. The best plays are complex enough that they cannot be reduced to simple "thesis statements" that sum up their meaning in a few words.

## Diction

Aristotle was also the author of the first important manual of public speaking, *The Art of Rhetoric,* so it should come as no surprise that he devotes considerable attention in the *Poetics* to the precise words, either alone or in combinations, that playwrights use. Instead of "diction," we would probably speak today of a playwright's "style," or discuss his or her handling of various levels of idiom in the dialogue. Much of what Aristotle has to say about parts of speech and the sounds of words in Greek is of little interest to us; of chief importance is his emphasis on clarity and originality in the choice of words. For Aristotle, the language of tragedy should be "poetic" in the best sense, somehow elevated above the level of ordinary speech but not so ornate that it loses the power to communicate feelings and ideas to an audience. Realism in speech is largely a matter of illusion, and close inspection of the actual lines of modern dramatists like Miller and Williams reveals a discrepancy between the carefully chosen words that characters speak in plays, often making up lengthy **monologues,** and the halting, often inarticulate ("Ya know what I mean?") manner in which we express ourselves in everyday life. The language of the theater has always been an artificial one. The idiom of plays, whether by Shakespeare or by August Wilson, *imitates* the language of life; it does not duplicate it.

Ancient Greek is a language with a relatively small vocabulary and, even in translation, we encounter a great deal of repetition of key words. *Polis,* the Greek word for city, appears many times in Sophocles' plays, stressing the communal fate that the protagonist and the chorus, representing the citizens, share. Shakespeare's use of the full resources of the English language has been the standard against which all subsequent writers in the language can measure themselves. Shakespeare's language presents some special difficulties to the modern reader. His vocabulary is essentially the same as ours, but many words have changed in meaning or become obsolete over the last four hundred years. Shakespeare is also a master of different **levels of diction.** In the space of a few lines he can range from self-consciously flowery heights ("If after every tempest come such calms, / May the winds blow till they have waken'd death! / And let the labouring bark climb hills of seas / Olympus-high and duck again as low / As hell's to heaven!" exults Othello on being reunited with his bride in Cyprus) to the slangy level of the streets—he is a master of the off-color joke and the sarcastic put-down. We should remember that Shakespeare's poetic drama lavishly uses figurative language; his lines abound with similes, metaphors, personifications, and hyperboles, all characteristic devices of the language of poetry. Shakespeare's theater had little in the way of scenery and no "special effects," so a passage from *Hamlet* like "But, look, the morn, in russet mantle clad / Walks o'er the dew of yon high eastward hill" is not merely pretty or picturesque; it has the dramatic function of helping the audience visualize the welcome end of a long, fearful night.

It is true that playwrights since the middle of the nineteenth century have striven for more fidelity to reality, more verisimilitude, in the language their characters use, but even realistic dramatists often rise to rhetorical peaks that have little relationship to the way people actually speak. Both Ibsen and Williams began their careers as poets and, surprisingly, the first draft of Miller's "realistic" tragedy *Death of a Salesman* was largely written in verse.

## Melody

Greek tragedy was accompanied by music. None of this music survives, and we cannot be certain how it was integrated into the drama.

Certainly the choral parts of the play were sung and danced, and it is likely that even the dialogue involved highly rhythmical chanting, especially in passages employing **stichomythia,** rapid alternation of single lines between two actors, a device often encountered during moments of high dramatic tension. In the original language, the different poetic rhythms used in Greek tragedy are still evident, although these are for the most part lost in English translation. At any rate it is apparent that the skillful manipulation of a variety of **poetic meters,** combinations of line lengths and rhythms, for different types of scenes was an important part of the tragic poet's repertoire.

Both tragedies and comedies have been written in verse throughout the ages, often employing rhyme as well as rhythm. *Oedipus the King* is written in a variety of poetic meters, some of which are appropriate for dialogue between actors and others for the choral odes. The greater part of the medieval morality play *Everyman* is written in rhyming pairs of lines, or **couplets.** Shakespeare's *Othello* is composed, like all of his plays, largely in **blank verse,** that is, unrhymed lines of iambic pentameter (lines of ten syllables, alternating unstressed and stressed syllables). He also uses rhymed couplets, particularly for emphasis at the close of scenes; songs (there are three in *Othello*); and even prose passages, especially when dealing with comic or "low" characters. A study of Shakespeare's versification is beyond the scope of this discussion, but suffice it to say that a trained actor must be aware of the rhythmical patterns that Shakespeare utilized if he or she is to deliver the lines with anything approaching accuracy.

Of course, not only verse drama has rhythm. The last sentences of Tennessee Williams's prose drama *The Glass Menagerie* can be easily recast as blank verse that would not have embarrassed Shakespeare himself:

> *Then all at once my sister touches my shoulder.*
> *I turn around and look into her eyes . . .*
> *Oh, Laura, Laura, I tried to leave you behind me,*
> *but I am more faithful than I intended to be!*
> *I reach for a cigarette, I cross the street,*
> *I run into the movies or a bar,*
> *I buy a drink, I speak to the nearest stranger—*
> *anything that can blow your candles out!*
> *—for nowadays the world is lit by lightning!*
> *Blow your candles out, Laura—and so good-bye . . .*

The ancient verse heritage of tragedy lingers on in the modern theater and has proved resistant to even the prosaic rhythms of what Williams calls a "world lit by lightning."

## Spectacle

Spectacle (sometimes called *mise en scène,* French for "putting on stage") is the last of Aristotle's elements of tragedy and, in his view, the least important. By spectacle we mean the purely visual dimension of a play; in ancient Greece, this meant costumes, a few props, and effects carried out by the use of the *mechane.* Costumes in Greek tragedy were simple but impressive. The tragic mask, or *persona,* and a high-heeled boot *(cothurnus)* were apparently designed to give characters a larger-than-life appearance. Historians also speculate that the mask might have additionally served as a crude megaphone to amplify the actors' voices, a necessary feature when we consider that the open-air theater in Athens could seat over 10,000 spectators.

Other elements of set decoration were kept to a minimum, although playwrights occasionally employed a few well-chosen spectacular effects like the triumphant entrance of the victorious king in Aeschylus's *Agamemnon.* Elizabethan drama likewise relied little on spectacular stage effects. Shakespeare's plays call for few props, and little attempt was made at historical accuracy in costumes, with a noble patron's cast-off clothing dressing Caesar one week, Othello the next.

Advances in technology since Shakespeare's day have obviously facilitated more elaborate effects in what we now call **staging** than patrons of earlier centuries could have envisioned. In the nineteenth century, first gas and then electric lighting not only made effects like sunrises possible but also, through the use of different combinations of color, added atmosphere to certain scenes. By Ibsen's day, realistic **box sets** were designed to resemble, in the smallest details, interiors of houses and apartments with an invisible "fourth wall" nearest the audience. Modern theater has experimented in all directions with set design, from the bare stage to barely suggested walls and furnishings, from revolving stages to scenes that "break the plane" by involving the audience in the drama. Tennessee Williams's *The Glass Menagerie* employs music, complicated lighting and sound effects, and semi-transparent **scrims** onto which images are projected, all to enhance the play's dream-like atmosphere. The most impressive uses of spectacle in today's Broadway productions may represent anything from the catacombs beneath the Paris Opera House to thirty-foot-high street barricades manned by soldiers firing muskets. Modern technology can create virtually any sort of stage illusion; the only limitations in today's professional theater are imagination and budget.

Before we leave our preliminary discussion, one further element should be mentioned—**setting**. Particular locales—Thebes, Corinth, and Mycenæ—are the sites of different tragedies, and each city has its own history; in the case of Thebes, this history involves a family curse that touches the members of three generations. But for the most part, specific locales in the greatest plays are less important than the universal currents that are touched. If we are interested in the particular features of middle-class marriage in Oslo in the late nineteenth century, we would perhaps do better going to sociology texts than to Ibsen's *A Doll House*.

Still, every play implies a larger sense of setting, a sense of history that is called the **enveloping action**. The "southern belle" youth of Amanda Wingfield, in Williams's *The Glass Menagerie,* is a fading dream as anachronistic as the "gentlemen callers" she still envisions knocking on her daughter's door. Even though a play from the past may still speak eloquently today, it also provides a "time capsule" whose contents tell us how people lived and what they most valued during the period when the play was written and first performed.

# Brief History and Description of Dramatic Conventions

## *Greek Tragedy*

By the time of Sophocles, tragedy had evolved into an art form with a complex set of conventions. Each playwright would submit a **tetralogy,** or set of four plays, to the yearly competition. The first three plays, or **trilogy,** would be tragedies, perhaps unified like those of Aeschylus's *Oresteia,* which deals with Agamemnon's tragic homecoming from the Trojan War. The fourth, called a **satyr-play,** was comic, with a chorus of goatmen engaging in bawdy revels that, oddly, mocked the serious content of the preceding tragedies. Only one complete trilogy, the *Oresteia* by Aeschylus, and one satyr-play, *The Cyclops* by Euripides, have survived. Three plays by Sophocles derived from the myths surrounding Oedipus and his family—*Oedipus the King, Oedipus at Colonus,* and *Antigone*—are still performed and read, but they were written at separate times and accompanied by other tragedies that are now lost. As tragedy developed in this period, it seems clear that playwrights thought increasingly of individual plays as complete in themselves; *Oedipus the King* does not leave the audience with the feeling that there is more to be told, even though Oedipus is still alive at the end of the play.

Each tragedy was composed according to a prescribed formula, as ritualized as the order of worship in a contemporary church service. The tragedy begins with a **prologue** *(prologos)*, "that which is said first." The prologue is an introductory scene that tells the audience important information about the play's setting, characters, and events immediately preceding the opening of the drama. The second part of the tragedy is called the *parodos,* the first appearance of the chorus in the play. As the members of the chorus enter the orchestra, they dance and sing more generally of the situation in which the city finds itself. Choral parts in some translations are divided into sections called **strophes** and **antistrophes,** indicating choral movements to left and right, respectively. The body of the play is made up of two types of alternating scenes. The first, an **episode** *(episodos)* is a passage of dialogue between two or more actors or between the actors and the chorus. Each of these "acts" of the tragedy is separated from the rest by a choral **ode** *(stasimon;* pl. *stasima)* during which the chorus is alone on the orchestra, commenting, as the voice of public opinion, about the course of action being taken by the main characters. Typically there are four pairs of episodes and odes in the play. The final scene of the play is called the *exodos.* During this part the climax occurs out of sight of the audience and a vivid description of this usually violent scene is sometimes delivered by a messenger or other witness. After the messenger's speech, the main character reappears and the resolution of his fate is determined. In some plays a wheeled platform called an *eccyclema* was used to move this fatal tableau into view of the spectators. A tragedy concludes with the exit of the main characters, sometimes leaving the chorus to deliver a brief speech or **epilogue,** a final summing up of the play's meaning.

While we may at first find such complicated rituals bizarre, we should keep in mind that dramatic conventions are primarily customary and artificial and have little to do with "reality" as we usually experience it. The role of the chorus (set by the time of Sophocles at fifteen members) may seem puzzling to modern readers, but in many ways, the conventions of Greek tragedy are no stranger than those of contemporary musical comedy, in which a pair of lovers burst into a duet and dance in the middle of a stroll in the park, soon to be joined by a host of other cast members. What is most remarkable about the history of drama is not how much these conventions have changed but how remarkably similar they have remained for over twenty-five centuries.

## Medieval Drama

Drama flourished during Greek and Roman times, but after the fall of the Roman Empire (A.D. 476) it declined during four centuries of eclipse, and was kept alive throughout Europe only by wandering troupes of actors performing various types of **folk drama.** The "Punch and Judy" puppet show, still popular in parts of Europe, is a late survivor of this tradition, as are the ancient slapstick routines of circus clowns. Even though drama was officially discouraged by the Church for a long period, when it did reemerge it was as an outgrowth of the Roman Catholic mass, in the form of **liturgical drama.** Around the ninth century, short passages of sung dialogue between the priest and choir, called **tropes,** were added on special holidays to commemorate the event. These tropes grew more elaborate over the years until full-fledged religious pageants were being performed in front of the altar. In 1210, Pope Innocent III, wishing to restore the dignity of the services, banned such performances from the interior of the church. Moving them outside, first to the church porch and later entirely off church property, provided greater opportunity for inventiveness in action and staging.

In the fourteenth and fifteenth centuries, much of the work of putting on plays passed to the guilds, organizations of skilled craftsmen, and their productions became part of city-wide festivals in many continental and British cities. Several types of plays evolved. **Mystery plays** were derived from holy scripture. **Passion plays** (some of which survive unchanged today) focused on the crucifixion of Christ. **Miracle plays** dramatized the lives of the saints. The last and most complex, **morality plays,** were dramatized sermons with allegorical characters (e.g., Everyman, Death, Good Deeds) representing various generalized aspects of human life.

## Elizabethan Drama

While the older morality plays were still performed throughout the sixteenth century, during the time of Queen Elizabeth I (b. 1533, reigned 1558–1603) a new type of drama, typical in many ways of other innovative types of literature developed during the Renaissance, began to be produced professionally by companies of actors not affiliated with any religious institutions. This **secular drama,** beginning in short pieces called **interludes** that may have been designed for entertainment during banquets or other public celebrations, eventually evolved into full-length tragedies and comedies designed for performance in large outdoor theaters like Shakespeare's famous Globe.

A full history of this fertile period would take many pages, but a few of its dramatic conventions are worth noting. We have already mentioned blank verse, the poetic line perfected by Shakespeare's contemporary Christopher Marlowe (1564–1593). Shakespeare wrote tragedies, comedies, and historical dramas with equal success, all characterized by passages that remain the greatest examples of poetic expression in English.

The raised platform stage in an Elizabethan theater used little or no scenery, with the author's descriptive talents setting the scene and indicating lighting and weather. The stage itself had two supporting columns, which might be used to represent trees or hiding places; a raised area at the rear, which could represent a balcony or upper story of a house; a small curtained alcove at its base; and a trap door, which could serve as a grave or hiding place. In contrast to the relatively bare stage, costumes were elaborate and acting was highly stylized. Female roles were played by young boys, and the same actor might play several different minor roles in the same play. The Oscar-winning film *Shakespeare in Love* reveals a great amount of information about Elizabethan staging.

A few more brief words about Shakespeare's plays are in order. First, drama in Shakespeare's time was intended for performance, with publication being of only secondary importance. The text of many of Shakespeare's plays were published in cheap editions called **quartos** which were full of misprints and often contained different versions of the same play. Any play by Shakespeare contains words and passages that different editors have trouble agreeing on. Second, originality, in the sense that we prize it, meant little to a playwright in a time before copyright laws; virtually every one of Shakespeare's plays is derived from an earlier source—Greek myth, history, another play or, the case of *Othello,* an Italian short story of questionable literary merit. The true test of Shakespeare's genius rests in his ability to transform these raw materials into art. Finally, we should keep in mind that Shakespeare's plays were designed to appeal to a wide audience—educated aristocrats and illiterate "groundlings" filled the theater—and this fact may account for the great diversity of tones and levels of language in the plays. Purists of later eras may have been dismayed by some of Shakespeare's wheezy clowns and bad puns, but for us the mixture of "high" and "low" elements gives his plays their remarkable texture.

## The Comic Genres

Shakespeare's ability to move easily between "high" and "low," between tragic and comic, should be a reminder that comedy has developed along lines parallel to tragedy and has never been wholly separate from it. Most of Aristotle's remarks on comedy are lost, but he does make the observation that comedy differs from tragedy in that comedy depicts men and women as worse than they are, whereas tragedy generally stresses their best qualities. During the great age of Greek tragedy, comedies were regularly performed at Athenian festivals. The greatest of the early comic playwrights was Aristophanes (450?–385? B.C.). The plays of Aristophanes are classified as **Old Comedy** and shared many of the same structural elements as tragedy. Old Comedy was always satirical and usually obscene; in *Lysistrata,* written during the devastating Athenian wars with Sparta, the men of both sides are brought to their knees by the women of the two cities, who engage in a sex strike until the men relent. Features of Old Comedy included the use of two semichoruses (in *Lysistrata,* old men and old women); an *agon,* an extended debate between the protagonist and an authority figure; and a *parabasis,* an ode sung by the chorus at an intermission in the action which reveals the author's own views on the play's subject. **New Comedy,** which evolved in the century after Aristophanes, tended to observe more traditional moral values and stressed romance. The New Comedy of Greece greatly influenced the writings of Roman playwrights like Plautus (254–184 B.C.) and Terence (190–159 B.C.). Plautus's *Pseudolus* (combined with elements from two of his other comedies) still finds favor in its modern musical adaptation, *A Funny Thing Happened on the Way to the Forum.*

Like other forms of drama, comedy virtually vanished during the early Middle Ages. Its spirit was kept alive primarily by roving companies of actors who staged improvisational dramas in the squares of towns throughout Europe. The popularity of these plays is evidenced by certain elements in the religious dramas of the same period; the *Second Shepherd's Play* (c. 1450) involves a sheep-rustler with three shepherds in an uproarious parody of the Nativity that still evokes laughter today. Even a serious play such as *Everyman* contains satirical elements in the involved excuses that Goods and other characters contrive for not accompanying the protagonist on his journey with Death.

On the continent, a highly stylized form of improvisational drama appeared in sixteenth century Italy, apparently an evolution from earlier types of folk drama. *Commedia dell'arte* involved a cast of masked stock characters (the miserly old man, the young wife, the ardent seducer) in situations involving mistaken identity and cuckoldry. *Commedia del-l'arte,* because it is an improvisational form, does not survive, but its popularity influenced the direction that comedy would take in the following century. The great French comic playwright Molière (1622–1673) incorporated many of its elements into his own plays, which combine elements of **farce,** a type of comedy which hinges on broadly drawn characters and embarrassing situations usually involving sexual misconduct, with serious social satire. Comedy such as Molière's, which exposes the hypocrisy and pretensions of people in social situations, is called **comedy of manners;** as Molière put it, the main purpose of his plays was "the correction of mankind's vices."

Other types of comedy have also been popular in different eras. Shakespeare's comedies begin with the farcical complications of *The Comedy of Errors,* progress through romantic **pastoral** comedies such as *As You Like It,* which present an idealized view of rural life, and end with the philosophical comedies of his final period, of which *The Tempest* is the greatest example. His contemporary Ben Jonson (1572–1637) favored a type known as **comedy of humours,** a type of comedy of manners in which the conduct of the characters is determined by their underlying dominant trait (the four humours were thought to be bodily fluids whose proportions determined personality). English plays of the late seventeenth and early eighteenth centuries tended to combine the hard-edged satire of comedy of manners with varying amounts of sentimental romance. A play of this type, usually hinging on matters of inheritance and marriage, is known as a **drawing-room comedy,** and its popularity, while peaking in the mid-nineteenth century, endures today.

Modern comedy in English can be said to begin with Oscar Wilde (1854–1900) and George Bernard Shaw (1856–1950). Wilde's brilliant wit and skillful incorporation of paradoxical **epigrams,** witty sayings that have made him one of the most quoted authors of the nineteenth century, have rarely been equaled. Shaw, who began his career as a drama critic, admired both Wilde and Ibsen, and succeeded in combining the best elements of the comedy of manners and the problem play in his works. *Major Barbara* (1905), a typical **comedy of ideas,** frames serious discussion of war, religion, and poverty with a search for an heir to a millionaire's fortune and a suitable husband for one of his daughters. Most subsequent writers of comedy, from Neil Simon to Wendy Wasserstein, reveal their indebtedness to Wilde and Shaw.

One striking development of comedy in recent times lies in its deliberate harshness. So-called **black humor,** an extreme type of satire in which barriers of taste are assaulted and pain seems the constant companion of laughter, has characterized much of the work of playwrights like Samuel Beckett (1906–1989), Eugene Ionesco (1912–1994), and Edward Albee (b. 1928).

## *Realistic Drama, the Modern Stage, and Beyond*

Realism is a term that is loosely employed as a synonym for "true to life," but in literary history it denotes a style of writing that developed in the mid-nineteenth century, first in the novels of such masters as Charles Dickens, Gustave Flaubert, and Leo Tolstoy, and later in the dramas of Ibsen and Anton Chekhov. Many of the aspects of dramatic realism have to do with staging and acting. The box set, with its invisible "fourth wall" facing the audience, could, with the added subtleties of artificial lighting, successfully mimic the interior of a typical middle-class home. Realistic prose drama dropped devices like the soliloquy in favor of more natural means of acting such as that championed by Konstantin Stanislavsky (1863–1938), the Russian director who worked closely with Chekhov (1860–1904) to perfect a method whereby actors learned to identify with their characters' psychological problems from "inside out." This "method" acting often tries, as is the case in Chekhov's plays and, later, in those of Williams and Miller, to develop a play's **subtext,** the crucial issue in the play that no one can bear to address directly. Stanislavsky's theories have influenced several generations of actors and have become standard throughout the world of the theater. Ibsen's plays, which in fact ushered in the modern era of the theater, are often called **problem plays** because they deal with serious, even controversial or taboo, issues in society. Shaw said that Ibsen's great originality as a playwright lay in his ability to shock the members of the audience into thinking about their own lives. As the barriers of censorship have fallen over the years, the capacity of the theater to shock has perhaps been diminished, but writers still find it a forum admirably suited for debating the controversial issues which divide society.

American and world drama in the twentieth and the present centuries has gone far beyond realism to experiment with the dream-like atmosphere of **expressionism** (which, like the invisible walls in Miller's *Death of a Salesman,* employs distorted sets to mirror the troubled, perhaps even unbalanced, psyches of the play's characters) or **theater of the absurd,** which depicts a world, like that of Samuel Beckett's *Waiting for*

*Godot* or the early plays of Edward Albee, without meaning in which everything seems ridiculous. Nevertheless, realism is still the dominant style of today's theater, even if our definition of it has to be modified to take into account plays as diverse as *The Glass Menagerie, Fences,* and *How I Learned to Drive.*

## Film Versions: A Note

Nothing can equal the experience of an actual stage production, but the many fine film versions of the plays in this anthology offer instructors and students the opportunity to explore, in some cases, two or three different cinematic approaches to the same material. I regularly teach a course in drama and film, and I have found that the differences between print and film versions of plays offer students many challenging topics for discussion, analysis, and writing. Of course, the two media differ radically; in some cases noted below, the film versions, especially those from past decades, badly compromise the original plays. To cite one notorious instance regarding a play not in this anthology, Elia Kazan's celebrated film of Tennessee Williams's *A Streetcar Named Desire,* so wonderful in its sets, direction, and the performances of Marlon Brando and Vivien Leigh, tampers with the play's ending (on orders from the Hollywood Production Code office) to give the impression that Stella will take her child and leave Stanley. Williams himself wrote the screenplay, and he was aware of, if not exactly happy with, the moral standards of the times.

The late O. B. Hardison, director of the Folger Shakespeare Library, once observed two important differences between plays and films. The first is that attending a play is a social function; the audience members and the performers are aware of one another's presence and respond to it. Applause can stir actors to new heights, and laughter in the wrong place can signal the beginning of a disaster. Film, on the contrary, is largely a private experience; it was with good reason that one film critic titled a collection of her reviews *A Year in the Dark.* The other chief difference, Hardison notes, is that drama is a realistic medium, whereas film is surrealistic. Watching a play, we see real persons who have a physical reality, and we see them from a uniform perspective. But film has conditioned us to its own vocabulary of close-ups, jump cuts, and panoramas, and we view a film from a variety of perspectives. These differences, as fundamental as they seem, are rarely noted by students until they are pointed out. Still, film versions provide us with a wonderful time capsule in which many treasures of the drama's past have been preserved. A reasoned list of some of these, most of them available on video, follows.

## *Oedipus the King*

Tyrone Guthrie's 1957 version, *Oedipus Rex,* is a filmed record of his famous Stratford, Ontario, production, and it retains the masks and choral movements of ancient Greek tragedy. Guthrie uses the William Butler Yeats translation, which sacrifices literal fidelity to rhetorical grandeur. Douglas Campbell and Eleanor Stuart are impressive as Oedipus and Jocasta, and the messenger is played by Douglas Rain, the voice of the HAL computer in *2001: A Space Odyssey.* The youthful William Shatner, hidden behind a mask, is a member of the chorus. Philip Savile's 1968 version, starring Christopher Plummer, is also worthwhile; this version opens up the play with scenes beautifully photographed in ancient settings. Orson Welles's performance as Tiresias is particularly striking, although some may protest at actually having to *watch* Oedipus blind himself while listening to the messenger's voiceover narration.

## *The Tragedy of Othello, the Moor of Venice*

*Othello* has proved to be one of Shakespeare's most popular plays on film. Orson Welles's 1952 version, thought lost for many years, was lovingly restored by his daughter Rebecca Welles and features a remastered soundtrack that remedies most of the original complaints about Welles's film. A fascinating film-noir study in Shakespeare, it features a bravura performance by Welles and an affecting one by Suzanne Cloutier as Desdemona. Less successful is Laurence Olivier's 1966 version, essentially a filmed version of his acclaimed Royal Shakespeare Company production. Olivier's controversial performance, which mimics West Indian speech patterns, and that of Maggie Smith as Desdemona are worth seeing, but Olivier's stage make-up, unconvincing in film close-ups, and minimal production values mar the effort. The 1980 version starring Anthony Hopkins as Othello and Bob Hoskins as Iago features interesting performances from the principals, despite Hopkins's strange hairpiece. This uncut version was part of the PBS Shakespeare series and is widely available in libraries. The 1995 film, directed by Oliver Parker, has excellent performances by Laurence Fishburne and Kenneth Branagh and a sumptuous, erotic style. Contemporary students will probably find it the most satisfying of the four. Tim Blake Nelson's 2001 film, *O,* transposed the plot (but precious little of the language) in a contemporary version exploring rivalries between basketball teammates at a southern prep school.

## A Doll House

For some inexplicable reason, *A Doll's House,* as it is titled in both films, was made into two films in the same year, 1973. Patrick Garland's version stars Claire Bloom as Nora and Anthony Hopkins as Torvald. Sir Ralph Richardson essays the role of Dr. Rank, and the reliable Denholm Elliott plays Krogstad. Joseph Losey's version features Jane Fonda as an energetic (and very young) Nora, David Warner as Torvald, and Trevor Howard as Dr. Rank. Most critics felt that the Losey version, which includes actual scenes only hinted at by Ibsen, tried too obviously to make the play relevant to contemporary audiences.

## The Glass Menagerie

The 1950 version, directed by Irving Rapper, has the advantage of Gertrude Lawrence, Arthur Kennedy, and Jane Wyman in the roles of the Wingfield family, but Kirk Douglas seems oddly out of place as Jim O'Connor. The film concludes with an absurd final shot of Amanda and Laura gleefully waving as a new gentleman caller approaches their door. The 1973 version, with Katharine Hepburn and Sam Waterston, surmounts the obvious problem of Hepburn, a New Englander if ever there was one, seeming plausible as a faded southern belle. In 1987, Paul Newman directed a well-received version with Joanne Woodward and John Malkovich in the leads.

## Death of a Salesman

Miller was not pleased with the 1951 film, in which Fredric March over-acted badly as Willy Loman. Still, Mildred Dunnock, Kevin McCarthy, and Cameron Mitchell provided excellent support. Volker Schlöndorff's 1985 version has been widely acclaimed, although some viewers have found Dustin Hoffman ill-suited to the role that Miller wrote with the large-boned Lee J. Cobb in mind. John Malkovich and Kate Reid are very good, and Schlöndorff's impressionistic set designs and seamless handling of flashbacks are impressive. A videotape of the final performance of the award-winning 1999 Broadway revival, starring Brian Dennehy and Elizabeth Franz, aired on Showtime in 2000. Dennehy brought to the role of Willy Loman a magnitude that many critics found impressive.

### *"Master Harold"* . . . *and the boys*

A young Matthew Broderick makes a believable Hallie in the 1984 film of *"Master Harold"* . . . *and the boys,* which was originally made for television. But Broderick, who displays ample evidence of his bright acting future, is matched step for step by the two supporting cast members, John Kani as Willie and Zakes Mokae as Sam. Mokae, as the elder of the two waiters, originated the part in 1982 and the dignity and patience he brings to the role are very moving. Essentially a photographed play, *"Master Harold"* . . . *and the boys* succeeds on the strength of Fugard's characterizations and the actors' skills.

# Writing About Drama

Writing assignments vary widely and your teacher's instructions may range from general ("Discuss any two scenes in the plays we have read") to very specific ("Write an explication, in not less than 1000 words, on Shakespeare's use of imagery and figurative language in Othello's speech to the Venetian Senate in which he describes his courtship of Desdemona"). Such processes as choosing, limiting, and developing a topic; "brainstorming" by taking notes on random ideas and refining those ideas further through group discussion or conferences with your instructor; using the library and the Internet to locate supporting secondary sources; and revising a first draft in light of critical remarks are undoubtedly techniques you have practiced in other composition classes. Basic types of organizational schemes learned in "theme-writing" courses can also be applied to writing about drama. Formal assignments of these types should avoid contractions and jargon, and should be written in a clear, straightforward style. Most literary essays are not of the personal experience type, and you should follow common sense in avoiding the first person and slang. It goes without saying that you should carefully proofread your rough and final drafts to eliminate errors in spelling, punctuation, usage, and grammar.

Typical writing assignments on plays fall into four main categories: reviews, explication or close reading, analysis, and comparison-contrast. A review, an evaluation of an actual performance of a play, will focus less on the play itself, particularly if it is a well-known one, than on the actors' performances, the overall direction of the production, and the elements of staging. Because reviews are primarily news stories, basic information about the time and place of production should be given at the beginning of the review. A short summary of the play's plot may follow, with perhaps some remarks on its stage history, and subsequent paragraphs will evaluate the performers and the production. Remember that a review is both a *report* and a *recommendation,* either positive or negative, to readers. You should strive for accuracy in such matters as spelling the actors' names correctly, and you should also try to be fair in pointing out the strong and weak points of the production. It is essential to support any general statements about the play's successes or shortcomings with specific references to the production, so it is a good idea to take notes during the performance. Because film versions of most of the plays in this book, sometimes in several different versions, are available on videotape, you might also be asked to review one of these films, paying attention perhaps to the innovative ways in which directors like Orson Welles or Volker Schlöndorff have "opened up" the action of the plays by utilizing the more complex technical resources of motion pictures. Two good reference sources providing examples of professional drama and film reviews, respectively, are *The New York Times Theater Reviews* (available in several volumes) and *The New York Times Film Reviews;* of course, *The New York Times* and other big-city newspapers may be searched online for reviews of recent productions. Popular magazines containing drama reviews include *Time, Newsweek, The New Yorker,* and others, and these reviews are indexed in the *Readers' Guide to Periodical Literature* (now available online at many libraries). Also, yearbooks like *Theatre World* provide useful information about New York productions of plays, and official websites of recent productions can be found on the Internet.

An explication assignment, on the other hand, requires that you pay close attention to selected passages, giving a detailed account of all the nuances of a speech from a play you have read. Because Shakespeare's poetry is often full of figurative language that may not be fully understood until it has been subjected to an "unfolding" (the literal meaning of explication), individual sections of *Othello*—speeches, scenes, soliloquies—would be likely choices for writing assignments. For example, you might be asked to compare the four different accounts of Othello's courtship of Desdemona—first by Iago and Roderigo, next by her father Brabantio, then by Othello and Desdemona themselves—that we hear in the first act of the play. Other passages that might yield more meaning under close reading include Iago's various explanations for his hatred of Othello or the several different references in the play to reputation and "good name."

Analysis assignments typically turn on definition and illustration, focusing on only one of the main elements of the play such as plot or characterization. You might be required to explain Aristotle's statements about peripety and then apply his terminology to a contemporary play like *Death of a Salesman.* Here you would attempt to locate relevant passages from the play to support Aristotle's contentions about the importance of these reversals in the best plots. Or you might be asked to provide a summary of his comments about the tragic hero and then apply this definition to a character like Willy Loman. In doing so, you might use other supporting materials such as Arthur Miller's essay "Tragedy and the Common Man," in which the author discusses the modern notion that the tragic hero need not be drawn from the upper strata of society.

Comparison and contrast assignments are also popular. You might be assigned to compare two or more characters in a single play (Willy Loman's sons Biff and Happy, for example, or male and female attitudes expressed by the two characters in David Ives's *Sure Thing*), or to contrast characters in two different plays (Oedipus and Othello as undeserving victims of fate, perhaps, or Willy Loman and Troy Maxson as protagonists embittered by failed dreams). Comparison and contrast assignments require careful planning, and it is essential to find both significant similarities and differences to support your thesis. Obviously, a proposed topic about two characters who have almost nothing in common, say, Iago and Tom Wingfield, would have little discernable purpose.

Supporting your statements about a play is necessary, either by quoting directly from the play or, if you are required, to use outside sources for additional critical opinion. You may be required to use secondary sources from the library or Internet in writing your paper. A subject search through your library's books is a good starting place, especially for older playwrights who have attracted extensive critical attention. Reference books like *Twentieth Century Authors, Contemporary Authors,* and the *Dictionary of Literary Biography* provide compact overviews of playwrights' careers. *Contemporary Literary Criticism, Critical Survey of Drama,* and *Drama Criticism* contain both original evaluations and excerpts from critical pieces on published works, and the *MLA Index* will direct you to articles on drama in scholarly journals. We have already mentioned the reference books from the *New York Times* as an excellent source of drama reviews. One scholarly journal that focuses on individual passages from literary works, the *Explicator*, is also worth inspecting. In recent years, the Internet has facilitated the chores of research, and many online databases, reference works, and periodicals may be quickly located using search engines like Yahoo (**www.yahoo.com**) and Google (**www.google.com**). The Internet also holds a wealth of information, ranging from corporate websites promoting play productions to sites on individual authors, many of which are run by universities or organizations. Navigating the Internet can be a forbidding task, and a book like Lester Faigley's *The Longman Guide to the Web* is an invaluable traveler's companion. Students should be aware, however, that websites vary widely in quality. Some are legitimate academic sources displaying sound scholarship; others are little more that "fan pages" that may contain erroneous or misleading information.

Careful documentation of your sources is essential; if you use any material other than what is termed "common knowledge," you must cite it in your paper. Common knowledge includes biographical information, an author's publications, prizes and awards received, and other information that can be found in more than one reference book. Anything else—direct quotes or material you have put in your own words by paraphrasing—requires both a parenthetical citation in the body of your paper and an entry on your works cited pages. Doing less than this is to commit an act of plagiarism, for which the penalties are usually severe. Internet materials, which are so easily cut and pasted into a manuscript, provide an easy temptation but are immediately noticeable. Nothing is easier to spot in a paper than an uncited "lift" from a source; in most cases the vocabulary and sentence structure will be radically different from the rest of the paper.

The current edition of the *MLA Handbook for Writers of Research Papers,* which is available in the reference section of almost any library and which, if you plan to write papers for other English or drama courses, is a good addition to your personal library, contains formats for bibliographies and manuscript form that most instructors consider standard; indeed, most of the handbooks of grammar and usage commonly used in college courses follow MLA style and may be sufficient for your needs. If you have doubts, ask your instructor about what format is preferred. The type of parenthetical citation used today is simple to learn and dispenses with such time-consuming and repetitive chores as footnotes and endnotes. In using parenthetical citations remember that your goal is to direct your reader from the quoted passage in the paper to its source in your bibliography and from there, if necessary, to the book or periodical from which the quote is taken. A good parenthetical citation gives only the *minimal* information needed to accomplish this. Here are a few examples from student papers on *Othello:*

> In a disarming display of modesty before the
> Venetian senators, Othello readily admits that his
> military background has not prepared him to act as an
> eloquent spokesman in his own defense: "[...] little
> of this great world can I speak / More than pertains
> to feats of broils and battle; / And therefore little
> shall I grace my cause / In speaking for myself"
> (1.3.86-89).

Quotations from Shakespeare's plays are cited by act, scene, and line numbers instead of by page numbers. Note that short quotes from poetic dramas require that line breaks be indicated by the virgule (/) or slash; quotes longer than five lines should be indented ten spaces and formatted to duplicate the line breaks of the original. Here, the reader knows that Shakespeare is the author, so the citation here will simply direct him or her to the anthology or the collected or single edition of Shakespeare listed in the works cited section at the end of the paper:

> Shakespeare, William. <u>The Complete Works of Shake-
> speare</u>. Ed. Hardin Craig. New York: Scott, 1961.
> Shakespeare, William. <u>Othello</u>. Ed. David Bevington.
> New York: Bantam, 1988.
> Shakespeare, William. <u>The Tragedy of Othello, the
> Moor of Venice</u>. <u>Literature: An Introduction to
> Fiction, Poetry, and Drama</u>. 7th ed. Ed. X. J.
> Kennedy and Dana Gioia. 9th ed. New York: Long-
> man, 2004. 1303-1400.

If, on the other hand, you are quoting from a prose drama, you would probably indicate a page number.

> In <u>A Doll House</u>, Ibsen wants to demonstrate im-
> mediately that Nora and Helmer share almost childlike
> attitudes towards each other. "Is that my little lark
> twittering out there?" is Helmer's initial line in
> the play (43).

The citation directs the reader to the works cited entry:

```
Ibsen, Henrik. Four Major Plays. Trans. Rolf Fjelde.
    New York: Signet, 1965.
```

Similarly, quotes from secondary critical sources should follow the same rules of common sense.

> One critic, providing a classic estimate of Shakespeare's skill in conceiving Othello's antagonist, notes, "Evil has nowhere else been portrayed with such mastery as in the character of Iago" (Bradley 173).

In this case, the critic is not named in the paper, so his name must be included in the parenthetical citation. The reader knows where to look in the works cited:

```
Bradley, A. C. Shakespearean Tragedy. New York:
    Fawcett, 1967.
```

If the writer provides the critic's name ("A. C. Bradley, providing a classic estimate . . ."), then the parentheses should contain only the page number.

Of course, different types of sources—reference book entries, articles in periodicals, newspaper reviews of plays—require different bibliographical information, so be sure to check the *MLA Handbook* if you have questions. Here are a few more of the most commonly used formats:

### AN EDITED COLLECTION OF ESSAYS

```
Snyder, Susan, ed. Othello: Critical Essays. New York:
    Garland, 1988.
```

### A CASEBOOK

```
Dean, Leonard Fellows, ed. A Casebook on Othello.
    New York: Crowell, 1961.
```

## Play Reprinted in an Anthology or Textbook

Wilson, August. <u>Fences</u>. <u>Literature: A Pocket Anthol-
ogy</u>. Ed. R. S. Gwynn. 2nd ed. New York: Addison-
Wesley, 2005. 1298-1361.

## Article in a Reference Book

"<u>Othello</u>." <u>The Oxford Companion to English
Literature</u>. Ed. Margaret Drabble. 5th ed.
New York: Oxford UP, 1985.

## Article in a Scholarly Journal

Berry, Edward. "Othello's Alienation." <u>Studies in
English Literature, 1500-1900</u> 30 (1990):
315-33.

## Review in a Newspaper

Evans, Everett. "Sturdy Staging of 'Equus' Raises In-
triguing Issues." <u>Houston Chronicle</u> 19 Jan.
2005: D1+.

## Play Production Website

"Monty Python's <u>Spamalot</u>." 2004. 22 Mar. 2005
<http:www.montypythonsspamalot.com>.

## Online Article or Review

Winship, Frederick M. "Nathan Lane Stars in Aristophanes' 'Frogs.'" 31 July 2004. <u>Washington
Times</u>. 11 Apr. 2005 <http://www.tdf.org/communi-
cations/wendy.htm>.

## Online Author Website

"August Wilson." 2001. <u>Literature Online</u>. 13 May
2005. <http://longman.awl.com/kennedy/wilson/
biography.html>.

## ONLINE REFERENCE WORK

"Sophocles." 2005. <u>Britannica Online</u>. Encyclopedia
Britannica. 12 Feb. 2005. <http://www.britan-
nica.com/bcom/eb/article/0/0,5716,118260+1+
109862,00.html?query=sophocles>.

# Drama

## Sophocles (496?–406 B.C.)

*Sophocles lived in Athens in the age of Pericles, during the city's greatest period of culture, power, and influence. Sophocles distinguished himself as an athlete, a musician, a military advisor, a politician and, most important, a dramatist. At sixteen, he was chosen to lead a chorus in reciting a poem on the Greek naval victory over the Persians at Salamis, and he won his first prizes as a playwright before he was thirty. Although both Aeschylus, his senior, and Euripides, his younger rival, have their champions, Sophocles, whose career spanned so long a period that he competed against both of them, is generally considered to be the most important Greek writer of tragedies; his thirty victories in the City Dionysia surpass the combined totals of his two great colleagues. Of his 123 plays, only seven survive intact, including two other plays relating to Oedipus and his children,* Antigone *and* Oedipus at Colonus, *which was produced after Sophocles' death by his grandson. He is generally credited with expanding the technical possibilities of drama by introducing a third actor in certain scenes (Aeschylus used only two) and by both reducing the number of lines given to the chorus and increasing its integration into his plays. Sophocles was intimately involved in both civic and military affairs, twice serving as a chief advisor to Pericles, and his sense of duty to the* polis *(Greek for city) is apparent in many of his plays.* Oedipus the King *was first performed in Athens in about 430 B.C. Its importance can be judged by the many references that Aristotle makes to it in his discussion of tragedy in the* Poetics.

# Oedipus the King
## Translated by Dudley Fitts and Robert Fitzgerald

### CHARACTERS °

Oedipus
A Priest
Creon
Teiresias
Iocastê
Messenger
Shepherd of Laïos
Second Messenger
Chorus of Theban Elders

**Characters:** Some of the characters' names are usually Anglicized: Jocasta, Laius. This translation uses spelling that reflects the original Greek.

*Scene: Before the palace of Oedipus, King of Thebes. A central door and two lateral doors open onto a platform which runs the length of the façade. On the platform, right and left, are altars; and three steps lead down into the "orchestra," or chorus-ground. At the beginning of the action these steps are crowded by suppliants° who have brought branches and chaplets of olive leaves and who lie in various attitudes of despair. Oedipus enters.*

## PROLOGUE °

OEDIPUS:  My children, generations of the living
    In the line of Kadmos,° nursed at his ancient hearth:
    Why have you strewn yourself before these altars
    In supplication, with your boughs and garlands?
    The breath of incense rises from the city          5
    With a sound of prayer and lamentation.
                               Children,
    I would not have you speak through messengers,
    And therefore I have come myself to hear you—
    I, Oedipus, who bear the famous name.
    (*To a Priest.*) You, there, since you are eldest in the company,    10
    Speak for them all, tell me what preys upon you,
    Whether you come in dread, or crave some blessing:
    Tell me, and never doubt that I will help you
    In every way I can; I should be heartless
    Were I not moved to find you suppliant here.    15
PRIEST:  Great Oedipus, O powerful King of Thebes!
    You see how all the ages of our people
    Cling to your altar steps: here are boys
    Who can barely stand alone, and here are priests
    By weight of age, as I am a priest of God,    20
    And young men chosen from those yet unmarried;
    As for the others, all that multitude,

---

**suppliants** persons who come to ask a favor.  **Prologue** first part of a tragedy, containing the exposition.  **2 line of Kadmos** Thebes had been founded by Cadmus.

They wait with olive chaplets in the squares,
At the two shrines of Pallas,° and where Apollo°
Speaks in the glowing embers.
                 Your own eyes          25
Must tell you: Thebes is tossed on a murdering sea
And can not lift her head from the death surge.
A rust consumes the buds and fruits of the earth;
The herds are sick; children die unborn,
And labor is vain. The god of plague and pyre     30
Raids like detestable lightning through the city,
And all the house of Kadmos is laid waste,
All emptied, and all darkened: Death alone
Battens upon the misery of Thebes.
You are not one of the immortal gods, we know;    35
Yet we have come to you to make our prayer
As to the man surest in mortal ways
And wisest in the ways of God. You saved us
From the Sphinx, that flinty singer, and the tribute
We paid to her so long; yet you were never    40
Better informed than we, nor could we teach you:
It was some god breathed in you to set us free.
Therefore, O mighty King, we turn to you:
Find us our safety, find us a remedy,
Whether by counsel of the gods or men.    45
A king of wisdom tested in the past
Can act in a time of troubles, and act well.
Noblest of men, restore
Life to your city! Think how all men call you
Liberator for your triumph long ago;    50
Ah, when your years of kingship are remembered,
Let them not say *We rose, but later fell—*
Keep the State from going down in the storm!
Once, years ago, with happy augury,
You brought us fortune; be the same again!    55

---

**24 Pallas** Athena, goddess of wisdom.   **Apollo** here the god of prophecy. At his shrine at Delphi, the future could be divined.

No man questions your power to rule the land:
But rule over men, not over a dead city!
Ships are only hulls, citadels are nothing,
When no life moves in the empty passageways.
OEDIPUS:   Poor children! You may be sure I know          60
All that you longed for in your coming here.
I know that you are deathly sick; and yet,
Sick as you are, not one is as sick as I.
Each of you suffers in himself alone
His anguish, not another's; but my spirit          65
Groans for the city, for myself, for you.
I was not sleeping, you are not waking me.
No, I have been in tears for a long while
And in my restless thought walked many ways.
In all my search, I found one helpful course,          70
And that I have taken: I have sent Creon,
Son of Menoikeus, brother of the Queen,
To Delphi, Apollo's place of revelation,
To learn there, if he can,
What act or pledge of mine may save the city.          75
I have counted the days, and now, this very day,
I am troubled, for he has overstayed his time.
What is he doing? He has been gone too long.
Yet whenever he comes back, I should do ill
To scant whatever duty God reveals.          80
PRIEST:   It is a timely promise. At this instant
They tell me Creon is here.
OEDIPUS:                    O Lord Apollo!
May his news be fair as his face is radiant!
PRIEST:   It could not be otherwise: he is crowned with bay,
The chaplet is thick with berries.
OEDIPUS:   We shall soon know;          85
He is near enough to hear us now.

*Enter Creon.*

O Prince:

Brother: son of Menoikeus:
What answer do you bring us from the god?
CREON: A strong one. I can tell you, great afflictions
Will turn out well, if they are taken well.                               90
OEDIPUS: What was the oracle? These vague words
Leave me still hanging between hope and fear.
CREON: Is it your pleasure to hear me with all these
Gathered around us? I am prepared to speak,
But should we not go in?
OEDIPUS:                           Let them all hear it               95
It is for them I suffer, more than for myself.
CREON: Then I will tell you what I heard at Delphi.
In plain words
The god commands us to expel from the land of Thebes
An old defilement we are sheltering.                                      100
It is a deathly thing, beyond cure.
We must not let it feed upon us longer.
OEDIPUS: What defilement? How shall we rid ourselves of it?
CREON: By exile or death, blood for blood. It was
Murder that brought the plague-wind on the city.                          105
OEDIPUS: Murder of whom? Surely the god has named him?
CREON: My lord: long ago Laïos was our king,
Before you came to govern us.
OEDIPUS:                           I know;
I learned of him from others; I never saw him.
CREON: He was murdered; and Apollo commands us now                        110
To take revenge upon whoever killed him.
OEDIPUS: Upon whom? Where are they? Where shall we
find a clue
To solve that crime, after so many years?
CREON: Here in this land, he said.
                                 If we make enquiry,
We may touch things that otherwise escape us.                             115
OEDIPUS: Tell me: Was Laïos murdered in his house,
Or in the fields, or in some foreign country?
CREON: He said he planned to make a pilgrimage.
He did not come home again.

OEDIPUS:                    And was there no one,
   No witness, no companion, to tell what happened?                    120
CREON:   They were all killed but one, and he got away
   So frightened that he could remember one thing only.
OEDIPUS:   What was that one thing? One may be the key
   To everything, if we resolve to use it.
CREON:   He said that a band of highwaymen attacked them,                    125
   Outnumbered them, and overwhelmed the King.
OEDIPUS:   Strange, that a highwayman should be so daring—
   Unless some faction here bribed him to do it.
CREON:   We thought of that. But after Laïos' death
   New troubles arose and we had no avenger.                    130
OEDIPUS:   What troubles could prevent your hunting down the
   killers?
CREON:   The riddling Sphinx's song
   Made us deaf to all mysteries but her own.
OEDIPUS:   Then once more I must bring what is dark to light.
   It is most fitting that Apollo shows,                    135
   As you do, this compunction for the dead.
   You shall see how I stand by you, as I should,
   To avenge the city and the city's god,
   And not as though it were for some distant friend,
   But for my own sake, to be rid of evil.                    140
   Whoever killed King Laïos might—who knows?—
   Decide at any moment to kill me as well.
   By avenging the murdered king I protect myself.
   Come, then, my children: leave the altar steps,
   Lift up your olive boughs!
                  One of you go                    145
   And summon the people of Kadmos to gather here.
   I will do all that I can; you may tell them that.

                         *Exit a Page.*

   So, with the help of God,
   We shall be saved—or else indeed we are lost.
PRIEST:   Let us rise, children. It was for this we came,                    150
   And now the King has promised it himself.

Phoibos° has sent us an oracle; may he descend
Himself to save us and drive out the plague.

*Exeunt Oedipus and Creon into the palace by the central door.*
*The Priest and the Suppliants disperse right and left. After a*
*short pause the Chorus enters the orchestra.*

## PÁRODOS °

### STROPHE° 1

CHORUS:   What is God singing in his profound
    Delphi of gold and shadow?
    What oracle for Thebes, the sunwhipped city?
    Fear unjoints me, the roots of my heart tremble.
    Now I remember, O Healer, your power, and wonder:    5
    Will you send doom like a sudden cloud, or weave it
    Like nightfall of the past?
    Speak, speak to us, issue of holy sound:
    Dearest to our expectancy: be tender!

### ANTISTROPHE° 1

    Let me pray to Athenê, the immortal daughter of Zeus,    10
    And to Artemis her sister
    Who keeps her famous throne in the market ring,
    And to Apollo, bowman at the far butts of heaven—
    O gods, descend! Like three streams leap against
    The fires of our grief, the fires of darkness;    15
    Be swift to bring us rest!
    As in the old time from the brilliant house
    Of air you stepped to save us, come again!

---

152 **Phoibos** that is, Apollo.
**Párodos** chanted by the chorus on its first entrance. A **strophe** was chanted while the chorus danced from stage right to stage left. An **antistrophe** was chanted while the chorus danced from left to right.

STROPHE 2

Now our afflictions have no end,
Now all our stricken host lies down                    20
And no man fights off death with his mind;
The noble plowland bears no grain,
And groaning mothers can not bear—
See, how our lives like birds take wing,
Like sparks that fly when a fire soars,                25
To the shore of the god of evening.

ANTISTROPHE 2

The plague burns on, it is pitiless,
Though pallid children laden with death
Lie unwept in the stony ways,
And old gray women by every path                       30
Flock to the strand about the altars
There to strike their breasts and cry
Worship of Phoibos in wailing prayers:
Be kind, God's golden child!

STROPHE 3

There are no swords in this attack by fire,            35
No shields, but we are ringed with cries.
Send the besieger plunging from our homes
Into the vast sea-room of the Atlantic
Or into the waves that foam eastward of Thrace—
For the day ravages what the night spares—             40
Destroy our enemy, lord of the thunder!
Let him be riven by lightning from heaven!

ANTISTROPHE 3

Phoibos Apollo, stretch the sun's bowstring,
That golden cord, until it sing for us,
Flashing arrows in heaven!
                              Artemis,° Huntress,       45
Race with flaring lights upon our mountains!

45 **Artemis** goddess of the hunt and female chastity.

O scarlet god, O golden-banded brow,
O Theban Bacchos in a storm of Maenads,°

*Enter Oedipus, center.*

Whirl upon Death, that all the Undying hate!
Come with blinding torches, come in joy!                    50

## SCENE I°

OEDIPUS:  Is this your prayer? It may be answered. Come,
Listen to me, act as the crisis demands,
And you shall have relief from all these evils.
Until now I was a stranger to this tale,
As I had been a stranger to the crime.                      5
Could I track down the murderer without a clue?
But now, friends,
As one who became a citizen after the murder,
I make this proclamation to all Thebans:
If any man knows by whose hand Laïos, son of Labdakos,      10
Met his death, I direct that man to tell me everything,
No matter what he fears for having so long withheld it.
Let it stand as promised that no further trouble
Will come to him, but he may leave the land in safety.
Moreover: If anyone knows the murderer to be foreign,       15
Let him not keep silent: he shall have his reward from me.
However, if he does conceal it; if any man
Fearing for his friend or for himself disobeys this edict,
Hear what I propose to do:
I solemnly forbid the people of this country,              20
Where power and throne are mine, ever to receive that man
Or speak to him, no matter who he is, or let him
Join in sacrifice, lustration, or in prayer.
I decree that he be driven from every house,
Being, as he is, corruption itself to us: the Delphic       25
Voice of Zeus has pronounced this revelation.
Thus I associate myself with the oracle

---

48 Bacchos . . . Maenads god of wine and his priestesses.    Scene in Greek, *episodos*

And take the side of the murdered king.
As for the criminal, I pray to God—
Whether it be a lurking thief, or one of a number— 30
I pray that that man's life be consumed in evil and
wretchedness.
And as for me, this curse applies no less
If it should turn out that the culprit is my guest here,
Sharing my hearth.
          You have heard the penalty.
I lay it on you now to attend to this 35
For my sake, for Apollo's, for the sick
Sterile city that heaven has abandoned.
Suppose the oracle had given you no command:
Should this defilement go uncleansed for ever?
You should have found the murderer: your king, 40
A noble king, had been destroyed!
          Now I,
Having the power that he held before me,
Having his bed, begetting children there
Upon his wife, as he would have, had he lived—
Their son would have been my children's brother, 45
If Laïos had had luck in fatherhood!
(But surely ill luck rushed upon his reign)—
I say I take the son's part, just as though
I were his son, to press the fight for him
And see it won! I'll find the hand that brought 50
Death to Labdakos' and Polydoros' child,
Heir of Kadmos' and Agenor's line.
And as for those who fail me,
May the gods deny them the fruit of the earth,
Fruit of the womb, and may they rot utterly! 55
Let them be wretched as we are wretched, and worse!
For you, for loyal Thebans, and for all
Who find my actions right, I pray the favor
Of justice, and of all the immortal gods.
CHORAGOS°:   Since I am under oath, my lord, I swear 60
I did not do the murder, I can not name

---

**60 Choragos** leader of the chorus.

The murderer. Might not the oracle
That has ordained the search tell where to find him?
OEDIPUS:   An honest question. But no man in the world
Can make the gods do more than the gods will.                    65
CHORAGOS:   There is one last expedient—
OEDIPUS:                                             Tell me what it is.
Though it seem slight, you must not hold it back.
CHORAGOS:   A lord clairvoyant to the lord Apollo,
As we all know, is the skilled Teiresias.
One might learn much about this from him, Oedipus.               70
OEDIPUS:   I am not wasting time:
Creon spoke of this, and I have sent for him—
Twice, in fact; it is strange that he is not here.
CHORAGOS:   The other matter—that old report—seems useless.
OEDIPUS:   Tell me. I am interested in all reports.                75
CHORAGOS:   The King was said to have been killed by
highwaymen.
OEDIPUS:   I know. But we have no witnesses to that.
CHORAGOS:   If the killer can feel a particle of dread,
Your curse will bring him out of hiding!
OEDIPUS:                                             No.
The man who dared that act will fear no curse.                    80

*Enter the blind seer Teiresias, led by a Page.*

CHORAGOS:   But there is one man who may detect the criminal.
This is Teiresias, this is the holy prophet
In whom, alone of all men, truth was born.
OEDIPUS:   Teiresias: seer: student of mysteries,
Of all that's taught and all that no man tells,                  85
Secrets of Heaven and secrets of the earth:
Blind though you are, you know the city lies
Sick with plague; and from this plague, my lord,
We find that you alone can guard or save us.
Possibly you did not hear the messengers?                        90
Apollo, when we sent to him,
Sent us back word that this great pestilence
Would lift, but only if we established clearly
The identity of those who murdered Laïos.
They must be killed or exiled.

Can you use                                                  95
Birdflight or any art of divination
To purify yourself, and Thebes, and me
From this contagion? We are in your hands.
There is no fairer duty
Than that of helping others in distress.                     100
TEIRESIAS:  How dreadful knowledge of the truth can be
When there's no help in truth! I knew this well,
But made myself forget. I should not have come.
OEDIPUS:  What is troubling you? Why are your eyes so cold?
TEIRESIAS:  Let me go home. Bear your own fate, and I'll     105
Bear mine. It is better so: trust what I say.
OEDIPUS:  What you say is ungracious and unhelpful
To your native country. Do not refuse to speak.
TEIRESIAS:  When it comes to speech, your own is neither
temperate
Nor opportune. I wish to be more prudent.                    110
OEDIPUS:  In God's name, we all beg you—
TEIRESIAS:  You are all ignorant.
No; I will never tell you what I know.
Now it is my misery; then, it would be yours.
OEDIPUS:  What! You do know something, and will not
tell us?
You would betray us all and wreck the State?                 115
TEIRESIAS:  I do not intend to torture myself, or you.
Why persist in asking? You will not persuade me.
OEDIPUS:  What a wicked old man you are! You'd try a stone's
Patience! Out with it! Have you no feeling at all?
TEIRESIAS:  You call me unfeeling. If you could only see      120
The nature of your own feelings . . .
OEDIPUS:                         Why,
Who would not feel as I do? Who could endure
Your arrogance toward the city?
TEIRESIAS:                         What does it matter!
Whether I speak or not; it is bound to come.
OEDIPUS:  Then, if "it" is bound to come, you are bound to
tell me.                                                     125
TEIRESIAS:  No, I will not go on. Rage as you please.

OEDIPUS:   Rage? Why not!
                    And I'll tell you what I think:
You planned it, you had it done, you all but
Killed him with your own hands: if you had eyes,
I'd say the crime was yours, and yours alone.                    130
TEIRESIAS:   So? I charge you, then,
Abide by the proclamation you have made:
From this day forth
Never speak again to these men or to me;
You yourself are the pollution of this country.                    135
OEDIPUS:   You dare say that! Can you possibly think you have
Some way of going free, after such insolence?
TEIRESIAS:   I have gone free. It is the truth sustains me.
OEDIPUS:   Who taught you shamelessness? It was not your
craft.
TEIRESIAS:   You did. You made me speak. I did not want to.                    140
OEDIPUS:   Speak what? Let me hear it again more clearly.
TEIRESIAS:   Was it not clear before? Are you tempting me?
OEDIPUS:   I did not understand it. Say it again.
TEIRESIAS:   I say that you are the murderer whom you seek.
OEDIPUS:   Now twice you have spat out infamy. You'll pay
for it!                    145
TEIRESIAS:   Would you care for more? Do you wish to be really
angry?
OEDIPUS:   Say what you will. Whatever you say is worthless.
TEIRESIAS:   I say you live in hideous shame with those
Most dear to you. You can not see the evil.
OEDIPUS:   It seems you can go on mouthing like this for ever.                    150
TEIRESIAS:   I can, if there is power in truth.
OEDIPUS:                    There is:
But not for you, not for you,
You sightless, witless, senseless, mad old man!
TEIRESIAS:   You are the madman. There is no one here
Who will not curse you soon, as you curse me.                    155
OEDIPUS:   You child of endless night! You can not hurt me
Or any other man who sees the sun.
TEIRESIAS:   True: it is not from me your fate will come.
That lies within Apollo's competence,

As it is his concern.

OEDIPUS:                    Tell me:                                            160
Are you speaking for Creon, or for yourself?

TEIRESIAS:   Creon is no threat. You weave your own doom.

OEDIPUS:   Wealth, power, craft of statesmanship!
Kingly position, everywhere admired!
What savage envy is stored up against these,                          165
If Creon, whom I trusted, Creon my friend,
For this great office which the city once
Put in my hands unsought—if for this power
Creon desires in secret to destroy me!
He has brought this decrepit fortune-teller, this                     170
Collector of dirty pennies, this prophet fraud—
Why, he is no more clairvoyant than I am!
                                                        Tell us:
Has your mystic mummery ever approached the truth?
When that hellcat the Sphinx was performing here,
What help were you to these people?                                   175
Her magic was not for the first man who came along:
It demanded a real exorcist. Your birds—
What good were they? or the gods, for the matter of that?
But I came by,
Oedipus, the simple man, who knows nothing—                           180
I thought it out for myself, no birds helped me!
And this is the man you think you can destroy,
That you may be close to Creon when he's king!
Well, you and your friend Creon, it seems to me,
Will suffer most. If you were not an old man,                         185
You would have paid already for your plot.

CHORAGOS:   We can not see that his words or yours
Have been spoken except in anger, Oedipus,
And of anger we have no need. How can God's will
Be accomplished best? That is what most concerns us.                  190

TEIRESIAS:   You are a king. But where argument's concerned
I am your man, as much a king as you.
I am not your servant, but Apollo's.
I have no need of Creon to speak for me.
Listen to me. You mock my blindness, do you?                          195

But I say that you, with both your eyes, are blind:
You can not see the wretchedness of your life,
Nor in whose house you live, no, nor with whom.
Who are your father and mother? Can you tell me?
You do not even know the blind wrongs                        200
That you have done them, on earth and in the world below.
But the double lash of your parents' curse will whip you
Out of this land some day, with only night
Upon your precious eyes.
Your cries then—where will they not be heard?              205
What fastness of Kithairon° will not echo them?
And that bridal-descant of yours—you'll know it then,
The song they sang when you came here to Thebes
And found your misguided berthing.
All this, and more, that you can not guess at now,         210
Will bring you to yourself among your children.
Be angry, then. Curse Creon. Curse my words.
I tell you, no man that walks upon the earth
Shall be rooted out more horribly than you.

OEDIPUS:  Am I to bear this from him?—Damnation              215
Take you! Out of this place! Out of my sight!

TEIRESIAS:  I would not have come at all if you had not
asked me.

OEDIPUS:  Could I have told that you'd talk nonsense, that
You'd come here to make a fool of yourself, and of me?

TEIRESIAS:  A fool? Your parents thought me sane enough.     220

OEDIPUS:  My parents again!—Wait: who were my parents?

TEIRESIAS:  This day will give you a father, and break your
heart.

OEDIPUS:  Your infantile riddles! Your damned abracadabra!

TEIRESIAS:  You were a great man once at solving riddles.

OEDIPUS:  Mock me with that if you like; you will find it true.  225

TEIRESIAS:  It was true enough. It brought about your ruin.

OEDIPUS:  But if it saved this town?

TEIRESIAS (*to the Page*):  Boy, give me your hand.

OEDIPUS:  Yes, boy; lead him away.

---

206 **Kithairon** a mountain near Thebes.

—While you are here
We can do nothing. Go; leave us in peace.

TEIRESIAS: I will go when I have said what I have to say.    230
How can you hurt me? And I tell you again:
The man you have been looking for all this time,
The damned man, the murderer of Laïos,
That man is in Thebes. To your mind he is foreignborn,
But it will soon be shown that he is a Theban,    235
A revelation that will fail to please.
                                    A blind man,
Who has his eyes now; a penniless man, who is rich now;
And he will go tapping the strange earth with his staff;
To the children with whom he lives now he will be
Brother and father—the very same; to her    240
Who bore him, son and husband—the very same
Who came to his father's bed, wet with his father's blood.
Enough. Go think that over.
If later you find error in what I have said,
You may say that I have no skill in prophecy.    245

*Exit Teiresias, led by his Page.*
*Oedipus goes into the palace.*

# *Ode*° *I*

### STROPHE 1

CHORUS:    The Delphic stone of prophecies
            Remembers ancient regicide
            And a still bloody hand.
            That killer's hour of flight has come.
            He must be stronger than riderless    5
            Coursers of untiring wind,
            For the son of Zeus° armed with his father's thunder
            Leaps in lightning after him;
            And the Furies° follow him, the sad Furies.

---

Ode also known as *stasimon*, a choral interlude.   **7 son of Zeus** Apollo.   **9 Furies** three female spirits who punished evildoers.

## ANTISTROPHE 1

Holy Parnassos' peak of snow 10
Flashes and blinds that secret man,
That all shall hunt him down:
Though he may roam the forest shade
Like a bull gone wild from pasture
To rage through glooms of stone. 15
Doom comes down on him; flight will not avail him;
For the world's heart calls him desolate,
And the immortal Furies follow, for ever follow.

## STROPHE 2

But now a wilder thing is heard
From the old man skilled at hearing Fate in the wingbeat 20
of a bird.
Bewildered as a blown bird, my soul hovers and can not find
Foothold in this debate, or any reason or rest of mind.
But no man ever brought—none can bring
Proof of strife between Thebes' royal house,
Labdakos' line,° and the son of Polybos;° 25
And never until now has any man brought word
Of Laïos' dark death staining Oedipus the King.

## ANTISTROPHE 2

Divine Zeus and Apollo hold
Perfect intelligence alone of all tales ever told;
And well though this diviner works, he works in his own night; 30
No man can judge that rough unknown or trust in second sight,
For wisdom changes hands among the wise.
Shall I believe my great lord criminal
At a raging word that a blind old man let fall?
I saw him, when the carrion woman faced him of old, 35
Prove his heroic mind! These evil words are lies.

---

25 **Labdakos' line** descendants of Laïos.  **Polybos** king of Corinth who adopted Oedipus.

## SCENE *II*

CREON:  Men of Thebes:
I am told that heavy accusations
Have been brought against me by King Oedipus.
I am not the kind of man to bear this tamely.
If in these present difficulties                                5
He holds me accountable for any harm to him
Through anything I have said or done—why, then,
I do not value life in this dishonor.
It is not as though this rumor touched upon
Some private indiscretion. The matter is grave.               10
The fact is that I am being called disloyal
To the State, to my fellow citizens, to my friends.
CHORAGOS:  He may have spoken in anger, not from his mind.
CREON:  But did you not hear him say I was the one
Who seduced the old prophet into lying?                       15
CHORAGOS:  The thing was said; I do not know how seriously.
CREON:  But you were watching him! Were his eyes steady?
Did he look like a man in his right mind?
CHORAGOS:                                    I do not know.
I can not judge the behavior of great men.
But here is the King himself.

*Enter Oedipus.*

OEDIPUS:                         So you dared come back.       20
Why? How brazen of you to come to my house,
You murderer!
              Do you think I do not know
That you plotted to kill me, plotted to steal my throne?
Tell me, in God's name: am I coward, a fool,
That you should dream you could accomplish this?              25
A fool who could not see your slippery game?
A coward, not to fight back when I saw it?
You are the fool, Creon, are you not? hoping
Without support or friends to get a throne?
Thrones may be won or bought: you could do neither.           30
CREON:  Now listen to me. You have talked; let me talk, too.

You can not judge unless you know the facts.

OEDIPUS:   You speak well: there is one fact; but I find it hard
To learn from the deadliest enemy I have.

CREON:   That above all I must dispute with you.                    35

OEDIPUS:   That above all I will not hear you deny.

CREON:   If you think there is anything good in being stubborn
Against all reason, then I say you are wrong.

OEDIPUS:   If you think a man can sin against his own kind
And not be punished for it, I say you are mad.                      40

CREON:   I agree. But tell me: what have I done to you?

OEDIPUS:   You advised me to send for that wizard, did you not?

CREON:   I did. I should do it again.

OEDIPUS:                                 Very well. Now tell me:
How long has it been since Laïos—

CREON:                                 What of Laïos?

OEDIPUS:   Since he vanished in that onset by the road?             45

CREON:   It was long ago, a long time.

OEDIPUS:                                 And this prophet,
Was he practicing here then?

CREON:                                 He was; and with honor, as now.

OEDIPUS:   Did he speak of me at that time?

CREON:                                 He never did;
At least, not when I was present.

OEDIPUS:                                 But . . . the enquiry?
I suppose you held one?

CREON:                                 We did, but we learned nothing.   50

OEDIPUS:   Why did the prophet not speak against me then?

CREON:   I do not know; and I am the kind of man
Who holds his tongue when he has no facts to go on.

OEDIPUS:   There's one fact that you know, and you could tell it.

CREON:   What fact is that? If I know it, you shall have it.        55

OEDIPUS:   If he were not involved with you, he could not say
That it was I who murdered Laïos.

CREON:   If he says that, you are the one that knows it!—
But now it is my turn to question you.

OEDIPUS:   Put your questions. I am no murderer.                    60

CREON:   First then: You married my sister?

OEDIPUS:                                 I married your sister.

CREON:    And you rule the kingdom equally with her?
OEDIPUS:    Everything that she wants she has from me.
CREON:    And I am the third, equal to both of you?
OEDIPUS:    That is why I call you a bad friend.                    65
CREON:    No. Reason it out, as I have done.
   Think of this first: Would any sane man prefer
   Power, with all a king's anxieties,
   To that same power and the grace of sleep?
   Certainly not I.                                              70
   I have never longed for the king's power—only his rights.
   Would any wise man differ from me in this?
   As matters stand, I have my way in everything
   With your consent, and no responsibilities.
   If I were king, I should be a slave to policy.                75
   How could I desire a scepter more
   Than what is now mine—untroubled influence?
   No, I have not gone mad; I need no honors,
   Except those with the perquisites I have now.
   I am welcome everywhere; every man salutes me,               80
   And those who want your favor seek my ear,
   Since I know how to manage what they ask.
   Should I exchange this ease for that anxiety?
   Besides, no sober mind is treasonable.
   I hate anarchy                                                85
   And never would deal with any man who likes it.
   Test what I have said. Go to the priestess
   At Delphi, ask if I quoted her correctly.
   And as for this other thing: if I am found
   Guilty of treason with Teiresias,                            90
   Then sentence me to death! You have my word
   It is a sentence I should cast my vote for—
   But not without evidence!
                        You do wrong
   When you take good men for bad, bad men for good.
   A true friend thrown aside—why, life itself                  95
   Is not more precious!
                        In time you will know this well:
   For time, and time alone, will show the just man,

Though scoundrels are discovered in a day.
CHORAGOS:   This is well said, and a prudent man would
ponder it.
Judgments too quickly formed are dangerous.                     100
OEDIPUS:   But is he not quick in his duplicity?
And shall I not be quick to parry him?
Would you have me stand still, hold my peace, and let
This man win everything, through my inaction?
CREON:   And you want—what is it, then? To banish me?         105
OEDIPUS:   No, not exile. It is your death I want,
So that all the world may see what treason means.
CREON:   You will persist, then? You will not believe me?
OEDIPUS:   How can I believe you?
CREON:                                   Then you are a fool.
OEDIPUS:   To save myself?
CREON:                              In justice, think of me.       110
OEDIPUS:   You are evil incarnate.
CREON:                                    But suppose that you are
wrong?
OEDIPUS:   Still I must rule.
CREON:                              But not if you rule badly.
OEDIPUS:   O city, city!
CREON:                       It is my city, too!
CHORAGOS:   Now, my lords, be still. I see the Queen,
Iocastê, coming from her palace chambers;                       115
And it is time she came, for the sake of you both.
This dreadful quarrel can be resolved through her.

*Enter Iocastê.*

IOCASTÊ:   Poor foolish men, what wicked din is this?
With Thebes sick to death, is it not shameful
That you should rake some private quarrel up?                   120
(*To Oedipus.*) Come into the house.
                              —And you, Creon,
go now:
Let us have no more of this tumult over nothing.
CREON:   Nothing? No, sister: what your husband plans for me
Is one of two great evils: exile or death.

OEDIPUS:  He is right.

                  Why, woman, I have caught him squarely   125
  Plotting against my life.

CREON:               No! Let me die
  Accurst if ever I have wished you harm!

IOCASTÊ:  Ah, believe it, Oedipus!
  In the name of the gods, respect this oath of his
  For my sake, for the sake of these people here!   130

STROPHE 1

CHORAGOS:  Open your mind to her, my lord. Be ruled by her, I
  beg you!

OEDIPUS:  What would you have me do?

CHORAGOS:  Respect Creon's word. He has never spoken like
  a fool,
  And now he has sworn an oath.

OEDIPUS:  You know what you ask?

CHORAGOS:              I do.

OEDIPUS:                 Speak on, then.

CHORAGOS:  A friend so sworn should not be baited so,   135
  In blind malice, and without final proof.

OEDIPUS:  You are aware, I hope, that what you say
  Means death for me, or exile at the least.

STROPHE 2

CHORAGOS:  No, I swear by Helios, first in Heaven!
  May I die friendless and accurst,   140
  The worst of deaths, if ever I meant that!
  It is the withering fields
  That hurt my sick heart:
  Must we bear all these ills,
  And now your bad blood as well?   145

OEDIPUS:  Then let him go. And let me die, if I must,
  Or be driven by him in shame from the land of Thebes.
  It is your unhappiness, and not his talk,
  That touches me.

As for him—
Wherever he goes, hatred will follow him.                    150
CREON:   Ugly in yielding, as you were ugly in rage!
   Natures like yours chiefly torment themselves.
OEDIPUS:   Can you not go? Can you not leave me?
CREON:                                    I can.
   You do not know me; but the city knows me,
   And in its eyes I am just, if not in yours.                155

                                        *Exit Creon.*

ANTISTROPHE 1

CHORAGOS:   Lady Iocastê, did you not ask the King to go to his
   chambers?
IOCASTÊ:   First tell me what has happened.
CHORAGOS:   There was suspicion without evidence; yet it rankled
   As even false charges will.
IOCASTÊ:   On both sides?
CHORAGOS:               On both.
IOCASTÊ:                                But what was said?
CHORAGOS:   Oh let it rest, let it be done with!                160
   Have we not suffered enough?
OEDIPUS:   You see to what your decency has brought you:
   You have made difficulties where my heart saw none.

ANTISTROPHE 2

CHORAGOS:   Oedipus, it is not once only I have told you—
   You must know I should count myself unwise            165
   To the point of madness, should I now forsake you—
   You, under whose hand,
   In the storm of another time,
   Our dear land sailed out free.
   But now stand fast at the helm!                        170
IOCASTÊ:   In God's name, Oedipus, inform your wife as well:
   Why are you so set in this hard anger?
OEDIPUS:   I will tell you, for none of these men deserves
   My confidence as you do. It is Creon's work,

His treachery, his plotting against me.                                    175
IOCASTÊ:   Go on, if you can make this clear to me.
OEDIPUS:   He charges me with the murder of Laïos.
IOCASTÊ:   Has he some knowledge? Or does he speak from
hearsay?
OEDIPUS:   He would not commit himself to such a charge,
But he has brought in that damnable soothsayer                             180
To tell his story.
IOCASTÊ:                Set your mind at rest.
If it is a question of soothsayers, I tell you
That you will find no man whose craft gives knowledge
Of the unknowable.
                          Here is my proof:
An oracle was reported to Laïos once                                       185
(I will not say from Phoibos himself, but from
His appointed ministers, at any rate)
That his doom would be death at the hands of his own son—
His son, born of his flesh and of mine!
Now, you remember the story: Laïos was killed                              190
By marauding strangers where three highways meet;
But his child had not been three days in this world
Before the King had pierced the baby's ankles
And left him to die on a lonely mountainside.
Thus, Apollo never caused that child                                       195
To kill his father, and it was not Laïos' fate
To die at the hands of his son, as he had feared.
This is what prophets and prophecies are worth!
Have no dread of them.
                          It is God himself
Who can show us what he wills, in his own way.                             200
OEDIPUS:   How strange a shadowy memory crossed my mind,
Just now while you were speaking; it chilled my heart.
IOCASTÊ:   What do you mean? What memory do you speak of?
OEDIPUS:   If I understand you, Laïos was killed
At a place where three roads meet.
IOCASTÊ:                              So it was said;                      205
We have no later story.
OEDIPUS:                    Where did it happen?

IOCASTÊ:   Phokis, it is called: at a place where the Theban Way
    Divides into the roads toward Delphi and Daulia.
OEDIPUS:   When?
IOCASTÊ:   We had the news not long before you came
    And proved the right to your succession here.              210
OEDIPUS:   Ah, what net has God been weaving for me?
IOCASTÊ:   Oedipus! Why does this trouble you?
OEDIPUS:                             Do not ask
    me yet.
    First, tell me how Laïos looked, and tell me
    How old he was.
IOCASTÊ:             He was tall, his hair just touched
    With white; his form was not unlike your own.        215
OEDIPUS:   I think that I myself may be accurst
    By my own ignorant edict.
IOCASTÊ:             You speak strangely.
    It makes me tremble to look at you, my King.
OEDIPUS:   I am not sure that the blind man can not see.
    But I should know better if you were to tell me—    220
IOCASTÊ:   Anything—though I dread to hear you ask it.
OEDIPUS:   Was the King lightly escorted, or did he ride
    With a large company, as a ruler should?
IOCASTÊ:   There were five men with him in all: one was a
    herald,
    And a single chariot, which he was driving.        225
OEDIPUS:   Alas, that makes it plain enough!
                               But who—
    Who told you how it happened?
IOCASTÊ:                A household servant,
    The only one to escape.
OEDIPUS:   And is he still
    A servant of ours?
IOCASTÊ:            No; for when he came back at last
    And found you enthroned in the place of the dead king,    230
    He came to me, touched my hand with his, and begged
    That I would send him away to the frontier district
    Where only the shepherds go—
    As far away from the city as I could send him.

I granted his prayer; for although the man was a slave,                235
He had earned more than this favor at my hands.
OEDIPUS:    Can he be called back quickly?
IOCASTÊ:                              Easily.
    But why?
OEDIPUS:    I have taken too much upon myself
Without enquiry; therefore I wish to consult him.
IOCASTÊ:    Then he shall come.
                        But am I not one also                         240
To whom you might confide these fears of yours?
OEDIPUS:    That is your right; it will not be denied you,
    Now least of all; for I have reached a pitch
    Of wild foreboding. Is there anyone
    To whom I should sooner speak?                                    245
    Polybos of Corinth is my father.
    My mother is a Dorian: Meropê.
    I grew up chief among the men of Corinth
    Until a strange thing happened—
    Not worth my passion, it may be, but strange.                    250
    At a feast, a drunken man maundering in his cups
    Cries out that I am not my father's son!
    I contained myself that night, though I felt anger
    And a sinking heart. The next day I visited
    My father and mother, and questioned them. They stormed,         255
    Calling it all the slanderous rant of a fool;
    And this relieved me. Yet the suspicion
    Remained always aching in my mind;
    I knew there was talk; I could not rest;
    And finally, saying nothing to my parents,                       260
    I went to the shrine at Delphi.
    The god dismissed my question without reply;
    He spoke of other things.
                        Some were clear,
    Full of wretchedness, dreadful, unbearable:
    As, that I should lie with my own mother, breed                  265
    Children from whom all men would turn their eyes;
    And that I should be my father's murderer.
    I heard all this, and fled. And from that day

Corinth to me was only in the stars
Descending in that quarter of the sky, 270
As I wandered farther and farther on my way
To a land where I should never see the evil
Sung by the oracle. And I came to this country
Where, so you say, King Laïos was killed.
I will tell you all that happened there, my lady. 275
There were three highways
Coming together at a place I passed;
And there a herald came towards me, and a chariot
Drawn by horses, with a man such as you describe
Seated in it. The groom leading the horses 280
Forced me off the road at his lord's command;
But as this charioteer lurched over towards me
I struck him in my rage. The old man saw me
And brought his double goad down upon my head
As I came abreast.

            He was paid back, and more! 285
Swinging my club in this right hand I knocked him
Out of his car, and he rolled on the ground.

                           I killed him.
I killed them all.
Now if that stranger and Laïos were—kin,
Where is a man more miserable than I? 290
More hated by the gods? Citizen and alien alike
Must never shelter me or speak to me—
I must be shunned by all.

                  And I myself
Pronounced this malediction upon myself!
Think of it: I have touched you with these hands, 295
These hands that killed your husband. What defilement!
Am I all evil, then? It must be so,
Since I must flee from Thebes, yet never again
See my own countrymen, my own country,
For fear of joining my mother in marriage 300
And killing Polybos, my father.

                       Ah,
If I was created so, born to this fate,

Who could deny the savagery of God?
O holy majesty of heavenly powers!
May I never see that day! Never! 305
Rather let me vanish from the race of men
Than know the abomination destined me!

CHORAGOS: We too, my lord, have felt dismay at this.
But there is hope: you have yet to hear the shepherd.

OEDIPUS: Indeed, I fear no other hope is left me. 310

IOCASTÊ: What do you hope from him when he
comes?

OEDIPUS: This much:
If his account of the murder tallies with yours,
Then I am cleared.

IOCASTÊ: What was it that I said
Of such importance?

OEDIPUS: Why, "marauders," you said,
Killed the King, according to this man's story. 315
If he maintains that still, if there were several,
Clearly the guilt is not mine: I was alone.
But if he says one man, singlehanded, did it,
Then the evidence all points to me.

IOCASTÊ: You may be sure that he said there were several; 320
And can he call back that story now? He cannot.
The whole city heard it as plainly as I.
But suppose he alters some detail of it:
He can not ever show that Laïos' death
Fulfilled the oracle: for Apollo said 325
My child was doomed to kill him; and my child—
Poor baby!—it was my child that died first.
No. From now on, where oracles are concerned,
I would not waste a second thought on any.

OEDIPUS: You may be right.
But come: let someone go 330
For the shepherd at once. This matter must be settled.

IOCASTÊ: I will send for him.
I would not wish to cross you in anything,
And surely not in this.—Let us go in.

                    *Exeunt into the palace.*

## ODE II

### STROPHE 1

CHORUS:   Let me be reverent in the ways of right,
    Lowly the paths I journey on;
    Let all my words and actions keep
    The laws of the pure universe
    From highest Heaven handed down.    5
    For Heaven is their bright nurse,
    Those generations of the realms of light;
    Ah, never of mortal kind were they begot,
    Nor are they slaves of memory, lost in sleep:
    Their Father is greater than Time, and ages not.    10

### ANTISTROPHE 1

    The tyrant is a child of Pride
    Who drinks from his great sickening cup
    Recklessness and vanity,
    Until from his high crest headlong
    He plummets to the dust of hope.    15
    That strong man is not strong.
    But let no fair ambition be denied;
    May God protect the wrestler for the State
    In government, in comely policy,
    Who will fear God, and on His ordinance wait.    20

### STROPHE 2

    Haughtiness and the high hand of disdain
    Tempt and outrage God's holy law;
    And any mortal who dares hold
    No immortal Power in awe
    Will be caught up in a net of pain:    25
    The price for which his levity is sold.
    Let each man take due earnings, then,
    And keep his hands from holy things,
    And from blasphemy stand apart—
    Else the crackling blast of heaven    30
    Blows on his head, and on his desperate heart;

Though fools will honor impious men,
In their cities no tragic poet sings.

### ANTISTROPHE 2

Shall we lose faith in Delphi's obscurities,
We who have heard the world's core                                    35
Discredited, and the sacred wood
Of Zeus at Elis praised no more?
The deeds and the strange prophecies
Must make a pattern yet to be understood.
Zeus, if indeed you are lord of all,                                   40
Throned in light over night and day,
Mirror this in your endless mind:
Our masters call the oracle
Words on the wind, and the Delphic vision blind!
Their hearts no longer know Apollo,                                    45
And reverence for the gods has died away.

## SCENE III

*Enter Iocastê.*

IOCASTÊ:   Princes of Thebes, it has occurred to me
To visit the altars of the gods, bearing
These branches as a suppliant, and this incense.
Our King is not himself: his noble soul
Is overwrought with fantasies of dread,                                5
Else he would consider
The new prophecies in the light of the old.
He will listen to any voice that speaks disaster,
And my advice goes for nothing.

*She approaches the altar, right.*

                              To you, then, Apollo,
Lycean lord, since you are nearest, I turn in prayer.                  10
Receive these offerings, and grant us deliverance
From defilement. Our hearts are heavy with fear
When we see our leader distracted, as helpless sailors

Are terrified by the confusion of their helmsman.

*Enter Messenger.*

MESSENGER:   Friends, no doubt you can direct me:                    15
Where shall I find the house of Oedipus,
Or, better still, where is the King himself?
CHORAGOS:   It is this very place, stranger; he is inside.
This is his wife and mother of his children.
MESSENGER:   I wish her happiness in a happy house,                 20
Blest in all the fulfillment of her marriage.
IOCASTÊ:   I wish as much for you: your courtesy
Deserves a like good fortune. But now, tell me:
Why have you come? What have you to say to us?
MESSENGER:   Good news, my lady, for your house and your
husband.                                                            25
IOCASTÊ:   What news? Who sent you here?
MESSENGER:                               I am from Corinth.
The news I bring ought to mean joy for you,
Though it may be you will find some grief in it.
IOCASTÊ:   What is it? How can it touch us in both ways?
MESSENGER:   The word is that the people of the Isthmus            30
Intend to call Oedipus to be their king.
IOCASTÊ:   But old King Polybos—is he not reigning still?
MESSENGER:   No. Death holds him in his sepulchre.
IOCASTÊ:   What are you saying? Polybos is dead?
MESSENGER:   If I am not telling the truth, may I die myself.       35
IOCASTÊ (*to a Maidservant*):   Go in, go quickly; tell this to your
master.
O riddlers of God's will, where are you now!
This was the man whom Oedipus, long ago,
Feared so, fled so, in dread of destroying him—
But it was another fate by which he died.                           40

*Enter Oedipus, center.*

OEDIPUS:   Dearest Iocastê, why have you sent for me?
IOCASTÊ:   Listen to what this man says, and then tell me
What has become of the solemn prophecies.
OEDIPUS:   Who is this man? What is his news for me?

IOCASTÊ:  He has come from Corinth to announce your father's
   death!                                                          45
OEDIPUS:  Is it true, stranger? Tell me in your own words.
MESSENGER:  I can not say it more clearly: the King is dead.
OEDIPUS:  Was it by treason? Or by an attack of illness?
MESSENGER:  A little thing brings old men to their rest.
OEDIPUS:  It was sickness, then?
MESSENGER:  Yes, and his many years.                               50
OEDIPUS:  Ah!
   Why should a man respect the Pythian hearth,° or
   Give heed to the birds that jangle above his head?
   They prophesied that I should kill Polybos,
   Kill my own father; but he is dead and buried,                  55
   And I am here—I never touched him, never,
   Unless he died of grief for my departure,
   And thus, in a sense, through me. No. Polybos
   Has packed the oracles off with him underground.
   They are empty words.
IOCASTÊ:  Had I not told you so?                                    60
OEDIPUS:  You had; it was my faint heart that betrayed me
IOCASTÊ:  From now on never think of those things again.
OEDIPUS:  And yet—must I not fear my mother's bed?
IOCASTÊ:  Why should anyone in this world be afraid,
   Since Fate rules us and nothing can be foreseen?                65
   A man should live only for the present day.
   Have no more fear of sleeping with your mother:
   How many men, in dreams, have lain with their mothers!
   No reasonable man is troubled by such things.
OEDIPUS:  That is true; only—                                      70
   If only my mother were not still alive!
   But she is alive. I can not help my dread.
IOCASTÊ:  Yet this news of your father's death is wonderful.
OEDIPUS:  Wonderful. But I fear the living woman.
MESSENGER:  Tell me, who is this woman that you fear?              75
OEDIPUS:  It is Meropê, man; the wife of King Polybos.
MESSENGER:  Meropê? Why should you be afraid of her?

---

52 **Pythian hearth** where burnt offerings were made at Delphi.

OEDIPUS:   An oracle of the gods, a dreadful saying.
MESSENGER:   Can you tell me about it or are you sworn to
      silence?
OEDIPUS:   I can tell you, and I will.                                    80
      Apollo said through his prophet that I was the man
      Who should marry his own mother, shed his father's blood
      With his own hands. And so, for all these years
      I have kept clear of Corinth, and no harm has come—
      Though it would have been sweet to see my parents again.   85
MESSENGER:   And is this the fear that drove you out of
      Corinth?
OEDIPUS:   Would you have me kill my father?
MESSENGER:                                            As for that
      You must be reassured by the news I gave you.
OEDIPUS:   If you could reassure me, I would reward you.
MESSENGER:   I had that in mind, I will confess: I thought    90
      I could count on you when you returned to Corinth.
OEDIPUS:   No: I will never go near my parents again.
MESSENGER:   Ah, son, you still do not know what you are
      doing—
OEDIPUS:   What do you mean? In the name of God tell me!
MESSENGER:   —If these are your reasons for not going home.    95
OEDIPUS:   I tell you, I fear the oracle may come true.
MESSENGER:   And guilt may come upon you through your
      parents?
OEDIPUS:   That is the dread that is always in my heart.
MESSENGER:   Can you not see that all your fears are
      groundless?
OEDIPUS:   How can you say that? They are my parents, surely?    100
MESSENGER:   Polybos was not your father.
OEDIPUS:                                      Not my father?
MESSENGER:   No more your father than the man speaking to
      you.
OEDIPUS:   But you are nothing to me!
MESSENGER:                                Neither was he.
OEDIPUS:   Then why did he call me son?
MESSENGER:                                  I will tell you:
      Long ago he had you from my hands, as a gift.              105

OEDIPUS:   Then how could he love me so, if I was not his?

MESSENGER:   He had no children, and his heart turned to you.

OEDIPUS:   What of you? Did you buy me? Did you find me by chance?

MESSENGER:   I came upon you in the crooked pass of Kithairon.

OEDIPUS:   And what were you doing there?

MESSENGER:                                   Tending my flocks.          110

OEDIPUS:   A wandering shepherd?

MESSENGER:                          But your savior, son, that day.

OEDIPUS:   From what did you save me?

MESSENGER:                                   Your ankles should tell you that.

OEDIPUS:   Ah, stranger, why do you speak of that childhood pain?

MESSENGER:   I cut the bonds that tied your ankles together.

OEDIPUS:   I have had the mark as long as I can remember.          115

MESSENGER:   That was why you were given the name you bear.

OEDIPUS:   God! Was it my father or my mother who did it? Tell me!

MESSENGER:   I do not know. The man who gave you to me Can tell you better than I.          120

OEDIPUS:   It was not you that found me, but another?

MESSENGER:   It was another shepherd gave you to me.

OEDIPUS:   Who was he? Can you tell me who he was?

MESSENGER:   I think he was said to be one of Laïos' people.

OEDIPUS:   You mean the Laïos who was king here years ago?          125

MESSENGER:   Yes; King Laïos; and the man was one of his herdsmen.

OEDIPUS:   Is he still alive? Can I see him?

MESSENGER:                                   These men here Know best about such things.

OEDIPUS:                          Does anyone here Know this shepherd that he is talking about? Have you seen him in the fields, or in the town?          130 If you have, tell me. It is time things were made plain.

CHORAGOS:   I think the man he means is that same shepherd

You have already asked to see. Iocastê perhaps
Could tell you something.
OEDIPUS:                    Do you know anything
About him, Lady? Is he the man we have summoned?          135
Is that the man this shepherd means?
IOCASTÊ:                           Why think of him?
Forget this herdsman. Forget it all.
This talk is a waste of time.
OEDIPUS:   How can you say that,
When the clues to my true birth are in my hands?
IOCASTÊ:   For God's love, let us have no more questioning!     140
Is your life nothing to you?
My own is pain enough for me to bear.
OEDIPUS:   You need not worry. Suppose my mother a slave,
And born of slaves: no baseness can touch you.
IOCASTÊ:   Listen to me, I beg you: do not do this thing!       145
OEDIPUS:   I will not listen; the truth must be made known.
IOCASTÊ:   Everything that I say is for your own good!
OEDIPUS:                                          My own
good
Snaps my patience, then; I want none of it.
IOCASTÊ:   You are fatally wrong! May you never learn who
you are!
OEDIPUS:   Go, one of you, and bring the shepherd here.        150
Let us leave this woman to brag of her royal name.
IOCASTÊ:   Ah, miserable!
That is the only word I have for you now.
That is the only word I can ever have.

*Exit into the palace.*

CHORAGOS:   Why has she left us, Oedipus? Why has she gone    155
In such a passion of sorrow? I fear this silence:
Something dreadful may come of it.
OEDIPUS:                            Let it come!
However base my birth, I must know about it.
The Queen, like a woman, is perhaps ashamed
To think of my low origin. But I                               160
Am a child of Luck; I can not be dishonored.

Luck is my mother; the passing months, my brothers,
Have seen me rich and poor.
                              If this is so,
How could I wish that I were someone else?
How could I not be glad to know my birth?                    165


## ODE III

### STROPHE

CHORUS:   If ever the coming time were known
          To my heart's pondering,
          Kithairon, now by Heaven I see the torches
          At the festival of the next full moon,
          And see the dance, and hear the choir sing          5
          A grace to your gentle shade:
          Mountain where Oedipus was found,
          O mountain guard of a noble race!
          May the god who heals us lend his aid,
          And let that glory come to pass                     10
          For our king's cradling-ground.


### ANTISTROPHE

          Of the nymphs that flower beyond the years,
          Who bore you, royal child,
          To Pan of the hills or the timberline Apollo,
          Cold in delight where the upland clears,            15
          Or Hermês for whom Kyllenê's° heights are piled?
          Or flushed as evening cloud,
          Great Dionysos, roamer of mountains,
          He—was it he who found you there,
          And caught you up in his own proud                  20
          Arms from the sweet god-ravisher
          Who laughed by the Muses' fountains?


16 **Kyllenê** a sacred mountain of Hermês, the messenger of the gods.

## SCENE IV

OEDIPUS:   Sirs: though I do not know the man,
I think I see him coming, this shepherd we want:
He is old, like our friend here, and the men
Bringing him seem to be servants of my house.
But you can tell, if you have ever seen him.                                5

*Enter Shepherd escorted by servants.*

CHORAGOS:   I know him, he was Laïos' man. You can trust
him.
OEDIPUS:   Tell me first, you from Corinth: is this the shepherd
We were discussing?
MESSENGER:              This is the very man.
OEDIPUS (*to Shepherd*):   Come here. No, look at me. You must
answer
Everything I ask.—You belonged to Laïos?                                10
SHEPHERD:   Yes: born his slave, brought up in his house.
OEDIPUS:   Tell me: what kind of work did you do for him?
SHEPHERD:   I was a shepherd of his, most of my life.
OEDIPUS:   Where mainly did you go for pasturage?
SHEPHERD:   Sometimes Kithairon, sometimes the hills near-by.   15
OEDIPUS:   Do you remember ever seeing this man out there?
SHEPHERD:   What would he be doing there? This man?
OEDIPUS:   This man standing here. Have you ever seen him
before?
SHEPHERD:   No. At least, not to my recollection.
MESSENGER:   And that is not strange, my lord. But I'll refresh   20
His memory: he must remember when we two
Spent three whole seasons together, March to September,
On Kithairon or thereabouts. He had two flocks;
I had one. Each autumn I'd drive mine home
And he would go back with his to Laïos' sheepfold.—              25
Is this not true, just as I have described it?
SHEPHERD:   True, yes; but it was all so long ago.
MESSENGER:   Well, then: do you remember, back in those days
That you gave me a baby boy to bring up as my own?
SHEPHERD:   What if I did? What are you trying to say?             30

MESSENGER:   King Oedipus was once that little child.

SHEPHERD:   Damn you, hold your tongue!

OEDIPUS:                                       No more of that!
It is your tongue needs watching, not this man's.

SHEPHERD:   My King, my Master, what is it I have done wrong?

OEDIPUS:   You have not answered his question about the boy.    35

SHEPHERD:   He does not know . . . He is only making
trouble . . .

OEDIPUS:   Come, speak plainly, or it will go hard with you.

SHEPHERD:   In God's name, do not torture an old man!

OEDIPUS:   Come here, one of you; bind his arms behind him.

SHEPHERD:   Unhappy king! What more do you wish to learn?    40

OEDIPUS:   Did you give this man the child he speaks of?

SHEPHERD:   I did.
And I would to God I had died that very day.

OEDIPUS:   You will die now unless you speak the truth.

SHEPHERD:   Yet if I speak the truth, I am worse than dead.

OEDIPUS:   Very well; since you insist upon delaying—    45

SHEPHERD:   No! I have told you already that I gave him the
boy.

OEDIPUS:   Where did you get him? From your house? From somewhere else?

SHEPHERD:   Not from mine, no. A man gave him to me.

OEDIPUS:   Is that man here? Do you know whose slave he was?

SHEPHERD:   For God's love, my King, do not ask me any more!    50

OEDIPUS:   You are a dead man if I have to ask you again.

SHEPHERD:   Then . . . Then the child was from the palace of
Laïos.

OEDIPUS:   A slave child? or a child of his own line?

SHEPHERD:   Ah, I am on the brink of dreadful speech!

OEDIPUS:   And I of dreadful hearing. Yet I must hear.    55

SHEPHERD:   If you must be told, then . . .
                                       They said it was
Laïos' child;
But it is your wife who can tell you about that.

OEDIPUS:   My wife!—Did she give it to you?

SHEPHERD:                                       My lord, she did.

OEDIPUS:   Do you know why?

SHEPHERD:                     I was told to get rid of it.

OEDIPUS:   An unspeakable mother!
SHEPHERD:                                There had been
     prophecies . . .                                                        60
OEDIPUS:   Tell me.
SHEPHERD:   It was said that the boy would kill his own father.
OEDIPUS:   Then why did you give him over to this old man?
SHEPHERD:   I pitied the baby, my King,
     And I thought that this man would take him far away        65
     To his own country.
     He saved him—but for what a fate!
     For if you are what this man says you are,
     No man living is more wretched than Oedipus.
OEDIPUS:   Ah God!
     It was true!
     All the prophecies!
     —Now,                                                                  70
     O Light, may I look on you for the last time!
     I, Oedipus,
     Oedipus, damned in his birth, in his marriage damned,
     Damned in the blood he shed with his own hand!

                                        *He rushes into the palace.*

## ODE IV

### STROPHE 1

CHORUS:   Alas for the seed of men.
     What measure shall I give these generations
     That breathe on the void and are void
     And exist and do not exist?
     Who bears more weight of joy                                    5
     Than mass of sunlight shifting in images,
     Or who shall make his thought stay on
     That down time drifts away?
     Your splendor is all fallen.
     O naked brow of wrath and tears,                               10
     O change of Oedipus!
     I who saw your days call no man blest—
     Your great days like ghosts gone.

## ANTISTROPHE 1

That mind was a strong bow.
Deep, how deep you drew it then, hard archer,                    15
At a dim fearful range,
And brought dear glory down!
You overcame the stranger—
The virgin with her hooking lion claws—
And though death sang, stood like a tower                        20
To make pale Thebes take heart.
Fortress against our sorrow!
True king, giver of laws,
Majestic Oedipus!
No prince in Thebes had ever such renown,                        25
No prince won such grace of power.

## STROPHE 2

And now of all men ever known
Most pitiful is this man's story:
His fortunes are most changed, his state
Fallen to a low slave's                                          30
Ground under bitter fate.
O Oedipus, most royal one!
The great door that expelled you to the light
Gave at night—ah, gave night to your glory:
As to the father, to the fathering son.                          35
All understood too late.
How could that queen whom Laïos won,
The garden that he harrowed at his height,
Be silent when that act was done?

## ANTISTROPHE 2

But all eyes fail before time's eye,                             40
All actions come to justice there.
Though never willed, though far down the deep past,
Your bed, your dread sirings,
Are brought to book at last.
Child by Laïos doomed to die,                                    45

Then doomed to lose that fortunate little death,
Would God you never took breath in this air
That with my wailing lips I take to cry:
For I weep the world's outcast.
I was blind, and now I can tell why:                              50
Asleep, for you had given ease of breath
To Thebes, while the false years went by.

## *ÉXODOS*°

*Enter, from the palace, Second Messenger.*

SECOND MESSENGER:   Elders of Thebes, most honored in this
    land,
    What horrors are yours to see and hear, what weight
    Of sorrow to be endured, if, true to your birth,
    You venerate the line of Labdakos!
    I think neither Istros nor Phasis, those great rivers,        5
    Could purify this place of the corruption
    It shelters now, or soon must bring to light—
    Evil not done unconsciously, but willed.
    The greatest griefs are those we cause ourselves.
CHORAGOS:   Surely, friend, we have grief enough already;         10
    What new sorrow do you mean?
SECOND MESSENGER:             The Queen is dead.
CHORAGOS:   Iocastê? Dead? But at whose hand?
SECOND MESSENGER:                            Her own.
    The full horror of what happened, you can not know,
    For you did not see it; but I, who did, will tell you
    As clearly as I can how she met her death.                    15

    When she had left us,
    In passionate silence, passing through the court,
    She ran to her apartment in the house,
    Her hair clutched by the fingers of both hands.
    She closed the doors behind her; then, by that bed            20

---

Éxodos final scene (or *episodos*).

Where long ago the fatal son was conceived—
That son who should bring about his father's death—
We heard her call upon Laïos, dead so many years,
And heard her wail for the double fruit of her marriage,
A husband by her husband, children by her child.                    25

Exactly how she died I do not know:
For Oedipus burst in moaning and would not let us
Keep vigil to the end: it was by him
As he stormed about the room that our eyes were caught.
From one to another of us he went, begging a sword,               30
Cursing the wife who was not his wife, the mother
Whose womb had carried his own children and himself.
I do not know: it was none of us aided him,
But surely one of the gods was in control!
For with a dreadful cry                                            35
He hurled his weight, as though wrenched out of himself,
At the twin doors: the bolts gave, and he rushed in.
And there we saw her hanging, her body swaying
From the cruel cord she had noosed about her neck.
A great sob broke from him, heartbreaking to hear,                40
As he loosed the rope and lowered her to the ground.

I would blot out from my mind what happened next!
For the King ripped from her gown the golden brooches
That were her ornament, and raised them, and plunged
them down
Straight into his own eyeballs, crying, "No more,                 45
No more shall you look on the misery about me,
The horrors of my own doing! Too long you have known
The faces of those whom I should never have seen,
Too long been blind to those for whom I was searching!
From this hour, go in darkness!" And as he spoke,                50
He struck at his eyes—not once, but many times;
And the blood spattered his beard,
Bursting from his ruined sockets like red hail.

So from the unhappiness of two this evil has sprung,
A curse on the man and woman alike. The old                      55
Happiness of the house of Labdakos

Was happiness enough: where is it today?
It is all wailing and ruin, disgrace, death—all
The misery of mankind that has a name—
And it is wholly and for ever theirs.                                    60
CHORAGOS:   Is he in agony still? Is there no rest for him?
SECOND MESSENGER:   He is calling for someone to lead him
    to the gates
So that all the children of Kadmos may look upon
His father's murderer, his mother's—no,
I can not say it!
                      And then he will leave Thebes,                     65
Self-exiled, in order that the curse
Which he himself pronounced may depart from the house.
He is weak, and there is none to lead him,
So terrible is his suffering.
                      But you will see:
Look, the doors are opening; in a moment                                 70
You will see a thing that would crush a heart of stone.

*The central door is opened; Oedipus, blinded, is led in.*

CHORAGOS:   Dreadful indeed for men to see.
    Never have my own eyes
    Looked on a sight so full of fear.
    Oedipus!                                                             75
    What madness came upon you, what daemon
    Leaped on your life with heavier
    Punishment than a mortal man can bear?
    No: I can not even
    Look at you, poor ruined one.                                       80
    And I would speak, question, ponder,
    If I were able. No.
    You make me shudder.
OEDIPUS:   God. God.
    Is there a sorrow greater?                                          85
    Where shall I find harbor in this world?
    My voice is hurled far on a dark wind.
    What has God done to me?
CHORAGOS:   Too terrible to think of, or to see.

## STROPHE 1

OEDIPUS:  O cloud of night,                                                     90
     Never to be turned away: night coming on,
     I can not tell how: night like a shroud!
     My fair winds brought me here.
                         Oh God. Again
     The pain of the spikes where I had sight,
     The flooding pain                                                          95
     Of memory, never to be gouged out.
CHORAGOS:  This is not strange.
     You suffer it all twice over, remorse in pain,
     Pain in remorse.

## ANTISTROPHE 1

OEDIPUS:  Ah dear friend                                                        100
     Are you faithful even yet, you alone?
     Are you still standing near me, will you stay here,
     Patient, to care for the blind?
                         The blind man!
     Yet even blind I know who it is attends me,
     By the voice's tone—                                                       105
     Though my new darkness hide the comforter.
CHORAGOS:  Oh fearful act!
     What god was it drove you to rake black
     Night across your eyes?

## STROPHE 2

OEDIPUS:  Apollo. Apollo. Dear                                                  110
     Children, the god was Apollo.
     He brought my sick, sick fate upon me.
     But the blinding hand was my own!
     How could I bear to see
     When all my sight was horror everywhere?                                   115
CHORAGOS:  Everywhere; that is true.
OEDIPUS:  And now what is left?
     Images? Love? A greeting even,
     Sweet to the senses? Is there anything?

Ah, no, friends: lead me away. 120
Lead me away from Thebes.
                  Lead the great wreck
And hell of Oedipus, whom the gods hate.
CHORAGOS:   Your fate is clear, you are not blind to that.
Would God you had never found it out!

### Antistrophe 2

OEDIPUS:   Death take the man who unbound 125
My feet on that hillside
And delivered me from death to life! What life?
If only I had died,
This weight of monstrous doom
Could not have dragged me and my darlings down. 130
CHORAGOS:   I would have wished the same.
OEDIPUS:   Oh never to have come here
With my father's blood upon me! Never
To have been the man they call his mother's husband!
Oh accurst! Oh child of evil, 135
To have entered that wretched bed—
                     the selfsame one!
More primal than sin itself, this fell to me.
CHORAGOS:   I do not know how I can answer you.
You were better dead than alive and blind.
OEDIPUS:   Do not counsel me any more. This punishment 140
That I have laid upon myself is just.
If I had eyes,
I do not know how I could bear the sight
Of my father, when I came to the house of Death,
Or my mother: for I have sinned against them both 145
So vilely that I could not make my peace
By strangling my own life.
                Or do you think my children,
Born as they were born, would be sweet to my eyes?
Ah never, never! Nor this town with its high walls,
Nor the holy images of the gods.
                   For I, 150
Thrice miserable!—Oedipus, noblest of all the line

Of Kadmos, have condemned myself to enjoy
These things no more, by my own malediction
Expelling that man whom the gods declared
To be a defilement in the house of Laïos.                      155
After exposing the rankness of my own guilt,
How could I look men frankly in the eyes?
No, I swear it,
If I could have stifled my hearing at its source,
I would have done it and made all this body                    160
A tight cell of misery, blank to light and sound:
So I should have been safe in a dark agony
Beyond all recollection.
                          Ah Kithairon!
Why did you shelter me? When I was cast upon you,
Why did I not die? Then I should never                         165
Have shown the world my execrable birth.
Ah Polybos! Corinth, city that I believed
The ancient seat of my ancestors: how fair
I seemed, your child! And all the while this evil
Was cancerous within me!
                          For I am sick                        170
In my daily life, sick in my origin.
O three roads, dark ravine, woodland and way
Where three roads met: you, drinking my father's blood,
My own blood, spilled by my own hand: can you remember
The unspeakable things I did there, and the things             175
I went on from there to do?
                          O marriage, marriage!
The act that engendered me, and again the act
Performed by the son in the same bed—
                          Ah, the net
Of incest, mingling fathers, brothers, sons,
With brides, wives, mothers: the last evil                     180
That can be known by men: no tongue can say
How evil!
          No. For the love of God, conceal me
Somewhere far from Thebes; or kill me; or hurl me
Into the sea, away from men's eyes for ever.

Come, lead me. You need not fear to touch me. 185
Of all men, I alone can bear this guilt.

*Enter Creon.*

CHORAGOS:  We are not the ones to decide; but Creon here
  May fitly judge of what you ask. He only
  Is left to protect the city in your place.
OEDIPUS:  Alas, how can I speak to him? What right have I 190
  To beg his courtesy whom I have deeply wronged?
CREON:  I have not come to mock you, Oedipus,
  Or to reproach you, either.
  (*To Attendants.*)          —You, standing there:
  If you have lost all respect for man's dignity,
  At least respect the flame of Lord Helios: 195
  Do not allow this pollution to show itself
  Openly here, an affront to the earth
  And Heaven's rain and the light of day. No, take him
  Into the house as quickly as you can.
  For it is proper 200
  That only the close kindred see his grief.
OEDIPUS:  I pray you in God's name, since your courtesy
  Ignores my dark expectation, visiting
  With mercy this man of all men most execrable:
  Give me what I ask—for your good, not for mine. 205
CREON:  And what is it that you would have me do?
OEDIPUS:  Drive me out of this country as quickly as may be
  To a place where no human voice can ever greet me.
CREON:  I should have done that before now—only,
  God's will had not been wholly revealed to me. 210
OEDIPUS:  But his command is plain: the parricide
  Must be destroyed. I am that evil man.
CREON:  That is the sense of it, yes; but as things are,
  We had best discover clearly what is to be done.
OEDIPUS:  You would learn more about a man like me? 215
CREON:  You are ready now to listen to the god.
OEDIPUS:  I will listen. But it is to you
  That I must turn for help. I beg you, hear me.
  The woman in there—

Give her whatever funeral you think proper:           220
She is your sister.
      —But let me go, Creon!
Let me purge my father's Thebes of the pollution
Of my living here, and go out to the wild hills,
To Kithairon, that has won such fame with me,
The tomb my mother and father appointed for me,           225
And let me die there, as they willed I should.
And yet I know
Death will not ever come to me through sickness
Or in any natural way: I have been preserved
For some unthinkable fate. But let that be.           230
As for my sons, you need not care for them.
They are men, they will find some way to live.
But my poor daughters, who have shared my table,
Who never before have been parted from their father—
Take care of them, Creon; do this for me.           235
And will you let me touch them with my hands
A last time, and let us weep together?
Be kind, my lord,
Great prince, be kind!
      Could I but touch them,
They would be mine again, as when I had my eyes.           240

*Enter Antigonê and Ismene, attended.*

Ah, God!
Is it my dearest children I hear weeping?
Has Creon pitied me and sent my daughters?
CREON:   Yes, Oedipus: I knew that they were dear to you
In the old days, and know you must love them still.           245
OEDIPUS:   May God bless you for this—and be a friendlier
Guardian to you than he has been to me!
Children, where are you?
Come quickly to my hands: they are your brother's—
Hands that have brought your father's once clear eyes           250
To this way of seeing—
      Ah dearest ones,
I had neither sight nor knowledge then, your father

By the woman who was the source of his own life!
And I weep for you—having no strength to see you—,
I weep for you when I think of the bitterness                    255
That men will visit upon you all your lives.
What homes, what festivals can you attend
Without being forced to depart again in tears?
And when you come to marriageable age,
Where is the man, my daughters, who would dare          260
Risk the bane that lies on all my children?
Is there any evil wanting? Your father killed
His father; sowed the womb of her who bore him;
Engendered you at the fount of his own existence!
That is what they will say of you.

Then, whom     265

Can you ever marry? There are no bridegrooms for you,
And your lives must wither away in sterile dreaming.
O Creon, son of Menoikeus!
You are the only father my daughters have,
Since we, their parents, are both of us gone for ever.    270
They are your own blood: you will not let them
Fall into beggary and loneliness;
You will keep them from the miseries that are mine!
Take pity on them; see, they are only children,
Friendless except for you. Promise me this,                    275
Great Prince, and give me your hand in token of it.

*Creon clasps his right hand.*

Children:
I could say much, if you could understand me,
But as it is, I have only this prayer for you:
Live where you can, be as happy as you can—             280
Happier, please God, than God has made your father!

CREON:   Enough. You have wept enough. Now go within.
OEDIPUS:   I must; but it is hard.
CREON:                Time eases all things.
OEDIPUS:   But you must promise—
CREON:                Say what you desire.
OEDIPUS:   Send me from Thebes!

CREON:                                    God grant that I may!                    285
OEDIPUS:    But since God hates me . . .
CREON:                                        No, he will grant your
    wish.
OEDIPUS:    You promise?
CREON:                        I cannot speak beyond my knowledge.
OEDIPUS:    Then lead me in.
CREON:                            Come now, and leave your children.
OEDIPUS:    No! Do not take them from me!
CREON:                                    Think no longer
    That you are in command here, but rather think          290
    How, when you were, you served your own destruction.

*Exeunt into the house all but the Chorus; the Choragos chants
directly to the audience.*

CHORAGOS:    Men of Thebes: look upon Oedipus.
    This is the king who solved the famous riddle
    And towered up, most powerful of men.
    No mortal eyes but looked on him with envy,          295
    Yet in the end ruin swept over him.
    Let every man in mankind's frailty
    Consider his last day; and let none
    Presume on his good fortune until he find
    Life, at his death, a memory without pain.          300

## William Shakespeare (1564–1616)

*William Shakespeare, the supreme writer of English, was born, baptized, and buried in the market town of Stratford-on-Avon, eighty miles from London. Son of a glove maker and merchant who was high bailiff (or mayor) of the town, he probably attended grammar school and learned to read Latin authors in the original. At eighteen he married Anne Hathaway, twenty-six, by whom he had three children, including twins. By 1592 he had become well-known and envied as an actor and playwright in London. From 1594 until he retired, he belonged to the same theatrical company, the Lord Chamberlain's Men (later renamed the King's Men in honor of their patron, James I), for whom he wrote thirty-six plays—some of them, such as* Hamlet *and* King Lear, *profound reworkings of old plays. As an actor, Shakespeare is believed to have played supporting roles, such as Hamlet's father's ghost. The company prospered, moved into the Globe Theater in 1599, and in 1608 bought the fashionable Blackfriars as well; Shakespeare owned an interest in both theaters. When plagues shut down the theaters from 1592 to 1594, Shakespeare turned to story poems; his great sonnets (published only in 1609) probably also date from the 1590s. Plays were regarded as entertainments of little literary merit and Shakespeare did not bother to supervise their publication. After* The Tempest *(1611), the last play entirely from his hand, he retired to Stratford, where since 1597 he had owned the second largest house in town. Most critics agree that when he wrote* Othello *(c. 1604), Shakespeare was at the height of his powers.*

# The Tragedy of Othello, The Moor of Venice

Edited by David Bevington

## CHARACTERS

*Othello*, the Moor
*Brabantio*, [a senator,] father to Desdemona
*Cassio*, an honorable lieutenant [to Othello]

NOTE ON THE TEXT: This text of *Othello* is based on that of the First Folio, or large collection, of Shakespeare's plays (1623). But there are many differences between the Folio text and that of the play's first printing in the Quarto, or small volume, of 1621 (eighteen or nineteen years after the play's first performance). Some readings from the Quarto are included. For the reader's convenience, some material has been added by the editor, David Bevington (some indications of scene, some stage directions). Such additions are enclosed in brackets. Mr. Bevington's text and notes were prepared for his book, *The Complete Works of Shakespeare*, 4th ed. (New York: HarperCollins, 1992).

*Iago*, [Othello's ancient,] a villain
*Roderigo*, a gulled gentleman
*Duke of Venice*
*Senators* [of Venice]
*Montano*, governor of Cyprus
*Gentlemen of Cyprus*
*Lodovico and Gratiano*, [kinsmen to Brabantio,] two noble Venetians
*Sailors*
*Clown*
*Desdemona*, [daughter to Brabantio and] wife to Othello
*Emilia*, wife to Iago
*Bianca*, a courtesan [and mistress to Cassio]
[*A Messenger*
*A Herald*
*A Musician*
*Servants, Attendants, Officers, Senators, Musicians, Gentlemen*]

[Scene: *Venice; a seaport in Cyprus*]

## ACT I

### SCENE I [VENICE. A STREET.]

*Enter Roderigo and Iago.*

RODERIGO:   Tush, never tell me!° I take it much unkindly
That thou, Iago, who hast had my purse
As if the strings were thine, shouldst know of this.°
IAGO:   'Sblood,° but you'll not hear me.
If ever I did dream of such a matter,                                  5
Abhor me.
RODERIGO:   Thou toldst me thou didst hold him in thy hate.
IAGO:   Despise me
If I do not. Three great ones of the city,
In personal suit to make me his lieutenant,                       10
Off-capped to him;° and by the faith of man,
I know my price, I am worth no worse a place.
But he, as loving his own pride and purposes,

---

**1 never tell me** (An expression of incredulity, like "tell me another one.")   **3 this** i.e., Desdemona's elopement   **4 'Sblood** by His (Christ's) blood   **11 him** i.e., Othello

Evades them with a bombast circumstance°
Horribly stuffed with epithets of war,°      15
And, in conclusion,
Nonsuits° my mediators. For, "Certes,"° says he,
"I have already chose my officer."
And what was he?
Forsooth, a great arithmetician,°      20
One Michael Cassio, a Florentine,
A fellow almost damned in a fair wife,°
That never set a squadron in the field
Nor the division of a battle° knows
More than a spinster°—unless the bookish theoric,°      25
Wherein the togaed° consuls° can propose°
As masterly as he. Mere prattle without practice
Is all his soldiership. But he, sir, had th' election;
And I, of whom his° eyes had seen the proof
At Rhodes, at Cyprus, and on other grounds      30
Christened° and heathen, must be beleed and calmed°
By debitor and creditor.° This countercaster,°
He, in good time,° must his lieutenant be,
And I—God bless the mark!°—his Moorship's ancient.°
RODERIGO: By heaven, I rather would have been his hangman.°      35
IAGO: Why, there's no remedy. 'Tis the curse of service;
Preferment° goes by letter and affection,°
And not by old gradation,° where each second
Stood heir to th' first. Now, sir, be judge yourself
Whether I in any just term° am affined°      40
To love the Moor.
RODERIGO: I would not follow him then.

---

14 **bombast circumstance** wordy evasion. (Bombast is cotton padding.)    15 **epithets of war** military expressions    17 **Nonsuits** rejects the petition of.    **Certes** certainly    20 **arithmetician** i.e., a man whose military knowledge is merely theoretical, based on books of tactics    22 **A . . . wife** (Cassio does not seem to be married, but his counterpart in Shakespeare's source does have a woman in his house. See also Act IV, Scene i, line 127.)    24 **division of a battle** disposition of a military unit    25 **a spinster** i.e., a housewife, one whose regular occupation is spinning.    **theoric** theory    26 **togaed** wearing the toga.    **consuls** counselors, senators.    **propose** discuss    29 **his** i.e., Othello's    31 **Christened** Christian.    **beleed and calmed** left to leeward without wind, becalmed. (A sailing metaphor.)    32 **debitor and creditor** (A name for a system of bookkeeping, here used as a contemptuous nickname for Cassio.)    **countercaster** i.e., bookkeeper, one who tallies with *counters*, or "metal disks." (Said contemptuously.)    33 **in good time** opportunely, i.e., forsooth    34 **God bless the mark** (Perhaps originally a formula to ward off evil; here an expression of impatience.) **ancient** standard-bearer, ensign    35 **his hangman** the executioner of him    37 **Preferment** promotion.    **letter and affection** personal influence and favoritism    38 **old gradation** step-by-step seniority, the traditional way    40 **term** respect    **affined** bound

IAGO:   O sir, content you.°
I follow him to serve my turn upon him.
We cannot all be masters, nor all masters                            45
Cannot be truly° followed. You shall mark
Many a duteous and knee-crooking knave
That, doting on his own obsequious bondage,
Wears out his time, much like his master's ass,
For naught but provender, and when he's old, cashiered.°           50
Whip me° such honest knaves. Others there are
Who, trimmed in forms and visages of duty,°
Keep yet their hearts attending on themselves,
And, throwing but shows of service on their lords,
Do well thrive by them, and when they have lined their coats,°       55
Do themselves homage.° These fellows have some soul,
And such a one do I profess myself. For, sir,
It is as sure as you are Roderigo,
Were I the Moor I would not be Iago.°
In following him, I follow but myself—                               60
Heaven is my judge, not I for love and duty,
But seeming so for my peculiar° end.
For when my outward action doth demonstrate
The native° act and figure° of my heart
In compliment extern,° 'tis not long after                          65
But I will wear my heart upon my sleeve
For daws° to peck at. I am not what I am.°
RODERIGO:   What a full° fortune does the thick-lips° owe°
If he can carry 't thus!°
IAGO:                            Call up her father.
Rouse him, make after him, poison his delight,                      70
Proclaim him in the streets; incense her kinsmen,

---

**43 content you** don't you worry about that    **46 truly** faithfully    **50 cashiered** dismissed from service    **51 Whip me** whip, as far as I'm concerned    **52 trimmed . . . duty** dressed up in the mere form and show of dutifulness    **55 lined their coats** i.e., stuffed their purses    **56 Do themselves homage** i.e., attend to self-interest solely    **59 Were . . . Iago** i.e., if I were able to assume command, I certainly would not choose to remain a subordinate, or, I would keep a suspicious eye on a flattering subordinate    **62 peculiar** particular, personal    **64 native** innate.  **figure** shape, intent    **65 compliment extern** outward show. (Conforming in this case to the inner workings and intention of the heart.)    **67 daws** small crowlike birds, proverbially stupid and avaricious.   **I am not what I am** i.e., I am not one who wears his heart on his sleeve    **68 full** swelling.  **thick-lips** (Elizabethans often applied the term "Moor" to Negroes.)  **owe** own    **69 carry 't thus** carry this off

And, though he in a fertile climate dwell,
Plague him with flies.° Though that his joy be joy,°
Yet throw such changes of vexation° on 't
As it may° lose some color.° 75
RODERIGO:  Here is her father's house. I'll call aloud.
IAGO:  Do, with like timorous° accent and dire yell
As when, by night and negligence,° the fire
Is spied in populous cities.
RODERIGO:  What ho, Brabantio! Signor Brabantio, ho! 80
IAGO:  Awake! What ho, Brabantio! Thieves, thieves, thieves!
Look to your house, your daughter, and your bags!
Thieves, thieves!

*Brabantio [enters] above [at a window].*°

BRABANTIO:  What is the reason of this terrible summons?
What is the matter° there? 85
RODERIGO:  Signor, is all your family within?
IAGO:  Are your doors locked?
BRABANTIO:                          Why, wherefore ask you this?
IAGO:  Zounds,° sir, you're robbed. For shame, put on your gown!
Your heart is burst; you have lost half your soul.
Even now, now, very now, an old black ram 90
Is tupping° your white ewe. Arise, arise!
Awake the snorting° citizens with the bell,
Or else the devil° will make a grandsire of you.
Arise, I say!
BRABANTIO:  What, have you lost your wits?
RODERIGO:  Most reverend signor, do you know my voice? 95
BRABANTIO:  Not I. What are you?
RODERIGO:  My name is Roderigo.
BRABANTIO:  The worser welcome.
I have charged thee not to haunt about my doors.
In honest plainness thou hast heard me say 100

---

72–73 **though . . . flies** though he seems prosperous and happy now, vex him with misery
73 **Though . . . be joy** although he seems fortunate and happy. (Repeats the idea of line 72.)
74 **changes of vexation** vexing changes    75 **As it may** that may cause it to.    **some color** some of its
fresh gloss    77 **timorous** frightening    78 **and negligence** i.e., by negligence    83 **[s.d.] at a window**
(This stage direction, from the Quarto, probably calls for an appearance on the gallery above and
rearstage.)    85 **the matter** your business    88 **Zounds** by His (Christ's) wounds    91 **tupping**
covering, copulating with. (Said of sheep.)    92 **snorting** snoring    93 **the devil** (The devil was
conventionally pictured as black.)

My daughter is not for thee; and now, in madness,
Being full of supper and distempering° drafts,
Upon malicious bravery° dost thou come
To start° my quiet.
RODERIGO:    Sir, sir, sir—
BRABANTIO:                    But thou must needs be sure    105
My spirits and my place° have in° their power
To make this bitter to thee.
RODERIGO:                    Patience, good sir.
BRABANTIO:   What tell'st thou me of robbing? This is Venice;
My house is not a grange.°
RODERIGO:                    Most grave Brabantio,
In simple° and pure soul I come to you.                    110
IAGO:   Zounds, sir, you are one of those that will not serve God if
the devil bid you. Because we come to do you service and you
think we are ruffians, you'll have your daughter covered with a
Barbary° horse; you'll have your nephews° neigh to you; you'll
have coursers° for cousins° and jennets° for germans.°    115
BRABANTIO:   What profane wretch art thou?
IAGO:   I am one, sir, that comes to tell you your daughter and
the Moor are now making the beast with two backs.
BRABANTIO:   Thou art a villain.
IAGO:                    You are—a senator.°
BRABANTIO:   This thou shalt answer.° I know thee, Roderigo.
RODERIGO:   Sir, I will answer anything. But I beseech you,    120
If't be your pleasure and most wise° consent—
As partly I find it is—that your fair daughter,
At this odd-even° and dull watch o' the night,
Transported with° no worse nor better guard
But with a knave° of common hire, a gondolier,    125
To the gross clasps of a lascivious Moor—
If this be known to you and your allowance°

---

102 **distempering** intoxicating    103 **Upon malicious bravery** with hostile intent to defy me
104 **start** startle, disrupt    106 **My spirits and my place** my temperament and my authority of office.
**have in** have it in    109 **grange** isolated country house    110 **simple** sincere    114 **Barbary** from
northern Africa (and hence associated with Othello).    **nephews** i.e., grandsons    115 **coursers**
powerful horses.    **cousins** kinsmen.    **jennets** small Spanish horses.    **germans** near relatives
118 **a senator** (Said with mock politeness, as though the word itself were an insult.)    119 **answer**
be held accountable for    121 **wise** well-informed    123 **odd-even** between one day and the next,
i.e., about midnight    124 **with** by    125 **But with a knave** than by a low fellow, a servant
127 **allowance** permission

We then have done you bold and saucy° wrongs.
But if you know not this, my manners tell me
We have your wrong rebuke. Do not believe                    130
That, from° the sense of all civility,°
I thus would play and trifle with your reverence.°
Your daughter, if you have not given her leave,
I say again, hath made a gross revolt,
Tying her duty, beauty, wit,° and fortunes                    135
In an extravagant° and wheeling° stranger°
Of here and everywhere. Straight° satisfy yourself.
If she be in her chamber or your house,
Let loose on me the justice of the state
For thus deluding you.                                        140
BRABANTIO:   Strike on the tinder,° ho!
Give me a taper! Call up all my people!
This accident° is not unlike my dream.
Belief of it oppresses me already.
Light, I say, light!                          *Exit [above].*
IAGO:   Farewell, for I must leave you.                       145
It seems not meet° nor wholesome to my place°
To be producted°—as, if I stay, I shall—
Against the Moor. For I do know the state,
However this may gall° him with some check,°
Cannot with safety cast° him, for he's embarked°             150
With such loud reason° to the Cyprus wars,
Which even now stands in act,° that, for their souls,°
Another of his fathom° they have none
To lead their business; in which regard,°
Though I do hate him as I do hell pains,                      155
Yet for necessity of present life°
I must show out a flag and sign of love,

---

128 **saucy** insolent   131 **from** contrary to.   **civility** good manners, decency   **132 your reverence**
the respect due to you   135 **wit** intelligence   136 **extravagant** expatriate, wandering far from
home.   **wheeling** roving about, vagabond.   **stranger** foreigner   137 **Straight** straightway   141
**tinder** charred linen ignited by a spark from flint and steel, used to light torches or tapers (lines
142, 167)   143 **accident** occurrence, event   146 **meet** fitting.   **place** position (as ensign)   147
**producted** produced (as a witness)   149 **gall** rub; oppress.   **check** rebuke   150 **cast** dismiss.
**embarked** engaged   151 **loud reason** unanimous shout of confirmation (in the Senate)   152 **stands
in act** are going on.   **for their souls** to save themselves   153 **fathom** i.e., ability, depth of
experience   154 **in which regard** out of regard for which   156 **life** livelihood

Which is indeed but sign. That you shall surely find him,
Lead to the Sagittary° the raisèd search,°
And there will I be with him. So farewell.                    *Exit.*    160

*Enter [below] Brabantio [in his nightgown°] with servants
and torches.*

BRABANTIO:   It is too true an evil. Gone she is;
And what's to come of my despisèd time°
Is naught but bitterness. Now, Roderigo,
Where didst thou see her?—O unhappy girl!—
With the Moor, sayst thou?—Who would be a father!—    165
How didst thou know 'twas she?—O, she deceives me
Past thought!—What said she to you?—Get more tapers.
Raise all my kindred.—Are they married, think you?
RODERIGO:   Truly, I think they are.
BRABANTIO:   O heaven! How got she out? O treason of the
   blood!                                                              170
Fathers, from hence trust not your daughters' minds
By what you see them act. Is there not charms°
By which the property° of youth and maidhood
May be abused?° Have you not read, Roderigo,
Of some such thing?
RODERIGO:                Yes, sir, I have indeed.                175
BRABANTIO:   Call up my brother.—O, would you had had her!—
Some one way, some another.—Do you know
Where we may apprehend her and the Moor?
RODERIGO:   I think I can discover° him, if you please
To get good guard and go along with me.                     180
BRABANTIO:   Pray you, lead on. At every house I'll call;
I may command° at most.—Get weapons, ho!
And raise some special officers of night.—
On, good Roderigo. I will deserve° your pains.

                                                          *Exeunt.*

---

159 **Sagittary** (An inn or house where Othello and Desdemona are staying, named for its sign of Sagittarius, or Centaur.) **raisèd search** search party roused out of sleep   160 [s.d.] **nightgown** dressing gown. (This costuming is specified in the Quarto text.)   162 **time** i.e., remainder of life   172 **charms** spells   173 **property** special quality, nature   174 **abused** deceived   179 **discover** reveal, uncover   182 **command** demand assistance   184 **deserve** show gratitude for

## Scene II [Venice. Another Street, Before Othello's Lodgings.]

*Enter Othello, Iago, attendants with torches.*

IAGO:   Though in the trade of war I have slain men,
    Yet do I hold it very stuff° o' the conscience
    To do no contrived° murder. I lack iniquity
    Sometimes to do me service. Nine or ten times
    I had thought t' have yerked° him° here under the ribs.          5
OTHELLO:   'Tis better as it is.
IAGO:                                   Nay, but he prated,
    And spoke such scurvy and provoking terms
    Against your honor
    That, with the little godliness I have,
    I did full hard forbear him.° But, I pray you, sir,          10
    Are you fast married? Be assured of this,
    That the magnifico° is much beloved,
    And hath in his effect° a voice potential°
    As double as the Duke's. He will divorce you,
    Or put upon you what restraint or grievance          15
    The law, with all his might to enforce it on,
    Will give him cable.°
OTHELLO:                                   Let him do his spite.
    My services which I have done the seigniory°
    Shall out-tongue his complaints. 'Tis yet to know°—
    Which, when I know that boasting is an honor,          20
    I shall promulgate—I fetch my life and being
    From men of royal siege,° and my demerits°
    May speak unbonneted° to as proud a fortune
    As this that I have reached. For know, Iago,
    But that I love the gentle Desdemona,          25
    I would not my unhousèd° free condition
    Put into circumscription and confine°
    For the sea's worth.° But look, what lights come yond?

---

**2 very stuff** essence, basic material (continuing the metaphor of *trade* from line 1)   **3 contrived** premeditated   **5 yerked** stabbed.   **him** i.e., Roderigo   **10 I . . . him** I restrained myself with great difficulty from assaulting him   **12 magnifico** Venetian grandee, i.e., Brabantio   **13 in his effect** at his command.   **potential** powerful   **17 cable** i.e., scope   **18 seigniory** Venetian government   **19 yet to know** not yet widely known   **22 siege** i.e., rank. (Literally, a seat used by a person of distinction.)   **demerits** deserts   **23 unbonneted** without removing the hat, i.e., on equal terms (? Or "with hat off," "in all due modesty.")   **26 unhousèd** unconfined, undomesticated   **27 circumscription and confine** restriction and confinement   **28 the sea's worth** all the riches at the bottom of the sea.

*Enter Cassio [and certain officers°] with torches.*

**IAGO:**  Those are the raisèd father and his friends.
You were best go in.

**OTHELLO:**          Not I. I must be found.                    30
My parts, my title, and my perfect soul°
Shall manifest me rightly. Is it they?

**IAGO:**  By Janus,° I think no.

**OTHELLO:**  The servants of the Duke? And my lieutenant?
The goodness of the night upon you, friends!          35
What is the news?

**CASSIO:**          The Duke does greet you, General,
And he requires your haste-post-haste appearance
Even on the instant.

**OTHELLO:**          What is the matter,° think you?

**CASSIO:**  Something from Cyprus, as I may divine.°
It is a business of some heat.° The galleys          40
Have sent a dozen sequent° messengers
This very night at one another's heels,
And many of the consuls,° raised and met,
Are at the Duke's already. You have been hotly called for;
When, being not at your lodging to be found,          45
The Senate hath sent about° three several° quests
To search you out.

**OTHELLO:**          'Tis well I am found by you.
I will but spend a word here in the house
And go with you.                              [*Exit.*]

**CASSIO:**          Ancient, what makes° he here?

**IAGO:**  Faith, he tonight hath boarded° a land carrack.°          50
If it prove lawful prize,° he's made forever.

**CASSIO:**  I do not understand.

**IAGO:**          He's married.

**CASSIO:**                    To who?

---

[s.d.] **officers** (The Quarto text calls for "Cassio with lights, officers with torches.")   **31 My . . .
soul** my natural gifts, my position or reputation, and my unflawed conscience   **33 Janus** Roman
two-faced god of beginnings   **38 matter** business   **39 divine** guess   **40 heat** urgency   **41 sequent**
successive   **43 consuls** senators   **46 about** all over the city.   **several** separate   **49 makes** does
**50 boarded** gone aboard and seized as an act of piracy (with sexual suggestion).   **carrack** large
merchant ship   **51 prize** booty

[*Enter Othello.*]

IAGO: Marry,° to—Come, Captain, will you go?
OTHELLO: Have with you.°
CASSIO: Here comes another troop to seek for you.                    55

*Enter Brabantio, Roderigo, with officers and torches.*°

IAGO: It is Brabantio. General, be advised.°
    He comes to bad intent.
OTHELLO:                          Holla! Stand there!
RODERIGO: Signor, it is the Moor.
BRABANTIO:                          Down with him, thief!

[*They draw on both sides.*]

IAGO: You, Roderigo! Come, sir, I am for you.
OTHELLO: Keep up° your bright swords, for the dew will rust
    them.                                                         60
    Good signor, you shall more command with years
    Than with your weapons.
BRABANTIO: O thou foul thief, where hast thou stowed my
    daughter?
    Damned as thou art, thou hast enchanted her!
    For I'll refer me° to all things of sense,°                    65
    If she in chains of magic were not bound
    Whether a maid so tender, fair, and happy,
    So opposite to marriage that she shunned
    The wealthy curlèd darlings of our nation,
    Would ever have, t' incur a general mock,                     70
    Run from her guardage° to the sooty bosom
    Of such a thing as thou—to fear, not to delight.
    Judge me the world if 'tis not gross in sense°
    That thou hast practiced on her with foul charms,
    Abused her delicate youth with drugs or minerals°            75

---

53 **Marry** (An oath, originally "by the Virgin Mary"; here used with wordplay on *married*.)
54 **Have with you** i.e., let's go   55 **[s.d.]** officers and torches (The Quarto text calls for "others with lights and weapons.")   56 **be advised** be on your guard   60 **Keep up** keep in the sheath
65 **refer me** submit my case.   **things of sense** commonsense understandings, or, creatures possessing common sense   71 **her guardage** my guardianship of her   73 **gross in sense** obvious   75 **minerals** i.e., poisons

That weakens motion.° I'll have 't disputed on;°
'Tis probable and palpable to thinking.
I therefore apprehend and do attach° thee
For an abuser of the world, a practicer
Of arts inhibited° and out of warrant.°—                    80
Lay hold upon him! If he do resist,
Subdue him at his peril.

OTHELLO:                    Hold your hands,
Both you of my inclining° and the rest.
Were it my cue to fight, I should have known it
Without a prompter.—Whither will you that I go       85
To answer this your charge?

BRABANTIO:   To prison, till fit time
Of law and course of direct session°
Call thee to answer.

OTHELLO:                    What if I do obey?
How may the Duke be therewith satisfied,                 90
Whose messengers are here about my side
Upon some present business of the state
To bring me to him?

OFFICER:                    'Tis true, most worthy signor.
The Duke's in council, and your noble self,
I am sure, is sent for.

BRABANTIO:                    How? The Duke in council?    95
In this time of the night? Bring him away.°
Mine's not an idle° cause. The Duke himself,
Or any of my brothers of the state,
Cannot but feel this wrong as 'twere their own;
For if such actions may have passage free,°               100
Bondslaves and pagans shall our statesmen be.

*Exeunt.*

---

76 **weakens motion** impair the vital faculties.   **disputed on** argued in court by professional counsel, debated by experts   78 **attach** arrest   80 **arts inhibited** prohibited arts, black magic.   **out of warrant** illegal   83 **inclining** following, party   88 **course of direct session** regular or specially convened legal proceedings   96 **away** right along   97 **idle** trifling   100 **have passage free** are allowed to go unchecked

## SCENE III [VENICE. A COUNCIL CHAMBER.]

*Enter Duke [and] Senators [and sit at a table, with lights], and Officers.° [The Duke and Senators are reading dispatches.]*

DUKE: There is no composition° in these news
That gives them credit.
FIRST SENATOR: Indeed, they are disproportioned.°
My letters say a hundred and seven galleys.
DUKE: And mine, a hundred forty.
SECOND SENATOR:       And mine, two hundred.    5
But though they jump° not on a just° account—
As in these cases, where the aim° reports
'Tis oft with difference—yet do they all confirm
A Turkish fleet, and bearing up to Cyprus.
DUKE: Nay, it is possible enough to judgment.    10
I do not so secure me in the error
But the main article I do approve°
In fearful sense.
SAILOR (*within*): What ho, what ho, what ho!

*Enter Sailor.*

OFFICER: A messenger from the galleys.
DUKE: Now, what's the business?    15
SAILOR: The Turkish preparation° makes for Rhodes.
So was I bid report here to the state
By Signor Angelo.
DUKE: How say you by° this change?
FIRST SENATOR:       This cannot be
By no assay° of reason. 'Tis a pageant°    20
To keep us in false gaze.° When we consider
Th' importancy of Cyprus to the Turk,
And let ourselves again but understand
That, as it more concerns the Turk than Rhodes,
So may he with more facile question bear it,°    25

---

[s.d.] Enter . . . Officers (The Quarto text calls for the Duke and senators to "sit at a table with lights and attendants.")  **1 composition** consistency  **3 disproportioned** inconsistent  **6 jump** agree.  **just** exact  **7 the aim** conjecture  **11–12 I do not . . . approve** I do not take such (false) comfort in the discrepancies that I fail to perceive the main point, i.e., that the Turkish fleet is threatening  **16 preparation** fleet prepared for battle  **19 by** about  **20 assay** test.  **pageant** mere show  **21 in false gaze** looking the wrong way  **25 So may . . . it** so also he (the Turk) can more easily capture it (Cyprus)

For that° it stands not in such warlike brace,°
But altogether lacks th' abilities°
That Rhodes is dressed in°—if we make thought of this,
We must not think the Turk is so unskillful°
To leave that latest° which concerns him first,                    30
Neglecting an attempt of ease and gain
To wake° and wage° a danger profitless.
DUKE:  Nay, in all confidence, he's not for Rhodes.
OFFICER:  Here is more news.

*Enter a Messenger.*

MESSENGER:  The Ottomites, reverend and gracious,         35
Steering with due course toward the isle of Rhodes,
Have there injointed them° with an after° fleet.
FIRST SENATOR:  Ay, so I thought. How many, as you guess?
MESSENGER:  Of thirty sail; and now they do restem
Their backward course,° bearing with frank appearance°     40
Their purposes toward Cyprus. Signor Montano,
Your trusty and most valiant servitor,°
With his free duty° recommends° you thus,
And prays you to believe him.
DUKE:  'Tis certain then for Cyprus.                              45
Marcus Luccicos, is not he in town?
FIRST SENATOR:  He's now in Florence.
DUKE:  Write from us to him, post-post-haste. Dispatch.
FIRST SENATOR:  Here comes Brabantio and the valiant Moor.

*Enter Brabantio, Othello, Cassio, Iago, Roderigo, and officers.*

DUKE:  Valiant Othello, we must straight° employ you         50
Against the general enemy° Ottoman.
[*To Brabantio.*] I did not see you; welcome, gentle° signor.
We lacked your counsel and your help tonight.
BRABANTIO:  So did I yours. Good Your Grace, pardon me;
Neither my place° nor aught I heard of business              55
Hath raised me from my bed, nor doth the general care

---

26 **For that** since.  **brace** state of defense    27 **abilities** means of self-defense    28 **dressed in**
equipped with    29 **unskillful** deficient in judgment    30 **latest** last    32 **wake** stir up.    **wage** risk
37 **injointed them** joined themselves.  **after** second, following    39–40 **restem . . . course** retrace
their original course    40 **frank appearance** undisguised intent    42 **servitor** officer under your
command    43 **free duty** freely given and loyal service.    **recommends** commends himself and reports
to    50 **. . . straight** straightway.    51 **general enemy** universal enemy to all Christendom    52 **gentle**
noble    55 **place** official position

Take hold on me, for my particular° grief
Is of so floodgate° and o'erbearing nature
That it engluts° and swallows other sorrows
And it is still itself.°
DUKE:                    Why, what's the matter?                    60
BRABANTIO:  My daughter! O, my daughter!
DUKE AND SENATORS:                    Dead?
BRABANTIO:                                        Ay, to me.
She is abused,° stol'n from me, and corrupted
By spells and medicines bought of mountebanks;
For nature so preposterously to err,
Being not deficient,° blind, or lame of sense,°                    65
Sans° witchcraft could not.
DUKE:  Whoe'er he be that in this foul proceeding
Hath thus beguiled your daughter of herself,
And you of her, the bloody book of law
You shall yourself read in the bitter letter                    70
After your own sense°—yea, though our proper° son
Stood in your action.°
BRABANTIO:                    Humbly I thank Your Grace.
Here is the man, this Moor, whom now it seems
Your special mandate for the state affairs
Hath hither brought.
ALL:                    We are very sorry for 't.                    75
DUKE [*to Othello*]:  What, in your own part, can you say to
    this?
BRABANTIO:  Nothing, but this is so.
OTHELLO:  Most potent, grave, and reverend signors,
My very noble and approved° good masters:
That I have ta'en away this old man's daughter,                    80
It is most true; true, I have married her.
The very head and front° of my offending
Hath this extent, no more. Rude° am I in my speech,
And little blessed with the soft phrase of peace;
For since these arms of mine had seven years' pith,°                    85
Till now some nine moons wasted,° they have used

---

57 **particular** personal   58 **floodgate** i.e., overwhelming (as when floodgates are opened)   59 **en-gluts** engulfs   60 **is still itself** remains undiminished   62 **abused** deceived   65 **deficient** defective. **fame of sense** deficient in sensory perception   66 **Sans** without   71 **After . . . sense** according to your own interpretation.   **our proper** my own   72 **Stood . . . action** were under your accusation   79 **approved** proved, esteemed   82 **head and front** height and breadth, entire extent   83 **Rude** unpolished   85 **since . . . pith** i.e., since I was seven.   **pith** strength, vigor   86 **Till . . . wasted** until some nine months ago (since when Othello has evidently not been on active duty, but in Venice); alternately, Othello may be revealing his age in saying that his life is nine-twelfths over (making him in his early 50s).

Their dearest° action in the tented field;
And little of this great world can I speak
More than pertains to feats of broils and battle,
And therefore little shall I grace my cause                              90
In speaking for myself. Yet, by your gracious patience,
I will a round° unvarnished tale deliver
Of my whole course of love—what drugs, what charms,
What conjuration, and what mighty magic,
For such proceeding I am charged withal,°                               95
I won his daughter.

BRABANTIO:                    A maiden never bold;
Of spirit so still and quiet that her motion
Blushed at herself;° and she, in spite of nature,
Of years,° of country, credit,° everything,
To fall in love with what she feared to look on!                       100
It is a judgment maimed and most imperfect
That will confess° perfection so could err
Against all rules of nature, and must be driven
To find out practices° of cunning hell
Why this should be. I therefore vouch° again                           105
That with some mixtures powerful o'er the blood,°
Or with some dram conjured to this effect,°
He wrought upon her.

DUKE:                              To vouch this is no proof,
Without more wider° and more overt test°
Than these thin habits° and poor likelihoods°                          110
Of modern seeming° do prefer° against him.

FIRST SENATOR:    But Othello, speak.
Did you by indirect and forcèd courses°
Subdue and poison this young maid's affections?
Or came it by request and such fair question°                          115
As soul to soul affordeth?

OTHELLO:                          I do beseech you,
Send for the lady to the Sagittary
And let her speak of me before her father.

---

**87 dearest** most valuable   **92 round** plain   **95 withal** with   **97–98 her . . . herself** i.e., she blushed easily at herself. (*Motion* can suggest the impulse of the soul or of the emotions, or physical movement.)   **99 years** i.e., difference in age.   **credit** virtuous reputation   **102 confess** concede (that)   **104 practices** plots   **105 vouch** assert   **106 blood** passions   **107 dram . . . effect** dose made by magical spells to have this effect   **109 more wider** fuller.   **test** testimony   **110 habits** garments, i.e., appearances.   **poor likelihoods** weak inferences   **111 modern seeming** commonplace assumption.   **prefer** bring forth   **113 forcèd courses** means used against her will   **115 question** conversation

If you do find me foul in her report,
The trust, the office I do hold of you                                120
Not only take away, but let your sentence
Even fall upon my life.
**DUKE:**                          Fetch Desdemona hither.
**OTHELLO:**   Ancient, conduct them. You best know the place.

> [*Exeunt Iago and attendants.*]

And, till she come, as truly as to heaven
I do confess the vices of my blood,°                                  125
So justly° to your grave ears I'll present
How I did thrive in this fair lady's love,
And she in mine.
**DUKE:**   Say it, Othello.
**OTHELLO:**   Her father loved me, oft invited me,                    130
Still° questioned me the story of my life
From year to year—the battles, sieges, fortunes
That I have passed.
I ran it through, even from my boyish days
To th' very moment that he bade me tell it,                           135
Wherein I spoke of most disastrous chances,
Of moving accidents° by flood and field,
Of hairbreadth scapes i' th' imminent deadly breach,°
Of being taken by the insolent foe
And sold to slavery, of my redemption thence,                        140
And portance° in my travels' history,
Wherein of antres° vast and deserts idle,°
Rough quarries,° rocks, and hills whose heads touch
   heaven,
It was my hint° to speak—such was my process—
And of the Cannibals that each other eat,                            145
The Anthropophagi,° and men whose heads
Do grow beneath their shoulders. These things to hear
Would Desdemona seriously incline;
But still the house affairs would draw her thence,
Which ever as she could with haste dispatch                          150
She'd come again, and with a greedy ear

125 **blood** passions, human nature   126 **justly** truthfully, accurately   131 **Still** continually
137 **moving accidents** stirring happenings   138 **imminent . . . breach** death-threatening gaps
made in a fortification   141 **portance** conduct   142 **antres** caverns.   **idle** barren, desolate
143 **Rough quarries** rugged rock formations   144 **hint** occasion, opportunity
146 **Anthropophagi** man-eaters. (A term from Pliny's *Natural History*.)

Devour up my discourse. Which I, observing,
Took once a pliant° hour, and found good means
To draw from her a prayer of earnest heart
That I would all my pilgrimage dilate,°                          155
Whereof by parcels° she had something heard,
But not intentively.° I did consent,
And often did beguile her of her tears,
When I did speak of some distressful stroke
That my youth suffered. My story being done,                    160
She gave me for my pains a world of sighs.
She swore, in faith, 'twas strange, 'twas passing° strange,
'Twas pitiful, 'twas wondrous pitiful.
She wished she had not heard it, yet she wished
That heaven had made her° such a man. She thanked me,           165
And bade me, if I had a friend that loved her,
I should but teach him how to tell my story,
And that would woo her. Upon this hint° I spake.
She loved me for the dangers I had passed,
And I loved her that she did pity them.                         170
This only is the witchcraft I have used.
Here comes the lady. Let her witness it.

*Enter Desdemona, Iago, [and] attendants.*

DUKE:   I think this tale would win my daughter too.
Good Brabantio,
Take up this mangled matter at the best.°                       175
Men do their broken° weapons rather use
Than their bare hands.
BRABANTIO:                          I pray you, hear her speak.
If she confess that she was half the wooer,
Destruction on my head if my bad blame
Light on the man!—Come hither, gentle mistress.                180
Do you perceive in all this noble company
Where most you owe obedience?
DESDEMONA:                          My noble Father,
I do perceive here a divided duty.
To you I am bound for life and education;°

153 **pliant** well-suiting  155 **dilate** relate in detail  156 **by parcels** piecemeal  157 **intentively**
with full attention, continuously  162 **passing** exceedingly  165 **made her** created her to be
168 **hint** opportunity. (Othello does not mean that she was dropping hints.)  175 **Take . . . best**
make the best of a bad bargain  184 **education** upbringing

My life and education both do learn° me                                185
How to respect you. You are the lord of duty;°
I am hitherto your daughter. But here's my husband,
And so much duty as my mother showed
To you, preferring you before her father,
So much I challenge° that I may profess                                190
Due to the Moor my lord.
BRABANTIO:   God be with you! I have done.
Please it Your Grace, on to the state affairs.
I had rather to adopt a child than get° it.
Come hither, Moor.                                                     195

[*He joins the hands of Othello and Desdemona.*]

I here do give thee that with all my heart°
Which, but thou hast already, with all my heart°
I would keep from thee.—For your sake,° jewel,
I am glad at soul I have no other child,
For thy escape° would teach me tyranny,                               200
To hang clogs° on them.—I have done, my lord.
DUKE:   Let me speak like yourself,° and lay a sentence°
Which, as a grece° or step, may help these lovers
Into your favor.
When remedies° are past, the griefs are ended                         205
By seeing the worst, which late on hopes depended.°
To mourn a mischief° that is past and gone
Is the next° way to draw new mischief on.
What° cannot be preserved when fortune takes,
Patience her injury a mockery makes.°                                 210
The robbed that smiles steals something from the thief;
He robs himself that spends a bootless grief.°
BRABANTIO:   So let the Turk of Cyprus us beguile,
We lose it not, so long as we can smile.
He bears the sentence well that nothing bears                          215
But the free comfort which from thence he hears,

---

185 **learn** teach   186 **of duty** to whom duty is due   190 **challenge** claim   194 **get** beget
196 **with all my heart** wherein my whole affection has been engaged   197 **with all my heart**
willingly, gladly   198 **For your sake** on your account   200 **escape** elopement   201 **clogs** (Literally,
blocks of wood fastened to the legs of criminals or convicts to inhibit escape.)   202 **like yourself**
i.e., as you would, in your proper temper.   **lay a sentence** apply a maxim   203 **grece** step   205
**remedies** hopes of remedy   206 **which . . . depended** which griefs were sustained until recently by
hopeful anticipation   207 **mischief** misfortune, injury   208 **next** nearest   209 **What** whatever
210 **Patience . . . makes** patience laughs at the injury inflicted by fortune (and thus eases the pain)
212 **spends a bootless grief** indulges in unavailing grief

But he bears both the sentence and the sorrow
That, to pay grief, must of poor patience borrow.°
These sentences, to sugar or to gall,
Being strong on both sides, are equivocal.°                                220
But words are words. I never yet did hear
That the bruised heart was piercèd through the ear.°
I humbly beseech you, proceed to th' affairs of state.

DUKE: The Turk with a most mighty preparation makes for
Cyprus. Othello, the fortitude° of the place is best known   225
to you; and though we have there a substitute° of most al-
lowed° sufficiency, yet opinion, a sovereign mistress of effects, throws a more safer voice on you.° You must therefore
be content to slubber° the gloss of your new fortunes with
this more stubborn° and boisterous expedition.

OTHELLO: The tyrant custom, most grave senators,              230
Hath made the flinty and steel couch of war
My thrice-driven° bed of down. I do agnize°
A natural and prompt alacrity
I find in hardness,° and do undertake
These present wars against the Ottomites.                          235
Most humbly therefore bending to your state,°
I crave fit disposition for my wife,
Due reference of place and exhibition,°
With such accommodation° and besort°
As levels° with her breeding.°                                      240

DUKE: Why, at her father's.

BRABANTIO:                          I will not have it so.

OTHELLO: Nor I.

DESDEMONA:          Nor I. I would not there reside,
To put my father in impatient thoughts
By being in his eye. Most gracious Duke,

---

215–218 **He bears . . . borrow** a person well bears out your maxim who can enjoy its platitudinous comfort, free of all genuine sorrow, but anyone whose grief bankrupts his poor patience is left with your saying and his sorrow, too. (*Bears the sentence* also plays on the meaning, "receives judicial sentence.")  219–220 **These . . . equivocal** these fine maxims are equivocal, either sweet or bitter in their application  222 **piercèd . . . ear** i.e., surgically lanced and cured by mere words of advice 225 **fortitude** strength  226 **substitute** deputy.  **allowed** acknowledged  226–227 **opinion . . . on you** general opinion, an important determiner of affairs, chooses you as the best man  228 **slubber** soil, sully.  **stubborn** harsh, rough  232 **thrice-driven** thrice sifted, winnowed.  **agnize** know in myself, acknowledge  234 **hardness** hardship  236 **bending . . . state** bowing or kneeling to your authority  238 **reference . . . exhibition** provision of appropriate place to live and allowance of money  239 **accommodation** suitable provision.  **besort** attendance  240 **levels** equals, suits. **breeding** social position, upbringing

To my unfolding° lend your prosperous° ear, 245
And let me find a charter° in your voice,
T' assist my simpleness.
DUKE: What would you, Desdemona?
DESDEMONA: That I did love the Moor to live with him,
My downright violence and storm of fortunes° 250
May trumpet to the world. My heart's subdued
Even to the very quality of my lord.°
I saw Othello's visage in his mind,
And to his honors and his valiant parts°
Did I my soul and fortunes consecrate. 255
So that, dear lords, if I be left behind
A moth° of peace, and he go to the war,
The rites° for why I love him are bereft me,
And I a heavy interim shall support
By his dear° absence. Let me go with him. 260
OTHELLO: Let her have your voice.°
Vouch with me, heaven, I therefor beg it not
To please the palate of my appetite,
Nor to comply with heat°—the young affects°
In me defunct—and proper° satisfaction, 265
But to be free° and bounteous to her mind.
And heaven defend° your good souls that you think°
I will your serious and great business scant
When she is with me. No, when light-winged toys
Of feathered Cupid seel° with wanton dullness 270
My speculative and officed instruments,°
That° my disports° corrupt and taint° my business,
Let huswives make a skillet of my helm,
And all indign° and base adversities
Make head° against my estimation!° 275

---

245 **unfolding** explanation, proposal. **prosperous** propitious  246 **charter** privilege, authorization  250 **My . . . fortunes** my plain and total breach of social custom, taking my future by storm and disrupting my whole life  251–252 **My heart's . . . lord** my heart is brought wholly into accord with Othello's virtues; I love him for his virtues  254 **parts** qualities  257 **moth** i.e., one who consumes merely  258 **rites** rites of love (with a suggestion, too, of "rights," sharing)  260 **dear** (1) heartfelt (2) costly  261 **voice** consent  264 **heat** sexual passion.  **young affects** passions of youth, desires  265 **proper** personal  266 **free** generous  267 **defend** forbid.  **think** should think  270 **seel** i.e., make blind (as in falconry, by sewing up the eyes of the hawk during training)  271 **speculative . . . instruments** eyes and other faculties used in the performance of duty  272 **That** so that.  **disports** sexual pastimes.  **taint** impair  274 **indign** unworthy, shameful  275 **Make head** raise an army.  **estimation** reputation

DUKE: Be it as you shall privately determine,
  Either for her stay or going. Th' affair cries haste,
  And speed must answer it.
A SENATOR:                You must away tonight.
DESDEMONA: Tonight, my lord?
DUKE:                        This night.
OTHELLO:                           With all my heart.
DUKE: At nine i' the morning here we'll meet again.          280
  Othello, leave some officer behind,
  And he shall our commission bring to you,
  With such things else of quality and respect°
  As doth import° you.
OTHELLO:           So please Your Grace, my ancient;
  A man he is of honesty and trust.                          285
  To his conveyance I assign my wife,
  With what else needful Your Good Grace shall think
  To be sent after me.
DUKE:             Let it be so.
  Good night to everyone. [*To Brabantio.*] And, noble signor,
  If virtue no delighted° beauty lack,                       290
  Your son-in-law is far more fair than black.
FIRST SENATOR: Adieu, brave Moor. Use Desdemona well.
BRABANTIO: Look to her, Moor, if thou hast eyes to see.
  She has deceived her father, and may thee.

  *Exeunt* [*Duke, Brabantio, Cassio, Senators, and officers*].

OTHELLO: My life upon her faith! Honest Iago,             295
  My Desdemona must I leave to thee.
  I prithee, let thy wife attend on her,
  And bring them after in the best advantage.°
  Come, Desdemona. I have but an hour
  Of love, of worldly matters and direction,°             300
  To spend with thee. We must obey the time.°

  *Exit* [*with Desdemona*].

RODERIGO: Iago—
IAGO: What sayst thou, noble heart?
RODERIGO: What will I do, think'st thou?

---

**283 of quality and respect** of importance and relevance  **284 import** concern  **290 delighted**
capable of delighting  **298 in . . . advantage** at the most favorable opportunity  **300 direction**
instructions  **301 the time** the urgency of the present crisis

IAGO:   Why, go to bed and sleep.                                                    305
RODERIGO:   I will incontinently° drown myself.
IAGO:   If thou dost, I shall never love thee after. Why, thou silly
gentleman?
RODERIGO:   It is silliness to live when to live is torment; and
then have we a prescription° to die when death is our
physician.
IAGO:   O villainous!° I have looked upon the world for four
times times seven years, and, since I could distinguish betwixt   310
a benefit and an injury, I never found man that knew how to
love himself. Ere I would say I would drown myself for the
love of a guinea hen,° I would change my humanity with a
baboon.
RODERIGO:   What should I do? I confess it is my shame to be so
fond,° but it is not in my virtue° to amend it.                        315
IAGO:   Virtue? A fig!° 'Tis in ourselves that we are thus or thus.
Our bodies are our gardens, to the which our wills are gar-
deners; so that if we will plant nettles or sow lettuce, set hys-
sop° and weed up thyme, supply it with one gender° of herbs
or distract it with° many, either to have it sterile with idleness°
or manured with industry—why, the power and corrigible au-
thority° of this lies in our wills. If the beam° of our lives had   320
not one scale of reason to poise° another of sensuality, the
blood° and baseness of our natures would conduct us to most
preposterous conclusions. But we have reason to cool our raging motions,° our carnal stings, our unbitted° lusts, whereof I
take this that you call love to be a sect or scion.°                    325
RODERIGO:   It cannot be.
IAGO:   It is merely a lust of the blood and a permission of the
will. Come, be a man. Drown thyself? Drown cats and blind
puppies. I have professed me thy friend, and I confess me knit
to thy deserving with cables of perdurable° toughness. I could

---

306 **incontinently** immediately, without self-restraint   308–309 **prescription** (1) right based on
long-established custom (2) doctor's prescription   310 **villainous** i.e., what perfect nonsense
313 **guinea hen** (A slang term for a prostitute.)   314 **fond** infatuated   315 **virtue** strength, nature
316 **fig** (To give a fig is to thrust the thumb between the first and second fingers in a vulgar and
insulting gesture.)   318 **hyssop** an herb of the mint family   319 **gender** kind.   **distract it with**
divide it among.   320 **idleness** want of cultivation.   **corrigible authority** power to correct
321 **beam** balance.   322 **poise** counterbalance.   **blood** natural passions   324 **motions** appetites.
**unbitted** unbridled, uncontrolled   325 **sect or scion** cutting or offshoot   329 **perdurable** very
durable

never better stead° thee than now. Put money in thy purse.
Follow thou the wars; defeat thy favor° with an usurped°   330
beard. I say, put money in thy purse. It cannot be long that
Desdemona should continue her love to the Moor—put
money in thy purse—nor he his to her. It was a violent com-
mencement in her, and thou shalt see an answerable seques-
tration°—put but money in thy purse. These Moors are
changeable in their wills°—fill thy purse with money. The   335
food that to him now is as luscious as locusts° shall be to him
shortly as bitter as coloquintida.° She must change for youth;
when she is sated with his body, she will find the error of her
choice. She must have change, she must. Therefore put
money in thy purse. If thou wilt needs damn thyself, do it a
more delicate way than drowning. Make° all the money thou   340
canst. If sanctimony° and a frail vow betwixt an erring° bar-
barian and a supersubtle Venetian be not too hard for my
wits and all the tribe of hell, thou shalt enjoy her. Therefore
make money. A pox of drowning thyself! It is clean out of the
way.° Seek thou rather to be hanged in compassing° thy joy
than to be drowned and go without her.                        345
RODERIGO:  Wilt thou be fast° to my hopes if I depend on the
   issue?°
IAGO:  Thou art sure of me. Go, make money. I have told thee often, and I retell thee again and again, I hate the Moor. My cause
   is hearted;° thine hath no less reason. Let us be conjunctive° in
   our revenge against him. If thou canst cuckold him, thou dost
   thyself a pleasure, me a sport. There are many events in the
   womb of time which will be delivered. Traverse,° go, provide   350
   thy money. We will have more of this tomorrow. Adieu.
RODERIGO:  Where shall we meet i' the morning?
IAGO:  At my lodging.
RODERIGO:  I'll be with thee betimes.° [*He starts to leave.*]      355

---

330 **stead** assist   331 **defeat thy favor** disguise your face.   **usurped** (The suggestion is that
Roderigo is not man enough to have a beard of his own.)   334–335 **an answerable sequestration** a
corresponding separation or estrangement   336 **wills** carnal appetites   337 **locusts** fruit of the
carob tree (see Matthew 3:4), or perhaps honeysuckle.   **coloquintida** colocynth or bitter apple,
a purgative   341 **Make** raise, collect.   **sanctimony** sacred ceremony   342 **erring** wandering,
vagabond, unsteady   344 **clean . . . way** entirely unsuitable as a course of action.   **compassing**
encompassing, embracing   346 **fast** true.   **issue** (successful) outcome   348 **hearted** fixed in the
heart, heartfelt   349 **conjunctive** united   351 **Traverse** (A military marching term.)   355 **betimes**
early

IAGO: Go to, farewell.—Do you hear, Roderigo?
RODERIGO: What say you?
IAGO: No more of drowning, do you hear?
RODERIGO: I am changed.
IAGO: Go to, farewell. Put money enough in your purse.          360
RODERIGO: I'll sell all my land.          *Exit.*
IAGO: Thus do I ever make my fool my purse;
    For I mine own gained knowledge should profane
    If I would time expend with such a snipe°
    But for my sport and profit. I hate the Moor;          365
    And it is thought abroad° that twixt my sheets
    He's done my office.° I know not if 't be true;
    But I, for mere suspicion in that kind,
    Will do as if for surety.° He holds me well;°
    The better shall my purpose work on him.          370
    Cassio's a proper° man. Let me see now:
    To get his place and to plume up° my will
    In double knavery—How, how?—Let's see:
    After some time, to abuse° Othello's ear
    That he° is too familiar with his wife.          375
    He hath a person and a smooth dispose°
    To be suspected, framed to make women false.
    The Moor is of a free° and open° nature,
    That thinks men honest that but seem to be so,
    And will as tenderly° be led by the nose          380
    As asses are.
    I have 't. It is engendered. Hell and night
    Must bring this monstrous birth to the world's light.

                                                 [*Exit.*]

---

364 **snipe** woodcock, i.e., fool   366 **it is thought abroad** it is rumored   367 **my office** i.e., my sexual function as husband   369 **do . . . surety** act as if on certain knowledge.   **holds me well** regards me favorably   371 **proper** handsome   372 **plume up** put a feather in the cap of, i.e., glorify, gratify   374 **abuse** deceive   375 **he** i.e., Cassio   376 **dispose** disposition   378 **free** frank, generous.   **open** unsuspicious   380 **tenderly** readily

## A C T  *II*

### Scene I [A Seaport in Cyprus. An Open Place Near the Quay.]

*Enter Montano and two Gentlemen.*

MONTANO: What from the cape can you discern at sea?

FIRST GENTLEMAN: Nothing at all. It is a high-wrought
    flood.°
    I cannot, twixt the heaven and the main,°
    Descry a sail.

MONTANO: Methinks the wind hath spoke aloud at land;    5
    A fuller blast ne'er shook our battlements.
    If it hath ruffianed° so upon the sea,
    What ribs of oak, when mountains° melt on them,
    Can hold the mortise?° What shall we hear of this?

SECOND GENTLEMAN: A segregation° of the Turkish fleet.    10
    For do but stand upon the foaming shore,
    The chidden° billow seems to pelt the clouds;
    The wind-shaked surge, with high and monstrous mane,°
    Seems to cast water on the burning Bear°
    And quench the guards of th' ever-fixèd pole.    15
    I never did like molestation° view
    On the enchafèd° flood.

MONTANO: If that° the Turkish fleet
    Be not ensheltered and embayed,° they are drowned;
    It is impossible to bear it out.°    20

*Enter a [Third] Gentleman.*

THIRD GENTLEMAN: News, lads! Our wars are done.
    The desperate tempest hath so banged the Turks
    That their designment° halts.° A noble ship of Venice

---

2 **high-wrought flood** very agitated sea  3 **main** ocean (also at line 41)
7 **ruffianed** raged
8 **mountains** i.e., of water  9 **hold the mortise** hold their joints together. (A *mortise* is the socket hollowed out in fitting timbers.)  10 **segregation** dispersal  12 **chidden** i.e., rebuked, repelled (by the shore), and thus shot into the air  13 **monstrous mane** (The surf is like the mane of a wild beast.)  14 **the burning Bear** i.e., the constellation Ursa Minor or the Little Bear, which includes the polestar (and hence regarded as the guards of *th' ever-fixèd pole* in the next line; sometimes the term *guards* is applied to the two "pointers" of the Big Bear or Dipper, which may be intended here.)  16 **like molestation** comparable disturbance  17 **enchafèd** angry  18 **If that** if  19 **embayed** sheltered by a bay  20 **bear it out** survive, weather the storm  23 **designment** design, enterprise.  **halts** is lame

Hath seen a grievous wreck° and sufferance°
On most part of their fleet.                                                          25
MONTANO:   How? Is this true?
THIRD GENTLEMAN:   The ship is here put in,
A Veronesa;° Michael Cassio,
Lieutenant to the warlike Moor Othello,
Is come on shore; the Moor himself at sea,                                  30
And is in full commission here for Cyprus.
MONTANO:   I am glad on 't. 'Tis a worthy governor.
THIRD GENTLEMAN:   But this same Cassio, though he speak
of comfort
Touching the Turkish loss, yet he looks sadly°
And prays the Moor be safe, for they were parted                    35
With foul and violent tempest.
MONTANO:                           Pray heaven he be,
For I have served him, and the man commands
Like a full° soldier. Let's to the seaside, ho!
As well to see the vessel that's come in
As to throw out our eyes for brave Othello,                              40
Even till we make the main and th' aerial blue°
An indistinct regard.°
THIRD GENTLEMAN:   Come, let's do so,
For every minute is expectancy°
Of more arrivance.°

*Enter Cassio.*

CASSIO:   Thanks, you the valiant of this warlike isle,                   45
That so approve° the Moor! O, let the heavens
Give him defense against the elements,
For I have lost him on a dangerous sea.
MONTANO:   Is he well shipped?
CASSIO:   His bark is stoutly timbered, and his pilot                      50
Of very expert and approved allowance;°
Therefore my hopes, not surfeited to death,°
Stand in bold cure.°

---

24 **wreck** shipwreck. **sufferance** damage, disaster   28 **Veronesa** i.e., fitted out in Verona for
Venetian service, or possibly *Verennessa* (the Folio spelling), i.e., *verrinessa*, a cutter (from
*verrinare*, "to cut through")   34 **sadly** gravely   38 **full** perfect   41 **the main . . . blue** the sea and
the sky   42 **An indistinct regard** indistinguishable in our view   43 **is expectancy** gives expectation
44 **arrivance** arrival   46 **approve** admire, honor   51 **approved allowance** tested reputation
52 **surfeited to death** i.e., overextended, worn thin through repeated application or delayed
fulfillment   53 **in bold cure** in strong hopes of fulfillment

[*A cry*] *within:* "A sail, a sail, a sail!"

CASSIO: What noise?

A GENTLEMAN: The town is empty. On the brow o' the sea° 55
Stand ranks of people, and they cry "A sail!"

CASSIO: My hopes do shape him for° the governor.

[*A shot within.*]

SECOND GENTLEMAN: They do discharge their shot of
courtesy;°
Our friends at least.

CASSIO: I pray you, sir, go forth,
And give us truth who 'tis that is arrived. 60

SECOND GENTLEMAN: I shall. *Exit.*

MONTANO: But, good Lieutenant, is your general wived?

CASSIO: Most fortunately. He hath achieved a maid
That paragons° description and wild fame,°
One that excels the quirks° of blazoning° pens, 65
And in th' essential vesture of creation
Does tire the enginer.°

*Enter* [*Second*] *Gentleman.*°

How now? Who has put in?°

SECOND GENTLEMAN: 'Tis one Iago, ancient to the General.

CASSIO: He's had most favorable and happy speed.
Tempests themselves, high seas, and howling winds, 70
The guttered° rocks and congregated sands—
Traitors ensteeped° to clog the guiltless keel—
As° having sense of beauty, do omit°
Their mortal° natures, letting go safely by
The divine Desdemona.

MONTANO: What is she? 75

CASSIO: She that I spake of, our great captain's captain,
Left in the conduct of the bold Iago,

---

55 **brow o' the sea** cliff-edge 57 **My . . . for** I hope it is 58 **discharge . . . courtesy** fire a salute in token of respect and courtesy 64 **paragons** surpasses. **wild fame** extravagant report 65 **quirks** witty conceits. **blazoning** setting forth as though in heraldic language 66–67 **in . . . enginer** in her real, God-given, beauty, (she) defeats any attempt to praise her. **enginer** engineer, i.e., poet, one who devises. [s.d.] **Second Gentleman** (So identified in the Quarto text here and in lines 58, 61, 68, and 96; the Folio calls him a gentleman.) 67 **put in** i.e., to harbor 71 **guttered** jagged, trenched 72 **ensteeped** lying under water 73 **As** as if. **omit** forbear to exercise 74 **mortal** deadly

Whose footing° here anticipates our thoughts
A sennight's° speed. Great Jove, Othello guard,
And swell his sail with thine own powerful breath,                    80
That he may bless this bay with his tall° ship,
Make love's quick pants in Desdemona's arms,
Give renewed fire to our extincted spirits,
And bring all Cyprus comfort!

*Enter Desdemona, Iago, Roderigo, and Emilia.*

                        O, behold,
The riches of the ship is come on shore!                    85
You men of Cyprus, let her have your knees.

[*The gentlemen make curtsy to Desdemona.*]

Hail to thee, lady! And the grace of heaven
Before, behind thee, and on every hand
Enwheel thee round!
DESDEMONA:               I thank you, valiant Cassio.
What tidings can you tell me of my lord?                    90
CASSIO:   He is not yet arrived, nor know I aught
But that he's well and will be shortly here.
DESDEMONA:   O, but I fear—How lost you company?
CASSIO:   The great contention of the sea and skies
Parted our fellowship.

               (*Within*) "*A sail, a sail!*" [*A shot.*]
               But hark. A sail!                    95
SECOND GENTLEMAN:   They give their greeting to the citadel.
This likewise is a friend.
CASSIO:               See for the news.

               [*Exit Second Gentleman.*]

Good Ancient, you are welcome. [*Kissing Emilia.*] Welcome,
   mistress.
Let it not gall your patience, good Iago,
That I extend° my manners; 'tis my breeding°                    100
That gives me this bold show of courtesy.
IAGO:   Sir, would she give you so much of her lips

---

**78 footing** landing   **79 sennight's** week's   **81 tall** splendid, gallant   **100 extend** give scope to.
**breeding** training in the niceties of etiquette

As of her tongue she oft bestows on me,
You would have enough.
DESDEMONA:   Alas, she has no speech!°                      105
IAGO:   In faith, too much.
I find it still,° when I have list° to sleep.
Marry, before your ladyship, I grant,
She puts her tongue a little in her heart
And chides with thinking.°
EMILIA:                         You have little cause to say so.   110
IAGO:   Come on, come on. You are pictures out of doors,°
Bells° in your parlors, wildcats in your kitchens,°
Saints° in your injuries, devils being offended,
Players° in your huswifery,° and huswives° in your beds.
DESDEMONA:   O, fie upon thee, slanderer!                    115
IAGO:   Nay, it is true, or else I am a Turk.°
You rise to play, and go to bed to work.
EMILIA:   You shall not write my praise.
IAGO:                                    No, let me not.
DESDEMONA:   What wouldst write of me, if thou shouldst
praise me?
IAGO:   O gentle lady, do not put me to 't,                  120
For I am nothing if not critical.°
DESDEMONA:   Come on, essay.°—There's one gone to the
harbor?
IAGO:   Ay, madam.
DESDEMONA:   I am not merry, but I do beguile
The thing I am° by seeming otherwise.                        125
Come, how wouldst thou praise me?
IAGO:   I am about it, but indeed my invention
Comes from my pate as birdlime° does from frieze°—
It plucks out brains and all. But my Muse labors,°
And thus she is delivered:                                   130
If she be fair and wise, fairness and wit,
The one's for use, the other useth it.°

---

105 **she has no speech** i.e., she's not a chatterbox, as you allege   107 **still** always.   **list** desire
110 **with thinking** i.e., in her thoughts only   111 **pictures out of doors** i.e., silent and well-behaved
in public   112 **Bells** i.e., jangling, noisy, and brazen.   **in your kitchens** i.e., in domestic affairs.
(Ladies would not do the cooking.)   113 **Saints** martyrs   114 **Players** idlers, triflers, or deceivers.
**huswifery** housekeeping.   **huswives** hussies (i.e., women are "busy" in bed, or unduly thrifty in
dispensing sexual favors)   116 **a Turk** an infidel, not to be believed   121 **critical** censorious
122 **essay** try   125 **The thing I am** i.e., my anxious self   128 **birdlime** sticky substance used to
catch small birds.   **frieze** coarse woolen cloth   129 **labors** (1) exerts herself (2) prepares to deliver
a child (with a following pun on *delivered* in line 130)   132 **The one's . . . it** i.e., her cleverness will
make use of her beauty

DESEMONA: Well praised! How if she be black° and witty?

IAGO: If she be black, and thereto have a wit,
She'll find a white° that shall her blackness fit.°                    135

DESEMONA: Worse and worse.

EMILIA:                              How if fair and foolish?

IAGO: She never yet was foolish that was fair,
For even her folly° helped her to an heir.°

DESEMONA: These are old fond° paradoxes to make fools
laugh i' th' alehouse.
What miserable praise hast thou for her that's foul and
foolish?                                                                 140

IAGO: There's none so foul° and foolish thereunto,°
But does foul° pranks which fair and wise ones do.

DESEMONA: O heavy ignorance! Thou praisest the worst best.
But what praise couldst thou bestow on a deserving woman indeed, one that, in the authority of her merit, did justly put on
the vouch° of very malice itself?                                        145

IAGO: She that was ever fair, and never proud,
Had tongue at will, and yet was never loud,
Never lacked gold and yet went never gay,°
Fled from her wish, and yet said, "Now I may,"°
She that being angered, her revenge being nigh,                          150
Bade her wrong stay° and her displeasure fly,
She that in wisdom never was so frail
To change the cod's head for the salmon's tail,°
She that could think and ne'er disclose her mind,
See suitors following and not look behind,                               155
She was a wight, if ever such wight were—

DESEMONA: To do what?

IAGO: To suckle fools° and chronicle small beer.°

DESEMONA: O most lame and impotent conclusion! Do not
learn of him, Emilia, though he be thy husband. How say you,    160
Cassio? Is he not a most profane° and liberal° counselor?

---

133 **black** dark-complexioned, brunette   135 **a white** a fair person (with word-play on "wight," a person)   **fit** (with sexual suggestion of mating)   138 **folly** (with added meaning of "lechery, wantonness")   **to an heir** i.e., to bear a child   139 **fond** foolish   141 **foul** ugly.   **thereunto** in addition   142 **foul** sluttish   145 **put . . . vouch** compel the approval   148 **gay** extravagantly clothed   149 **Fled . . . may** avoided temptation where the choice was hers   151 **Bade . . . stay** i.e., resolved to put up with her injury patiently   153 **To . . . tail** i.e., to exchange a lackluster husband for a sexy lover (?) (**Cod's head** is slang for "penis," and tail, for "pudendum.")   158 **suckle fools** breastfeed babies   **chronicle small beer** i.e., keep petty household accounts; keep track of trivial matters   161 **profane** irreverent, ribald   **liberal** licentious free-spoken

CASSIO: He speaks home,° madam. You may relish° him more
in° the soldier than in the scholar.

[*Cassio and Desdemona stand together, conversing intimately.*]

IAGO [*aside*]: He takes her by the palm. Ay, well said,° whisper.
With as little a web as this will I ensnare as great a fly as Cas- 165
sio. Ay, smile upon her, do; I will gyve° thee in thine own
courtship.° You say true;° 'tis so, indeed. If such tricks as these
strip you out of your lieutenantry, it had been better you had
not kissed your three fingers so oft, which now again you are
most apt to play the sir° in. Very good; well kissed! An excellent courtesy! 'Tis so, indeed. Yet again your fingers to your
lips? Would they were clyster pipes° for your sake! [*Trumpet* 170
*within.*] The Moor! I know his trumpet.
CASSIO: 'Tis truly so.
DESDEMONA: Let's meet him and receive him.
CASSIO: Lo, where he comes!

*Enter Othello and attendants.*

OTHELLO: O my fair warrior!
DESDEMONA:              My dear Othello! 175
OTHELLO: It gives me wonder great as my content
   To see you here before me. O my soul's joy,
   If after every tempest come such calms,
   May the winds blow till they have wakened death,
   And let the laboring bark climb hills of seas 180
   Olympus-high, and duck again as low
   As hell's from heaven! If it were now to die,
   'Twere now to be most happy, for I fear
   My soul hath her content so absolute
   That not another comfort like to this 185
   Succeeds in unknown fate.°
DESDEMONA:             The heavens forbid
   But that our loves and comforts should increase
   Even as our days do grow!
OTHELLO: Amen to that, sweet powers!
   I cannot speak enough of this content. 190

---

162 **home** right to the target (a term from fencing)   **relish** appreciate   **in** in the character of   164
**well said** well done   166 **gyve** fetter, shackle.   **courtship** courtesy, show of courtly manners.   **You
say true** i.e., that's right, go ahead   169 **the sir** i.e., the fine gentleman   170 **clyster pipes** tubes
used for enemas and douches   186 **Succeeds . . . fate** i.e., can follow in the unknown future

It stops me here; it is too much of joy.
And this, and this, the greatest discords be

[*They kiss.*]°

That e'er our hearts shall make!
IAGO [*aside*]:   O, you are well tuned now!
But I'll set down° the pegs that make this music,                    195
As honest as I am.°
OTHELLO:   Come, let us to the castle.
News, friends! Our wars are done, the Turks are drowned.
How does my old acquaintance of this isle?—
Honey, you shall be well desired° in Cyprus;                         200
I have found great love amongst them. O my sweet,
I prattle out of fashion,° and I dote
In mine own comforts.—I prithee, good Iago,
Go to the bay and disembark my coffers.°
Bring thou the master° to the citadel;                               205
He is a good one, and his worthiness
Does challenge° much respect.—Come, Desdemona.—
Once more, well met at Cyprus!

> *Exeunt Othello and Desdemona [and all
> but Iago and Roderigo].*

IAGO [*to an attendant*]:   Do thou meet me presently at the harbor.
[*To Roderigo.*] Come hither. If thou be'st valiant—as, they say,
base men° being in love have then a nobility in their natures   210
more than is native to them—list° me. The Lieutenant tonight
watches on the court of guard.° First, I must tell thee this: Desdemona is directly in love with him.
RODERIGO:   With him? Why, 'tis not possible.
IAGO:   Lay thy finger thus,° and let thy soul be instructed. Mark   215
me with what violence she first loved the Moor, but° for brag-
ging and telling her fantastical lies. To love him still for prat-
ing? Let not thy discreet heart think it. Her eye must be fed;
and what delight shall she have to look on the devil? When the

---

192 [s.d.] **They kiss** (The direction is from the Quarto.)   195 **set down** loosen (and hence untune
the instrument)   196 **As . . . I am** for all my supposed honesty   200 **desired** welcomed   202 **out
of fashion** irrelevantly, incoherently (?)   204 **coffers** chests, baggage   205 **master** ship's captain
207 **challenge** lay claim to, deserve   210 **base men** even lowly born men   211 **list** listen to
212 **court of guard** guardhouse. (Cassio is in charge of the watch.)   215 **thus** i.e., on your lips
216 **but** only

blood is made dull with the act of sport,° there should be, again to inflame it and to give satiety a fresh appetite, loveliness in favor,° sympathy° in years, manners,and beauties—all 220 which the Moor is defective in. Now, for want of these required conveniences,° her delicate tenderness will find itself abused,° begin to heave the gorge,° disrelish and abhor the Moor. Very nature° will instruct her in it and compel her to some second choice. Now, sir, this granted—as it is a most pregnant° and unforced position—who stands so eminent in 225 the degree of° this fortune as Cassio does? A knave very voluble,° no further conscionable° than in putting on the mere form of civil and humane° seeming for the better compassing of his salt° and most hidden loose affection.° Why, none, why, none. A slipper° and subtle knave, a finder out of occasions, that has an eye can stamp° and counterfeit advantages,° 230 though true advantage never present itself; a devilish knave. Besides, the knave is handsome, young, and hath all those requisites in him that folly° and green° minds look after. A pestilent complete knave, and the woman hath found him° already.

RODERIGO:   I cannot believe that in her. She's full of most blessed condition.° 235

IAGO:   Blessed fig's end!° The wine she drinks is made of grapes. If she had been blessed, she would never have loved the Moor. Blessed pudding!° Didst thou not see her paddle with the palm of his hand? Didst not mark that?

RODERIGO:   Yes, that I did; but that was but courtesy.

IAGO:   Lechery, by this hand. An index° and obscure° prologue to 240 the history of lust and foul thoughts. They met so near with their lips that their breaths embraced together. Villainous thoughts, Roderigo! When these mutualities° so marshal the way, hard at hand° comes the master and main exercise, th' in-

---

219 **the act of sport** sex   220 **favor** appearance.   **sympathy** correspondence, similarity   222 **required conveniences** things conducive to sexual compatibility   223 **abused** cheated, revolted. **heave the gorge** experience nausea   224 **Very nature** her very instincts   225 **pregnant** evident, cogent   226 **in . . . of** next in line for   227 **voluble** facile, glib.   **conscionable** conscientious, conscience-bound   228 **humane** polite, courteous.   **salt** licentious   229 **affection** passion. **slipper** slippery   230 **an eye can stamp** an eye that can coin, create   231 **advantages** favorable opportunities   233 **folly** wantonness.   **green** immature   234 **found him** sized him up, perceived his intent   235 **condition** disposition   236 **fig's end** (See Act I, Scene iii, line 316 for the vulgar gesture of the fig.)   237 **pudding** sausage   240 **index** table of contents.   **obscure** (i.e., the *lust and foul thoughts* in line 241 are secret, hidden from view)   243 **mutualities** exchanges, intimacies.   **hard at hand** closely following

corporate° conclusion. Pish! But, sir, be you ruled by me. I
have brought you from Venice. Watch you° tonight; for the  245
command, I'll lay 't upon you.° Cassio knows you not. I'll not
be far from you. Do you find some occasion to anger Cassio,
either by speaking too loud, or tainting° his discipline, or from
what other course you please, which the time shall more favorably minister.°
RODERIGO:  Well.  250
IAGO:  Sir, he's rash and very sudden in choler,° and haply° may
strike at you. Provoke him that he may, for even out of that
will I cause these of Cyprus to mutiny,° whose qualification°
shall come into no true taste° again but by the displanting of
Cassio. So shall you have a shorter journey to your desires by
the means I shall then have to prefer° them, and the impedi-  255
ment most profitably removed, without the which there were
no expectation of our prosperity.
RODERIGO:  I will do this, if you can bring it to any
opportunity.
IAGO:  I warrant° thee. Meet me by and by° at the citadel. I
must fetch his necessaries ashore. Farewell.  260
RODERIGO:  Adieu.                                    *Exit.*
IAGO:  That Cassio loves her, I do well believe 't;
That she loves him, 'tis apt° and of great credit.°
The Moor, howbeit that I endure him not,
Is of a constant, loving, noble nature,  265
And I dare think he'll prove to Desdemona
A most dear husband. Now, I do love her too,
Not out of absolute lust—though peradventure
I stand accountant° for as great a sin—
But partly led to diet° my revenge  270
For that I do suspect the lusty Moor
Hath leaped into my seat, the thought whereof
Doth, like a poisonous mineral, gnaw my innards;
And nothing can or shall content my soul
Till I am evened with him, wife for wife,  275
Or failing so, yet that I put the Moor
At least into a jealousy so strong

244 incorporate carnal   245 Watch you stand watch   245–246 for the command . . . you I'll
arrange for you to be appointed, given orders   247 tainting disparaging   249 minister provide
251 choler wrath   haply perhaps   253 mutiny riot.   qualification appeasement.   true taste i.e.,
acceptable state   255 prefer advance   259 warrant assure.   by and by immediately   263 apt
probable.   credit credibility   269 accountant accountable   270 diet feed

That judgment cannot cure. Which thing to do,
If this poor trash of Venice, whom I trace°
For° his quick hunting, stand the putting on,°          280
I'll have our Michael Cassio on the hip,°
Abuse° him to the Moor in the rank garb—°
For I fear Cassio with my nightcap° too—
Make the Moor thank me, love me, and reward me
For making him egregiously an ass                       285
And practicing upon° his peace and quiet
Even to madness. 'Tis here, but yet confused.
Knavery's plain face is never seen till used.

                                                 *Exit.*

## SCENE II [CYPRUS. A STREET.]

*Enter Othello's Herald with a proclamation.*

HERALD:  It is Othello's pleasure, our noble and valiant general,
that, upon certain tidings now arrived, importing the mere
perdition° of the Turkish fleet, every man put himself into triumph:° some to dance, some to make bonfires, each man to
what sport and revels his addiction° leads him. For, besides
these beneficial news, it is the celebration of his nuptial. So    5
much was his pleasure should be proclaimed. All offices° are
open, and there is full liberty of feasting from this present hour
of five till the bell have told eleven. Heaven bless the isle of
Cyprus and our noble general Othello!

                                                 *Exit.*

## SCENE III [CYPRUS. THE CITADEL.]

*Enter Othello, Desdemona, Cassio, and attendants.*

OTHELLO:  Good Michael, look you to the guard tonight.
Let's teach ourselves that honorable stop°
Not to outsport° discretion.

---

279 **trace** i.e., train, or follow (?), or perhaps *trash,* a hunting term, meaning to put weights on a
hunting dog in order to slow him down    280 **For** to make more eager.  **stand . . . on** respond
properly when I incite him to quarrel    281 **on the hip** at my mercy, where I can throw him. (A
wrestling term.)  282 **Abuse** slander.  **rank garb** coarse manner, gross fashion    283 **with my
nightcap** i.e., as a rival in my bed, as one who gives me cuckold's horns    286 **practicing upon**
plotting against
2 **mere perdition** complete destruction    3 **triumph** public celebration    4 **addiction** inclination
6 **offices** rooms where food and drink are kept    2 **stop** restraint    3 **outsport** celebrate beyond the
bounds of

CASSIO:  Iago hath direction what to do,
But notwithstanding, with my personal eye                    5
Will I look to 't.
OTHELLO:            Iago is most honest.
Michael, good night. Tomorrow with your earliest°
Let me have speech with you. [*To Desdemona.*]
     Come, my dear love,
The purchase made, the fruits are to ensue;
That profit's yet to come 'tween me and you.°—               10
Good night.

*Exit [Othello, with Desdemona and attendants].*

*Enter Iago.*

CASSIO:  Welcome, Iago. We must to the watch.
IAGO:  Not this hour,° Lieutenant; 'tis not yet ten o' the clock.
Our general cast° us thus early for the love of his Desdemona;
who° let us not therefore blame. He hath not yet made wanton
the night with her, and she is sport for Jove.                15
CASSIO:  She's a most exquisite lady.
IAGO:  And, I'll warrant her, full of game.
CASSIO:  Indeed, she's a most fresh and delicate creature.
IAGO:  What an eye she has! Methinks it sounds a parley° to
provocation.
CASSIO:  An inviting eye, and yet methinks right modest.        20
IAGO:  And when she speaks, is it not an alarum° to love?
CASSIO:  She is indeed perfection.
IAGO:  Well, happiness to their sheets! Come, Lieutenant, I have a
stoup° of wine, and here without° are a brace° of Cyprus gal-
lants that would fain have a measure° to the health of black
Othello.                                                       25
CASSIO:  Not tonight, good Iago. I have very poor and unhappy
brains for drinking. I could well wish courtesy would invent
some other custom of entertainment.
IAGO:  O, they are our friends. But one cup! I'll drink for you.°

---

7 **with your earliest** at your earliest convenience   9–10 **The purchase . . . you** i.e., though married,
we haven't yet consummated our love   13 **Not this hour** not for an hour yet.   **cast** dismissed
14 **who** i.e., Othello   19 **sounds a parley** calls for a conference, issues an invitation   21 **alarum**
signal calling men to arms (continuing the military metaphor of *parley,* line 19)   23 **stoup** measure
of liquor, two quarts   24 **without** outside.   **brace** pair   24–25 **fain have a measure** gladly drink a
toast   28 **for you** in your place. (Iago will do the steady drinking to keep the gallants company
while Cassio has only one cup.)

CASSIO: I have drunk but one cup tonight, and that was craftily
   qualified° too, and behold what innovation° it makes here.° I   30
   am unfortunate in the infirmity and dare not task my weakness
   with any more.
IAGO: What, man? 'Tis a night of revels. The gallants desire it.
CASSIO: Where are they?
IAGO: Here at the door. I pray you, call them in.
CASSIO: I'll do 't, but it dislikes me.°                      *Exit.*   35
IAGO: If I can fasten but one cup upon him,
   With that which he hath drunk tonight already,
   He'll be as full of quarrel and offense°
   As my young mistress' dog. Now, my sick fool Roderigo,
   Whom love hath turned almost the wrong side out,        40
   To Desdemona hath tonight caroused°
   Potations pottle-deep;° and he's to watch.°
   Three lads of Cyprus—noble swelling° spirits,
   That hold their honors in a wary distance,°
   The very elements° of this warlike isle—                45
   Have I tonight flustered with flowing cups,
   And they watch° too. Now, 'mongst this flock of drunkards
   Am I to put our Cassio in some action
   That may offend the isle.—But here they come.

*Enter Cassio, Montano, and gentlemen; [servants following
with wine].*

   If consequence do but approve my dream,°                50
   My boat sails freely both with wind and stream.°
CASSIO: 'Fore God, they have given me a rouse° already.
MONTANO: Good faith, a little one; not past a pint, as I am a
   soldier.
IAGO: Some wine, ho! [He *sings.*]

      "And let me the cannikin° clink, clink,
      And let me the cannikin clink.                       55
      A soldier's a man,
      O, man's life's but a span;°

29 **qualified** diluted   30 **innovation** disturbance, insurrection.   **here** i.e., in my head   35 **it
dislikes me** i.e., I'm reluctant   38 **offense** readiness to take offense   41 **caroused** drunk off
42 **pottle-deep** to the bottom of the tankard.   **watch** stand watch   43 **swelling** proud   44 **hold . . .
distance** i.e., are extremely sensitive of their honor   45 **very elements** typical sort   47 **watch** are
members of the guard   50 **If . . . dream** if subsequent events will only substantiate my scheme
51 **stream** current   52 **rouse** full draft of liquor   55 **cannikin** small drinking vessel   58 **span** brief
span of time. (Compare Psalm 39:6 as rendered in the 1928 *Book of Common Prayer*: "Thou hast
made my days as it were a span long.")

Why, then, let a soldier drink."

Some wine, boys!                                                                   60

CASSIO:  'Fore God, an excellent song.

IAGO:  I learned it in England, where indeed they are most potent
in potting.° Your Dane, your German, and your swag-bellied
Hollander—drink, ho!—are nothing to your English.

CASSIO:  Is your Englishman so exquisite in his drinking?             65

IAGO:  Why, he drinks you,° with facility, your Dane° dead
drunk; he sweats not° to overthrow your Almain;° he gives
your Hollander a vomit ere the next pottle can be filled.

CASSIO:  To the health of our general!

MONTANO:  I am for it, Lieutenant, and I'll do you justice.°          70

IAGO:  O sweet England! [*He sings.*]

> "King Stephen was and—a worthy peer,
>    His breeches cost him but a crown;
> He held them sixpence all too dear,
>    With that he called the tailor lown.°                            75
> He was a wight of high renown,
>    And thou art but of low degree.
> 'Tis pride° that pulls the country down;
>    Then take thy auld° cloak about thee."

Some wine, ho!                                                                    80

CASSIO:  'Fore God, this is a more exquisite song than the
other.

IAGO:  Will you hear 't again?

CASSIO:  No, for I hold him to be unworthy of his place that does
those things. Well, God's above all; and there be souls must be
saved, and there be souls must not be saved.                          85

IAGO:  It's true, good Lieutenant.

CASSIO:  For mine own part—no offense to the General, nor any
man of quality°—I hope to be saved.

IAGO:  And so do I too, Lieutenant.

CASSIO:  Ay, but, by your leave, not before me; the lieutenant is
to be saved before the ancient. Let's have no more of this;          90
let's to our affairs.—God forgive us our sins!—Gentlemen,
let's look to our business. Do not think, gentlemen, I am
drunk. This is my ancient; this is my right hand, and this is

---

62 **potting** drinking  66 **drinks you** drinks.  **your Dane** your typical Dane.  **sweats not** i.e., need
not exert himself  67 **Almain** German  70 **I'll . . . justice** i.e., I'll drink as much as you  75 **lown**
lout, rascal  78 **pride** i.e., extravagance in dress  79 **auld** old  88 **quality** rank

my left. I am not drunk now. I can stand well enough, and
speak well enough.

GENTLEMEN: Excellent well. 95

CASSIO: Why, very well then; you must not think then that I
am drunk. *Exit.*

MONTANO: To th' platform, masters. Come, let's set the
watch.°

[*Exeunt Gentlemen.*]

IAGO: You see this fellow that is gone before.
He's a soldier fit to stand by Caesar
And give direction; and do but see his vice. 100
'Tis to his virtue a just equinox,°
The one as long as th' other. 'Tis pity of him.
I fear the trust Othello puts him in,
On some odd time of his infirmity,
Will shake this island.

MONTANO: But is he often thus? 105

IAGO: 'Tis evermore the prologue to his sleep.
He'll watch the horologe a double set,°
If drink rock not his cradle.

MONTANO: It were well
The General were put in mind of it.
Perhaps he sees it not, or his good nature 110
Prizes the virtue that appears in Cassio
And looks not on his evils. Is not this true?

*Enter Roderigo.*

IAGO [aside to him]: How now, Roderigo?
I pray you, after the Lieutenant; go. [*Exit Roderigo.*]

MONTANO: And 'tis great pity that the noble Moor 115
Should hazard such a place as his own second
With° one of an engraffed° infirmity.
It were an honest action to say so
To the Moor.

IAGO: Not I, for this fair island.
I do love Cassio well and would do much 120

---

**97 set the watch** mount the guard **101 just equinox** exact counterpart. (*Equinox* is a day on which daylight and nighttime hours are equal.) **107 watch . . . set** stay awake twice around the clock or *horologe* **116–117 hazard . . . With** risk giving such an important position as his second in command to **117 engraffed** engrafted, inveterate

To cure him of this evil.        [*Cry within:* "Help! Help!"]
            But, hark! What noise?

*Enter Cassio, pursuing° Roderigo.*

CASSIO:  Zounds, you rogue! You rascal!
MONTANO:  What's the matter, Lieutenant?
CASSIO:  A knave teach me my duty? I'll beat the knave into a
    twiggen° bottle.
RODERIGO:  Beat me?                                              125
CASSIO:  Dost thou prate, rogue? [*He strikes Roderigo.*]
MONTANO:  Nay, good Lieutenant. [*Restraining him.*] I pray
    you, sir, hold your hand.
CASSIO:  Let me go, sir, or I'll knock you o'er the mazard.°
MONTANO:  Come, come, you're drunk.
CASSIO:  Drunk?                                    [*They fight.*]    130
IAGO [*aside to Roderigo*]:  Away, I say. Go out and cry a
    mutiny.°

                                                        [*Exit Roderigo.*]

Nay, good Lieutenant—God's will, gentlemen—
Help, ho!—Lieutenant—sir—Montano—sir—
Help, masters!°—Here's a goodly watch indeed!

[*A bell rings.*]°

Who's that which rings the bell?—Diablo,° ho!                    135
The town will rise.° God's will, Lieutenant, hold!
You'll be ashamed forever.

*Enter Othello and attendants [with weapons].*

OTHELLO:  What is the matter here?
MONTANO:                                Zounds, I bleed still.
    I am hurt to th' death. He dies! [*He thrusts at Cassio.*]
OTHELLO:                                Hold, for your lives!
IAGO:  Hold, ho! Lieutenant—sir—Montano—gentlemen—            140
    Have you forgot all sense of place and duty?
    Hold! The General speaks to you. Hold, for shame!

---

121 [s.d.] **pursuing** (The Quarto text reads, "driving in.")   124 **twiggen** wicker-covered. (Cassio
vows to assail Roderigo until his skin resembles wickerwork or until he has driven Roderigo through
the holes in a wickerwork.)   128 **mazard** i.e., head (literally, a drinking vessel)   131 **mutiny** riot
134 **masters** sirs   [s.d.] **A bell rings** (This direction is from the Quarto, as are *Exit Roderigo* at line
114, *They fight* at line 130, and *with weapons* at line 137.)   135 **Diablo** the devil   136 **rise** grow
riotous

OTHELLO: Why, how now, ho! From whence ariseth this?
Are we turned Turks, and to ourselves do that
Which heaven hath forbid the Ottomites?° 145
For Christian shame, put by this barbarous brawl!
He that stirs next to carve for° his own rage
Holds his soul light;° he dies upon his motion.°
Silence that dreadful bell. It frights the isle
From her propriety.° What is the matter, masters? 150
Honest Iago, that looks dead with grieving,
Speak. Who began this? On thy love, I charge thee.
IAGO: I do not know. Friends all but now, even now,
In quarter° and in terms° like bride and groom
Devesting them° for bed; and then, but now— 155
As if some planet had unwitted men—
Swords out, and tilting one at others' breasts
In opposition bloody. I cannot speak°
Any beginning to this peevish odds;°
And would in action glorious I had lost 160
Those legs that brought me to a part of it!
OTHELLO: How comes it, Michael, you are thus forgot?°
CASSIO: I pray you, pardon me. I cannot speak.
OTHELLO: Worthy Montano, you were wont be° civil;
The gravity and stillness° of your youth 165
The world hath noted, and your name is great
In mouths of wisest censure.° What's the matter
That you unlace° your reputation thus
And spend your rich opinion° for the name
Of a night-brawler? Give me answer to it. 170
MONTANO: Worthy Othello, I am hurt to danger.
Your officer, Iago, can inform you—
While I spare speech, which something° now offends° me—
Of all that I do know; nor know I aught
By me that's said or done amiss this night, 175
Unless self-charity be sometimes a vice,

---

144–145 **to ourselves . . . Ottomites** inflict on ourselves the harm that heaven has prevented the
Turks from doing (by destroying their fleet) 147 **carve for** i.e., indulge, satisfy with his sword 148
**Holds . . . light** i.e., places little value on his life **upon his motion** if he moves 150 **propriety**
proper state or condition 154 **In quarter** in friendly conduct, within bounds. **in terms** on good
terms 155 **Devesting them** undressing themselves 158 **speak** explain 159 **peevish** odds childish
quarrel 162 **are thus forgot** have forgotten yourself thus 164 **wont be** accustomed to be 165
**stillness** sobriety 167 **censure** judgment 168 **unlace** undo, lay open (as one might loose the
strings of a purse containing reputation) 169 **opinion** reputation 173 **something** somewhat
**offends** pains

And to defend ourselves it be a sin
When violence assails us.
OTHELLO:                    Now, by heaven,
My blood° begins my safer guides° to rule,
And passion, having my best judgment collied,°                    180
Essays° to lead the way. Zounds, if I stir,
Or do but lift this arm, the best of you
Shall sink in my rebuke. Give me to know
How this foul rout° began, who set it on;
And he that is approved in° this offense,                    185
Though he had twinned with me, both at a birth,
Shall lose me. What? In a town of° war
Yet wild, the people's hearts brim full of fear,
To manage° private and domestic quarrel?
In night, and on the court and guard of safety?°                    190
'Tis monstrous. Iago, who began 't?
MONTANO [*to Iago*]:   If partially affined,° or leagued in office,°
Thou dost deliver more or less than truth,
Thou art no soldier.
IAGO:                    Touch me not so near.
I had rather have this tongue cut from my mouth                    195
Than it should do offense to Michael Cassio;
Yet, I persuade myself, to speak the truth
Shall nothing wrong him. Thus it is, General.
Montano and myself being in speech,
There comes a fellow crying out for help,                    200
And Cassio following him with determined sword
To execute° upon him. Sir, this gentleman

[*indicating Montano*]

Steps in to Cassio and entreats his pause.°
Myself the crying fellow did pursue,
Lest by his clamor—as it so fell out—                    205
The town might fall in fright. He, swift of foot,
Outran my purpose, and I returned, the rather°
For that I heard the clink and fall of swords

---

179 **blood** passion (of anger)   **guides** i.e., reason   180 **collied** darkened   181 **Essays** undertakes
184 **rout** riot   185 **approved in** found guilty of   187 **town of** town garrisoned for   189 **manage**
undertake   190 **on . . . safety** at the main guardhouse or headquarters and on watch   192 **partially**
**affined** made partial by some personal relationship   **leagued in office** in league as fellow officers
202 **execute** give effect to (his anger)   203 **his pause** him to stop   207 **rather** sooner

And Cassio high in oath, which till tonight
I ne'er might say before. When I came back—                    210
For this was brief—I found them close together
At blow and thrust, even as again they were
When you yourself did part them.
More of this matter cannot I report.
But men are men; the best sometimes forget.°                  215
Though Cassio did some little wrong to him,
As men in rage strike those that wish them best,°
Yet surely Cassio, I believe, received
From him that fled some strange indignity,
Which patience could not pass.°
OTHELLO:                      I know, Iago,                    220
Thy honesty and love doth mince this matter,
Making it light to Cassio. Cassio, I love thee,
But nevermore be officer of mine.

*Enter Desdemona, attended.*

Look if my gentle love be not raised up.
I'll make thee an example.                                    225
DESDEMONA:   What is the matter, dear?
OTHELLO:                             All's well now,
    sweeting;
Come away to bed. [*To Montano.*] Sir, for your hurts,
Myself will be your surgeon.°—Lead him off.

[*Montano is led off.*]

Iago, look with care about the town
And silence those whom this vile brawl distracted.            230
Come, Desdemona. 'Tis the soldiers' life
To have their balmy slumbers waked with strife.

                    *Exit [with all but Iago and Cassio].*

IAGO:   What, are you hurt, Lieutenant?
CASSIO:   Ay, past all surgery.
IAGO:   Marry, God forbid!                                    235

---

**215 forget** forget themselves   **217 those . . . best** i.e., even those who are well disposed   **220 pass** pass over, overlook   **228 be your surgeon** i.e., make sure you receive medical attention

**CASSIO:** Reputation, reputation, reputation! O, I have lost my reputation! I have lost the immortal part of myself, and what remains is bestial. My reputation, Iago, my reputation!

**IAGO:** As I am an honest man, I thought you had received some bodily wound; there is more sense in that than in reputation. 240 Reputation is an idle and most false imposition,° oft got without merit and lost without deserving. You have lost no reputation at all, unless you repute yourself such a loser. What, man, there are more ways to recover° the General again. You are but now cast in his mood°—a punishment more in policy° than in malice, even so as one would beat his offenseless dog to affright an imperious lion.° Sue° to him again and he's yours. 245

**CASSIO:** I will rather sue to be despised than to deceive so good a commander with so slight,° so drunken, and so indiscreet an officer. Drunk? And speak parrot?° And squabble? Swagger? Swear? And discourse fustian with one's own shadow? O thou invisible spirit of wine, if thou hast no name to be known by, 250 let us call thee devil!

**IAGO:** What was he that you followed with your sword? What had he done to you?

**CASSIO:** I know not.

**IAGO:** Is 't possible?

**CASSIO:** I remember a mass of things, but nothing distinctly; a 255 quarrel, but nothing wherefore.° O God, that men should put an enemy in their mouths to steal away their brains! That we should, with joy, pleasance, revel, and applause° transform ourselves into beasts!

**IAGO:** Why, but you are now well enough. How came you thus recovered?

**CASSIO:** It hath pleased the devil drunkenness to give place to the devil wrath. One unperfectness shows me another, to make me 260 frankly despise myself.

**IAGO:** Come, you are too severe a moraler.° As the time, the place, and the condition of this country stands, I could heartily

---

241 **false imposition** thing artificially imposed and of no real value   243 **recover** regain favor with
244 **cast in his mood** dismissed in a moment of anger.   **in policy** done for expediency's sake and
as a public gesture   245 **would . . . lion** i.e., would make an example of a minor offender in order
to deter more important and dangerous offenders   246 **Sue** petition   248 **slight** worthless
248–249 **speak parrot** talk nonsense, rant   256 **wherefore** why   258 **applause** desire for
applause   262 **moraler** moralizer

wish this had not befallen; but since it is as it is, mend it for
your own good.

CASSIO: I will ask him for my place again; he shall tell me I am a  265
drunkard. Had I as many mouths as Hydra,° such an answer
would stop them all. To be now a sensible man, by and by a
fool, and presently a beast! O, strange! Every inordinate cup is
unblessed, and the ingredient is a devil.

IAGO: Come, come, good wine is a good familiar creature, if it be
well used. Exclaim no more against it. And, good Lieutenant, I  270
think you think I love you.

CASSIO: I have well approved° it, sir. I drunk!

IAGO: You or any man living may be drunk at a time,° man. I'll
tell you what you shall do. Our general's wife is now the general—I may say so in this respect, for that° he hath devoted
and given up himself to the contemplation, mark, and denote-  275
ment° of her parts and graces. Confess yourself freely to her;
importune her help to put you in your place again. She is of so
free,° so kind, so apt, so blessed a disposition, she holds it a
vice in her goodness not to do more than she is requested. This
broken joint between you and her husband entreat her to
splinter;° and, my fortunes against any lay° worth naming, this  280
crack of your love shall grow stronger than it was before.

CASSIO: You advise me well.

IAGO: I protest,° in the sincerity of love and honest kindness.

CASSIO: I think it freely;° and betimes in the morning I will beseech the virtuous Desdemona to undertake for me. I am des-  285
perate of my fortunes if they check° me here.

IAGO: You are in the right. Good night, Lieutenant. I must to
the watch.

CASSIO: Good night, honest Iago.                        *Exit Cassio.*

IAGO: And what's he then that says I play the villain,
When this advice is free° I give, and honest,                        290
Probal° to thinking, and indeed the course
To win the Moor again? For 'tis most easy

---

266 **Hydra** the Lernaean Hydra, a monster with many heads and the ability to grow two heads
when one was cut off, slain by Hercules as the second of his twelve labors    272 **approved** proved
273 **at a time** at one time or another    274–275 **in . . . that** in view of this fact, that    275–276
**mark, and denotement** (Both words mean "observation.")    276 **parts** qualities    277 **free** generous
280 **splinter** bind with splints    **lay** stake, wager    283 **protest** insist, declare    284 **freely**
unreservedly    286 **check** repulse    290 **free** (1) free from guile (2) freely given    291 **Probal**
probable, reasonable

Th' inclining° Desdemona to subdue°
In any honest suit; she's framed as fruitful°
As the free elements.° And then for her                              295
To win the Moor—were 't to renounce his baptism,
All seals and symbols of redeemèd sin—
His soul is so enfettered to her love
That she may make, unmake, do what she list,
Even as her appetite° shall play the god                           300
With his weak function.° How am I then a villain,
To counsel Cassio to this parallel° course
Directly to his good? Divinity of hell!°
When devils will the blackest sins put on,°
They do suggest° at first with heavenly shows,                     305
As I do now. For whiles this honest fool
Plies Desdemona to repair his fortune,
And she for him pleads strongly to the Moor,
I'll pour this pestilence into his ear,
That she repeals him° for her body's lust;                         310
And by how much she strives to do him good,
She shall undo her credit with the Moor.
So will I turn her virtue into pitch,°
And out of her own goodness make the net
That shall enmesh them all.

*Enter Roderigo.*

                        How now, Roderigo?                                  315
RODERIGO:   I do follow here in the chase, not like a hound that
hunts, but one that fills up the cry.° My money is almost spent;
I have been tonight exceedingly well cudgeled; and I think the
issue will be I shall have so much° experience for my pains,
and so, with no money at all and a little more wit, return again
to Venice.                                                          320
IAGO:   How poor are they that have not patience!

---

293 **inclining** favorably disposed.  **subdue** persuade  294 **framed as fruitful** created as generous
295 **free elements** i.e., earth, air, fire, and water, unrestrained and spontaneous  300 **her appetite**
her desire, or, perhaps, his desire for her  301 **function** exercise of faculties (weakened by his
fondness for her)  302 **parallel** corresponding to these facts and to his best interests  303 **Divinity
of hell** inverted theology of hell (which seduces the soul to its damnation)  304 **put on** further,
instigate  305 **suggest** tempt  310 **repeals him** attempts to get him restored  313 **pitch** i.e., (1) foul
blackness (2) a snaring substance  317 **fills up the cry** merely takes part as one of the pack  318 **so
much** just so much and no more

What wound did ever heal but by degrees?
Thou know'st we work by wit, and not by witchcraft,
And wit depends on dilatory time.
Does 't not go well? Cassio hath beaten thee,                    325
And thou, by that small hurt, hast cashiered° Cassio.
Though other things grow fair against the sun,
Yet fruits that blossom first will first be ripe.°
Content thyself awhile. By the Mass, 'tis morning!
Pleasure and action make the hours seem short.                  330
Retire thee; go where thou art billeted.
Away, I say! Thou shalt know more hereafter.
Nay, get thee gone.                          *Exit Roderigo.*
          Two things are to be done.
My wife must move° for Cassio to her mistress;
I'll set her on;                                                335
Myself the while to draw the Moor apart
And bring him jump° when he may Cassio find
Soliciting his wife. Ay, that's the way.
Dull not device° by coldness° and delay.            *Exit.*

## Act III

### Scene I [Before the Chamber of Othello and Desdemona.]

*Enter Cassio [and] Musicians.*

CASSIO:  Masters, play here—I will content your pains°—
Something that's brief, and bid "Good morrow, General."

[*They play.*]

[*Enter*] *Clown.*

CLOWN:  Why, masters, have your instruments been in Naples,
that they speak i' the nose° thus?

---

326 **cashiered** dismissed from service   327–328 **Though . . . ripe** i.e., plans that are well-prepared
and set expeditiously in motion will soonest ripen into success   334 **move** plead   337 **jump**
precisely   339 **device** plot   **coldness** lack of zeal
1 **content your pains** reward your efforts   3–4 **speak i' the nose** (1) sound nasal (2) sound like one
whose nose has been attacked by syphilis. (Naples was popularly supposed to have a high incidence
of venereal disease.)

A MUSICIAN:  How, sir, how?                                                    5
CLOWN:  Are these, I pray you, wind instruments?
A MUSICIAN:  Ay, marry, are they, sir.
CLOWN:  O, thereby hangs a tail.
A MUSICIAN:  Whereby hangs a tale, sir?
CLOWN:  Marry, sir, by many a wind instrument° that I know.     10
   But, masters, here's money for you. [*He gives money.*] And the
   General so likes your music that he desires you, for love's
   sake,° to make no more noise with it.
A MUSICIAN:  Well, sir, we will not.
CLOWN:  If you have any music that may not° be heard, to 't
   again; but, as they say, to hear music the General does not
   greatly care.                                                             15
A MUSICIAN:  We have none such, sir.
CLOWN:  Then put up your pipes in your bag, for I'll away.°
   Go, vanish into air, away!                      *Exeunt Musicians.*
CASSIO:  Dost thou hear, mine honest friend?
CLOWN:  No, I hear not your honest friend; I hear you.          20
CASSIO:  Prithee, keep up° thy quillets.° There's a poor piece of
   gold for thee. [*He gives money.*] If the gentle-woman that at-
   tends the General's wife be stirring, tell her there's one Cassio
   entreats her a little favor of speech.° Wilt thou do this?
CLOWN:  She is stirring, sir. If she will stir° hither, I shall seem°
   to notify unto her.                                                      25
CASSIO:  Do, good my friend.                            *Exit Clown.*

   *Enter Iago.*

                          In happy time,° Iago.
IAGO:  You have not been abed, then?
CASSIO:  Why, no. The day had broke
   Before we parted. I have made bold, Iago,
   To send in to your wife. My suit to her                                  30
   Is that she will to virtuous Desdemona
   Procure me some access.

---

10 **wind instrument** (With a joke on flatulence. The *tail,* line 8, that hangs nearby the *wind instrument* suggests the penis.)  12 **for love's sake** (1) out of friendship and affection (2) for the sake of lovemaking in Othello's marriage  14 **may not** cannot  17 **I'll away** (Possibly a misprint, or a snatch of song?)  21 **keep up** do not bring out, do not use.  **quillets** quibbles, puns  23 **a little . . . speech** the favor of a brief talk  25 **stir** bestir herself (with a play on *stirring,* "rousing herself from rest")  **seem** deem it good, think fit  26 **In happy time** i.e., well-met

IAGO:   I'll send her to you presently;
And I'll devise a means to draw the Moor
Out of the way, that your converse and business          35
May be more free.

CASSIO:   I humbly thank you for 't.                    *Exit [Iago].*
                              I never knew
A Florentine° more kind and honest.

*Enter Emilia.*

EMILIA:   Good morrow, good Lieutenant. I am sorry
For your displeasure;° but all will sure be well.        40
The General and his wife are talking of it,
And she speaks for you stoutly.° The Moor replies
That he you hurt is of great fame° in Cyprus
And great affinity,° and that in wholesome wisdom
He might not but refuse you; but he protests° he loves you   45
And needs no other suitor but his likings
To take the safest occasion by the front°
To bring you in again.

CASSIO:                       Yet I beseech you,
If you think fit, or that it may be done,
Give me advantage of some brief discourse                50
With Desdemona alone.

EMILIA:                       Pray you, come in.
I will bestow you where you shall have time
To speak your bosom° freely.

CASSIO:   I am much bound to you.          *[Exeunt.]*

SCENE II [THE CITADEL.]

*Enter Othello, Iago, and Gentlemen.*

OTHELLO *[giving letters]:*   These letters give, Iago, to the pilot.
And by him do my duties° to the Senate.
That done, I will be walking on the works;°
Repair° there to me.

---

38 **Florentine** i.e., even a fellow Florentine. (Iago is a Venetian; Cassio is a Florentine.)   40
**displeasure** fall from favor   42 **stoutly** spiritedly   43 **fame** reputation, importance   44 **affinity**
kindred, family connection   45 **protests** insists   47 **occasion . . . front** opportunity by the forelock
53 **bosom** inmost thoughts
2 **do my duties** convey my respects   3 **works** breastworks, fortifications   4 **Repair** return, come

IAGO:                     Well, my good lord, I'll do 't.
OTHELLO:   This fortification, gentlemen, shall we see 't?                     5
GENTLEMEN:   We'll wait upon° your lordship.                     *Exeunt.*

## SCENE III [THE GARDEN OF THE CITADEL.]

*Enter Desdemona, Cassio, and Emilia.*

DESDEMONA:   Be thou assured, good Cassio, I will do
All my abilities in thy behalf.
EMILIA:   Good madam, do. I warrant it grieves my husband
As if the cause were his.
DESDEMONA:   O, that's an honest fellow. Do not doubt, Cassio,      5
But I will have my lord and you again
As friendly as you were.
CASSIO:                     Bounteous madam,
Whatever shall become of Michael Cassio,
He's never anything but your true servant.
DESDEMONA:   I know 't. I thank you. You do love my lord;      10
You have known him long, and be you well assured
He shall in strangeness° stand no farther off
Than in a politic° distance.
CASSIO:                     Ay, but, lady,
That policy may either last so long,
Or feed upon such nice and waterish diet,°                     15
Or breed itself so out of circumstance,°
That, I being absent and my place supplied,°
My general will forget my love and service.
DESDEMONA:   Do not doubt° that. Before Emilia here
I give thee warrant° of thy place. Assure thee,                     20
If I do vow a friendship I'll perform it
To the last article. My lord shall never rest.
I'll watch him tame° and talk him out of patience;°
His bed shall seem a school, his board° a shrift;°
I'll intermingle everything he does                     25

6 **wait upon** attend
12 **strangeness** aloofness   13 **politic** required by wise policy   15 **Or . . . diet** or sustain itself at
length upon such trivial and meager technicalities   16 **breed . . . circumstance** continually renew
itself so out of chance events, or yield so few chances for my being pardoned   17 **supplied** filled by
another person   19 **doubt** fear   20 **warrant** guarantee   23 **watch him tame** tame him by keeping
him from sleeping (a term from falconry)   **out of patience** past his endurance   24 **board** dining
table.   **shrift** confessional

With Cassio's suit. Therefore be merry, Cassio,
For thy solicitor° shall rather die
Than give thy cause away.°

*Enter Othello and Iago [at a distance].*

EMILIA:   Madam, here comes my lord.
CASSIO:   Madam, I'll take my leave.                                        30
DESDEMONA:   Why, stay, and hear me speak.
CASSIO:   Madam, not now. I am very ill at ease,
Unfit for mine own purposes.
DESDEMONA:   Well, do your discretion.°         *Exit Cassio.*
IAGO:   Ha? I like not that.                                               35
OTHELLO:   What dost thou say?
IAGO:   Nothing, my lord; or if—I know not what.
OTHELLO:   Was not that Cassio parted from my wife?
IAGO:   Cassio, my lord? No, sure, I cannot think it,
That he would steal away so guiltylike,                                    40
Seeing you coming.
OTHELLO:   I do believe 'twas he.
DESDEMONA:   How now, my lord?
I have been talking with a suitor here,
A man that languishes in your displeasure.                                 45
OTHELLO:   Who is 't you mean?
DESDEMONA:   Why, your lieutenant, Cassio. Good my lord,
If I have any grace or power to move you,
His present reconciliation take;°
For if he be not one that truly loves you,                                 50
That errs in ignorance and not in cunning,°
I have no judgment in an honest face.
I prithee, call him back.
OTHELLO:   Went he hence now?
DESDEMONA:   Yes, faith, so humbled                                        55
That he hath left part of his grief with me
To suffer with him. Good love, call him back.
OTHELLO:   Not now, sweet Desdemon. Some other time.
DESDEMONA:   But shall 't be shortly?
OTHELLO:   The sooner, sweet, for you.                                     60
DESDEMONA:   Shall 't be tonight at supper?

---

27 **solicitor** advocate   28 **away** up   34 **do your discretion** act according to your own discretion
49 **His . . . take** let him be reconciled to you right away   51 **in cunning** wittingly

OTHELLO:  No, not tonight.
DESDEMONA:  Tomorrow dinner,° then?
OTHELLO:  I shall not dine at home.
I meet the captains at the citadel.                                            65
DESDEMONA:  Why, then, tomorrow night, or Tuesday morn,
On Tuesday noon, or night, on Wednesday morn.
I prithee, name the time, but let it not
Exceed three days. In faith, he's penitent;
And yet his trespass, in our common reason°—                                   70
Save that, they say, the wars must make example
Out of her best°—is not almost° a fault
T' incur a private check.° When shall he come?
Tell me, Othello. I wonder in my soul
What you would ask me that I should deny,                                      75
Or stand so mammering on.° What? Michael Cassio,
That came a-wooing with you, and so many a time,
When I have spoke of you dispraisingly,
Hath ta'en your part—to have so much to do
To bring him in!° By 'r Lady, I could do much—                                 80
OTHELLO:  Prithee, no more. Let him come when he will;
I will deny thee nothing.
DESDEMONA:  Why, this is not a boon.
'Tis as I should entreat you wear your gloves,
Or feed on nourishing dishes, or keep you warm,                               85
Or sue to you to do a peculiar° profit
To your own person. Nay, when I have a suit
Wherein I mean to touch° your love indeed,
It shall be full of poise° and difficult weight,
And fearful to be granted.                                                     90
OTHELLO:  I will deny thee nothing.
Whereon,° I do beseech thee, grant me this,
To leave me but a little to myself.
DESDEMONA:  Shall I deny you? No. Farewell, my lord.
OTHELLO:  Farewell, my Desdemona. I'll come to thee straight.°               95
DESDEMONA:  Emilia, come.—Be as your fancies° teach you;
Whate'er you be, I am obedient.          *Exit [with Emilia].*

---

63 **dinner** (The noontime meal.)  70 **common reason** everyday judgments  71–72 **Save . . . best** were
it not that, as the saying goes, military discipline requires making an example of the very best men.
(*Her* refers to wars as a singular concept.)  72 **not almost** scarcely  73 **private check** even a private
reprimand  76 **mammering on** wavering about  80 **bring him in** restore him to favor  86 **peculiar**
particular, personal  88 **touch** test  89 **poise** weight, heaviness; or equipoise, delicate balance
involving hard choice  92 **Whereon** in return for which  95 **straight** straightway  96 **fancies**
inclinations

OTHELLO: Excellent wretch!° Perdition catch my soul
But I do love thee! And when I love thee not,
Chaos is come again.°                                           100
IAGO: My noble lord—
OTHELLO: What dost thou say, Iago?
IAGO: Did Michael Cassio, when you wooed my lady,
Know of your love?
OTHELLO: He did, from first to last. Why dost thou ask?    105
IAGO: But for a satisfaction of my thought;
No further harm.
OTHELLO:                Why of thy thought, Iago?
IAGO: I did not think he had been acquainted with her.
OTHELLO: O, yes, and went between us very oft.
IAGO: Indeed?                                                    110
OTHELLO: Indeed? Ay, indeed. Discern'st thou aught in that?
Is he not honest?
IAGO: Honest, my lord?
OTHELLO: Honest. Ay, honest.
IAGO: My lord, for aught I know.                                115
OTHELLO: What dost thou think?
IAGO: Think, my lord?
OTHELLO: "Think, my lord?" By heaven, thou echo'st me,
As if there were some monster in thy thought
Too hideous to be shown. Thou dost mean something.            120
I heard thee say even now, thou lik'st not that,
When Cassio left my wife. What didst not like?
And when I told thee he was of my counsel°
In my whole course of wooing, thou criedst "Indeed?"
And didst contract and purse° thy brow together              125
As if thou then hadst shut up in thy brain
Some horrible conceit.° If thou dost love me,
Show me thy thought.
IAGO: My lord, you know I love you.
OTHELLO: I think thou dost;                                     130
And, for° I know thou'rt full of love and honesty,
And weigh'st thy words before thou giv'st them breath,
Therefore these stops° of thine fright me the more;

---

**98 wretch** (A term of affectionate endearment.)   **99–100 And . . . again** i.e., my love for you will last forever, until the end of time when chaos will return. (But with an unconscious, ironic suggestion that, if anything should induce Othello to cease loving Desdemona, the result would be chaos.)   **123 of my counsel** in my confidence   **125 purse** knit   **127 conceit** fancy   **131 for** because   **133 stops** pauses

For such things in a false disloyal knave
Are tricks of custom,° but in a man that's just          135
They're close dilations,° working from the heart
That passion cannot rule.°
IAGO:                    For° Michael Cassio,
I dare be sworn I think that he is honest.
OTHELLO:   I think so too.
IAGO:                    Men should be what they seem;
Or those that be not, would they might seem none!°       140
OTHELLO:   Certain, men should be what they seem.
IAGO:   Why, then, I think Cassio's an honest man.
OTHELLO:   Nay, yet there's more in this.
I prithee, speak to me as to thy thinkings,
As thou dost ruminate, and give thy worst of thoughts     145
The worst of words.
IAGO:                    Good my lord, pardon me.
Though I am bound to every act of duty,
I am not bound to that° all slaves are free to.°
Utter my thoughts? Why, say they are vile and false,
As where's the palace whereinto foul things              150
Sometimes intrude not? Who has that breast so pure
But some uncleanly apprehensions
Keep leets and law days,° and in sessions sit
With° meditations lawful?°
OTHELLO:   Thou dost conspire against thy friend,° Iago,   155
If thou but think'st him wronged and mak'st his ear
A stranger to thy thoughts.
IAGO:                         I do beseech you,
Though I perchance am vicious° in my guess—
As I confess it is my nature's plague
To spy into abuses, and oft my jealousy°                 160
Shapes faults that are not—that your wisdom then,°
From one° that so imperfectly conceits,°
Would take no notice, nor build yourself a trouble

135 **of custom** customary   136 **close dilations** secret or involuntary expressions or delays
137 **That passion cannot rule** i.e., that are too passionately strong to be restrained (referring to the
workings), or . . . that cannot rule its own passions (referring to the heart).   137 **For** as for
140 **none** i.e., not to be men, or not seem to be honest   148 **that** that which.   **free to** free with
respect to   153 **Keep leets and law days** i.e., hold court, set up their authority in one's heart. (*Leets*
are a kind of manor court; *law days* are the days courts sit in session, or those sessions.)   154 **With**
along with.   **lawful** innocent   155 **thy friend** i.e., Othello   158 **vicious** wrong   160 **jealousy**
suspicious nature   161 **then** on that account   162 **one** i.e., myself, Iago.   **conceits** judges,
conjectures

Out of his scattering° and unsure observance.
It were not for your quiet nor your good,                    165
Nor for my manhood, honesty, and wisdom,
To let you know my thoughts.
OTHELLO:                         What dost thou mean?
IAGO:   Good name in man and woman, dear my lord,
Is the immediate° jewel of their souls.
Who steals my purse steals trash; 'tis something, nothing;    170
'Twas mine, 'tis his, and has been slave to thousands;
But he that filches from me my good name
Robs me of that which not enriches him
And makes me poor indeed.
OTHELLO:   By heaven, I'll know thy thoughts.              175
IAGO:   You cannot, if° my heart were in your hand,
Nor shall not, whilst 'tis in my custody.
OTHELLO:   Ha?
IAGO:   O, beware, my lord, of jealousy.
It is the green-eyed monster which doth mock
The meat it feeds on.° That cuckold lives in bliss          180
Who, certain of his fate, loves not his wronger;°
But O, what damnèd minutes tells° he o'er
Who dotes, yet doubts, suspects, yet fondly loves!
OTHELLO:   O misery!
IAGO:   Poor and content is rich, and rich enough,°        185
But riches fineless° is as poor as winter
To him that ever fears he shall be poor.
Good God, the souls of all my tribe defend
From jealousy!
OTHELLO:   Why, why is this?                                190
Think'st thou I'd make a life of jealousy,
To follow still the changes of the moon
With fresh suspicions?° No! To be once in doubt
Is once° to be resolved.° Exchange me for a goat
When I shall turn the business of my soul                   195

---

164 **scattering** random   169 **immediate** essential, most precious   176 **if** even if   179–180 **doth mock . . . on** mocks and torments the heart of its victim, the man who suffers jealousy   181 **his wronger** i.e., his faithless wife. (The unsuspecting cuckold is spared the misery of loving his wife only to discover she is cheating on him.)   182 **tells** counts   185 **Poor . . . enough** to be content with what little one has is the greatest wealth of all. (Proverbial.)   186 **fineless** boundless   192–193 **To follow . . . suspicions** to be constantly imagining new causes for suspicion, changing incessantly like the moon   194 **once** once and for all.   **resolved** free of doubt, having settled the matter

To such exsufflicate and blown° surmises
Matching thy inference.° 'Tis not to make me jealous
To say my wife is fair, feeds well, loves company,
Is free of speech, sings, plays, and dances well;
Where virtue is, these are more virtuous.                                    200
Nor from mine own weak merits will I draw
The smallest fear or doubt of her revolt,°
For she had eyes, and chose me. No, Iago,
I'll see before I doubt; when I doubt, prove;
And on the proof, there is no more but this—                                 205
Away at once with love or jealousy.
IAGO:   I am glad of this, for now I shall have reason
To show the love and duty that I bear you
With franker spirit. Therefore, as I am bound,
Receive it from me. I speak not yet of proof.                                210
Look to your wife; observe her well with Cassio.
Wear your eyes thus, not° jealous nor secure.°
I would not have your free and noble nature,
Out of self-bounty,° be abused.° Look to 't.
I know our country disposition well;                                         215
In Venice they do let God see the pranks
They dare not show their husbands; their best conscience
Is not to leave 't undone, but keep 't unknown.
OTHELLO:   Dost thou say so?
IAGO:   She did deceive her father, marrying you;                            220
And when she seemed to shake and fear your looks,
She loved them most.
OTHELLO:                          And so she did.
IAGO:                                        Why, go to,° then!
She that, so young, could give out such a seeming,°
To seel° her father's eyes up close as oak,°
He thought 'twas witchcraft! But I am much to blame.                         225
I humbly do beseech you of your pardon
For too much loving you.
OTHELLO:   I am bound° to thee forever.
IAGO:   I see this hath a little dashed your spirits.

---

196 **exsufflicate and blown** inflated and blown up, rumored about, or, spat out and flyblown, hence,
loathsome, disgusting   197 **inference** description or allegation   202 **doubt . . . revolt** fear of her
unfaithfulness   212 **not** neither.   **secure** free from uncertainty   214 **self-bounty** inherent or
natural goodness and generosity.   **abused** deceived   222 **go to** (An expression of impatience.)
223 **seeming** false appearance   224 **seel** blind (a term from falconry)   **oak** (A close-grained wood.)
228 **bound** indebted (but perhaps with ironic sense of "tied")

OTHELLO: Not a jot, not a jot.
IAGO:                                        I' faith, I fear it has.                230
I hope you will consider what is spoke
Comes from my love. But I do see you're moved.
I am to pray you not to strain my speech
To grosser issues° nor to larger reach°
Than to suspicion.                                                                     235
OTHELLO: I will not.
IAGO: Should you do so, my lord,
My speech should fall into such vile success°
Which my thoughts aimed not. Cassio's my worthy friend.
My lord, I see you're moved.
OTHELLO:                                  No, not much moved.            240
I do not think but Desdemona's honest.°
IAGO: Long live she so! And long live you to think so!
OTHELLO: And yet, how nature erring from itself—
IAGO: Ay, there's the point! As—to be bold with you—
Not to affect° many proposèd matches                                    245
Of her own clime, complexion, and degree,°
Whereto we see in all things nature tends—
Foh! One may smell in such a will° most rank,
Foul disproportion,° thoughts unnatural.
But pardon me. I do not in position°                                         250
Distinctly speak of her, though I may fear
Her will, recoiling° to her better° judgment,
May fall to match you with her country forms°
And happily repent.°
OTHELLO:                           Farewell, farewell!
If more thou dost perceive, let me know more.                       255
Set on thy wife to observe. Leave me, Iago.
IAGO [*going*]: My lord, I take my leave.
OTHELLO: Why did I marry? This honest creature doubtless
Sees and knows more, much more, than he unfolds.
IAGO [*returning*]: My Lord, I would I might entreat your honor   260
To scan° this thing no farther. Leave it to time.
Although 'tis fit that Cassio have his place—

---

234 **issues** significances.   **reach** meaning, scope   238 **success** effect, result   241 **honest** chaste   245 **affect** prefer, desire   246 **clime** . . . **degree** country, color, and social position   248 **will** sensuality, appetite   249 **disproportion** abnormality   250 **position** argument, proposition   252 **recoiling** reverting.   **better** i.e., more natural and reconsidered   253 **fall** . . . **forms** undertake to compare you with Venetian norms of handsomeness   254 **happily repent** haply repent her marriage   261 **scan** scrutinize

For, sure, he fills it up with great ability—
Yet, if you please to hold him off awhile,
You shall by that perceive him and his means.°          265
Note if your lady strain his entertainment°
With any strong or vehement importunity;
Much will be seen in that. In the meantime,
Let me be thought too busy° in my fears—
As worthy cause I have to fear I am—          270
And hold her free,° I do beseech your honor.
OTHELLO:   Fear not my government.°
IAGO:   I once more take my leave.          *Exit.*
OTHELLO:   This fellow's of exceeding honesty,
And knows all qualities,° with a learnèd spirit,          275
Of human dealings. If I do prove her haggard,°
Though that her jesses° were my dear heartstrings,
I'd whistle her off and let her down the wind°
To prey at fortune.° Haply, for° I am black
And have not those soft parts of conversation°          280
That chamberers° have, or for I am declined
Into the vale of years—yet that's not much—
She's gone. I am abused,° and my relief
Must be to loathe her. O curse of marriage,
That we can call these delicate creatures ours          285
And not their appetites! I had rather be a toad
And live upon the vapor of a dungeon
Than keep a corner in the thing I love
For others' uses. Yet, 'tis the plague of great ones;
Prerogatived° are they less than the base.°          290
'Tis destiny unshunnable, like death.
Even then this forkèd° plague is fated to us
When we do quicken.° Look where she comes.

---

265 **his means** the method he uses (to regain his post)   266 **strain his entertainment** urge his
reinstatement   269 **busy** interfering   271 **hold her free** regard her as innocent   272 **government**
self-control, conduct   275 **qualities** natures, types   276 **haggard** wild (like a wild female hawk)
277 **jesses** straps fastened around the legs of a trained hawk   278 **I'd . . . wind** i.e., I'd let her go
forever. (To release a hawk downwind was to invite it not to return.)   279 **prey at fortune** fend for
herself in the wild.   **Haply, for** perhaps because   280 **soft . . . conversation** pleasing graces of
social behavior   281 **chamberers** gallants   283 **abused** deceived   290 **Prerogatived** privileged (to
have honest wives).   **the base** ordinary citizens. (Socially prominent men are especially prone to the
unavoidable destiny of being cuckolded and to the public shame that goes with it.)   292 **forkèd** (An
allusion to the horns of the cuckold.)   293 **quicken** receive life. (Quicken may also mean to swarm
with maggots as the body festers, as in Act IV, Scene ii, line 69, in which case lines 292–293 suggest
that *even then,* in death, we are cuckolded by *forkèd* worms.)

*Enter Desdemona and Emilia.*

If she be false, O, then heaven mocks itself!
I'll not believe 't.
DESDEMONA:   How now, my dear Othello?                          295
Your dinner, and the generous° islanders
By you invited, do attend° your presence.
OTHELLO:   I am to blame.
DESDEMONA:                    Why do you speak so faintly?
Are you not well?
OTHELLO:   I have a pain upon my forehead here.                 300
DESDEMONA:   Faith, that's with watching.° 'Twill away again.

[*She offers her handkerchief.*]

Let me but bind it hard, within this hour
It will be well.
OTHELLO:          Your napkin° is too little.
Let it alone.° Come, I'll go in with you.

[*He puts the handkerchief from him, and it drops.*]

DESDEMONA:   I am very sorry that you are not well.             305

                                        *Exit [with Othello].*

EMILIA   [*picking up the handkerchief*]: I am glad I have found
   this napkin.
This was her first remembrance from the Moor.
My wayward° husband hath a hundred times
Wooed me to steal it, but she so loves the token—
For he conjured her she should ever keep it—              310
That she reserves it evermore about her
To kiss and talk to. I'll have the work ta'en out,°
And give 't Iago. What he will do with it
Heaven knows, not I;
I nothing but to please his fantasy.°                     315

---

296 **generous** noble   297 **attend** await   301 **watching** too little sleep   303 **napkin** handkerchief
304 **Let it alone** i.e., never mind   308 **wayward** capricious   312 **work ta'en out** design of the
embroidery copied   315 **fantasy** whim

*Enter Iago.*

IAGO: How now? What do you here alone?
EMILIA: Do not you chide. I have a thing for you.
IAGO: You have a thing for me? It is a common thing°—
EMILIA: Ha?
IAGO: To have a foolish wife.                                            320
EMILIA: O, is that all? What will you give me now
For that same handkerchief?
IAGO: What handkerchief?
EMILIA: What handkerchief?
Why, that the Moor first gave to Desdemona;                    325
That which so often you did bid me steal.
IAGO: Hast stolen it from her?
EMILIA: No, faith. She let it drop by negligence,
And to th' advantage° I, being here, took 't up.
Look, here 'tis.
IAGO:               A good wench! Give it me.                     330
EMILIA: What will you do with 't, that you have been so
earnest
To have me filch it?
IAGO [*snatching it*]: Why, what is that to you?
EMILIA: If it be not for some purpose of import,
Give 't me again. Poor lady, she'll run mad
When she shall lack° it.
IAGO:                    Be not acknown on't.°                    335
I have use for it. Go, leave me.          *Exit Emilia.*
I will in Cassio's lodging lose° this napkin
And let him find it. Trifles light as air
Are to the jealous confirmations strong
As proofs of Holy Writ. This may do something.           340
The Moor already changes with my poison.
Dangerous conceits° are in their natures poisons,
Which at the first are scarce found to distaste,°
But with a little act° upon the blood
Burn like the mines of sulfur.

---

318 common thing (With bawdy suggestion; *common* suggests coarseness and availability to all comers, and *thing* is a slang term for the pudendum.)   329 to th' advantage taking the opportunity   335 lack miss.   Be . . . on't do not confess knowledge of it   337 lose (The Folio spelling, *loose*, is a normal spelling for "lose," but it may also contain the idea of "let go," "release.")   342 conceits fancies, ideas   343 distaste be distasteful   344 act action, working

*Enter Othello.*

I did say so. 345
Look where he comes! Not poppy nor mandragora°
Nor all the drowsy syrups of the world
Shall ever medicine thee to that sweet sleep
Which thou owedst° yesterday.
OTHELLO:                          Ha, ha, false to me?
IAGO:   Why, how now, General? No more of that. 350
OTHELLO:   Avaunt! Begone! Thou hast set me on the rack.
I swear 'tis better to be much abused
Than but to know 't a little.
IAGO:                          How now, my lord?
OTHELLO:   What sense had I of her stolen hours of lust?
I saw 't not, thought it not, it harmed not me. 355
I slept the next night well, fed well, was free° and merry;
I found not Cassio's kisses on her lips.
He that is robbed, not wanting° what is stolen,
Let him not know 't and he's not robbed at all.
IAGO:   I am sorry to hear this. 360
OTHELLO:   I had been happy if the general camp,
Pioners° and all, had tasted her sweet body,
So° I had nothing known. O, now, forever
Farewell the tranquil mind! Farewell content!
Farewell the plumèd troops and the big° wars 365
That makes ambition virtue! O, farewell!
Farewell the neighing steed and the shrill trump,
The spirit-stirring drum, th' ear-piercing fife,
The royal banner, and all quality,°
Pride,° pomp, and circumstance° of glorious war! 370
And O, you mortal engines,° whose rude throats
Th' immortal Jove's dread clamors° counterfeit,
Farewell! Othello's occupation's gone.
IAGO:   Is 't possible, my lord?
OTHELLO:   Villain, be sure thou prove my love a whore! 375
Be sure of it. Give me the ocular proof,
Or, by the worth of mine eternal soul,

---

346 **mandragora** an opiate made of the mandrake root   349 **thou owedst** you did own   356 **free** carefree   358 **wanting** missing   362 **Pioners** diggers of mines, the lowest grade of soldiers   363 **So** provided   365 **big** stately   369 **quality** character, essential nature   370 **Pride** rich display. **circumstance** pageantry   371 **mortal engines** i.e., cannon. (*Mortal* means "deadly.")   372 **Jove's dread clamors** i.e., thunder

Thou hadst been better have been born a dog
Than answer my waked wrath!

IAGO:                                    Is 't come to this?

OTHELLO:   Make me to see 't, or at the least so prove it                    380
That the probation° bear no hinge nor loop
To hang a doubt on, or woe upon thy life!

IAGO:   My noble lord—

OTHELLO:   If thou dost slander her and torture me,
Never pray more; abandon all remorse;°                                         385
On horror's head horrors accumulate;°
Do deeds to make heaven weep, all earth amazed;°
For nothing canst thou to damnation add
Greater than that.

IAGO:                    O grace! O heaven forgive me!
Are you a man? Have you a soul or sense?                                        390
God b' wi' you; take mine office. O wretched fool,°
That lov'st to make thine honesty a vice!°
O monstrous world! Take note, take note, O world,
To be direct and honest is not safe.
I thank you for this profit,° and from hence°                                  395
I'll love no friend, sith° love breeds such offense.°

OTHELLO:   Nay, stay. Thou shouldst be° honest.

IAGO:   I should be wise, for honesty's a fool
And loses that° it works for.

OTHELLO:                    By the world,
I think my wife be honest and think she is not;                                400
I think that thou art just and think thou art not.
I'll have some proof. My name, that was as fresh
As Dian's° visage, is now begrimed and black
As mine own face. If there be cords, or knives,
Poison, or fire, or suffocating streams,                                       405
I'll not endure it. Would I were satisfied!

IAGO:   I see, sir, you are eaten up with passion.
I do repent me that I put it to you.
You would be satisfied?

---

381 **probation** proof   385 **remorse** pity, penitent hope for salvation   386 **horrors accumulate** add
still more horrors   387 **amazed** confounded with horror   391 **O wretched fool** (Iago addresses
himself as a fool for having carried honesty too far.)   392 **vice** failing, something overdone
395 **profit** profitable instruction. **hence** henceforth   396 **sith** since. **offense** i.e., harm to the one
who offers help and friendship   397 **Thou shouldst be** it appears that you are. (But Iago replies in
the sense of "ought to be.")   399 **that** what   403 **Dian** Diana, goddess of the moon and of chastity

OTHELLO:                    Would? Nay, and I will.
IAGO:   And may; but how? How satisfied, my lord?          410
Would you, the supervisor,° grossly gape on?
Behold her topped?
OTHELLO:                    Death and damnation! O!
IAGO:   It were a tedious difficulty, I think,
To bring them to that prospect. Damn them then,°
If ever mortal eyes do see them bolster°                       415
More° than their own.° What then? How then?
What shall I say? Where's satisfaction?
It is impossible you should see this,
Were they as prime° as goats, as hot as monkeys,
As salt° as wolves in pride,° and fools as gross         420
As ignorance made drunk. But yet I say,
If imputation and strong circumstances°
Which lead directly to the door of truth
Will give you satisfaction, you might have 't.
OTHELLO:   Give me a living reason she's disloyal.          425
IAGO:   I do not like the office.
But sith° I am entered in this cause so far,
Pricked° to 't by foolish honesty and love,
I will go on. I lay with Cassio lately,
And being troubled with a raging tooth                      430
I could not sleep. There are a kind of men
So loose of soul that in their sleeps will mutter
Their affairs. One of this kind is Cassio.
In sleep I heard him say, "Sweet Desdemona,
Let us be wary, let us hide our loves!"                       435
And then, sir, would he grip and wring my hand,
Cry "O sweet creature!", then kiss me hard,
As if he plucked up kisses by the roots
That grew upon my lips; then laid his leg
Over my thigh, and sighed, and kissed, and then             440
Cried, "Cursèd fate that gave thee to the Moor!"
OTHELLO:   O monstrous! Monstrous!
IAGO:                              Nay, this was but his dream.

---

**411 supervisor** onlooker   **414 Damn them then** i.e., they would have to be really incorrigible
**415 bolster** go to bed together, share a bolster   **416 More** other.   **own** own eyes   **419 prime**
lustful   **420 salt** wanton, sensual. **pride** heat   **422 imputation . . . circumstances** strong
circumstantial evidence   **427 sith** since   **428 Pricked** spurred

OTHELLO:   But this denoted a foregone conclusion.°
'Tis a shrewd doubt,° though it be but a dream.
IAGO:   And this may help to thicken other proofs                    445
That do demonstrate thinly.
OTHELLO:                              I'll tear her all to pieces.
IAGO:   Nay, but be wise. Yet we see nothing done;
She may be honest yet. Tell me but this:
Have you not sometimes seen a handkerchief
Spotted with strawberries° in your wife's hand?                       450
OTHELLO:   I gave her such a one. 'Twas my first gift.
IAGO:   I know not that; but such a handkerchief—
I am sure it was your wife's—did I today
See Cassio wipe his beard with.
OTHELLO:                              If it be that—
IAGO:   If it be that, or any that was hers,                          455
It speaks against her with the other proofs.
OTHELLO:   O, that the slave° had forty thousand lives!
One is too poor, too weak for my revenge.
Now do I see 'tis true. Look here, Iago,
All my fond° love thus do I blow to heaven.                           460
'Tis gone.
Arise, black vengeance, from the hollow hell!
Yield up, O love, thy crown and hearted° throne
To tyrannous hate! Swell, bosom, with thy freight,
For 'tis of aspics'° tongues!                                         465
IAGO:   Yet be content.°
OTHELLO:   O, blood, blood, blood!
IAGO:   Patience, I say. Your mind perhaps may change.
OTHELLO:   Never, Iago. Like to the Pontic Sea,°
Whose icy current and compulsive course                              470
Ne'er feels retiring ebb, but keeps due on
To the Propontic° and the Hellespont,°
Even so my bloody thoughts with violent pace
Shall ne'er look back, ne'er ebb to humble love,
I that a capable° and wide revenge                                    475

---

443 **foregone conclusion** concluded experience or action    444 **shrewd doubt** suspicious circumstance
450 **Spotted with strawberries** embroidered with a strawberry pattern    457 **the slave** i.e.,
Cassio    460 **fond** foolish (but also suggesting "affectionate")    463 **hearted** fixed in the heart
464 **freight** burden    465 **aspics'** venomous serpents'    466 **content** calm    469 **Pontic Sea** Black Sea
472 **Propontic** Sea of Marmara, between the Black Sea and the Aegean.    **Hellespont** Dardanelles,
straits where the Sea of Marmara joins with the Aegean    475 **capable** ample, comprehensive

Swallow them up. Now, by yond marble° heaven,
[*Kneeling*] In the due reverence of a sacred vow
I here engage my words.
IAGO:                              Do not rise yet.
[*He kneels.*]° Witness, you ever-burning lights above,
You elements that clip° us round about,                                480
Witness that here Iago doth give up
The execution° of his wit,° hands, heart,
To wronged Othello's service. Let him command,
And to obey shall be in me remorse,°
What bloody business ever.° [*They rise.*]
OTHELLO:                        I greet thy love,                        485
Not with vain thanks, but with acceptance bounteous,
And will upon the instant put thee to 't.°
Within these three days let me hear thee say
That Cassio's not alive.
IAGO:                              My friend is dead;
'Tis done at your request. But let her live.                          490
OTHELLO:   Damn her, lewd minx!° O, damn her, damn her!
Come, go with me apart. I will withdraw
To furnish me with some swift means of death
For the fair devil. Now art thou my lieutenant.
IAGO:   I am your own forever.                  *Exeunt.*            495


Scene IV [Before the Citadel.]

*Enter Desdemona, Emilia, and Clown.*

DESDEMONA:   Do you know, sirrah,° where Lieutenant Cassio
lies?°
CLOWN:   I dare not say he lies anywhere.
DESDEMONA:   Why, man?
CLOWN:   He's a soldier, and for me to say a soldier lies, 'tis
stabbing.
DESDEMONA:   Go to. Where lodges he?                                  5
CLOWN:   To tell you where he lodges is to tell you where I lie.
DESDEMONA:   Can anything be made of this?

---

476 **marble** i.e., gleaming like marble and unrelenting   479 **[s.d.] He kneels** (In the Quarto text,
Iago kneels here after Othello has knelt at line 477.)   480 **clip** encompass   482 **execution** exercise,
action.   **wit** mind   484 **remorse** pity (for Othello's wrongs)   485 **ever** soever   487 **to 't** to the
proof   491 **minx** wanton
1 **sirrah** (A form of address to an inferior.)   **lies** lodges. (But the Clown makes the obvious pun.)

CLOWN: I know not where he lodges, and for me to devise a lodging and say he lies here, or he lies there, were to lie in mine own throat.°

DESDEMONA: Can you inquire him out, and be edified by report? 10

CLOWN: I will catechize the world for him; that is, make questions, and by them answer.

DESDEMONA: Seek him, bid him come hither. Tell him I have moved° my lord on his behalf and hope all will be well.

CLOWN: To do this is within the compass of man's wit, and therefore I will attempt the doing it. 15

*Exit Clown.*

DESDEMONA: Where should I lose that handkerchief, Emilia?

EMILIA: I know not, madam.

DESDEMONA: Believe me, I had rather have lost my purse
Full of crusadoes;° and but my noble Moor 20
Is true of mind and made of no such baseness
As jealous creatures are, it were enough
To put him to ill thinking.

EMILIA:                              Is he not jealous?

DESDEMONA: Who, he? I think the sun where he was born
Drew all such humors° from him.

EMILIA:                              Look where he comes. 25

*Enter Othello.*

DESDEMONA: I will not leave him now till Cassio
Be called to him.—How is 't with you, my lord?

OTHELLO: Well, my good lady. [*Aside.*] O, hardness to
dissemble!—
How do you, Desdemona?

DESDEMONA:                         Well, my good lord.

OTHELLO: Give me your hand. [*She gives her hand.*] This hand
is moist, my lady.

DESDEMONA: It yet hath felt no age nor known no sorrow.

OTHELLO: This argues° fruitfulness° and liberal° heart. 30
Hot, hot, and moist. This hand of yours requires
A sequester° from liberty, fasting and prayer,
Much castigation,° exercise devout;° 35

---

9 lie . . . throat (1) lie egregiously and deliberately (2) use the windpipe to speak a lie   13 moved petitioned   20 crusadoes Portuguese gold coins   25 humors (Refers to the four bodily fluids thought to determine temperament.)   32 argues gives evidence of.   fruitfulness generosity, amorousness, and fecundity.   liberal generous and sexually free   34 sequester separation, sequestration   35 castigation corrective discipline.   exercise devout i.e., prayer, religious meditation, etc.

For here's a young and sweating devil here
That commonly rebels. 'Tis a good hand,
A frank° one.
DESDEMONA: You may indeed say so,
For 'twas that hand that gave away my heart.
OTHELLO: A liberal hand. The hearts of old gave hands,°          40
But our new heraldry is hands, not hearts.°
DESDEMONA: I cannot speak of this. Come now, your promise.
OTHELLO: What promise, chuck?°
DESDEMONA: I have sent to bid Cassio come speak with you.
OTHELLO: I have a salt and sorry rheum° offends me;          45
Lend me thy handkerchief.
DESDEMONA: Here, my lord. [*She offers a handkerchief.*]
OTHELLO: That which I gave you.
DESDEMONA:                          I have it not about me.
OTHELLO: Not?
DESDEMONA: No, faith, my lord.          50
OTHELLO: That's a fault. That handkerchief
Did an Egyptian to my mother give.
She was a charmer,° and could almost read
The thoughts of people. She told her, while she kept it
'Twould make her amiable° and subdue my father          55
Entirely to her love, but if she lost it
Or made a gift of it, my father's eye
Should hold her loathèd and his spirits should hunt
After new fancies.° She, dying, gave it me,
And bid me, when my fate would have me wived,          60
To give it her.° I did so; and take heed on 't;
Make it a darling like your precious eye.
To lose 't or give 't away were such perdition°
As nothing else could match.
DESDEMONA:                          Is 't possible?
OTHELLO: 'Tis true. There's magic in the web° of it.          65
A sibyl, that had numbered in the world
The sun to course two hundred compasses,°
In her prophetic fury° sewed the work;°

---

38 **frank** generous, open (with sexual suggestion)   40 **The hearts . . . hands** i.e., in former times, people would give their hearts when they gave their hands to something   41 **But . . . hearts** i.e., in our decadent times, the joining of hands is no longer a badge to signify the giving of hearts   43 **chuck** (A term of endearment.)   45 **salt . . . rheum** distressful head cold or watering of the eyes   53 **charmer** sorceress   55 **amiable** desirable   59 **fancies** loves   61 **her** i.e., to my wife   63 **perdition** loss   65 **web** fabric, weaving   67 **compasses** annual circlings. (The *sibyl*, or prophetess, was two-hundred years old.)   68 **prophetic fury** frenzy of prophetic inspiration.   **work** embroidered pattern

The worms were hallowed that did breed the silk,
And it was dyed in mummy° which the skillful          70
Conserved of° maidens' hearts.
DESDEMONA:                    I' faith! Is 't true?
OTHELLO:   Most veritable. Therefore look to 't well.
DESDEMONA:   Then would to God that I had never seen 't!
OTHELLO:   Ha? Wherefore?
DESDEMONA:   Why do you speak so startingly and rash?°          75
OTHELLO:   Is 't lost? Is 't gone? Speak, is 't out o' the way?°
DESDEMONA:   Heaven bless us!
OTHELLO:   Say you?
DESDEMONA:   It is not lost; but what an if° it were?
OTHELLO:   How?          80
DESDEMONA:   I say it is not lost.
OTHELLO:                    Fetch 't, let me see 't.
DESDEMONA:   Why, so I can, sir, but I will not now.
   This is a trick to put me from my suit.
   Pray you, let Cassio be received again.
OTHELLO:   Fetch me the handkerchief! My mind misgives.          85
DESDEMONA:   Come, come,
   You'll never meet a more sufficient° man.
OTHELLO:   The handkerchief!
DESDEMONA:                    I pray, talk° me of Cassio.
OTHELLO:   The handkerchief!
DESDEMONA:                    A man that all his time°
   Hath founded his good fortunes on your love,          90
   Shared dangers with you—
OTHELLO:   The handkerchief!
DESDEMONA:   I' faith, you are to blame.
OTHELLO:   Zounds!                    *Exit Othello.*
EMILIA:   Is not this man jealous?          95
DESDEMONA:   I ne'er saw this before.
   Sure, there's some wonder in this handkerchief.
   I am most unhappy in the loss of it.
EMILIA:   'Tis not a year or two shows us a man.°
   They are all but stomachs, and we all but° food;          100

---

70 **mummy** medicinal or magical preparation drained from mummified bodies   71 **Conserved of**
prepared or preserved out of   75 **startingly and rash** disjointedly and impetuously excitedly
76 **out o' the way** lost, misplaced   79 **an if** if   87 **sufficient** able, complete   88 **talk** talk to
89 **all his time** throughout his career   99 **'Tis . . . man** i.e., you can't really know a man even in a
year or two of experience (?), or, real men come along seldom (?)   100 **but** nothing but

They eat us hungerly,° and when they are full
They belch us.

*Enter Iago and Cassio.*

              Look you, Cassio and my husband.
IAGO [*to Cassio*]:   There is no other way; 'tis she must do 't.
And, lo, the happiness!° Go and importune her.
DESDEMONA:   How now, good Cassio? What's the news with    105
you?
CASSIO:   Madam, my former suit. I do beseech you
    That by your virtuous° means I may again
    Exist and be a member of his love
    Whom I, with all the office° of my heart,
    Entirely honor. I would not be delayed.    110
    If my offense be of such mortal° kind
    That nor my service past, nor° present sorrows,
    Nor purposed merit in futurity
    Can ransom me into his love again,
    But to know so must be my benefit;°    115
    So shall I clothe me in a forced content,
    And shut myself up in° some other course,
    To fortune's alms.°
DESDEMONA:         Alas, thrice-gentle Cassio,
    My advocation° is not now in tune.
    My lord is not my lord; nor should I know him,    120
    Were he in favor° as in humor° altered.
    So help me every spirit sanctified
    As I have spoken for you all my best
    And stood within the blank° of his displeasure
    For my free speech! You must awhile be patient.    125
    What I can do I will, and more I will
    Than for myself I dare. Let that suffice you.
IAGO:   Is my lord angry?
EMILIA:         He went hence but now,
    And certainly in strange unquietness.
IAGO:   Can he be angry? I have seen the cannon    130
    When it hath blown his ranks into the air,

101 **hungerly** hungrily  104 **the happiness** in happy time, fortunately met  107 **virtuous** efficacious
109 **office** loyal service  111 **mortal** fatal  112 **nor . . . nor** neither . . . nor  115 **But . . . benefit**
merely to know that my case is hopeless will have to content me (and will be better than
uncertainty)  117 **shut . . . in** confine myself to  118 **To fortune's alms** throwing myself on the
mercy of fortune  119 **advocation** advocacy  121 **favor** appearance. **humor** mood  124 **within
the blank** within point-blank range. (The *blank* is the center of the target.)

And like the devil from his very arm
Puffed his own brother—and is he angry?
Something of moment° then. I will go meet him.
There's matter in 't indeed, if he be angry.                    135
DESDEMONA:   I prithee, do so.                 *Exit [Iago].*
                Something, sure, of state,°
Either from Venice, or some unhatched practice°
Made demonstrable here in Cyprus to him,
Hath puddled° his clear spirit; and in such cases
Men's natures wrangle with inferior things,                     140
Though great ones are their object. 'Tis even so;
For let our finger ache, and it indues°
Our other, healthful members even to a sense
Of pain. Nay, we must think men are not gods,
Nor of them look for such observancy°                           145
As fits the bridal.° Beshrew me° much, Emilia,
I was, unhandsome° warrior as I am,
Arraigning his unkindness with° my soul;
But now I find I had suborned the witness,°
And he's indicted falsely.
EMILIA:                Pray heaven it be                        150
State matters, as you think, and no conception
Nor no jealous toy° concerning you.
DESDEMONA:   Alas the day! I never gave him cause.
EMILIA:   But jealous souls will not be answered so;
They are not ever jealous for the cause,                        155
But jealous for° they're jealous. It is a monster
Begot upon itself,° born on itself.
DESDEMONA:   Heaven keep that monster from Othello's mind!
EMILIA:   Lady, amen.
DESDEMONA:   I will go seek him. Cassio, walk hereabout.        160
If I do find him fit, I'll move your suit
And seek to effect it to my uttermost.
CASSIO:   I humbly thank your ladyship.

                *Exit [Desdemona with Emilia].*

---

134 **of moment** of immediate importance, momentous   136 **of state** concerning state affairs
137 **unhatched practice** as yet unexecuted or undiscovered plot   139 **puddled** muddied   142 **indues**
brings to the same condition   145 **observancy** attentiveness   146 **bridal** wedding (when a bride-
groom is newly attentive to his bride).   **Beshrew me** (A mild oath.)   147 **unhandsome** insufficient,
unskillful   148 **with** before the bar of   149 **suborned the witness** induced the witness to give false
testimony   152 **toy** fancy   156 **for** because   157 **Begot upon itself** generated solely from itself

*Enter Bianca.*

BIANCA: Save° you, friend Cassio!
CASSIO:                 What make° you from home?
How is 't with you, my most fair Bianca?             165
I' faith, sweet love, I was coming to your house.
BIANCA: And I was going to your lodging, Cassio.
What, keep a week away? Seven days and nights?
Eightscore-eight° hours? And lovers' absent hours
More tedious than the dial° eightscore times?         170
O weary reckoning!
CASSIO:            Pardon me, Bianca.
I have this while with leaden thoughts been pressed;
But I shall, in a more continuate° time,
Strike off this score° of absence. Sweet Bianca,

[*giving her Desdemona's handkerchief*]

Take me this work out.°
BIANCA:          O Cassio, whence came this?       175
This is some token from a newer friend.°
To the felt absence now I feel a cause.
Is 't come to this? Well, well.
CASSIO:            Go to, woman!
Throw your vile guesses in the devil's teeth,
From whence you have them. You are jealous now     180
That this is from some mistress, some remembrance.
No, by my faith, Bianca.
BIANCA:           Why, whose is it?
CASSIO: I know not, neither. I found it in my chamber.
I like the work well. Ere it be demanded°—
As like° enough it will—I would have it copied.      185
Take it and do 't, and leave me for this time.
BIANCA: Leave you? Wherefore?
CASSIO: I do attend here on the General,
And think it no addition,° nor my wish,
To have him see me womaned.                 190

---

**164 Save** God save.   **make** do   **169 Eightscore-eight** one hundred sixty-eight, the number of
hours in a week   **170 the dial** a complete revolution of the clock   **173 continuate** uninterrupted
**174 Strike . . . score** settle this account   **175 Take . . . out** copy this embroidery for me
**176 friend** mistress   **184 demanded** inquired for   **185 like** likely   **189 addition** i.e., addition to my
reputation

BIANCA: Why, I pray you?
CASSIO: Not that I love you not.
BIANCA: But that you do not love me.
    I pray you, bring° me on the way a little,
    And say if I shall see you soon at night.                      195
CASSIO: 'Tis but a little way that I can bring you,
    For I attend here; but I'll see you soon.
BIANCA: 'Tis very good. I must be circumstanced.°

                                        *Exeunt omnes.*

## A C T  *IV*

### S C E N E  I [B E F O R E  T H E  C I T A D E L.]

*Enter Othello and Iago.*

IAGO: Will you think so?
OTHELLO:                    Think so, Iago?
IAGO:                                What,
    To kiss in private?
OTHELLO:             An unauthorized kiss!
IAGO: Or to be naked with her friend in bed
    An hour or more, not meaning any harm?
OTHELLO: Naked in bed, Iago, and not mean harm?            5
    It is hypocrisy against the devil.
    They that mean virtuously and yet do so,
    The devil their virtue tempts, and they tempt heaven.
IAGO: If they do nothing, 'tis a venial° slip.
    But if I give my wife a handkerchief—                        10
OTHELLO: What then?
IAGO: Why then, 'tis hers, my lord, and being hers,
    She may, I think, bestow 't on any man.
OTHELLO: She is protectress of her honor too.
    May she give that?                                           15
IAGO: Her honor is an essence that's not seen;
    They have it° very oft that have it not.
    But, for the handkerchief—

---

**194 bring** accompany   **198 be circumstanced** be governed by circumstance, yield to your conditions
**9 venial** pardonable   **17 They have it** i.e., they enjoy a reputation for it

OTHELLO: By heaven, I would most gladly have forgot it.
Thou saidst—O, it comes o'er my memory                                    20
As doth the raven o'er the infectious house,°
Boding to all—he had my handkerchief.
IAGO: Ay, what of that?
OTHELLO:                          That's not so good now.
IAGO:                                               What
If I had said I had seen him do you wrong?
Or heard him say—as knaves be such abroad,°                               25
Who having, by their own importunate suit,
Or voluntary dotage° of some mistress,
Convincèd or supplied° them, cannot choose
But they must blab—
OTHELLO:                          Hath he said anything?
IAGO: He hath, my lord; but, be you well assured,                        30
No more than he'll unswear.
OTHELLO:                          What hath he said?
IAGO: Faith, that he did—I know not what he did.
OTHELLO: What? What?
IAGO: Lie—
OTHELLO: With her?
IAGO:                    With her, on her; what you will.
OTHELLO: Lie with her? Lie on her? We say "lie on her" when
they belie° her. Lie with her? Zounds, that's fulsome.°—Hand-       35
kerchief—confessions—handkerchief!—To confess and be
hanged for his labor—first to be hanged and then to
confess.°—I tremble at it. Nature would not invest herself in
such shadowing passion without some instruction.° It is not
words° that shakes me thus. Pish! Noses, ears, and lips.—Is 't
possible?—Confess—handkerchief!—O devil!                                 40

*Falls in a trance.*

IAGO: Work on,
My medicine, work! Thus credulous fools are caught,
And many worthy and chaste dames even thus,

---

21 **raven . . . house** (Allusion to the belief that the raven hovered over a house of sickness or
infection, such as one visited by the plague.)  25 **abroad** around about  27 **voluntary dotage**
willing infatuation  28 **Convincèd or supplied** seduced or sexually gratified  35 **belie** slander  36
**fulsome** foul  37–38 **first . . . to confess** (Othello reverses the proverbial *confess* and *be hanged;*
Cassio is to be given no time to confess before he dies.)  38–39 **Nature . . . instruction** i.e., without
some foundation in fact, nature would not have dressed herself in such an overwhelming passion
that comes over me now and fills my mind with images, or in such a lifelike fantasy as Cassio had
in his dream of lying with Desdemona  39 **words** mere words

All guiltless, meet reproach.—What, ho! My lord!    45
My lord, I say! Othello!

*Enter Cassio.*

How now, Cassio?
CASSIO:   What's the matter?
IAGO:   My lord is fall'n into an epilepsy.
This is his second fit. He had one yesterday.
CASSIO:   Rub him about the temples.
IAGO:                                     No, forbear.    50
The lethargy° must have his° quiet course.
If not, he foams at mouth, and by and by
Breaks out to savage madness. Look, he stirs.
Do you withdraw yourself a little while.
He will recover straight. When he is gone,    55
I would on great occasion° speak with you.

[*Exit Cassio.*]

How is it, General? Have you not hurt your head?
OTHELLO:   Dost thou mock me?°
IAGO:                          I mock you not, by heaven.
Would you would bear your fortune like a man!
OTHELLO:   A hornèd man's a monster and a beast.    60
IAGO:   There's many a beast then in a populous city,
And many a civil° monster.
OTHELLO:   Did he confess it?
IAGO:   Good sir, be a man.
Think every bearded fellow that's but yoked°    65
May draw with you.° There's millions now alive
That nightly lie in those unproper° beds
Which they dare swear peculiar.° Your case is better.°
O, 'tis the spite of hell, the fiend's arch-mock,
To lip° a wanton in a secure° couch    70
And to suppose her chaste! No, let me know,
And knowing what I am,° I know what she shall be.°

---

51 **lethargy** coma.   **his** its   56 **on great occasion** on a matter of great importance   58 **mock me**
(Othello takes Iago's question about hurting his head to be a mocking reference to the cuckold's
horns.)   62 **civil** i.e., dwelling in a city   65 **yoked** (1) married (2) put into the yoke of infamy and
cuckoldry   66 **draw with you** pull as you do, like oxen who are yoked, i.e., share your fate as
cuckold   67 **unproper** not exclusively their own   68 **peculiar** private, their own.   **better** i.e.,
because you know the truth   70 **lip** kiss.   **secure** free from suspicion   72 **what I am** i.e., a cuckold.
**she shall be** will happen to her

OTHELLO: O, thou art wise. 'Tis certain.

IAGO: Stand you awhile apart;
    Confine yourself but in a patient list.°                      75
    Whilst you were here o'erwhelmèd with your grief—
    A passion most unsuiting such a man—
    Cassio came hither. I shifted him away,°
    And laid good 'scuse upon your ecstasy,°
    Bade him anon return and here speak with me,          80
    The which he promised. Do but encave° yourself
    And mark the fleers,° the gibes, and notable° scorns
    That dwell in every region of his face;
    For I will make him tell the tale anew,
    Where, how, how oft, how long ago, and when        85
    He hath and is again to cope° your wife.
    I say, but mark his gesture. Marry, patience!
    Or I shall say you're all-in-all in spleen,°
    And nothing of a man.

OTHELLO:               Dost thou hear, Iago?
    I will be found most cunning in my patience;         90
    But—dost thou hear?—most bloody.

IAGO:                    That's not amiss;
    But yet keep time° in all. Will you withdraw?

[*Othello stands apart.*]

    Now will I question Cassio of Bianca,
    A huswife° that by selling her desires
    Buys herself bread and clothes. It is a creature       95
    That dotes on Cassio—as 'tis the strumpet's plague
    To beguile many and be beguiled by one.
    He, when he hears of her, cannot restrain°
    From the excess of laughter. Here he comes.

*Enter Cassio.*

    As he shall smile, Othello shall go mad;            100
    And his unbookish° jealousy must conster°
    Poor Cassio's smiles, gestures, and light behaviors

---

75 **in . . . list** within the bounds of patience   78 **shifted him away** used a dodge to get rid of him
79 **ecstasy** trance   81 **encave** conceal   82 **fleers** sneers.  **notable** obvious   86 **cope** encounter with,
have sex with   88 **all-in-all in spleen** utterly governed by passionate impulses   92 **keep time** keep
yourself steady (as in music)   94 **huswife** hussy   98 **restrain** refrain   101 **unbookish** uninstructed.
**conster** construe

Quite in the wrong.—How do you now, Lieutenant?
CASSIO:   The worser that you give me the addition°
Whose want° even kills me.                                               105
IAGO:   Ply Desdemona well and you are sure on 't.
[*Speaking lower.*] Now, if this suit lay in Bianca's power,
How quickly should you speed!
CASSIO [*laughing*]:   Alas, poor caitiff!°
OTHELLO [*aside*]:   Look how he laughs already!                          110
IAGO:   I never knew a woman love man so.
CASSIO:   Alas, poor rogue! I think, i' faith, she loves me.
OTHELLO:   Now he denies it faintly, and laughs it out.
IAGO:   Do you hear, Cassio?
OTHELLO:                         Now he importunes him
To tell it o'er. Go to!° Well said,° well said.                          115
IAGO:   She gives it out that you shall marry her.
Do you intend it?
CASSIO:   Ha, ha, ha!
OTHELLO:   Do you triumph, Roman?° Do you triumph?
CASSIO:   I marry her? What? A customer?° Prithee, bear some               120
charity to my wit;° do not think it so unwholesome. Ha, ha, ha!

OTHELLO:   So, so, so, so! They laugh that win.°
IAGO:   Faith, the cry° goes that you shall marry her.
CASSIO:   Prithee, say true.
IAGO:   I am a very villain else.°                                        125
OTHELLO:   Have you scored me?° Well.
CASSIO:   This is the monkey's own giving out. She is persuaded I
will marry her out of her own love and flattery,° not out of my
promise.
OTHELLO:   Iago beckons me.° Now he begins the story.
CASSIO:   She was here even now; she haunts me in every place. I          130
was the other day talking on the seabank° with certain Vene-
tians, and thither comes the bauble,° and, by this hand,° she
falls me thus about my neck—

[*He embraces Iago.*]

---

104 addition title   105 Whose want the lack of which   109 caitiff wretch   115 Go to (An
expression of remonstrance.)   Well said well done   119 Roman (The Romans were noted for
their *triumphs* or triumphal processions.)   120 customer i.e., prostitute.   bear . . . wit be more
charitable to my judgment   122 They . . . win i.e., they that laugh last laugh best   123 cry rumor
125 I . . . else call me a complete rogue if I'm not telling the truth   126 scored me scored off
me, beaten me, made up my reckoning, branded me   128 flattery self-flattery, self-deception
129 beckons signals   131 seabank seashore   132 bauble plaything   by this hand I make my vow

OTHELLO: Crying, "O dear Cassio!" as it were; his gesture
   imports it.
CASSIO: So hangs and lolls and weep upon me, so shakes and
   pulls me. Ha, ha, ha!
OTHELLO: Now he tells how she plucked him to my chamber.   135
   O, I see that nose of yours, but not that dog I shall throw
   it to.°
CASSIO: Well, I must leave her company.
IAGO: Before me,° look where she comes.

*Enter Bianca [with Othello's handkerchief].*

CASSIO: 'Tis such another fitchew!° Marry, a perfumed one.—
   What do you mean by this haunting of me?   140
BIANCA: Let the devil and his dam° haunt you! What did you
   mean by that same handkerchief you gave me even now? I was
   a fine fool to take it. I must take out the work? A likely piece
   of work,° that you should find it in your chamber and know
   not who left it there! This is some minx's token, and I must
   take out the work? There; give it your hobbyhorse.° [*She gives*  145
   *him the handkerchief.*] Wheresoever you had it, I'll take out no
   work on 't.
CASSIO: How now, my sweet Bianca? How now? How now?
OTHELLO: By heaven, that should be° my handkerchief!
BIANCA: If you'll come to supper tonight, you may; if you will
   not, come when you are next prepared for.°   150

                                    *Exit.*

IAGO: After her, after her.
CASSIO: Faith, I must. She'll rail in the streets else.
IAGO: Will you sup there?
CASSIO: Faith, I intend so.
IAGO: Well, I may chance to see you, for I would very fain
   speak with you.   155
CASSIO: Prithee, come. Will you?
IAGO: Go to.° Say no more.             [*Exit Cassio.*]

---

**136 not . . . to** (Othello imagines himself cutting off Cassio's nose and throwing it to a dog.)
**138 Before me** i.e., on my soul  **139 'Tis . . . fitchew** what a polecat she is! Just like all the others.
(Polecats were often compared with prostitutes because of their rank smell and presumed lechery.)
**141 dam** mother  **143 A likely . . . work** a fine story  **145 hobbyhorse** harlot  **148 should be**
must be  **149–150 when . . . for** when I'm ready for you (i.e., never)  **157 Go to** (an expression of
remonstrance)

OTHELLO [*advancing*]:  How shall I murder him, Iago?
IAGO:  Did you perceive how he laughed at his vice?
OTHELLO:  O, Iago!                                                                    160
IAGO:  And did you see the handkerchief?
OTHELLO:  Was that mine?
IAGO:  Yours, by this hand. And to see how he prizes the foolish
woman your wife! She gave it him, and he hath given it his
whore.
OTHELLO:  I would have him nine years a-killing. A fine woman!
A fair woman! A sweet woman!                                      165
IAGO:  Nay, you must forget that.
OTHELLO:  Ay, let her rot and perish, and be damned tonight, for
she shall not live. No, my heart is turned to stone; I strike it,
and it hurts my hand. O, the world hath not a sweeter creature!
She might lie by an emperor's side and command him tasks.   170
IAGO:  Nay, that's not your way.°
OTHELLO:  Hang her! I do but say what she is. So delicate with
her needle! An admirable musician! O, she will sing the savage-
ness out of a bear. Of so high and plenteous wit and invention!° 175
IAGO:  She's the worse for all this.
OTHELLO:  O, a thousand, a thousand times! And then, of so
gentle a condition!°
IAGO:  Ay, too gentle.°
OTHELLO:  Nay, that's certain. But yet the pity of it, Iago! O,
Iago, the pity of it, Iago!                                                    180
IAGO:  If you are so fond° over her iniquity, give her patent° to
offend, for if it touch not you it comes near nobody.
OTHELLO:  I will chop her into messes.° Cuckold me?
IAGO:  O, 'tis foul in her.
OTHELLO:  With mine officer?                                              185
IAGO:  That's fouler.
OTHELLO:  Get me some poison, Iago, this night. I'll not ex-
postulate with her, lest her body and beauty unprovide° my
mind again. This night, Iago.
IAGO:  Do it not with poison. Strangle her in her bed, even the
bed she hath contaminated.                                               190
OTHELLO:  Good, good! The justice of it pleases. Very good.

---

172 **your way** i.e., the way you should think of her  175 **invention** imagination  177 **gentle a
condition** well-born and well-bred  178 **gentle** generous, yielding (to other men)  181 **fond** foolish.
**patent** license  183 **messes** portions of meat, i.e., bits  188 **unprovide** weaken, render unfit

IAGO: And for Cassio, let me be his undertaker.° You shall hear
more by midnight.

OTHELLO: Excellent good. [*A trumpet within.*] What trumpet is
that same?

IAGO: I warrant, something from Venice.

*Enter Lodovico, Desdemona, and attendants.*

'Tis Lodovico. This comes from the Duke.                                    195
See, your wife's with him.

LODOVICO: God save you, worthy General!

OTHELLO:                                     With all my heart,° sir.

LODOVICO [*giving him a letter*]: The Duke and the senators of
Venice greet you.

OTHELLO: I kiss the instrument of their pleasures.

[*He opens the letter, and reads.*]

DESDEMONA: And what's the news, good cousin Lodovico?         200

IAGO: I am very glad to see you, signor.
Welcome to Cyprus.

LODOVICO: I thank you. How does Lieutenant Cassio?

IAGO: Lives, sir.

DESDEMONA: Cousin, there's fall'n between him and my lord      205
An unkind° breach; but you shall make all well.

OTHELLO: Are you sure of that?

DESDEMONA: My lord?

OTHELLO [*reads*]: "This fail you not to do, as you will—"

LODOVICO: He did not call; he's busy in the paper.               210
Is there division twixt my lord and Cassio?

DESDEMONA: A most unhappy one. I would do much
T' atone° them, for the love I bear to Cassio.

OTHELLO: Fire and brimstone!

DESDEMONA: My lord?                                              215

OTHELLO: Are you wise?

DESDEMONA: What, is he angry?

LODOVICO:                       Maybe the letter moved him;
For, as I think, they do command him home,
Deputing Cassio in his government.°

DESDEMONA: By my troth, I am glad on 't.°                        220

---

192 **be his undertaker** undertake to dispatch him   197 **With all my heart** i.e., I thank you most
heartily   206 **unkind** unnatural, contrary to their natures; hurtful   213 **atone** reconcile
219 **government** office   220 **on 't** of it

OTHELLO: Indeed?
DESDEMONA: My lord?
OTHELLO: I am glad to see you mad.°
DESDEMONA: Why, sweet Othello—
OTHELLO [*striking her*]: Devil!                                      225
DESDEMONA: I have not deserved this.
LODOVICO: My lord, this would not be believed in Venice,
    Though I should swear I saw 't. 'Tis very much.°
    Make her amends; she weeps.
OTHELLO:                                     O devil, devil!
    If that the earth could teem° with woman's tears,               230
    Each drop she falls would prove a crocodile.°
    Out of my sight!
DESDEMONA: I will not stay to offend you. [*Going.*]
LODOVICO: Truly, an obedient lady.
    I do beseech your lordship, call her back.
OTHELLO: Mistress!                                                    235
DESDEMONA [*returning*]: My lord?
OTHELLO: What would you with her, sir?°
LODOVICO: Who, I, my lord?
OTHELLO: Ay, you did wish that I would make her turn.
    Sir, she can turn, and turn, and yet go on                      240
    And turn again; and she can weep, sir, weep;
    And she's obedient,° as you say, obedient,
    Very obedient.—Proceed you in your tears.—
    Concerning this, sir—O well-painted passion!°—
    I am commanded home.—Get you away;                              245
    I'll send for you anon.—Sir, I obey the mandate
    And will return to Venice.—Hence, avaunt!

                          [*Exit Desdemona.*]

    Cassio shall have my place. And, sir, tonight
    I do entreat that we may sup together.
    You are welcome, sir, to Cyprus.—Goats and monkeys!° *Exit.*   250
LODOVICO: Is this the noble Moor whom our full Senate

---

223 I am . . . mad i.e., I am glad to see that you are insane enough to rejoice in Cassio's promotion
(? Othello bitterly plays on Desdemona's *I am glad.*)   228 very much too much, outrageous
230 teem breed, be impregnated   231 falls . . . crocodile (Crocodiles were supposed to weep
hypocritical tears for their victims.)   237 What . . . sir (Othello implies that Desdemona is pliant
and will do a *turn*, lines 239–241, for any man.)   242 obedient (with much the same sexual
connotation as *turn* in lines 239–241)   244 passion i.e., grief   250 Goats and monkeys (See Act
III, Scene iii, line 419.)

Call all in all sufficient? Is this the nature
Whom passion could not shake? Whose solid virtue
The shot of accident nor dart of chance
Could neither graze nor pierce?
IAGO:                                     He is much changed.                    255
LODOVICO:   Are his wits safe? Is he not light of brain?
IAGO:   He's that he is. I may not breathe my censure
What he might be. If what he might he is not,
I would to heaven he were!°
LODOVICO:                         What, strike his wife?
IAGO:   Faith, that was not so well; yet would I knew        260
That stroke would prove the worst!
LODOVICO:                                   Is it his use?°
Or did the letters work upon his blood°
And new-create his fault?
IAGO:                            Alas, alas!
It is not honesty in me to speak
What I have seen and known. You shall observe him,        265
And his own courses will denote° him so
That I may save my speech. Do but go after,
And mark how he continues.
LODOVICO:   I am sorry that I am deceived in him.        *Exeunt.*

SCENE II [THE CITADEL.]

*Enter Othello and Emilia.*

OTHELLO:   You have seen nothing then?
EMILIA:   Nor ever heard, nor ever did suspect.
OTHELLO:   Yes, you have seen Cassio and she together.
EMILIA:   But then I saw no harm, and then I heard
Each syllable that breath made up between them.        5
OTHELLO:   What, did they never whisper?
EMILIA:   Never, my lord.
OTHELLO:   Nor send you out o' the way?
EMILIA:   Never.
OTHELLO:   To fetch her fan, her gloves, her mask, nor nothing?        10
EMILIA:   Never, my lord.

257-259 I may . . . were i.e., I dare not venture an opinion as to whether he's of unsound mind, as
you suggest, but, if he isn't, then it might be better to wish he were in fact insane, since only that
could excuse his wild behavior   261 use custom   262 blood passions   266 courses will denote
actions will reveal

OTHELLO: That's strange.

EMILIA: I durst, my lord, to wager she is honest,
Lay down my soul at stake.° If you think other,
Remove your thought; it doth abuse your bosom.°                    15
If any wretch have put this in your head,
Let heaven requite it with the serpent's curse!°
For if she be not honest, chaste, and true,
There's no man happy; the purest of their wives
Is foul as slander.

OTHELLO:                    Bid her come hither. Go.                    20

                                        *Exit Emilia.*

She says enough; yet she's a simple bawd
That cannot say as much.° This° is a subtle whore,
A closet lock and key° of villainous secrets.
And yet she'll kneel and pray; I have seen her do 't.

*Enter Desdemona and Emilia.*

DESDEMONA: My lord, what is your will?                    25

OTHELLO: Pray you, chuck, come hither.

DESDEMONA: What is your pleasure?

OTHELLO:                    Let me see your eyes.
Look in my face.

DESDEMONA:                    What horrible fancy's this?

OTHELLO [*to Emilia*]: Some of your function,° mistress.
Leave procreants° alone and shut the door;                    30
Cough or cry "hem" if anybody come.
Your mystery, your mystery!° Nay, dispatch.

                                        *Exit Emilia.*

DESDEMONA [*kneeling*]: Upon my knees, what doth your
    speech import?
I understand a fury in your words,
But not the words.                    35

OTHELLO: Why, what art thou?

---

14 at stake as the wager   15 abuse your bosom deceive you   17 the serpent's curse the curse
pronounced by God on the serpent for deceiving Eve, just as some man has done to Othello and
Desdemona. (See Genesis 3:14.)   21-22 she's . . . much i.e., any procuress or go-between who
couldn't make up as plausible a story as Emilia's would have to be pretty stupid   22 This i.e.,
Desdemona   23 closet lock and key i.e., concealer   29 Some . . . function i.e., practice your chosen
profession, that of bawd (by guarding the door)   30 procreants mating couples   32 mystery trade,
occupation

DESEMONA:                    Your wife, my lord, your true
    And loyal wife.
OTHELLO:          Come, swear it, damn thyself,
    Lest, being like one of heaven,° the devils themselves
    Should fear to seize thee. Therefore be double damned:
    Swear thou art honest.
DESEMONA:           Heaven doth truly know it.          40
OTHELLO:   Heaven truly knows that thou art false as hell.
DESEMONA:   To whom, my lord? With whom? How am I false?
OTHELLO [weeping]:   Ah, Desdemon! Away, away, away!
DESEMONA:   Alas the heavy day! Why do you weep?
    Am I the motive° of these tears, my lord?          45
    If haply you my father do suspect
    An instrument of this your calling back,
    Lay not your blame on me. If you have lost him,
    I have lost him too.
OTHELLO:          Had it pleased heaven
    To try me with affliction, had they° rained          50
    All kinds of sores and shames on my bare head,
    Steeped me in poverty to the very lips,
    Given to captivity me and my utmost hopes,
    I should have found in some place of my soul
    A drop of patience. But, alas, to make me          55
    A fixèd figure for the time of scorn°
    To point his° slow and moving finger° at!
    Yet could I bear that too, well, very well.
    But there where I have garnered° up my heart,
    Where either I must live or bear no life,          60
    The fountain° from the which my current runs
    Or else dries up—to be discarded thence!
    Or keep it as a cistern° for foul toads
    To knot° and gender° in! Turn thy complexion there,°
    Patience, thou young and rose-lipped cherubin—          65
    Ay, there look grim as hell!°
DESEMONA:   I hope my noble lord esteems me honest.°

---

38 being . . . heaven looking like an angel   45 motive cause   50 they i.e., heavenly powers
56 time of scorn i.e., scornful world   57 his its.   slow and moving finger i.e., hour hand of the
clock, moving so slowly it seems hardly to move at all. (Othello envisages himself as being eternally
pointed at by the scornful world as the numbers on a clock are pointed at by the hour hand.)
59 garnered stored   61 fountain spring   63 cistern cesspool   64 knot couple.   gender engender.
Turn . . . there change your color, grow pale, at such a sight   65–66 Patience . . . hell (Even
Patience, that rose-lipped cherub, will look grim and pale at this spectacle.)   67 honest chaste

OTHELLO:   O, ay, as summer flies are in the shambles,°
That quicken° even with blowing.° O thou weed,
Who art so lovely fair and smell'st so sweet                              70
That the sense aches at thee, would thou hadst ne'er been born!
DESDEMONA:   Alas, what ignorant° sin have I committed?
OTHELLO:   Was this fair paper, this most goodly book,
Made to write "whore" upon? What committed?
Committed? O thou public commoner!°                                       75
I should make very forges of my cheeks,
That would to cinders burn up modesty,
Did I but speak thy deeds. What committed?
Heaven stops the nose at it and the moon winks;°
The bawdy° wind, that kisses all it meets,                                80
Is hushed within the hollow mine° of earth
And will not hear 't. What committed?
Impudent strumpet!
DESDEMONA:                 By heaven, you do me wrong.
OTHELLO:   Are not you a strumpet?
DESDEMONA:   No, as I am a Christian.                                     85
If to preserve this vessel° for my lord
From any other foul unlawful touch
Be not to be a strumpet, I am none.
OTHELLO:   What, not a whore?
DESDEMONA:   No, as I shall be saved.                                     90
OTHELLO:   Is 't possible?
DESDEMONA:   O, heaven forgive us!
OTHELLO:                          I cry you mercy,° then.
I took you for that cunning whore of Venice
That married with Othello. [*Calling out.*] You, mistress,
That have the office opposite to Saint Peter                             95
And keep the gate of hell!

*Enter Emilia.*

                         You, you, ay, you!
We have done our course.° There's money for your
pains. [*He gives money.*]

---

68 **shambles** slaughterhouse   69 **quicken** come to life.   **with blowing** i.e., with the puffing up of
something rotten in which maggots are breeding   72 **ignorant sin** sin in ignorance   75 **commoner**
prostitute   79 **winks** closes her eyes. (The moon symbolizes chastity.)   80 **bawdy** kissing one and
all   81 **mine** cave (where the winds were thought to dwell)   86 **vessel** body   92 **cry you mercy** beg
your pardon   97 **course** business (with an indecent suggestion of "trick," turn at sex)

I pray you, turn the key and keep our counsel.    *Exit.*
EMILIA: Alas, what does this gentleman conceive?°
  How do you, madam? How do you, my good lady?    100
DESDEMONA: Faith, half asleep.°
EMILIA: Good madam, what's the matter with my lord?
DESDEMONA: With who?
EMILIA: Why, with my lord, madam.
DESDEMONA: Who is thy lord?
EMILIA:                    He that is yours, sweet lady.    105
DESDEMONA: I have none. Do not talk to me, Emilia.
  I cannot weep, nor answers have I none
  But what should go by water.° Prithee, tonight
  Lay on my bed my wedding sheets, remember;
  And call thy husband hither.    110
EMILIA: Here's a change indeed!    *Exit.*
DESDEMONA: 'Tis meet I should be used so, very meet.°
  How have I been behaved, that he might stick°
  The small'st opinion° on my least misuse?°

*Enter Iago and Emilia.*

IAGO: What is your pleasure, madam? How is 't with you?    115
DESDEMONA: I cannot tell. Those that do teach young babes
  Do it with gentle means and easy tasks.
  He might have chid me so, for, in good faith,
  I am a child to chiding.
IAGO: What is the matter, lady?    120
EMILIA: Alas, Iago, my lord hath so bewhored her,
  Thrown such despite and heavy terms upon her,
  That true hearts cannot bear it.
DESDEMONA: Am I that name, Iago?
IAGO: What name, fair lady?    125
DESDEMONA: Such as she said my lord did say I was.
EMILIA: He called her whore. A beggar in his drink
  Could not have laid such terms upon his callet.°
IAGO: Why did he so?
DESDEMONA [*weeping*]: I do not know. I am sure I am none
  such.    130
IAGO: Do not weep, do not weep. Alas the day!

---

**99 conceive** suppose, think   **101 half asleep** i.e., dazed   **108 go by water** be expressed by tears
**112 meet** fitting   **113 stick** attach   **114 opinion** censure.  **least misuse** slightest misconduct   **128 callet** whore

EMILIA:   Hath she forsook so many noble matches,
   Her father and her country and her friends,
   To be called whore? Would it not make one weep?
DESDEMONA:   It is my wretched fortune.
IAGO:                              Beshrew° him for 't!          135
   How comes this trick° upon him?
DESDEMONA:                       Nay, heaven doth know.
EMILIA:   I will be hanged if some eternal° villain,
   Some busy and insinuating° rogue,
   Some cogging,° cozening° slave, to get some office,
   Have not devised this slander. I will be hanged else.     140
IAGO:   Fie, there is no such man. It is impossible.
DESDEMONA:   If any such there be, heaven pardon him!
EMILIA:   A halter° pardon him! And hell gnaw his bones!
   Why should he call her whore? Who keeps her company?
   What place? What time? What form?° What likelihood?     145
   The Moor's abused by some most villainous knave,
   Some base notorious knave, some scurvy fellow.
   O heaven, that° such companions° thou'dst unfold,°
   And put in every honest hand a whip
   To lash the rascals naked through the world              150
   Even from the east to th' west!
IAGO:                              Speak within door.°
EMILIA:   O, fie upon them! Some such squire° he was
   That turned your wit the seamy side without°
   And made you to suspect me with the Moor.
IAGO:   You are a fool. Go to.°
DESDEMONA:                      Alas, Iago,                   155
   What shall I do to win my lord again?
   Good friend, go to him; for, by this light of heaven,
   I know not how I lost him. Here I kneel. [*She kneels.*]
   If e'er my will did trespass 'gainst his love,
   Either in discourse° of thought or actual deed,          160
   Or that° mine eyes, mine ears, or any sense
   Delighted them° in any other form;
   Or that I do not yet,° and ever did,

---

**135 Beshrew** curse   **136 trick** strange behavior, delusion   **137 eternal** inveterate   **138 insinuating** ingratiating, fawning, wheedling   **139 cogging** cheating.   **cozening** defrauding   **143 halter** hangman's noose   **145 form** appearance, circumstance   **148 that** would that   **companions** fellows **unfold** expose   **151 within door** i.e., not so loud   **152 squire** fellow   **153 seamy side without** wrong side out   **155 Go to** i.e., that's enough   **160 discourse of thought** process of thinking **161 that** if (also in line 163)   **162 Delighted them** took delight   **163 yet** still

And ever will—though he do shake me off
To beggarly divorcement—love him dearly,                    165
Comfort forswear° me! Unkindness may do much,
And his unkindness may defeat° my life,
But never taint my love. I cannot say "whore."
It does abhor° me now I speak the word;
To do the act that might the addition° earn                  170
Not the world's mass of vanity° could make me.

[*She rises.*]

IAGO:  I pray you, be content. 'Tis but his humor.°
The business of the state does him offense,
And he does chide with you.
DESDEMONA:  If 'twere no other—                              175
IAGO:  It is but so, I warrant. [*Trumpets within.*]
Hark, how these instruments summon you to supper!
The messengers of Venice stays the meat.°
Go in, and weep not. All things shall be well.

                *Exeunt Desdemona and Emilia.*

*Enter Roderigo.*

How now, Roderigo?                                           180
RODERIGO:  I do not find that thou deal'st justly with me.
IAGO:  What in the contrary?
RODERIGO:  Every day thou daff'st me° with some device,° Iago,
and rather, as it seems to me now, keep'st from me all conve-
niency° than suppliest me with the least advantage° of hope. I   185
will indeed no longer endure it, nor am I yet persuaded to put
up° in peace what already I have foolishly suffered.
IAGO:  Will you hear me, Roderigo?
RODERIGO:  Faith, I have heard too much, for your words and
performances are no kin together.
IAGO:  You charge me most unjustly.                          190
RODERIGO:  With naught but truth. I have wasted myself out of
my means. The jewels you have had from me to deliver°

---

166 **Comfort forswear** may heavenly comfort forsake   167 **defeat** destroy   169 **abhor** (1) fill me
with abhorrence (2) make me whorelike   170 **addition** title   171 **vanity** showy splendor
172 **humor** mood   178 **stays the meat** are waiting to dine   183 **thou daff'st me** you put me off.
**device** excuse, trick   184 **conveniency** advantage, opportunity   185 **advantage** increase   186 **put
up** submit to, tolerate   192 **deliver** deliver to

Desdemona would half have corrupted a votarist.° You have
told me she hath received them and returned me expectations
and comforts of sudden respect° and acquaintance, but I find
none.                                                                                    195
IAGO: Well, go to, very well.
RODERIGO: "Very well"! "Go to"! I cannot go to,° man, nor 'tis
not very well. By this hand, I think it is scurvy, and begin to
find myself fopped° in it.
IAGO: Very well.
RODERIGO: I tell you 'tis not very well.° I will make myself   200
known to Desdemona. If she will return me my jewels, I will
give over my suit and repent my unlawful solicitation; if not,
assure yourself I will seek satisfaction° of you.
IAGO: You have said now?°
RODERIGO: Ay, and said nothing but what I protest intendment°
of doing.
IAGO: Why, now I see there's mettle in thee, and even from this   205
instant do build on thee a better opinion than ever before. Give
me thy hand, Roderigo. Thou hast taken against me a most
just exception; but yet I protest I have dealt most directly in
thy affair.
RODERIGO: It hath not appeared.
IAGO: I grant indeed it hath not appeared, and your suspicion is   210
not without wit and judgment. But, Roderigo, if thou hast that
in thee indeed which I have greater reason to believe now than
ever—I mean purpose, courage, and valor—this night show it.
If thou the next night following enjoy not Desdemona, take me
from this world with treachery and devise engines for° my life.   215
RODERIGO: Well, what is it? Is it within reason and compass?
IAGO: Sir, there is especial commission come from Venice to de-
pute Cassio in Othello's place.
RODERIGO: Is that true? Why, then Othello and Desdemona re-
turn again to Venice.                                                                    220
IAGO: O, no; he goes into Mauritania and takes away with him
the fair Desdemona, unless his abode be lingered here by some

---

193 **votarist** nun   194 **sudden respect** immediate consideration   197 **I cannot go to** (Roderigo
changes Iago's go to, an expression urging patience, to *I cannot go to,* "I have no opportunity for
success in wooing.")   198 **fopped** fooled, duped   200 **not very well** (Roderigo changes Iago's *very
well,* "all right, then," to *not very well,* "not at all good.")   202 **satisfaction** repayment. (The term
normally means settling of accounts in a duel.)   203 **You . . . now** have you finished?
204 **intendment** intention   214 **engines for** plots against

accident; wherein none can be so determinate° as the removing of Cassio.

RODERIGO: How do you mean, removing of him?

IAGO: Why, by making him uncapable of Othello's place— 225
knocking out his brains.

RODERIGO: And that you would have me to do?

IAGO: Ay, if you dare do yourself a profit and a right. He sups tonight with a harlotry,° and thither will I go to him. He knows not yet of his honorable fortune. If you will watch his going thence, which I will fashion to fall out° between twelve 230 and one, you may take him at your pleasure. I will be near to second your attempt, and he shall fall between us. Come, stand not amazed at it, but go along with me. I will show you such a necessity in his death that you shall think yourself bound to put it on him. It is now high° suppertime, and the night grows to waste.° About it. 235

RODERIGO: I will hear further reason for this.

IAGO: And you shall be satisfied. *Exeunt.*

SCENE III [THE CITADEL.]

*Enter Othello, Lodovico, Desdemona, Emilia, and attendants.*

LODOVICO: I do beseech you, sir, trouble yourself no further.

OTHELLO: O, pardon me; 'twill do me good to walk.

LODOVICO: Madam, good night. I humbly thank your ladyship.

DESDEMONA: Your honor is most welcome.

OTHELLO: Will you walk, sir?
O, Desdemona! 5

DESDEMONA: My lord?

OTHELLO: Get you to bed on th' instant. I will be returned forthwith. Dismiss your attendant there. Look 't be done.

DESDEMONA: I will, my lord. 10

*Exit [Othello, with Lodovico and attendants].*

EMILIA: How goes it now? He looks gentler than he did.

---

223 **determinate** conclusive    229 **harlotry** slut    230 **fall out** occur    234 **high** fully    235 **grows to waste** wastes away

DESDEMONA:   He says he will return incontinent,°
And hath commanded me to go to bed,
And bid me to dismiss you.
EMILIA:   Dismiss me?                                                    15
DESDEMONA:   It was his bidding. Therefore, good Emilia,
Give me my nightly wearing, and adieu.
We must not now displease him.
EMILIA:   I would you had never seen him!
DESDEMONA:   So would not I. My love doth so approve him     20
That even his stubbornness,° his checks,° his frowns—
Prithee, unpin me—have grace and favor in them.

[*Emilia prepares Desdemona for bed.*]

EMILIA:   I have laid those sheets you bade me on the bed.
DESDEMONA:   All's one.° Good faith, how foolish are our minds!
If I do die before thee, prithee shroud me                              25
In one of these same sheets.
EMILIA:                              Come, come, you talk.°
DESDEMONA:   My mother had a maid called Barbary.
She was in love, and he she loved proved mad°
And did forsake her. She had a song of "Willow."
An old thing 'twas, but it expressed her fortune,                        30
And she died singing it. That song tonight
Will not go from my mind; I have much to do
But to go hang° my head all at one side
And sing it like poor Barbary. Prithee, dispatch.
EMILIA:   Shall I go fetch your nightgown?°                              35
DESDEMONA:   No, unpin me here.
This Lodovico is a proper° man.
EMILIA:   A very handsome man.
DESDEMONA:   He speaks well.
EMILIA:   I know a lady in Venice would have walked barefoot            40
to Palestine for a touch of his nether lip.
DESDEMONA [*singing*]:
          "The poor soul sat sighing by a sycamore tree,
          Sing all a green willow;°
          Her hand on her bosom, her head on her knee,

---

12 **incontinent** immediately   21 **stubbornness** roughness   **checks** rebukes   24 **All's one** all right. It
doesn't really matter   26 **talk** i.e., prattle   28 **mad** wild, i.e., faithless   32-33 **I . . . hang** I can
scarcely keep myself from hanging   35 **nightgown** dressing gown   37 **proper** handsome
43 **willow** (A conventional emblem of disappointed love.)

Sing willow, willow, willow. 45
The fresh streams ran by her and murmured her moans;
Sing willow, willow, willow;
Her salt tears fell from her, and softened the stones—"
Lay by these.
　　　[*Singing.*] "Sing willow, willow, willow—" 50
Prithee, hie thee.° He'll come anon.°
　　　[*Singing.*] "Sing all a green willow must be my
　　　　garland.
Let nobody blame him; his scorn I approve—"
Nay, that's not next.—Hark! Who is 't that knocks?
EMILIA:　It's the wind.
DESDEMONA [*singing*]:
　　　"I called my love false love; but what said he then? 55
　　　Sing willow, willow, willow;
　　　If I court more women, you'll couch with more men."
So, get thee gone. Good night. Mine eyes do itch;
Doth that bode weeping?
EMILIA:　　　　　　　'Tis neither here nor there. 60
DESDEMONA:　I have heard it said so. O, these men, these men!
Dost thou in conscience think—tell me, Emilia—
That there be women do abuse° their husbands
In such gross kind?
EMILIA:　　　　　There be some such, no question.
DESDEMONA:　Wouldst thou do such a deed for all the world? 65
EMILIA:　Why, would not you?
DESDEMONA:　　　　　　　No, by this heavenly light!
EMILIA:　Nor I neither by this heavenly light;
I might do 't as well i' the dark.
DESDEMONA:　Wouldst thou do such a deed for all the world?
EMILIA:　The world's a huge thing. It is a great price 70
For a small vice.
DESDEMONA:　Good troth, I think thou wouldst not.
EMILIA:　By my troth, I think I should, and undo 't when I had
　　done. Marry, I would not do such a thing for a joint ring,° nor
　　for measures of lawn,° nor for gowns, petticoats, nor caps, nor
　　any petty exhibition.° But for all the whole world! Uds° pity, 75
　　who would not make her husband a cuckold to make him a
　　monarch? I should venture purgatory for 't.

---

51 **hie thee** hurry. **anon** right away　63 **abuse** deceive　74 **joint ring** a ring made in separate
halves. **lawn** fine linen　75 **exhibition** gift　76 **Uds** God's

DESDEMONA:   Beshrew me if I would do such a wrong
For the whole world.
EMILIA:   Why, the wrong is but a wrong i' the world, and having
the world for your labor, 'tis a wrong in your own world, and
you might quickly make it right.                                        80
DESDEMONA:   I do not think there is any such woman.
EMILIA:   Yes, a dozen, and as many
To th' vantage° as would store° the world they played° for.            85
But I do think it is their husbands' faults
If wives do fall. Say that they slack their duties°
And pour our treasures into foreign laps,°
Or else break out in peevish jealousies,
Throwing restraint upon us? Or say they strike us,°                     90
Or scant our former having in despite?°
Why, we have galls,° and though we have some grace,
Yet have we some revenge. Let husbands know
Their wives have sense° like them. They see, and smell,
And have their palates both for sweet and sour,                        95
As husbands have. What is it that they do
When they change us for others? Is it sport?°
I think it is. And doth affection° breed it?
I think it doth. Is 't frailty that thus errs?
It is so, too. And have not we affections,                             100
Desires for sport, and frailty, as men have?
Then let them use us well; else let them know,
The ills we do, their ills instruct us so.
DESDEMONA:   Good night, good night. God me such uses° send
Not to pick bad from bad, but by bad mend!°                            105

*Exeunt.*

---

85 **To th' vantage** in addition, to boot   **store** populate   **played** (1) gambled (2) sported sexually
87 **duties** marital duties   88 **pour . . . laps** i.e., are unfaithful, give what is rightfully ours (semen)
to other women   90 **Throwing . . . us** i.e., jealously restricting our freedom to see other men
91 **scant . . . despite** reduce our allowance to spite us   92 **have galls** i.e., are capable of resenting
injury and insult   94 **sense** physical sense   97 **sport** sexual pastime   98 **affection** passion
104 **uses** habit, practice   105 **Not . . . mend** i.e., not to learn bad conduct from others' badness (as
Emilia has suggested women learn from men), but to mend my ways by perceiving what badness is,
making spiritual benefit out of evil and adversity

# ACT V

## SCENE I [A STREET IN CYPRUS.]

*Enter Iago and Roderigo.*

IAGO:   Here stand behind this bulk.° Straight will he come.
Wear thy good rapier bare,° and put it home.
Quick, quick! Fear nothing. I'll be at thy elbow.
It makes us or it mars us. Think on that,
And fix most firm thy resolution.                                  5
RODERIGO:   Be near at hand. I may miscarry in 't.
IAGO:   Here, at thy hand. Be bold, and take thy stand.

*[Iago stands aside. Roderigo conceals himself.]*

RODERIGO:   I have no great devotion to the deed;
And yet he hath given me satisfying reasons.
'Tis but a man gone. Forth, my sword! He dies.                     10

*[He draws.]*

IAGO:   I have rubbed this young quat° almost to the sense,°
And he grows angry. Now, whether he kill Cassio
Or Cassio him, or each do kill the other,
Every way makes my gain. Live Roderigo,°
He calls me to a restitution large                                 15
Of gold and jewels that I bobbed° from him
As gifts to Desdemona.
It must not be. If Cassio do remain,
He hath a daily beauty in his life
That makes me ugly; and besides, the Moor                          20
May unfold° me to him; there stand I in much peril.
No, he must die. Be 't so. I hear him coming.

*Enter Cassio.*

RODERIGO *[coming forth]*:   I know his gait, 'tis he.—Villain,
thou diest!

*[He attacks Cassio.]*

---

1 **bulk** framework projecting from the front of a shop   2 **bare** unsheathed   11 **quat** pimple,
pustule.   **to the sense** to the quick   14 **Live Roderigo** if Roderigo lives   16 **bobbed** swindled
21 **unfold** expose

**CASSIO:** That thrust had been mine enemy indeed,
But that my coat° is better than thou know'st.       25
I will make proof° of thine.

[*He draws, and wounds Roderigo.*]

**RODERIGO:**               O, I am slain! [*He falls.*]

[*Iago, from behind, wounds Cassio in the leg, and exits.*]

**CASSIO:** I am maimed forever. Help, ho! Murder! Murder!

*Enter Othello.*

**OTHELLO:** The voice of Cassio! Iago keeps his word.
**RODERIGO:** O, villain that I am!
**OTHELLO:** It is even so.       30
**CASSIO:** O, help, ho! Light! A surgeon!
**OTHELLO:** 'Tis he. O brave Iago, honest and just,
That hast such noble sense of thy friend's wrong!
Thou teachest me. Minion,° your dear lies dead,
And your unblest fate hies.° Strumpet, I come.      35
Forth of° my heart those charms, thine eyes, are blotted;
Thy bed, lust-stained, shall with lust's blood be spotted.

*Exit Othello.*

*Enter Lodovico and Gratiano.*

**CASSIO:** What ho! No watch? No passage?° Murder! Murder!
**GRATIANO:** 'Tis some mischance. The voice is very direful.
**CASSIO:** O, help!      40
**LODOVICO:** Hark!
**RODERIGO:** O wretched villain!
**LODOVICO:** Two or three groan. 'Tis heavy° night;
These may be counterfeits. Let's think 't unsafe
To come in to° the cry without more help.      45

[*They remain near the entrance.*]

**RODERIGO:** Nobody come? Then shall I bleed to death.

---

25 **coat** (Possibly a garment of mail under the outer clothing, or simply a tougher coat than Roderigo expected.)  **26 proof** a test  **34 Minion** hussy (i.e., Desdemona)  **35 hies** hastens on  **36 Forth of** from out  **38 passage** people passing by  **43 heavy** thick, dark  **45 come in to** approach

*Enter Iago [in his shirtsleeves, with a light].*

**LODOVICO:** Hark!
**GRATIANO:** Here's one comes in his shirt, with light and
weapons.
**IAGO:** Who's there? Whose noise is this that cries on° murder?
**LODOVICO:** We do not know.
**IAGO:** Did not you hear a cry? 50
**CASSIO:** Here, here! For heaven's sake, help me!
**IAGO:** What's the matter?

*[He moves toward Cassio.]*

**GRATIANO** *[to Lodovico]:* This is Othello's ancient, as I take it.
**LODOVICO** *[to Gratiano]:* The same indeed, a very valiant
fellow.
**IAGO** *[to Cassio]:* What° are you here that cry so grievously?
**CASSIO:** Iago? O, I am spoiled,° undone by villains! 55
Give me some help.
**IAGO:** O me, Lieutenant! What villains have done this?
**CASSIO:** I think that one of them is hereabout,
And cannot make° away.
**IAGO:** O treacherous villains!

*[To Lodovico and Gratiano.]*

What are you there? Come in, and give some help. *[They
advance.]* 60
**RODERIGO:** O, help me there!
**CASSIO:** That's one of them.
**IAGO:** O murderous slave! O villain!

*[He stabs Roderigo.]*

**RODERIGO:** O damned Iago! O inhuman dog!
**IAGO:** Kill men i' the dark?—Where be these bloody
thieves?—
How silent is this town!—Ho! Murder, murder!— 65
*[To Lodovico and Gratiano.]* What may you be? Are you of
good or evil?

**LODOVICO:** As you shall prove us, praise° us.

**49 cries on** cries out   **54 What** who (also at lines 60 and 66)   **55 spoiled** ruined, done for
**59 make** get   **67 praise** appraise

**IAGO:** Signor Lodovico?
**LODOVICO:** He, sir.
**IAGO:** I cry you mercy.° Here's Cassio hurt by villains.　　　70
**GRATIANO:** Cassio?
**IAGO:** How is 't, brother?
**CASSIO:** My leg is cut in two.
**IAGO:** Marry, heaven forbid!
　Light, gentlemen! I'll bind it with my shirt.　　　75

[*He hands them the light, and tends to Cassio's wound.*]

*Enter Bianca.*

**BIANCA:** What is the matter, ho? Who is 't that cried?
**IAGO:** Who is 't that cried?
**BIANCA:**　　　　　　　　O my dear Cassio!
　My sweet Cassio! O Cassio, Cassio, Cassio!
**IAGO:** O notable strumpet! Cassio, may you suspect
　Who they should be that have thus mangled you?　　　80
**CASSIO:** No.
**GRATIANO:** I am sorry to find you thus. I have been to seek
　you.
**IAGO:** Lend me a garter. [*He applies a tourniquet.*] So.—O,
　for a chair,°
To bear him easily hence!
**BIANCA:** Alas, he faints! O Cassio, Cassio, Cassio!　　　85
**IAGO:** Gentlemen all, I do suspect this trash
　To be a party in this injury.—
　Patience awhile, good Cassio.—Come, come;
　Lend me a light. [*He shines the light on Roderigo.*] Know
　we this face or no?
　Alas, my friend and my dear countryman　　　90
　Roderigo! No.—Yes, sure.—O heaven! Roderigo!
**GRATIANO:** What, of Venice?
**IAGO:** Even he, sir. Did you know him?
**GRATIANO:** Know him? Ay.
**IAGO:** Signor Gratiano? I cry your gentle° pardon.　　　95
　These bloody accidents° must excuse my manners
　That so neglected you.
**GRATIANO:**　　　　　　　I am glad to see you.

---

70 **I cry you mercy** I beg your pardon　83 **chair** litter　95 **gentle** noble　96 **accidents** sudden events

IAGO: How do you, Cassio? O, a chair, a chair!
GRATIANO: Roderigo!
IAGO: He, he, 'tis he. [*A litter is brought in.*] O, that's well
    said;° the chair.                                                    100
    Some good man bear him carefully from hence;
    I'll fetch the General's surgeon. [*To Bianca.*] For you,
    mistress,
    Save you your labor.°—He that lies slain here, Cassio,
    Was my dear friend. What malice° was between you?
CASSIO: None in the world, nor do I know the man.                       105
IAGO [*to Bianca*]: What, look you pale?—O, bear him out o'
    th' air.°

> [*Cassio and Roderigo are borne off.*]

    Stay you,° good gentlemen.—Look you pale, mistress?—
    Do you perceive the gastness° of her eye?—
    Nay, if you stare,° we shall hear more anon.—
    Behold her well; I pray you, look upon her.                         110
    Do you see, gentlemen? Nay, guiltiness
    Will speak, though tongues were out of use.

[*Enter Emilia.*]

EMILIA: 'Las, what's the matter? What's the matter, husband?
IAGO: Cassio hath here been set on in the dark
    By Roderigo and fellows that are scaped.                            115
    He's almost slain, and Roderigo dead.
EMILIA: Alas, good gentleman! Alas, good Cassio!
IAGO: This is the fruits of whoring. Prithee, Emilia,
    Go know° of Cassio where he supped tonight.
    [*To Bianca.*] What, do you shake at that?                          120
BIANCA: He supped at my house, but I therefore shake not.
IAGO: O, did he so? I charge you go with me.
EMILIA: O, fie upon thee, strumpet!
BIANCA: I am no strumpet, but of life as honest°
    As you that thus abuse me.                                          125
EMILIA: As I? Faugh! Fie upon thee!

---

100 **well said** well done   103 **Save . . . labor** i.e., never you mind tending Cassio
104 **malice** enmity   106 **bear . . . air** (Fresh air was thought to be dangerous for a wound.)
107 **Stay you** (Lodovico and Gratiano are evidently about to leave.)   108 **gastness** terror
109 **stare** (Iago pretends to interpret Bianca's wild looks as an involuntary confession of guilt.)
119 **know** learn   124 **honest** chaste

IAGO:   Kind gentlemen, let's go see poor Cassio dressed.°—
Come, mistress, you must tell's another tale.
Emilia, run you to the citadel
And tell my lord and lady what hath happed.—                    130
Will you go on afore? [*Aside.*] This is the night
That either makes me or fordoes° me quite.          *Exeunt.*

SCENE II [A BEDCHAMBER IN THE CITADEL.]

*Enter Othello [with a light], and Desdemona in her bed.°*

OTHELLO:   It is the cause,° it is the cause, my soul.
Let me not name it to you, you chaste stars!
It is the cause. Yet I'll not shed her blood,
Nor scar that whiter skin of hers than snow,
And smooth as monumental° alabaster.                              5
Yet she must die, else she'll betray more men.
Put out the light, and then put out the light.°
If I quench thee, thou flaming minister,°
I can again thy former light restore,
Should I repent me;° but once put out thy light,                 10
Thou cunning'st pattern° of excelling nature,
I know not where is that Promethean heat°
That can thy light relume.° When I have plucked thy rose,
I cannot give it vital growth again;
It needs must wither. I'll smell thee on the tree.               15

[*He kisses her.*]

O balmy breath, that dost almost persuade
Justice to break her sword! One more, one more.
Be thus when thou art dead, and I will kill thee,
And love thee after. One more, and that's the last.

---

127 **Cassio dressed** Cassio's wounds dressed    132 **fordoes** undoes, ruins       [**s.d.**] **in her bed** (Either the curtains are drawn back to reveal the bed in a recessed area backstage, or the bed is "thrust out" onstage as the scene begins.)
1 **cause** i.e., cause of justice, the offense itself, which Othello must correct as an agent of justice
5 **monumental** i.e., used in making tombs and funeral monuments    7 **the light . . . light** the torch or lamp . . . Desdemona's life    8 **flaming minister** torch or lamp that serves me    10 **repent me** change my mind    11 **Thou . . . pattern** you skillfully wrought perfect example    12 **Promethean heat** divine fire (alluding to the theft of fire from heaven by Prometheus)    13 **relume** rekindle

[*He kisses her.*]

So sweet was ne'er so fatal. I must weep,                    20
But they are cruel° tears. This sorrow's heavenly;
It strikes where it doth love.° She wakes.
DESDEMONA:  Who's there? Othello?
OTHELLO:  Ay, Desdemona.
DESDEMONA:  Will you come to bed, my lord?                   25
OTHELLO:  Have you prayed tonight, Desdemon?
DESDEMONA:  Ay, my lord.
OTHELLO:  If you bethink yourself of any crime°
Unreconciled as yet to heaven and grace,
Solicit° for it straight.°                                    30
DESDEMONA:  Alack, my lord, what may you mean by that?
OTHELLO:  Well, do it, and be brief. I will walk by.
I would not kill thy unprepared spirit.
No, heaven forfend!° I would not kill thy soul.
DESDEMONA:  Talk you of killing?
OTHELLO:                          Ay, I do.
DESDEMONA:                                  Then heaven       35
Have mercy on me!
OTHELLO:  Amen, with all my heart!
DESDEMONA:  If you say so, I hope you will not kill me.
OTHELLO:  Humh!
DESDEMONA:  And yet I fear you; for you're fatal then
When your eyes roll so. Why I should fear I know not,        40
Since guiltiness I know not; but yet I feel I fear.
OTHELLO:  Think on thy sins.
DESDEMONA:                    They are loves I bear to you.°
OTHELLO:  Ay, and for that thou diest.
DESDEMONA:  That death's unnatural that kills for loving.
Alas, why gnaw you so your nether lip?                        45
Some bloody passion shakes your very frame.
These are portents; but yet I hope, I hope,
They do not point on° me.

---

21 **cruel** unrelenting   22 **It . . . love** (Compare Hebrews 12:6: "For whom the Lord loveth he chasteneth.")   28 **crime** sin   30 **Solicit** petition, pray.   **straight** immediately   34 **forfend** forbid   42 **They are . . . you** i.e., if I sinned, it was in loving you more than my father or more than God   48 **point on** point at, predict what is to happen to

OTHELLO:   Peace, and be still!
DESDEMONA:   I will so. What's the matter?                                  50
OTHELLO:   That handkerchief which I so loved and gave thee
   Thou gav'st to Cassio.
DESDEMONA:                  No, by my life and soul!
   Send for the man and ask him.
OTHELLO:   Sweet soul, take heed, take heed of perjury.
   Thou art on thy deathbed.                                                55
DESDEMONA:   Ay, but not yet to die.
OTHELLO:                            Yes, presently.°
   Therefore confess thee freely of thy sin;
   For to deny each article with oath
   Cannot remove nor choke the strong conception°
   That I do groan withal.° Thou art to die.                               60
DESDEMONA:   Then Lord have mercy on me!
OTHELLO:                                  I say, amen.
DESDEMONA:   And have you mercy too! I never did
   Offend° you in my life; never loved Cassio
   But with such general warranty° of heaven
   As I might love. I never gave him token.                                65
OTHELLO:   By heaven, I saw my handkerchief in 's hand.
   O perjured woman! Thou dost stone° my heart,
   And makes me call what I intend to do
   A murder, which I thought a sacrifice.
   I saw the handkerchief.
DESDEMONA:                  He found it, then.                              70
   I never gave it him. Send for him hither;
   Let him confess a truth.
OTHELLO:                    He hath confessed.
DESDEMONA:   What, my lord?
OTHELLO:   That he hath used thee.
DESDEMONA:                          How? Unlawfully?
OTHELLO:                                            Ay.
DESDEMONA:   He will not say so.
OTHELLO:                        No, his mouth is stopped;                   75
   Honest Iago hath ta'en order° for 't.

---

56 **presently** immediately   59 **conception** (1) belief in your guilt (2) plan in my mind   60 **groan withal** (1) groan at in sorrow (2) as in giving birth   63 **Offend** wrong   64 **warranty** sanction   67 **stone** turn to stone, harden   76 **ta'en order** taken measures

DESDEMONA:   O, my fear interprets. What, is he dead?
OTHELLO:   Had all his hairs been lives, my great revenge
Had stomach for them all.
DESDEMONA:   Alas, he is betrayed and I undone! [*She weeps.*]     80
OTHELLO:   Out, strumpet! Weep'st thou for him to my face?
DESDEMONA:   O, banish me, my lord, but kill me not!
OTHELLO:   Down, strumpet!
DESDEMONA:   Kill me tomorrow; let me live tonight!
OTHELLO:   Nay, if you strive—     85
DESDEMONA:   But half an hour!
OTHELLO:                              Being done,° there is no pause.
DESDEMONA:   But while I say one prayer!
OTHELLO:                                          It is too late.

*Smothers her.*

EMILIA [*at the door*]:   My lord, my lord! What, ho! My lord,
my lord!
OTHELLO:   What noise is this? Not dead? Not yet quite dead?
I that am cruel am yet merciful;     90
I would not have thee linger in thy pain.

[*He dispatches her.*]

                                          So, so.
EMILIA [*within*]:   What, ho! My lord, my lord!
OTHELLO:                                          Who's there?
EMILIA [*within*]:   O, good my lord, I would speak a word with
you!
OTHELLO:   Yes, 'tis Emilia.—By and by.—She's dead.
'Tis like° she comes to speak of Cassio's death.—     95
The noise was here.° Ha! No more moving?
Still as the grave. Shall she come in? Were 't good?—
I think she stirs again. No. What's best to do?
If she come in, she'll sure speak to my wife.
My wife! My wife! What wife? I have no wife.     100
O, insupportable! O heavy hour!

---

**86 Being done** i.e., since justice has begun its relentless course   **95 like** likely that   **96 here** (The
Folio's *high* is possible, suggesting that the commotion of the attack on Cassio was loud.)

Methinks it should be now a huge eclipse
Of sun and moon, and that th' affrighted globe
Should yawn° at alteration.°
EMILIA [*within*]:                 I do beseech you
That I may speak with you, O, good my lord!                    105
OTHELLO:   I had forgot thee. O, come in, Emilia.—
Soft,° by and by. Let me the curtains draw.—

[*He closes the bed-curtains and opens the door.*]

Where art thou?

*Enter Emilia.*

                 What's the matter with thee now?
EMILIA:   O, my good lord, yonder's foul murders done!
OTHELLO:   What, now?                                         110
EMILIA:   But now, my lord.
OTHELLO:   It is the very error° of the moon;
She comes more nearer earth than she was wont,
And makes men mad.
EMILIA:   Cassio, my lord, hath killed a young Venetian       115
Called Roderigo.
OTHELLO:             Roderigo killed?
And Cassio killed?
EMILIA:             No, Cassio is not killed.
OTHELLO:   Not Cassio killed? Then murder's out of tune,
And sweet revenge grows harsh.
DESDEMONA:   O, falsely, falsely murdered!                    120
EMILIA:   O Lord, what cry is that?
OTHELLO:   That? What?
EMILIA:   Out° and alas, that was my lady's voice.

[*She opens the bed-curtains.*]

Help, help, ho, help! O lady, speak again!
Sweet Desdemona! O sweet mistress, speak!                     125

---

104 yawn gape in amazement, i.e., move in an earthquake. (According to Pliny, earthquakes often
happen during eclipses.)   at alteration at these cataclysmic events in nature, well-suited to express
the horror of Desdemona's death   107 Soft wait a minute   112 error aberration, irregularity   123
Out (A cry of dismay, intensifying *alas.*)

DESDEMONA:  A guiltless death I die.
EMILIA:  O, who hath done this deed?
DESDEMONA:  Nobody; I myself. Farewell.
    Commend me to my kind lord. O, farewell!    [*She dies.*]
OTHELLO:  Why, how should she be murdered?
EMILIA:                                    Alas, who knows?   130
OTHELLO:  You heard her say herself it was not I.
EMILIA:  She said so. I must needs report the truth.
OTHELLO:  She's like a liar gone to burning hell!
    'Twas I that killed her.
EMILIA:                O, the more angel she,
    And you the blacker devil!   135
OTHELLO:  She turned to folly,° and she was a whore.
EMILIA:  Thou dost belie° her, and thou art a devil.
OTHELLO:  She was false as water.
EMILIA:             Thou art rash as fire to say
    That she was false. O, she was heavenly true!   140
OTHELLO:  Cassio did top her. Ask thy husband else.°
    O, I were damned beneath all depth in hell
    But that I did proceed upon just grounds
    To this extremity. Thy husband knew it all.
EMILIA:  My husband?   145
OTHELLO:  Thy husband.
EMILIA:  That she was false to wedlock?
OTHELLO:  Ay, with Cassio. Nay, had she been true,
    If heaven would make me such another world
    Of one entire and perfect chrysolite,°   150
    I'd not have sold her for it.
EMILIA:  My husband?
OTHELLO:  Ay, 'twas he that told me on her first.
    An honest man he is, and hates the slime
    That sticks on filthy deeds.   155
EMILIA:  My husband?
OTHELLO:  What needs this iterance,° woman? I say thy
    husband.

---

136 **folly** i.e., wantonness, fleshly sin   137 **belie** slander   141 **else** i.e., if you don't believe me
150 **chrysolite** precious topaz   157 **iterance** iteration, repetition

EMILIA:  O mistress, villainy hath made mocks with° love!
  My husband say she was false?
OTHELLO:                He, woman;
  I say thy husband. Dost understand the word?                    160
  My friend, thy husband, honest, honest Iago.
EMILIA:  If he say so, may his pernicious soul
  Rot half a grain a day! He lies to th' heart.
  She was too fond of her most filthy bargain.
OTHELLO:  Ha?                          [*He draws.*]    165
EMILIA:  Do thy worst!
  This deed of thine is no more worthy heaven
  Than thou wast worthy her.
OTHELLO:                Peace, you were best.°
EMILIA:  Thou hast not half that power to do me harm
  As I have to be hurt.° O gull!° O dolt!                         170
  As ignorant as dirt! Thou hast done a deed—
  I care not for thy sword; I'll make thee known,
  Though I lost twenty lives.—Help! Help, ho, help!
  The Moor hath killed my mistress! Murder, murder!

*Enter Montano, Gratiano, and Iago.*

MONTANO:  What is the matter? How now, General?                  175
EMILIA:  O, are you come, Iago? You have done well,
  That men must lay their murders on your neck.
GRATIANO:  What is the matter?
EMILIA [*to Iago*]:  Disprove this villain, if thou be'st a man.
  He says thou toldst him that his wife was false.               180
  I know thou didst not; thou'rt not such a villain.
  Speak, for my heart is full.
IAGO:  I told him what I thought, and told no more
  Than what he found himself was apt° and true.
EMILIA:  But did you ever tell him she was false?               185
IAGO:  I did.
EMILIA:  You told a lie, an odious, damnèd lie!
  Upon my soul, a lie, a wicked lie.
  She false with Cassio? Did you say with Cassio?

---

158 made mocks with derided, made sport of  168 you were best it would be best for you  170 to
be hurt i.e., to endure hurt.  gull dupe  184 apt plausible

IAGO:  With Cassio, mistress. Go to, charm° your tongue.          190
EMILIA:  I will not charm my tongue; I am bound to speak.
   My mistress here lies murdered in her bed—
ALL:  O heavens forfend!
EMILIA:  And your reports have set the murder on.
OTHELLO:  Nay, stare not, masters. It is true indeed.          195
GRATIANO:  'Tis a strange truth.
MONTANO:  O monstrous act!
EMILIA:                 Villainy, villainy, villainy!
   I think upon 't—I think I smell 't! O villainy!
   I thought so then°—I'll kill myself for grief—
   O villainy, villainy!          200
IAGO:  What, are you mad? I charge you, get you home.
EMILIA:  Good gentlemen, let me have leave to speak.
   'Tis proper I obey him, but not now.
   Perchance, Iago, I will ne'er go home.
   Othello: O! O! O!     [*Othello falls on the bed.*°]
EMILIA:             Nay, lay thee down and roar,          205
   For thou hast killed the sweetest innocent
   That e'er did lift up eye.°
OTHELLO [*rising*]:       O, she was foul!
   I scarce did know you, uncle. There lies your niece,
   Whose breath indeed these hands have newly stopped.
   I know this act shows° horrible and grim.          210
GRATIANO:  Poor Desdemona! I am glad thy father's dead.
   Thy match was mortal to him, and pure grief
   Shore his old thread° in twain. Did he live now,
   This sight would make him do a desperate turn,°
   Yea, curse his better angel from his side,          215
   And fall to reprobance.°
OTHELLO:  'Tis pitiful. But yet Iago knows
   That she with Cassio hath the act of shame
   A thousand times committed. Cassio confessed it;

---

190 **charm** keep silent (as though by a magic spell)  199 **then** (Perhaps at Act III, Scene iii, lines 331–332 and Act IV, Scene ii, lines 137–154.)  205 [s.d.] **Othello . . . bed** (This direction is from the Quarto, as also *He kisses her* at line 19 and *She dies* at line 129.)  207 **lift up eye** i.e., lift her eyes to heaven  210 **shows** looks  213 **Shore . . . thread** sheared the thread of his old age (as Atropos, one of the three Fates, was thought to do)  214 **turn** deed  216 **reprobance** damnation, i.e., suicide

And she did gratify° his amorous works                          220
With that recognizance° and pledge of love
Which I first gave her. I saw it in his hand;
It was a handkerchief, an antique token
My father gave my mother.
EMILIA:   O God! O heavenly God!                                225
IAGO:   Zounds, hold your peace.
EMILIA:                               'Twill out, 'twill out! I peace?
No, I will speak as liberal as the north.°
Let heaven and men and devils, let them all,
All, all, cry shame against me, yet I'll speak.
IAGO:   Be wise, and get you home.
EMILIA:                          I will not.

[*Iago threatens Emilia.*]

GRATIANO:                               Fie                      230
Your sword upon a woman?
EMILIA:   O thou dull Moor! That handkerchief thou speak'st of
I found by fortune and did give my husband;
For often, with a solemn earnestness,
More than indeed belonged° to such a trifle,                    235
He begged of me to steal 't.
IAGO:                          Villainous whore!
EMILIA:   She give it Cassio? No, alas! I found it,
And I did give 't my husband.
IAGO:                          Filth, thou liest!
EMILIA:   By heaven, I do not, I do not, gentlemen.
O murderous coxcomb!° What should such a fool                   240
Do with so good a wife?
OTHELLO:   Are there no stones° in heaven
But what serves for the thunder?—Precious° villain!

[*He runs at Iago; Montano disarms Othello. Iago, from behind,
stabs Emilia.°*]

GRATIANO:   The woman falls! Sure he hath killed his wife.

---

220 **gratify** reward   221 **recognizance** token   227 **liberal as the north** freely as the north wind
(blows)   235 **belonged** was appropriate   240 **coxcomb** fool. (Addressed to Othello.)   242 **stones**
bolts, such as those used for thunderbolts   243 **Precious** i.e., arrant, utter.   [s.d.] **He . . . Emilia**
(The Quarto text reads, "The Moor runs at Iago. Iago kills his wife." The Quarto also specifies the
exit of Iago at line 245 and the death of Emilia at line 260.)

EMILIA:  Ay, ay. O, lay me by my mistress' side.    245

*Exit* [*Iago.*]

GRATIANO:  He's gone, but his wife's killed.
MONTANO:  'Tis a notorious villain. Take you this weapon,
Which I have here recovered from the Moor.
Come, guard the door without. Let him not pass,
But kill him rather. I'll after that same villain,    250
For 'tis a damnèd slave.

*Exit* [*with all but Othello and Emilia, who has been laid by
Desdemona's side*].

OTHELLO:  I am not valiant neither,
But every puny whipster° gets my sword.
But why should honor° outlive honesty?°
Let it go all.
EMILIA:         What did thy song bode, lady?    255
Hark, canst thou hear me? I will play the swan,
And die in music. [*She sings.*] "Willow, willow, willow."
Moor, she was chaste. She loved thee, cruel Moor.
So come my soul to bliss as I speak true.
So speaking as I think, alas, I die.         [*She dies.*]    260
OTHELLO:  I have another weapon in this chamber;
It was a sword of Spain, the ice-brook's temper°—
O, here it is. [*He finds a sword.*] Uncle, I must come forth.
GRATIANO [*within*]:  If thou attempt it, it will cost thee dear.
Thou hast no weapon, and perforce must suffer.    265
OTHELLO:  Look in upon me then and speak with me,
Or, naked° as I am, I will assault thee.

[*Enter Gratiano.*]

GRATIANO:  What is the matter?
OTHELLO:                    Behold, I have a weapon;
A better never did itself sustain
Upon a soldier's thigh. I have seen the day    270
That, with this little arm and this good sword,

---

**253 whipster** contemptible fellow (one who is always ready to whip out his sword)  **254 honor** i.e.,
the bravery for which one enjoys a soldier's reputation.  **honesty** true integrity  **262 the ice-
brook's temper** tempered in ice-cold water  **267 naked** unarmed

I have made my way through more impediments
Than twenty times your stop.° But O, vain boast!
Who can control his fate? 'Tis not so now.
Be not afraid, though you do see me weaponed;          275
Here is my journey's end, here is my butt°
And very seamark° of my utmost sail.

[*Gratiano steps back.*]

Do you go back dismayed? 'Tis a lost° fear;
Man but a rush° against Othello's breast
And he retires. Where should Othello go?          280

[*He turns to Desdemona.*]

Now, how dost thou look now? O ill-starred wench!
Pale as thy smock! When we shall meet at compt,°
This look of thine will hurl my soul from heaven,
And fiends will snatch at it. Cold, cold, my girl?
Even like thy chastity. O cursèd, cursèd slave!°          285
Whip me, ye devils,
From the possession of this heavenly sight!
Blow me about in winds! Roast me in sulfur!
Wash me in steep-down gulfs of liquid fire!
O Desdemon! Dead, Desdemon! Dead! O! O!          290

*Enter Lodovico, Cassio [carried in a litter°], Montano, and Iago
[prisoner], with officers.*

LODOVICO:   Where is this rash and most unfortunate man?
OTHELLO:   That's he that was Othello. Here I am.
LODOVICO:   Where is that viper? Bring the villain forth.

[*Iago is led forward.*]

---

273 **stop** power (to stop)   276 **butt** goal, limit (an archery term)   277 **seamark** beacon (marking
his destination or limit)   278 **lost** wasted, unneeded   279 **Man . . . rush** wield no more than a reed
282 **compt** account, judgment day   285 **slave** i.e., Othello himself   290 **[s.d.]** in a litter (The
Quarto specifies that Cassio is "in a chair.")

OTHELLO:   I look down towards his feet;° but that's a fable.
If that thou be'st a devil, I cannot kill thee.                    295

[*He wounds Iago.*]

LODOVICO:   Wrench his sword from him.

[*Othello is disarmed.*]

IAGO:                                    I bleed, sir, but not
killed.
OTHELLO:   I am not sorry neither. I'd have thee live,
For in my sense° 'tis happiness to die.
LODOVICO:   O thou Othello, that was once so good,
Fall'n in the practice° of a cursèd slave,°                        300
What shall be said to thee?
OTHELLO:                        Why, anything.
An honorable murderer, if you will,
For naught I did in hate, but all in honor.
LODOVICO:   This wretch hath part confessed his villainy.
Did you and he consent° in Cassio's death?                        305
OTHELLO:   Ay.
CASSIO:   Dear General, I never gave you cause.
OTHELLO:   I do believe it, and I ask your pardon.
Will you, I pray, demand that demi-devil
Why he hath thus ensnared my soul and body?                       310
IAGO:   Demand me nothing. What you know, you know.
From this time forth I never will speak word.
LODOVICO:   What, not to pray?
GRATIANO:   Torments° will ope your lips.
OTHELLO:   Well, thou dost best.                                  315
LODOVICO:   Sir, you shall understand what hath befall'n,
Which, as I think, you know not. Here is a letter
Found in the pocket of the slain Roderigo;
And here another. [*He produces letters.*] The one of them
imports

---

**294 towards his feet** i.e., to see if they are cloven, as the devil's are fabled to be   **298 in my sense** to
one who feels as I do   **300 in the practice** through the plotting, into the snare.   **slave** villain   **305
consent** agree   **314 Torments** torture

The death of Cassio, to be undertook                    320
By Roderigo.
OTHELLO:   O villain!
CASSIO:                  Most heathenish and most gross!°
LODOVICO [*showing another paper*]:   Now here's another
    discontented° paper
    Found in his pocket too. And this, it seems,
    Roderigo meant t' have sent this damnèd villain;        325
    But that belike° Iago in the interim
    Came in and satisfied him.°
OTHELLO:   O thou pernicious caitiff!—
    How came you, Cassio, by that handkerchief
    That was my wife's?
CASSIO:                    I found it in my chamber;        330
    And he himself confessed but even now
    That there he dropped it for a special purpose
    Which wrought to his desire.°
OTHELLO:                  O fool, fool, fool!
CASSIO:   There is besides in Roderigo's letter
    How he upbraids Iago, that he made him               335
    Brave° me upon the watch, whereon it came°
    That I was cast;° and even but now he spake,
    After long seeming dead, Iago hurt him,
    Iago set him on.
LODOVICO [*to Othello*]:   You must forsake this room and go   340
    with us.
    Your power and your command is taken off,°
    And Cassio rules in Cyprus. For this slave,
    If there be any cunning cruelty
    That can torment him much and hold him long,°
    It shall be his. You shall close prisoner rest°        345
    Till that the nature of your fault be known
    To the Venetian state.—Come, bring away.
OTHELLO:   Soft you;° a word or two before you go.
    I have done the state some service, and they know 't.

---

322 **gross** monstrous   323 **discontented** full of discontent   326 **belike** most likely   327 **Came . . . him** interposed and gave him satisfactory explanation   333 **wrought . . . desire** worked out as he wished, fitted in with his plan   336 **Brave** defy.  **whereon it came** whereof it came about   337 **cast** dismissed   341 **taken off** taken away   344 **hold him long** keep him alive a long time (during his torture)   345 **rest** remain   348 **Soft you** one moment

No more of that. I pray you, in your letters,          350
When you shall these unlucky° deeds relate,
Speak of me as I am; nothing extenuate,
Nor set down aught in malice. Then must you speak
Of one that loved not wisely but too well;
Of one not easily jealous but, being wrought,°          355
Perplexed° in the extreme; of one whose hand,
Like the base Indian,° threw a pearl away
Richer than all his tribe; of one whose subdued° eyes,
Albeit unusèd to the melting mood,
Drops tears as fast as the Arabian trees          360
Their medicinable gum.° Set you down this;
And say besides that in Aleppo once,
Where a malignant and a turbaned Turk
Beat a Venetian and traduced the state,
I took by th' throat the circumcisèd dog          365
And smote him, thus.          [*He stabs himself.*°]
LODOVICO:   O bloody period!°
GRATIANO:   All that is spoke is marred.
OTHELLO:   I kissed thee ere I killed thee. No way but this,
Killing myself, to die upon a kiss.          370

[*He kisses Desdemona and*] *dies.*

CASSIO:   This did I fear, but thought he had no weapon;
For he was great of heart.
LODOVICO [*to Iago*]:          O Spartan dog,°
More fell° than anguish, hunger, or the sea!
Look on the tragic loading of this bed.
This is thy work. The object poisons sight;          375
Let it be hid.° Gratiano, keep° the house,

[*The bed curtains are drawn*]

---

351 **unlucky** unfortunate   355 **wrought** worked upon, worked into a frenzy   356 **Perplexed** distraught   357 **Indian** (This reading from the Quarto pictures an ignorant savage who cannot recognize the value of a precious jewel. The Folio reading, *Iudean* or *Judean*, i.e., infidel or disbeliever, may refer to Herod, who slew Mariamne in a fit of jealousy, or to Judas Iscariot, the betrayer of Christ.)   358 **subdued** i.e., overcome by grief   361 **gum** i.e., myrrh   366 [s.d.] **He stabs himself** (This direction is in the Quarto text.)   367 **period** termination, conclusion   372 **Spartan dog** (Spartan dogs were noted for their savagery and silence.)   373 **fell** cruel   376 **Let it be hid** i.e., draw the bed curtains. (No stage direction specifies that the dead are to be carried offstage at the end of the play.) **keep** remain in

And seize upon° the fortunes of the Moor,
For they succeed on° you. [*To Cassio.*] To you, Lord
Governor,
Remains the censure° of this hellish villain,
The time, the place, the torture. O, enforce it!                    380
Myself will straight aboard, and to the state
This heavy act with heavy heart relate.                    *Exeunt.*

*—1604?*

---

**377 seize upon** take legal possession of   **378 succeed on** pass as though by inheritance to   **379 censure** sentencing

# Henrik Ibsen (1828–1906)

*Henrik Ibsen, universally acknowledged as the first of the great modern playwrights, was born in Skien, a small town in Norway, the son of a merchant who went bankrupt during Ibsen's childhood. Ibsen first trained for a medical career, but drifted into the theatre, gaining, like Shakespeare and Molière, important dramatic training through a decade's service as a stage manager and director. Ibsen was unsuccessful in establishing a theater in Oslo, and he spent almost thirty years living and writing in Germany and Italy. The fame he won through early poetic dramas like* Peer Gynt *(1867), which is considered the supreme exploration of the Norwegian national character, was overshadowed by the realistic prose plays he began writing with* Pillars of Society *(1877).* A Doll House *(1879) and* Ghosts *(1881), which deal, respectively, with a woman's struggle for independence and self-respect and with the taboo subject of venereal disease, made Ibsen an internationally famous, if controversial, figure. Although Ibsen's type of realism, displayed in "problem plays" such as these and later psychological dramas like* The Wild Duck *(1885) and* Hedda Gabler *(1890), has become so fully assimilated into our literary heritage that now it is difficult to think of him as an innovator, his marriage of the tightly constructed plots of the conventional "well-made play" to serious discussion of social issues was one of the most significant developments in the history of drama. Interestingly, the conclusion of* A Doll House *proved so unsettling that Ibsen was forced to write an alternate ending in which Nora states her case but does not slam the door on her marriage. His most influential advocate in English-speaking countries was George Bernard Shaw, whose* The Quintessence of Ibsenism *(1891) is one of the earliest and most influential studies of Ibsen's dramatic methods and ideas.*

# A Doll House

### Translated by Rolf Fjelde

## CHARACTERS

Torvald Helmer, *a lawyer*
Nora, *his wife*
Dr. Rank
Mrs. Linde
Nils Krogstad, *a bank clerk*
The Helmers' Three Small Children

Anne-Marie, *their nurse*
Helene, *a maid*
A Delivery Boy

The action takes place in Helmer's residence.

## ACT I

A comfortable room, tastefully but not expensively furnished. A door to the right in the back wall leads to the entryway; another to the left leads to Helmer's study. Between these doors, a piano. Midway in the left-hand wall a door, and farther back a window. Near the window a round table with an armchair and a small sofa. In the right-hand wall, toward the rear, a door, and nearer the foreground a porcelain stove with two armchairs and a rocking chair beside it. Between the stove and the side door, a small table. Engravings on the walls. An étagère with china figures and other small art objects; small bookcase with richly bound books; the floor carpeted; a fire burning in the stove. It is a winter day.

A bell rings in the entryway; shortly after we hear the door being unlocked. Nora comes into the room, humming happily to herself; she is wearing street clothes and carries an armload of packages, which she puts down on the table to the right. She has left the hall door open and through it a Delivery Boy is seen, holding a Christmas tree and a basket, which he gives to the Maid who let them in.

NORA: Hide the tree well, Helene. The children mustn't get a glimpse of it till this evening, after it's trimmed. (*To the Delivery Boy, taking out her purse.*) How much?

DELIVERY BOY: Fifty, ma'am.

NORA: There's a crown. No, keep the change. (*The Boy thanks her and leaves. Nora shuts the door. She laughs softly to herself while taking off her street things. Drawing a bag of macaroons from her pocket, she eats a couple, then steals over and listens at her husband's study door.*) Yes, he's home. (*Hums again as she moves to the table, right.*)

HELMER (*from the study*): Is that my little lark twittering out there?

NORA (*busy opening some packages*): Yes, it is.

HELMER: Is that my squirrel rummaging around?

NORA: Yes!

HELMER: When did my squirrel get in?

NORA: Just now. (*Putting the macaroon bag in her pocket and wiping her mouth.*) Do come in, Torvald, and see what I've bought.

HELMER: Can't be disturbed. (*After a moment he opens the door and peers in, pen in hand.*) Bought, you say? All that there? Has the little spendthrift been out throwing money around again?

NORA: Oh, but Torvald, this year we really should let ourselves go a bit. It's the first Christmas we haven't had to economize.

HELMER: But you know we can't go squandering.

NORA: Oh yes, Torvald, we can squander a little now. Can't we? Just a tiny, wee bit. Now that you've got a big salary and are going to make piles and piles of money.

HELMER: Yes—starting New Year's. But then it's a full three months till the raise comes through.

NORA: Pooh! We can borrow that long.

HELMER: Nora! (*Goes over and playfully takes her by the ear.*) Are your scatter-brains off again? What if today I borrowed a thousand crowns, and you squandered them over Christmas week, and then on New Year's Eve a roof tile fell on my head, and I lay there—

NORA (*putting her hand on his mouth*): Oh! Don't say such things!

HELMER: Yes, but what if it happened—then what?

NORA: If anything so awful happened, then it just wouldn't matter if I had debts or not.

HELMER: Well, but the people I'd borrowed from?

NORA: Them? Who cares about them? They're strangers.

HELMER: Nora, Nora, how like a woman! No, but seriously, Nora, you know what I think about that. No debts! Never borrow! Something of freedom's lost—and something of beauty, too—from a home that's founded on borrowing and debt. We've made a brave stand up to now, the two of us; and we'll go right on like that the little while we have to.

NORA (*going toward the stove*): Yes, whatever you say, Torvald.

HELMER (*following her*): Now, now, the little lark's wings mustn't droop. Come on, don't be a sulky squirrel. (*Taking out his wallet.*) Nora, guess what I have here.

NORA (*turning quickly*): Money!

HELMER: There, see. (*Hands her some notes.*) Good grief, I know how costs go up in a house at Christmastime.

NORA: Ten—twenty—thirty—forty. Oh, thank you, Torvald; I can manage no end on this.

HELMER: You really will have to.

NORA: Oh yes, I promise I will! But come here so I can show you everything I bought. And so cheap! Look, new clothes for Ivar here—and a sword. Here a horse and a trumpet for Bob. And a doll and a doll's bed here for Emmy; they're nothing much, but she'll tear them to bits in no time anyway. And here I have dress material and handkerchiefs for the maids. Old Anne-Marie really deserves something more.

HELMER: And what's in that package there?

NORA (*with a cry*): Torvald, no! You can't see that till tonight!

HELMER: I see. But tell me now, you little prodigal, what have you thought of for yourself?

NORA: For myself? Oh, I don't want anything at all.

HELMER: Of course you do. Tell me just what—within reason— you'd most like to have.

NORA: I honestly don't know. Oh, listen, Torvald—

HELMER: Well?

NORA (*fumbling at his coat buttons, without looking at him*): If you want to give me something, then maybe you could—you could—

HELMER: Come on, out with it.

NORA (*hurriedly*): You could give me money, Torvald. No more than you think you can spare; then one of these days I'll buy something with it.

HELMER: But Nora—

NORA: Oh, please, Torvald darling, do that! I beg you, please. Then I could hang the bills in pretty gilt paper on the Christmas tree. Wouldn't that be fun?

HELMER: What are those little birds called that always fly through their fortunes?

NORA: Oh yes, spendthrifts; I know all that. But let's do as I say, Torvald; then I'll have time to decide what I really need most. That's very sensible, isn't it?

HELMER (*smiling*): Yes, very—that is, if you actually hung onto the money I give you, and you actually used it to buy yourself something. But it goes for the house and for all sorts of foolish things, and then I only have to lay out some more.

NORA: Oh, but Torvald—

HELMER: Don't deny it, my dear little Nora. (*Putting his arm around her waist.*) Spendthrifts are sweet, but they use up a frightful amount of money. It's incredible what it costs a man to feed such birds.

NORA: Oh, how can you say that! Really, I save everything I can.

HELMER (*laughing*): Yes, that's the truth. Everything you can. But that's nothing at all.

NORA (*humming, with a smile of quiet satisfaction*): Hm, if you only knew what expenses we larks and squirrels have, Torvald.

HELMER: You're an odd little one. Exactly the way your father was. You're never at a loss for scaring up money; but the moment you have it, it runs right out through your fingers; you never know what you've done with it. Well, one takes you as you are. It's deep in your blood. Yes, these things are hereditary, Nora.

NORA: Ah, I could wish I'd inherited many of Papa's qualities.

HELMER: And I couldn't wish you anything but just what you are, my sweet little lark. But wait; it seems to me you have a very— what should I call it?—a very suspicious look today—

NORA: I do?

HELMER: You certainly do. Look me straight in the eye.

NORA (*looking at him*): Well?

HELMER (*shaking an admonitory finger*): Surely my sweet tooth hasn't been running riot in town today, has she?

NORA: No. Why do you imagine that?

HELMER: My sweet tooth really didn't make a little detour through the confectioner's?

NORA: No, I assure you, Torvald—

HELMER: Hasn't nibbled some pastry?

NORA: No, not at all.

HELMER: Nor even munched a macaroon or two?

NORA: No, Torvald, I assure you, really—

HELMER: There, there now. Of course I'm only joking.

NORA (*going to the table, right*): You know I could never think of going against you.

HELMER: No, I understand that; and you *have* given me your word. (*Going over to her.*) Well, you keep your little Christmas secrets to yourself, Nora darling I expect they'll come to light this evening, when the tree is lit.

NORA: Did you remember to ask Dr. Rank?

HELMER: No. But there's no need for that; it's assumed he'll be dining with us. All the same, I'll ask him when he stops by here this morning. I've ordered some fine wine. Nora, you can't imagine how I'm looking forward to this evening.

NORA: So am I—And what fun for the children, Torvald!

HELMER: Ah, it's so gratifying to know that one's gotten a safe, secure job, and with a comfortable salary. It's a great satisfaction, isn't it?

NORA: Oh, it's wonderful!

HELMER: Remember last Christmas? Three whole weeks before, you shut yourself in every evening till long after midnight, making flowers for the Christmas tree, and all the other decorations to surprise us. Ugh, that was the dullest time I've ever lived through.

NORA: It wasn't at all dull for me.

HELMER (*smiling*): But the outcome *was* pretty sorry, Nora.

NORA: Oh, don't tease me with that again. How could I help it that the cat came in and tore everything to shreds.

HELMER: No, poor thing, you certainly couldn't. You wanted so much to please us all, and that's what counts. But it's just as well that the hard times are past.

NORA: Yes, it's really wonderful.

HELMER: Now I don't have to sit here alone, boring myself, and you don't have to tire your precious eyes and your fair little delicate hands—

NORA (*clapping her hands*): No, is it really true, Torvald, I don't have to? Oh, how wonderfully lovely to hear! (*Taking his arm.*) Now I'll tell you just how I've thought we should plan things. Right after Christmas—(*The doorbell rings.*) Oh, the bell. (*Straightening the room up a bit.*) Somebody would have to come. What a bore!

HELMER: I'm not at home to visitors, don't forget.

MAID (*from the hall doorway*): Ma'am, a lady to see you—

NORA: All right, let her come in.

MAID (*to Helmer*): And the doctor's just come too.

HELMER: Did he go right to my study?

MAID: Yes, he did.

*Helmer goes into his room. The Maid shows in Mrs. Linde, dressed in traveling clothes, and shuts the door after her.*

MRS. LINDE (*in a dispirited and somewhat hesitant voice*): Hello, Nora.

NORA (*uncertain*): Hello—

MRS. LINDE: You don't recognize me.

NORA: No, I don't know—but wait, I think—(*Exclaiming.*) What! Kristine! Is it really you?

MRS. LINDE: Yes, it's me.

NORA: Kristine! To think I didn't recognize you. But then, how could I? (*More quietly.*) How you've changed, Kristine!

MRS. LINDE: Yes, no doubt I have. In nine—ten long years.

NORA: Is it so long since we met! Yes, it's all of that. Oh, these last eight years have been a happy time, believe me. And so now you've come to town, too. Made the long trip in the winter. That took courage.

MRS. LINDE: I just got here by ship this morning.

NORA: To enjoy yourself over Christmas, of course. Oh, how lovely! Yes, enjoy ourselves, we'll do that. But take your coat off. You're not still cold? (*Helping her.*) There now, let's get cozy here by the stove. No, the easy chair there! I'll take the rocker here. (*Seizing her hands.*) Yes, now you have your old look again; it was only in that first moment. You're a bit more pale, Kristine—and maybe a bit thinner.

MRS. LINDE: And much, much older, Nora.

NORA: Yes, perhaps a bit older; a tiny, tiny bit; not much at all. (*Stopping short; suddenly serious.*) Oh, but thoughtless me, to sit here, chattering away. Sweet good Kristine, can you forgive me?

MRS. LINDE: What do you mean, Nora?

NORA (*softly*): Poor Kristine, you've become a widow.

MRS. LINDE: Yes, three years ago.

NORA: Oh, I knew it, of course; I read it in the papers. Oh, Kristine, you must believe me; I often thought of writing you then, but I kept postponing it, and something always interfered.

MRS. LINDE: Nora dear, I understand completely.

NORA: No, it was awful of me, Kristine. You poor thing, how much you must have gone through. And he left you nothing?

MRS. LINDE: No.

NORA: And no children?

MRS. LINDE: No.

NORA: Nothing at all, then?

MRS. LINDE: Not even a sense of loss to feed on.

NORA (*looking incredulously at her*): But Kristine, how could that be?

MRS. LINDE (*smiling wearily and smoothing her hair*): Oh, sometimes it happens, Nora.

NORA: So completely alone. How terribly hard that must be for you. I have three lovely children. You can't see them now; they're out with the maid. But now you must tell me everything—

MRS. LINDE: No, no, no, tell me about yourself.

NORA: No, you begin. Today I don't want to be selfish. I want to think only of you today. But there *is* something I must tell you. Did you hear of the wonderful luck we had recently?

MRS. LINDE: No, what's that?

NORA: My husband's been made manager in the bank, just think!

MRS. LINDE: Your husband? How marvelous!

NORA: Isn't it? Being a lawyer is such an uncertain living, you know, especially if one won't touch any cases that aren't clean and decent. And of course Torvald would never do that, and I'm with him completely there. Oh, we're simply delighted, believe me! He'll join the bank right after New Year's and start getting a huge salary and lots of commissions. From now on we can live quite differently— just as we want. Oh, Kristine, I feel so light and happy! Won't it be lovely to have stacks of money and not a care in the world?

MRS. LINDE: Well, anyway, it would be lovely to have enough for necessities.

NORA: No, not just for necessities, but stacks and stacks of money!

MRS. LINDE (*smiling*): Nora, Nora, aren't you sensible yet? Back in school you were such a free spender.

NORA (*With a quiet laugh*): Yes, that's what Torvald still says. (*Shaking her finger.*) But "Nora, Nora" isn't as silly as you all think. Really, we've been in no position for me to go squandering. We've had to work, both of us.

MRS. LINDE: You too?

NORA: Yes, at odd jobs—needlework, crocheting, embroidery, and such—(*casually*) and other things too. You remember that Torvald left the department when we were married? There was no chance of promotion in his office, and of course he needed to earn more money. But that first year he drove himself terribly. He took on all kinds of extra work that kept him going morning and night. It wore him down, and then he fell deathly ill. The doctors said it was essential for him to travel south.

MRS. LINDE: Yes, didn't you spend a whole year in Italy?

NORA: That's right. It wasn't easy to get away, you know. Ivar had just been born. But of course we had to go. Oh, that was a beautiful trip, and it saved Torvald's life. But it cost a frightful sum, Kristine.

MRS. LINDE: I can well imagine.

NORA: Four thousand, eight hundred crowns it cost. That's really a lot of money.

MRS. LINDE: But it's lucky you had it when you needed it.

NORA: Well, as it was, we got it from Papa.

MRS. LINDE: I see. It was just about the time your father died.

NORA: Yes, just about then. And, you know, I couldn't make that trip out to nurse him. I had to stay here, expecting Ivar any moment, and with my poor sick Torvald to care for. Dearest Papa, I never saw him again, Kristine. Oh, that was the worst time I've known in all my marriage.

MRS. LINDE: I know how you loved him. And then you went off to Italy?

NORA: Yes. We had the means now, and the doctors urged us. So we left a month after.

MRS. LINDE: And your husband came back completely cured?

NORA: Sound as a drum!

MRS. LINDE: But—the doctor?

NORA: Who?

MRS. LINDE: I thought the maid said he was a doctor, the man who came in with me.

NORA: Yes, that was Dr. Rank—but he's not making a sick call. He's our closest friend, and he stops by at least once a day. No, Torvald hasn't had a sick moment since, and the children are healthy and strong, and I am, too. (*Jumping up and clapping her hands.*) Oh, dear God, Kristine, what a lovely thing to live and be happy! But how disgusting of me—I'm talking of nothing but my own affairs. (*Sits on a stool close by Kristine, arms resting across her knees.*) Oh, don't be angry with me! Tell me, is it really true that you weren't in love with your husband? Why did you marry him, then?

MRS. LINDE: My mother was still alive, but bedridden and helpless— and I had my two younger brothers to look after. In all conscience, I didn't think I could turn him down.

NORA: No, you were right there. But was he rich at the time?

MRS. LINDE: He was very well off, I'd say. But the business was shaky, Nora. When he died, it all fell apart, and nothing was left.

NORA: And then—?

MRS. LINDE: Yes, so I had to scrape up a living with a little shop and a little teaching and whatever else I could find. The last three years have been like one endless workday without a rest for me. Now it's over, Nora. My poor mother doesn't need me, for she's passed on. Nor the boys, either; they're working now and can take care of themselves.

NORA: How free you must feel—

MRS. LINDE: No—only unspeakably empty. Nothing to live for now. (*Standing up anxiously.*) That's why I couldn't take it any longer out in that desolate hole. Maybe here it'll be easier to find something to do and keep my mind occupied. If I could only be lucky enough to get a steady job, some office work—

NORA: Oh, but Kristine, that's so dreadfully tiring, and you already look so tired. It would be much better for you if you could go off to a bathing resort.

MRS. LINDE (*going toward the window*):   I have no father to give me travel money, Nora.

NORA (*rising*):   Oh, don't be angry with me.

MRS. LINDE (*going to her*):   Nora dear, don't you be angry with me. The worst of my kind of situation is all the bitterness that's stored away. No one to work for, and yet you're always having to snap up your opportunities. You have to live; and so you grow selfish. When you told me the happy change in your lot, do you know I was delighted less for your sakes than for mine?

NORA:   How so? Oh, I see. You think Torvald could do something for you.

MRS. LINDE:   Yes, that's what I thought.

NORA:   And he will, Kristine! Just leave it to me; I'll bring it up so delicately—find something attractive to humor him with. Oh, I'm so eager to help you.

MRS. LINDE:   How very kind of you, Nora, to be so concerned over me—doubly kind, considering you really know so little of life's burdens yourself.

NORA:   I—? I know so little—?

MRS. LINDE (*smiling*):   Well my heavens—a little needlework and such—Nora, you're just a child.

NORA (*tossing her head and pacing the floor*):   You don't have to act so superior.

MRS. LINDE:   Oh?

NORA:   You're just like the others. You all think I'm incapable of anything serious—

MRS. LINDE:   Come now—

NORA:   That I've never had to face the raw world.

MRS. LINDE:   Nora dear, you've just been telling me all your troubles.

NORA:   Hm! Trivia! (*Quietly.*) I haven't told you the big thing.

MRS. LINDE:   Big thing? What do you mean?

NORA:   You look down on me so, Kristine, but you shouldn't. You're proud that you worked so long and hard for your mother.

MRS. LINDE:   I don't look down on a soul. But it *is* true: I'm proud—and happy, too—to think it was given to me to make my mother's last days almost free of care.

NORA:   And you're also proud thinking of what you've done for your brothers.

MRS. LINDE:   I feel I've a right to be.

NORA:   I agree. But listen to this, Kristine—I've also got something to be proud and happy for.

MRS. LINDE:   I don't doubt it. But whatever do you mean?

NORA: Not so loud. What if Torvald heard! He mustn't, not for anything in the world. Nobody must know, Kristine. No one but you.

MRS. LINDE: But what is it, then?

NORA: Come here. (*Drawing her down beside her on the sofa.*) It's true—I've also got something to be proud and happy for. I'm the one who saved Torvald's life.

MRS. LINDE: Saved—? Saved how?

NORA: I told you about the trip to Italy. Torvald never would have lived if he hadn't gone south—

MRS. LINDE: Of course; your father gave you the means—

NORA (*smiling*): That's what Torvald and all the rest think, but—

MRS. LINDE: But—?

NORA: Papa didn't give us a pin. I was the one who raised the money.

MRS. LINDE: You? That whole amount?

NORA: Four thousand, eight hundred crowns. What do you say to that?

MRS. LINDE: But Nora, how was it possible? Did you win the lottery?

NORA (*disdainfully*): The lottery? Pooh! No art to that.

MRS. LINDE: But where did you get it from then?

NORA (*humming, with a mysterious smile*): Hmm, tra-la-la-la.

MRS. LINDE: Because you couldn't have borrowed it.

NORA: No? Why not?

MRS. LINDE: A wife can't borrow without her husband's consent.

NORA (*tossing her head*): Oh, but a wife with a little business sense, a wife who knows how to manage—

MRS. LINDE: Nora, I simply don't understand—

NORA: You don't have to. Whoever said I *borrowed* the money? I could have gotten it other ways. (*Throwing herself back on the sofa.*) I could have gotten it from some admirer or other. After all, a girl with my ravishing appeal—

MRS. LINDE: You lunatic.

NORA: I'll bet you're eaten up with curiosity, Kristine.

MRS. LINDE: Now listen here, Nora—you haven't done something indiscreet?

NORA (*sitting up again*): Is it indiscreet to save your husband's life?

MRS. LINDE: I think it's indiscreet that without his knowledge you—

NORA: But that's the point: he mustn't know! My Lord, can't you understand? He mustn't ever know the close call he had. It was to *me* the doctors came to say his life was in danger—that nothing could save him but a stay in the south. Didn't I try strategy then! I began talking about how lovely it would be for me to travel abroad like other young wives; I begged and I cried; I told him please to remember my condition, to be kind and indulge me; and then I dropped a hint that he could easily take out a loan. But at that, Kristine, he nearly exploded. He said I was frivolous, and it was his duty as man of the house not to indulge me in whims and fancies—as I think he called them. Aha, I thought now, you'll just have to be saved—and that's when I saw my chance.

MRS. LINDE: And your father never told Torvald the money wasn't from him?

NORA: No, never. Papa died right about then. I'd considered bringing him into my secret and begging him never to tell. But he was too sick at the time—and then, sadly, it didn't matter.

MRS. LINDE: And you've never confided in your husband since?

NORA: For heaven's sake, no! Are you serious? He's so strict on that subject. Besides—Torvald, with all his masculine pride—how painfully humiliating for him if he ever found out he was in debt to me. That would just ruin our relationship. Our beautiful, happy home would never be the same.

MRS. LINDE: Won't you ever tell him?

NORA (*thoughtfully, half smiling*): Yes—maybe sometime, years from now, when I'm no longer so attractive. Don't laugh! I only mean when Torvald loves me less than now, when he stops enjoying my dancing and dressing up and reciting for him. Then it might be wise to have something in reserve—(*Breaking off.*) How ridiculous! That'll never happen—Well, Kristine, what do you think of my big secret? I'm capable of something too, hm? You can imagine, of course, how this thing hangs over me. It really hasn't been easy meeting the payments on time. In the business world there's what they call quarterly interest and what they call amortization, and these are always so terribly hard to manage. I've had to skimp a little here and there, wherever I could, because Torvald has to live well. I couldn't let the children go poorly dressed; whatever I got for them, I felt I had to use up completely—the darlings!

MRS. LINDE: Poor Nora, so it had to come out of your own budget, then?

NORA: Yes, of course. But I was the one most responsible, too. Every time Torvald gave me money for new clothes and such, I never used more than half; always bought the simplest, cheapest outfits. It was a godsend that everything looks so well on me that Torvald never noticed. But it did weigh me down at times, Kristine. It *is* such a joy to wear fine things. You understand.

MRS. LINDE: Oh, of course.

NORA: And then I found other ways of making money. Last winter I was lucky enough to get a lot of copying to do. I locked myself in and sat writing every evening till late in the night. Ah, I was tired so often, dead tired. But still it was wonderful fun, sitting and working like that, earning money. It was almost like being a man.

MRS. LINDE: But how much have you paid off this way so far?

NORA: That's hard to say, exactly. These accounts, you know, aren't easy to figure. I only know that I've paid out all I could scrape together. Time and again I haven't known where to turn. (*Smiling.*) Then I'd sit here dreaming of a rich old gentleman who had fallen in love with me—

MRS. LINDE: What! Who is he?

NORA: Oh, really! And that he'd died, and when his will was opened, there in big letters it said, "All my fortune shall be paid over in cash, immediately to that enchanting Mrs. Nora Helmer."

MRS. LINDE: But Nora dear—who *was* this gentleman?

NORA: Good grief, can't you understand? The old man never existed; that was only something I'd dream up time and again whenever I was at my wits' end for money. But it makes no difference now; the old fossil can go where he pleases for all I care; I don't need him or his will—because now I'm free. (*Jumping up.*) Oh, how lovely to think of that, Kristine! Carefree! To know you're carefree, utterly carefree; to be able to romp and play with the children, and to keep up a beautiful, charming home—everything just the way Torvald likes it! And think, spring is coming, with big blue skies. Maybe we can travel a little then. Maybe I'll see the ocean again. Oh yes, it *is* so marvelous to live and be happy!

*The front doorbell rings.*

MRS. LINDE (*rising*): There's the bell. It's probably best that I go.

NORA: No, stay. No one's expected. It must be for Torvald.

MAID (*from the hall doorway*): Excuse me, ma'am—there's a gentleman here to see Mr. Helmer, but I didn't know—since the doctor's with him.

NORA: Who is the gentleman?

KROGSTAD (*from the doorway*): It's me, Mrs. Helmer.

*Mrs. Linde starts and turns away toward the window.*

NORA (*stepping toward him, tense, her voice a whisper*): You? What is it? Why do you want to speak to my husband?

KROGSTAD: Bank business—after a fashion. I have a small job in the investment bank and I hear now your husband is going to be our chief—

NORA: In other words, it's—

KROGSTAD: Just dry business, Mrs. Helmer. Nothing but that.
NORA: Yes, then please be good enough to step into the study. (*She nods indifferently as she sees him out by the hall door, then returns and begins stirring up the stove.*)
MRS. LINDE: Nora—who was that man?
NORA: That was a Mr. Krogstad—a lawyer.
MRS. LINDE: Then it really was him.
NORA: Do you know that person?
MRS. LINDE: I did once—many years ago. For a time he was a law clerk in our town.
NORA: Yes, he's been that.
MRS. LINDE: How he's changed.
NORA: I understand he had a very unhappy marriage.
MRS. LINDE: He's a widower now.
NORA: With a number of children. There now, it's burning. (*She closes the stove and moves the rocker a bit to one side.*)
MRS. LINDE: They say he has a hand in all kinds of business.
NORA: That may be true: I wouldn't know. But let's not think about business. It's so dull.

*Dr. Rank enters from Helmer's study.*

RANK (*still in the doorway*): No, no, really—I don't want to intrude, I'd just as soon talk a little while with your wife. (*Shuts the door, then notices Mrs. Linde.*) Oh, beg pardon. I'm intruding here, too.
NORA: No, not at all. (*Introducing him.*) Dr. Rank, Mrs. Linde.
RANK: Well now, that's a name much heard in this house. I believe I passed the lady on the stairs as I came.
MRS. LINDE: Yes, I take the stairs very slowly. They're rather hard on me.
RANK: Uh-hm, some touch of internal weakness?
MRS. LINDE: More overexertion, I'd say.
RANK: Nothing else? Then you're probably here in town to rest up in a round of parties?
MRS. LINDE: I'm here to look for work.
RANK: Is that the best cure for overexertion?
MRS. LINDE: One has to live, Doctor.
RANK: Yes, there's a common prejudice to that effect.
NORA: Oh, come on, Dr. Rank—you really do want to live yourself.
RANK: Yes, I really do. Wretched as I am, I'll gladly prolong my torment indefinitely. All my patients feel like that. And it's quite the same, too, with the morally sick. Right at this moment there's one of those moral invalids in there with Helmer—

MRS. LINDE (*softly*):  Ah!

NORA:  What do you mean?

RANK:  Oh, it's a lawyer, Krogstad, a type you wouldn't know. His character is rotten to the root—but even he began chattering all-importantly about how he had to *live*.

NORA:  Oh? What did he want to talk to Torvald about?

RANK:  I really don't know. I only heard something about the bank.

NORA:  I didn't know that Krog—that this man Krogstad had anything to do with the bank.

RANK:  Yes, he's gotten some kind of berth down there. (*To Mrs. Linde.*) I don't know if you also have, in your neck of the woods, a type of person who scuttles about breathlessly, sniffing out hints of moral corruption, and then maneuvers his victim into some sort of key position where he can keep an eye on him. It's the healthy these days that are out in the cold.

MRS. LINDE:  All the same, it's the sick who most need to be taken in.

RANK (*with a shrug*):  Yes, there we have it. That's the concept that's turning society into a sanatorium.

*Nora, lost in her thoughts, breaks out into quiet laughter and claps her hands.*

RANK:  Why do you laugh at that? Do you have any real idea of what society is?

NORA:  What do I care about dreary old society? I was laughing at something different—something terribly funny. Tell me, Doctor—is everyone who works in the bank dependent now on Torvald?

RANK:  Is that what you find so terribly funny?

NORA (*smiling and humming*):  Never mind, never mind! (*Pacing the floor.*) Yes, that's really immensely amusing: that we—that Torvald has so much power now over all those people. (*Taking the bag out of her pocket.*) Dr. Rank, a little macaroon on that?

RANK:  See here, macaroons! I thought they were contraband here.

NORA:  Yes, but these are some that Kristine gave me.

MRS. LINDE:  What? I—?

NORA:  Now, now, don't be afraid. You couldn't possibly know that Torvald had forbidden them. You see, he's worried they'll ruin my teeth. But hmp! Just this once! Isn't that so, Dr. Rank? Help yourself! (*Puts a macaroon in his mouth.*) And you too, Kristine. And I'll also have one, only a little one—or two, at the most. (*Walking about again.*) Now I'm really tremendously happy. Now there's just one last thing in the world that I have an enormous desire to do.

RANK:  Well! And what's that?

NORA:  It's something I have such a consuming desire to say so Torvald could hear.

RANK:  And why can't you say it?

NORA:  I don't dare. It's quite shocking.

MRS. LINDE:  Shocking?

RANK:  Well, then it isn't advisable. But in front of us you certainly can. What do you have such a desire to say so Torvald could hear?

NORA:  I have such a huge desire to say—to hell and be damned!

RANK:  Are you crazy?

MRS. LINDE:  My goodness, Nora!

RANK:  Go on, say it. Here he is.

NORA (*hiding the macaroon bag*):  Shh, shh, shh!

*Helmer comes in from his study, hat in hand, overcoat over his arm.*

NORA (*going toward him*):  Well, Torvald dear, are you through with him?

HELMER:  Yes, he just left.

NORA:  Let me introduce you—this is Kristine, who's arrived here in town.

HELMER:  Kristine—? I'm sorry, but I don't know—

NORA:  Mrs. Linde, Torvald dear. Mrs. Kristine Linde.

HELMER:  Of course. A childhood friend of my wife's, no doubt?

MRS. LINDE:  Yes, we knew each other in those days.

NORA:  And just think, she made the long trip down here in order to talk with you.

HELMER:  What's this?

MRS. LINDE:  Well, not exactly—

NORA:  You see, Kristine is remarkably clever in office work, and so she's terribly eager to come under a capable man's supervision and add more to what she already knows—

HELMER:  Very wise, Mrs. Linde.

NORA:  And then when she heard that you'd become a bank manager—the story was wired out to the papers—then she came in as fast as she could and—Really, Torvald, for my sake you can do a little something for Kristine, can't you?

HELMER:  Yes, it's not at all impossible. Mrs. Linde, I suppose you're a widow?

MRS. LINDE:  Yes.

HELMER:  Any experience in office work?

MRS. LINDE:  Yes, a good deal.

HELMER: Well, it's quite likely that I can make an opening for you.

NORA (*clapping her hands*): You see, you see!

HELMER: You've come at a lucky moment, Mrs. Linde.

MRS. LINDE: Oh, how can I thank you?

HELMER: Not necessary. (*Putting his overcoat on.*) But today you'll have to excuse me—

RANK: Wait, I'll go with you. (*He fetches his coat from the hall and warms it at the stove.*)

NORA: Don't stay out long, dear.

HELMER: An hour; no more.

NORA: Are you going too, Kristine?

MRS. LINDE (*putting on her winter garments*): Yes, I have to see about a room now.

HELMER: Then perhaps we can all walk together.

NORA (*helping her*): What a shame we're so cramped here, but it's quite impossible for us to—

MRS. LINDE: Oh, don't even think of it! Good-bye, Nora dear, and thanks for everything.

NORA: Good-bye for now. Of course you'll be back this evening. And you too, Dr. Rank. What? If you're well enough? Oh, you've got to be! Wrap up tight now.

*In a ripple of small talk the company moves out into the hall; children's voices are heard outside on the steps.*

NORA: There they are! There they are! (*She runs to open the door. The children come in with their nurse, Anne-Marie.*) Come in, come in! (*Bends down and kisses them.*) Oh, you darling—! Look at them, Kristine. Aren't they lovely!

RANK: No loitering in the draft here.

HELMER: Come, Mrs. Linde—this place is unbearable now for anyone but mothers.

*Dr. Rank, Helmer, and Mrs. Linde go down the stairs. Anne-Marie goes into the living room with the children. Nora follows, after closing the hall door.*

NORA: How fresh and strong you look. Oh, such red cheeks you have! Like apples and roses. (*The children interrupt her throughout the following.*) And it was so much fun? That's wonderful. Really? You pulled both Emmy and Bob on the sled? Imagine, all together! Yes, you're a clever boy, Ivar. Oh, let me hold her a bit, Anne-Marie. My sweet little doll baby! (*Takes the smallest from the nurse and dances with her.*) Yes, yes, Mama will dance with Bob as well. What? Did you throw snowballs? Oh, if I'd only been there! No, don't bother, Anne-Marie: I'll undress them myself. Oh yes, let me. It's such fun. Go in and rest; you look half frozen. There's hot coffee waiting for you on the stove. (*The nurse goes into the room to the left. Nora takes the children's winter things off, throwing them about, while the children talk to her all at once.*) Is that so? A big dog chased you? But it didn't bite? No, dogs never bite little, lovely doll babies. Don't peek in the packages, Ivar! What is it? Yes, wouldn't you like to know. No, no, it's an ugly something. Well? Shall we play? What shall we play? Hide-and-seek? Yes, let's play hide-and-seek. Bob must hide first. I must? Yes, let me hide first. (*Laughing and shouting, she and the children play in and out of the living room and the adjoining room to the right. At last Nora hides under the table. The children come storming in, search, but cannot find her, then hear her muffled laughter, dash over to the table, lift the cloth up and find her. Wild shouting. She creeps forward as if to scare them. More shouts. Meanwhile, a knock at the hall door; no one has noticed it. Now the door half opens, and Krogstad appears. He waits a moment; the game goes on.*)

KROGSTAD:  Beg pardon, Mrs. Helmer—

NORA (*with a strangled cry, turning and scrambling to her knees*): Oh! What do you want?

KROGSTAD:  Excuse me. The outer door was ajar; it must be someone forgot to shut it—

NORA (*rising*):  My husband isn't home, Mr. Krogstad.

KROGSTAD:  I know that.

NORA:  Yes—then what do you want here?

KROGSTAD:  A word with you.

NORA:  With—? (*To the children, quietly.*) Go in to Anne-Marie. What? No, the strange man won't hurt Mama. When he's gone, we'll play some more. (*She leads the children into the room to the left and shuts the door after them. Then, tense and nervous*): You want to speak to me?

KROGSTAD:  Yes, I want to.

NORA:  Today? But it's not yet the first of the month—

KROGSTAD:  No, it's Christmas Eve. It's going to be up to you how merry a Christmas you have.

NORA:  What is it you want? Today I absolutely can't—

KROGSTAD:  We won't talk about that till later. This is something else. You do have a moment to spare, I suppose?

NORA:  Oh yes, of course—I do, except—

KROGSTAD:   Good. I was sitting over at Olsen's Restaurant when I saw your husband go down the street.

NORA:   Yes?

KROGSTAD:   With a lady.

NORA:   Yes. So?

KROGSTAD:   If you'll pardon my asking: wasn't that lady a Mrs. Linde?

NORA:   Yes.

KROGSTAD:   Just now come into town?

NORA:   Yes, today.

KROGSTAD:   She's a good friend of yours?

NORA:   Yes, she is. But I don't see—

KROGSTAD:   I also knew her once.

NORA:   I'm aware of that.

KROGSTAD:   Oh! You know all about it. I thought so. Well, then let me ask you short and sweet: is Mrs. Linde getting a job in the bank?

NORA:   What makes you think you can cross-examine me, Mr. Krogstad—you, one my husband's employees? But since you ask, you might as well know—yes, Mrs. Linde's going to be taken on at the bank. And I'm the one who spoke for her, Mr. Krogstad. Now you know.

KROGSTAD:   So I guessed right.

NORA (*pacing up and down*):   Oh, one does have a tiny bit of influence, I should hope. Just because I am a woman, don't think it means that—: When one has a subordinate position, Mr. Krogstad, one really ought to be careful about pushing somebody who—hm—

KROGSTAD:   Who has influence?

NORA:   That's right.

KROGSTAD (*in a different tone*):   Mrs. Helmer, would you be good enough to use your influence on my behalf?

NORA:   What? What do you mean?

KROGSTAD:   Would you please make sure that I keep my subordinate position in the bank?

NORA:   What does that mean? Who's thinking of taking away your position?

KROGSTAD:   Oh, don't play the innocent with me. I'm quite aware that your friend would hardly relish the chance of running into me again; and I'm also aware now whom I can thank for being turned out.

NORA:   But I promise you—

KROGSTAD:   Yes, yes, yes, to the point: there's still time, and I'm advising you to use your influence to prevent it.

NORA:   But Mr. Krogstad, I have absolutely no influence.

KROGSTAD: You haven't? I thought you were just saying—

NORA: You shouldn't take me so literally. I! How can you believe that I have any such influence over my husband?

KROGSTAD: Oh, I've known your husband from our student days. I don't think the great bank manager's more steadfast than any other married man.

NORA: You speak insolently about my husband, and I'll show you the door.

KROGSTAD: The lady has spirit.

NORA: I'm not afraid of you any longer. After New Year's, I'll soon be done with the whole business.

KROGSTAD (*restraining himself*): Now listen to me, Mrs. Helmer. If necessary, I'll fight for my little job in the bank as if it were life itself.

NORA: Yes, so it seems.

KROGSTAD: It's not just a matter of income; that's the least of it. It's something else—All right, out with it! Look, this is the thing. You know, just like all the others, of course, that once, a good many years ago, I did something rather rash.

NORA: I've heard rumors to that effect.

KROGSTAD: The case never got into court; but all the same, every door was closed in my face from then on. So I took up those various activities you know about. I had to grab hold somewhere; and I dare say I haven't been among the worst. But now I want to drop all that. My boys are growing up. For their sakes, I'll have to win back as much respect as possible here in town. That job in the bank was like the first rung in my ladder. And now your husband wants to kick me right back down in the mud again.

NORA: But for heaven's sake, Mr. Krogstad, it's simply not in my power to help you.

KROGSTAD: That's because you haven't the will to—but I have the means to make you.

NORA: You certainly won't tell my husband that I owe you money?

KROGSTAD: Hm—what if I told him that?

NORA: That would be shameful of you. (*Nearly in tears.*) This secret—my joy and my pride—that he should learn it in such a crude and disgusting way—learn it from you. You'd expose me to the most horrible unpleasantness—

KROGSTAD: Only unpleasantness?

NORA (*vehemently*): But go on and try. It'll turn out the worse for you, because then my husband will really see what a crook you are, and then you'll *never* be able to hold your job.

KROGSTAD: I asked if it was just domestic unpleasantness you were afraid of?

NORA: If my husband finds out, then of course he'll pay what I owe at once, and then we'd be through with you for good.

KROGSTAD (*a step closer*): Listen, Mrs. Helmer—you've either got a very bad memory or else no head at all for business. I'd better put you a little more in touch with the facts.

NORA: What do you mean?

KROGSTAD: When your husband was sick, you came to me for a loan of four thousand, eight hundred crowns.

NORA: Where else could I go?

KROGSTAD: I promised to get you that sum—

NORA: And you got it.

KROGSTAD: I promised to get you that sum, on certain conditions. You were so involved in your husband's illness, and so eager to finance your trip, that I guess you didn't think out all the details. It might just be a good idea to remind you. I promised you the money on the strength of a note I drew up.

NORA: Yes, and that I signed.

KROGSTAD: Right. But at the bottom I added some lines for your father to guarantee the loan. He was supposed to sign down there.

NORA: Supposed to? He did sign.

KROGSTAD: I left the date blank. In other words, your father would have dated his signature himself. Do you remember that?

NORA: Yes, I think—

KROGSTAD: Then I gave you the note for you to mail to your father. Isn't that so?

NORA: Yes.

KROGSTAD: And naturally you sent it at once—because only some five, six days later you brought me the note, properly signed. And with that, the money was yours.

NORA: Well, then; I've made my payments regularly, haven't I?

KROGSTAD: More or less. But—getting back to the point—those were hard times for you then, Mrs. Helmer.

NORA: Yes, they were.

KROGSTAD: Your father was very ill, I believe.

NORA: He was near the end.

KROGSTAD: He died soon after?

NORA: Yes.

KROGSTAD: Tell me, Mrs. Helmer, do you happen to recall the date of your father's death? The day of the month, I mean.

NORA: Papa died the twenty-ninth of September.

KROGSTAD: That's quite correct; I've already looked into that. And now we come to a curious thing—(*taking out a paper*) which I simply cannot comprehend.

NORA: Curious thing? I don't know—

KROGSTAD: This is the curious thing: that your father co-signed the note for your loan three days after his death.

NORA: How—? I don't understand.

KROGSTAD: Your father died the twenty-ninth of September. But look. Here your father dated his signature October second. Isn't that curious, Mrs. Helmer? (*Nora is silent*). Can you explain it to me? (*Nora remains silent.*) It's also remarkable that the words "October second" and the year aren't written in your father's hand, but rather in one that I think I know. Well, it's easy to understand. Your father forgot perhaps to date his signature, and then someone or other added it, a bit sloppily, before anyone knew of his death. There's nothing wrong in that. It all comes down to the signature. And there's no question about *that,* Mrs. Helmer. It really *was* your father who signed his own name here, wasn't it?

NORA (*after a short silence, throwing her head back and looking squarely at him*): No it wasn't. *I:* signed Papa's name.

KROGSTAD: Wait, now—are you fully aware that this is a dangerous confession?

NORA: Why? You'll soon get your money.

KROGSTAD: Let me ask you a question—why didn't you send the paper to your father?

NORA: That was impossible. Papa was so sick. If I'd asked him for his signature, I also would have had to tell him what the money was for. But I couldn't tell him, sick as he was, that my husband's life was in danger. That was just impossible.

KROGSTAD: Then it would have been better if you'd given up the trip abroad.

NORA: I couldn't possibly. The trip was to save my husband's life. I couldn't give that up.

KROGSTAD: But didn't you ever consider that this was a fraud against me?

NORA: I couldn't let myself be bothered by that. You weren't any concern of mine. I couldn't stand you, with all those cold complications you made, even though you knew how badly off my husband was.

KROGSTAD: Mrs. Helmer, obviously you haven't the vaguest idea of what you've involved yourself in. But I can tell you this: it was nothing more and nothing worse than I once did—and it wrecked my whole reputation.

NORA: You? Do you expect me to believe that you ever acted bravely to save your wife's life?

KROGSTAD: Laws don't inquire into motives.

NORA: Then they must be very poor laws.

KROGSTAD: Poor or not—if I introduce this paper in court, you'll be judged according to law.

NORA: This I refuse to believe. A daughter hasn't a right to protect her dying father from anxiety and care? A wife hasn't a right to save her husband's life? I don't know much about laws, but I'm sure that somewhere in the books these things are allowed. And you don't know anything about it—you who practice law? You must be an awful lawyer, Mr. Krogstad.

KROGSTAD: Could be. But business—the kind of business we two are mixed up in—don't you think I know about that? All right. Do what you want now. But I'm telling you *this:* if I get shoved down a second time, you're going to keep me company. (*He bows and goes out through the hall.*)

NORA (*pensive for a moment, then tossing her head*): Oh, really! Trying to frighten me! I'm not so silly as all that. (*Begins gathering up the children's clothes, but soon stops.*) But—? No, but that's impossible! I did it out of love.

THE CHILDREN (*in the doorway, left*): Mama: that strange man's gone out the door.

NORA: Yes, yes, I know it. But don't tell anyone about the strange man. Do you hear? Not even Papa!

THE CHILDREN: No, Mama. But now will you play again?

NORA: No, not now.

THE CHILDREN: Oh, but Mama, you promised.

NORA: Yes, but I can't now. Go inside; I have too much to do. Go in, go in, my sweet darlings. (*She herds them gently back in the room and shuts the door after them. Settling on the sofa, she takes up a piece of embroidery and makes some stitches, but soon stops abruptly.*) No! (*Throws the work aside, rises, goes to the hall door and calls out.*) Helene! Let me have the tree in here. (*Goes to the table, left, opens the table drawer, and stops again.*) No, but that's utterly impossible!

MAID: (*with the Christmas tree*): Where should I put it, ma'am?

NORA: There. The middle of the floor.

MAID: Should I bring anything else?

NORA: No, thanks. I have what I need.

*The Maid, who has set the tree down, goes out.*

NORA (*absorbed in trimming the tree*): Candles here—and flowers here. That terrible creature! Talk, talk, talk! There's nothing to it at all. The tree's going to be lovely. I'll do anything to please you, Torvald. I'll sing for you, dance for you—

*Helmer comes in from the hall, with a sheaf of papers under his arm.*

NORA: Oh! You're back so soon?

HELMER: Yes. Has anyone been here?

NORA: Here? No.

HELMER: That's odd. I saw Krogstad leaving the front door.

NORA: So? Oh yes, that's true. Krogstad was here a moment.

HELMER: Nora, I can see by your face that he's been here, begging you to put in a good word for him.

NORA: Yes.

HELMER: And it was supposed to seem like your own idea? You were to hide it from me that he'd been here. He asked you that, too, didn't he?

NORA: Yes, Torvald, but—

HELMER: Nora, Nora, and you could fall for that? Talk with that sort of person and promise him anything? And then in the bargain, tell me an untruth.

NORA: An untruth—?

HELMER: Didn't you say that no one had been here? (*Wagging his finger.*) My little songbird must never do that again. A songbird needs a clean beak to warble with. No false notes. (*Putting his arm about her waist.*) That's the way it should be, isn't it? Yes, I'm sure of it. (*Releasing her.*) And so, enough of that. (*Sitting by the stove.*) Ah, how snug and cozy it is here. (*Leafing among his papers.*)

NORA (*busy with the tree, after a short pause*): Torvald!

HELMER: Yes.

NORA: I'm so much looking forward to the Stenborgs' costume party, day after tomorrow.

HELMER: And I can't wait to see what you'll surprise me with.

NORA: Oh, that stupid business!

HELMER: What?

NORA: I can't find anything that's right. Everything seems so ridiculous, so inane.

HELMER:  So my little Nora's come to *that* recognition?

NORA (*going behind his chair, her arms resting on its back*):  Are you very busy, Torvald?

HELMER:  Oh—

NORA:  What papers are those?

HELMER:  Bank matters.

NORA:  Already?

HELMER:  I've gotten full authority from the retiring management to make all necessary changes in personnel and procedure. I'll need Christmas week for that. I want to have everything in order by New Year's.

NORA:  So that was the reason this poor Krogstad—

HELMER:  Hm.

NORA (*still leaning on the chair and slowly stroking the nape of his neck*):  If you weren't so very busy, I would have asked you an enormous favor, Torvald.

HELMER:  Let's hear. What is it?

NORA:  You know, there isn't anyone who has your good taste—and I want so much to look well at the costume party. Torvald, couldn't you take over and decide what I should be and plan my costume?

HELMER:  Ah, is my stubborn little creature calling for a lifeguard?

NORA:  Yes, Torvald, I can't get anywhere without your help.

HELMER:  All right—I'll think it over. We'll hit on something.

NORA:  Oh, how sweet of you. (*Goes to the tree again. Pause.*) Aren't the red flowers pretty—? But tell me, was it really such a crime that this Krogstad committed?

HELMER:  Forgery. Do you have any idea what that means?

NORA:  Couldn't he have done it out of need?

HELMER:  Yes, or thoughtlessness, like so many others. I'm not so heartless that I'd condemn a man categorically for just one mistake.

NORA:  No, of course not, Torvald!

HELMER:  Plenty of men have redeemed themselves by openly confessing their crime and taking their punishment.

NORA:  Punishment—?

HELMER:  But now Krogstad didn't go that way. He got himself out by sharp practices, and that's the real cause of his moral breakdown.

NORA:  Do you really think that would—?

HELMER:  Just imagine how a man with that sort of guilt in him has to lie and cheat and deceive on all sides, has to wear a mask even with the nearest and dearest he has, even with his own wife and children. And with the children, Nora—that's where it's most horrible.

NORA: Why?

HELMER: Because that kind of atmosphere of lies infects the whole life of a home. Every breath the children take in is filled with the germs of something degenerate.

NORA (*coming closer behind him*): Are you sure of that?

HELMER: Oh, I've seen it often enough as a lawyer. Almost everyone who goes bad early in life has a mother who's a chronic liar.

NORA: Why just—the mother?

HELMER: It's usually the mother's influence that's dominant, but the father's works in the same way, of course. Every lawyer is quite familiar with it. And still this Krogstad's been going home year in, year out, poisoning his own children with lies and pretense; that's why I call him morally lost. (*Reaching his hands out toward her.*) So my sweet little Nora must promise me never to plead his cause. Your hand on it. Come, come, what's this? Give me your hand. There, now. All settled. I can tell you it'd be impossible for me to work alongside of him. I literally feel physically revolted when I'm anywhere near such a person.

NORA (*withdraws her hand and goes to the other side of the Christmas tree*): How hot it is here! And I've got so much to do.

HELMER (*getting up and gathering his papers*): Yes, and I have to think about getting some of these read through before dinner. I'll think about your costume, too. And something to hang on the tree in gilt paper, I may even see about that. (*Putting his hand on her head.*) Oh you, my darling little songbird. (*He goes into his study and closes the door after him.*)

NORA (*softly, after a silence*): Oh, really! It isn't so. It's impossible. It must be impossible.

ANNE-MARIE (*in the doorway, left*): The children are begging so hard to come in to Mama.

NORA: No, no, no, don't let them in to me! You stay with them, Anne-Marie.

ANNE-MARIE: Of course, ma'am. (*Closes the door.*)

NORA (*pale with terror*): Hurt my children—! Poison my home? (*A moment's pause; she tosses her head.*) That's not true. Never. Never in all the world.

## *ACT II*

*Same room. Beside the piano the Christmas tree now stands stripped of ornaments, burned-down candle stubs on its ragged branches. Nora's street clothes lie on the sofa. Nora, alone in the room, moves restlessly about; at last she stops at the sofa and picks up her coat.*

NORA (*dropping the coat again*): Someone's coming! (*Goes toward the door, listens.*) No—there's no one. Of course—nobody's coming today, Christmas Day—or tomorrow, either. But maybe— (*Opens the door and looks out.*) No, nothing in the mailbox. Quite empty. (*Coming forward.*) What nonsense! He won't do anything serious. Nothing terrible could happen. It's impossible. Why, I have three small children.

*Anne-Marie, with a large carton, comes in from the room to the left.*

ANNE-MARIE: Well, at last I found the box with the masquerade clothes.
NORA: Thanks. Put it on the table.
ANNE-MARIE (*does so*): But they're all pretty much of a mess.
NORA: Ahh! I'd love to rip them in a million pieces!
ANNE-MARIE: Oh, mercy, they can be fixed right up. Just a little patience.
NORA: Yes, I'll go get Mrs. Linde to help me.
ANNE-MARIE: Out again now? In this nasty weather? Miss Nora will catch cold.
NORA: Oh, worse things could happen—How are the children?
ANNE-MARIE: The poor mites are playing with their Christmas presents, but—
NORA: Do they ask for me much?
ANNE-MARIE: They're so used to having Mama around, you know.
NORA: But Anne-Marie, I *can't* be together with them as much as I was.
ANNE-MARIE: Well, small children get used to anything.
NORA: You think so? Do you think they'd forget their mother if she was gone for good?
ANNE-MARIE: Oh, mercy—gone for good!
NORA: Wait, tell me, Anne-Marie—I've wondered so often—how could you ever have the heart to give your child over to strangers?
ANNE-MARIE: But I had to, you know, to become little Nora's nurse.
NORA: Yes, but how could you *do* it?
ANNE-MARIE: When I could get such a good place? A girl who's poor and who's gotten in trouble is glad enough for that. Because that slippery fish, he didn't do a thing for me, you know.

NORA: But your daughter's surely forgotten you.

ANNE-MARIE: Oh, she certainly has not. She's written to me, both when she was confirmed and when she was married.

NORA (*clasping her about the neck*): You old Anne-Marie, you were a good mother for me when I was little.

ANNE-MARIE: Poor little Nora, with no other mother but me.

NORA: And if the babies didn't have one, then I know that you'd— What silly talk! (*Opening the carton.*) Go in to them. Now I'll have to—Tomorrow you can see how lovely I'll look.

ANNE-MARIE: Oh, there won't be anyone at the party as lovely as Miss Nora. (*She goes off into the room, left.*)

NORA (*begins unpacking the box, but soon throws it aside*): Oh, if I dared to go out. If only nobody would come. If only nothing would happen here while I'm out. What craziness—nobody's coming. Just don't think. This muff—needs a brushing. Beautiful gloves, beautiful gloves. Let it go. Let it go! One, two, three, four, five, six—(*With a cry.*) Oh, there they are! (*Poises to move toward the door, but remains irresolutely standing. Mrs. Linde enters from the hall, where she has removed her street clothes.*)

NORA: Oh, it's you, Kristine. There's no one else out there? How good that you've come.

MRS. LINDE: I hear you were up asking for me.

NORA: Yes, I just stopped by. There's something you really can help me with. Let's get settled on the sofa. Look, there's going to be a costume party tomorrow evening at the Stenborgs' right above us, and now Torvald wants me to go as a Neapolitan peasant girl and dance the tarantella that I learned in Capri.

MRS. LINDE: Really, are you giving a whole performance?

NORA: Torvald says yes, I should. See, here's the dress. Torvald had it made for me down there; but now it's all so tattered that I just don't know—

MRS. LINDE: Oh, we'll fix that up in no time. It's nothing more than the trimmings—they're a bit loose here and there. Needle and thread? Good, now we have what we need.

NORA: Oh, how sweet of you!

MRS. LINDE (*sewing*): So you'll be in disguise tomorrow, Nora. You know what? I'll stop by then for a moment and have a look at you all dressed up. But listen, I've absolutely forgotten to thank you for that pleasant evening yesterday.

NORA (*getting up and walking about*): I don't think it was as pleasant as usual yesterday. You should have come to town a bit sooner,

Kristine—Yes, Torvald really knows how to give a home elegance and charm.

**MRS. LINDE:** And you do, too, if you ask me. You're not your father's daughter for nothing. But tell me, is Dr. Rank always so down in the mouth as yesterday?

**NORA:** No, that was quite an exception. But he goes around critically ill all the time—tuberculosis of the spine, poor man. You know, his father was a disgusting thing who kept mistresses and so on—and that's why the son's been sickly from birth.

**MRS. LINDE** (*lets her sewing fall to her lap*): But my dearest Nora, how do you know about such things?

**NORA** (*walking more jauntily*): Hmp! When you've had three children, then you've had a few visits from—from women who know something of medicine, and they tell you this and that.

**MRS. LINDE** (*resumes sewing; a short pause*): Does Dr. Rank come here every day?

**NORA:** Every blessed day. He's Torvald's best friend from childhood, and my good friend, too. Dr. Rank almost belongs to this house.

**MRS. LINDE:** But tell me—is he quite sincere? I mean, doesn't he rather enjoy flattering people?

**NORA:** Just the opposite. Why do you think that?

**MRS. LINDE:** When you introduced us yesterday, he was proclaiming that he'd often heard my name in this house; but later I noticed that your husband hadn't the slightest idea who I really was. So how could Dr. Rank—?

**NORA:** But it's all true, Kristine. You see, Torvald loves me beyond words and, as he puts it, he'd like to keep me all to himself. For a long time he'd almost be jealous if I even mentioned any of my old friends back home. So of course I dropped that. But with Dr. Rank I talk a lot about such things, because he likes hearing about them.

**MRS. LINDE:** Now listen, Nora; in many ways you're still like a child. I'm a good deal older than you, with a little more experience. I'll tell you something: you ought to put an end to all this with Dr. Rank.

**NORA:** What should I put an end to?

**MRS. LINDE:** Both parts of it, I think. Yesterday you said something about a rich admirer who'd provide you with money—

**NORA:** Yes, one who doesn't exist—worse luck. So?

**MRS. LINDE:** Is Dr. Rank well off?

**NORA:** Yes, he is.

**MRS. LINDE:** With no dependents?

**NORA:** No, no one. But—

MRS. LINDE: And he's over here every day?

NORA: Yes, I told you that.

MRS. LINDE: How can a man of such refinement be so grasping?

NORA: I don't follow you at all.

MRS. LINDE: Now don't try to hide it, Nora. You think I can't guess who loaned you the forty-eight hundred crowns?

NORA: Are you out of your mind? How could you think such a thing! A friend of ours, who comes here every single day. What an intolerable situation that would have been!

MRS. LINDE: Then it really wasn't him.

NORA: No, absolutely not. It never even crossed my mind for a moment—And he had nothing to lend in those days; his inheritance came later.

MRS. LINDE: Well, I think that was a stroke of luck for you, Nora dear.

NORA: No, it never would have occurred to me to ask Dr. Rank— Still, I'm quite sure that if I had asked him—

MRS. LINDE: Which you won't, of course.

NORA: No, of course not. I can't see that I'd ever need to. But I'm quite positive that if I talked to Dr. Rank—

MRS. LINDE: Behind your husband's back?

NORA: I've got to clear up this other thing; *that's* also behind his back. I've *got to* clear it all up.

MRS. LINDE: Yes, I was saying that yesterday, but—

NORA (*pacing up and down*): A man handles these problems so much better than a woman—

MRS. LINDE: One's husband does, yes.

NORA: Nonsense. (*Stopping.*) When you pay everything you owe, then you get your note back, right?

MRS. LINDE: Yes, naturally.

NORA: And can rip it into a million pieces and burn it up—that filthy scrap of paper!

MRS. LINDE (*looking hard at her, laying her sewing aside, and rising slowly*): Nora, you're hiding something from me.

NORA: You can see it in my face?

MRS. LINDE: Something's happened to you since yesterday morning. Nora, what is it?

NORA (*hurrying toward her*): Kristine! (*Listening.*) Shh! Torvald's home. Look, go in with the children a while. Torvald can't bear all this snipping and stitching. Let Anne-Marie help you.

MRS. LINDE (*gathering up some of the things*): All right, but I'm not leaving here until we've talked this out. (*She disappears into the room, left, as Torvald enters from the hall.*)

NORA: Oh, how I've been waiting for you, Torvald dear.

HELMER: Was that the dressmaker?

NORA: No, that was Kristine. She's helping me fix up my costume. You know, it's going to be quite attractive.

HELMER: Yes, wasn't that a bright idea I had?

NORA: Brilliant! But then wasn't I good as well to give in to you?

HELMER: Good—because you give in to your husband's judgment? All right, you little goose, I know you didn't mean it like that. But I won't disturb you. You'll want to have a fitting, I suppose.

NORA: And you'll be working?

HELMER: Yes. (*Indicating a bundle of papers.*) See. I've been down to the bank. (*Starts toward his study.*)

NORA: Torvald.

HELMER (*stops*): Yes.

NORA: If your little squirrel begged you, with all her heart and soul, for something—?

HELMER: What's that?

NORA: Then would you do it?

HELMER: First, naturally, I'd have to know what it was.

NORA: Your squirrel would scamper about and do tricks, if you'd only be sweet and give in.

HELMER: Out with it.

NORA: Your lark would be singing high and low in every room—

HELMER: Come on, she does that anyway.

NORA: I'd be a wood nymph and dance for you in the moonlight.

HELMER: Nora—don't tell me it's that same business from this morning!

NORA (*coming closer*): Yes, Torvald, I beg you, please!

HELMER: And you actually have the nerve to drag that up again?

NORA: Yes, yes, you've got to give in to me; you *have* to let Krogstad keep his job in the bank.

HELMER: My dear Nora, I've slated his job for Mrs. Linde.

NORA: That's awfully kind of you. But you could just fire another clerk instead of Krogstad.

HELMER: This is the most incredible stubbornness! Because you go and give an impulsive promise to speak up for him, I'm expected to—

NORA: That's not the reason, Torvald. It's for your own sake. That man does writing for the worst papers; you said it yourself. He could do you any amount of harm. I'm scared to death of him—

HELMER: Ah, I understand. It's the old memories haunting you.

NORA: What do you mean by that?

HELMER: Of course, you're thinking about your father.

NORA: Yes, all right. Just remember how those nasty gossips wrote in the papers about Papa and slandered him so cruelly. I think they'd have had him dismissed if the department hadn't sent you up to investigate, and if you hadn't been so kind and open-minded toward him.

HELMER: My dear Nora, there's a notable difference between your father and me. Your father's official career was hardly above reproach. But mine is; and I hope it'll stay that way as long as I hold my position.

NORA: Oh, who can ever tell what vicious minds can invent? We could be so snug and happy now in our quiet, carefree home—you and I and the children, Torvald! That's why I'm pleading with you so—

HELMER: And just by pleading for him you make it impossible for me to keep him on. It's already known at the bank that I'm firing Krogstad. What if it's rumored around now that the new bank manager was vetoed by his wife—

NORA: Yes, what then—?

HELMER: Oh yes—as long as our little bundle of stubbornness gets her way—! I should go and make myself ridiculous in front of the whole office—give people the idea I can be swayed by all kinds of outside pressure. Oh, you can bet I'd feel the effects of that soon enough! Besides—there's something that rules Krogstad right out at the bank as long as I'm the manager.

NORA: What's that?

HELMER: His moral failings I could maybe overlook if I had to—

NORA: Yes, Torvald, why not?

HELMER: And I hear he's quite efficient on the job. But he was a crony of mine back in my teens—one of those rash friendships that crop up again and again to embarrass you later in life. Well, I might as well say it straight out: we're on a first-name basis. And that tactless fool makes no effort at all to hide it in front of others. Quite the contrary—he thinks that entitles him to take a familiar air around me, and so every other second he comes booming out with his "Yes, Torvald!" and "Sure thing, Torvald!" I tell you, it's been excruciating for me. He's out to make my place in the bank unbearable.

NORA: Torvald, you can't be serious about all this.

HELMER: Oh no? Why not?

NORA: Because these are such petty considerations.

HELMER: What are you saying? Petty? You think I'm petty!

NORA: No, just the opposite, Torvald dear. That's exactly why—

HELMER: Never mind. You call my motives petty; then I might as well be just that. Petty! All right! We'll put a stop to this for good. (*Goes to the hall door and calls.*) Helene!

NORA: What do you want?

HELMER (*searching among his papers*): A decision. (*The Maid comes in.*) Look here; take this letter; go out with it at once. Get hold of a messenger and have him deliver it. Quick now. It's already addressed. Wait, here's some money.

MAID: Yes, sir. (*She leaves with the letter.*)

HELMER (*straightening his papers*): There, now, little Miss Willful.

NORA (*breathlessly*): Torvald, what was that letter?

HELMER: Krogstad's notice.

NORA: Call it back, Torvald! There's still time. Oh, Torvald, call it back! Do it for my sake—for your sake, for the children's sake! Do you hear, Torvald; do it! You don't know how this can harm us.

HELMER: Too late.

NORA: Yes, too late.

HELMER: Nora dear, I can forgive you this panic, even though basically you're insulting me. Yes, you are! Or isn't it an insult to think that *I* should be afraid of a courtroom hack's revenge? But I forgive you anyway, because this shows so beautifully how much you love me. (*Takes her in his arms.*) This is the way it should be, my darling Nora. Whatever comes, you'll see: when it really counts, I have strength and courage enough as a man to take on the whole weight myself.

NORA (*terrified*): What do you mean by that?

HELMER: The whole weight, I said.

NORA (*resolutely*): No, never in all the world.

HELMER: Good. So we'll share it, Nora, as man and wife. That's as it should be. (*Fondling her.*) Are you happy now? There, there, there—not these frightened dove's eyes. It's nothing at all but empty fantasies—Now you should run through your tarantella and practice your tambourine. I'll go to the inner office and shut both doors, so I won't hear a thing; you can make all the noise you like. (*Turning in the doorway.*) And when Rank comes, just tell him where he can find me. (*He nods to her and goes with his papers into the study, closing the door.*)

NORA (*standing as though rooted, dazed with fright, in a whisper*): He really could do it. He will do it. He'll do it in spite of everything.

No, not that, never, never! Anything but that! Escape! A way out—
(*The doorbell rings.*) Dr. Rank! Anything but that! *Anything, what-*
ever it is! (*Her hands pass over her face, smoothing it; she pulls her-*
*self together, goes over and opens the hall door. Dr. Rank stands*
*outside, hanging his fur coat up. During the following scene, it be-*
*gins getting dark.*)

NORA:  Hello, Dr. Rank. I recognized your ring. But you mustn't go in
to Torvald yet; I believe he's working.

RANK:  And you?

NORA:  For you, I always have an hour to spare—you know that. (*He*
*has entered, and she shuts the door after him.*)

RANK:  Many thanks. I'll make use of these hours while I can.

NORA:  What do you mean by that? While you can?

RANK:  Does that disturb you?

NORA:  Well, it's such an odd phrase. Is anything going to happen?

RANK:  What's going to happen is what I've been expecting so long—
but I honestly didn't think it would come so soon.

NORA (*gripping his arm*):  What is it you've found out? Dr. Rank, you
have to tell me!

RANK (*sitting by the stove*):  It's all over with me. There's nothing to
be done about it.

NORA (*breathing easier*):  Is it you—then—?

RANK:  Who else? There's no point in lying to one's self. I'm the most
miserable of all my patients, Mrs. Helmer. These past few days I've
been auditing my internal accounts. Bankrupt! Within a month I'll
probably be laid out and rotting in the churchyard.

NORA:  Oh, what a horrible thing to say.

RANK:  The thing itself is horrible. But the worst of it is all the other horror before it's over. There's only one final examination left; when I'm
finished with that, I'll know about when my disintegration will begin.
There's something I want to say. Helmer with his sensitivity has a
sharp distaste for anything ugly. I don't want him near my sickroom.

NORA:  Oh, but Dr. Rank—

RANK:  I won't have him in there. Under no condition. I'll lock my
door to him—As soon as I'm completely sure of the worst, I'll send
you my calling card marked with a black cross, and you'll know
then the wreck has started to come apart.

NORA:  No, today you're completely unreasonable. And I wanted you
so much to be in a really good humor.

RANK:  With death up my sleeve? And then to suffer this way for
somebody else's sins. Is there any justice in that? And in every sin-

gle family, in some way or another, this inevitable retribution of nature goes on—

**NORA** (*her hands pressed over her eyes*): Oh, stuff! Cheer up! Please—be gay!

**RANK:** Yes, I'd just as soon laugh at it all. My poor, innocent spine, serving time for my father's gay army days.

**NORA** (*by the table, left*): He was so infatuated with asparagus tips and *pâté de foie gras,*: wasn't that it?

**RANK:** Yes—and with truffles.

**NORA:** Truffles, yes. And then with oysters, I suppose?

**RANK:** Yes, tons of oysters, naturally.

**NORA:** And then the port and champagne to go with it. It's so sad that all these delectable things have to strike at our bones.

**RANK:** Especially when they strike at the unhappy bones that never shared in the fun.

**NORA:** Oh, that's the saddest of all.

**RANK** (*looks searchingly at her*): Hm.

**NORA** (*after a moment*): Why did you smile?

**RANK:** No, it was you who laughed.

**NORA:** No, it was you who smiled, Dr. Rank!

**RANK** (*getting up*): You're even a bigger tease than I'd thought.

**NORA:** I'm full of wild ideas today.

**RANK:** That's obvious.

**NORA** (*putting both hands on his shoulders*): Dear, dear Dr. Rank, you'll never die for Torvald and me.

**RANK:** Oh, that loss you'll easily get over. Those who go away are soon forgotten.

**NORA** (*looks fearfully at him*): You believe that?

**RANK:** One makes new connections, and then—

**NORA:** Who makes new connections?

**RANK:** Both you and Torvald will when I'm gone. I'd say you're well under way already. What was that Mrs. Linde doing here last evening?

**NORA:** Oh, come—you can't be jealous of poor Kristine?

**RANK:** Oh yes, I am. She'll be my successor here in the house. When I'm down under, that woman will probably—

**NORA:** Shh! Not so loud. She's right in there.

**RANK:** Today as well. So you see.

**NORA:** Only to sew on my dress. Good gracious, how unreasonable you are. (*Sitting on the sofa.*) Be nice now, Dr. Rank. Tomorrow you'll see how beautifully I'll dance, and you can imagine then that

I'm dancing only for you—yes, and of course for Torvald, too—
that's understood. (*Takes various items out of the carton.*) Dr. Rank,
sit over here and I'll show you something.

RANK (*sitting*):   What's that?

NORA:   Look here. Look.

RANK:   Silk stockings.

NORA:   Flesh-colored. Aren't they lovely? Now it's so dark here, but
tomorrow. No, no, no, just look at the feet. Oh well, you might as
well look at the rest.

RANK:   Hm—

NORA:   Why do you look so critical? Don't you believe they'll fit?

RANK:   I've never had any chance to form an opinion on that.

NORA (*glancing at him a moment*):   Shame on you. (*Hits him lightly
on the ear with the stockings*) That's for you. (*Puts them away
again.*)

RANK:   And what other splendors am I going to see now?

NORA:   Not the least bit more, because you've been naughty. (*She
hums a little and rummages among her things.*)

RANK (*after a short silence*):   When I sit here together with you like
this, completely easy and open, then I don't know—I simply can't
imagine—whatever would have become of me if I'd never come
into this house.

NORA (*smiling*):   Yes, I really think you feel completely at ease with us.

RANK (*more quietly, staring straight ahead*):   And then to have to go
away from it all—

NORA:   Nonsense, you're not going away.

RANK (*his voice unchanged*):—And not even be able to leave some
poor show of gratitude behind, scarcely a fleeting regret—no more
than a vacant place that anyone can fill.

NORA:   And if I asked you now for—? No—

RANK:   For what?

NORA:   No, I mean—for an exceptionally big favor—

RANK:   Would you really, for once, make me so happy?

NORA:   Oh, you haven't the vaguest idea what it is.

RANK:   All right, then tell me.

NORA:   No, but I can't, Dr. Rank—it's all out of reason. It's advice
and help, too—and a favor—

RANK:   So much the better. I can't fathom what you're hinting at. Just
speak out. Don't you trust me?

NORA:   Of course. More than anyone else. You're my best and truest
friend, I'm sure. That's why I want to talk to you. All right, then,
Dr. Rank: there's something you can help me prevent. You know

how deeply, how inexpressibly dearly Torvald loves me; he'd never hesitate a second to give up his life for me.

RANK (*leaning close to her*): Nora—do you think he's the only one—

NORA (*with a slight start*): Who—?

RANK: Who'd gladly give up his life for you.

NORA (*heavily*): I see.

RANK: I swore to myself you should know this before I'm gone. I'll never find a better chance. Yes, Nora, now you know. And also you know now that you can trust me beyond anyone else.

NORA (*rising, natural and calm*): Let me by.

RANK (*making room for her, but still sitting*): Nora—

NORA (*in the hall doorway*): Helene, bring the lamp in. (*Goes over to the stove.*) Ah dear Dr. Rank, that was really mean of you.

RANK (*getting up*): That I've loved you just as deeply as somebody else? Was *that* mean?

NORA: No, but that you came out and told me. That was quite unnecessary—

RANK: What do you mean? Have you known—?

*The Maid comes in with the lamp, sets it on the table, and goes out again.*

RANK: Nora—Mrs. Helmer—I'm asking you: have you known about it?

NORA: Oh, how can I tell what I know or don't know? Really, I don't know what to say—Why did you have to be so clumsy, Dr. Rank! Everything was so good.

RANK: Well, in any case, you now have the knowledge that my body and soul are at your command. So won't you speak out?

NORA (*looking at him*): After that?

RANK: Please, just let me know what it is.

NORA: You can't know anything now.

RANK: I have to. You mustn't punish me like this. Give me the chance to do whatever is humanly possible for you.

NORA: Now there's nothing you can do for me. Besides, actually, I don't need any help. You'll see—it's only my fantasies. That's what it is. Of course! (*Sits in the rocker, looks at him, and smiles.*) What a nice one you are, Dr. Rank. Aren't you a little bit ashamed, now that the lamp is here?

RANK: No, not exactly. But perhaps I'd better go—for good?

NORA: No, you certainly can't do that. You must come here just as you always have. You know Torvald can't do without you.

RANK: Yes, but *you*?

NORA: You know how much I enjoy it when you're here.

RANK: That's precisely what threw me off. You're a mystery to me. So many times I've felt you'd almost rather be with me than with Helmer.

NORA: Yes—you see, there are some people that one loves most and other people that one would almost prefer being with.

RANK: Yes, there's something to that.

NORA: When I was back home, of course I loved Papa most. But I always thought it was so much fun when I could sneak down to the maids' quarters, because they never tried to improve me, and it was always so amusing, the way they talked to each other.

RANK: Aha, so it's *their* place that I've filled.

NORA (*Jumping up and going to him*): Oh, dear, sweet Dr. Rank, that's not what I mean at all. But you can understand that with Torvald it's just the same as with Papa—

*The Maid enters from the hall.*

MAID: Ma'am—please! (*She whispers to Nora and hands her a calling card.*)

NORA (*glancing at the card*): Ah! (*Slips it into her pocket.*)

RANK: Anything wrong?

NORA: No, no, not at all. It's only some—it's my new dress—

RANK: Really? But—there's your dress.

NORA: Oh, that. But this is another one—I ordered it—Torvald mustn't know—

RANK: Ah, now we have the big secret.

NORA: That's right. Just go in with him—he's back in the inner study. Keep him there as long as—

RANK: Don't worry. He won't get away. (*Goes into the study.*)

NORA (*to the Maid*): And he's standing waiting in the kitchen?

MAID: Yes, he came up by the back stairs.

NORA: But didn't you tell him somebody was here?

MAID: Yes, but that didn't do any good.

NORA: He won't leave?

MAID: No, he won't go till he's talked with you, ma'am.

NORA: Let him come in, then—but quietly. Helene, don't breathe a word about this. It's a surprise for my husband.

MAID: Yes, yes, I understand—(*Goes out.*)

NORA: This horror—it's going to happen. No, no, no, it can't happen, it mustn't. (*She goes and bolts Helmer's door. The Maid opens the hall door for Krogstad and shuts it behind him. He is dressed for travel in a fur coat, boots, and a fur cap.*)

NORA (*going toward him*): Talk softly. My husband's home.

KROGSTAD: Well, good for him.

NORA: What do you want?

KROGSTAD: Some information.

NORA: Hurry up, then. What is it?

KROGSTAD: You know, of course, that I got my notice.

NORA: I couldn't prevent it, Mr. Krogstad. I fought for you to the bitter end, but nothing worked.

KROGSTAD: Does your husband's love for you run so thin? He knows everything I can expose you to, and all the same he dares to—

NORA: How can you imagine he knows anything about this?

KROGSTAD: Ah, no—I can't imagine it either, now. It's not at all like my fine Torvald Helmer to have so much guts.

NORA: Mr. Krogstad, I demand respect for my husband!

KROGSTAD: Why, of course—all due respect. But since the lady's keeping it so carefully hidden, may I presume to ask if you're also a bit better informed than yesterday about what you've actually done?

NORA: More than you ever could teach me.

KROGSTAD: Yes, I *am* such an awful lawyer.

NORA: What is it you want from me?

KROGSTAD: Just a glimpse of how you are, Mrs. Helmer. I've been thinking about you all day long. A cashier, a night-court scribbler, a—well, a type like me also has a little of what they call a heart, you know.

NORA: Then show it. Think of my children.

KROGSTAD: Did you or your husband ever think of mine? But never mind. I wanted to tell you that you don't need to take this thing too seriously. For the present, I'm not proceeding with any action.

NORA: Oh no, really! Well—I knew that.

KROGSTAD: Everything can be settled in a friendly spirit. It doesn't have to get around town at all; it can stay just among us three.

NORA: My husband must never know anything of this.

KROGSTAD: How can you manage that? Perhaps you can pay me the balance?

NORA: No, not right now.

KROGSTAD: Or you know some way of raising the money in a day or two?

NORA: No way that I'm willing to use.

KROGSTAD:  Well, it wouldn't have done you any good, anyway. If you stood in front of me with a fistful of bills, you still couldn't buy your signature back.

NORA:  Then tell me what you're going to do with it.

KROGSTAD:  I'll just hold onto it—keep it on file. There's no outsider who'll even get wind of it. So if you've been thinking of taking some desperate step—

NORA:  I have.

KROGSTAD:  Been thinking of running away from home—

NORA:  I have!

KROGSTAD:  Or even of something worse—

NORA:  How could you guess that?

KROGSTAD:  You can drop those thoughts.

NORA:  How could you guess I was thinking of that?

KROGSTAD:  Most of us think about *that* at first. I thought about it too, but I discovered I hadn't the courage—

NORA (*lifelessly*):  I don't either.

KROGSTAD (*relieved*):  That's true, you haven't the courage? You too?

NORA:  I don't have it—I don't have it.

KROGSTAD:  It would be terribly stupid, anyway. After that first storm at home blows out, why, then—I have here in my pocket a letter for your husband—

NORA:  Telling everything?

KROGSTAD:  As charitably as possible.

NORA (*quickly*):  He mustn't ever get that letter. Tear it up. I'll find some way to get money.

KROGSTAD:  Beg pardon, Mrs. Helmer, but I think I just told you—

NORA:  Oh, I don't mean the money I owe you. Let me know how much you want from my husband, and I'll manage it.

KROGSTAD:  I don't want any money from your husband.

NORA:  What do you want, then?

KROGSTAD:  I'll tell you what I want to recoup, Mrs. Helmer; I want to get on in the world—and there's where your husband can help me. For a year and a half I've kept myself clean of anything disreputable—all that time struggling with the worst conditions; but I was satisfied, working my way up step by step. Now I've been written right off, and I'm just not in the mood to come crawling back. I tell you, I want to move on. I want to get back in the bank—in a better position. Your husband can set up a job for me—

NORA:  He'll never do that!

KROGSTAD: He'll do it. I know him. He won't dare breathe a word of protest. And once I'm in there together with him, you just wait and see! Inside of a year, I'll be the manager's right-hand man. It'll be Nils Krogstad, not Torvald Helmer who runs the bank.

NORA: You'll never see the day!

KROGSTAD: Maybe you think you can—

NORA: I have the courage now—for *that*.

KROGSTAD: Oh, you don't scare me. A smart, spoiled lady like you—

NORA: You'll see; you'll see!

KROGSTAD: Under the ice, maybe? Down in the freezing, coal-black water? There, till you float up in the spring, ugly, unrecognizable, with your hair falling out—

NORA: You don't frighten me!

KROGSTAD: Nor do you frighten me. One doesn't do these things, Mrs. Helmer. Besides, what good would it be? I'd still have him safe in my pocket.

NORA: Afterwards? When I'm no longer—?

KROGSTAD: Are you forgetting that *I'll* be in control then over your final reputation? (*Nora stands speechless, staring at him.*) Good; now I've warned you. Don't do anything stupid. When Helmer's read my letter, I'll be waiting for his reply. And bear in mind that it's your husband himself who's forced me back to my old ways. I'll never forgive him for that. Good-bye, Mrs. Helmer. (*He goes out through the hall.*)

NORA (*goes to the hall door, opens it a crack, and listens*): He's gone. Didn't leave the letter. Oh no, no, that's impossible too! (*Opening the door more and more.*) What's that? He's standing outside—not going downstairs. He's thinking it over? Maybe he'll—? (*A letter falls in the mailbox; then Krogstad's footsteps are heard, dying away down a flight of stairs. Nora gives a muffled cry and runs over toward the sofa table. A short pause.*) In the mailbox. (*Slips warily over to the hall door.*) It's lying there. Torvald, Torvald—now we're lost!

MRS. LINDE (*entering with the costume from the room, left*): There now. I can't see anything else to mend. Perhaps you'd like to try.

NORA (*in a hoarse whisper*): Kristine, come here.

MRS. LINDE (*tossing the dress on the sofa*): What's wrong? You look upset.

NORA: Come here. See that letter? *There!* Look—through the glass in the mailbox.

MRS. LINDE: Yes, yes, I see it.

NORA: That letter's from Krogstad—

MRS. LINDE: Nora—it's Krogstad who loaned you the money!

NORA: Yes, and now Torvald will find out everything.

MRS. LINDE: Believe me, Nora, it's best for both of you.

NORA: There's more you don't know. I forged a name.

MRS. LINDE: But for heaven's sake—?

NORA: I only want to tell you that, Kristine, so that you can be my witness.

MRS. LINDE: Witness? Why should I—?

NORA: If I should go out of my mind—it could easily happen—

MRS. LINDE: Nora!

NORA: Or anything else occurred—so I couldn't be present here—

MRS. LINDE: Nora, Nora, you aren't yourself at all!

NORA: And someone should try to take on the whole weight, all of the guilt, you follow me—

MRS. LINDE: Yes, of course, but why do you think—?

NORA: Then you're the witness that it isn't true, Kristine. I'm very much myself; my mind right now is perfectly clear; and I'm telling you: nobody else has known about this; I alone did everything. Remember that.

MRS. LINDE: I will. But I don't understand all this.

NORA: Oh, how could you ever understand it? It's the miracle now that's going to take place.

MRS. LINDE: The miracle?

NORA: Yes, the miracle. But it's so awful, Kristine. It mustn't take place, not for anything in the world.

MRS. LINDE: I'm going right over and talk with Krogstad.

NORA: Don't go near him; he'll do you some terrible harm!

MRS. LINDE: There was a time once when he'd gladly have done anything for me.

NORA: He?

MRS. LINDE: Where does he live?

NORA: Oh, how do I know? Yes. (*Searches in her pocket.*) Here's his card. But the letter, the letter—!

HELMER (*from the study, knocking on the door*): Nora!

NORA (*with a cry of fear*): Oh! What is it? What do you want?

HELMER: Now, now, don't be so frightened. We're not coming in. You locked the door—are you trying on the dress?

NORA: Yes, I'm trying it. I'll look just beautiful, Torvald.

MRS. LINDE (*who has read the card*): He's living right around the corner.

NORA: Yes, but what's the use? We're lost. The letter's in the box.

MRS. LINDE: And your husband has the key?

NORA: Yes, always.

MRS. LINDE: Krogstad can ask for his letter back unread; he can find some excuse—

NORA: But it's just this time that Torvald usually—

MRS. LINDE: Stall him. Keep him in there. I'll be back as quick as I can. (*She hurries out through the hall entrance.*)

NORA (*goes to Helmer's door, opens it, and peers in*): Torvald!

HELMER (*from the inner study*): Well—does one dare set foot in one's own living room at last? Come on, Rank, now we'll get a look—(*In the doorway.*) But what's this?

NORA: What, Torvald dear?

HELMER: Rank had me expecting some grand masquerade.

RANK (*in the doorway*): That was my impression, but I must have been wrong.

NORA: No one can admire me in my splendor—not till tomorrow.

HELMER: But Nora dear, you look so exhausted. Have you practiced too hard?

NORA: No, I haven't practiced at all yet.

HELMER: You know, it's necessary—

NORA: Oh, it's absolutely necessary, Torvald. But I can't get anywhere without your help. I've forgotten the whole thing completely.

HELMER: Ah, we'll soon take care of that.

NORA: Yes, take care of me, Torvald, please! Promise me that? Oh, I'm so nervous. That big party—You must give up everything this evening for me. No business—don't even touch your pen. Yes? Dear Torvald, promise?

HELMER: It's a promise. Tonight I'm totally at your service—you little helpless thing—but first there's one thing I want to—(*Goes toward the hall door.*)

NORA: What are you looking for?

HELMER: Just to see if there's any mail.

NORA: No, no, don't do that, Torvald!

HELMER: Now what?

NORA: Torvald, please. There isn't any.

HELMER: Let me look, though. (*Starts out. Nora, at the piano, strikes the first notes of the tarantella. Helmer, at the door, stops.*) Aha!

NORA: I can't dance tomorrow if I don't practice with you.

HELMER (*going over to her*): Nora dear, are you really so frightened?

NORA:   Yes, so terribly frightened. Let me practice right now; there's still time before dinner. Oh, sit down and play for me, Torvald. Direct me. Teach me, the way you always have.

HELMER:   Gladly, if it's what you want. (*Sits at the piano.*)

NORA (*snatches the tambourine up from the box, then a long, varicolored shawl, which she throws around herself, whereupon she springs forward and cries out*):   Play for me now! Now I'll dance!

*Helmer plays and Nora dances. Rank stands behind Helmer at the piano and looks on.*

HELMER (*as he plays*):   Slower. Slow down.

NORA:   Can't change it.

HELMER:   Not so violent, Nora!

NORA:   Has to be just like this.

HELMER (*stopping*):   No, no, that won't do at all.

NORA (*laughing and swinging her tambourine*):   Isn't that what I told you?

RANK:   Let me play for her.

HELMER (*getting up*):   Yes, go on. I can teach her more easily then.

*Rank sits at the piano and plays; Nora dances more and more wildly. Helmer has stationed himself by the stove and repeatedly gives her directions; she seems not to hear them; her hair loosens and falls over her shoulders; she does not notice, but goes on dancing. Mrs. Linde enters.*

MRS. LINDE (*standing dumbfounded at the door*):   Ah—!

NORA (*still dancing*):   See what fun, Kristine!

HELMER:   But Nora darling, you dance as if your life were at stake.

NORA:   And it is.

HELMER:   Rank, stop! This is pure madness. Stop it, I say!

*Rank breaks off playing, and Nora halts abruptly.*

HELMER (*going over to her*):   I never would have believed it. You've forgotten everything I taught you.

NORA (*throwing away the tambourine*):   You see for yourself.

HELMER:   Well, there's certainly room for instruction here.

NORA:   Yes, you see how important it is. You've got to teach me to the very last minute. Promise me that, Torvald?

HELMER:   You can bet on it.

NORA:   You mustn't, either today or tomorrow, think about anything else but you mustn't open any letters—or the mailbox—

HELMER: Ah, it's still the fear of that man—

NORA: Oh yes, yes, that too.

HELMER: Nora, it's written all over you—there's already a letter from him out there.

NORA: I don't know. I guess so. But you mustn't read such things now; there mustn't be anything ugly between us before it's all over.

RANK (*quietly to Helmer*): You shouldn't deny her.

HELMER (*putting his arm around her*): The child can have her way. But tomorrow night, after you've danced—

NORA: Then you'll be free.

MAID (*in the doorway, right*): Ma'am, dinner is served.

NORA: We'll be wanting champagne, Helene.

MAID: Very good, ma'am. (*Goes out.*)

HELMER: So—a regular banquet, hm?

NORA: Yes, a banquet—champagne till daybreak! (*Calling out.*) And some macaroons, Helene. Heaps of them—just this once.

HELMER (*taking her hands*): Now, now, now—no hysterics. Be my own little lark again.

NORA: Oh, I will soon enough. But go on in—and you, Dr. Rank. Kristine, help me put up my hair.

RANK (*whispering, as they go*): There's nothing wrong—really wrong, is there?

HELMER: Oh, of course not. It's nothing more than this childish anxiety I was telling you about. (*They go out, right.*)

NORA: Well?

MRS. LINDE: Left town.

NORA: I could see by your face.

MRS. LINDE: He'll be home tomorrow evening. I wrote him a note.

NORA: You shouldn't have. Don't try to stop anything now. After all, it's a wonderful joy, this waiting here for the miracle.

MRS. LINDE: What is it you're waiting for?

NORA: Oh, you can't understand that. Go in to them: I'll be along in a moment.

*Mrs. Linde goes into the dining room. Nora stands a short while as if composing herself; then she looks at her watch.*

NORA: Five. Seven hours to midnight. Twenty-four hours to the midnight after, and then the tarantella's done. Seven and twenty-four? Thirty-one hours to live.

HELMER (*in the doorway, right*): What's become of the little lark?

NORA (*going toward him with open arms*): Here's your lark!

# ACT III

*Same scene. The table, with chairs around it, has been moved to the center of the room. A lamp on the table is lit. The hall door stands open. Dance music drifts down from the floor above. Mrs. Linde sits at the table, absently paging through a book trying to read, but apparently unable to focus her thoughts. Once or twice she pauses, tensely listening for a sound at the outer entrance.*

MRS. LINDE (*glancing at her watch*):   Not yet—and there's hardly any time left. If only he's not—(*Listening again.*) Ah, there he is. (*She goes out in the hall and cautiously opens the outer door. Quiet footsteps are heard on the stairs. She whispers.*) Come in. Nobody's here.

KROGSTAD (*in the doorway*):   I found a note from you at home. What's back of all this?

MRS. LINDE:   I just *had* to talk to you.

KROGSTAD:   Oh! And it just *had* to be here in this house?

MRS. LINDE:   At my place it was impossible; my room hasn't a private entrance. Come in; we're all alone. The maid's asleep, and the Helmers are at the dance upstairs.

KROGSTAD (*entering the room*):   Well, well, the Helmers are dancing tonight? Really?

MRS. LINDE:   Yes, why not?

KROGSTAD:   How true—why not?

MRS. LINDE:   All right, Krogstad, let's talk.

KROGSTAD:   Do we two have anything more to talk about?

MRS. LINDE:   We have a great deal to talk about.

KROGSTAD:   I wouldn't have thought so.

MRS. LINDE:   No, because you've never understood me, really.

KROGSTAD:   Was there anything more to understand—except what's all too common in life? A calculating woman throws over a man the moment a better catch comes by.

MRS. LINDE:   You think I'm so thoroughly calculating? You think I broke it off lightly?

KROGSTAD:   Didn't you?

MRS. LINDE:   Nils—is that what you really thought?

KROGSTAD:   If you cared, then why did you write me the way you did?

MRS. LINDE:   What else could I do? If I had to break off with you, then it was my job as well to root out everything you felt for me.

KROGSTAD (*wringing his hands*): So that was it. And this—all this, simply for money!

MRS. LINDE: Don't forget I had a helpless mother and two small brothers. We couldn't wait for you, Nils; you had such a long road ahead for you then.

KROGSTAD: That may be; but you still hadn't the right to abandon me for somebody else's sake.

MRS. LINDE: Yes—I don't know. So many, many times I've asked myself if I did have that right.

KROGSTAD (*more softly*): When I lost you, it was as if all the solid ground dissolved from under my feet. Look at me; I'm a half-drowned man now, hanging onto a wreck.

MRS. LINDE: Help may be near.

KROGSTAD: It was near—but then you came and blocked it off.

MRS. LINDE: Without my knowing it, Nils. Today for the first time I learned that it's you I'm replacing at the bank.

KROGSTAD: All right—I believe you. But now that you know, will you step aside?

MRS. LINDE: No, because that wouldn't benefit you in the slightest.

KROGSTAD: Not "benefit" me, hm! I'd step aside anyway.

MRS. LINDE: I've got to be realistic. Life and hard, bitter necessity have taught me that.

KROGSTAD: And life's taught me never to trust fine phrases.

MRS. LINDE: Then life's taught you a very sound thing. But you do have to trust in actions, don't you?

KROGSTAD: What does that mean?

MRS. LINDE: You said you were hanging on like a half-drowned man to a wreck.

KROGSTAD: I've good reason to say that.

MRS. LINDE: I'm also like a half-drowned woman on a wreck. No one to suffer with; no one to care for.

KROGSTAD: You made your choice.

MRS. LINDE: There wasn't any choice then.

KROGSTAD: So—what of it?

MRS. LINDE: Nils, if only we two shipwrecked people could reach across to each other.

KROGSTAD: What are you saying?

MRS. LINDE: Two on one wreck are at least better off than each on his own.

KROGSTAD: Kristine!

MRS. LINDE: Why do you think I came into town?

KROGSTAD:   Did you really have some thought of me?

MRS. LINDE:   I have to work to go on living. All my born days, as long as I can remember, I've worked, and it's been my best and my only joy. But now I'm completely alone in the world; it frightens me to be so empty and lost. To work for yourself—there's no joy in that. Nils, give me something—someone to work for.

KROGSTAD:   I don't believe all this. It's just some hysterical feminine urge to go out and make a noble sacrifice.

MRS. LINDE:   Have you ever found me to be hysterical?

KROGSTAD:   Can you honestly mean this? Tell me—do you know everything about my past?

MRS. LINDE:   Yes.

KROGSTAD:   And you know what they think I'm worth around here.

MRS. LINDE:   From what you were saying before, it would seem that with me you could have been another person.

KROGSTAD:   I'm positive of that.

MRS. LINDE:   Couldn't it happen still?

KROGSTAD:   Kristine—you're saying this in all seriousness? Yes, you are! I can see it in you. And do you really have the courage, then—?

MRS. LINDE:   I need to have someone to care for; and your children need a mother. We both need each other. Nils, I have faith that you're good at heart—I'll risk everything together with you.

KROGSTAD (*gripping her hands*):   Kristine, thank you, thank you— Now I know I can win back a place in their eyes. Yes—but I forgot—

MRS. LINDE (*listening*):   Shh! The tarantella. Go now! Go on!

KROGSTAD:   Why? What is it?

MRS. LINDE:   Hear the dance up there? When that's over, they'll be coming down.

KROGSTAD:   Oh, then I'll go. But—it's all pointless. Of course, you don't know the move I made against the Helmers.

MRS. LINDE:   Yes, Nils, I know.

KROGSTAD:   And all the same, you have the courage to—?

MRS. LINDE:   I know how far despair can drive a man like you.

KROGSTAD:   Oh, if I only could take it all back.

MRS. LINDE:   You easily could—your letter's still lying in the mailbox.

KROGSTAD:   Are you sure of that?

MRS. LINDE:   Positive. But—

KROGSTAD (*looks at her searchingly*):   Is that the meaning of it, then? You'll save your friend at any price. Tell me straight out. Is that it?

MRS. LINDE:   Nils—anyone who's sold herself for somebody else once isn't going to do it again.

KROGSTAD:  I'll demand my letter back.

MRS. LINDE:  No, no.

KROGSTAD:  Yes, of course. I'll stay here till Helmer comes down; I'll tell him to give me my letter again—that it only involves my dismissal—that he shouldn't read it—

MRS. LINDE:  No, Nils, don't call the letter back.

KROGSTAD:  But wasn't that exactly why you wrote me to come here?

MRS. LINDE:  Yes, in that first panic. But it's been a whole day and night since then, and in that time I've seen such incredible things in this house. Helmer's got to learn everything; this dreadful secret has to be aired; those two have to come to a full understanding; all these lies and evasions can't go on.

KROGSTAD:  Well, then, if you want to chance it. But at least there's one thing I can do, and do right away.

MRS. LINDE (*listening*):  Go now, go, quick! The dance is over. We're not safe another second.

KROGSTAD:  I'll wait for you downstairs.

MRS. LINDE:  Yes, please do; take me home.

KROGSTAD:  I can't believe it; I've never been so happy. (*He leaves by way of the outer door; the door between the room and hall stays open.*)

MRS. LINDE (*straightening up a bit and getting together her street clothes*):  How different now! How different! Someone to work for, to live for—a home to build. Well, it is worth the try! Oh, if they'd only come! (*Listening.*) Ah, there they are. Bundle up. (*She picks up her hat and coat. Nora's and Helmer's voices can be heard outside; a key turns in the lock, and Helmer brings Nora into the hall almost by force. She is wearing the Italian costume with a large black shawl about her; he has on evening dress, with a black domino open over it.*)

NORA (*struggling in the doorway*):  No, no, no, not inside! I'm going up again. I don't want to leave so soon.

HELMER:  But Nora dear—

NORA:  Oh, I beg you, please, Torvald. From the bottom of my heart, *please*—only an hour more!

HELMER:  Not a single minute, Nora darling. You know our agreement. Come on, in we go; you'll catch cold out here. (*In spite of her resistance, he gently draws her into the room.*)

MRS. LINDE:  Good evening.

NORA:  Kristine!

HELMER:  Why, Mrs. Linde—are you here so late?

MRS. LINDE: Yes, I'm sorry, but I did want to see Nora in costume.

NORA: Have you been sitting here, waiting for me?

MRS. LINDE: Yes. I didn't come early enough; you were all upstairs; and then I thought I really couldn't leave without seeing you.

HELMER (*removing Nora's shawl*): Yes, take a good look. She's worth looking at, I can tell you that, Mrs. Linde. Isn't she lovely?

MRS. LINDE: Yes, I should say—

HELMER: A dream of loveliness, isn't she? That's what everyone thought at the party, too. But she's horribly stubborn—this sweet little thing. What's to be done with her? Can you imagine, I almost had to use force to pry her away.

NORA: Oh, Torvald, you're going to regret you didn't indulge me, even for just a half hour more.

HELMER: There, you see. She danced the tarantella and got a tumultuous hand—which was well earned, although the performance may have been a bit too naturalistic—I mean it rather overstepped the proprieties of art. But never mind—what's important is, she made a success, an overwhelming success. You think I could let her stay on after that and spoil the effect? Oh no; I took my lovely little Capri girl—my capricious little Capri girl, I should say—took her under my arm; one quick tour of the ballroom, a curtsy to every side, and then—as they say in novels—the beautiful vision disappeared. An exit should always be effective, Mrs. Linde, but that's what I can't get Nora to grasp. Phew, it's hot in here. (*Flings the domino on a chair and opens the door to his room.*) Why's it dark in here? Oh yes, of course. Excuse me. (*He goes in and lights a couple of candles.*)

NORA (*in a sharp, breathless whisper*): So?

MRS. LINDE (*quietly*): I talked with him.

NORA: And—?

MRS. LINDE: Nora—you must tell your husband everything.

NORA (*dully*): I knew it.

MRS. LINDE: You've got nothing to fear from Krogstad, but you have to speak out.

NORA: I won't tell.

MRS. LINDE: Then the letter will.

NORA: Thanks, Kristine. I know now what's to be done. Shh!

HELMER (*reentering*): Well, then, Mrs. Linde—have you admired her?

MRS. LINDE: Yes, and now I'll say good night.

HELMER: Oh, come, so soon? Is this yours, this knitting?

MRS. LINDE: Yes, thanks. I nearly forgot it.

HELMER:  Do you knit, then?

MRS. LINDE:  Oh yes.

HELMER:  You know what? You should embroider instead.

MRS. LINDE:  Really? Why?

HELMER:  Yes, because it's a lot prettier. See here, one holds the embroidery so, in the left hand, and then one guides the needle with the right—so—in an easy, sweeping curve—right?

MRS. LINDE:  Yes, I guess that's—

HELMER:  But, on the other hand, knitting—it can never be anything but ugly. Look, see here, the arms tucked in, the knitting needles going up and down—there's something Chinese about it. Ah, that was really a glorious champagne they served.

MRS. LINDE:  Yes, good night, Nora, and don't be stubborn any more.

HELMER:  Well put, Mrs. Linde!

MRS. LINDE:  Good night, Mr. Helmer.

HELMER (*accompanying her to the door*):  Good night, good night. I hope you get home all right. I'd be very happy to—but you don't have far to go. Good night, good night. (*She leaves. He shuts the door after her and returns.*) There, now, at last we got her out the door. She's a deadly bore, that creature.

NORA:  Aren't you pretty tired, Torvald?

HELMER:  No, not a bit.

NORA:  You're not sleepy?

HELMER:  Not at all. On the contrary, I'm feeling quite exhilarated. But you? Yes, you really look tired and sleepy.

NORA:  Yes, I'm very tired. Soon now I'll sleep.

HELMER:  See! You see! I was right all along that we shouldn't stay longer.

NORA:  Whatever you do is always right.

HELMER (*kissing her brow*):  Now my little lark talks sense. Say, did you notice what a time Rank was having tonight?

NORA:  Oh, was he? I didn't get to speak with him.

HELMER:  I scarcely did either, but it's a long time since I've seen him in such high spirits. (*Gazes at her a moment, then comes nearer her.*) Hm—it's marvelous, though, to be back home again—to be completely alone with you. Oh, you bewitchingly lovely young woman!

NORA:  Torvald, don't look at me like that!

HELMER:  Can't I look at my richest treasure? At all that beauty that's mine, mine alone—completely and utterly.

NORA (*moving around to the other side of the table*):  You mustn't talk to me that way tonight.

HELMER (*following her*): The tarantella is still in your blood, I can see—and it makes you even more enticing. Listen. The guests are beginning to go. (*Dropping his voice.*) Nora—it'll soon be quiet through this whole house.

NORA: Yes, I hope so.

HELMER: You do, don't you, my love? Do you realize—when I'm out at a party like this with you—do you know why I talk to you so little, and keep such a distance away; just send you a stolen look now and then—you know why I do it? It's because I'm imagining then that you're my secret darling, my secret young bride-to-be, and that no one suspects there's anything between us.

NORA: Yes, yes; oh, yes, I know you're always thinking of me.

HELMER: And then when we leave and I place the shawl over those fine young rounded shoulders—over that wonderful curving neck—then I pretend that you're my young bride, that we're just coming from the wedding, that for the first time I'm bringing you into my house—that for the first time I'm alone with you—completely alone with you, your trembling young beauty! All this evening I've longed for nothing but you. When I saw you turn and sway in the tarantella—my blood was pounding till I couldn't stand it—that's why I brought you down here so early—

NORA: Go away, Torvald! Leave me alone. I don't want all this.

HELMER: What do you mean? Nora, you're teasing me. You will, won't you? Aren't I your husband—?

*A knock at the outside door.*

NORA (*startled*): What's that?

HELMER (*going toward the hall*): Who is it?

RANK (*outside*): It's me. May I come in a moment?

HELMER (*with quiet irritation*): Oh, what does he want now? (*Aloud.*) Hold on. (*Goes and opens the door.*) Oh, how nice that you didn't just pass us by!

RANK: I thought I heard your voice, and then I wanted so badly to have a look in. (*Lightly glancing about.*) Ah, me, these old familiar haunts. You have it snug and cozy in here, you two.

HELMER: You seemed to be having it pretty cozy upstairs, too.

RANK: Absolutely. Why shouldn't I? Why not take in everything in life? As much as you can, anyway, and as long as you can. The wine was superb—

HELMER: The champagne especially.

RANK: You noticed that too? It's amazing how much I could guzzle down.

NORA: Torvald also drank a lot of champagne this evening.

RANK: Oh?

NORA: Yes, and that always makes him so entertaining.

RANK: Well, why shouldn't one have a pleasant evening after a well-spent day?

HELMER: Well spent? I'm afraid I can't claim that.

RANK (*slapping him on the back*): But I can, you see!

NORA: Dr. Rank, you must have done some scientific research today.

RANK: Quite so.

HELMER: Come now—little Nora talking about scientific research!

NORA: And can I congratulate you on the results?

RANK: Indeed you may.

NORA: Then they were good?

RANK: The best possible for both doctor and patient—certainty.

NORA (*quickly and searching*): Certainty?

RANK: Complete certainty. So don't I owe myself a gay evening afterwards?

NORA: Yes, you're right, Dr. Rank.

HELMER: I'm with you—just so long as you don't have to suffer for it in the morning.

RANK: Well, one never gets something for nothing in life.

NORA: Dr. Rank—are you very fond of masquerade parties?

RANK: Yes, if there's a good array of odd disguises—

NORA: Tell me, what should we two go as at the next masquerade?

HELMER: You little featherhead—already thinking of the next!

RANK: We two? I'll tell you what: you must go as Charmed Life—

HELMER: Yes, but find a costume for *that*!

RANK: Your wife can appear just as she looks every day.

HELMER: That was nicely put. But don't you know what you're going to be?

RANK: Yes, Helmer, I've made up my mind.

HELMER: Well?

RANK: At the next masquerade I'm going to be invisible.

HELMER: That's a funny idea.

RANK: They say there's a hat—black, huge—have you never heard of the hat that makes you invisible? You put it on, and then no one on earth can see you.

HELMER (*suppressing a smile*): Ah, of course.

RANK: But I'm quite forgetting what I came for. Helmer, give me a cigar, one of the dark Havanas.

HELMER: With the greatest pleasure. (*Holds out his case.*)

RANK: Thanks. (*Takes one and cuts off the tip.*)

NORA (*striking a match*): Let me give you a light.

RANK: Thank you. (*She holds the match for him; he lights the cigar.*) And now good-bye.

HELMER: Good-bye, good-bye, old friend.

NORA: Sleep well, Doctor.

RANK: Thanks for that wish.

NORA: Wish me the same.

RANK: You? All right, if you like—Sleep well. And thanks for the light. (*He nods to them both and leaves.*)

HELMER (*his voice subdued*): He's been drinking heavily.

NORA (*absently*): Could be. (*Helmer takes his keys from his pocket and goes out in the hall.*) Torvald—what are you after?

HELMER: Got to empty the mailbox; it's nearly full. There won't be room for the morning papers.

NORA: Are you working tonight?

HELMER: You know I'm not. Why—what's this? Someone's been at the lock.

NORA: At the lock—?

HELMER: Yes, I'm positive. What do you suppose—? I can't imagine one of the maids—? Here's a broken hairpin. Nora, it's yours—

NORA (*quickly*): Then it must be the children—

HELMER: You'd better break them of that. Hm, hm—well, opened it after all. (*Takes the contents out and calls into the kitchen.*) Helene! Helene, would you put out the lamp in the hall. (*He returns to the room, shutting the hall door, then displays the handful of mail.*) Look how it's piled up. (*Sorting through them.*) Now what's this?

NORA (*at the window*): The letter! Oh, Torvald, no!

HELMER: Two calling cards—from Rank.

NORA: From Dr. Rank?

HELMER (*examining them*): "Dr. Rank, Consulting Physician." They were on top. He must have dropped them in as he left.

NORA: Is there anything on them?

HELMER: There's a black cross over the name. See? That's a gruesome notion. He could almost be announcing his own death.

NORA: That's just what he's doing.

HELMER: What! You've heard something? Something he's told you?

NORA: Yes. That when those cards came, he'd be taking his leave of us. He'll shut himself in now and die.

HELMER: Ah, my poor friend! Of course I knew he wouldn't be here much longer. But so soon—And then to hide himself away like a wounded animal.

NORA: If it has to happen, then it's best it happens in silence—don't you think so, Torvald?

HELMER (*pacing up and down*): He'd grown right into our lives. I simply can't imagine him gone. He with his suffering and loneliness—like a dark cloud setting off our sunlit happiness. Well, maybe it's best this way. For him, at least. (*Standing still.*) And maybe for us too, Nora. Now we're thrown back on each other, completely. (*Embracing her.*) Oh you, my darling wife, how can I hold you close enough? You know what, Nora—time and again I've wished you were in some terrible danger, just so I could stake my life and soul and everything, for your sake.

NORA (*tearing herself away, her voice firm and decisive*): Now you must read your mail, Torvald.

HELMER: No, no, not tonight. I want to stay with you, dearest.

NORA: With a dying friend on your mind?

HELMER: You're right. We've both had a shock. There's ugliness between us—these thoughts of death and corruption. We'll have to get free of them first. Until then—we'll stay apart.

NORA (*clinging about his neck*): Torvald—good night! Good night!

HELMER (*kissing her on the cheek*): Good night, little songbird. Sleep well, Nora. I'll be reading my mail now. (*He takes the letters into his room and shuts the door after him.*)

NORA (*with bewildered glances, groping about, seizing Helmer's domino, throwing it around her, and speaking in short, hoarse, broken whispers*): Never see him again. Never, never. (*Putting her shawl over her head.*) Never see the children either—them, too. Never, never. Oh, the freezing black water! The depths—down— Oh, I wish it were over—He has it now; he's reading it—now. Oh no, no, not yet. Torvald, good-bye, you and the children—(*She starts for the hall; as she does, Helmer throws open his door and stands with an open letter in his hand.*)

HELMER: Nora!

NORA (*screams*): Oh—!

HELMER: What is this? You know what's in this letter?

NORA: Yes, I know. Let me go! Let me out!

HELMER (*holding her back*): Where are you going?

NORA (*struggling to break loose*): You can't save me, Torvald!

HELMER (*slumping back*): True! Then it's true what he writes? How horrible! No, no, it's impossible—it can't be true.

NORA: It is true. I've loved you more than all this world.

HELMER: Ah, none of your slippery tricks.

NORA (*taking one step toward him*): Torvald—!

HELMER: What is this you've blundered into?

NORA: Just let me loose. You're not going to suffer for my sake. You're not going to take on my guilt.

HELMER: No more playacting. (*Locks the hall door.*) You stay right here and give me a reckoning. You understand what you've done? Answer! You understand?

NORA (*looking squarely at him, her face hardening*): Yes. I'm beginning to understand everything now.

HELMER (*striding about*): Oh, what an awful awakening! In all these eight years—she who was my pride and joy—a hypocrite, a liar— worse, worse—a criminal! How infinitely disgusting it all is! The shame! (*Nora says nothing and goes looking straight at him. He stops in front of her.*) I should have suspected something of the kind. I should have known. All your father's flimsy values have come out in you. No religion, no morals, no sense of duty—Oh, how I'm punished for letting him off! I did it for your sake, and you repay me like this.

NORA: Yes, like this.

HELMER: Now you've wrecked all my happiness—ruined my whole future. Oh, it's awful to think of. I'm in a cheap little grafter's hands; he can do anything he wants with me, ask for anything, play with me like a puppet—and I can't breathe a word. I'll be swept down miserably into the depths on account of a featherbrained woman.

NORA: When I'm gone from this world, you'll be free.

HELMER: Oh, quit posing. Your father had a mess of those speeches too. What good would that ever do me if you were gone from this world, as you say? Not the slightest. He can still make the whole thing known; and if he does, I could be falsely suspected as your accomplice. They might even think that I was behind it—that I put you up to it. And all that I can thank you for—you that I've coddled the whole of our marriage. Can you see now what you've done to me?

NORA (*icily calm*): Yes.

HELMER: It's so incredible, I just can't grasp it. But we'll have to patch up whatever we can. Take off the shawl. I said, take it off! I've got to appease him somehow or other. The thing has to be hushed up at any cost. And as for you and me, it's got to seem like everything between us is just as it was—to the outside world, that is. You'll go right on living in this house, of course. But you can't be allowed to bring up the children; I don't dare trust you with them—Oh, to have to say this to someone I've loved so much! Well, that's done with. From now on happiness doesn't matter; all that matters is saving the bits and pieces, the appearance—(*The doorbell rings. Helmer starts.*) What's that? And so late. Maybe the worst—? You think he'd—? Hide, Nora! Say you're sick. (*Nora remains standing motionless. Helmer goes and opens the door.*)

MAID (*fully dressed, in the hall*): A letter for Mrs. Helmer.

HELMER: I'll take it. (Snatches the letter and shuts the door.) Yes, it's from him. You don't get it; I'm reading it myself.

NORA: Then read it.

HELMER (*by the lamp*): I hardly dare. We may be ruined, you and I. But—I've got to know. (*Rips open the letter, skims through a few lines, glances at an enclosure, then cries out joyfully.*) Nora! (*Nora looks inquiringly at him.*) Nora! Wait—better check it again—Yes, yes, it's true. I'm saved. Nora, I'm saved!

NORA: And I?

HELMER: You too, of course. We're both saved, both of us. He's sent back your note. He says he's sorry and ashamed—that a happy development in his life—oh, who cares what he says! Nora, we're saved! No one can hurt you. Oh, Nora, Nora—but first, this ugliness all has to go. Let me see—(*Takes a look at the note.*) No, I don't want to see it; I want the whole thing to fade like a dream. (*Tears the note and both the letters to pieces, throws them into the stove and watches them burn.*) There—now there's nothing left—He wrote that since Christmas Eve you—Oh, they must have been three terrible days for you, Nora.

NORA: I fought a hard fight.

HELMER: And suffered pain and saw no escape but—No, we're not going to dwell on anything unpleasant. We'll just be grateful and keep on repeating: it's over now, it's over! You hear me, Nora? You don't seem to realize—it's over. What's it mean—that frozen look? Oh, poor little Nora, I understand. You can't believe I've forgiven you. But I have, Nora; I swear I have. I know that what you did, you did out of love for me.

NORA: That's true.

HELMER: You loved me the way a wife ought to love her husband. It's simply the means that you couldn't judge. But you think I love you any the less for not knowing how to handle your affairs? No, no— just lean on me; I'll guide you and teach you. I wouldn't be a man if this feminine helplessness didn't make you twice as attractive to me.

You mustn't mind those sharp words I said—that was all in the first confusion of thinking my world had collapsed. I've forgiven you, Nora; I swear I've forgiven you.

NORA: My thanks for your forgiveness. (*She goes out through the door, right.*)

HELMER: No, wait—(*Peers in.*) What are you doing in there?

NORA (*inside*): Getting out of my costume.

HELMER (*by the open door*): Yes, do that. Try to calm yourself and collect your thoughts again, my frightened little songbird. You can rest easy now; I've got wide wings to shelter you with. (*Walking about close by the door.*) How snug and nice our home is, Nora. You're safe here; I'll keep you like a hunted dove I've rescued out of a hawk's claws. I'll bring peace to your poor, shuddering heart. Gradually it'll happen, Nora; you'll see. Tomorrow all this will look different to you; then everything will be as it was. I won't have to go on repeating I forgive you; you'll feel it for yourself. How can you imagine I'd ever conceivably want to disown you—or even blame you in any way? Ah, you don't know a man's heart, Nora. For a man there's something indescribably sweet and satisfying in knowing he's forgiven his wife—and forgiven her out of a full and open heart. It's as if she belongs to him in two ways now: in a sense he's given her fresh into the world again, and she's become his wife and his child as well. From now on that's what you'll be to me—you little, bewildered, helpless thing. Don't be afraid of anything, Nora; just open your heart to me, and I'll be conscience and will to you both—(*Nora enters in her regular clothes.*) What's this? Not in bed? You've changed your dress?

NORA: Yes, Torvald, I've changed my dress.

HELMER: But why now, so late?

NORA: Tonight I'm not sleeping.

HELMER: But Nora dear—

NORA (*looking at her watch*): It's still not so very late. Sit down, Torvald; we have a lot to talk over. (*She sits at one side of the table.*)

HELMER: Nora—what is this? That hard expression—

NORA: Sit down. This'll take some time. I have a lot to say.

HELMER (*sitting at the table directly opposite her*): You worry me, Nora. And I don't understand you.

NORA: No, that's exactly it. You don't understand me. And I've never understood you either—until tonight. No, don't interrupt. You can just listen to what I say. We're closing our accounts, Torvald.

HELMER: How do you mean that?

NORA (*after a short pause*): Doesn't anything strike you about our sitting here like this?

HELMER: What's that?

NORA: We've been married now eight years. Doesn't it occur to you that this is the first time we two, you and I, man and wife, have ever talked seriously together?

HELMER: What do you mean—seriously?

NORA: In eight whole years—longer even—right from our first acquaintance, we've never exchanged a serious word on any serious thing.

HELMER: You mean I should constantly go and involve you in problems you couldn't possibly help me with?

NORA: I'm not talking of problems. I'm saying that we've never sat down seriously together and tried to get to the bottom of anything.

HELMER: But dearest, what good would that ever do you?

NORA: That's the point right there: you've never understood me. I've been wronged greatly, Torvald—first by Papa, and then by you.

HELMER: What! By us—the two people who've loved you more than anyone else?

NORA (*shaking her head*): You never loved me. You've thought it fun to be in love with me, that's all.

HELMER: Nora, what a thing to say!

NORA: Yes, it's true now, Torvald. When I lived at home with Papa, he told me all his opinions, so I had the same ones too; or if they were different I hid them, since he wouldn't have cared for that. He used to call me his doll-child, and he played with me the way I played with my dolls. Then I came into your house—

HELMER: How can you speak of our marriage like that?

NORA (*unperturbed*): I mean, then I went from Papa's hands into yours. You arranged everything to your own taste, and so I got the same taste as you—or I pretended to; I can't remember. I guess a little of both, first one, then the other. Now when I look back, it seems as if I'd lived here like a beggar—just from hand to mouth. I've lived by doing tricks for you, Torvald. But that's the way you wanted it. It's a great sin what you and Papa did to me. You're to blame that nothing's become of me.

HELMER: Nora, how unfair and ungrateful you are! Haven't you been happy here?

NORA: No, never. I thought so—but I never have.

HELMER: Not—not happy!

NORA: No, only lighthearted. And you've always been so kind to me. But our home's been nothing but a playpen. I've been your doll-wife here, just as at home I was Papa's doll-child. And in turn the children have been my dolls. I thought it was fun when you played with me, just as they thought it fun when I played with them. That's been our marriage, Torvald.

HELMER: There's some truth in what you're saying—under all the raving exaggeration. But it'll all be different after this. Playtime's over; now for the schooling.

NORA: Whose schooling—mine or the children's?

HELMER: Both yours and the children's, dearest.

NORA: Oh, Torvald, you're not the man to teach me to be a good wife to you.

HELMER: And you can say that?

NORA: And I—how am I equipped to bring up children?

HELMER: Nora!

NORA: Didn't you say a moment ago that that was no job to trust me with?

HELMER: In a flare of temper! Why fasten on that?

NORA: Yes, but you were so very right. I'm not up to the job. There's another job I have to do first. I have to try to educate myself. You can't help me with that. I've got to do it alone. And that's why I'm leaving you now.

HELMER (*jumping up*): What's that?

NORA: I have to stand completely alone, if I'm ever going to discover myself and the world out there. So I can't go on living with you.

HELMER: Nora, Nora!

NORA: I want to leave right away. Kristine should put me up for the night—

HELMER: You're insane! You've no right! I forbid you!

NORA: From here on, there's no use forbidding me anything. I'll take with me whatever is mine. I don't want a thing from you, either now or later.

HELMER: What kind of madness is this!

NORA: Tomorrow I'm going home—I mean, home where I came from. It'll be easier up there to find something to do.

HELMER: Oh, you blind, incompetent child!

NORA: I must learn to be competent, Torvald.

HELMER: Abandon your home, your husband, your children! And you're not even thinking what people will say.

NORA: I can't be concerned about that. I only know how essential this is.

HELMER: Oh, it's outrageous. So you'll run out like this on your most sacred vows.

NORA: What do you think are my most sacred vows?

HELMER: And I have to tell you that! Aren't they your duties to your husband and children?

NORA: I have other duties equally sacred.

HELMER: That isn't true. What duties are they?

NORA: Duties to myself.

HELMER: Before all else, you're a wife and a mother.

NORA: I don't believe in that any more. I believe that, before all else, I'm a human being, no less than you—or anyway, I ought to try to become one. I know the majority thinks you're right, Torvald, and plenty of books agree with you, too. But I can't go on believing what the majority says, or what's written in books. I have to think over these things myself and try to understand them.

HELMER: Why can't you understand your place in your own home? On a point like that, isn't there one everlasting guide you can turn to? Where's your religion?

NORA: Oh, Torvald, I'm really not sure what religion is.

HELMER: What—?

NORA: I only know what the minister said when I was confirmed. He told me religion was this thing and that. When I get clear and away by myself, I'll go into that problem too. I'll see if what the minister said was right, or, in any case, if it's right for me.

HELMER: A young woman your age shouldn't talk like that. If religion can't move you, I can try to rouse your conscience. You do have some moral feeling? Or, tell me—has that gone too?

NORA: It's not easy to answer that, Torvald. I simply don't know. I'm all confused about these things. I just know I see them so differently from you. I find out, for one thing, that the law's not at all what I'd thought—but I can't get it through my head that the law is fair. A woman hasn't a right to protect her dying father or save her husband's life! I can't believe that.

HELMER: You talk like a child. You don't know anything of the world you live in.

NORA: No, I don't. But now I'll begin to learn for myself. I'll try to discover who's right, the world or I.

HELMER: Nora, you're sick; you've got a fever. I almost think you're out of your head.

NORA: I've never felt more clearheaded and sure in my life.

HELMER: And—clearheaded and sure—you're leaving your husband and children?

NORA: Yes.

HELMER: Then there's only one possible reason.

NORA: What?

HELMER: You no longer love me.

NORA: No. That's exactly it.

HELMER: Nora! You can't be serious!

NORA: Oh, this is so hard, Torvald—you've been so kind to me always. But I can't help it. I don't love you any more.

HELMER (*struggling for composure*): Are you also clearheaded and sure about that?

NORA: Yes, completely. That's why I can't go on staying here.

HELMER: Can you tell me what I did to lose your love?

NORA: Yes, I can tell you. It was this evening when the miraculous thing didn't come—then I knew you weren't the man I'd imagined.

HELMER: Be more explicit; I don't follow you.

NORA: I've waited now so patiently eight long years—for, my Lord, I know miracles don't come every day. Then this crisis broke over me, and such a certainty filled me: *now* the miraculous event would occur. While Krogstad's letter was lying out there, I never for an instant dreamed that you could give in to his terms. I was so utterly sure you'd say to him: go on, tell your tale to the whole wide world. And when he'd done that—

HELMER: Yes, what then? When I'd delivered my own wife into shame and disgrace—!

NORA: When he'd done that, I was so utterly sure that you'd step forward, take the blame on yourself and say: I am the guilty one.

HELMER: Nora—!

NORA: You're thinking I'd never accept such a sacrifice from you? No, of course not. But what good would my protests be against you? That was the miracle I was waiting for, in terror and hope. And to stave that off, I would have taken my life.

HELMER: I'd gladly work for you day and night, Nora—and take on pain and deprivation. But there's no one who gives up honor for love.

NORA: Millions of women have done just that.

HELMER: Oh, you think and talk like a silly child.

NORA: Perhaps. But you neither think nor talk like the man I could join myself to. When your big fright was over—and it wasn't from any threat against me, only for what might damage you—when all the danger was past, for you it was just as if nothing had happened. I was exactly the same, your little lark, your doll, that you'd have to handle with double care now that I'd turned out so brittle and frail. (*Gets up.*) Torvald—in that instant it dawned on me that for eight years I've been living here with a stranger, and that I'd even conceived three children—oh, I can't stand the thought of it! I could tear myself to bits.

HELMER (*heavily*): I see. There's a gulf that's opened between us— that's clear. Oh but Nora, can't we bridge it somehow?

NORA: The way I am now, I'm no wife for you.

HELMER: I have the strength to make myself over.

NORA: Maybe—if your doll gets taken away.

HELMER: But to part! To part from you! No, Nora, no—I can't imagine it.

NORA (*going out, right*): All the more reason why it has to be. (*She reenters with her coat and a small overnight bag, which she puts on a chair by the table.*)

HELMER: Nora, Nora, not now! Wait till tomorrow.

NORA: I can't spend the night in a strange man's room.

HELMER: But couldn't we live here like brother and sister—

NORA: You know very well how long that would last. (*Throws her shawl about her.*) Good-bye, Torvald. I won't look in on the children. I know they're in better hands than mine. The way I am now, I'm no use to them.

HELMER: But someday, Nora—someday—?

NORA: How can I tell? I haven't the least idea what'll become of me.

HELMER: But you're my wife, now and wherever you go.

NORA: Listen, Torvald—I've heard that when a wife deserts her husband's house just as I'm doing, then the law frees him from all responsibility. In any case, I'm freeing you from being responsible. Don't feel yourself bound, any more than I will. There has to be absolute freedom for us both. Here, take your ring back. Give me mine.

HELMER: That too?

NORA: That too.

HELMER: There it is.

NORA: Good. Well, now it's all over. I'm putting the keys here. The maids know all about keeping up the house—better than I do. Tomorrow, after I've left town, Kristine will stop by to pack up everything that's mine from home. I'd like those things shipped up to me.

HELMER: Over! All over! Nora, won't you ever think about me?

NORA: I'm sure I'll think of you often, and about the children and the house here.

HELMER: May I write you?

NORA: No—never. You're not to do that.

HELMER: Oh, but let me send you—

NORA: Nothing. Nothing.

HELMER: Or help you if you need it.

NORA: No. I accept nothing from strangers.

HELMER: Nora—can I never be more than a stranger to you?

NORA (*picking up the overnight bag*): Ah, Torvald—it would take the greatest miracle of all—

HELMER: Tell me the greatest miracle!

NORA: You and I both would have to transform ourselves to the point that—Oh, Torvald, I've stopped believing in miracles.

HELMER: But I'll believe. Tell me! Transform ourselves to the point that—?

NORA: That our living together could be a true marriage. (*She goes out down the hall.*)

HELMER (*sinks down on a chair by the door, face buried in his hands*): Nora! Nora! (*Looking about and rising.*): Empty. She's gone. (*A sudden hope leaps in him.*) The greatest miracle—?

*From below, the sound of a door slamming shut.*

*—1879*

# *Susan Glaspell*  (1882–1948)

*Susan Glaspell was born in Iowa and educated at Drake University. Glaspell was one of the founders, with her husband George Cram Cook, of the Provincetown Players. This company, founded in the Cape Cod resort village, was committed to producing experimental drama, an alternative to the standard fare playing in Broadway theaters. Eventually it was relocated to New York. Along with Glaspell, Eugene O'Neill, America's only Nobel Prize–winning dramatist, wrote plays for this group. Trained as a journalist and the author of short stories and novels, Glaspell wrote* Trifles *(1916), her first play, shortly after the founding of the Players, basing her plot on an Iowa murder case she had covered. The one-act play, with both Glaspell and her husband in the cast, premiered during the Players' second season and also exists in a short-story version. Glaspell won the Pulitzer Prize for Drama in 1930 for* Alison's House, *basing the title character on poet Emily Dickinson. A socialist and feminist, Glaspell lived in Provincetown in her last years, writing* The Road to the Temple, *a memoir of her husband's life, and novels.*

# Trifles

## CHARACTERS

George Henderson, County Attorney
Mrs. Peters
Henry Peters, Sheriff
Lewis Hale, a neighbor
Mrs. Hale

SCENE: The kitchen in the now abandoned farmhouse of John Wright, a gloomy kitchen, and left without having been put in order— unwashed pans under the sink, a loaf of bread outside the breadbox, a dish towel on the table—other signs of incompleted work. At the rear the outer door opens, and the Sheriff comes in, followed by the County Attorney and Hale. The Sheriff and Hale are men in middle life, the County Attorney is a young man; all are much bundled up and go at once to the stove. They are followed by the two women—the Sheriff's Wife first; she is a slight wiry woman, a thin nervous face. Mrs. Hale is larger and would ordinarily be called more comfortable looking, but she is disturbed now and looks fearfully about as she enters. The women have come in slowly and stand close together near the door.

COUNTY ATTORNEY (*rubbing his hands*):   This feels good. Come up to the fire, ladies.

MRS. PETERS (*after taking a step forward*):   I'm not—cold.

SHERIFF (*unbuttoning his overcoat and stepping away from the stove as if to the beginning of official business*):   Now, Mr. Hale, before we move things about, you explain to Mr. Henderson just what you saw when you came here yesterday morning.

COUNTY ATTORNEY:   By the way, has anything been moved? Are things just as you left them yesterday?

SHERIFF (*looking about*):   It's just the same. When it dropped below zero last night, I thought I'd better send Frank out this morning to make a fire for us—no use getting pneumonia with a big case on; but I told him not to touch anything except the stove—and you know Frank.

COUNTY ATTORNEY:   Somebody should have been left here yesterday.

SHERIFF:   Oh—yesterday. When I had to send Frank to Morris Center for that man who went crazy—I want you to know I had my hands full yesterday. I knew you could get back from Omaha by today, and as long as I went over everything here myself—

COUNTY ATTORNEY:   Well, Mr. Hale, tell just what happened when you came here yesterday morning.

HALE:   Harry and I had started to town with a load of potatoes. We came along the road from my place; and as I got here, I said, "I'm going to see if I can't get John Wright to go in with me on a party telephone." I spoke to Wright about it once before, and he put me off, saying folks talked too much anyway, and all he asked was peace and quiet—I guess you know about how much he talked himself; but I thought maybe if I went to the house and talked about it before his wife, though I said to Harry that I didn't know as what his wife wanted made much difference to John—

COUNTY ATTORNEY:   Let's talk about that later, Mr. Hale. I do want to talk about that, but tell now just what happened when you got to the house.

HALE:   I didn't hear or see anything; I knocked at the door, and still it was all quiet inside. I knew they must be up, it was past eight o'clock. So I knocked again, and I thought I heard somebody say, "Come in." I wasn't sure, I'm not sure yet, but I opened the door— this door (*indicating the door by which the two women are still standing*), and there in that rocker—(*pointing to it*) sat Mrs. Wright. (*They all look at the rocker.*)

COUNTY ATTORNEY: What—was she doing?

HALE: She was rockin' back and forth. She had her apron in her hand and was kind of—pleating it.

COUNTY ATTORNEY: And how did she—look?

HALE: Well, she looked queer.

COUNTY ATTORNEY: How do you mean—queer?

HALE: Well, as if she didn't know what she was going to do next. And kind of done up.

COUNTY ATTORNEY: How did she seem to feel about your coming?

HALE: Why, I don't think she minded—one way or other. She didn't pay much attention. I said, "How do, Mrs. Wright, it's cold, ain't it?" And she said, "Is it?"—and went on kind of pleating at her apron. Well, I was surprised; she didn't ask me to come up to the stove, or to set down, but just sat there, not even looking at me, so I said, "I want to see John." And then she—laughed. I guess you would call it a laugh. I thought of Harry and the team outside, so I said a little sharp: "Can't I see John?" "No," she says, kind o' dull like. "Ain't he home?" says I. "Yes," says she, "he's home." "Then why can't I see him?" I asked her, out of patience. "'Cause he's dead," says she. "*Dead?*" says I. She just nodded her head, not getting a bit excited, but rockin' back and forth. "Why—where is he?" says I, not knowing what to say. She just pointed upstairs—like that (*himself pointing to the room above*). I got up, with the idea of going up there. I walked from there to here—then I says, "Why, what did he die of?" "He died of a rope around his neck," says she, and just went on pleatin' at her apron. Well, I went out and called Harry. I thought I might—need help. We went upstairs, and there he was lyin'—

COUNTY ATTORNEY: I think I'd rather have you go into that upstairs, where you can point it all out. Just go on now with the rest of the story.

HALE: Well, my first thought was to get that rope off. I looked . . . (*Stops, his face twitches.*) . . . but Harry, he went up to him, and he said, "No, he's dead all right, and we'd better not touch anything." So we went back downstairs. She was still sitting that same way. "Has anybody been notified?" I asked. "No," says she, unconcerned. "Who did this, Mrs. Wright?" said Harry. He said it businesslike—and she stopped pleatin' of her apron. "I don't know," she says. "You don't *know?*" says Harry. "No," says she, "Weren't you sleepin' in the bed with him?" says Harry. "Yes," says she, "but

I was on the inside." "Somebody slipped a rope round his neck and strangled him, and you didn't wake up?" says Harry. "I didn't wake up," she said after him. We must 'a looked as if we didn't see how that could be, for after a minute she said, "I sleep sound." Harry was going to ask her more questions, but I said maybe we ought to let her tell her story first to the coroner, or the sheriff, so Harry went fast as he could to Rivers' place, where there's a telephone.

COUNTY ATTORNEY:  And what did Mrs. Wright do when she knew that you had gone for the coroner?

HALE:  She moved from that chair to this over here . . . (*Pointing to a small chair in the corner.*) . . . and just sat there with her hands held together and looking down. I got a feeling that I ought to make some conversation, so I said I had come in to see if John wanted to put in a telephone, and at that she started to laugh, and then she stopped and looked at me—scared. (*The County Attorney, who has had his notebook out, makes a note.*) I dunno, maybe it wasn't scared. I wouldn't like to say it was. Soon Harry got back, and then Dr. Lloyd came, and you, Mr. Peters, and so I guess that's all I know that you don't.

COUNTY ATTORNEY (*looking around*):  I guess we'll go upstairs first—and then out to the barn and around there. (*To the Sheriff.*) You're convinced that there was nothing important here—nothing that would point to any motive?

SHERIFF:  Nothing here but kitchen things.

(*The County Attorney, after again looking around the kitchen, opens the door of a cupboard closet. He gets up on a chair and looks on a shelf. Pulls his hand away, sticky.*)

COUNTY ATTORNEY:  Here's a nice mess.

(*The women draw nearer.*)

MRS. PETERS (*to the other woman*):  Oh, her fruit; it did freeze. (*To the Lawyer.*) She worried about that when it turned so cold. She said the fir'd go out and her jars would break.

SHERIFF:  Well, can you beat the women! Held for murder and worryin' about her preserves.

COUNTY ATTORNEY:  I guess before we're through she may have something more serious than preserves to worry about.

HALE:  Well, women are used to worrying over trifles.

(*The two women move a little closer together.*)

COUNTY ATTORNEY (*with the gallantry of a young politician*): And yet, for all their worries, what would we do without the ladies? (*The women do not unbend. He goes to the sink, takes a dipperful of water from the pail and, pouring it into a basin, washes his hands. Starts to wipe them on the roller towel, turns it for a cleaner place.*) Dirty towels! (*Kicks his foot against the pans under the sink.*) Not much of a housekeeper, would you say, ladies?

MRS. HALE (*stiffly*): There's a great deal of work to be done on a farm.

COUNTY ATTORNEY: To be sure. And yet . . . (*With a little bow to her.*) . . . I know there are some Dickson county farmhouses which do not have such roller towels. (*He gives it a pull to expose its full length again.*)

MRS. HALE: Those towels get dirty awful quick. Men's hands aren't always as clean as they might be.

COUNTY ATTORNEY: Ah, loyal to your sex, I see. But you and Mrs. Wright were neighbors. I suppose you were friends, too.

MRS. HALE (*shaking her head*): I've not seen much of her of late years. I've not been in this house—it's more than a year.

COUNTY ATTORNEY: And why was that? You didn't like her?

MRS. HALE: I liked her all well enough. Farmers' wives have their hands full, Mr. Henderson. And then—

COUNTY ATTORNEY: Yes—?

MRS. HALE (*looking about*): It never seemed a very cheerful place.

COUNTY ATTORNEY: No—it's not cheerful. I shouldn't say she had the homemaking instinct.

MRS. HALE: Well, I don't know as Wright had, either.

COUNTY ATTORNEY: You mean that they didn't get on very well?

MRS. HALE: No, I don't mean anything. But I don't think a place'd be any cheerfuler for John Wright's being in it.

COUNTY ATTORNEY: I'd like to talk more of that a little later. I want to get the lay of things upstairs now. (*He goes to the left, where three steps lead to a stair door.*)

SHERIFF: I suppose anything Mrs. Peters does'll be all right. She was to take in some clothes for her, you know, and a few little things. We left in such a hurry yesterday.

COUNTY ATTORNEY: Yes, but I would like to see what you take, Mrs. Peters, and keep an eye out for anything that might be of use to us.

MRS. PETERS: Yes, Mr. Henderson.

(*The women listen to the men's steps on the stairs, then look about the kitchen.*)

MRS. HALE:   I'd hate to have men coming into my kitchen, snooping around and criticizing. (*She arranges the pans under sink which the Lawyer had shoved out of place.*)

MRS. PETERS:   Of course it's no more than their duty.

MRS. HALE:   Duty's all right, but I guess that deputy sheriff that came out to make the fire might have got a little of this on. (*Gives the roller towel a pull.*) Wish I'd thought of that sooner. Seems mean to talk about her for not having things slicked up when she had to come away in such a hurry.

MRS. PETERS (*who has gone to a small table in the left rear corner of the room, and lifted one end of a towel that covers a pan*):   She had bread set. (*Stands still.*)

MRS. HALE (*eyes fixed on a loaf of bread beside the breadbox, which is on a low shelf at the other side of the room. Moves slowly toward it*):   She was going to put this in there. (*Picks up loaf, then abruptly drops it. In a manner of returning to familiar things.*) It's a shame about her fruit. I wonder if it's all gone. (*Gets up on the chair and looks.*) I think there's some here that's all right, Mrs. Peters. Yes—here; (*Holding it toward the window.*) this is cherries, too. (*Looking again.*) I declare I believe that's the only one. (*Gets down, bottle in her hand. Goes to the sink and wipes it off on the outside.*) She'll feel awful bad after all her hard work in the hot weather. I remember the afternoon I put up my cherries last summer. (*She puts the bottle on the big kitchen table, center of the room, front table. With a sigh, is about to sit down in the rocking chair. Before she is seated realizes what chair it is; with a slow look at it, steps back. The chair, which she has touched, rocks back and forth.*)

MRS. PETERS:   Well, I must get those things from the front room closet. (*She goes to the door at the right, but after looking into the other room steps back.*) You coming with me, Mrs. Hale? You could help me carry them. (*They go into the other room; reappear, Mrs. Peters carrying a dress and skirt, Mrs. Hale following with a pair of shoes.*)

MRS. PETERS:   My, it's cold in there. (*She puts the cloth on the big table, and hurries to the stove.*)

MRS. HALE (*examining the skirt*):   Wright was close. I think maybe that's why she kept so much to herself. She didn't even belong to the Ladies' Aid. I suppose she felt she couldn't do her part, and then you don't enjoy things when you feel shabby. She used to wear pretty clothes and be lively, when she was Minnie Foster, one of the town girls singing in the choir. But that—oh, that was thirty years ago. This all you was to take in?

MRS. PETERS: She said she wanted an apron. Funny thing to want, for there isn't much to get you dirty in jail, goodness knows. But I suppose just to make her feel more natural. She said they was in the top drawer in this cupboard. Yes, here. And then her little shawl that always hung behind the door. (*Opens stair door and looks.*) Yes, here it is. (*Quickly shuts door leading upstairs.*)

MRS. HALE (*abruptly moving toward her*): Mrs. Peters?

MRS. PETERS: Yes, Mrs. Hale?

MRS. HALE: Do you think she did it?

MRS. PETERS (*in a frightened voice*): Oh, I don't know.

MRS. HALE: Well, I don't think she did. Asking for an apron and her little shawl. Worrying about her fruit.

MRS. PETERS (*starts to speak, glances up, where footsteps are heard in the room above. In a low voice*): Mr. Peters says it looks bad for her. Mr. Henderson is awful sarcastic in speech, and he'll make fun of her sayin' she didn't wake up.

MRS. HALE: Well, I guess John Wright didn't wake when they was slipping that rope under his neck.

MRS. PETERS: No, it's strange. It must have been done awful crafty and still. They say it was such a—funny way to kill a man, rigging it all up like that.

MRS. HALE: That's just what Mr. Hale said. There was a gun in the house. He says that's what he can't understand.

MRS. PETERS: Mr. Henderson said coming out that what was needed for the case was a motive; something to show anger, or—sudden feeling.

MRS. HALE (*who is standing by the table*): Well, I don't see any signs of anger around here. (*She puts her hand on the dish towel which lies on the table, stands looking down at the table, one half of which is clean, the other half messy.*) It's wiped here. (*Makes a move as if to finish work, then turns and looks at loaf of bread outside the breadbox. Drops towel. In that voice of coming back to familiar things.*) Wonder how they are finding things upstairs? I hope she had it a little more red-up there. You know, it seems kind of *sneaking*. Locking her up in town and then coming out here and trying to get her own house to turn against her!

MRS. PETERS: But, Mrs. Hale, the law is the law.

MRS. HALE: I s'pose 'tis. (*Unbuttoning her coat.*) Better loosen up your things, Mrs. Peters. You won't feel them when you go out.

*(Mrs. Peters takes off her fur tippet, goes to hang it on hook at the back of room, stands looking at the under part of the small corner table.)*

MRS. PETERS:   She was piecing a quilt. (*She brings the large sewing basket, and they look at the bright pieces.*)

MRS. HALE:   It's log cabin pattern. Pretty, isn't it? I wonder if she was goin' to quilt or just knot it?

*(Footsteps have been heard coming down the stairs. The Sheriff enters, followed by Hale and the County Attorney.)*

SHERIFF:   They wonder if she was going to quilt it or just knot it. (*The men laugh, the women look abashed.*)

COUNTY ATTORNEY (*rubbing his hands over the stove*):   Frank's fire didn't do much up there, did it? Well, let's go out to the barn and get that cleared up.

*(The men go outside.)*

MRS. HALE (*resentfully*):   I don't know as there's anything so strange, our takin' up our time with little things while we're waiting for them to get the evidence. (*She sits down at the big table, smoothing out a block with decision.*) I don't see as it's anything to laugh about.

MRS. PETERS (*apologetically*):   Of course they've got awful important things on their minds. (*Pulls up a chair and joins Mrs. Hale at the table.*)

MRS. HALE (*examining another block*):   Mrs. Peters, look at this one. Here, this is the one she was working on, and look at the sewing! All the rest of it has been so nice and even. And look at this! It's all over the place! Why, it looks as if she didn't know what she was about! (*After she has said this, they look at each other, then started to glance back at the door. After an instant Mrs. Hale has pulled at a knot and ripped the sewing.*)

MRS. PETERS:   Oh, what are you doing, Mrs. Hale?

MRS. HALE (*mildly*):   Just pulling out a stitch or two that's not sewed very good. (*Threading a needle.*) Bad sewing always made me fidgety.

MRS. PETERS (*nervously*):   I don't think we ought to touch things.

MRS. HALE:   I'll just finish up this end. (*Suddenly stopping and leaning forward.*) Mrs. Peters?

MRS. PETERS:   Yes, Mrs. Hale?

MRS. HALE:   What do you suppose she was so nervous about?

MRS. PETERS: Oh—I don't know. I don't know as she was nervous. I sometimes sew awful queer when I'm just tired. (*Mrs. Hale starts to say something, looks at Mrs. Peters, then goes on sewing.*) Well, I must get these things wrapped up. They may be through sooner than we think. (*Putting apron and other things together.*) I wonder where I can find a piece of paper, and string.

MRS. HALE: In that cupboard, maybe.

MRS. PETERS (*looking in cupboard*): Why, here's a birdcage. (*Holds it up.*) Did she have a bird, Mrs. Hale?

MRS. HALE: Why, I don't know whether she did or not—I've not been here for so long. There was a man around last year selling canaries cheap, but I don't know as she took one; maybe she did. She used to sing real pretty herself.

MRS. PETERS (*glancing around*): Seems funny to think of a bird here. But she must have had one, or why should she have a cage? I wonder what happened to it?

MRS. HALE: I s'pose maybe the cat got it.

MRS. PETERS: No, she didn't have a cat. She's got that feeling some people have about cats—being afraid of them. My cat got in her room, and she was real upset and asked me to take it out.

MRS. HALE: My sister Bessie was like that. Queer, ain't it?

MRS. PETERS (*examining the cage*): Why, look at this door. It's broke. One hinge is pulled apart.

MRS. HALE (*looking, too*): Looks as if someone must have been rough with it.

MRS. PETERS: Why, yes. (*She brings the cage forward and puts it on the table.*)

MRS. HALE: I wish if they're going to find any evidence they'd be about it. I don't like this place.

MRS. PETERS: But I'm awful glad you came with me, Mrs. Hale. It would be lonesome for me sitting here alone.

MRS. HALE: It would, wouldn't it? (*Dropping her sewing.*) But I tell you what I do wish, Mrs. Peters. I wish I had come over sometimes when *she* was here. I—(*Looking around the room.*)—wish I had.

MRS. PETERS: But of course you were awful busy, Mrs. Hale—your house and your children.

MRS. HALE: I could've come. I stayed away because it weren't cheerful—and that's why I ought to have come. I—I've never liked this place. Maybe because it's down in a hollow, and you don't see the road. I dunno what it is, but it's a lonesome place and always was.

I wish I had come over to see Minnie Foster sometimes. I can see now—(*Shakes her head.*)

MRS. PETERS:  Well, you mustn't reproach yourself, Mrs. Hale. Somehow we just don't see how it is with other folks until—something comes up.

MRS. HALE:  Not having children makes less work—but it makes a quiet house, and Wright out to work all day, and no company when he did come in. Did you know John Wright, Mrs. Peters?

MRS. PETERS:  Not to know him; I've seen him in town. They say he was a good man.

MRS. HALE:  Yes—good; he didn't drink, and kept his word as well as most, I guess, and paid his debts. But he was a hard man, Mrs. Peters. Just to pass the time of day with him. (*Shivers.*) Like a raw wind that gets to the bone. (*Pauses, her eye falling on the cage.*) I should think she would 'a wanted a bird. But what do you suppose went with it?

MRS. PETERS:  I don't know, unless it got sick and died. (*She reaches over and swings the broken door, swings it again; both women watch it.*)

MRS. HALE:  You weren't raised round here, were you? (*Mrs. Peters shakes her head.*) You didn't know—her?

MRS. PETERS:  Not till they brought her yesterday.

MRS. HALE:  She—come to think of it, she was kind of like a bird herself—real sweet and pretty, but kind of timid and—fluttery. How—she—did—change. (*Silence; then as if struck by a happy thought and relieved to get back to everyday things.*) Tell you what, Mrs. Peters, why don't you take the quilt in with you? It might take up her mind.

MRS. PETERS:  Why, I think that's a real nice idea, Mrs. Hale. There couldn't possibly be any objection to it, could there? Now, just what would I take? I wonder if her patches are in here—and her things. (*They look in the sewing basket.*)

MRS. HALE:  Here's some red. I expect this has got sewing things in it (*Brings out a fancy box.*) What a pretty box. Looks like something somebody would give you. Maybe her scissors are in here. (*Opens box. Suddenly puts her hand to her nose.*) Why—(*Mrs. Peters bends nearer, then turns her face away.*) There's something wrapped up in this piece of silk.

MRS. PETERS:  Why, this isn't her scissors.

MRS. HALE (*lifting the silk*):  Oh, Mrs. Peters—it's—(*Mrs. Peters bends closer.*)

MRS. PETERS:  It's the bird.

MRS. HALE (*jumping up*): But, Mrs. Peters—look at it. Its neck! Look at its neck! It's all—other side *to*.

MRS. PETERS: Somebody—wrung—its neck.

(*Their eyes meet. A look of growing comprehension of horror. Steps are heard outside. Mrs. Hale slips box under quilt pieces, and sinks into her chair. Enter Sheriff and County Attorney. Mrs. Peters rises.*)

COUNTY ATTORNEY (*as one turning from serious things to little pleasantries*): Well, ladies, have you decided whether she was going to quilt it or knot it?

MRS. PETERS: We think she was going to—knot it.

COUNTY ATTORNEY: Well, that's interesting, I'm sure. (*Seeing the birdcage.*) Has the bird flown?

MRS. HALE (*putting more quilt pieces over the box*): We think the—cat got it.

COUNTY ATTORNEY (*preoccupied*): Is there a cat?

(*Mrs. Hale glances in a quick covert way at Mrs. Peters.*)

MRS. PETERS: Well, not now. They're superstitious, you know. They leave.

COUNTY ATTORNEY (*to Sheriff Peters, continuing an interrupted conversation*): No sign at all of anyone having come from the outside. Their own rope. Now let's go up again and go over it piece by piece. (*They start upstairs.*) It would have to have been someone who knew just the—

(*Mrs. Peters sits down. The two women sit there not looking at one another, but as if peering into something and at the same time holding back. When they talk now, it is the manner of feeling their way over strange ground, as if afraid of what they are saying, but as if they cannot help saying it.*)

MRS. HALE: She liked the bird. She was going to bury it in that pretty box.

MRS. PETERS (*in a whisper*): When I was a girl—my kitten—there was a boy took a hatchet, and before my eyes—and before I could get there—(*Covers her face an instant.*) If they hadn't held me back, I would have—(*Catches herself, looks upstairs where steps are heard, falters weakly.*)—hurt him.

MRS. HALE (*with a slow look around her*): I wonder how it would seem never to have had any children around. (*Pause.*) No, Wright wouldn't like the bird—a thing that sang. She used to sing. He killed that, too.

MRS. PETERS (*moving uneasily*): We don't know who killed the bird.

MRS. HALE: I knew John Wright.

MRS. PETERS: It was an awful thing was done in this house that night, Mrs. Hale. Killing a man while he slept, slipping a rope around his neck that choked the life out of him.

MRS. HALE: His neck. Choked the life out of him.

*(Her hand goes out and rests on the birdcage.)*

MRS. PETERS (*with a rising voice*): We don't know who killed him. We don't *know*.

MRS. HALE (*her own feeling not interrupted*): If there'd been years and years of nothing, then a bird to sing to you, it would be awful—still, after the bird was still.

MRS. PETERS (*something within her speaking*): I know what stillness is. When we homesteaded in Dakota, and my first baby died—after he was two years old, and me with no other then—

MRS. HALE (*moving*): How soon do you suppose they'll be through, looking for evidence?

MRS. PETERS: I know what stillness is. (*Pulling herself back.*) The law has got to punish crime, Mrs. Hale.

MRS. HALE (*not as if answering that*): I wish you'd seen Minnie Foster when she wore a white dress with blue ribbons and stood up there in the choir and sang. (*A look around the room.*) Oh, I *wish* I'd come over here once in a while! That was a crime! That was a crime! Who's going to punish that?

MRS. PETERS (*looking upstairs*): We mustn't—take on.

MRS. HALE: I might have known she needed help! I know how things can be—for women. I tell you, it's queer, Mrs. Peters. We live close together and we live far apart. We all go through the same things—it's all just a different kind of the same thing. (*Brushes her eyes, noticing the bottle of fruit, reaches out for it.*) If I was you, I wouldn't tell her her fruit was gone. Tell her it *ain't*. Tell her it's all right. Take this in to prove it to her. She—she may never know whether it was broke or not.

MRS. PETERS (*takes the bottle, looks about for something to wrap it in; takes petticoat from the clothes brought from the other room, very nervously begins winding this around the bottle. In a false voice*): My, it's a good thing the men couldn't hear us. Wouldn't they just laugh! Getting all stirred up over a little thing like a—

dead canary. As if that could have anything to do with—with—
wouldn't they *laugh!*

*(The men are heard coming downstairs.)*

MRS. HALE *(under her breath)*: Maybe they would—maybe they
wouldn't.

COUNTY ATTORNEY: No, Peters, it's all perfectly clear except a reason for doing it. But you know juries when it comes to women. If
there was some definite thing. Something to show—something to
make a story about—a thing that would connect up with this
strange way of doing it.

*(The women's eyes meet for an instant. Enter Hale from
outer door.)*

HALE: Well, I've got the team around. Pretty cold out there.

COUNTY ATTORNEY: I'm going to stay here awhile by myself. *(To
the Sheriff.)* You can send Frank out for me, can't you? I want to
go over everything. I'm not satisfied that we can't do better.

SHERIFF: Do you want to see what Mrs. Peters is going to take in?

*(The Lawyer goes to the table, picks up the apron, laughs.)*

COUNTY ATTORNEY: Oh I guess they're not very dangerous things
the ladies have picked up. *(Moves a few things about, disturbing
the quilt pieces which cover the box. Steps back.)* No, Mrs. Peters
doesn't need supervising. For that matter, a sheriff's wife is married
to the law. Ever think of it that way, Mrs. Peters?

MRS. PETERS: Not—just that way.

SHERIFF *(chuckling)*: Married to the law. *(Moves toward the other
room.)* I just want you to come in here a minute, George. We ought
to take a look at these windows.

COUNTY ATTORNEY *(scoffingly)*: Oh, windows!

SHERIFF: We'll be right out, Mr. Hale.

*(Hale goes outside. The Sheriff follows the County Attorney
into the other room. Then Mrs. Hale rises, hands tight together, looking intensely at Mrs. Peters, whose eyes take a
slow turn, finally meeting, Mrs. Hale's. A moment Mrs. Hale
holds her, then her own eyes point the way to where the box is
concealed. Suddenly Mrs. Peters throws back quilt pieces and
tries to put the box in the bag she is wearing. It is too big. She*

*opens box, starts to take the bird out, cannot touch it, goes to pieces, stands there helpless. Sound of a knob turning in the other room. Mrs. Hale snatches the box and puts it in the pocket of her big coat. Enter County Attorney and Sheriff.)*

COUNTY ATTORNEY (*facetiously*): Well, Henry, at least we found out that she was not going to quilt it. She was going to—what is it you call it, ladies?

MRS. HALE (*her hand against her pocket*): We call it—knot it, Mr. Henderson.

CURTAIN

—*1917*

## *Tennessee Williams* (1911–1983)

*Tennessee Williams was the first important American playwright to emerge in the post–World War II period. Born Thomas Lanier Williams and raised in St. Louis, he took his professional name from his mother's southern forebears. Williams studied at the University of Missouri and Washington University, ultimately completing a degree in drama at the University of Iowa. After staging some of his early one-act plays with the Group Theater (later known as the Actors Studio), Williams first came to larger public attention with* The Glass Menagerie, *which won a Drama Critics Circle award in 1945.* The Glass Menagerie *is clearly autobiographical, drawing on Williams's memories of life with his faded southern belle mother and his tragically disturbed sister, Rose, who ultimately had to be institutionalized; and subsequent plays draw on Williams's life and his southern roots. In 1947* A Streetcar Named Desire *received the Pulitzer Prize, the first of two Williams would win in a forty-year career.* A Streetcar Named Desire, *which starred the young Marlon Brando on stage and film, is, in contrast to* The Glass Menagerie, *a brutally naturalistic tragedy in which no romantic illusions are allowed to survive. Both Jessica Tandy, who originated the stage role, and Vivien Leigh, who starred in the film, were acclaimed for their portrayals of Blanche DuBois. Williams's plays are constantly revived in little theaters and on Broadway. In the last decade both* A Streetcar Named Desire, *with Alec Baldwin, and* Cat on a Hot Tin Roof, *starring Kathleen Turner, completed successful New York engagements, and 2005 saw yet another Broadway revival of* The Glass Menagerie, *starring Jessica Lange. Some of the film adaptations of Williams's plays, several of which have screenplays written by the author, remain classics, especially Elia Kazan's version of* A Streetcar Named Desire. *Williams published his autobiography in 1975. A fascinating collection of his correspondence, which gives insight into both his concerns as a writer and his intensely troubled personal life, appeared in 2000.*

# The Glass Menagerie

*nobody, not even the rain, has such small hand.*

*e.e. cummings*

## List of Characters

Amanda Wingfield, *the mother.—A little woman of great but confused vitality clinging frantically to another time and place. Her characterization must be carefully created, not copied from type. She is not paranoiac, but her life is paranoia. There is much to admire in Amanda, and as much to love and pity as there is to laugh at. Certainly she has endurance and a kind of heroism, and though her foolishness makes her unwittingly cruel at times, there is tenderness in her slight person.*

Laura Wingfield, *her daughter.—Amanda, having failed to establish contact with reality, continues to live vitally in her illusions, but Laura's situation is even graver. A childhood illness has left her crippled, one leg slightly shorter than the other, and held in a brace. This defect need not be more than suggested on the stage. Stemming from this, Laura's separation increases till she is like a piece of her own glass collection, too exquisitely fragile to move from the shelf.*

Tom Wingfield, *her son.—And the narrator of the play. A poet with a job in a warehouse. His nature is not remorseless, but to escape from a trap he has to act without pity.*

Jim O'Connor, *the gentleman caller.—A nice, ordinary young man.*

Scene: *An alley in St. Louis.*

Part 1. *Preparation for a Gentleman Caller.*

Part 2. *The Gentleman Calls.*

Part 3. *Now and the Past.*

## Scene 1

*The Wingfield apartment is in the rear of the building, one of those vast hive-like conglomerations of cellular living-units that flower as warty growths in overcrowded urban centers of lower middle-class population and are symptomatic of the impulse of this largest and fundamentally enslaved section of American society to avoid fluidity and differentiation and to exist and function as one interfused mass of automatism.*

*The apartment faces an alley and is entered by a fire-escape, a structure whose name is a touch of accidental poetic truth, for all of these huge buildings are always burning with the slow and implacable fires of human desperation. The fire escape is included in the set—that is, the landing of it and steps descending from it.*

*The scene is memory and is therefore non-realistic. Memory takes a lot of poetic license. It omits some details; others are exaggerated, according to the emotional value of the articles it touches, for memory is seated predominantly in the heart. The interior is therefore rather dim and poetic.*

*At the rise of the curtain, the audience is faced with the dark, grim rear wall of the Wingfield tenement. This building, which runs parallel to the footlights, is flanked on both sides by dark, narrow alleys which run into murky canyons of tangled clotheslines, garbage cans and the sinister latticework of neighboring fire-escapes. It is up and down these side alleys that exterior entrances and exits are made, during the play. At the end of Tom's opening commentary, the dark tenement wall slowly reveals (by means of a transparency) the interior of the ground floor Wingfield apartment.*

*Downstage is the living room, which also serves as a sleeping room for Laura, the sofa unfolding to make her bed. Upstage, center, and divided by a wide arch or second proscenium with transparent faded portieres (or second curtain), is the dining room. In an old-fashioned what-not in the living room are seen scores of transparent glass animals. A blown-up photograph of the father hangs on the wall of the living room, facing the audience, to the left of the archway. It is the face of a very handsome young man in a doughboy's First World War cap. He is gallantly smiling, ineluctably smiling, as if to say, "I will be smiling forever."*

*The audience hears and sees the opening scene in the dining room through both the transparent wall of the building and the transparent gauze portieres of the diningroom arch. It is during this revealing scene that the fourth wall slowly ascends, out of sight.*

*This transparent exterior wall is not brought down again until the very end of the play, during Tom's final speech.*

*The narrator is an undisguised convention of the play. He takes whatever license with dramatic convention as is convenient to his purposes.*

*Tom enters dressed as a merchant sailor from alley, stage left, and strolls across the front of the stage to the fire-escape. There he stops and lights a cigarette. He addresses the audience.*

TOM: Yes, I have tricks in my pocket, I have things up my sleeve. But I am the opposite of a stage magician. He gives you the illusion that has the appearance of truth. I give you truth in the pleasant disguise of illusion. To begin with, I turn back time. I reverse it to that quaint period, the thirties, when the huge middle class of America was matriculating in a school for the blind. Their eyes had failed them, or they had failed their eyes, and so they were having their fingers pressed forcibly down on the fiery Braille alphabet of a dissolving economy. In Spain there was revolution. Here there was only shouting and confusion. In Spain there was Guernica. Here there were disturbances of labor, sometimes pretty violent, in otherwise peaceful cities such as Chicago, Cleveland, Saint Louis. . . . This is the social background of the play.

(Music.)

The play is memory. Being a memory play, it is dimly lighted, it is sentimental, it is not realistic. In memory everything seems to happen to music. That explains the fiddle in the wings. I am the narrator of the play, and also a character in it. The other characters are my mother, Amanda, my sister, Laura, and a gentleman caller who appears in the final scenes. He is the most realistic character in the play, being an emissary from a world of reality that we were somehow set apart from. But since I have a poet's weakness for symbols, I am using this character also as a symbol; he is the long delayed but always expected something that we live for. There is a fifth character in the play who doesn't appear except in this larger-than-life photograph over the mantel. This is our father who left us a long time ago. He was a telephone man who fell in love with long distances; he gave up his job with the telephone company and skipped the light fantastic out of town. . . . The last we heard of him was a picture post-card from Mazatlan, on the Pacific coast of Mexico, containing a message of two words—"Hello—Good-bye!" and no address. I think the rest of the play will explain itself. . . .

*Amanda's voice becomes audible through the portieres.*

(Legend on Screen: "Où Sont Les Neiges?")°

---

**Où Sont Les Neiges** refrain from a poem by François Villion (1431–1463?): "Where are the snows of yesteryear?"

*He divides the portieres and enters the upstage area. Amanda and Laura are seated at a drop-leaf table. Eating is indicated by gestures without food or utensils. Amanda faces the audience. Tom and Laura are seated in profile. The interior has lit up softly and through the scrim we see Amanda and Laura seated at the table in the upstage area.*

AMANDA (*calling*): Tom?

TOM: Yes, Mother.

AMANDA: We can't say grace until you come to the table!

TOM: Coming, Mother. (*He bows slightly and withdraws, reappearing a few moments later in his place at the table.*)

AMANDA (*to her son*): Honey, don't *push* with your *fingers*. If you have to push with something, the thing to push with is a crust of bread. And chew—chew! Animals have sections in their stomachs which enable them to digest food without mastication, but human beings are supposed to chew their food before they swallow it down. Eat food leisurely, son, and really enjoy it. A well-cooked meal has lots of delicate flavors that have to be held in the mouth for appreciation. So chew your food and give your salivary glands a chance to function!

*(Tom deliberately lays his imaginary fork down and pushes his chair back from the table.)*

TOM: I haven't enjoyed one bite of this dinner because of your constant directions on how to eat it. It's you that makes me rush through meals with your hawk-like attention to every bite I take. Sickening—spoils my appetite—all this discussion of animals' secretion—salivary glands—mastication!

AMANDA (*lightly*): Temperament like a Metropolitan star! (*He rises and crosses downstage.*) You're not excused from the table.

TOM: I am getting a cigarette.

AMANDA: You smoke too much. (*Laura rises.*)

LAURA: I'll bring in the blanc mange.

*(He remains standing with cigarette by the portieres during the following.)*

AMANDA (*rising*): No, sister, no, sister—you be the lady this time and I'll be the darky.

LAURA: I'm already up.

AMANDA: Resume your seat, little sister—I want you to stay fresh and pretty—for gentlemen callers!

LAURA: I'm not expecting any gentlemen callers.

AMANDA (*crossing out to kitchenette. Airily.*): Sometimes they come when they are least expected! Why, I remember one Sunday afternoon in the Blue Mountain—(*Enters kitchenette.*)

TOM: I know what's coming!

LAURA: Yes. But let her tell it.

TOM: Again?

LAURA: She loves to tell it.

*(Amanda returns with bowl of dessert.)*

AMANDA: One Sunday afternoon in Blue Mountain—your mother received—*seventeen!*—gentlemen callers! Why sometimes there weren't chairs enough to accommodate them all. We had to send the nigger over to bring in folding chairs from the parish house.

TOM (*remaining at portieres*): How did you entertain those gentlemen callers?

AMANDA: I understood the art of conversation!

TOM: I bet you could talk.

AMANDA: Girls in those days *knew* how to talk, I can tell you.

TOM: Yes?

(Image: Amanda as a Girl on a Porch Greeting Callers.)

AMANDA: They knew how to entertain their gentlemen callers. It wasn't enough for a girl to be possessed of a pretty face and a graceful figure—although I wasn't slighted in either respect. She also needed to have a nimble wit and a tongue to meet all occasions.

TOM: What did you talk about?

AMANDA: Things of importance going on in the world! Never anything coarse or common or vulgar. (*She addresses Tom as though he were seated in the vacant chair at the table though he remains by portieres. He plays this scene as though he held the book.*) My callers were gentlemen—all! Among my callers were some of the most prominent young planters of the Mississippi Delta—planters and sons of planters!

*(Tom motions for music and a spot of light on Amanda. Her eyes lift, her face glows, her voice becomes rich and elegiac.)*

(Screen Legend: "Où Sont Les Neiges?")

There was young Champ Laughlin who later became vice-president of the Delta Planters Bank. Hadley Stevenson who was drowned in Moon Lake and left his widow one hundred and fifty thousand in Government bonds. There were the Cutrere brothers, Wesley and Bates. Bates was one of my bright particular beaux! He got in a quarrel with that wild Wainright boy. They shot it out on the floor of Moon Lake Casino. Bates was shot through the stomach. Died in the ambulance on his way to Memphis. His widow was also well provided for, came into eight or ten thousand acres, that's all. She married him on the rebound—never loved her—carried my picture on him the night he died! And there was that boy that every girl in the Delta had set her cap for! That beautiful, brilliant young Fitzhugh boy from Green County!

TOM: What did he leave his widow?

AMANDA: He never married! Gracious, you talk as though all of my old admirers had turned up their toes to the daisies!

TOM: Isn't this the first you mentioned that still survives?

AMANDA: That Fitzhugh boy went North and made a fortune—came to be known as the Wolf of Wall Street! He had the Midas touch, whatever he touched turned to gold! And I could have been Mrs. Duncan J. Fitzhugh, mind you! But—I picked your *father!*

LAURA (*rising*): Mother, let me clear the table.

AMANDA: No dear, you go in front and study your typewriter chart. Or practice your shorthand a little. Stay fresh and pretty!—It's almost time for our gentlemen callers to start arriving. (*She flounces girlishly toward the kitchenette.*) How many do you suppose we're going to entertain this afternoon?

(*Tom throws down the paper and jumps up with a groan.*)

LAURA (*alone in the dining room*): I don't believe we're going to receive any, Mother.

AMANDA (*reappearing, airily*): What? No one—not one? You must be joking! (*Laura nervously echoes her laugh. She slips in a fugitive manner through the half-open portieres and draws them gently behind her. A shaft of very clear light is thrown on her face against the faded tapestry of the curtain.*) (*Music: "The Glass Menagerie" Under Faintly.*) (*Lightly*) Not one gentleman caller? It can't be true! There must be a flood, there must have been a tornado!

LAURA: It isn't a flood, it's not a tornado, Mother. I'm just not popular like you were in Blue Mountain. . . . (*Tom utters another groan. Laura glances at him with a faint, apologetic smile. Her voice catching a little*) Mother's afraid I'm going to be an old maid.

(The Scene Dims Out with "Glass Menagerie" Music.)

## SCENE 2

### "LAURA, HAVEN'T YOU EVER LIKED SOME BOY?"

*On the dark stage the screen is lighted with the image of blue roses. Gradually Laura's figure becomes apparent and the screen goes out. The music subsides. Laura is seated in the delicate ivory chair at the small clawfoot table. She wears a dress of soft violet material for a kimono—her hair tied back from her forehead with a ribbon. She is washing and polishing her collection of glass.*

*Amanda appears on the fire-escape steps. At the sound of her ascent, Laura catches her breath, thrusts the bowl of ornaments away and seats herself stiffly before the diagram of the typewriter keyboard as though it held her spellbound. Something has happened to Amanda. It is written in her face as she climbs to the landing: a look that is grim and hopeless and a little absurd.*

*She has one of those cheap or imitation velvety-looking cloth coats with imitation fur collar. Her hat is five or six years old, one of those dreadful cloche hats that were worn in the late twenties, and she is clasping an enormous black patent-leather pocketbook with nickel clasp and initials. This is her full-dress outfit, the one she usually wears to the D.A.R.*

*Before entering she looks through the door. She purses her lips, opens her eyes wide, rolls them upward and shakes her head. Then she slowly lets herself in the door. Seeing her mother's expression Laura touches her lips with a nervous gesture.*

LAURA: Hello, Mother, I was—(*She makes a nervous gesture toward the chart on the wall. Amanda leans against the shut door and stares are Laura with a martyred look.*)

AMANDA: Deception? Deception? (*She slowly removes her hat and gloves, continuing the swift suffering stare. She lets the hat and gloves fall on the floor—a bit of acting.*)

LAURA (*shakily*): How was the D.A.R. meeting? (*Amanda slowly opens her purse and removes a dainty white handkerchief which she shakes out delicately and delicately touches to her lips and nostrils.*) Didn't you go to the D.A.R. meeting, Mother?

AMANDA (*faintly, almost inaudibly*): —No.—No. (*Then more forcibly*) I did not have the strength—to go to the D.A.R. In fact, I did not have the courage. I waited to find a hole in the ground and hide myself in it forever! (*She crosses slowly to the wall and removes the diagram of the typewriter keyboard. She holds it in front of her for a second, starting at it sweetly and sorrowfully— then bites her lips and tears it in two pieces.*)

LAURA (*faintly*): Why did you do that, Mother? (*Amanda repeats the same procedure with the chart of the Gregg Alphabet.*) Why are you—

AMANDA: Why? Why? How old are you, Laura?

LAURA: Mother, you know my age.

AMANDA: I thought that you were an adult; it seems that I was mistaken. (*She crosses slowly to the sofa and sinks down and stares at Laura.*)

LAURA: Please don't stare at me, Mother.

(*Amanda closes her eyes and lowers her head. Count ten.*)

AMANDA: What are we going to do, what is going to become of us, what is the future?

(*Count ten.*)

LAURA: Has something happened, Mother? (*Amanda draws a long breath and takes out the handkerchief again. Dabbing process.*) Mother, has—something happened?

AMANDA: I'll be right in a minute. I'm just bewildered—(*count five*) —by life. . . .

LAURA: Mother, I wish you would tell me what's happened.

AMANDA: As you know, I was supposed to be inducted into my office at the D.A.R. this afternoon. (*Image: A Swarm of Typewriters.*) But I stopped off at Rubicam's Business College to speak to your teachers about your having a cold and ask them what progress they thought you were making down there.

LAURA: Oh. . . .

AMANDA: I went to the typing instructor and introduced myself as your mother. She didn't know who you were. Wingfield, she said. We don't have any such student enrolled at the school! I assured her she did, that you had been going to classes since early in January.

"I wonder," she said, "if you could be talking about that terribly shy little girl who dropped out of school after only a few days' attendance?" "No," I said, "Laura, my daughter, has been going to school every day for the past six weeks!" "Excuse me," she said. She took the attendance book out and there was your name, unmistakably printed, and all the dates you were absent until they decided that you had dropped out of school. I still said, "No, there must have been some mistake! There must have been some mix-up in the records!" And she said, "No—I remember her perfectly now. Her hand shook so that she couldn't hit the right keys! The first time we gave a speed-test, she broke down completely—was sick at the stomach and almost had to be carried into the wash-room! After that morning she never showed up any more. We phoned the house but never got any answer"—while I was working at Famous and Barr, I suppose demonstrating those—Oh! I felt so weak I could barely keep on my feet. I had to sit down while they got me a glass of water! Fifty dollars' tuition, all of our plans—my hopes and ambitions for you—just gone up the spout, just gone up the spout like that. (*Laura draws a long breath and gets awkwardly to her feet. She crosses to the victrola and winds it up.*) What are you doing?

LAURA:  Oh! (*She releases the handle and returns to her seat.*)

AMANDA:  Laura, where have you been going when you've gone out pretending that you were going to business college?

LAURA:  I've just been going out walking.

AMANDA:  That's not true.

LAURA:  It is. I just went walking.

AMANDA:  Walking? Walking? In winter? Deliberately courting pneumonia in that light coat? Where did you walk to, Laura?

LAURA:  It was the lesser of two evils, Mother. (*Image: Winter Scene in Park.*) I couldn't go back up. I—threw up—on the floor!

AMANDA:  From half past seven till after five thirty every day you mean to tell me you walked around in the park, because you wanted to make me think that you were still going to Rubicam's Business College?

LAURA:  It wasn't as bad as it sounds. I went inside places to get warmed up.

AMANDA:  Inside where?

LAURA:  I went in the art museum and the birdhouses at the Zoo. I visited the penguins every day! Sometimes I did without lunch and went to the movies. Lately I've been spending most of my afternoons in the Jewel-box, that big glass house where they raise the tropical flowers.

AMANDA:  You did all this to deceive me, just for the deception? (*Laura looks down.*) Why?

LAURA:  Mother, when you're disappointed, you get that awful suffering look on your face. Like the picture of Jesus' mother in the museum!

AMANDA:  Hush!

LAURA:  I couldn't face it.

(*Pause: A whisper of strings.*)

(Legend: "The Crust of Humility.")

AMANDA (*hopelessly fingering the huge pocketbook*):  So what are we going to do the rest of our lives? Stay home and watch the parades go by? Amuse ourselves with the glass menagerie, darling? Eternally play those worn-out phonograph records your father left as a painful reminder of him? We won't have a business career— we've given that up because it gave us nervous indigestion! (*Laughs wearily.*) What is there left but dependency all our lives? I know so well what becomes of unmarried women who aren't prepared to occupy a position. I've seen such pitiful cases in the South—barely tolerated spinsters living upon the grudging patronage of sister's husband or brother's wife!—stuck away in some little mousetrap of a room—encouraged by one inlaw to visit another— little birdlike women without any nest—eating the crust of humility all their life! Is that the future that we've mapped out for ourselves? I swear it's the only alternative I can think of! It isn't a very pleasant alternative, is it? Of course—some girls *do marry*. (*Laura twists her hands nervously.*) Haven't you ever liked some boy?

LAURA:  Yes, I liked one once. (*Rises.*) I came across his picture a while ago.

AMANDA (*with some interest*):  He gave you his picture?

LAURA:  No, it's in the year-book.

AMANDA (*disappointed*):  Oh—a high-school boy.

(Screen Image: Jim as a High-School Hero Bearing a Silver Cup.)

LAURA:  Yes. His name was Jim. (*Laura lifts the heavy annual from the clawfoot table.*) Here he is in *The Pirates of Penzance*.

AMANDA (*absently*):  The what?

LAURA:  The operetta the senior class put on. He had a wonderful voice and we sat across the aisle from each other Mondays, Wednesdays, and Fridays in the Aud. Here he is with the silver cup for debating! See his grin?

AMANDA (*absently*):  He must have had a jolly disposition.

LAURA: He used to call me—Blue Roses.

(Image: Blue Roses.)

AMANDA: Why did he call you such a name as that?

LAURA: When I had that attack of pleurosis—he asked me what was the matter when I came back. I said pleurosis—he thought I said Blue Roses! So that's what he always called me after that. Whenever he saw me, he'd holler, "Hello, Blue Roses!" I didn't care for the girl that he went out with. Emily Meisenbach. Emily was the best-dressed girl at Soldan. She never struck me, though, as being sincere. . . . It says in the Personal Section—they're engaged. That's—six years ago! They must be married by now.

AMANDA: Girls that aren't cut out for business careers usually wind up married to some nice man. (*Gets up with a spark of revival.*) Sister, that's what you'll do!

(*Laura utters a startled, doubtful laugh. She reaches quickly for a piece of glass.*)

LAURA: But, Mother—

AMANDA: Yes? (*Crossing to photograph.*)

LAURA (*in a tone of frightened apology*): I'm—crippled!

(Image: Screen.)

AMANDA: Nonsense! Laura, I've told you never, never to use that word. Why, you're not crippled, you just have a little defect— hardly noticeable, even! When people have some slight disadvantage like that, they cultivate other things to make up for it—develop charm—and vivacity—and—*charm!* That's all you have to do! (*She turns again to the photograph.*) One thing your father had plenty of—was *charm!*

(*Tom motions to the fiddle in the wings.*)

(The Scene Fades Out with Music.)

## SCENE 3

(LEGEND ON THE SCREEN: "AFTER THE FIASCO—")

*Tom speaks from the fire-escape landing.*

TOM: After the fiasco at Rubicam's Business College, the idea of getting a gentleman caller for Laura began to play a more important part in Mother's calculations. It became an obsession. Like some archetype of the universal unconscious, the image of the gentleman caller haunted our small apartment. . . . (*Image: Young Man at Door with Flowers.*) An evening at home rarely passed without some allusion to this image, this specter, this hope. . . . Even when he wasn't mentioned, his presence hung in Mother's preoccupied look and in my sister's frightened, apologetic manner—hung like a sentence passed upon the Wingfields! Mother was a woman of action as well as words. She began to take logical steps in the planned direction. Late that winter and in the early spring—realizing that extra money would be needed to properly feather the nest and plume the bird—she conducted a vigorous campaign on the telephone, roping in subscribers to one of those magazines for matrons called *The Home-maker's Companion,* the type of journal that features the serialized sublimation of ladies of letters who think in terms of delicate cup-like breasts, slim, tapering waists, rich, creamy thighs, eyes like wood-smoke in autumn, fingers that soothe and caress like strains of music, bodies as powerful as Etruscan sculpture.

(Screen Image: Glamour Magazine Cover.)

*(Amanda enters with phone on long extension cord. She is spotted in the dim stage.)*

**AMANDA:** Ida Scott? This is Amanda Wingfield! We *missed* you at the D.A.R. last Monday! I said to myself: She's probably suffering with that sinus condition! How is that sinus condition? Horrors! Heaven have mercy!—You're a Christian martyr, yes, that's what you are, a Christian martyr! Well, I just now happened to notice that your subscription to the *Companion's* about to expire! Yes, it expires with the next issue, honey!—just when that wonderful new serial by Bessie Mae Hopper is getting off to such an exciting start. Oh, honey, it's something that you can't miss! You remember how *Gone With the Wind* took everybody by storm? You simply couldn't go out if you hadn't read it. All everybody *talked* was Scarlett O'Hara. Well, this is a book that critics already compare to *Gone With the Wind.* It's the *Gone With the Wind* of the post-World War generation!—What?—Burning? Oh, honey, don't let them burn, go take a look in the oven and I'll hold the wire! Heavens—I think she's hung up!

(Dim Out.)

(Legend on Screen: "You Think I'm in Love with Continental Shoemakers?")

*(Before the stage is lighted, the violent voices of Tom and Amanda are heard. They are quarreling behind the portieres. In front of them stands Laura with clenched hands and panicky expression. A clear pool of light on her figure throughout this scene.)*

**TOM:**   What in Christ's name am I—

**AMANDA** *(shrilly)*:   Don't you use that—

**TOM:**   Supposed to do!

**AMANDA:**   Expression! Not in my—

**TOM:**   Ohhh!

**AMANDA:**   Presence! Have you gone out of your senses?

**TOM:**   I have, that's true, *driven* out!

**AMANDA:**   What is the mater with you, you—big—big—IDIOT!

**TOM:**   Look—I've got *no thing,* no single thing—

**AMANDA:**   Lower your voice?

**TOM:**   In my life here that I can call my OWN! Everything is—

**AMANDA:**   Stop that shouting!

**TOM:**   Yesterday you confiscated my books! You had the nerve to—

**AMANDA:**   I took that horrible novel back to the library—yes! That hideous book by that insane Mr. Lawrence. *(Tom laughs wildly.)* I cannot control the output of diseased minds or people who cater to them—*(Tom laughs still more wildly.)* BUT I WON'T ALLOW SUCH FILTH BROUGHT INTO MY HOUSE! No, no, no, no, no!

**TOM:**   House, house! Who pays rent on it, who makes a slave of himself to—

**AMANDA** *(fairly screeching)*:   Don't you DARE to—

**TOM:**   No, no, *I* musn't say things! *I've* got to just—

**AMANDA:**   Let me tell you—

**TOM:**   I don't want to hear any more! *(He tears the portieres open. The upstage area is lit with a turgid smoky red glow.)*

*Amanda's hair is in metal curlers and she wears a very old bathrobe, much too large for her slight figure, a relic of the faithless Mr. Wingfield. An upright typewriter and a mild disarray of manuscripts are on the drop-leaf table. The quarrel was probably precipitated by Amanda's interruption of his creative labor. A chair lying overthrown on the floor. Their gesticulating shadows are cast on the ceiling by the fiery glow.*

AMANDA: You *will* hear more, you—

TOM: No, I won't hear more, I'm going out!

AMANDA: You come right back in—

TOM: Out, out out! Because I'm—

AMANDA: Come back here, Tom Wingfield! I'm not through talking to you!

TOM: Oh, go—

LAURA (*desperately*): Tom!

AMANDA: You're going to listen, and no more insolence from you! I'm at the end of my patience! (*He comes back toward her.*)

TOM: What do you think I'm at? Aren't I supposed to have any patience to reach the end of, Mother? I know, I know. It seems unimportant to you, what I'm *doing*—what I *want* to do—having a little *difference* between them! You don't think that—

AMANDA: I think you've been doing things that you're ashamed of. That's why you act like this. I don't believe that you go every night to movies. Nobody goes to the movies night after night. Nobody in their right minds goes to movies as often as you pretend to. People don't go to the movies at nearly midnight, and movies don't let out at two A.M. Come in stumbling. Muttering to yourself like a maniac! You get three hours' sleep and then go to work. Oh, I can picture the way you're doing down there. Moping, doping, because you're in no condition.

TOM (*wildly*): No, I'm in no condition!

AMANDA: What right have you got to jeopardize your job? Jeopardize the security of us all? How do you think we'd manage if you were—

TOM: Listen! You think I'm crazy *about the warehouse?* (*He bends fiercely toward her slight figure.*) You think I'm in love with the Continental Shoemakers? You think I want to spend fifty-five *years* down there in that—*celotex interior!* with—*fluorescent—tubes!* Look! I'd rather somebody picked up a crowbar and battered out my brains than go back mornings! I *go!* Every time you come in yelling that God damn *"Rise and Shine!"* *"Rise and Shine!"* I say to myself "How *lucky dead* people are!" But I get up. I *go!* For sixty-five dollars a month I gave up all that I dream of doing and being *ever!* And you say self—*self's* all I ever think of. Why, listen, if self is what I thought of, Mother, I'd be where he is—GONE! (*Pointing to father's picture.*) As far as the system of transportation reaches! (*He starts past her. She grabs his arm.*) Don't grab at me, Mother!

AMANDA: Where are you going?

TOM: I'm going to the *movies!*

AMANDA: I don't believe that lie!

TOM (*crouching toward her, overtowering her tiny figure. She backs away, gasping*): I'm going to opium dens! Yes, opium dens, dens of vice and criminals' hang-outs, Mother. I've joined the Hogan gang, I'm a hired assassin, I carry a tommy-gun in a violin case! I run a string of cat-houses in the Valley. They call me Killer, Killer Wingfield, I'm leading a double-life, a simple, honest warehouse worker by day, by night a dynamic *czar* of the *underworld, Mother.* I go to gambling casinos, I spin away fortunes on the roulette table! I wear a patch over one eye and a false mustache, sometimes I put on green whiskers. On those occasions they call me—*El Diablo!* Oh, I could tell you things to make you sleepless! My enemies plan to dynamite this place. They're going to blow us all sky-high some night! I'll be glad, very happy, and so will you! You'll go up, up on a broomstick, over Blue Mountain with seventeen gentlemen callers! You ugly—babbling old—*witch.* . . . (*He goes through a series of violent, clumsy movements, seizing his overcoat, lunging to the door, pulling it fiercely open. The women watch him, aghast. His arm catches in the sleeve of the coat as he struggles to pull it on. For a moment he is pinioned by the bulky garment. With an outraged groan he tears the coat off again, splitting the shoulders of it, and hurls it across the room. It strikes against the shelf of Laura's glass collection, there is a tinkle of shattering glass. Laura cries out as if wounded.*)

(Music Legend: "The Glass Menagerie.")

LAURA (*shrilly*): My glass! —menagerie. . . . (*She covers her face and turns away.*)

(*But Amanda is still stunned and stupefied by the "ugly witch" so that she barely notices this occurrence. Now she recovers her speech.*)

AMANDA (*in an awful voice*): I won't speak to you—until you apologize! (*She crosses through the portieres and draws them together behind her. Tom is left with Laura. Laura clings weakly to the mantel with her face averted. Tom stares at her stupidly for a moment. Then he crosses to shelf. Drops awkwardly to his knees to collect the fallen glass, glancing at Laura as if he would speak but couldn't.*)

("The Glass Menagerie" steals in as the Scene Dims Out.)

## SCENE 4

*The interior is dark. Faint light in the alley. A deep-voiced bell in a church is tolling the hour by five as the scene commences.*

*Tom appears at the top of the alley. After each solemn boom of the bell in the tower, he shakes a little noise-maker or rattle as if to express the tiny spasm of man in contrast to the sustained power and dignity of the Almighty. This and the unsteadiness of his advance make it evident that he has been drinking.*

*As he climbs the few steps to the fire-escape landing light steals up inside. Laura appears in night-dress, observing Tom's empty bed in the front room.*

*Tom fishes in his pockets for the door-key, removing a motley assortment of articles in the search, including a perfect shower of movie-ticket stubs and an empty bottle. At last he finds the key, but just as he about to insert it, it slips from his fingers. He strikes a match and crouches below the door.*

TOM (*bitterly*):   One crack—and it falls through!

*(Laura opens the door.)*

LAURA:   Tom! Tom, what are you doing?
TOM:   Looking for a door-key.
LAURA:   Where have you been all this time?
TOM:   I have been to the movies.
LAURA:   All this time at the movies?
TOM:   There was a very long program. There was a Garbo picture and a Mickey Mouse and a travelogue and a newsreel and a preview of coming attractions. And there was an organ solo and a collection for the milk-fund—simultaneously—which ended up in a terrible fight between a fat lady and an usher!
LAURA (*innocently*):   Did you have to stay through everything?
TOM:   Of course! And, oh, I forgot! There was a big stage show! The headliner on this stage show was Malvolio the Magician. He performed wonderful tricks, many of them, such as pouring water back and forth between pitchers. First it turned to wine and then it turned to beer and then it turned to whiskey. I know it was whiskey it finally turned into because he needed somebody to come

up out of the audience to help him, and I came up—both shows! It was Kentucky Straight Bourbon. A very generous fellow, he gave souvenirs. (*He pulls from his back pocket a shimmering rainbow-colored scarf.*) He gave me this. This is his magic scarf. You can have it, Laura. You wave it over a canary cage and you get a bowl of gold-fish. You wave it over the goldfish bowl and they fly away canaries. . . . But the wonderfulest trick of all was the coffin trick. We nailed him into a coffin and he got out of the coffin without removing one nail. (*He has come inside.*) There is a trick that would come in handy for me—get me out of this 2 by 4 situation! (*Flops onto bed and starts removing shoes.*)

LAURA:  Tom—Shhh!

TOM:  What you shushing me for?

LAURA:  You'll wake up Mother.

TOM:  Goody, goody! Pay 'er back for those "Rise an' Shines." (*Lies down, groaning.*) You know it don't take much intelligence to get yourself into a nailed-up coffin, Laura. But who in hell ever got himself out of one without removing one nail?

(*As if in answer, the father's grinning photograph lights up.*)

(Scene Dims Out.)

*Immediately following: The church bell is heard striking six. At the sixth stroke the alarm clock goes off in Amanda's room, and after a few moments we hear her calling: "Rise and Shine! Rise and Shine! Laura, go tell your brother to rise and shine!"*

TOM (*sitting up slowly*):  I'll rise—but I won't shine.

*(The light increases.)*

AMANDA:  Laura, tell your brother his coffee is ready.

*(Laura slips into front room.)*

LAURA:  Tom! it's nearly seven. Don't make Mother nervous. (*He stares at her stupidly. Beseechingly.*) Tom, speak to Mother this morning. Make up with her, apologize, speak to her!

TOM:  She won't to me. It's her that started not speaking.

LAURA:  If you just say you're sorry she'll start speaking.

TOM:  Her not speaking—is that such a tragedy?

LAURA:  Please—please!

AMANDA (*calling from kitchenette*):   Laura, are you going to do what I asked you to do, or do I have to get dressed and go out myself?

LAURA:   Going, going—soon as I get on my coat! (*She pulls on a shapeless felt hat with nervous, jerky movement, pleadingly glancing at Tom. Rushes awkwardly for coat. The coat is one of Amanda's, inaccurately made-over, the sleeves too short for Laura.*) Butter and what else?

AMANDA (*entering upstage*):   Just butter. Tell them to charge it.

LAURA:   Mother, they make such faces when I do that.

AMANDA:   Sticks and stones may break my bones, but the expression of Mr. Garfinkel's face won't harm me! Tell your brother his coffee is getting cold.

LAURA (*at door*):   Do what I asked you, will you, will you, Tom?

(*He looks sullenly away.*)

AMANDA:   Laura, go now or just don't go at all!

LAURA (*rushing out*):   Going—going! (*A second later she cries out. Tom springs up and crosses to the door. Amanda rushes anxiously in. Tom opens the door.*)

TOM:   Laura?

LAURA:   I'm all right. I slipped, but I'm all right.

AMANDA (*peering anxiously after her*):   If anyone breaks a leg on those fire-escape steps, the landlord ought to be sued for every cent he possesses! (*She shuts door. Remembers she isn't speaking and returns to the other room.*)

(*As Tom enters listlessly for his coffee, she turns her back to him and stands rigidly facing the widow on the gloomy gray vault of the areaway. Its light on her face with its aged but childish features is cruelly sharp, satirical as a Daumier print.*)

(Music Under: "Ave Maria.")

(*Tom glances sheepishly but sullenly at her averted figure and slumps at the table. The coffee is scalding hot; he sips it and gasps and spits it back in the cup. At his gasp, Amanda catches breath and half turns. Then catches herself and turns back to window.*

*Tom blows on his coffee, glancing sidewise at his mother. She clears her throat. Tom clears his. He starts to rise. Sinks back down again, scratches his head, clears his throat again. Amanda coughs. Tom raises his cup in both hands to blow on it, his eyes staring over the rim of it at his mother for several moments. Then he slowly sets the cup down and awkwardly and hesitantly rises from the chair.)*

TOM (*hoarsely*): Mother. I—I apologize. Mother. (*Amanda draws a quick, shuddering breath. Her face works grotesquely. She breaks into childlike tears.*) I'm sorry for that I said, for everything that I said, I didn't mean it.

AMANDA (*sobbingly*): My devotion has made me a witch and so I make myself hateful to my children!

TOM: No, you *don't.*

AMANDA: I worry so much, don't sleep, it makes me nervous!

TOM (*gently*): I understand that.

AMANDA: I've had to put up a solitary battle all these years. But you're my right-hand bower! Don't fall down, don't fail!

TOM (*gently*): I try, Mother.

AMANDA (*with great enthusiasm*): Try and you will SUCCEED! (*The notion makes her breathless.*) Why, you—you're just *full* of natural endowments! Both of my children—they're *unusual* children! Don't you think I know it? I'm so—*proud!* Happy and—feel I've— so much to be thankful for but—Promise me one thing, son!

TOM: What, Mother?

AMANDA: Promise, son, you'll—never be a drunkard!

TOM (*turns to her grinning*): I will never be a drunkard!

AMANDA: That's what frightened me so, that you'd be drinking! Eat a bowl of Purina!

TOM: Just coffee, Mother.

AMANDA: Shredded wheat biscuit?

TOM: No. No, Mother, just coffee.

AMANDA: You can't put in a day's work on an empty stomach. You've got ten minutes—don't gulp! Drinking too-hot liquids makes cancer of the stomach. . . . Put cream in.

TOM: No, thank you.

AMANDA: To cool it.

TOM: No! No, thank you, I want it black.

AMANDA: I know, but it's not good for you. We have to do all that we can to build ourselves up. In these trying times we live in, all that we have to cling to is each other. . . . That's why it's so important to—Tom, I—I sent out your sister so I could discuss something with you. If you hadn't spoken I would have spoken to you. (*Sits down.*)

TOM (*gently*): What is it, Mother, that you want to discuss?

AMANDA: Laura!

*(Tom puts his cup down slowly.)*

(Legend on Screen: "Laura.")

(Music: "The Glass Menagerie.")

TOM: —Oh.—Laura . . .

AMANDA (*touching his sleeve*): You know how Laura is. So quiet but—still water runs deep! She notices things and I think she—broods about them. (*Tom looks up.*) A few days ago I came in and she was crying.

TOM: What about?

AMANDA: You.

TOM: Me?

AMANDA: She has an idea that you're not happy here.

TOM: What gave her that idea?

AMANDA: What gives her any idea? However, you do act strangely. I—I'm not criticizing, understand *that!* I know your ambitions do not lie in the warehouse, that like everybody in the whole wide world—you've had to—make sacrifices, but—Tom—Tom—life's not easy, it calls for—Spartan endurance! There's so many things in my heart that I cannot describe to you! I've never told you but I— *loved* your father. . . .

TOM (*gently*): I know that, Mother.

AMANDA: And you—when I see you taking after his ways! Staying out late—and—well, you *had* been drinking the night you were in that—terrifying condition! Laura says that you hate the apartment and that you go out nights to get away from it! Is that true, Tom?

TOM: No. You say there's so much in your heart that you can't describe to me. That's true of me, too. There's so much in my heart that I can't describe to *you!* So let's respect each other's—

AMANDA: But, why—*why,* Tom—are you always so *restless?* Where do you go to, nights?

TOM: I—go to the movies.

AMANDA: Why do you go to the movies so much, Tom?

TOM: I go to the movies because—I like adventure. Adventure is something I don't have much of at work, so I go to the movies.

AMANDA: But, Tom, you go to the movies *entirely too much!*

TOM:   I like a lot of adventure.

(*Amanda looks baffled, then hurt. As the familiar inquisition resumes he becomes hard and impatient again. Amanda slips back into her querulous attitude toward him.*)

(Image on Screen: Sailing Vessel with Jolly Roger.)

AMANDA:   Most young men find adventure in their careers.

TOM:   Then most young men are not employed in a warehouse.

AMANDA:   The world is full of young men employed in warehouses and offices and factories.

TOM:   Do all of them find adventure in their careers?

AMANDA:   They do or they do without it! Not everybody has a craze for adventure.

TOM:   Man is by instinct a lover, a hunter, a fighter, and none of these instincts are given much play at the warehouse!

ARMANDA:   Man is by instinct! Don't quote instinct to me! Instinct is something that people have got away from! It belongs to animals! Christian adults don't want it!

TOM:   What do Christian adults want, then, Mother?

AMANDA:   Superior things! Things of the mind and the spirit! Only animals have to satisfy instincts! Surely your aims are somewhat higher than theirs! Than monkeys—pigs—

TOM:   I reckon they're not.

AMANDA:   You're joking. However, that isn't what I wanted to discuss.

TOM (*rising*):   I haven't much time.

AMANDA (*pushing his shoulders*):   Sit down.

TOM:   You want me to punch in red at the warehouse, Mother?

AMANDA:   You have five minutes. I want to talk about Laura.

(Legend: "Plans and Provisions.")

TOM:   All right! What about Laura?

AMANDA:   We have to be making plans and provisions for her. She's older than you, two years, and nothing has happened. She just drifts along doing nothing. It frightens me terribly how she just drifts along.

TOM:   I guess she's the type that people call home girls.

AMANDA:   There's no such type, and if there is, it's a pity! That is unless the home is hers, with a husband!

TOM:   What?

AMANDA:   Oh, I can see the handwriting on the wall as plain as I see the nose in front of my face! It's terrifying! More and more you remind me of your father! He was out all hours without explanation—Then *left! Good-bye!* And me with the bag to hold. I saw that letter you got from the Merchant Marine. I know what you're dreaming of. I'm not standing here blindfolded. Very well, then. Then *do* it! But not till there's somebody to take your place.

TOM: What do you mean?

AMANDA: I mean that as soon as Laura has got somebody to take care of her, married, a home of her own, independent—why, then you'll be free to go wherever you please, on land, on sea, whichever way the wind blows! But until that time you've got to look out for your sister. I don't say me because I'm old and don't matter! I say for your sister because she's young and dependent. I put her in business college—a dismal failure! Frightened her so it made her sick to her stomach. I took her over to the Young People's League at the church. Another fiasco. She spoke to nobody, nobody spoke to her. Now all she does is fool with those pieces of glass and play those worn-out records. What kind of life is that for a girl to lead!

TOM: What can I do about it?

AMANDA: Overcome selfishness! Self, self, self is all that you ever think of! (*Tom springs up and crosses to get his coat. It is ugly and bulky. He pulls on a cap with earmuffs.*) Where is your muffler? Put your wool muffler on! (*He snatches it angrily from the closet and tosses it around his neck and pulls both ends tight.*) Tom! I haven't said what I had in mind to ask you.

TOM: I'm too late to—

AMANDA (*catching his arms very importunately. Then shyly.*): Down the warehouse, aren't there some—nice young men?

TOM: No!

AMANDA: There *must* be—*some.*

TOM: Mother—

(*Gesture.*)

AMANDA: Find out one that's clean-living—doesn't drink and—ask him out for sister?

TOM: What?

AMANDA: For *sister!* To *meet!* Get acquainted!

TOM (*stamping to door*): Oh, my go-osh!

AMANDA: Will you? (*He opens door. Imploringly*) Will you? (*He starts down.*) Will you? *Will* you, dear?

TOM (*calling back*): YES!

*(Amanda closes the door hesitantly and with a troubled but faintly hopeful expression.)*

(Screen Image: Glamor Magazine Cover.)

*(Spot Amanda at phone.)*

AMANDA: Ella Cartwright? This is Amanda Wingfield! How are you, honey? How is that kidney condition? *(Count five.)* Horrors! *(Count five.)* You're a Christian martyr, yes, honey, that's what you are, a Christian martyr! Well, I just happened to notice in my little red book that your subscription to the *Companion* has just run out! I knew that you wouldn't want to miss out on the wonderful serial starting in this new issue. It's by Bessie Mae Hopper, the first thing she's written since *Honeymoon for Three*. Wasn't that a strange and interesting story? Well, this one is even lovelier, I believe. It has a sophisticated society background. It's all about the horsey set on Long Island!

(Fade Out.)

## SCENE 5

(LEGEND ON SCREEN: "ANNUNCIATION.") FADE WITH MUSIC.

*It is early dusk of a spring evening. Supper has just been finished in the Wingfield apartment. Amanda and Laura in light-colored dresses are removing dishes from the table, in the upstage area, which is shadowy, their movements formalized almost as a dance or ritual, their moving forms as pale and silent as moths. Tom, in white shirt and trousers, rises from the table and crosses toward the fire-escape.*

AMANDA *(as he passes her)*: Son, will you do me a favor?
TOM: What?
AMANDA: Comb your hair! You look so pretty when your hair is combed! *(Tom slouches on sofa with evening paper. Enormous caption "Franco Triumphs.")* There is only one respect in which I would like you to emulate your father.
TOM: What respect is that?
AMANDA: The care he always took of his appearance. He never allowed himself to look untidy. *(He throws down the paper and crosses to fire-escape.)* Where are you going?

TOM: I'm going out to smoke.

AMANDA: You smoke too much. A pack a day at fifteen cents a pack. How much would that amount to in month? Thirty times fifteen is how much, Tom? Figure it out and you will be astounded at what you could save. Enough to give you a night-school course in accounting at Washington U! Just think what a wonderful thing that would be for you, son!

*(Tom is unmoved by the thought.)*

TOM: I'd rather smoke. *(He steps out on landing, letting the screen door slam.)*

AMANDA *(sharply)*: I know! That's the tragedy of it. . . . *(Alone, she turns to look at her husband's picture.)*

(Dance Music: "All the World Is Waiting for the Sunrise!")

TOM *(to the audience)*: Across the alley from us was the Paradise Dance Hall. On evenings in spring the windows and doors were open and the music came outdoors. Sometimes the lights were turned out except for a large glass sphere that hung from the ceiling. It would turn slowly about and filter the dusk with delicate rainbow colors. Then the orchestra played a waltz or a tango, something that had a slow and sensuous rhythm. Couples would come outside, to the relative privacy of the alley. You could see them kissing behind ashpits and telephone poles. This was the compensation for lives that passed like mine, without any change or adventure. Adventure and change were imminent in this year. They were waiting around the corner for all these kinds. Suspended in the mist over Berchtesgaden, caught in the folds of Chamberlain's umbrella—In Spain there was Guernica! But here there was only hot swing music and liquor, dance halls, bars, and movies, and sex that hung in the gloom like a chandelier and flooded the world with brief, deceptive rainbows. . . . All the world was waiting for bombardments!

*(Amanda turns from the picture and comes outside.)*

AMANDA *(sighing)*: A fire-escape landing's a poor excuse for a porch. *(She spreads a newspaper on a step and sits down, gracefully and demurely as if she were settling into a swing on a Mississippi veranda.)* What are you looking at?

TOM: The moon.

AMANDA: Is there a moon this evening?

TOM: It's rising over Garfinkel's Delicatessen.

AMANDA: So it is! A little silver slipper of a moon. Have you made a wish on it yet?

TOM: Um-hum.

AMANDA: What did you wish for.

TOM: That's a secret.

AMANDA: A secret, huh? Well, I won't tell you mine either. I will be just as mysterious as you.

TOM: I bet I can guess what yours is.

AMANDA: Is my head so transparent?

TOM: You're not a sphinx.

AMANDA: No, I don't have secrets. I'll tell you what I wished for on the moon. Success and happiness for my precious children! I wish for that whenever there's a moon, and when there isn't a moon, I wish for it, too.

TOM: I thought perhaps you wished for a gentleman caller.

AMANDA: Why do you say that?

TOM: Don't you remember asking me to fetch one?

AMANDA: I remember suggesting that it would be nice for your sister if you brought home some nice young man from the warehouse. I think I've made that suggestion more than once.

TOM: Yes, you have made it repeatedly.

AMANDA: Well?

TOM: We are going to have one.

AMANDA: What?

TOM: A gentleman caller!

(The Annunciation Is Celebrated with Music.)

*(Amanda rises.)*

(Image on Screen: Caller with Bouquet.)

AMANDA: You mean you have asked some nice young man to come over?

TOM: Yep. I've asked him to dinner.

AMANDA: You really did?

TOM: I did!

AMANDA: You did, and did he—*accept?*

TOM: He did!

AMANDA: Well, well—well, well! That's—lovely!

TOM: I thought that you would be pleased.

AMANDA: It's definite, then?

TOM: Very definite.

AMANDA: Soon?

TOM: Very soon.

AMANDA: For heaven's sake, stop putting on and tell me some things, will you?

TOM: What things do you want me to tell you?

AMANDA: Naturally I would like to know when he's *coming!*

TOM: He's coming tomorrow.

AMANDA: Tomorrow?

TOM: Yep. Tomorrow.

AMANDA: But, Tom!

TOM: Yes, Mother?

AMANDA: Tomorrow gives me no time!

TOM: Time for what?

AMANDA: Preparations! Why didn't you phone me at once, as soon as you asked him, the minute that he accepted? Then, don't you see, I could have been getting ready!

TOM: You don't have to make any fuss.

AMANDA: Oh, Tom, Tom, Tom, of course I have to make a fuss! I want things nice, not sloppy! Not thrown together. I'll certainly have to do some fast thinking, won't I?

TOM: I don't see why you have to think at all.

AMANDA: You just don't know. We can't have a gentleman caller in a pig-sty! All my wedding silver has to be polished, the mono-grammed table linen ought to be laundered! The windows have to be washed and fresh curtains put up. And how about clothes? We have to *wear* something, don't we?

TOM: Mother, this boy is no one to make a fuss over!

AMANDA: Do you realize he's the first young man we've had intro-duced to your sister? It's terrible, dreadful, disgraceful that poor little sister has never received a single gentleman caller! Tom, come inside! (*She opens the screen door.*)

TOM: What for?

AMANDA: I want to ask you some things.

TOM: If you're going to make such a fuss, I'll call it off, I'll tell him not to come.

AMANDA: You certainly won't do anything of the kind. Nothing of-fends people worse than broken engagements. It simply means I'll have to work like a Turk! We won't be brilliant, but we'll pass in-spection. Come on inside. (*Tom follows, groaning.*) Sit down.

TOM: Any particular place you would like me to sit?

AMANDA: Thank heavens I've got that new sofa! I'm also making payments on a floor lamp I'll have sent out! And put the chintz covers on, they'll brighten things up! Of course I'd hoped to have these walls re-papered. . . . What is the young man's name?

TOM: His name is O'Connor.

AMANDA: That, of course, means fish—tomorrow is Friday! I'll have that salmon loaf—with Durkee's dressing! What does he do? He works at the warehouse?

TOM: Of course! How else would I—

AMANDA: Tom, he—doesn't drink?

TOM: Why do you ask me that?

AMANDA: Your father *did!*

TOM: Don't get started on that!

AMANDA: He *does* drink, then?

TOM: Not that I know of!

AMANDA: Make sure, be certain! The last thing I want for my daughter's a boy who drinks?

TOM: Aren't you being a little premature? Mr. O'Connor has not yet appeared on the scene!

AMANDA: But will tomorrow. To meet your sister, and what do I know about his character? Nothing! Old maids are better off than wives of drunkards!

TOM: Oh, my God.

AMANDA: Be still!

TOM (*leaning forward to whisper*): Lots of fellows meet girls whom they don't marry!

AMANDA: Oh, talk sensibly, Tom—and don't be sarcastic! (*She has gotten a hairbrush.*)

TOM: What are you doing?

AMANDA: I'm brushing that cow-lick down! What is this young man's position at the warehouse?

TOM (*submitting grimly to the brush and the interrogation*): This young man's position is that of a shipping clerk, Mother.

AMANDA: Sounds to me like a fairly responsible job, the sort of a job *you* would be in if you just had more *get-up*. What is his salary? Have you got any idea?

TOM: I would judge it to be approximately eighty-five dollars a month.

AMANDA: Well—not princely, but—

TOM: Twenty more than I make.

AMANDA: Yes, how well I know! But for a family man, eighty-five dollars a month is not much more than you can just get by on. . . .

TOM: Yes, but Mr. O'Connor is not a family man.

AMANDA: He might be, mightn't he? Some time in the future?

TOM: I see. Plans and provisions.

AMANDA: You are the only young man that I know of who ignores the fact that the future becomes the present, the present the past, and the past turns into everlasting regret if you don't plan for it!

TOM: I will think that over and see what I can make of it.

AMANDA: Don't be supercilious with your mother! Tell me some more about this—what do you call him?

TOM: James D. O'Connor. The D. is for Delaney.

AMANDA: Irish on *both* sides! *Gracious!* And doesn't drink?

TOM: Shall I call him up and ask him right this minute?

AMANDA: The only way to find out about those things is to make discreet inquiries at the proper moment. When I was a girl in Blue Mountain and it was suspected that a young man drank, the girl whose attentions he had been receiving, if any girl *was,* would sometimes speak to the minister of his church, or rather her father would if her father was living, and sort of feel him out on the young man's character. That is the way such things are discreetly handled to keep a young woman from making a tragic mistake!

TOM: Then how did you happen to make a tragic mistake?

AMANDA: That innocent look of your father's had everyone fooled! He *smiled*—the world was *enchanted!* No girl can do worse than put herself at the mercy of a handsome appearance! I hope that Mr. O'Connor is not too good-looking.

TOM: No, he's not too good-looking. He's covered with freckles and hasn't too much of a nose.

AMANDA: He's not right-down homely, though?

TOM: Not right-down homely. Just medium homely, I'd say.

AMANDA: Character's what to look for in a man.

TOM: That's what I've always said, Mother.

AMANDA: You've never said anything of the kind and I suspect you would never give it a thought.

TOM: Don't be suspicious of me.

AMANDA: At least I hope he's the type that's up and coming.

TOM: I think he really goes in for self-improvement.

AMANDA: What reason have you to think so?

TOM: He goes to night school.

AMANDA (*beaming*): Splendid! What does he do, I mean study?

TOM: Radio engineering and public speaking!

AMANDA: Then he has visions of being advanced in the world! Any young man who studies public speaking is aiming to have an executive job some day! And radio engineering? A thing for the future! Both of these facts are very illuminating. Those are the sort of things that a mother should know concerning any young man who comes to call on her daughter. Seriously or—not.

TOM: One little warning. He doesn't know about Laura. I didn't let on that we had dark ulterior motives. I just said, why don't you come have dinner with us? He said okay and that was the whole conversation.

AMANDA: I bet it was! You're eloquent as an oyster. However, he'll know about Laura when he gets here. When we sees how lovely and sweet and pretty she is, he'll thank his lucky stars he was asked to dinner.

TOM: Mother, you mustn'toexpect too much of Laura.

AMANDA: What do you mean?

TOM: Laura seems all those things to you and me because she's ours and we love her. We don't even notice she's crippled any more.

AMANDA: Don't say crippled! You know that I never allow that word to be used!

TOM: But face facts, Mother. She is and—that's not all—

AMANDA: What do you mean "not all"?

TOM: Laura is very different from other girls.

AMANDA: I think the difference is all to her advantage.

TOM: Not quite all—in the eyes of others—strangers—she's terribly shy and lives in a world of her own and those things make her seem a little peculiar to people outside the house.

AMANDA: Don't say peculiar.

TOM: Face the facts. She is.

(*The Dance-Hall Music Changes to a Tango That Has a Minor and Somewhat Ominous Tone.*)

AMANDA: In what way is she peculiar—may I ask?

TOM (*gently*): She lives in a world of her own—a world of—little glass ornaments, Mother. . . . (*Gets up, Amanda remains holding brush, looking at him, troubled.*) She plays old phonograph records and—that's about all—(*He glances at himself in the mirror and crosses to door.*)

AMANDA (*sharply*): Where are you going?

TOM: I'm going to the movies. (*Out screen door.*)

AMANDA: Not to the movies, every night to the movies! (*Follows quickly to screen door.*) I don't believe you always go to the movies! (*He is gone. Amanda looks worriedly after him for a moment. Then vitality and optimism return and she turns from the door. Crossing to portieres.*) Laura! Laura! (*Laura answers from kitchenette.*)

LAURA: Yes, Mother.

AMANDA: Let those dishes go and come in front! (*Laura appears with dish towel. Gaily*) Laura, come here and make a wish on the moon!

LAURA (*entering*): Moon—moon?

AMANDA: A little silver slipper of a moon. Look over your left shoulder, Laura, and make a wish! (*Laura looks faintly puzzled as if called out of sleep. Amanda seizes her shoulders and turns her at angle by the door.*) Now! Now, darling, *wish!*

LAURA: What shall I wish for, Mother?

AMANDA (*her voice trembling and her eyes suddenly filling with tears*): Happiness! Good Fortune!

*(The violin rises and the stage dims out.)*

## SCENE 6

(IMAGE: HIGH SCHOOL HERO.)

TOM: And so the following evening I brought Jim home to dinner. I had known Jim slightly in high school. In high school Jim was a hero. He had tremendous Irish good nature and vitality with the scrubbed and polished look of white chinaware. He seemed to move in a continual spotlight. He was a star in basketball, captain of the debating club, president of the senior class and the glee club and he sang the male lead in the annual light operas. He was always running or bounding, never just walking. He seemed always at the point of defeating the law of gravity. He was shooting with such velocity through his adolescence that you would logically expect him to arrive at nothing short of the White House by the time he was thirty. But Jim apparently ran into more interference after his graduation from Soldan. His speed had definitely slowed. Six years after he left high school he was holding a job that wasn't much better than mine.

(Image: Clerk.)

He was the only one at the warehouse with whom I was on friendly terms. I was valuable to him as someone who could remember his former glory, who had seen him win basketball games and the silver cup in debating. He knew of my secret practice of retiring to a cabinet of the washroom to work on poems when business was slack in the warehouse. He called me Shakespeare. And while the other boys in the warehouse regarded me with suspicious hostility, Jim took a humorous attitude toward me. Gradually his attitude affected the others, their hostility wore off and they also began to smile at me as people smile at an oddly fashioned dog who trots across their path at some distance.

I knew that Jim and Laura had known each other at Soldan, and I had heard Laura speak admiringly of his voice. I didn't know if Jim remembered her or not. In high school Laura had been as unobtrusive as Jim had been astonishing. If he did remember Laura, it was not as my sister for when I asked him to dinner, he grinned and said, "You know, Shakespeare, I never thought of you as having folks!" He was about to discover that I did. . . .

(Light upstage.)

(Legend on Screen: "The Accent of a Coming Foot.")

*(Friday evening. It is about five o'clock of a late spring evening which comes "scattering poems in the sky." A delicate lemony light is in the Wingfield apartment. Amanda has worked like a Turk in preparation for the gentleman caller. The results are astonishing. The new floor lamp with its rose-silk shade is in place, a colored paper lantern conceals the broken light fixture in the ceiling, new billowing white curtains are at the windows, chintz covers are on chairs, and sofa, a pair of new sofa pillows make their initial appearance.*

*Open boxes and tissue paper are scattered on the floor.*

*Laura stands in the middle with lifted arms while Amanda crouches before her, adjusting the hem of the new dress, devout and ritualistic. The dress is colored and designed by memory. The arrangement of Laura's hair is changed; it is softer and more becoming. A fragile, unearthly prettiness has come out in Laura: she is like a piece of translucent glass touched by light, given a momentary radiance, not actual, not lasting.)*

**AMANDA** (*impatiently*):   Why are you trembling?

LAURA:   Mother, you've made me so nervous!

AMANDA:   How have I made you nervous?

LAURA:   By all this fuss! You make it seem so important?

AMANDA:   I don't understand you, Laura. You couldn't be satisfied with just sitting home, and yet whenever I try to arrange something for you, you seem to resist it. (*She gets up.*) Now take a look at yourself. No, wait! Wait just a moment—I have an idea!

LAURA:   What is it now?

*(Amanda produces two powder puffs which she wraps in handkerchiefs and stuffs in Laura's bosom.)*

LAURA:   Mother, what are you doing?

AMANDA:   They call them "Gay Deceivers"!

LAURA:   I won't wear them!

AMANDA:   You will!

LAURA:   Why should I?

AMANDA:   Because, to be painfully honest, your chest is flat.

LAURA:   You make it seem like we were setting a trap.

AMANDA:   All pretty girls are a trap, a pretty trap, and men expect them to be.

(Legend: "A Pretty Trap.")

Now look at yourself, young lady. This is the prettiest you will ever be! I've got to fix myself now! You're going to be surprised by your mother's appearance.

*(She crosses through portieres, humming gaily.)*

*(Laura moves slowly to the long mirror and stares solemnly at herself. A wind blows the white curtains inward in a slow, graceful motion and with a faint, sorrowful sighing.)*

AMANDA (*offstage*):   It isn't dark enough yet. (*She turns slowly before the mirror with a troubled look.*)

(Legend on Screen: "This Is My Sister: Celebrate Her with Strings!" Music.)

AMANDA (*laughing, off*):   I'm going to show you something. I'm going to make a spectacular appearance!

LAURA:   What is it, Mother?

AMANDA:   Possess your soul in patience—you will see! Something I've resurrected from that old trunk! Styles haven't changed so terribly much after all. . . . (*She parts the portieres.*) Now just look at your mother! (*She wears a girlish frock of yellowed voile with a blue silk sash. She carries a bunch of jonquils—the legend of her youth is nearly revived. Feverishly)* This is the dress in which I led the cotillion. Won the cakewalk twice at Sunset Hill, wore one spring to the Governor's ball in Jackson! See how I sashayed around the ballroom, Laura? (*She raises her skirt and does a mincing step around the room.*) I wore it on Sundays for my gentleman callers! I had it on the day I met your father—I had malaria fever all that spring. The change of climate from East Tennessee to the Delta—weakened resistance—I had a little temperature all the time—not enough to be serious—just enough to make me restless and giddy! Invitations poured in parties all over the Delta!—"Stay in bed," said Mother, "you have fever!"—but I just wouldn't.—I took quinine but kept on going, going!—Evenings, dances!—Afternoon, long, long rides! Picnics—lovely!—So lovely, that country in May.—All lacy with dogwood, literally flooded with jonquils.— That was the spring I had the craze for jonquils. Jonquils became an absolute obsession. Mother said, "Honey, there's no more room for jonquils." And still I kept bringing in more jonquils. Whenever, wherever I saw them, I'd say, "Stop! Stop! I see jonquils!" I made the young men help me gather the jonquils! It was a joke, Amanda and her jonquils! Finally there were no more vases to hold them, every available space was filled with jonquils. No vases to hold them? All right, I'll hold them myself! And then I—(*She stops in front of the picture.*) (*Music.*) met your father! Malaria fever and jonquils and then—this—boy. . . . (*She switches on the rose-colored lamp.*) I hope they get here before it starts to rain. (*She crosses upstage and places the jonquils in bowl on table.*) I gave your brother a little extra change so he and Mr. O'Connor could take the service car home.

LAURA (*with altered look*): What did you say his name was?

AMANDA: O'Connor.

LAURA: What is his first name?

AMANDA: I don't remember. Oh, yes, I do. It was—Jim!

*(Laura sways slightly and catches hold of a chair.)*

(Legend on Screen: "Not Jim!")

LAURA (*faintly*): Not—Jim!

AMANDA: Yes, that was it, it was Jim! I've never know a Jim that wasn't nice!

(Music: Ominous.)

LAURA: Are you sure his name is Jim O'Connor?

AMANDA: Yes. Why?

LAURA: Is he the one that Tom used to know in high school?

AMANDA: He didn't say so. I think he just got to know him at the warehouse.

LAURA: There was a Jim O'Connor we both knew in high school— (*Then, with effort.*) If that is the one that Tom is bringing to dinner—you'll have to excuse me, I won't come to the table.

AMANDA: What sort of nonsense is this?

LAURA: You asked me once if I'd ever liked a boy. Don't you remember I showed you this boy's picture?

AMANDA: You mean the boy you showed me in the year book?

LAURA: Yes, that boy.

AMANDA: Laura, Laura, were you in love with that boy?

LAURA: I don't know, Mother. All I know is I couldn't sit at the table if it was him!

AMANDA: It won't be him! It isn't the least bit likely. But whether it is or not, you will come to the table. You will not be excused.

LAURA: I'll have to be, Mother.

AMANDA: I don't intend to humor your silliness, Laura. I've had too much from you and your brother, both! So just sit down and compose yourself till they come. Tom has forgotten his key so you'll have to let them in, when they arrive.

LAURA (*panicky*): Oh, Mother—*you* answer the door!

AMANDA (*lightly*): I'll be in the kitchen—busy!

LAURA: Oh, Mother, please answer the door, don't make me do it!

AMANDA (*crossing into kitchenette*): I've got to fix the dressing for the salmon. Fuss, fuss—silliness!—over a gentleman caller!

*(Door swings shut. Laura is left alone.)*

(Legend: "Terror!")

*(She utters a low moan and turns off the lamp—sits stiffly on the edge of the sofa, knotting her fingers together.)*

(Legend on Screen: "The Opening of a Door!")

*(Tom and Jim appear on the fire-escape steps and climb to landing. Hearing their approach, Laura rises with a panicky gesture. She retreats to the portieres.*

*The doorbell. Laura catches her breath and touches her throat. Low drums.)*

AMANDA (*calling*): Laura, sweetheart! The door!

(*Laura stares at it without moving.*)

JIM: I think we just beat the rain.

TOM: Uh-huh. (*He rings again, nervously, Jim whistles and fishes for a cigarette.*)

AMANDA (*very, very gaily*): Laura, that is your brother and Mr. O'Connor! Will you let them in, darling?

(*Laura crosses toward kitchenette door*).

LAURA (*breathlessly*): Mother—you go to the door!

(*Amanda steps out of the kitchenette and stares furiously at Laura. She points imperiously at the door.*)

LAURA: Please, please!

AMANDA (*in a fierce whisper*): What is the matter with you, you silly thing?

LAURA (*desperately*): Please, you answer it, *please!*

AMANDA: I told you I wasn't going to humor you, Laura. Why have you chosen this time to lose your mind?

LAURA: Please, please, please, you go!

AMANDA: You'll have to go to the door because I can't.

LAURA (*despairingly*): I can't either!

AMANDA: Why?

LAURA: I'm *sick?*

AMANDA: I'm sick, too—of your nonsense! Why can't you and your brother be normal people? Fantastic whims and behavior! (*Tom gives a long ring.*) Preposterous goings on! Can you give me one reason—(*Calls out lyrically.*) COMING! JUST ONE SECOND!—why should you be afraid to open a door? Now you answer it, Laura!

LAURA: Oh, oh, oh . . . (*She returns through the portieres. Darts to the victrola and winds it frantically and turns it on.*)

AMANDA: Laura Wingfield, you march right to that door!

LAURA: Yes—yes, Mother.

(*A faraway, scratchy rendition of "Dardanella" softens the air and gives her strength to move through it. She slips to the door and draws it cautiously open. Tom enters with the caller, Jim O'Connor.*)

TOM: Laura, this is Jim. Jim, this is my sister, Laura.

JIM (*stepping inside*): I didn't know that Shakespeare had a sister!

LAURA (*retreating stiff and trembling from the door*):   How—how do you do?

JIM (*heartily extending his hand*):   Okay!

(*Laura touches it hesitantly with hers.*)

JIM:   Your hand's *cold*, Laura!

LAURA:   Yes, well—I've been playing the victrola. . . .

JIM:   Must have been playing classical music on it! You ought to play a little hot swing music to warm you up!

LAURA:   Excuse me—I haven't finished playing the victrola. . . .

(*She turns awkwardly and hurries onto the front room. She pauses a second by the victrola. Then catches her breath and darts through the portieres like a frightened deer.*)

JIM (*grinning*):   What was the matter?

TOM:   Oh—with Laura? Laura is—terribly shy.

JIM:   Shy, huh? It's unusual to meet a shy girl nowadays. I don't believe you ever mentioned you had a sister.

TOM:   Well, now you know. I have one. Here is the *Post Dispatch*. You want a piece of it?

JIM:   Uh-huh.

TOM:   What piece? The comics?

JIM:   Sports! (*Glances at it.*) Ole Dizzy Dean is on his bad behavior.

TOM (*disinterest*):   Yeah? (*Lights cigarette and crosses back to fire-escape door.*)

JIM:   Where are *you* going?

TOM:   I'm going out on the terrace.

JIM (*goes after him*):   You know, Shakespeare—I'm going to sell you a bill of goods!

TOM:   What goods?

JIM:   A course I'm taking.

TOM:   Huh?

JIM:   In public speaking! You and me, we're not the warehouse type.

TOM:   Thanks—that's good news. But what has public speaking got to do with it?

JIM:   It fits you for—executive positions!

TOM:   Awww.

JIM:   I tell you it's done a helluva lot for me.

(Image: Executive at Desk.)

TOM:   In what respect?

JIM: In every! Ask yourself what is the difference between you an' me in the office down front? Brains?—No!—Ability?—No! Then what? Just one little thing—

TOM: What is that one little thing?

JIM: Primarily it amounts to—social poise! Being able to square up to people and hold your own on any social level!

AMANDA (*off stage*): Tom?

TOM: Yes, Mother?

AMANDA: Is that you and Mr. O'Connor?

TOM: Yes, Mother.

AMANDA: Well, you just make yourselves comfortable in there.

TOM: Yes, Mother.

AMANDA: Ask Mr. O'Connor if he would like to wash his hands.

JIM: Aw—no—no—thank you—I took care of that at the warehouse. Tom—

TOM: Yes?

JIM: Mr. Mendoza was speaking to me about you.

TOM: Favorably?

JIM: What do you think?

TOM: Well—

JIM: You're going to be out of a job if you don't wake up.

TOM: I am waking up—

JIM: You show no signs.

TOM: The signs are interior.

(Image on Screen: The Sailing Vessel with Jolly Roger Again.)

TOM: I'm planning to change. (*He leans over the rail speaking with quiet exhilaration. The incandescent marquees and signs of the first-run movie houses light his face from across the alley. He looks like a voyager.*) I'm right at the point of committing myself to a future that doesn't include the warehouse and Mr. Mendoza or even a night-school course in public speaking.

JIM: What are you gassing about?

TOM: I'm tired of the movies.

JIM: Movies!

TOM: Yes, movies! Look at them—(*A wave toward the marvels of Grand Avenue.*) All of those glamorous people—having adventures—hogging it all, gobbling the whole thing up! You know what happens? People go to the *movies* instead of *moving!* Hollywood characters are supposed to have all the adventures for everybody in America, while everybody in America sits in a dark room and watches them have them! Yes, until there's a war. That's when adventure becomes available to the masses! *Everyone's* dish, not only Gable's! Then the people in the dark room come out of the dark room to have some adventures themselves—Goody, goody—It's our turn now, to go to the South Sea Island—to make a safari—to be exotic, far-off—But I'm not patient. I don't want to wait till then. I'm tired of the *movies* and I am *about* to move!

JIM (*incredulously*):  Move?

TOM:  Yes.

JIM:  When?

TOM:  Soon!

JIM:  Where? Where?

*(Theme Three: Music Seems to Answer the Question, While Tom Thinks It Over. He Searches Among His Pockets.)*

TOM:  I'm starting to boil inside. I know I seem dreamy, but inside— well, I'm boiling! Whenever I pick up a shoe, I shudder a little thinking how short life is and what I am doing!—Whatever that means. I know it doesn't mean shoes—except as something to wear on a traveler's feet! (*Finds paper.*) Look—

JIM:  What?

TOM:  I'm a member.

JIM (*reading*):  The Union of Merchant Seamen.

TOM:  I paid my dues this month, instead of the light bill.

JIM:  You will regret it when they turn the lights off.

TOM:  I won't be here.

JIM:  How about your mother?

TOM:  I'm like my father. The bastard son of a bastard! See how he grins? And he's been absent going on sixteen years!

JIM:  You're just talking, you drip. How does you mother feel about it?

TOM:  Shhh—Here comes Mother! Mother is not acquainted with my plans.

AMANDA (*enters portiere*):  Where are you all?

TOM:  On the terrace, Mother.

*(They start inside. She advances to them. Tom is distinctly shocked at her appearance. Even Jim blinks a little. He is making his first contact with girlish Southern vivacity and in spite of the night-school course in public speaking is somewhat*

*thrown off the beam by the unexpected outlay of social charm. Certain responses are attempted by Jim but are swept aside by Amanda's gay laughter and chatter. Tom is embarrassed but after the first shock Jim reacts very warmly. Grins and chuckles, is altogether won over.)*

(Image: Amanda as a Girl.)

AMANDA (*coyly smiling, shaking her girlish ringlets*): Well, well, well, so this is Mr. O'Connor. Introductions entirely unnecessary. I've heard so much about you from my boy. I finally said to him, Tom—good gracious!—why don't you bring this paragon to supper? I'd like to meet this nice young man at the warehouse!—Instead of just hearing him sing your praises so much! I don't know why my son is so stand-offish—that's not Southern behavior! Let's sit down and—I think we could stand a little more air in here! Tom, leave the door open. I felt a nice fresh breeze a moment ago. Where has it gone? Mmm, so warm already! And not quite summer, even. We're going to burn up when summer really gets started. However, we're having—we're having a very light supper. I think light things are better fo' this time of year. The same as light clothes are. Light clothes an' light food are what warm weather calls fo'. You know our blood gets so thick during th' winter—it takes a while fo' us to *adjust* ou'selves!—when the season changes . . . It's come so quick this year. I wasn't prepared. All of a sudden—heavens! Already summer!—I ran to the trunk an' pulled out this light dress—Terribly old! Historical almost! But feels so good—so good an' co-ol, y'know. . . .

TOM: Mother—

AMANDA: Yes, honey?

TOM: How about—supper?

AMANDA: Honey, you go ask Sister if supper is ready! You know that Sister is in full charge of supper! Tell her you hungry boys are waiting for it. (*To Jim*) Have you met Laura?

JIM: She—

AMANDA: Let you in? Oh, good, you've met already! It's rare for a girl as sweet an' pretty as Laura to be domestic! But Laura is, thank heavens, not only pretty but also very domestic. I'm not at all. I never was a bit. I never could make a thing but angel-food cake. Well, in the South we had so many servants. Gone, gone, gone. All vestiges of gracious living! Gone completely! I wasn't prepared for what the future brought me. All of my gentleman callers were sons of planters and so of course I assumed that I would be married to one and raise my family on a large piece of land with plenty of servants. But man proposes—and woman accepts the proposal!—To vary that old, old saying a little bit—I married no planter! I married a man who worked for the telephone company!—that gallantly smiling gentleman over there! (*Points to the picture.*) A telephone man who—fell in love with long distance!—Now he travels and I don't even know where!—But what am I going on for about my—tribulations! Tell me yours—I hope you don't have any! Tom?

TOM (*returning*): Yes, Mother?

AMANDA: Is supper nearly ready?

TOM: It looks to me like supper is on the table.

AMANDA: Let me look—(*She rises prettily and looks through portieres.*) Oh, lovely—but where is Sister?

TOM: Laura is not feeling well and she says that she thinks she'd better not come to the table.

AMANDA: What?—Nonsense!—Laura? Oh, Laura!

LAURA (*off stage, faintly*): Yes, Mother.

AMANDA: You really must come to the table. We won't be seated until you come to the table! Come in, Mr. O'Connor. You sit over there and I'll—Laura? Laura Wingfield! You're keeping us waiting, honey! We can't say grace until you come to the table!

(*The back door is pushed weakly open and Laura comes in. She is obviously quite faint, her lips trembling, her eyes wide and staring. She moves unsteadily toward the table.*)

(Legend: "Terror!")

(*Outside a summer storm is coming abruptly. The white curtains billow inward at the windows and there is a sorrowful murmur and deep blue dusk. Laura suddenly stumbles—She catches at a chair with a faint moan.*)

TOM: Laura!

AMANDA: Laura! (*There's a clap of thunder*). (*Legend: "Ah!"*) (*Despairingly*) Why, Laura, you *are* sick, darling! Tom, help your sister into the living room, dear! Sit in the living room, Laura—rest on the sofa. Well! (*To the gentleman caller*) Standing over the hot stove made her ill! I told her that it was just too warm this evening, but—(*Tom comes back in. Laura is on the sofa.*) Is Laura all right now?

TOM: Yes.

AMANDA: What is that? Rain? A nice cool rain has come up? (*She gives the gentleman caller a frightened look.*) I think we may— have grace—now . . . (*Tom looks at her stupidly.*) Tom, honey— you say grace!

TOM: Oh . . . "For these and all thy mercies—" (*They bow their heads. Amanda stealing a nervous glance at Jim. In the living room Laura, stretched on the sofa, clenches her hands to her lips, to hold back a shuddering sob.*) God's Holy Name be praised—

(The Scene Dims Out.)


## Scene 7

### A Souvenir

*Half an hour later. Dinner is just being finished in the upstage area which is concealed by the drawn portieres.*

*As the curtain rises Laura is still huddled upon the sofa, her feet drawn under her, her head resting on a pale blue pillow, her eyes wide and mysteriously watchful. The new floor lamp with its shade of rose-colored silk gives a soft, becoming light to her face, bringing out the fragile, unearthly prettiness which usually escapes attention. There is a steady murmur of rain, but it is slackening and stops soon after the scene begins; the air outside becomes pale and luminous as the moon breaks out.*

*A moment after the curtain rises, the lights in both rooms flicker and go out.*

JIM: Hey, there, Mr. Light Bulb!

(*Amanda laughs nervously.*)

(Legend: "Suspension of a Public Service.")

AMANDA: Where was Moses when the lights went out? Ha-ha. Do you know the answer to that one, Mr. O'Connor?

JIM: No, Ma'am, what's the answer?

AMANDA: In the dark! (*Jim laughs appreciatively.*) Everybody sit still. I'll light the candles. Isn't it lucky we have them on the table? Where's a match. Which of you gentlemen can provide a match?

JIM: Here.

AMANDA: Thank you, sir.

JIM: Not at all, Ma'am!

AMANDA: I guess the fuse has burnt out. Mr. O'Connor, can you tell a burnt-out fuse? I know I can't and Tom is a total loss when it comes to mechanics. (*Sound: Getting Up: Voices Recede a Little to Kitchenette.*) Oh, be careful, you don't bump into something. We don't want our gentleman caller to break his neck. Now wouldn't that be a fine howdy-do?

JIM: Ha-ha! Where is the fuse-box?

AMANDA: Right there next to the stove. Can you see anything?

JIM: Just a minute.

AMANDA: Isn't electricity a mysterious thing? Wasn't it Benjamin Franklin who tied a key to a kite? We live in such a mysterious universe, don't we? Some people say that science clears up all the mysteries for us. In my opinion it only creates more! Have you found it yet?

JIM: No, Ma'am. All these fuses look okay to me.

AMANDA: Tom!

TOM: Yes, Mother?

AMANDA: That light bill I gave you several days ago. The one I told you we got the notices about?

TOM: Oh.—Yeah.

(Legend: "Ha!")

AMANDA: You didn't neglect to pay it by any chance.

TOM: Why, I—

AMANDA: Didn't! I might have known it!

JIM: Shakespeare probably wrote a poem on the light bill, Mrs. Wingfield.

AMANDA: I might have known better than to trust him with it! There's such a high price for negligence in this world!

JIM: Maybe the poem will win a ten-dollar prize.

AMANDA: We'll just have to spend the remainder of the evening in the nineteenth century, before Mr. Edison made the Mazda lamp!

JIM: Candlelight is my favorite kind of light.

AMANDA: That shows you're romantic! But that's no excuse for Tom. Well, we got through dinner. Very considerate of them to let us get through dinner before they plunged us into everlasting darkness, wasn't it, Mr. O'Connor?

JIM: Ha-ha!

AMANDA: Tom, as a penalty for your carelessness you can help me with the dishes.

JIM: Let me give you a hand.

AMANDA: Indeed you will not!

JIM: I ought to be good for something.

AMANDA: Good for something? (*Her tone is rhapsodic.*) You? Why, Mr. O'Connor, nobody, *nobody's* given me this much entertainment in years—as you have!

JIM: Aw, now, Mrs. Wingfield!

AMANDA: I'm not exaggerating, not one bit! But Sister is all by her lonesome. You go keep her company in the parlor! I'll give you this lovely old candelabrum that used to be on the altar at the church of the Heavenly Rest. It was melted a little out of shape when the church burnt down. Lightning struck it one spring. Gypsy Jones was holding a revival at the time and he estimated that the church was destroyed because the Episcopalians gave card parties.

JIM: Ha-ha.

AMANDA: And how about coaxing Sister to drink a little wine? I think it would be good for her! Can you carry both at once?

JIM: Sure, I'm Superman!

AMANDA: Now, Thomas, get into this apron!

(*The door of kitchenette swings closed on Amanda's gay laughter; the flickering light approaches the portieres. Laura sits up nervously as he enters. Her speech at first is low and breathless from the almost intolerable strain of being alone with a stranger.*)

(Legend: "I Don't Suppose You Remember Me at All!")

(*In her first speeches in this scene, before Jim's warmth overcomes her paralyzing shyness, Laura's voice is thin and breathless as though she has run up a steep flight of stairs. Jim's attitude is gently humorous. In playing this scene it should be stressed that while the incident is apparently unimportant, it is to Laura the climax of her secret life.*)

JIM: Hello, there, Laura.

LAURA (*faintly*):   Hello. (*She clears her throat.*)

JIM:   How are you feeling now? Better?

LAURA:   Yes. Yes, thank you.

JIM:   This is for you. A little dandelion wine. (*He extends it toward her with extravagant gallantry.*)

LAURA:   Thank you.

JIM:   Drink it—but don't get drunk! (*He laughs heartily. Laura takes the glass uncertainly; laughs shyly.*) Where shall I set the candles?

LAURA:   Oh—oh, anywhere . . .

JIM:   How about here on the floor? Any objections?

LAURA:   No.

JIM:   I'll spread a newspaper under to catch the drippings. I like to sit on the floor. Mind if I do?

LAURA:   Oh, no.

JIM:   Give me a pillow?

LAURA:   What?

JIM:   A pillow!

LAURA:   Oh . . . (*Hands him one quickly.*)

JIM:   How about you? Don't you like to sit on the floor?

LAURA:   Oh—yes.

JIM:   Why don't you, then?

LAURA:   I—will.

JIM:   Take a pillow! (*Laura does. Sits on the other side of the candelabrum. Jim crosses his legs and smiles engagingly at her.*) I can't hardly see you sitting way over there.

LAURA:   I can—see you.

JIM:   I know, but that's not fair, I'm in the limelight. (*Laura moves her pillow closer.*) Good! Now I can see you! Comfortable?

LAURA:   Yes.

JIM:   So am I. Comfortable as a cow. Will you have some gum?

LAURA:   No, thank you.

JIM:   I think that I will indulge, with your permission. (*Musingly unwraps it and holds it up.*) Think of the fortune made by the guy that invented the first piece of chewing gum. Amazing, huh? The Wrigley Building is one of the sights of Chicago.—I saw it summer before last when I went up to the Century of Progress. Did you take in the Century of Progress?

LAURA:   No, I didn't.

JIM:   Well, it was quite a wonderful exposition. What impressed me most was the Hall of Science. Gives you an idea of what the future will be in America, even more wonderful than the present time is!

(*Pause. Smiling at her*) Your brother tells me you're shy. Is that right, Laura?

LAURA: I—don't know.

JIM: I judge you to be an old-fashioned type of girl. Well, I think that's a pretty good type to be. Hope you don't think I'm being too personal—do you?

LAURA (*hastily, out of embarrassment*): I believe I *will* take a piece of gum, if you—don't mind. (*Clearing her throat*) Mr. O'Connor, have you—kept up with your singing?

JIM: Singing? Me?

LAURA: Yes. I remember what a beautiful voice you had.

JIM: When did you hear me sing?

(Voice Offstage in the Pause.)

VOICE (*offstage*):
O blow, ye winds, heigh-ho,
A-roving I will go!
I'm off to my love
With a boxing glove—
Ten thousand miles away!

JIM: You say you've heard me sing?

LAURA: Oh, yes! Yes, very often . . . I—don't suppose you remember me—at all?

JIM (*smiling doubtfully*): You know I have an idea I've seen you before. I had that idea soon as I opened the door. It seemed almost like I was about to remember your name. But the name that I started to call you—wasn't a name! And so I stopped myself before I said it.

LAURA: Wasn't it—Blue Roses?

JIM (*springs up, grinning*): Blue Roses! My gosh, yes—Blue Roses! That's what I had on my tongue when you opened the door! Isn't it funny what tricks your memory plays? I didn't connect you with the high school somehow or other. But that's where it was; it was high school. I didn't even know you were Shakespeare's sister! Gosh, I'm sorry.

LAURA: I didn't expect you to. You—barely knew me!

JIM: But we did have a speaking acquaintance, huh?

LAURA: Yes, we—spoke to each other.

JIM: When did you recognize me?

LAURA: Oh, right away!

JIM: Soon as I came in the door?

LAURA: When I heard your name I thought it was probably you. I knew that Tom used to know you a little in high school. So when you came in the door—Well, then I was—sure.

JIM: Why didn't you say something, then?

LAURA (*breathlessly*): I didn't know what to say, I was—too surprised!

JIM: For goodness' sakes! You know, this sure is funny!

LAURA: Yes! Yes, isn't it, though . . .

JIM: Didn't we have a class in something together?

LAURA: Yes, we did.

JIM: What class was that?

LAURA: It was—singing—Chorus!

JIM: Aw!

LAURA: I sat across the aisle from you in the Aud.

JIM: Aw.

LAURA: Mondays, Wednesdays and Fridays.

JIM: Now I remember—you always came in late.

LAURA: Yes, it was so hard for me, getting upstairs. I had that brace on my leg—it clumped so loud!

JIM: I never heard any clumping.

LAURA (*wincing at the recollection*): To me it sounded like—thunder!

JIM: Well, well, well. I never even noticed.

LAURA: And everybody was seated before I came in. I had to walk in front of all those people. My seat was in the back row. I had to go clumping all the way up the aisle with everyone watching!

JIM: You shouldn't have been self-conscious.

LAURA: I know, but I was. It was always such a relief when the singing started.

JIM: Aw, yes. I've placed you now! I used to call you Blue Roses. How was it that I got started calling you that?

LAURA: I was out of school a little while with pleurosis. When I came back you asked me what was the matter. I said I had pleurosis—you thought I said Blue Roses. That's what you always called me after that!

JIM: I hope you didn't mind.

LAURA: Oh, no—I liked it. You see, I wasn't acquainted with many—people. . . .

JIM: As I remember you sort of stuck by yourself.

LAURA: I—I—never had much luck at—making friends.

JIM: I don't see why you wouldn't.

LAURA: Well, I—started out badly.

JIM: You mean being—

LAURA: Yes, it sort of—stood between me—

JIM: You shouldn't have let it!

LAURA: I know but it did, and—

JIM: You were shy with people!

LAURA: I tried not to be but never could—

JIM: Overcome it?

LAURA: No, I—I never could!

JIM: I guess being shy is something you have to work out of kind of gradually.

LAURA (*sorrowfully*): Yes—I guess it—

JIM: Takes time!

LAURA: Yes.

JIM: People are not so dreadful when you know them. That's what you have to remember! And everybody has problems, not just you, but practically everybody has got some problems. You think of yourself as having the only problems, as being the only one who is disappointed. But just look around you and you will see lots of people as disappointed as you are. For instance, I hoped when I was going to high school that I would be further along at this time, six years later, than I am now—You remember that wonderful write-up I had in *The Torch?*

LAURA: Yes! (*She rises and crosses to table.*)

JIM: It said I was bound to succeed in anything I went into! (*Laura returns with the annual.*) Holy Jeez! *The Torch!* (*He accepts it reverently. They smiled across it with mutual wonder. Laura crouches beside him and they begin to turn through it. Laura's shyness is dissolving in his warmth.*)

LAURA: Here you are in *Pirates of Penzance!*

JIM (*wistfully*): I sang the baritone lead in that operatta.

LAURA (*rapidly*): So—*beautifully!*

JIM (*protesting*): Aw—

LAURA: Yes, yes—beautifully—beautifully!

JIM: You heard me?

LAURA: All three times!

JIM: No!

LAURA: Yes!

JIM: All three performances?

LAURA (*looking down*): Yes.

JIM: Why?

LAURA: I—wanted to ask you to—autograph my program.

JIM: Why didn't you ask me to?

LAURA: You were always surrounded by your own friends so much that I never had a chance to.

JIM: You should have just—

LAURA: Well, I—thought you might think I was—

JIM: Thought I might think you was—what?

LAURA: Oh—

JIM (*with reflective relish*): I was beleaguered by females in those days.

LAURA: You were terribly popular!

JIM: Yeah—

LAURA: You had such a—friendly way—

JIM: I was spoiled in high school.

LAURA: Everybody—liked you!

JIM: Including you?

LAURA: I—yes, I—I did, too—(*She gently closes the book in her lap.*)

JIM: Well, well, well!—Give me that program, Laura. (*She hands it to him. He signs it with a flourish.*) There you are—better late then never!

LAURA: Oh, I—what a—surprise!

JIM: My signature isn't worth very much right now. But some day—maybe—it will increase in value! Being disappointed is one thing and being discouraged is something else. I am disappointed but I'm not discouraged. I'm twenty-three years old. How old are you?

LAURA: I'll be twenty-four in June.

JIM: That's not old age!

LAURA: No, but—

JIM: You finished high school?

LAURA (*with difficulty*): I didn't go back.

JIM: You mean you dropped out?

LAURA: I made bad grades in my final examinations. (*She rises and replaces the book and the program. Her voice strained.*) How is—Emily Meisenbach getting along?

JIM: Oh, that kraut-head!

LAURA: Why do you call her that?

JIM: That's what she was.

LAURA: You're not still—going with her?

JIM: I never see her.

LAURA: It said in the Personal Section that you were—engaged!
JIM: I know, but I wasn't impressed by that—propaganda!
LAURA: It wasn't—the truth?
JIM: Only in Emily's optimistic opinion!
LAURA: Oh—

(Legend: "What Have You Done Since High School?")

*(Jim lights a cigarette and leans indolently back on his elbows smiling at Laura with a warmth and charm which light her inwardly with altar candles. She remains by the table and turns in her hands a piece of glass to cover her tumult.)*

JIM *(after several reflective puffs on a cigarette)*: What have you done since high school? *(She seems not to hear him.)* Huh? *(Laura looks up.)* I said what have you done since high school, Laura?
LAURA: Nothing much.
JIM: You must have been doing something these six long years.
LAURA: Yes.
JIM: Well, then, such as what?
LAURA: I took a business course at business college—
JIM: How did that work out?
LAURA: Well, not very—well—I had to drop out, it gave me—indigestion—

*(Jim laughs gently.)*

JIM: What are you doing now?
LAURA: I don't do anything—much. Oh, please don't think I sit around doing nothing! My glass collection takes up a good deal of my time. Glass is something you have to take good care of.
JIM: What did you say—about glass?
LAURA: Collection I said—I have one—*(She clears her throat and turns away again, acutely shy.)*
JIM *(abruptly)*: You know what I judge to be the trouble with you? Inferiority complex! Know what that is? That's what they call it when someone low-rates himself? I understand it because I had it, too. Although my case was not so aggravated as yours seems to be. I had it until I took up public speaking, developed my voice, and learned that I had an aptitude for science. Before that time I never thought of myself as being outstanding in any way whatso-ever! Now I've never made a regular study of it, but I have a

friend who says I can analyze people better than doctors that make a profession of it. I don't claim that to be necessarily true, but I can sure guess a person's psychology, Laura. (*Takes out his gum.*) Excuse me, Laura. I always take it out when the flavor is gone. I'll use this scrap of paper to wrap it in. I know how it is to get it stuck on a shoe. Yep—that's what I judge to be your principal trouble. A lack of confidence in yourself as a person. You don't have the proper amount of faith in yourself. I'm basing that fact on a number of your remarks and also on certain observations I've made. For instance that clumping you thought was so awful in high school. You say that you even dreaded to walk into class. You see what you did? You dropped out of school, you gave up an education because of a clump, which as far as I know was practically nonexistent! A little physical defect is what you have? Hardly noticeable even! Magnified thousands of times by imagination! You know what my strong advice to you is? Think of yourself as superior in some way!

LAURA: In what way would I think?

JIM: Why, man alive, Laura! Just look about you a little. What do you see? A world full of common people! All of 'em born and all of 'em going to die! Which of them has one-tenth of your good points! Or mine! Or anyone else's, as far as that goes—Gosh! Everybody excels in some one thing. Some in many! (*Unconsciously glances at himself in the mirror.*) All you've got to do is discover in what! Take me, for instance. (*He adjusts his tie at the mirror.*) My interest happens to lie in electrodynamics. I'm taking a course in radio engineering at night school, Laura, on top of a fairly responsible job at the warehouse. I'm taking that course and studying public speaking.

LAURA: Ohhhh.

JIM: Because I believe in the future of television! (*Turning back to her.*) I wish to be ready to go up right along with it. Therefore I'm planning to get in on the ground floor. In fact, I've already made the right connections and all that remains is for the industry itself to get under way! Full steam—(*His eyes are starry.*) Knowledge—Zzzzzp! Money—Zzzzzzp! Power! That's the cycle democracy is built on! (*His attitude is convincingly dynamic. Laura stares at him, even her shyness eclipsed in her absolute wonder. He suddenly grins.*) I guess you think I think a lot of myself!

LAURA: No—o-o-o, I—

JIM: Now how about you? Isn't there something you take more interest in than anything else?

LAURA: Well, I do—as I said—have my—glass collection—

(*A peal of girlish laughter from the kitchen.*)

JIM: I'm not right sure I know what you're talking about. What kind of glass is it?

LAURA: Little articles of it, they're ornaments mostly! Most of them are little animals made out of glass, the tiniest little animals in the world. Mother calls them a glass menagerie! Here's an example of one, if you'd like to see it! This one is one of the oldest. It's nearly thirteen. (*He stretches out his hand.*) (*Music: "The Glass Menagerie."*) Oh, be careful—if you breathe, it breaks!

JIM: I'd better not take it. I'm pretty clumsy with things.

LAURA: Go on. I trust you with him! (*Places it in his palm.*) There now—you're holding him gently! Hold him over the light, he loves the light! You see how the light shines through him?

JIM: It sure does shine!

LAURA: I shouldn't be partial, but he is my favorite one.

JIM: What kind of thing is this one supposed to be?

LAURA: Haven't you noticed the single horn on his forehead?

JIM: A unicorn, huh?

LAURA: Mmm-hmmm!

JIM: Unicorns, aren't they extinct in the modern world?

LAURA: I know!

JIM: Poor little fellow, he must feel sort of lonesome.

LAURA (*smiling*): Well, if he does he doesn't complain about it. He stays on a shelf with some horses that don't have horns and all of them seem to get along nicely together.

JIM: How do you know?

LAURA (*lightly*): I haven't heard any arguments among them!

JIM (*grinning*): No arguments, huh? Well, that's a pretty good sign! Where shall I set him?

LAURA: Put him on the table. They all like a change of scenery once in a while!

JIM (*stretching*): Well, well, well, well—Look how big my shadow is when I stretch!

LAURA: Oh, oh, yes—it stretches across the ceiling!

JIM (*crossing to door*): I think it's stopped raining. (*Opens fire-escape door*) Where does the music come from?

LAURA: From the Paradise Dance Hall across the alley.

JIM: How about cutting the rug a little, Miss Wingfield?

LAURA: Oh, I—

JIM: Or is your program filled up? Let me have a look at it. (*Grasps imaginary card.*) Why, every dance is taken! I'll just have to scratch some out. (*Waltz Music: "La Golondrina."*) Ahhh, a waltz! (*He executes some sweeping turns by himself then holds his arms toward Laura.*)

LAURA (*breathlessly*): I—can't dance!

JIM: There you go, that inferiority stuff!

LAURA: I've never danced in my life!

JIM: Come on, try!

LAURA: Oh, but I'd step on you!

JIM: I'm not made out of glass.

LAURA: How—how—how do we start?

JIM: Just leave it to me. You hold your arms out a little.

LAURA: Like this?

JIM: A little bit higher. Right. Now don't tighten up, that's the main thing about it—relax.

LAURA (*laughing breathlessly*): It's hard not to.

JIM: Okay.

LAURA: I'm afraid you can't budge me.

JIM: What do you bet I can't? (*He swings her into motion.*)

LAURA: Goodness, yes, you can!

JIM: Let yourself go, now, Laura, just let yourself go.

LAURA: I'm—

JIM: Come on!

LAURA: Trying!

JIM: Not so stiff—Easy does it!

LAURA: I know but I'm—

JIM: Loosen th' backbone! There now, that's a lot better.

LAURA: Am I?

JIM: Lots, lots better! (*He moves her about the room in a clumsy waltz.*)

LAURA: Oh, my!

JIM: Ha-ha!

LAURA: Goodness, yes you can!

JIM: Ha-ha-ha! (*They suddenly bump into the table, Jim stops.*) What did we hit on?

LAURA: Table.

JIM: Did something fall off it? I think—

LAURA: Yes.

JIM: I hope that it wasn't the little glass horse with the horn!

LAURA: Yes.

JIM: Aw, aw, aw. Is it broken?

LAURA: Now it is just like all the other horses.

JIM: It's lost its—

LAURA: Horn! It doesn't matter. Maybe it's a blessing in disguise.

JIM: You'll never forgive me. I bet that was your favorite piece of glass.

LAURA: I don't have favorites much. It's no tragedy, Freckles. Glass breaks so easily. No matter how careful you are. The traffic jars the shelves and things fall off them.

JIM: Still I'm awfully sorry that I was the cause.

LAURA (*smiling*): I'll just imagine he had an operation. The horn was removed to make him feel less—freakish! (*They both laugh.*) Now he will feel more at home with the other horses, the ones that don't have horns . . .

JIM: Ha-ha, that's very funny! (*Suddenly serious.*) I'm glad to see that you have a sense of humor. You know—you're—well—very different! Surprisingly different from anyone else I know! (*His voice becomes soft and hesitant with a genuine feeling.*) Do you mind me telling you that? (*Laura is abashed beyond speech.*) You make me feel sort of—I don't know how to put it! I'm usually pretty good at expressing things, but—This is something that I don't know how to say! (*Laura touches her throat, clears it—turns the broken unicorn in her hands.*) (*Even softer.*) Has anyone ever told you that you were pretty? (*Pause: Music.*) (*Laura looks up slowly, with wonder, and shakes her head.*) Well, you are! In a very different way from anyone else. And all the nicer because of the difference, too. (*His voice becomes low and husky. Laura turns away, nearly faint with the novelty of her emotions.*) I wish that you were my sister. I'd teach you to have some confidence in yourself. The different people are not like other people, but being different is nothing to be ashamed of. Because other people are not such wonderful people. They're one hundred times one thousand. You're one times one! They walk all over the earth. You just stay here. They're common as—weeds, but—you—well, you're—Blue Roses!

(Image on Screen: Blue Roses.)

(Music Changes.)

LAURA: But blue is wrong for—roses . . .

JIM: It's right for you—You're—pretty!

LAURA: In what respect am I pretty?

JIM: In all respects—believe me! Your eyes—your hair—are pretty! Your hands are pretty! (*He catches hold of her hand.*) You think I'm making this up because I'm invited to dinner and have to be nice. Oh, I could do that! I could put on an act for you, Laura, and say lots of things without being very sincere. But this time I am. I'm talking to you sincerely. I happened to notice you had this inferiority complex that keeps you from feeling comfortable with people. Somebody needs to build your confidence up and make you proud instead of shy and turning away and—blushing—Somebody ought to—ought to—*kiss* you, Laura!

(*His hand slips slowly up her arm to her shoulder.*) (*Music Swells Tumultuously.*) (*He suddenly turns her about and kisses her on the lips. When he releases her Laura sinks on the sofa with a bright, dazed look. Jim backs away and fishes in his pocket for a cigarette.*) (*Legend on Screen: "Souvenir."*) Stumble-john! (*He lights the cigarette, avoiding her look. There is a peal of girlish laughter from Amanda in the kitchen. Laura slowly raises and opens her hand. It still contains the little broken glass animal. She looks at it with a tender, bewildered expression.*) Stumble-john! I shouldn't have done that—That was way off the beam. You don't smoke, do you? (*She looks up, smiling, not hearing the question. He sits besides her a little gingerly. She looks at him speechlessly— waiting. He coughs decorously and moves a little farther aside as he considers the situation and senses her feelings, dimly, with perturbation. Gently.*) Would you—care for a— mint? (*She doesn't seem to hear him but her look grows brighter even.*) Peppermint—Life Saver? My pocket's a regular drug store—wherever I go . . . (*He pops a mint in his mouth. Then gulps and decides to make a clean breast of it. He speaks slowly and gingerly.*) Laura, you know, if I had a sister like you, I'd do the same thing as Tom. I'd bring out fellows—introduce her to them. The right type of boys of a type to—appreciate her. Only—well—he made a mistake about me. Maybe I've got no call to be saying this. This may not have been the idea in having me over. But what if it was?

*There's nothing wrong about that. The only trouble is that in my case—I'm not in a situation to—do the right thing. I can't take down your number and say I'll phone. I can't call up next week and—ask for a date. I thought I had better explain the situation in case you misunderstood it and—hurt your feelings. . . . (Pause. Slowly, very slowly, Laura's look changes, her eyes returning slowly from his to the ornament in her palm.)*

*(Amanda utters another gay laugh in the kitchen.)*

LAURA *(faintly)*:   You—won't—call again?

JIM:   No, Laura. I can't. *(He rises from the sofa.)* As I was just explaining, I've—got strings on me, Laura, I've—been going steady! I go out all the time with a girl named Betty. She's a home-girl like you, and Catholic, and Irish, and in a great many ways we—get along fine. I met her last summer on a moonlight boat trip up the river to Alton, on the Majestic. Well—right away from the start it was—love! *(Legend: "Love!")* *(Laura sways slightly forward and grips the arm of the sofa. He fails to notice, now enrapt in his own comfortable being.)* Being in love has made a new man of me! *(Leaning stiffly forward, clutching the arm of the sofa, Laura struggles visibly with her storm. But Jim is oblivious, she is a long way off.)* The power of love is really pretty tremendous! Love is something that—changes the whole world, Laura! *(The storm abates a little and Laura leans back. He notices her again.)* It happened that Betty's aunt took sick, she got a wire and had to go to Centralia. So Tom—when he asked me to dinner—I naturally just accepted the invitation, not knowing that you—that he—that I—(He stops awkwardly.)* Huh—I'm a stumble-john! *(He flops back on the sofa. The holy candles in the altar of Laura's face have been snuffed out! There is a look of almost infinite desolation. Jim glances at her uneasily.)* I wish that you would—say something. *(She bites her lip which was trembling and then bravely smiles. She opens her hand again on the broken glass ornament. Then she gently takes his hand and raises it level to her own. She carefully places the unicorn in the palm of his hand, then pushes his fingers closed upon it.)* What are you—doing that for? You want me to have him?—Laura? *(She nods.)* What for?

LAURA:   A—souvenir . . .

*(She rises unsteadily and crouches beside the victrola to wind it up.)*

(Legend on Screen: "Things Have a Way of Turning Out So Badly.")

(Or Image: "Gentleman Caller Waving Good-Bye—Gaily.")

*(At this moment Amanda rushes brightly back in the front room. She bears a pitcher of fruit punch in an old-fashioned cut-glass pitcher and a plate of macaroons. The plate has a gold border and poppies painted on it.)*

AMANDA: Well, well, well! Isn't the air delightful after the shower? I've made you children a little liquid refreshment. *(Turns gaily to the gentleman caller.)* Jim, do you know that song about lemonade?
"Lemonade, lemonade
Made in the shade and stirred with a spade—
Good enough for any old maid!"

JIM *(uneasily)*: Ha-ha! No—I never heard it.

AMANDA: Why, Laura! You look so serious!

JIM: We were having a serious conversation.

AMANDA: Good! Now you're better acquainted!

JIM *(uncertainly)*: Ha-ha! Yes.

AMANDA: You modern young people are much more serious-minded than my generation. I was so gay as a girl!

JIM: You haven't changed, Mrs. Wingfield.

AMANDA: Tonight I'm rejuvenated! The gaiety of the occasion, Mr. O'Connor! *(She tosses her head with a peal of laughter. Spills lemonade.)* Oooo! I'm baptizing myself!

JIM: Here—let me—

AMANDA *(setting the pitcher down.)*: There now. I discovered we had some maraschino cherries. I dumped them in, juice and all!

JIM: You shouldn't have gone to that trouble, Mrs. Wingfield.

AMANDA: Trouble, trouble? Why it was loads of fun! Didn't you hear me cutting up in the kitchen? I bet your ears were burning! I told Tom how outdone with him I was for keeping you to himself so long a time! He should have brought you over much, much sooner! Well, now that you've found your way, I want you to be a very frequent caller! Not just occasional but all the time. Oh, we're going to have a lot of gay times together! I see them coming! Mmm, just breathe that air! So fresh, and the moon's so pretty! I'll skip back out—I know where my place is when young folks are having a—serious conversation!

JIM: Oh, don't go out, Mrs. Wingfield. The fact of the matter is I've got to be going.

AMANDA: Going, now? You're joking! Why, it's only the shank of the evening, Mr. O'Connor.

JIM: Well, you now how it is.

AMANDA: You mean you're a young workingman and have to keep workingmen's hours. We'll let you off early tonight. But only on the condition that next time you stay later. What's the best night for you? Isn't Saturday night the best night for you workingmen?

JIM: I have a couple of time-clocks to punch, Mrs. Wingfield. One at morning, another one at night.

AMANDA: My, but you are ambitious! You work at night, too?

JIM: No, Ma'am, not work but—Betty! (*He crosses deliberately to pick up his hat. The band at the Paradise Dance Hall goes into a tender waltz.*)

AMANDA: Betty? Betty? Who's—Betty! (*There is an ominous cracking sound in the sky.*)

JIM: Oh, just a girl. The girl I go steady with! (*He smiles charmingly. The sky falls.*)

(Legend: "The Sky Falls")

AMANDA (*a long-drawn exhalation*): Ohhhh . . . Is it a serious romance, Mr. O'Connor?

JIM: We're going to be married the second Sunday in June.

AMANDA: Ohhhh—how nice! Tom didn't mention that you were engaged to be married.

JIM: The cat's not out of the bag at the warehouse yet. You know how they are. They call you Romeo and stuff like that. (*He stops at the oval mirror to put on his hat. He carefully shapes the brim and the crown to give a discreetly dashing effect.*) It's been a wonderful evening, Mrs. Wingfield. I guess this is what they mean by Southern hospitality.

AMANDA: It really wasn't anything at all.

JIM: I hope it don't seem like I'm rushing off. But I promised Betty I'd pick her up at the Wabash depot, an' by the time I get my jalopy down there her train'll be in. Some women are pretty upset if you keep 'em waiting.

AMANDA: Yes, I know—The tyranny of women! (*Extends her hand.*) Goodbye, Mr. O'Connor. I wish you luck—and happiness—and success! All three of them, and so does Laura!—Don't you, Laura?

LAURA: Yes!

JIM (*taking her hand*):   Goodbye, Laura. I'm certainly going to treasure that souvenir. And don't you forget the good advice I gave you. (*Raises his voice to a cheery shout.*) So long, Shakespeare! Thanks again, ladies—Good night!

(*He grins and ducks jauntily out. Still bravely grimacing, Amanda closes the door on the gentleman caller. Then she turns back to the room with a puzzled expression. She and Laura don't dare to face each other. Laura crouches beside the victrola to wind it.*)

AMANDA (*faintly*):   Things have a way of turning out so badly. I don't believe that I would play the victrola. Well, well—well—Our gentleman caller was engaged to be married! Tom!

TOM (*from back*):   Yes, Mother?

AMANDA:   Come in here a minute. I want to tell you something awfully funny.

TOM (*enters with macaroon and a glass of the lemonade*):   Has the gentleman caller gotten away already?

AMANDA:   The gentleman caller has made an early departure. What a wonderful joke you played on us!

TOM:   How do you mean?

AMANDA:   You didn't mention that he was engaged to be married.

TOM:   Jim? Engaged?

AMANDA:   That's what he just informed us.

TOM:   I'll be jiggered! I didn't know about that.

AMANDA:   That seems very peculiar.

TOM:   What's peculiar about it?

AMANDA:   Didn't you call him your best friend down at the warehouse?

TOM:   He is, but how did I know?

AMANDA:   It seems extremely peculiar that you wouldn't know your best friend was going to be married!

TOM:   The warehouse is where I work, not where I know things about people!

AMANDA:   You don't know things anywhere! You live in a dream; you manufacture illusions! (*He crosses to door.*) Where are you going?

TOM:   I'm going to the movies.

AMANDA:   That's right, now that you've had us make such fools of ourselves. The effort, the preparations, all the expense! The new

floor lamp, the rug, the clothes for Laura! All for what? To entertain some other girl's fiancé! Go to the movies, go! Don't think
about us, a mother deserted, an unmarried sister who's crippled
and has no job! Don't let anything interfere with your selfish pleasure! Just go, go, go—to the movies!

TOM:   All right, I will! The more you shout about my selfishness to
me the quicker I'll go, and I won't go to the movies!

AMANDA:   Go, then! Then go to the moon—you selfish dreamer!

*Tom smashes his glass on the floor. He plunges out on the
fire-escape, slamming the door. Laura screams—cut by door.*

*Dance-hall music up. Tom goes to the rail and grips it desper-
ately, lifting his face in the chill white moonlight penetrating
the narrow abyss of the alley.*

(Legend on Screen: "And So Good-Bye . . .")

*(Tom's closing speech is timed with the interior pantomime.
The interior scene is played as though viewed through sound-
proof glass. Amanda appears to be making a comforting
speech to Laura who is huddled upon the sofa. Now that we
cannot hear the mother's speech, her silliness is gone and she
has dignity and tragic beauty. Laura's dark hair hides her face
until at the end of the speech she lifts it to smile at her
mother. Amanda's gestures are slow and graceful, almost
dancelike, as she comforts her daughter. At the end of her
speech she glances a moment at the father's picture—then
withdraws through the portieres. At close of Tom's speech,
Laura blows out the candles, ending the play.)*

TOM:   I didn't go to the moon, I went much further—for time is the
longest distance between two places—Not long after that I was
fired for writing a poem on the lid of a shoe-box. I left Saint Louis.
I descended the steps of this fire-escape for a last time and followed, from then on, in my father's footsteps, attempting to find in
motion what was lost in space—I traveled around a great deal. The
cities swept about me like dead leaves, leaves that were brightly
colored but torn away from the branches. I would have stopped,
but I was pursued by something. It always came upon me un-
awares, taking me altogether by surprise. Perhaps it was a familiar
bit of music. Perhaps it was only a piece of transparent glass—

Perhaps I am walking along a street at night, in some strange city, before I have found companions. I pass the lighted window of a shop where perfume is sold. The window is filled with pieces of colored glass, tiny transparent bottles in delicate colors, like bits of a shattered rainbow. Then all at once my sister touches my shoulder. I turn around and look into her eyes . . . Oh, Laura, Laura, I tried to leave you behind me, but I am more faithful than I intended to be! I reach for a cigarette, I cross the street, I run into the movies or a bar, I buy a drink, I speak to the nearest stranger—anything that can blow your candles out! (*Laura bends over the candles.*)—for nowadays the world is lit by lightning! Blow out your candles, Laura—and so goodbye . . .

(*She blows the candles out.*)

(The Scene Dissolves.)

*—1944*

# *Arthur Miller* (1915–2005)

*Arthur Miller, gained a reputation as a major American dramatist with his second play, and continues to be productive in his mid 80s. Miller was born in Harlem, the son of prosperous Jewish immigrants who suffered badly during the depression. He studied drama at the University of Michigan and was for a time employed by the Federal Theatre Project, a Roosevelt-era government program dedicated to bringing drama with social themes to audiences in areas outside New York. His first success was* All My Sons *(1947), an Ibsenesque problem play (Miller later adapted Ibsen's* An Enemy of the People *for the New York stage) about a manufacturer who profited during World War II by knowingly supplying defective parts which caused airplanes to crash.* All My Sons, *following closely on the heels of investigations of wartime profiteering, easily found appreciative audiences.* Death of a Salesman *(1949) won Miller a Pulitzer Prize. Originally a short story based to some degree on one of Miller's uncles,* Death of a Salesman *evolved into its final form over many years. When Miller finally sat down at the typewriter to write the play, he said, "All I had was the first two lines and a death." During the height of the play's success, Miller wrote a famous essay titled "Tragedy and the Common Man," in which he dismisses the ancient "rule" that true tragedy can concern only the lives and fates of the famous. "I believe," he said, "that the common man is an apt a subject for tragedy in its highest sense as knigs were. . . . If the exaltation of tragic action were truly a property of the high-bred character alone, it is inconceivable that the mass of mankind should cherish tragedy above all other forms, let alone be capable of understanding it." Miller's fame was further increased by* The Crucible *(1953), a play about the Salem witch trials that had obvious contemporary political overtones, drawing on Miller's own McCarthy-era investigations by the House Un-Amerian Activities Committee into his past political affiliations. Miller risked a jail term for his refusal to cooperate with the committee. His marriage to Marilyn Monroe, which is in part the subject of* After the Fall *(1964), ended unhappily shortly after Miller completed work on the screenplay of* The Misfits, *which proved to be her final film. Other important plays include* A View from the Bridge *(1955), which has been revived several times on Broadway and also exists in an operatic version;* Incident at Vichy *(1964), a play about the Holocaust;* The Price *(1968);* Broken Glass, *another play about anti-Semetism; and* Ride Down Mount Morgan *(1998), which starred Patrick Stewart in its Broadway production. Miller's autobiography,* Timebends, *was published in 1987. In it he proudly recounts his experiences in 1983 directing a Chinese production of* Death of a Salesman *in Beijing, the first contemporary American play produced in China. Like Tennessee Williams's plays, Miller's are frequently revived; the final performance of the 1999 award-winning production of* Death of a Salesman *was televised on Showtime. Miller's last play,* Finishing the Picture, *enjoyed a successful run in Chicago in the fall of 2004, only months before the playwright's death at 89 in February of 2005.*

# Death of a Salesman

## CHARACTERS

Willy Loman
Linda
Biff
Happy
Bernard
The Woman
Charley
Uncle Ben
Howard Wagner
Jenny
Stanley
Miss Forsythe
Letta

*Scene: The action takes place in Willy Loman's house and yard and in various places he visits in the New York and Boston of today.*

## ACT 1

*Scene: A melody is heard, played upon a flute. It is small and fine, telling of grass and trees and the horizon. The curtain rises.*

*Before us is the Salesman's house. We are aware of towering, angular shapes behind it, surrounding it on all sides. Only the blue light of the sky falls upon the house and forestage; the surrounding area shows an angry glow of orange. As more light appears, we see a solid vault of apartment houses around the small, fragile-seeming home. An air of the dream clings to the place, a dream rising out of reality. The kitchen at center seems actual enough, for there is a kitchen table with three chairs, and a refrigerator. But no other fixtures are seen. At the back of the kitchen there is a draped entrance, which leads to the living room. To the right of the kitchen, on a level raised two feet, is a bedroom furnished only with a brass bedstead and a straight chair. On a shelf over the bed a silver athletic trophy stands. A window opens onto the apartment house at the side.*

*Behind the kitchen, on a level raised six and a half feet, is the boys' bedroom, at present barely visible. Two beds are dimly seen, and at the back of the room a dormer window. (This bedroom is above the un-seen living room.) At the left a stairway curves up to it from the kitchen.*

*The entire setting is wholly or, in some places, partially transparent. The roof-line of the house is one-dimensional; under and over it we see the apartment buildings. Before the house lies an apron, curving be-yond the forestage into the orchestra. This forward area serves as the back yard as well as the locale of all Willy's imaginings and of his city scenes. Whenever the action is in the present the actors observe the imaginary wall-lines, entering the house only through its door at the left. But in the scenes of the past these boundaries are broken, and characters enter or leave a room by stepping "through" a wall onto the forestage.*

*From the right, Willy Loman, the Salesman, enters, carrying two large sample cases. The flute plays on. He hears but is not aware of it. He is past sixty years of age, dressed quietly. Even as he crosses the stage to the doorway of the house, his exhaustion is apparent. He unlocks the door, comes into the kitchen, and thankfully lets his burden down, feel-ing the soreness of his palms. A word-sigh escapes his lips—it might be "Oh, boy, oh, boy." He closes the door, then carries his cases out into the living room, through the draped kitchen doorway.*

*Linda, his wife, has stirred in her bed at the right. She gets out and puts on a robe, listening. Most often jovial, she has developed an iron re-pression of her exceptions to Willy's behavior—she more than loves him, she admires him, as though his mercurial nature, his temper, his massive dreams and little cruelties, served her only as sharp reminders of the turbulent longings within him, longings which she shares but lacks the temperament to utter and follow to their end.*

LINDA [*hearing Willy outside the bedroom, calls with some trepi-dation*]: Willy!

WILLY: It's all right. I came back.

LINDA: Why? What happened? (*Slight pause.*) Did something hap-pen, Willy?

WILLY: No, nothing happened.

LINDA: You didn't smash the car, did you?

WILLY (*with casual irritation*): I said nothing happened. Didn't you hear me?

LINDA:   Don't you feel well?

WILLY:   I'm tired to the death. (*The flute has faded away. He sits on the bed beside her, a little numb.*) I couldn't make it. I just couldn't make it, Linda.

LINDA (*very carefully, delicately*):   Where were you all day? You look terrible.

WILLY:   I got as far as a little above Yonkers. I stopped for a cup of coffee. Maybe it was the coffee.

LINDA:   What?

WILLY (*after a pause*):   I suddenly couldn't drive any more. The car kept going off onto the shoulder, y'know?

LINDA (*helpfully*):   Oh. Maybe it was the steering again. I don't think Angelo knows the Studebaker.

WILLY:   No, it's me, it's me. Suddenly I realize I'm goin' sixty miles an hour and I don't remember the last five minutes. I'm—I can't seem to—keep my mind to it.

LINDA:   Maybe it's your glasses. You never went for your new glasses.

WILLY:   No, I see everything. I came back ten miles an hour. It took me nearly four hours from Yonkers.

LINDA (*resigned*):   Well, you'll just have to take a rest, Willy, you can't continue this way.

WILLY:   I just got back from Florida.

LINDA:   But you didn't rest your mind. Your mind is overactive, and the mind is what counts, dear.

WILLY:   I'll start out in the morning. Maybe I'll feel better in the morning. (*She is taking off his shoes.*) These goddam arch supports are killing me.

LINDA:   Take an aspirin. Should I get you an aspirin? It'll soothe you.

WILLY (*with wonder*):   I was driving along, you understand? And I was fine. I was even observing the scenery. You can imagine, me looking at scenery, on the road every week of my life. But it's so beautiful up there, Linda, the trees are so thick, and the sun is warm. I opened the windshield and just let the warm air bathe over me. And then all of a sudden I'm goin' off the road! I'm tellin' ya, I absolutely forgot I was driving. If I'd've gone the other way over the white line I might've killed somebody. So I went on again—and five minutes later I'm dreamin' again, and I nearly . . . (*He presses two fingers against his eyes.*) I have such thoughts, I have such strange thoughts.

LINDA:   Willy, dear. Talk to them again. There's no reason why you can't work in New York.

WILLY: They don't need me in New York. I'm the New England man. I'm vital in New England.

LINDA: But you're sixty years old. They can't expect you to keep traveling every week.

WILLY: I'll have to send a wire to Portland. I'm supposed to see Brown and Morrison tomorrow morning at ten o'clock to show the line. Goddammit, I could sell them! (*He starts putting on his jacket.*)

LINDA (*taking the jacket from him*): Why don't you go down to the place tomorrow and tell Howard you've simply got to work in New York? You're too accommodating, dear.

WILLY: If old man Wagner was alive I'd a been in charge of New York now! That man was a prince, he was a masterful man. But that boy of his, that Howard, he don't appreciate. When I went north the first time, the Wagner Company didn't know where New England was!

LINDA: Why don't you tell those things to Howard, dear?

WILLY (*encouraged*): I will, I definitely will. Is there any cheese?

LINDA: I'll make you a sandwich.

WILLY: No, go to sleep. I'll take some milk. I'll be up right away. The boys in?

LINDA: They're sleeping. Happy took Biff on a date tonight.

WILLY (*interested*): That so?

LINDA: It was so nice to see them shaving together, one behind the other, in the bathroom. And going out together. You notice? The whole house smells of shaving lotion.

WILLY: Figure it out. Work a lifetime to pay off a house. You finally own it, and there's nobody to live in it.

LINDA: Well, dear, life is a casting off. It's always that way.

WILLY: No, no, some people—some people accomplish something. Did Biff say anything after I went this morning?

LINDA: You shouldn't have criticized him, Willy, especially after he just got off the train. You mustn't lose your temper with him.

WILLY: When the hell did I lose my temper? I simply asked him if he was making any money. Is that a criticism?

LINDA: But, dear, how could he make any money?

WILLY (*worried and angered*): There's such an undercurrent in him. He became a moody man. Did he apologize when I left this morning?

LINDA: He was crestfallen, Willy. You know how he admires you. I think if he finds himself, then you'll both be happier and not fight any more.

WILLY: How can he find himself on a farm? Is that a life? A farm hand? In the beginning, when he was young, I thought, well, a young man, it's good for him to tramp around, take a lot of different jobs. But it's more than ten years now and he has yet to make thirty-five dollars a week!

LINDA: He's finding himself, Willy.

WILLY: Not finding yourself at the age of thirty-four is a disgrace!

LINDA: Shh!

WILLY: The trouble is he's lazy, goddammit!

LINDA: Willy, please!

WILLY: Biff is a lazy bum!

LINDA: They're sleeping. Get something to eat. Go on down.

WILLY: Why did he come home? I would like to know what brought him home.

LINDA: I don't know. I think he's still lost, Willy. I think he's very lost.

WILLY: Biff Loman is lost. In the greatest country in the world a young man with such—personal attractiveness, gets lost. And such a hard worker. There's one thing about Biff—he's not lazy.

LINDA: Never.

WILLY (*with pity and resolve*): I'll see him in the morning; I'll have a nice talk with him. I'll get him a job selling. He could be big in no time. My God! Remember how they used to follow him around in high school? When he smiled at one of them their faces lit up. When he walked down the street . . . (*He loses himself in reminiscences.*)

LINDA (*trying to bring him out of it*): Willy, dear, I got a new kind of American-type cheese today. It's whipped.

WILLY: Why do you get American when I like Swiss?

LINDA: I just thought you'd like a change . . .

WILLY: I don't want a change! I want Swiss cheese. Why am I always being contradicted?

LINDA (*with a covering laugh*): I thought it would be a surprise.

WILLY: Why don't you open a window in here, for God's sake?

LINDA (*with infinite patience*): They're all open, dear.

WILLY: The way they boxed us in here. Bricks and windows, windows and bricks.

LINDA: We should've bought the land next door.

WILLY: The street is lined with cars. There's not a breath of fresh air in the neighborhood. The grass don't grow any more, you can't raise a carrot in the back yard. They should've had a law against apartment houses. Remember those two beautiful elm trees out there? When I and Biff hung the swing between them?

LINDA: Yeah, like being a million miles from the city.

WILLY: They should've arrested the builder for cutting those down. They massacred the neighborhood. (*Lost.*) More and more I think of those days, Linda. This time of year it was lilac and wisteria. And then the peonies would come out, and the daffodils. What fragrance in this room!

LINDA: Well, after all, people had to move somewhere.

WILLY: No, there's more people now.

LINDA: I don't think there's more people. I think . . .

WILLY: There's more people! That's what's ruining this country! Population is getting out of control. The competition is maddening! Smell the stink from that apartment house! And another one on the other side . . . How can they whip cheese?

*On Willy's last line, Biff and Happy raise themselves up in their beds, listening.*

LINDA: Go down, try it. And be quiet.

WILLY (*turning to Linda, guiltily*): You're not worried about me, are you, sweetheart?

BIFF: What's the matter?

HAPPY: Listen!

LINDA: You've got too much on the ball to worry about.

WILLY: You're my foundation and my support, Linda.

LINDA: Just try to relax, dear. You make mountains out of molehills.

WILLY: I won't fight with him any more. If he wants to go back to Texas, let him go.

LINDA: He'll find his way.

WILLY: Sure. Certain men just don't get started till later in life. Like Thomas Edison, I think. Or B. F. Goodrich. One of them was deaf. (*He starts for the bedroom doorway.*) I'll put my money on Biff.

LINDA: And Willy—if it's warm Sunday we'll drive in the country. And we'll open the windshield, and take lunch.

WILLY: No, the windshields don't open on the new cars.

LINDA: But you opened it today.

WILLY: Me? I didn't. (*He stops.*) Now isn't that peculiar! Isn't that a remarkable . . . (*He breaks off in amazement and fright as the flute is heard distantly.*)

LINDA: What, darling?

WILLY: That is the most remarkable thing.

LINDA: What, dear?

WILLY: I was thinking of the Chevvy. (*Slight pause.*) Nineteen twenty-eight . . . when I had that red Chevvy . . . (*Breaks off:*) That funny? I coulda sworn I was driving that Chevvy today.

LINDA: Well, that's nothing. Something must've reminded you.

WILLY: Remarkable. Ts. Remember those days? The way Biff used to simonize that car? The dealer refused to believe there was eighty thousand miles on it. (*He shakes his head.*) Heh! (*To Linda.*) Close your eyes, I'll be right up. (*He walks out of the bedroom.*)

HAPPY (*to Biff*): Jesus, maybe he smashed up the car again!

LINDA (*calling after Willy*): Be careful on the stairs, dear! The cheese is on the middle shelf. (*She turns, goes over to the bed, takes his jacket, and goes out of the bedroom.*)

*Light has risen on the boys' room. Unseen, Willy is heard talking to himself; "Eighty thousand miles," and a little laugh. Biff gets out of bed, comes downstage a bit, and stands attentively. Biff is two years older than his brother Happy, well built, but in these days bears a worn air and seems less self-assured. He has succeeded less, and his dreams are stronger and less acceptable than Happy's. Happy is tall, powerfully made. Sexuality is like a visible color on him, or a scent that many women have discovered. He, like his brother, is lost, but in a different way, for he has never allowed himself to turn his face toward defeat and is thus more confused and hard-skinned, although seemingly more content.*

HAPPY (*getting out of bed*): He's going to get his license taken away if he keeps that up. I'm getting nervous about him, y'know, Biff?

BIFF: His eyes are going.

HAPPY: No, I've driven with him. He sees all right. He just doesn't keep his mind on it. I drove into the city with him last week. He stops at a green light and then it turns red and he goes. (*He laughs.*)

BIFF: Maybe he's color-blind.

HAPPY: Pop? Why he's got the finest eye for color in the business. You know that.

BIFF (*sitting down on his bed*): I'm going to sleep.

HAPPY: You're not still sour on Dad, are you, Biff?

BIFF: He's all right, I guess.

WILLY (*underneath them, in the living room*): Yes, sir, eighty thousand miles—eighty-two thousand!

BIFF: You smoking?

HAPPY (*holding out a pack of cigarettes*): Want one?

BIFF (*taking a cigarette*): I can never sleep when I smell it.

WILLY: What a simonizing job, heh!

HAPPY (*with deep sentiment*): Funny, Biff, y'know? Us sleeping in here again? The old beds. (*He pats his bed affectionately.*) All the talk that went across those beds, huh? Our whole lives.

BIFF: Yeah. Lotta dreams and plans.

HAPPY (*with a deep and masculine laugh*): About five hundred women would like to know what was said in this room. (*They share a soft laugh.*)

BIFF: Remember that big Betsy something—what the hell was her name—over on Bushwick Avenue?

HAPPY (*combing his hair*): With the collie dog!

BIFF: That's the one. I got you in there, remember?

HAPPY: Yeah, that was my first time—I think. Boy, there was a pig. (*They laugh, almost crudely.*) You taught me everything I know about women. Don't forget that.

BIFF: I bet you forgot how bashful you used to be. Especially with girls.

HAPPY: Oh, I still am, Biff.

BIFF: Oh, go on.

HAPPY: I just control it, that's all. I think I got less bashful and you got more so. What happened, Biff? Where's the old humor, the old confidence? (*He shakes Biff's knee. Biff gets up and moves restlessly about the room.*) What's the matter?

BIFF: Why does Dad mock me all the time?

HAPPY: He's not mocking you, he . . .

BIFF: Everything I say there's a twist of mockery on his face. I can't get near him.

HAPPY: He just wants you to make good, that's all. I wanted to talk to you about Dad for a long time, Biff. Something's—happening to him. He—talks to himself.

BIFF: I noticed that this morning. But he always mumbled.

HAPPY: But not so noticeable. It got so embarrassing I sent him to Florida. And you know something? Most of the time he's talking to you.

BIFF: What's he say about me?

HAPPY: I can't make it out.

BIFF: What's he say about me?

HAPPY: I think the fact that you're not settled, that you're still kind of up in the air . . .

BIFF: There's one or two other things depressing him, Happy.

HAPPY: What do you mean?

BIFF: Never mind. Just don't lay it all to me.

HAPPY: But I think if you just got started—I mean—is there any future for you out there?

BIFF: I tell ya, Hap, I don't know what the future is. I don't know—what I'm supposed to want.

HAPPY: What do you mean?

BIFF: Well, I spent six or seven years after high school trying to work myself up. Shipping clerk, salesman, business of one kind or another. And it's a measly manner of existence. To get on that subway on the hot mornings in summer. To devote your whole life to keeping stock, or making phone calls, or selling or buying. To suffer fifty weeks of the year for the sake of a two-week vacation, when all you really desire is to be outdoors, with your shirt off. And always to have to get ahead of the next fella. And still—that's how you build a future.

HAPPY: Well, you really enjoy it on a farm? Are you content out there?

BIFF (*with rising agitation*): Hap, I've had twenty or thirty different kinds of jobs since I left home before the war, and it always turns out the same. I just realized it lately. In Nebraska when I herded cattle, and the Dakotas, and Arizona, and now in Texas. It's why I came home now, I guess, because I realized it. This farm I work on, it's spring there now, see? And they've got about fifteen new colts. There's nothing more inspiring or—beautiful than the sight of a mare and a new colt. And it's cool there now, see? Texas is cool now, and it's spring. And whenever spring comes to where I am, I suddenly get the feeling, my God, I'm not gettin' anywhere! What the hell am I doing, playing around with horses, twenty-eight dollars a week! I'm thirty-four years old, I oughta be makin' my future. That's when I come running home. And now, I get here, and I don't know what to do with myself. (*After a pause.*) I've always made a point of not wasting my life, and everytime I come back here I know that all I've done is to waste my life.

HAPPY: You're a poet, you know that, Biff? You're a—you're an idealist!

BIFF: No, I'm mixed up very bad. Maybe I oughta get married. Maybe I oughta get stuck into something. Maybe that's my trouble. I'm like a boy. I'm not married, I'm not in business, I just—I'm like a boy. Are you content, Hap? You're a success, aren't you? Are you content?

HAPPY: Hell, no!

**BIFF:** Why? You're making money, aren't you?

**HAPPY** (*moving about with energy, expressiveness*): All I can do now is wait for the merchandise manager to die. And suppose I get to be merchandise manager? He's a good friend of mine, and he just built a terrific estate on Long Island. And he lived there about two months and sold it, and now he's building another one. He can't enjoy it once it's finished. And I know that's just what I would do. I don't know what the hell I'm workin' for. Sometimes I sit in my apartment—all alone. And I think of the rent I'm paying. And it's crazy. But then, it's what I always wanted. My own apartment, a car, and plenty of women. And still, goddammit, I'm lonely.

**BIFF** (*with enthusiasm*): Listen, why don't you come out West with me?

**HAPPY:** You and I, heh?

**BIFF:** Sure, maybe we could buy a ranch. Raise cattle, use our muscles. Men built like we are should be working out in the open.

**HAPPY** (*avidly*): The Loman Brothers, heh?

**BIFF** (*with vast affection*): Sure, we'd be known all over the counties!

**HAPPY** (*enthralled*): That's what I dream about, Biff. Sometimes I want to just rip my clothes off in the middle of the store and outbox that goddam merchandise manager. I mean I can outbox, outrun, and outlift anybody in that store, and I have to take orders from those common, petty sons-of-bitches till I can't stand it any more.

**BIFF:** I'm tellin' you, kid, if you were with me I'd be happy out there.

**HAPPY** (*enthused*): See, Biff, everybody around me is so false that I'm constantly lowering my ideals . . .

**BIFF:** Baby, together we'd stand up for one another, we'd have someone to trust.

**HAPPY:** If I were around you . . .

**BIFF:** Hap, the trouble is we weren't brought up to grub for money. I don't know how to do it.

**HAPPY:** Neither can I!

**BIFF:** Then let's go!

**HAPPY:** The only thing is—what can you make out there?

**BIFF:** But look at your friend. Builds an estate and then hasn't the peace of mind to live in it.

**HAPPY:** Yeah, but when he walks into the store the waves part in front of him. That's fifty-two thousand dollars a year coming through the revolving door, and I got more in my pinky finger than he's got in his head.

BIFF: Yeah, but you just said . . .

HAPPY: I gotta show some of those pompous, self-important executives over there that Hap Loman can make the grade. I want to walk into the store the way he walks in. Then I'll go with you, Biff. We'll be together yet, I swear. But take those two we had tonight. Now weren't they gorgeous creatures?

BIFF: Yeah, yeah, most gorgeous I've had in years.

HAPPY: I get that any time I want, Biff. Whenever I feel disgusted. The only trouble is, it gets like bowling or something. I just keep knockin' them over and it doesn't mean anything. You still run around a lot?

BIFF: Naa. I'd like to find a girl—steady, somebody with substance.

HAPPY: That's what I long for.

BIFF: Go on! You'd never come home.

HAPPY: I would! Somebody with character, with resistance! Like Mom, y'know? You're gonna call me a bastard when I tell you this. That girl Charlotte I was with tonight is engaged to be married in five weeks. (*He tries on his new hat.*)

BIFF: No kiddin'!

HAPPY: Sure, the guy's in line for the vice-presidency of the store. I don't know what gets into me, maybe I just have an over-developed sense of competition or something, but I went and ruined her, and furthermore I can't get rid of her. And he's the third executive I've done that to. Isn't that a crummy characteristic? And to top it all, I go to their weddings! (*Indignantly, but laughing.*) Like I'm not supposed to take bribes. Manufacturers offer me a hundred-dollar bill now and then to throw an order their way. You know how honest I am, but it's like this girl, see. I hate myself for it. Because I don't want the girl, and, still, I take it and—I love it!

BIFF: Let's go to sleep.

HAPPY: I guess we didn't settle anything, heh?

BIFF: I just got one idea that I think I'm going to try.

HAPPY: What's that?

BIFF: Remember Bill Oliver?

HAPPY: Sure, Oliver is very big now. You want to work for him again?

BIFF: No, but when I quit he said something to me. He put his arm on my shoulder, and he said, "Biff, if you ever need anything, come to me."

HAPPY: I remember that. That sounds good.

BIFF: I think I'll go to see him. If I could get ten thousand or even seven or eight thousand dollars I could buy a beautiful ranch.

HAPPY: I bet he'd back you. 'Cause he thought highly of you, Biff. I mean, they all do. You're well liked, Biff. That's why I say to come back here, and we both have the apartment. And I'm tellin' you, Biff, any babe you want . . .

BIFF: No, with a ranch I could do the work I like and still be something. I just wonder though. I wonder if Oliver still thinks I stole that carton of basketballs.

HAPPY: Oh, he probably forgot that long ago. It's almost ten years. You're too sensitive. Anyway, he didn't really fire you.

BIFF: Well, I think he was going to. I think that's why I quit. I was never sure whether he knew or not. I know he thought the world of me, though. I was the only one he'd let lock up the place.

WILLY (below): You gonna wash the engine, Biff?

HAPPY: Shh!

*Biff looks at Happy, who is gazing down, listening. Willy is mumbling in the parlor.*

HAPPY: You hear that?

*They listen. Willy laughs warmly.*

BIFF (growing angry): Doesn't he know Mom can hear that?

WILLY: Don't get your sweater dirty, Biff!

*A look of pain crosses Biff's face.*

HAPPY: Isn't that terrible? Don't leave again, will you? You'll find a job here. You gotta stick around. I don't know what to do about him, it's getting embarrassing.

WILLY: What a simonizing job!

BIFF: Mom's hearing that!

WILLY: No kiddin', Biff, you got a date? Wonderful!

HAPPY: Go on to sleep. But talk to him in the morning, will you?

BIFF (reluctantly getting into bed): With her in the house. Brother!

HAPPY (getting into bed): I wish you'd have a good talk with him.

*The light on their room begins to fade.*

BIFF (to himself in bed): That selfish, stupid . . .

HAPPY: Sh . . . Sleep, Biff.

*Their light is out. Well before they have finished speaking, Willy's form is dimly seen below in the darkened kitchen. He opens the refrigerator, searches in there, and takes out a bottle of milk. The apartment houses are fading out, and the entire house and surroundings become covered with leaves. Music insinuates itself as the leaves appear.*

WILLY: Just wanna be careful with those girls, Biff, that's all. Don't make any promises. No promises of any kind. Because a girl, y'know, they always believe what you tell 'em, and you're very young, Biff, you're too young to be talking seriously to girls.

*Light rises on the kitchen. Willy, talking, shuts the refrigerator door and comes downstage to the kitchen table. He pours milk into a glass. He is totally immersed in himself, smiling faintly.*

WILLY: Too young entirely, Biff. You want to watch your schooling first. Then when you're all set, there'll be plenty of girls for a boy like you. (*He smiles broadly at a kitchen chair.*) That so? The girls pay for you? (*He laughs.*) Boy, you must really be makin' a hit.

*Willy is gradually addressing—physically—a point offstage, speaking through the wall of the kitchen, and his voice has been rising in volume to that of a normal conversation.*

WILLY: I been wondering why you polish the car so careful. Ha! Don't leave the hubcaps, boys. Get the chamois to the hubcaps. Happy, use newspaper on the windows, it's the easiest thing. Show him how to do it, Biff! You see, Happy? Pad it up, use it like a pad. That's it, that's it, good work. You're doin' all right, Hap. (*He pauses, then nods in approbation for a few seconds, then looks upward.*) Biff, first thing we gotta do when we get time is clip that big branch over the house. Afraid it's gonna fall in a storm and hit the roof. Tell you what. We get a rope and sling her around, and then we climb up there with a couple of saws and take her down. Soon as you finish the car, boys, I wanna see ya. I got a surprise for you, boys.

BIFF (*offstage*): Whatta ya got, Dad?

WILLY: No, you finish first. Never leave a job till you're finished—remember that. (*Looking toward the "big trees."*) Biff, up in Albany I saw a beautiful hammock. I think I'll buy it next trip, and we'll hang it right between those two elms. Wouldn't that be something? Just swingin' there under those branches. Boy, that would be . . .

*Young Biff and Young Happy appear from the direction Willy was addressing. Happy carries rags and a pail of water. Biff, wearing a sweater with a block "S," carries a football.*

BIFF (*pointing in the direction of the car offstage*): How's that, Pop, professional?

WILLY: Terrific. Terrific job, boys. Good work, Biff.

HAPPY: Where's the surprise, Pop?

WILLY: In the back seat of the car.

HAPPY: Boy! (*He runs off.*)

BIFF: What is it, Dad? Tell me, what'd you buy?

WILLY (*laughing, cuffs him*): Never mind, something I want you to have.

BIFF (*turns and starts off*): What is it, Hap?

HAPPY (*offstage*): It's a punching bag!

BIFF: Oh, Pop!

WILLY: It's got Gene Tunney's signature on it!

*Happy runs onstage with a punching bag.*

BIFF: Gee, how'd you know we wanted a punching bag?

WILLY: Well, it's the finest thing for the timing.

HAPPY (*lies down on his back and pedals with his feet*): I'm losing weight, you notice, Pop?

WILLY (*to Happy*): Jumping rope is good too.

BIFF: Did you see the new football I got?

WILLY (*examining the ball*): Where'd you get a new ball?

BIFF: The coach told me to practice my passing.

WILLY: That so? And he gave you the ball, heh?

BIFF: Well, I borrowed it from the locker room. (*He laughs confidentially.*)

WILLY (*laughing with him at the theft*): I want you to return that.

HAPPY: I told you he wouldn't like it!

BIFF (*angrily*): Well, I'm bringing it back!

WILLY (*stopping the incipient argument, to Happy*): Sure, he's gotta practice with a regulation ball, doesn't he? (*To Biff.*) Coach'll probably congratulate you on your initiative!

BIFF: Oh, he keeps congratulating my initiative all the time, Pop.

WILLY: That's because he likes you. If somebody else took that ball there'd be an uproar. So what's the report, boys, what's the report?

BIFF: Where'd you go this time, Dad? Gee we were lonesome for you.

WILLY (*pleased, puts an arm around each boy and they come down to the apron*): Lonesome, heh?

BIFF: Missed you every minute.

WILLY: Don't say? Tell you a secret, boys. Don't breathe it to a soul. Someday I'll have my own business, and I'll never have to leave home any more.

**HAPPY:** Like Uncle Charley, heh?

**WILLY:** Bigger than Uncle Charley! Because Charley is not—liked. He's liked, but he's not—well liked.

**BIFF:** Where'd you go this time, Dad?

**WILLY:** Well, I got on the road, and I went north to Providence. Met the Mayor.

**BIFF:** The Mayor of Providence!

**WILLY:** He was sitting in the hotel lobby.

**BIFF:** What'd he say?

**WILLY:** He said, "Morning!" And I said, "Morning!" And I said, "You got a fine city here, Mayor." And then he had coffee with me. And then I went to Waterbury. Waterbury is a fine city. Big clock city, the famous Waterbury clock. Sold a nice bill there. And then Boston—Boston is the cradle of the Revolution. A fine city. And a couple of other towns in Mass., and on to Portland and Bangor and straight home!

**BIFF:** Gee, I'd love to go with you sometime, Dad.

**WILLY:** Soon as summer comes.

**HAPPY:** Promise?

**WILLY:** You and Hap and I, and I'll show you all the towns. America is full of beautiful towns and fine, upstanding people. And they know me, boys, they know me up and down New England. The finest people. And when I bring you fellas up, there'll be open sesame for all of us, 'cause one thing, boys: I have friends. I can park my car in any street in New England, and the cops protect it like their own. This summer, heh?

**BIFF AND HAPPY** (*together*): Yeah! You bet!

**WILLY:** We'll take our bathing suits.

**HAPPY:** We'll carry your bags, Pop!

**WILLY:** Oh, won't that be something! Me comin' into the Boston stores with you boys carryin' my bags. What a sensation!

*Biff is prancing around, practicing passing the ball.*

**WILLY:** You nervous, Biff, about the game?

**BIFF:** Not if you're gonna be there.

**WILLY:** What do they say about you in school, now that they made you captain?

**HAPPY:** There's a crowd of girls behind him everytime the classes change.

**BIFF** (*taking Willy's hand*): This Saturday, Pop, this Saturday—just for you, I'm going to break through for a touchdown.

**HAPPY:** You're supposed to pass.

BIFF:  I'm takin' one play for Pop. You watch me, Pop, and when I take off my helmet, that means I'm breakin' out. Then you watch me crash through that line!

WILLY (*kisses Biff*):  Oh, wait'll I tell this in Boston!

*Bernard enters in knickers. He is younger than Biff, earnest and loyal, a worried boy.*

BERNARD:  Biff, where are you? You're supposed to study with me today.

WILLY:  Hey, looka Bernard. What're you lookin' so anemic about, Bernard?

BERNARD:  He's gotta study, Uncle Willy. He's got Regents next week.

HAPPY (*tauntingly, spinning Bernard around*):  Let's box, Bernard!

BERNARD:  Biff! (*He gets away from Happy.*) Listen, Biff, I heard Mr. Birnbaum say that if you don't start studyin' math he's gonna flunk you, and you won't graduate. I heard him!

WILLY:  You better study with him, Biff. Go ahead now.

BERNARD:  I heard him!

BIFF:  Oh, Pop, you didn't see my sneakers! (*He holds up a foot for Willy to look at.*)

WILLY:  Hey, that's a beautiful job of printing!

BERNARD (*wiping his glasses*):  Just because he printed University of Virginia on his sneakers doesn't mean they've got to graduate him, Uncle Willy!

WILLY (*angrily*):  What're you talking about? With scholarships to three universities they're gonna flunk him?

BERNARD:  But I heard Mr. Birnbaum say . . .

WILLY:  Don't be a pest, Bernard! (*To his boys.*) What an anemic!

BERNARD:  Okay, I'm waiting for you in my house, Biff.

*Bernard goes off. The Lomans laugh.*

WILLY:  Bernard is not well liked, is he?

BIFF:  He's liked, but he's not well liked.

HAPPY:  That's right, Pop.

WILLY:  That's just what I mean. Bernard can get the best marks in school, y'understand, but when he gets out in the business world, y'understand, you are going to be five times ahead of him. That's why I thank Almighty God you're both built like Adonises. Because the man who makes an appearance in the business world, the man who creates personal interest, is the man who gets ahead. Be liked and you will never want. You take me, for instance. I never have to wait in line to see a buyer. "Willy Loman is here!" That's all they have to know, and I go right through.

BIFF: Did you knock them dead, Pop?

WILLY: Knocked 'em cold in Providence, slaughtered 'em in Boston.

HAPPY (*on his back, pedaling again*): I'm losing weight, you notice, Pop?

*Linda enters as of old, a ribbon in her hair, carrying a basket of washing.*

LINDA (*with youthful energy*): Hello, dear!

WILLY: Sweetheart!

LINDA: How'd the Chevvy run?

WILLY: Chevrolet, Linda, is the greatest car ever built. (*To the boys.*) Since when do you let your mother carry wash up the stairs?

BIFF: Grab hold there, boy!

HAPPY: Where to, Mom?

LINDA: Hang them up on the line. And you better go down to your friends, Biff. The cellar is full of boys. They don't know what to do with themselves.

BIFF: Ah, when Pop comes home they can wait!

WILLY (*laughs appreciatively*): You better go down and tell them what to do. Biff.

BIFF: I think I'll have them sweep out the furnace room.

WILLY: Good work, Biff.

BIFF (*goes through wall-line of kitchen to doorway at back and calls down*): Fellas! Everybody sweep out the furnace room! I'll be right down!

VOICES: All right! Okay, Biff.

BIFF: George and Sam and Frank, come out back! We're hangin' up the wash! Come on, Hap, on the double! (*He and Happy carry out the basket.*)

LINDA: The way they obey him!

WILLY: Well, that's training, the training. I'm tellin' you, I was sellin' thousands and thousands, but I had to come home.

LINDA: Oh, the whole block'll be at that game. Did you sell anything?

WILLY: I did five hundred gross in Providence and seven hundred gross in Boston.

LINDA: No! Wait a minute. I've got a pencil. (*She pulls pencil and paper out of her apron pocket.*) That makes your commission . . . Two hundred—my God! Two hundred and twelve dollars!

WILLY: Well, I didn't figure it yet, but . . .

LINDA: How much did you do?

WILLY: Well, I—I did—about a hundred and eighty gross in Providence. Well, no—it came to—roughly two hundred gross on the whole trip.

LINDA (*without hesitation*): Two hundred gross. That's . . . (*She figures.*)

WILLY: The trouble was that three of the stores were half-closed for inventory in Boston. Otherwise I woulda broke records.

LINDA: Well, it makes seventy dollars and some pennies. That's very good.

WILLY: What do we owe?

LINDA: Well, on the first there's sixteen dollars on the refrigerator . . .

WILLY: Why sixteen?

LINDA: Well, the fan belt broke, so it was a dollar eighty.

WILLY: But it's brand new.

LINDA: Well, the man said that's the way it is. Till they work themselves in, y'know.

*They move through the wall-line into the kitchen.*

WILLY: I hope we didn't get stuck on that machine.

LINDA: They got the biggest ads of any of them!

WILLY: I know, it's a fine machine. What else?

LINDA: Well, there's nine-sixty for the washing machine. And for the vacuum cleaner there's three and a half due on the fifteenth. Then the roof, you got twenty-one dollars remaining.

WILLY: It don't leak, does it?

LINDA: No, they did a wonderful job. Then you owe Frank for the carburetor.

WILLY: I'm not going to pay that man! That goddam Chevrolet, they ought to prohibit the manufacture of that car!

LINDA: Well, you owe him three and a half. And odds and ends, comes to around a hundred and twenty dollars by the fifteenth.

WILLY: A hundred and twenty dollars! My God, if business don't pick up I don't know what I'm gonna do!

LINDA: Well, next week you'll do better.

WILLY: Oh, I'll knock 'em dead next week. I'll go to Hartford. I'm very well liked in Hartford. You know, the trouble is, Linda, people don't seem to take to me.

*They move onto the forestage.*

LINDA:  Oh, don't be foolish.

WILLY:  I know it when I walk in. They seem to laugh at me.

LINDA:  Why? Why would they laugh at you? Don't talk that way, Willy.

*Willy moves to the edge of the stage. Linda goes into the kitchen and starts to darn stockings.*

WILLY:  I don't know the reason for it, but they just pass me by. I'm not noticed.

LINDA:  But you're doing wonderful, dear. You're making seventy to a hundred dollars a week.

WILLY:  But I gotta be at it ten, twelve hours a day. Other men—I don't know—they do it easier. I don't know why—I can't stop myself—I talk too much. A man oughta come in with a few words. One thing about Charley. He's a man of few words, and they respect him.

LINDA:  You don't talk too much, you're just lively.

WILLY (*smiling*):  Well, I figure, what the hell, life is short, a couple of jokes. (*To himself:*) I joke too much! (*The smile goes.*)

LINDA:  Why? You're . . .

WILLY:  I'm fat. I'm very—foolish to look at, Linda. I didn't tell you, but Christmas time I happened to be calling on F. H. Stewarts, and a salesman I know, as I was going in to see the buyer I heard him say something about—walrus. And I—I cracked him right across the face. I won't take that. I simply will not take that. But they do laugh at me. I know that.

LINDA:  Darling . . .

WILLY:  I gotta overcome it. I know I gotta overcome it. I'm not dressing to advantage, maybe.

LINDA:  Willy, darling, you're the handsomest man in the world . . .

WILLY:  Oh, no, Linda.

LINDA:  To me you are. (*Slight pause.*) The handsomest.

*From the darkness is heard the laughter of a woman. Willy doesn't turn to it, but it continues through Linda's lines.*

LINDA:  And the boys, Willy. Few men are idolized by their children the way you are.

*Music is heard as behind a scrim, to the left of the house; The Woman, dimly seen, is dressing.*

WILLY (*with great feeling*):  You're the best there is. Linda, you're a pal, you know that? On the road—on the road I want to grab you sometimes and just kiss the life outa you.

*The laughter is loud now, and he moves into a brightening area at the left, where The Woman has come from behind the scrim and is standing, putting on her hat, looking into a "mirror" and laughing.*

WILLY: 'Cause I get so lonely—especially when business is bad and there's nobody to talk to. I get the feeling that I'll never sell anything again, that I won't make a living for you, or a business, a business for the boys. (*He talks through The Woman's subsiding laughter; The Woman primps at the "mirror."*) There's so much I want to make for . . .

THE WOMAN: Me? You didn't make me, Willy. I picked you.

WILLY (*pleased*): You picked me?

THE WOMAN (*who is quite proper-looking, Willy's age*): I did. I've been sitting at that desk watching all the salesmen go by, day in, day out. But you've got such a sense of humor, and we do have such a good time together, don't we?

WILLY: Sure, sure. (*He takes her in his arms.*) Why do you have to go now?

THE WOMAN: It's two o'clock . . .

WILLY: No, come on in! (*He pulls her.*)

THE WOMAN: . . . my sisters'll be scandalized. When'll you be back?

WILLY: Oh, two weeks about. Will you come up again?

THE WOMAN: Sure thing. You do make me laugh. It's good for me. (*She squeezes his arm, kisses him.*) And I think you're a wonderful man.

WILLY: You picked me, heh?

THE WOMAN: Sure. Because you're so sweet. And such a kidder.

WILLY: Well, I'll see you next time I'm in Boston.

THE WOMAN: I'll put you right through to the buyers.

WILLY (*slapping her bottom*): Right. Well, bottoms up!

THE WOMAN (*slaps him gently and laughs*): You just kill me, Willy. (*He suddenly grabs her and kisses her roughly.*) You kill me. And thanks for the stockings. I love a lot of stockings. Well, good night.

WILLY: Good night. And keep your pores open!

THE WOMAN: Oh, Willy!

*The Woman bursts out laughing, and Linda's laughter blends in. The Woman disappears into the dark. Now the area at the kitchen table brightens. Linda is sitting where she was at the kitchen table, but now is mending a pair of her silk stockings.*

LINDA:  You are, Willy. The handsomest man. You've got no reason to feel that . . .

WILLY (*coming out of The Woman's dimming area and going over to Linda*):  I'll make it all up to you, Linda, I'll . . .

LINDA:  There's nothing to make up, dear. You're doing fine, better than . . .

WILLY (*noticing her mending*):  What's that?

LINDA:  Just mending my stockings. They're so expensive . . .

WILLY (*angrily, taking them from her*):  I won't have you mending stockings in this house! Now throw them out!

*Linda puts the stockings in her pocket.*

BERNARD (*entering on the run*):  Where is he? If he doesn't study!

WILLY (*moving to the forestage, with great agitation*):  You'll give him the answers!

BERNARD:  I do, but I can't on a Regents! That's a state exam! They're liable to arrest me!

WILLY:  Where is he? I'll whip him, I'll whip him!

LINDA:  And he'd better give back that football, Willy, it's not nice.

WILLY:  Biff! Where is he? Why is he taking everything?

LINDA:  He's too rough with the girls, Willy. All the mothers are afraid of him!

WILLY:  I'll whip him!

BERNARD:  He's driving the car without a license!

*The Woman's laugh is heard.*

WILLY:  Shut up!

LINDA:  All the mothers . . .

WILLY:  Shut up!

BERNARD (*backing quietly away and out*):  Mr. Birnbaum says he's stuck up.

WILLY:  Get outa here!

BERNARD:  If he doesn't buckle down he'll flunk math! (*He goes off.*)

LINDA:  He's right, Willy, you've gotta . . .

WILLY (*exploding at her*):  There's nothing the matter with him! You want him to be a worm like Bernard? He's got spirit, personality . . .

*As he speaks, Linda, almost in tears, exits into the living room. Willy is alone in the kitchen, wilting and staring. The*

*leaves are gone. It is night again, and the apartment houses
look down from behind.*

WILLY: Loaded with it. Loaded! What is he stealing? He's giving it
back, isn't he? Why is he stealing? What did I tell him? I never in
my life told him anything but decent things.

*Happy in pajamas has come down the stairs; Willy suddenly
becomes aware of Happy's presence.*

HAPPY: Let's go now, come on.

WILLY (*sitting down at the kitchen table*): Huh! Why did she have to
wax the floors herself? Everytime she waxes the floors she keels
over. She knows that!

HAPPY: Shh! Take it easy. What brought you back tonight?

WILLY: I got an awful scare. Nearly hit a kid in Yonkers. God! Why
didn't I go to Alaska with my brother Ben that time! Ben! That
man was a genius, that man was success incarnate! What a mistake! He begged me to go.

HAPPY: Well, there's no use in . . .

WILLY: You guys! There was a man started with the clothes on his
back and ended up with diamond mines!

HAPPY: Boy, someday I'd like to know how he did it.

WILLY: What's the mystery? The man knew what he wanted and went
out and got it! Walked into a jungle, and comes out, the age of
twenty-one, and he's rich! The world is an oyster, but you don't
crack it open on a mattress!

HAPPY: Pop, I told you I'm gonna retire you for life.

WILLY: You'll retire me for life on seventy goddam dollars a week?
And your women and your car and your apartment, and you'll retire me for life! Christ's sake, I couldn't get past Yonkers today!
Where are you guys, where are you? The woods are burning! I
can't drive a car!

*Charley has appeared in the doorway. He is a large man,
slow of speech, laconic, immovable. In all he says, despite
what he says, there is pity, and, now, trepidation. He has a
robe over pajamas, slippers on his feet. He enters the kitchen.*

CHARLEY: Everything all right?

HAPPY: Yeah, Charley, everything's . . .

WILLY: What's the matter?

CHARLEY: I heard some noise. I thought something happened. Can't we do something about the walls? You sneeze in here, and in my house hats blow off.

HAPPY: Let's go to bed, Dad. Come on.

*Charley signals to Happy to go.*

WILLY: You go ahead, I'm not tired at the moment.

HAPPY (*to Willy*): Take it easy, huh? (*He exits.*)

WILLY: What're you doin' up?

CHARLEY (*sitting down at the kitchen table opposite Willy*): Couldn't sleep good. I had a heartburn.

WILLY: Well, you don't know how to eat.

CHARLEY: I eat with my mouth.

WILLY: No, you're ignorant. You gotta know about vitamins and things like that.

CHARLEY: Come on, let's shoot. Tire you out a little.

WILLY (*hesitantly*): All right. You got cards?

CHARLEY (*taking a deck from his pocket*): Yeah, I got them. Someplace. What is it with those vitamins?

WILLY (*dealing*): They build up your bones. Chemistry.

CHARLEY: Yeah, but there's no bones in a heartburn.

WILLY: What are you talkin' about? Do you know the first thing about it?

CHARLEY: Don't get insulted.

WILLY: Don't talk about something you don't know anything about.

*They are playing. Pause.*

CHARLEY: What're you doin' home?

WILLY: A little trouble with the car.

CHARLEY: Oh. (*Pause.*) I'd like to take a trip to California.

WILLY: Don't say.

CHARLEY: You want a job?

WILLY: I got a job, I told you that. (*After a slight pause.*) What the hell are you offering me a job for?

CHARLEY: Don't get insulted.

WILLY: Don't insult me.

CHARLEY: I don't see no sense in it. You don't have to go on this way.

WILLY: I got a good job. (*Slight pause.*) What do you keep comin' in here for?

CHARLEY: You want me to go?

WILLY (*after a pause, withering*): I can't understand it. He's going back to Texas again. What the hell is that?

CHARLEY: Let him go.

WILLY: I got nothin' to give him, Charley, I'm clean, I'm clean.

CHARLEY: He won't starve. None a them starve. Forget about him.

WILLY: Then what have I got to remember?

CHARLEY: You take it too hard. To hell with it. When a deposit bottle is broken you don't get your nickel back.

WILLY: That's easy enough for you to say.

CHARLEY: That ain't easy for me to say.

WILLY: Did you see the ceiling I put up in the living room?

CHARLEY: Yeah, that's a piece of work. To put up a ceiling is a mystery to me. How do you do it?

WILLY: What's the difference?

CHARLEY: Well, talk about it.

WILLY: You gonna put up a ceiling?

CHARLEY: How could I put up a ceiling?

WILLY: Then what the hell are you bothering me for?

CHARLEY: You're insulted again.

WILLY: A man who can't handle tools is not a man. You're disgusting.

CHARLEY: Don't call me disgusting, Willy.

*Uncle Ben, carrying a valise and an umbrella, enters the fore-stage from around the right corner of the house. He is a stolid man, in his sixties, with a mustache and an authoritative air. He is utterly certain of his destiny, and there is an aura of far places about him. He enters exactly as Willy speaks.*

WILLY: I'm getting awfully tired, Ben.

*Ben's music is heard. Ben looks around at everything.*

CHARLEY: Good, keep playing; you'll sleep better. Did you call me Ben?

*Ben looks at his watch.*

WILLY: That's funny. For a second there you reminded me of my brother Ben.

BEN: I only have a few minutes. (*He strolls, inspecting the place. Willy and Charley continue playing.*)

CHARLEY: You never heard from him again, heh? Since that time?

WILLY:   Didn't Linda tell you? Couple of weeks ago we got a letter from his wife in Africa. He died.

CHARLEY:   That so.

BEN (*chuckling*):   So this is Brooklyn, eh?

CHARLEY:   Maybe you're in for some of his money.

WILLY:   Naa, he had seven sons. There's just one opportunity I had with that man . . .

BEN:   I must make a train, William. There are several properties I'm looking at in Alaska.

WILLY:   Sure, sure! If I'd gone with him to Alaska that time, everything would've been totally different.

CHARLEY:   Go on, you'd froze to death up there.

WILLY:   What're you talking about?

BEN:   Opportunity is tremendous in Alaska, William. Surprised you're not up there.

WILLY:   Sure, tremendous.

CHARLEY:   Heh?

WILLY:   There was the only man I ever met who knew the answers.

CHARLEY:   Who?

BEN:   How are you all?

WILLY (*taking a pot, smiling*):   Fine, fine.

CHARLEY:   Pretty sharp tonight.

BEN:   Is Mother living with you?

WILLY:   No, she died a long time ago.

CHARLEY:   Who?

BEN:   That's too bad. Fine specimen of a lady, Mother.

WILLY (*to Charley*):   Heh?

BEN:   I'd hoped to see the old girl.

CHARLEY:   Who died?

BEN:   Heard anything from Father, have you?

WILLY (*unnerved*):   What do you mean, who died?

CHARLEY (*taking a pot*):   What're you talkin' about?

BEN (*looking at his watch*):   William, it's half-past eight!

WILLY (*as though to dispel his confusion he angrily stops Charley's hand*):   That's my build!

CHARLEY:   I put the ace . . .

WILLY:   If you don't know how to play the game I'm not gonna throw my money away on you!

CHARLEY (*rising*):   It was my ace, for God's sake!

WILLY:   I'm through, I'm through!

BEN: When did Mother die?

WILLY: Long ago. Since the beginning you never knew how to play cards.

CHARLEY (*picks up the cards and goes to the door*): All right! Next time I'll bring a deck with five aces.

WILLY: I don't play that kind of game!

CHARLEY (*turning to him*): You ought to be ashamed of yourself!

WILLY: Yeah?

CHARLEY: Yeah! (*He goes out.*)

WILLY (*slamming the door after him*): Ignoramus!

BEN (*as Willy comes toward him through the wall-line of the kitchen*): So you're William.

WILLY (*shaking Ben's hand*): Ben! I've been waiting for you so long! What's the answer? How did you do it?

BEN: Oh, there's a story in that.

*Linda enters the forestage, as of old, carrying the wash basket.*

LINDA: Is this Ben?

BEN (*gallantly*): How do you do, my dear.

LINDA: Where've you been all these years? Willy's always wondered why you . . .

WILLY (*pulling Ben away from her impatiently*): Where is Dad? Didn't you follow him? How did you get started?

BEN: Well, I don't know how much you remember.

WILLY: Well, I was just a baby, of course, only three or four years old . . .

BEN: Three years and eleven months.

WILLY: What a memory, Ben!

BEN: I have many enterprises, William, and I have never kept books.

WILLY: I remember I was sitting under the wagon in—was it Nebraska?

BEN: It was South Dakota, and I gave you a bunch of wild flowers.

WILLY: I remember you walking away down some open road.

BEN (*laughing*): I was going to find Father in Alaska.

WILLY: Where is he?

BEN: At that age I had a very faulty view of geography, William. I discovered after a few days that I was heading due south, so instead of Alaska, I ended up in Africa.

LINDA: Africa!

WILLY: The Gold Coast!

BEN: Principally diamond mines.

LINDA: Diamond mines!

BEN: Yes, my dear. But I've only a few minutes . . .

WILLY: No! Boys! Boys! (*Young Biff and Happy appear.*) Listen to this. This is your Uncle Ben, a great man! Tell my boys, Ben!

BEN: Why, boys, when I was seventeen I walked into the jungle, and when I was twenty-one I walked out. (*He laughs.*) And by God I was rich.

WILLY (*to the boys*): You see what I been talking about? The greatest things can happen!

BEN (*glancing at his watch*): I have an appointment in Ketchikan Tuesday week.

WILLY: No, Ben! Please tell about Dad. I want my boys to hear. I want them to know the kind of stock they spring from. All I remember is a man with a big beard, and I was in Mamma's lap, sitting around a fire, and some kind of high music.

BEN: His flute. He played the flute.

WILLY: Sure, the flute, that's right!

*New music is heard, a high, rollicking tune.*

BEN: Father was a very great and a very wild-hearted man. We would start in Boston, and he'd toss the whole family into the wagon, and then he'd drive the team right across the country; through Ohio, and Indiana, Michigan, Illinois, and all the Western states. And we'd stop in the towns and sell the flutes that he'd made on the way. Great inventor, Father. With one gadget he made more in a week than a man like you could make in a lifetime.

WILLY: That's just the way I'm bringing them up, Ben—rugged, well liked, all-around.

BEN: Yeah? (*To Biff.*) Hit that, boy—hard as you can. (*He pounds his stomach.*)

BIFF: Oh, no, sir!

BEN (*taking boxing stance*): Come on, get to me! (*He laughs.*)

WILLY: Go to it. Biff! Go ahead, show him!

BIFF: Okay! (*He cocks his fists and starts in.*)

LINDA (*to Willy*): Why must he fight, dear?

BEN (*sparring with Biff*): Good boy! Good boy!

WILLY: How's that, Ben, heh?

HAPPY: Give him the left, Biff!

LINDA: Why are you fighting?

BEN: Good boy! (*Suddenly comes in, trips Biff, and stands over him, the point of his umbrella poised over Biff's eye.*)

LINDA:  Look out, Biff!

BIFF:  Gee!

BEN (*patting Biff's knee*):  Never fight fair with a stranger, boy. You'll never get out of the jungle that way. (*Taking Linda's hand and bowing.*) It was an honor and a pleasure to meet you, Linda.

LINDA (*withdrawing her hand coldly, frightened*):  Have a nice—trip.

BEN (*to Willy*):  And good luck with your—what do you do?

WILLY:  Selling.

BEN:  Yes. Well . . . (*He raises his hand in farewell to all.*)

WILLY:  No, Ben, I don't want you to think . . . (*He takes Ben's arm to show him.*) It's Brooklyn, I know, but we hunt too.

BEN:  Really, now.

WILLY:  Oh, sure, there's snakes and rabbits and—that's why I moved out here. Why, Biff can fell any one of these trees in no time! Boys! Go right over to where they're building the apartment house and get some sand. We're gonna rebuild the entire front stoop right now! Watch this, Ben!

BIFF:  Yes, sir! On the double, Hap!

HAPPY (*as he and Biff run off*):  I lost weight, Pop, you notice?

*Charley enters in knickers, even before the boys are gone.*

CHARLEY:  Listen, if they steal any more from that building the watchman'll put the cops on them!

LINDA (*to Willy*):  Don't let Biff . . .

*Ben laughs lustily.*

WILLY:  You shoulda seen the lumber they brought home last week. At least a dozen six-by-tens worth all kinds a money.

CHARLEY:  Listen, if that watchman . . .

WILLY:  I gave them hell, understand. But I got a couple of fearless characters there.

CHARLEY:  Willy, the jails are full of fearless characters.

BEN (*clapping Willy on the back, with a laugh at Charley*):  And the stock exchange, friend!

WILLY (*joining in Ben's laughter*):  Where are the rest of your pants?

CHARLEY:  My wife bought them.

WILLY:  Now all you need is a golf club and you can go upstairs and go to sleep. (*To Ben.*) Great athlete! Between him and his son Bernard they can't hammer a nail!

BERNARD (*rushing in*):  The watchman's chasing Biff!

WILLY (*angrily*):  Shut up! He's not stealing anything!

LINDA (*alarmed, hurrying off left*):   Where is he? Biff, dear! (*She exits.*)
WILLY (*moving toward the left, away from Ben*):   There's nothing wrong. What's the matter with you?
BEN:   Nervy boy. Good!
WILLY (*laughing*):   Oh, nerves of iron, that Biff!
CHARLEY:   Don't know what it is. My New England man comes back and he's bleedin', they murdered him up there.
WILLY:   It's contacts, Charley, I got important contacts!
CHARLEY (*sarcastically*):   Glad to hear it, Willy. Come in later, we'll shoot a little casino. I'll take some of your Portland money. (*He laughs at Willy and exits.*)
WILLY (*turning to Ben*):   Business is bad, it's murderous. But not for me, of course.
BEN:   I'll stop by on my way back to Africa.
WILLY (*longingly*):   Can't you stay a few days? You're just what I need, Ben, because I—I have a fine position here, but I—well, Dad left when I was such a baby and I never had a chance to talk to him and I still feel—kind of temporary about myself.
BEN:   I'll be late for my train.

*They are at opposite ends of the stage.*

WILLY:   Ben, my boys—can't we talk? They'd go into the jaws of hell for me, see, but I . . .
BEN:   William, you're being first-rate with your boys. Outstanding, manly chaps!
WILLY (*hanging on to his words*):   Oh, Ben, that's good to hear! Because sometimes I'm afraid that I'm not teaching them the right kind of—Ben, how should I teach them?
BEN (*giving great weight to each word, and with a certain vicious audacity*):   William, when I walked into the jungle, I was seventeen. When I walked out I was twenty-one. And, by God, I was rich! (*He goes off into darkness around the right corner of the house.*)
WILLY:   . . . was rich! That's just the spirit I want to imbue them with! To walk into a jungle! I was right! I was right! I was right!

*Ben is gone, but Willy is still speaking to him as Linda, in nightgown and robe, enters the kitchen, glances around for Willy, then goes to the door of the house, looks out and sees him. Comes down to his left. He looks at her.*

LINDA:   Willy, dear? Willy?
WILLY:   I was right!

LINDA: Did you have some cheese? (*He can't answer.*) It's very late, darling. Come to bed, heh?

WILLY (*looking straight up*): Gotta break your neck to see a star in this yard.

LINDA: You coming in?

WILLY: Whatever happened to that diamond watch fob? Remember? When Ben came from Africa that time? Didn't he give me a watch fob with a diamond in it?

LINDA: You pawned it, dear. Twelve, thirteen years ago. For Biff's radio correspondence course.

WILLY: Gee, that was a beautiful thing. I'll take a walk.

LINDA: But you're in your slippers.

WILLY (*starting to go around the house at the left*): I was right! I was! (*Half to Linda, as he goes, shaking his head.*) What a man! There was a man worth talking to. I was right!

LINDA (*calling after Willy*): But in your slippers, Willy!

*Willy is almost gone when Biff, in his pajamas, comes down the stairs and enters the kitchen.*

BIFF: What is he doing out there?

LINDA: Sh!

BIFF: God Almighty, Mom, how long has he been doing this?

LINDA: Don't, he'll hear you.

BIFF: What the hell is the matter with him?

LINDA: It'll pass by morning.

BIFF: Shouldn't we do anything?

LINDA: Oh, my dear, you should do a lot of things, but there's nothing to do, so go to sleep.

*Happy comes down the stair and sits on the steps.*

HAPPY: I never heard him so loud, Mom.

LINDA: Well, come around more often; you'll hear him. (*She sits down at the table and mends the lining of Willy's jacket.*)

BIFF: Why didn't you ever write me about this, Mom?

LINDA: How would I write to you? For over three months you had no address.

BIFF: I was on the move. But you know I thought of you all the time. You know that, don't you, pal?

LINDA: I know, dear, I know. But he likes to have a letter. Just to know that there's still a possibility for better things.

BIFF: He's not like this all the time, is he?

LINDA: It's when you come home he's always the worst.

BIFF: When I come home?

LINDA: When you write you're coming, he's all smiles, and talks about the future, and—he's just wonderful. And then the closer you seem to come, the more shaky he gets, and then, by the time you get here, he's arguing, and he seems angry at you. I think it's just that maybe he can't bring himself to—to open up to you. Why are you so hateful to each other? Why is that?

BIFF (*evasively*): I'm not hateful, Mom.

LINDA: But you no sooner come in the door than you're fighting!

BIFF: I don't know why. I mean to change. I'm tryin', Mom, you understand?

LINDA: Are you home to stay now?

BIFF: I don't know. I want to look around, see what's doin'.

LINDA: Biff, you can't look around all your life, can you?

BIFF: I just can't take hold, Mom. I can't take hold of some kind of a life.

LINDA: Biff, a man is not a bird, to come and go with the spring time.

BIFF: Your hair . . . (*He touches her hair.*) Your hair got so gray.

LINDA: Oh, it's been gray since you were in high school. I just stopped dyeing it, that's all.

BIFF: Dye it again, will ya? I don't want my pal looking old.

(*He smiles.*)

LINDA: You're such a boy! You think you can go away for a year and . . . You've got to get it into your head now that one day you'll knock on this door and there'll be strange people here . . .

BIFF: What are you talking about? You're not even sixty, Mom.

LINDA: But what about your father?

BIFF (*lamely*): Well, I meant him too.

HAPPY: He admires Pop.

LINDA: Biff, dear, if you don't have any feeling for him, then you can't have any feeling for me.

BIFF: Sure I can, Mom.

LINDA: No. You can't just come to see me, because I love him. (*With a threat, but only a threat, of tears.*) He's the dearest man in the world to me, and I won't have anyone making him feel unwanted and low and blue. You've got to make up your mind now, darling, there's no leeway any more. Either he's your father and you pay him that respect, or else you're not to come here. I know he's not easy to get along with—nobody knows that better than me but . . .

**WILLY** (*from the left, with a laugh*): Hey, hey, Biffo!

**BIFF** (*starting to go out after Willy*): What the hell is the matter with him? (*Happy stops him.*)

**LINDA:** Don't—don't go near him!

**BIFF:** Stop making excuses for him! He always, always wiped the floor with you. Never had an ounce of respect for you.

**HAPPY:** He's always had respect for . . .

**BIFF:** What the hell do you know about it?

**HAPPY** (*surlily*): Just don't call him crazy!

**BIFF:** He's got no character—Charley wouldn't do this. Not in his own house—spewing out that vomit from his mind.

**HAPPY:** Charley never had to cope with what he's got to.

**BIFF:** People are worse off than Willy Loman. Believe me, I've seen them!

**LINDA:** Then make Charley your father, Biff. You can't do that, can you? I don't say he's a great man. Willy Loman never made a lot of money. His name was never in the paper. He's not the finest character that ever lived. But he's a human being, and a terrible thing is happening to him. So attention must be paid. He's not to be allowed to fall into his grave like an old dog. Attention, attention must be finally paid to such a person. You called him crazy . . .

**BIFF:** I didn't mean . . .

**LINDA:** No, a lot of people think he's lost his—balance. But you don't have to be very smart to know what his trouble is. The man is exhausted.

**HAPPY:** Sure!

**LINDA:** A small man can be just as exhausted as a great man. He works for a company thirty-six years this March, opens up unheard-of territories to their trademark, and now in his old age they take his salary away.

**HAPPY** (*indignantly*): I didn't know that, Mom.

**LINDA:** You never asked, my dear! Now that you get your spending money someplace else you don't trouble your mind with him.

**HAPPY:** But I gave you money last . . .

**LINDA:** Christmas time, fifty dollars! To fix the hot water it cost ninety-seven fifty! For five weeks he's been on straight commission, like a beginner, an unknown!

**BIFF:** Those ungrateful bastards!

LINDA: Are they any worse than his sons? When he brought them business, when he was young, they were glad to see him. But now his old friends, the old buyers that loved him so and always found some order to hand him in a pinch—they're all dead, retired. He used to be able to make six, seven calls a day in Boston. Now he takes his valises out of the car and puts them back and takes them out again and he's exhausted. Instead of walking he talks now. He drives seven hundred miles, and when he gets there no one knows him any more, no one welcomes him. And what goes through a man's mind, driving seven hundred miles home without having earned a cent? Why shouldn't he talk to himself? Why? When he has to go to Charley and borrow fifty dollars a week and pretend to me that it's his pay? How long can that go on? How long? You see what I'm sitting here and waiting for? And you tell me he has no character? The man who never worked a day but for your benefit? When does he get the medal for that? Is this his reward—to turn around at the age of sixty-three and find his sons, who he loved better than his life, one a philandering bum . . .

HAPPY: Mom!

LINDA: That's all you are, my baby! (*To Biff.*) And you! What happened to the love you had for him? You were such pals! How you used to talk to him on the phone every night! How lonely he was till he could come home to you!

BIFF: All right, Mom. I'll live here in my room, and I'll get a job. I'll keep away from him, that's all.

LINDA: No, Biff. You can't stay here and fight all the time.

BIFF: He threw me out of this house, remember that.

LINDA: Why did he do that? I never knew why.

BIFF: Because I know he's a fake and he doesn't like anybody around who knows!

LINDA: Why a fake? In what way? What do you mean?

BIFF: Just don't lay it all at my feet. It's between me and him—that's all I have to say. I'll chip in from now on. He'll settle for half my paycheck. He'll be all right. I'm going to bed. (*He starts for the stairs.*)

LINDA: He won't be all right.

BIFF (*turning on the stairs, furiously*): I hate this city and I'll stay here. Now what do you want?

LINDA: He's dying, Biff.

*Happy turns quickly to her, shocked.*

BIFF (*after a pause*): Why is he dying?

LINDA: He's been trying to kill himself.

BIFF (*with great horror*): How?

LINDA: I live from day to day.

BIFF: What're you talking about?

LINDA: Remember I wrote you that he smashed up the car again? In February?

BIFF: Well?

LINDA: The insurance inspector came. He said that they have evidence. That all these accidents in the last year—weren't—weren't—accidents.

HAPPY: How can they tell that? That's a lie.

LINDA: It seems there's a woman . . . (*She takes a breath as:*)

BIFF (*sharply but contained*): What woman?

LINDA (*simultaneously*): . . .and this woman . . .

LINDA: What?

BIFF: Nothing. Go ahead.

LINDA: What did you say?

BIFF: Nothing. I just said what woman?

HAPPY: What about her?

LINDA: Well, it seems she was walking down the road and saw his car. She says that he wasn't driving fast at all, and that he didn't skid. She says he came to that little bridge, and then deliberately smashed into the railing, and it was only the shallowness of the water that saved him.

BIFF: Oh, no, he probably just fell asleep again.

LINDA: I don't think he fell asleep.

BIFF: Why not?

LINDA: Last month . . . (*With great difficulty.*) Oh, boys, it's so hard to say a thing like this! He's just a big stupid man to you, but I tell you there's more good in him than in many other people. (*She chokes, wipes her eyes.*) I was looking for a fuse. The lights blew out, and I went down the cellar. And behind the fuse box—it happened to fall out—was a length of rubber pipe—just short.

HAPPY: No kidding!

LINDA: There's a little attachment on the end of it. I knew right away. And sure enough, on the bottom of the water heater there's a new little nipple on the gas pipe.

HAPPY (*angrily*): That—jerk.

BIFF: Did you have it taken off?

LINDA: I'm—I'm ashamed to. How can I mention it to him? Every day I go down and take away that little rubber pipe. But, when he comes home, I put it back where it was. How can I insult him that way? I don't know what to do. I live from day to day, boys. I tell you, I know every thought in his mind. It sounds so old-fashioned and silly, but I tell you he put his whole life into you and you've turned your backs on him. (*She is bent over in the chair, weeping, her face in her hands.*) Biff, I swear to God! Biff, his life is in your hands!

HAPPY (*to Biff*): How do you like that damned fool!

BIFF (*kissing her*): All right, pal, all right. It's all settled now. I've been remiss. I know that, Mom. But now I'll stay, and I swear to you, I'll apply myself. (*Kneeling in front of her, in a fever of self-reproach.*) It's just—you see, Mom, I don't fit in business. Not that I won't try. I'll try, and I'll make good.

HAPPY: Sure you will. The trouble with you in business was you never tried to please people.

BIFF: I know, I . . .

HAPPY: Like when you worked for Harrison's. Bob Harrison said you were tops, and then you go and do some damn fool thing like whistling whole songs in the elevator like a comedian.

BIFF (*against Happy*): So what? I like to whistle sometimes.

HAPPY: You don't raise a guy to a responsible job who whistles in the elevator!

LINDA: Well, don't argue about it now.

HAPPY: Like when you'd go off and swim in the middle of the day instead of taking the line around.

BIFF (*his resentment rising*): Well, don't you run off? You take off sometimes, don't you? On a nice summer day?

HAPPY: Yeah, but I cover myself!

LINDA: Boys!

HAPPY: If I'm going to take a fade the boss can call any number where I'm supposed to be and they'll swear to him that I just left. I'll tell you something that I hate to say, Biff, but in the business world some of them think you're crazy.

BIFF (*angered*): Screw the business world!

HAPPY: All right, screw it! Great, but cover yourself!

LINDA: Hap, Hap!

BIFF: I don't care what they think! They've laughed at Dad for years, and you know why? Because we don't belong in this nuthouse of a city! We should be mixing cement on some open plain or—or carpenters. A carpenter is allowed to whistle!

*Willy walks in from the entrance of the house, at left.*

WILLY: Even your grandfather was better than a carpenter. (*Pause. They watch him.*) You never grew up. Bernard does not whistle in the elevator, I assure you.

BIFF (*as though to laugh Willy out of it*): Yeah, but you do, Pop.

WILLY: I never in my life whistled in an elevator! And who in the business world thinks I'm crazy?

BIFF: I didn't mean it like that, Pop. Now don't make a whole thing out of it, will ya?

WILLY: Go back to the West! Be a carpenter, a cowboy, enjoy yourself!

LINDA: Willy, he was just saying . . .

WILLY: I heard what he said!

HAPPY (*trying to quiet Willy*): Hey, Pop, come on now . . .

WILLY (*continuing over Happy's line*): They laugh at me, heh? Go to Filene's, go to the Hub, go to Slattery's, Boston. Call out the name Willy Loman and see what happens! Big shot!

BIFF: All right, Pop.

WILLY: Big!

BIFF: All right!

WILLY: Why do you always insult me?

BIFF: I didn't say a word. (*To Linda.*) Did I say a word?

LINDA: He didn't say anything, Willy.

WILLY (*going to the doorway of the living room*): All right, good night, good night.

LINDA: Willy, dear, he just decided . . .

WILLY (*to Biff*): If you get tired hanging around tomorrow, paint the ceiling I put up in the living room.

BIFF: I'm leaving early tomorrow.

HAPPY: He's going to see Bill Oliver, Pop.

WILLY (*interestedly*): Oliver? For what?

BIFF (*with reserve, but trying; trying*): He always said he'd stake me. I'd like to go into business, so maybe I can take him up on it.

LINDA: Isn't that wonderful?

WILLY: Don't interrupt. What's wonderful about it? There's fifty men in the City of New York who'd stake him. (*To Biff.*) Sporting goods?

BIFF: I guess so. I know something about it and . . .

WILLY: He knows something about it! You know sporting goods better than Spalding, for God's sake! How much is he giving you?

BIFF: I don't know, I didn't even see him yet, but . . .

WILLY: Then what're you talkin' about?

BIFF (*getting angry*): Well, all I said was I'm gonna see him, that's all!

WILLY (*turning away*): Ah, you're counting your chickens again.

BIFF (*starting left for the stairs*): Oh, Jesus, I'm going to sleep!

WILLY (*calling after him*): Don't curse in this house!

BIFF (*turning*): Since when did you get so clean?

HAPPY (*trying to stop them*): Wait a . . .

WILLY: Don't use that language to me! I won't have it!

HAPPY (*grabbing Biff, shouts*): Wait a minute! I got an idea. I got a feasible idea. Come here, Biff, let's talk this over now, let's talk some sense here. When I was down in Florida last time, I thought of a great idea to sell sporting goods. It just came back to me. You and I, Biff—we have a line, the Loman Line. We train a couple of weeks, and put on a couple of exhibitions, see?

WILLY: That's an idea!

HAPPY: Wait! We form two basketball teams, see? Two water-polo teams. We play each other. It's a million dollars' worth of publicity. Two brothers, see? The Loman Brothers. Displays in the Royal Palms—all the hotels. And banners over the ring and the basketball court: "Loman Brothers." Baby, we could sell sporting goods!

WILLY: That is a one-million-dollar idea!

LINDA: Marvelous!

BIFF: I'm in great shape as far as that's concerned.

HAPPY: And the beauty of it is, Biff, it wouldn't be like a business. We'd be out playin' ball again.

BIFF (*enthused*): Yeah, that's . . .

WILLY: Million-dollar . . .

HAPPY: And you wouldn't get fed up with it, Biff. It'd be the family again. There'd be the old honor, and comradeship, and if you wanted to go off for a swim or somethin'—well, you'd do it! Without some smart cooky gettin' up ahead of you!

WILLY: Lick the world! You guys together could absolutely lick the civilized world.

BIFF: I'll see Oliver tomorrow. Hap, if we could work that out . . .

LINDA: Maybe things are beginning to . . .

WILLY (*widely enthused, to Linda*): Stop interrupting! (*To Biff.*) But don't wear sport jacket and slacks when you see Oliver.

BIFF: No, I'll . . .

WILLY: A business suit, and talk as little as possible, and don't crack any jokes.

BIFF: He did like me. Always liked me.

LINDA: He loved you!

WILLY (*to Linda*): Will you stop! (*To Biff.*) Walk in very serious. You are not applying for a boy's job. Money is to pass. Be quiet, fine, and serious. Everybody likes a kidder, but nobody lends him money.

HAPPY: I'll try to get some myself, Biff. I'm sure I can.

WILLY: I see great things for you kids, I think your troubles are over. But remember, start big and you'll end big. Ask for fifteen. How much you gonna ask for?

BIFF: Gee, I don't know . . .

WILLY: And don't say "Gee." "Gee" is a boy's word. A man walking in for fifteen thousand dollars does not say "Gee!"

BIFF: Ten, I think, would be top though.

WILLY: Don't be so modest. You always started too low. Walk in with a big laugh. Don't look worried. Start off with a couple of your good stories to lighten things up. It's not what you say, it's how you say it—because personality always wins the day.

LINDA: Oliver always thought the highest of him . . .

WILLY: Will you let me talk?

BIFF: Don't yell at her, Pop, will ya?

WILLY (*angrily*): I was talking, wasn't I?

BIFF: I don't like you yelling at her all the time, and I'm tellin' you, that's all.

WILLY: What're you, takin' over this house?

LINDA: Willy . . .

WILLY (*turning to her*): Don't take his side all the time, goddammit!

BIFF (*furiously*): Stop yelling at her!

WILLY (*suddenly pulling on his cheek, beaten down, guilt ridden*): Give my best to Bill Oliver—he may remember me. (*He exits through the living room doorway.*)

LINDA (*her voice subdued*): What'd you have to start that for? (*Biff turns away.*) You see how sweet he was as soon as you talked hopefully? (*She goes over to Biff.*) Come up and say good night to him. Don't let him go to bed that way.

HAPPY: Come on, Biff, let's buck him up.

LINDA: Please, dear. Just say good night. It takes so little to make him happy. Come. (*She goes through the living room doorway, calling upstairs from within the living room.*) Your pajamas are hanging in the bathroom, Willy!

HAPPY (*looking toward where Linda went out*): What a woman! They broke the mold when they made her. You know that, Biff.

BIFF: He's off salary. My God, working on commission!

HAPPY: Well, let's face it: he's no hot-shot selling man. Except that sometimes, you have to admit, he's a sweet personality.

BIFF (*deciding*): Lend me ten bucks, will ya? I want to buy some new ties.

HAPPY: I'll take you to a place I know. Beautiful stuff. Wear one of my striped shirts tomorrow.

BIFF: She got gray. Mom got awful old. Gee, I'm gonna go in to Oliver tomorrow and knock him for a . . .

HAPPY: Come on up. Tell that to Dad. Let's give him a whirl. Come on.

BIFF (*steamed up*): You know, with ten thousand bucks, boy!

HAPPY (*as they go into the living room*): That's the talk, Biff, that's the first time I've heard the old confidence out of you! (*From within the living room, fading off*) You're gonna live with me, kid, and any babe you want just say the word . . . (*The last lines are hardly heard. They are mounting the stairs to their parents' bedroom.*)

LINDA (*entering her bedroom and addressing Willy, who is in the bathroom. She is straightening the bed for him*): Can you do anything about the shower? It drips.

WILLY (*from the bathroom*): All of a sudden everything falls to pieces. Goddam plumbing, oughta be sued, those people. I hardly finished putting it in and the thing . . . (*His words rumble off.*)

LINDA: I'm just wondering if Oliver will remember him. You think he might?

WILLY (*coming out of the bathroom in his pajamas*): Remember him? What's the matter with you, you crazy? If he'd've stayed with Oliver he'd be on top by now! Wait'll Oliver gets a look at him. You don't know the average caliber any more. The average young man today—(*he is getting into bed*)—is got a caliber of zero. Greatest thing in the world for him was to bum around.

*Biff and Happy enter the bedroom. Slight pause.*

WILLY (*stops short, looking at Biff*): Glad to hear it, boy.

HAPPY: He wanted to say good night to you, sport.

WILLY (*to Biff*): Yeah. Knock him dead, boy. What'd you want to tell me?

BIFF: Just take it easy, Pop. Good night. (*He turns to go.*)

WILLY (*unable to resist*): And if anything falls off the desk while you're talking to him—like a package or something—don't you pick it up. They have office boys for that.

LINDA: I'll make a big breakfast . . .

WILLY: Will you let me finish? (*To Biff.*) Tell him you were in the business in the West. Not farm work.

BIFF: All right, Dad.

LINDA: I think everything . . .

WILLY (*going right through her speech*): And don't undersell yourself. No less than fifteen thousand dollars.

BIFF (*unable to bear him*): Okay. Good night, Mom. (*He starts moving.*)

WILLY: Because you got a greatness in you, Biff, remember that. You got all kinds of greatness . . . (*He lies back, exhausted. Biff walks out.*)

LINDA (*calling after Biff*): Sleep well, darling!

HAPPY: I'm gonna get married, Mom. I wanted to tell you.

LINDA: Go to sleep, dear.

HAPPY (*going*): I just wanted to tell you.

WILLY: Keep up the good work. (*Happy exits.*) God . . . remember that Ebbets Field game? The championship of the city?

LINDA: Just rest. Should I sing to you?

WILLY: Yeah. Sing to me. (*Linda hums a soft lullaby.*) When that team came out—he was the tallest, remember?

LINDA: Oh, yes. And in gold.

*Biff enters the darkened kitchen, takes a cigarette, and leaves the house. He comes downstage into a golden pool of light. He smokes, staring at the night.*

WILLY: Like a young god. Hercules—something like that. And the sun, the sun all around him. Remember how he waved to me? Right up from the field, with the representatives of three colleges standing by? And the buyers I brought, and the cheers when he came out—Loman, Loman, Loman! God Almighty, he'll be great yet. A star like that, magnificent, can never really fade away!

*The light on Willy is fading. The gas heater begins to glow through the kitchen wall, near the stairs, a blue flame beneath red coils.*

LINDA (*timidly*): Willy dear, what has he got against you?

WILLY: I'm so tired. Don't talk any more.

*Biff slowly returns to the kitchen. He stops, stares toward the heater.*

**LINDA:** Will you ask Howard to let you work in New York?

**WILLY:** First thing in the morning. Everything'll be all right.

*Biff reaches behind the heater and draws out a length of rubber tubing. He is horrified and turns his head toward Willy's room, still dimly lit, from which the strains of Linda's desperate but monotonous humming rise.*

**WILLY** (*staring through the window into the moonlight*): Gee, look at the moon moving between the buildings! (*Biff wraps the tubing around his hand and quickly goes up the stairs.*)

## *A C T 2*

*Scene: Music is heard, gay and bright. The curtain rises as the music fades away. Willy, in shirt sleeves, is sitting at the kitchen table, sipping coffee, his hat in his lap. Linda is filling his cup when she can.*

**WILLY:** Wonderful coffee. Meal in itself.

**LINDA:** Can I make you some eggs?

**WILLY:** No. Take a breath.

**LINDA:** You look so rested, dear.

**WILLY:** I slept like a dead one. First time in months. Imagine, sleeping till ten on a Tuesday morning. Boys left nice and early, heh?

**LINDA:** They were out of here by eight o'clock.

**WILLY:** Good work!

**LINDA:** It was so thrilling to see them leaving together. I can't get over the shaving lotion in this house!

**WILLY** (*smiling*): Mmm . . .

**LINDA:** Biff was very changed this morning. His whole attitude seemed to be hopeful. He couldn't wait to get downtown to see Oliver.

**WILLY:** He's heading for a change. There's no question, there simply are certain men that take longer to get—solidified. How did he dress?

**LINDA:** His blue suit. He's so handsome in that suit. He could be a— anything in that suit!

*Willy gets up from the table. Linda holds his jacket for him.*

WILLY: There's no question, no question at all. Gee, on the way home tonight I'd like to buy some seeds.

LINDA (*laughing*): That'd be wonderful. But not enough sun gets back there. Nothing'll grow any more.

WILLY: You wait, kid, before it's all over we're gonna get a little place out in the country, and I'll raise some vegetables, a couple of chickens . . .

LINDA: You'll do it yet, dear.

*Willy walks out of his jacket. Linda follows him.*

WILLY: And they'll get married, and come for a weekend. I'd build a little guest house. 'Cause I got so many fine tools, all I'd need would be a little lumber and some peace of mind.

LINDA (*joyfully*): I sewed the lining . . .

WILLY: I could build two guest houses, so they'd both come. Did he decide how much he's going to ask Oliver for?

LINDA (*getting him into the jacket*): He didn't mention it, but I imagine ten or fifteen thousand. You going to talk to Howard today?

WILLY: Yeah. I'll put it to him straight and simple. He'll just have to take me off the road.

LINDA: And Willy, don't forget to ask for a little advance, because we've got the insurance premium. It's the grace period now.

WILLY: That's a hundred . . . ?

LINDA: A hundred and eight, sixty-eight. Because we're a little short again.

WILLY: Why are we short?

LINDA: Well, you had the motor job on the car . . .

WILLY: That goddam Studebaker!

LINDA: And you got one more payment on the refrigerator . . .

WILLY: But it just broke again!

LINDA: Well, it's old, dear.

WILLY: I told you we should've bought a well-advertised machine. Charley bought a General Electric and it's twenty years old and it's still good, that son-of-a-bitch.

LINDA: But, Willy . . .

WILLY: Whoever heard of a Hastings refrigerator? Once in my life I would like to own something outright before it's broken! I'm always in a race with the junkyard! I just finished paying for the car and it's on its last legs. The refrigerator consumes belts like a goddam maniac. They time those things. They time them so when you finally paid for them, they're used up.

LINDA (*buttoning up his jacket as he unbuttons it*): All told, about two hundred dollars would carry us, dear. But that includes the last payment on the mortgage. After this payment, Willy, the house belongs to us.

WILLY: It's twenty-five years!

LINDA: Biff was nine years old when we bought it.

WILLY: Well, that's a great thing. To weather a twenty-five year mortgage is . . .

LINDA: It's an accomplishment.

WILLY: All the cement, the lumber, the reconstruction I put in this house! There ain't a crack to be found in it any more.

LINDA: Well, it served its purpose.

WILLY: What purpose? Some stranger'll come along, move in, and that's that. If only Biff would take this house, and raise a family . . . (*He starts to go.*) Good-by, I'm late.

LINDA (*suddenly remembering*): Oh, I forgot! You're supposed to meet them for dinner.

WILLY: Me?

LINDA: At Frank's Chop House on Forty-eighth near Sixth Avenue.

WILLY: Is that so! How about you?

LINDA: No, just the three of you. They're gonna blow you to a big meal!

WILLY: Don't say! Who thought of that?

LINDA: Biff came to me this morning, Willy, and he said, "Tell Dad, we want to blow him to a big meal." Be there six o'clock. You and your two boys are going to have dinner.

WILLY: Gee whiz! That's really somethin'. I'm gonna knock Howard for a loop, kid. I'll get an advance, and I'll come home with a New York job. Goddammit, now I'm gonna do it!

LINDA: Oh, that's the spirit, Willy!

WILLY: I will never get behind a wheel the rest of my life!

LINDA: It's changing, Willy, I can feel it changing!

WILLY: Beyond a question. G'by, I'm late. (*He starts to go again.*)

LINDA (*calling after him as she runs to the kitchen table for a handkerchief*): You got your glasses?

WILLY (*feels for them, then comes back in*): Yeah, yeah, got my glasses.

LINDA (*giving him the handkerchief*): And a handkerchief.

WILLY: Yeah, handkerchief.

LINDA: And your saccharine?

WILLY: Yeah, my saccharine.

LINDA:   Be careful on the subway stairs.

*She kisses him, and a silk stocking is seen hanging from her hand. Willy notices it.*

WILLY:   Will you stop mending stockings? At least while I'm in the house. It gets me nervous. I can't tell you. Please.

*Linda hides the stocking in her hand as she follows Willy across the forestage in front of the house.*

LINDA:   Remember, Frank's Chop House.

WILLY (*passing the apron*):   Maybe beets would grow out there.

LINDA (*laughing*):   But you tried so many times.

WILLY:   Yeah. Well, don't work hard today. (*He disappears around the right corner of the house.*)

LINDA:   Be careful!

*As Willy vanishes, Linda waves to him. Suddenly the phone rings. She runs across the stage and into the kitchen and lifts it.*

LINDA:   Hello? Oh, Biff! I'm so glad you called, I just . . . Yes, sure, I just told him. Yes, he'll be there for dinner at six o'clock, I didn't forget. Listen, I was just dying to tell you. You know that little rubber pipe I told you about? That he connected to the gas heater? I finally decided to go down the cellar this morning and take it away and destroy it. But it's gone! Imagine? He took it away himself, it isn't there! (*She listens.*) When? Oh, then you took it. Oh— nothing, it's just that I'd hoped he'd taken it away himself. Oh, I'm not worried, darling, because this morning he left in such high spirits, it was like the old days! I'm not afraid any more. Did Mr. Oliver see you?. . . Well, you wait there then. And make a nice impression on him, darling. Just don't perspire too much before you see him. And have a nice time with Dad. He may have big news too!. . . That's right, a New York job. And be sweet to him tonight, dear. Be loving to him. Because he's only a little boat looking for a harbor. (*She is trembling with sorrow and joy.*) Oh, that's wonderful, Biff, you'll save his life. Thanks, darling. Just put your arm around him when he comes into the restaurant. Give him a smile. That's the boy . . . Good-by, dear. . . . You got your comb?. . . That's fine. Good-by, Biff dear.

*In the middle of her speech, Howard Wagner, thirty-six, wheels in a small typewriter table on which is a wire-recording machine and proceeds to plug it in. This is on the left forestage. Light slowly fades on Linda as it rises on Howard. Howard is intent on threading the machine and only glances over his shoulder as Willy appears.*

WILLY:  Pst! Pst!

HOWARD:  Hello, Willy, come in.

WILLY:  Like to have a little talk with you, Howard.

HOWARD:  Sorry to keep you waiting. I'll be with you in a minute.

WILLY:  What's that, Howard?

HOWARD:  Didn't you ever see one of these? Wire recorder.

WILLY:  Oh. Can we talk a minute?

HOWARD:  Records things. Just got delivery yesterday. Been driving me crazy, the most terrific machine I ever saw in my life. I was up all night with it.

WILLY:  What do you do with it?

HOWARD:  I bought it for dictation, but you can do anything with it. Listen to this. I had it home last night. Listen to what I picked up. The first one is my daughter. Get this. (*He flicks the switch and "Roll Out the Barrel" is heard being whistled.*) Listen to that kid whistle.

WILLY:  That is lifelike, isn't it?

HOWARD:  Seven years old. Get that tone.

WILLY:  Ts, ts. Like to ask a little favor if you . . .

*The whistling breaks off, and the voice of Howard's daughter is heard.*

HIS DAUGHTER:  "Now you, Daddy."

HOWARD:  She's crazy for me! (*Again the same song is whistled.*) That's me! Ha! (*He winks.*)

WILLY:  You're very good!

*The whistling breaks off again. The machine runs silent for a moment.*

HOWARD:  Sh! Get this now, this is my son.

HIS SON:  "The capital of Alabama is Montgomery; the capital of Arizona is Phoenix; the capital of Arkansas is Little Rock; the capital of California is Sacramento . . ." (*and on, and on.*)

HOWARD (*holding up five fingers*):  Five years old, Willy!

WILLY:  He'll make an announcer some day!

HIS SON (*continuing*):  "The capital . . ."

HOWARD:  Get that—alphabetical order! (*The machine breaks off suddenly.*) Wait a minute. The maid kicked the plug out.

**WILLY:** It certainly is a . . .

**HOWARD:** Sh, for God's sake!

**HIS SON:** "It's nine o'clock, Bulova watch time. So I have to go to sleep."

**WILLY:** That really is . . .

**HOWARD:** Wait a minute! The next is my wife.

*They wait.*

**HOWARD'S VOICE:** "Go on, say something." (*Pause.*) "Well, you gonna talk?"

**HIS WIFE:** "I can't think of anything."

**HOWARD'S VOICE:** "Well, talk—it's turning."

**HIS WIFE** (*shyly, beaten*): "Hello." (*Silence.*) "Oh, Howard, I can't talk into this . . ."

**HOWARD** (*snapping the machine off*): That was my wife.

**WILLY:** That is a wonderful machine. Can we . . .

**HOWARD:** I tell you, Willy, I'm gonna take my camera, and my bandsaw, and all my hobbies, and out they go. This is the most fascinating relaxation I ever found.

**WILLY:** I think I'll get one myself.

**HOWARD:** Sure, they're only a hundred and a half. You can't do without it. Supposing you wanna hear Jack Benny, see? But you can't

be at home at that hour. So you tell the maid to turn the radio on when Jack Benny comes on, and this automatically goes on with the radio . . .

**WILLY:** And when you come home you . . .

**HOWARD:** You can come home twelve o'clock, one o'clock, any time you like, and you get yourself a Coke and sit yourself down, throw the switch, and there's Jack Benny's program in the middle of the night!

**WILLY:** I'm definitely going to get one. Because lots of times I'm on the road, and I think to myself, what I must be missing on the radio!

**HOWARD:** Don't you have a radio in the car?

**WILLY:** Well, yeah, but who ever thinks of turning it on?

**HOWARD:** Say, aren't you supposed to be in Boston?

**WILLY:** That's what I want to talk to you about, Howard. You got a minute? (*He draws a chair in from the wing.*)

**HOWARD:** What happened? What're you doing here?

**WILLY:** Well . . .

HOWARD:   You didn't crack up again, did you?

WILLY:   Oh, no. No . . .

HOWARD:   Geez, you had me worried there for a minute. What's the trouble?

WILLY:   Well, tell you the truth, Howard. I've come to the decision that I'd rather not travel any more.

HOWARD:   Not travel! Well, what'll you do?

WILLY:   Remember, Christmas time, when you had the party here? You said you'd try to think of some spot for me here in town.

HOWARD:   With us?

WILLY:   Well, sure.

HOWARD:   Oh, yeah, yeah. I remember. Well, I couldn't think of anything for you, Willy.

WILLY:   I tell ya, Howard. The kids are all grown up, y'know. I don't need much any more. If I could take home—well, sixty-five dollars a week, I could swing it.

HOWARD:   Yeah, but Willy, see I . . .

WILLY:   I tell ya why, Howard. Speaking frankly and between the two of us, y'know—I'm just a little tired.

HOWARD:   Oh, I could understand that, Willy. But you're a road man, Willy, and we do a road business. We've only got a half-dozen salesmen on the floor here.

WILLY:   God knows, Howard. I never asked a favor of any man. But I was with the firm when your father used to carry you in here in his arms.

HOWARD:   I know that, Willy, but . . .

WILLY:   Your father came to me the day you were born and asked me what I thought of the name Howard, may he rest in peace.

HOWARD:   I appreciate that, Willy, but there just is no spot here for you. If I had a spot I'd slam you right in, but I just don't have a single solitary spot.

*He looks for his lighter. Willy has picked it up and gives it to him. Pause.*

WILLY (*with increasing anger*):   Howard, all I need to set my table is fifty dollars a week.

HOWARD:   But where am I going to put you, kid?

WILLY:   Look, it isn't a question of whether I can sell merchandise, is it?

HOWARD:   No, but it's business, kid, and everybody's gotta pull his own weight.

WILLY (*desperately*):   Just let me tell you a story, Howard . . .

HOWARD: 'Cause you gotta admit, business is business.

WILLY (*angrily*): Business is definitely business, but just listen for a minute. You don't understand this. When I was a boy—eighteen, nineteen—I was already on the road. And there was a question in my mind as to whether selling had a future for me. Because in those days I had a yearning to go to Alaska. See, there were three gold strikes in one month in Alaska, and I felt like going out. Just for the ride, you might say.

HOWARD (*barely interested*): Don't say.

WILLY: Oh, yeah, my father lived many years in Alaska. He was an adventurous man. We've got quite a little streak of self-reliance in our family. I thought I'd go out with my older brother and try to locate him, and maybe settle in the North with the old man. And I was almost decided to go, when I met a salesman in the Parker House. His name was Dave Singleman. And he was eighty-four years old, and he'd drummed merchandise in thirty-one states. And old Dave, he'd go up to his room, y'understand, put on his green velvet slippers—I'll never forget—and pick up his phone and call the buyers, and without ever leaving his room, at the age of eighty-four, he made his living. And when I saw that, I realized that selling was the greatest career a man could want. 'Cause what could be more satisfying than to be able to go, at the age of eight-four, into twenty or thirty different cities, and pick up a phone, and be re-membered and loved and helped by so many different people? Do you know? when he died—and by the way he died the death of a salesman, in his green velvet slippers in the smoker of the New York, New Haven and Hartford, going into Boston—when he died, hundreds of salesmen and buyers were at his funeral. Things were sad on a lotta trains for months after that. (*He stands up, Howard has not looked at him.*) In those days there was personal-ity in it, Howard. There was respect, and comradeship, and grati-tude in it. Today, it's all cut and dried, and there's no chance for bringing friendship to bear—or personality. You see what I mean? They don't know me any more.

HOWARD (*moving away, to the right*): That's just the thing, Willy.

WILLY: If I had forty dollars a week—that's all I'd need. Forty dollars, Howard.

HOWARD: Kid, I can't take blood from a stone, I . . .

WILLY (*desperation is on him now*): Howard, the year Al Smith was nominated, your father came to me and . . .

HOWARD (*starting to go off*): I've got to see some people, kid.

WILLY (*stopping him*): I'm talking about your father! There were promises made across this desk! You mustn't tell me you've got people to see—I put thirty-four years into this firm, Howard, and now I can't pay my insurance! You can't eat the orange and throw the peel away—a man is not a piece of fruit! (*After a pause.*) Now pay attention. Your father—in 1928 I had a big year. I averaged a hundred and seventy dollars a week in commissions.

HOWARD (*impatiently*): Now, Willy, you never averaged . . .

WILLY (*banging his hand on the desk*): I averaged a hundred and seventy dollars a week in the year of 1928! And your father came to me—or rather, I was in the office here—it was right over this desk—and he put his hand on my shoulder . . .

HOWARD (*getting up*): You'll have to excuse me, Willy, I gotta see some people. Pull yourself together. (*Going out.*) I'll be back in a little while.

*On Howard's exit, the light on his chair grows very bright and strange.*

WILLY: Pull myself together! What the hell did I say to him? My God, I was yelling at him! How could I? (*Willy breaks off, staring at the light, which occupies the chair, animating it. He approaches this chair, standing across the desk from it.*) Frank, Frank, don't you remember what you told me that time? How you put your hand on my shoulder, and Frank . . . (*He leans on the desk and as he speaks the dead man's name he accidentally switches on the recorder, and instantly*)

HOWARD'S SON: ". . . of New York is Albany. The capital of Ohio is Cincinnati, the capital of Rhode Island is . . ." (*The recitation continues.*)

WILLY (*leaping away with fright, shouting*): Ha! Howard! Howard! Howard!

HOWARD (*rushing in*): What happened?

WILLY (*pointing at the machine, which continues nasally, childishly, with the capital cities*): Shut it off! Shut it off!

HOWARD (*pulling the plug out*): Look, Willy . . .

WILLY (*pressing his hands to his eyes*): I gotta get myself some coffee. I'll get some coffee . . .

*Willy starts to walk out. Howard stops him.*

HOWARD (*rolling up the cord*): Willy, look . . .

WILLY: I'll go to Boston.

HOWARD: Willy, you can't go to Boston for us.

WILLY: Why can't I go?

HOWARD: I don't want you to represent us. I've been meaning to tell you for a long time now.

WILLY: Howard, are you firing me?

HOWARD: I think you need a good long rest, Willy.

WILLY: Howard . . .

HOWARD: And when you feel better, come back, and we'll see if we can work something out.

WILLY: But I gotta earn money, Howard. I'm in no position to . . .

HOWARD: Where are your sons? Why don't your sons give you a hand?

WILLY: They're working on a very big deal.

HOWARD: This is no time for false pride, Willy. You go to your sons and you tell them that you're tired. You've got two great boys, haven't you?

WILLY: Oh, no question, no question, but in the meantime . . .

HOWARD: Then that's that, heh?

WILLY: All right, I'll go to Boston tomorrow.

HOWARD: No, no.

WILLY: I can't throw myself on my sons. I'm not a cripple!

HOWARD: Look, kid, I'm busy this morning.

WILLY (*grasping Howard's arm*): Howard, you've got to let me go to Boston!

HOWARD (*hard, keeping himself under control*): I've got a line of people to see this morning. Sit down, take five minutes, and pull yourself together, and then go home, will ya? I need the office, Willy. (*He starts to go, turns, remembering the recorder, starts to push off the table holding the recorder.*) Oh, yeah. Whenever you can this week, stop by and drop off the samples. You'll feel better, Willy, and then come back and we'll talk. Pull yourself together, kid, there's people outside.

*Howard exits, pushing the table off left. Willy stares into space, exhausted. Now the music is heard—Ben's music— first distantly, then closer, closer. As Willy speaks, Ben enters from the right. He carries valise and umbrella.*

WILLY: Oh, Ben, how did you do it? What is the answer? Did you wind up the Alaska deal already?

BEN: Doesn't take much time if you know what you're doing. Just a short business trip. Boarding ship in an hour. Wanted to say good-by.

WILLY:   Ben, I've got to talk to you.

BEN (*glancing at his watch*):   Haven't the time, William.

WILLY (*crossing the apron to Ben*):   Ben, nothing's working out. I don't know what to do.

BEN:   Now, look here, William. I've bought timberland in Alaska and I need a man to look after things for me.

WILLY:   God, timberland! Me and my boys in those grand outdoors!

BEN:   You've a new continent at your doorstep, William. Get out of these cities, they're full of talk and time payments and courts of law. Screw on your fists and you can fight for a fortune up there.

WILLY:   Yes, yes! Linda, Linda!

*Linda enters as of old, with the wash.*

LINDA:   Oh, you're back?

BEN:   I haven't much time.

WILLY:   No, wait! Linda, he's got a proposition for me in Alaska.

LINDA:   But you've got . . . (*To Ben.*) He's got a beautiful job here.

WILLY:   But in Alaska, kid, I could . . .

LINDA:   You're doing well enough, Willy!

BEN (*to Linda*):   Enough for what, my dear?

LINDA (*frightened of Ben and angry at him*):   Don't say those things to him! Enough to be happy right here, right now. (*To Willy, while Ben laughs.*) Why must everybody conquer the world? You're well liked, and the boys love you, and someday—(*To Ben*)—why, old man Wagner told him just the other day that if he keeps it up he'll be a member of the firm, didn't he, Willy?

WILLY:   Sure, sure. I am building something with this firm, Ben, and if a man is building something he must be on the right track, mustn't he?

BEN:   What are you building? Lay your hand on it. Where is it?

WILLY (*hesitantly*):   That's true, Linda, there's nothing.

LINDA:   Why? (*To Ben.*) There's a man eighty-four years old . . .

WILLY:   That's right, Ben, that's right. When I look at that man I say, what is there to worry about?

BEN:   Bah!

WILLY:   It's true, Ben. All he has to do is go into any city, pick up the phone, and he's making his living and you know why?

BEN (*picking up his valise*):   I've got to go.

WILLY (*HOLDING BEN BACK*):   Look at this boy!

*Biff, in his high school sweater, enters carrying suitcase. Happy carries Biff's shoulder guards, gold helmet, and football pants.*

WILLY: Without a penny to his name, three great universities are begging for him, and from there the sky's the limit, because it's not what you do, Ben. It's who you know and the smile on your face! It's contacts, Ben, contacts! The whole wealth of Alaska passes over the lunch table at the Commodore Hotel, and that's the wonder, the wonder of this country, that a man can end with diamonds here on the basis of being liked! (*He turns to Biff.*) And that's why when you get out on that field today it's important. Because thousands of people will be rooting for you and loving you. (*To Ben, who has again begun to leave.*) And Ben! when he walks into a business office his name will sound out like a bell and all the doors will open to him! I've seen it, Ben, I've seen it a thousand times! You can't feel it with your hand like timber, but it's there!

BEN: Good-by, William.

WILLY: Ben, am I right? Don't you think I'm right? I value your advice.

BEN: There's a new continent at your doorstep, William. You could walk out rich. Rich! (*He is gone.*)

WILLY: We'll do it here, Ben! You hear me? We're gonna do it here!

*Young Bernard rushes in. The gay music of the Boys is heard.*

BERNARD: Oh, gee, I was afraid you left already!

WILLY: Why? What time is it?

BERNARD: It's half-past one!

WILLY: Well, come on, everybody! Ebbets Field next stop! Where's the pennants? (*He rushes through the wall-line of the kitchen and out into the living room.*)

LINDA (*to Biff*): Did you pack fresh underwear?

BIFF (*who has been limbering up*): I want to go!

BERNARD: Biff, I'm carrying your helmet, ain't I?

HAPPY: No, I'm carrying the helmet.

BERNARD: Oh, Biff, you promised me.

HAPPY: I'm carrying the helmet.

BERNARD: How am I going to get in the locker room?

LINDA: Let him carry the shoulder guards. (*She puts her coat and hat on in the kitchen.*)

BERNARD: Can I, Biff? 'Cause I told everybody I'm going to be in the locker room.

HAPPY: In Ebbets Field it's the clubhouse.

BERNARD: I meant the clubhouse. Biff!

HAPPY: Biff!

BIFF (*grandly, after a slight pause*):   Let him carry the shoulder guards.

HAPPY (*as he gives Bernard the shoulder guards*):   Stay close to us now.

*Willy rushes in with the pennants.*

WILLY (*handing them out*):   Everybody wave when Biff comes out on the field. (*Happy and Bernard run off.*) You set now, boy?

*The music has died away.*

BIFF:   Ready to go, Pop. Every muscle is ready.

WILLY (*at the edge of the apron*):   You realize what this means?

BIFF:   That's right, Pop.

WILLY (*feeling Biff's muscles*):   You're comin' home this afternoon captain of the All-Scholastic Championship Team of the City of New York.

BIFF:   I got it, Pop. And remember, pal, when I take off my helmet, that touchdown is for you.

WILLY:   Let's go! (*He is starting out, with his arm around Biff, when Charley enters, as of old, in knickers.*) I got no room for you, Charley.

CHARLEY:   Room? For what?

WILLY:   In the car.

CHARLEY:   You goin' for a ride? I wanted to shoot some casino.

WILLY (*furiously*):   Casino! (*Incredulously.*) Don't you realize what today is?

LINDA:   Oh, he knows, Willy. He's just kidding you.

WILLY:   That's nothing to kid about!

CHARLEY:   No, Linda, what's goin' on?

LINDA:   He's playing in Ebbets Field.

CHARLEY:   Baseball in this weather?

WILLY:   Don't talk to him. Come on, come on! (*He is pushing them out.*)

CHARLEY:   Wait a minute, didn't you hear the news?

WILLY:   What?

CHARLEY:   Don't you listen to the radio? Ebbets Field just blew up.

WILLY:   You go to hell! (*Charley laughs. Pushing them out.*) Come on, come on! We're late.

CHARLEY (*as they go*):   Knock a homer, Biff, knock a homer!

WILLY (*the last to leave, turning to Charley*):   I don't think that was funny, Charley. This is the greatest day of his life.

CHARLEY:   Willy, when are you going to grow up?

WILLY:   Yeah, heh? When this game is over, Charley, you'll be laughing out of the other side of your face. They'll be calling him another Red Grange. Twenty-five thousand a year.

CHARLEY (*kidding*):   Is that so?

WILLY:   Yeah, that's so.

CHARLEY:   Well, then, I'm sorry, Willy. But tell me something.

WILLY:   What?

CHARLEY:   Who is Red Grange?

WILLY:   Put up your hands. Goddam you, put up your hands!

*Charley, chuckling, shakes his head and walks away, around the left corner of the stage. Willy follows him. The music rises to a mocking frenzy.*

WILLY:   Who the hell do you think you are, better than everybody else? You don't know everything, you big, ignorant, stupid . . . Put up your hands!

*Light rises, on the right side of the forestage, on a small table in the reception room of Charley's office. Traffic sounds are heard. Bernard, now mature, sits whistling to himself. A pair of tennis rackets and an old overnight bag are on the floor beside him.*

WILLY (*offstage*):   What are you walking away for? Don't walk away! If you're going to say something say it to my face! I know you laugh at me behind my back. You'll laugh out of the other side of your goddam face after this game. Touchdown! Touchdown! Eighty thousand people! Touchdown! Right between the goal posts.

*Bernard is a quiet, earnest, but self-assured young man. Willy's voice is coming from right upstage now. Bernard lowers his feet off the table and listens. Jenny, his father's secretary, enters.*

JENNY (*distressed*):   Say, Bernard, will you go out in the hall?

BERNARD:   What is that noise? Who is it?

JENNY:   Mr. Loman. He just got off the elevator.

BERNARD (*getting up*):   Who's he arguing with?

JENNY:   Nobody. There's nobody with him. I can't deal with him any more, and your father gets all upset every time he comes. I've got a lot of typing to do, and your father's waiting to sign it. Will you see him?

WILLY (*entering*): Touchdown! Touch—(*He sees Jenny.*) Jenny, Jenny, good to see you. How're ya? Workin'? Or still honest?

JENNY: Fine. How've you been feeling?

WILLY: Not much any more, Jenny. Ha, ha! (*He is surprised to see the rackets.*)

BERNARD: Hello, Uncle Willy.

WILLY (*almost shocked*): Bernard! Well, look who's here! (*He comes quickly, guiltily, to Bernard and warmly shakes his hand.*)

BERNARD: How are you? Good to see you.

WILLY: What are you doing here?

BERNARD: Oh, just stopped by to see Pop. Get off my feet till my train leaves. I'm going to Washington in a few minutes.

WILLY: Is he in?

BERNARD: Yes, he's in his office with the accountant. Sit down.

WILLY (*sitting down*): What're you going to do in Washington?

BERNARD: Oh, just a case I've got there, Willy.

WILLY: That so? (*Indicating the rackets.*) You going to play tennis there?

BERNARD: I'm staying with a friend who's got a court.

WILLY: Don't say. His own tennis court. Must be fine people, I bet.

BERNARD: They are, very nice. Dad tells me Biff's in town.

WILLY (*with a big smile*): Yeah, Biff's in. Working on a very big deal, Bernard.

BERNARD: What's Biff doing?

WILLY: Well, he's been doing very big things in the West. But he decided to establish himself here. Very big. We're having dinner. Did I hear your wife had a boy?

BERNARD: That's right. Our second.

WILLY: Two boys! What do you know!

BERNARD: What kind of a deal has Biff got?

WILLY: Well, Bill Oliver—very big sporting-goods man—he wants Biff very badly. Called him in from the West. Long distance, carte blanche, special deliveries. Your friends have their own private tennis court?

BERNARD: You still with the old firm, Willy?

WILLY (*after a pause*): I'm—I'm overjoyed to see how you made the grade, Bernard, overjoyed. It's an encouraging thing to see a young man really—really . . . Looks very good for Biff—very . . . (*He breaks off, then.*) Bernard . . . (*He is so full of emotion, he breaks off again.*)

BERNARD: What is it, Willy?

WILLY (*small and alone*): What—what's the secret?

BERNARD: What secret?

WILLY: How—how did you? Why didn't he ever catch on?

BERNARD: I wouldn't know that, Willy.

WILLY (*confidentially, desperately*): You were his friend, his boyhood friend. There's something I don't understand about it. His life ended after that Ebbets Field game. From the age of seventeen nothing good ever happened to him.

BERNARD: He never trained himself for anything.

WILLY: But he did, he did. After high school he took so many correspondence courses. Radio mechanics; television; God knows what, and never made the slightest mark.

BERNARD (*taking off his glasses*): Willy, do you want to talk candidly?

WILLY (*rising, faces Bernard*): I regard you as a very brilliant man, Bernard. I value your advice.

BERNARD: Oh, the hell with the advice, Willy. I couldn't advise you. There's just one thing I've always wanted to ask you. When he was supposed to graduate, and the math teacher flunked him . . .

WILLY: Oh, that son-of-a-bitch ruined his life.

BERNARD: Yeah, but, Willy, all he had to do was go to summer school and make up that subject.

WILLY: That's right, that's right.

BERNARD: Did you tell him not to go to summer school?

WILLY: Me? I begged him to go. I ordered him to go!

BERNARD: Then why wouldn't he go?

WILLY: Why? Why! Bernard, that question has been trailing me like a ghost for the last fifteen years. He flunked the subject, and laid down and died like a hammer hit him!

BERNARD: Take it easy, kid.

WILLY: Let me talk to you—I got nobody to talk to. Bernard, Bernard, was it my fault? Y'see? It keeps going around in my mind, maybe I did something to him. I got nothing to give him.

BERNARD: Don't take it so hard.

WILLY: Why did he lay down? What is the story there? You were his friend!

BERNARD: Willy, I remember, it was June, and our grades came out. And he'd flunked math.

WILLY: That son-of-a-bitch!

BERNARD: No, it wasn't right then. Biff just got very angry, I remember, and he was ready to enroll in summer school.

WILLY (*surprised*): He was?

BERNARD:   He wasn't beaten by it at all. But then, Willy, he disappeared from the block for almost a month. And I got the idea that he'd gone up to New England to see you. Did he have a talk with you then?

*Willy stares in silence.*

BERNARD:   Willy?

WILLY (*with a strong edge of resentment in his voice*):   Yeah, he came to Boston. What about it?

BERNARD:   Well, just that when he came back—I'll never forget this, it always mystifies me. Because I'd thought so well of Biff, even though he'd always taken advantage of me. I loved him, Willy, y'know? And he came back after that month and took his sneakers—remember those sneakers with "University of Virginia" printed on them? He was so proud of those, wore them every day. And he took them down in the cellar, and burned them up in the furnace. We had a fist fight. It lasted at least half an hour. Just the two of us, punching each other down the cellar, and crying right through it. I've often thought of how strange it was that I knew he'd given up his life. What happened in Boston, Willy?

*Willy looks at him as at an intruder.*

BERNARD:   I just bring it up because you asked me.

WILLY (*angrily*):   Nothing. What do you mean, "What happened?" What's that got to do with anything?

BERNARD:   Well, don't get sore.

WILLY:   What are you trying to do, blame it on me? If a boy lays down is that my fault?

BERNARD:   Now, Willy, don't get . . .

WILLY:   Well, don't—don't talk to me that way! What does that mean, "What happened?"

*Charley enters. He is in his vest, and he carries a bottle of bourbon.*

CHARLEY:   Hey, you're going to miss that train. (*He waves the bottle.*)

BERNARD:   Yeah, I'm going. (*He takes the bottle.*) Thanks, Pop. (*He picks up his rackets and bag.*) Good-by, Willy, and don't worry about it. You know, "If at first you don't succeed . . ."

WILLY:   Yes, I believe in that.

BERNARD:   But sometimes, Willy, it's better for a man just to walk away.

**WILLY:** Walk away?

**BERNARD:** That's right.

**WILLY:** But if you can't walk away?

**BERNARD** (*after a slight pause*): I guess that's when it's tough. (*Extending his hand.*) Good-by, Willy.

**WILLY** (*shaking Bernard's hand*): Good-by, boy.

**CHARLEY** (*an arm on Bernard's shoulder*): How do you like this kid? Gonna argue a case in front of the Supreme Court.

**BERNARD** (*protesting*): Pop!

**WILLY** (*genuinely shocked, pained, and happy*): No! The Supreme Court!

**BERNARD:** I gotta run. 'By, Dad!

**CHARLEY:** Knock 'em dead, Bernard!

*Bernard goes off.*

**WILLY** (*as Charley takes out his wallet*): The Supreme Court! And he didn't even mention it!

**CHARLEY** (*counting out money on the desk*): He don't have to—he's gonna do it.

**WILLY:** And you never told him what to do, did you? You never took any interest in him.

**CHARLEY:** My salvation is that I never took any interest in anything. There's some money—fifty dollars. I got an accountant inside.

**WILLY:** Charley, look . . . (*with difficulty.*) I got my insurance to pay. If you can manage it—I need a hundred and ten dollars.

*Charley doesn't reply for a moment; merely stops moving.*

**WILLY:** I'd draw it from my bank but Linda would know, and I . . .

**CHARLEY:** Sit down, Willy.

**WILLY** (*moving toward the chair*): I'm keeping an account of everything, remember. I'll pay every penny back. (*He sits.*)

**CHARLEY:** Now listen to me, Willy.

**WILLY:** I want you to know I appreciate . . .

**CHARLEY** (*sitting down on the table*): Willy, what're you doin'? What the hell is going on in your head?

**WILLY:** Why? I'm simply . . .

**CHARLEY:** I offered you a job. You make fifty dollars a week. And I won't send you on the road.

**WILLY:** I've got a job.

**CHARLEY:** Without pay? What kind of a job is a job without pay?

(*He rises.*) Now, look, kid, enough is enough. I'm no genius but I know when I'm being insulted.

WILLY: Insulted!

CHARLEY: Why don't you want to work for me?

WILLY: What's the matter with you? I've got a job.

CHARLEY: Then what're you walkin' in here every week for?

WILLY (*getting up*): Well, if you don't want me to walk in here . . .

CHARLEY: I'm offering you a job.

WILLY: I don't want your goddam job!

CHARLEY: When the hell are you going to grow up?

WILLY (*furiously*): You big ignoramus, if you say that to me again I'll rap you one! I don't care how big you are! (*He's ready to fight.*)

*Pause.*

CHARLEY (*kindly, going to him*): How much do you need, Willy?

WILLY: Charley, I'm strapped. I'm strapped. I don't know what to do. I was just fired.

CHARLEY: Howard fired you?

WILLY: That snotnose. Imagine that? I named him. I named him Howard.

CHARLEY: Willy, when're you gonna realize that them things don't mean anything? You named him Howard, but you can't sell that. The only thing you got in this world is what you can sell. And the funny thing is that you're a salesman, and you don't know that.

WILLY: I've always tried to think otherwise, I guess. I always felt that if a man was impressive, and well liked, that nothing . . .

CHARLEY: Why must everybody like you? Who liked J. P. Morgan? Was he impressive? In a Turkish bath he'd look like a butcher. But with his pockets on he was very well liked. Now listen, Willy, I know you don't like me, and nobody can say I'm in love with you, but I'll give you a job because—just for the hell of it, put it that way. Now what do you say?

WILLY: I—I just can't work for you, Charley.

CHARLEY: What're you, jealous of me?

WILLY: I can't work for you, that's all, don't ask me why.

CHARLEY (*angered, takes out more bills*): You been jealous of me all your life, you damned fool! Here, pay your insurance. (*He puts the money in Willy's hand.*)

WILLY: I'm keeping strict accounts.

CHARLEY: I've got some work to do. Take care of yourself. And pay your insurance.

WILLY (*moving to the right*):   Funny, y'know? After all the highways, and the trains, and the appointments, and the years, you end up worth more dead than alive.

CHARLEY:   Willy, nobody's worth nothin' dead. (*After a slight pause.*) Did you hear what I said?

*Willy stands still, dreaming.*

CHARLEY:   Willy!

WILLY:   Apologize to Bernard for me when you see him. I didn't mean to argue with him. He's a fine boy. They're all fine boys, and they'll end up big—all of them. Someday they'll all play tennis together. Wish me luck, Charley. He saw Bill Oliver today.

CHARLEY:   Good luck.

WILLY (*on the verge of tears*):   Charley, you're the only friend I got. Isn't that a remarkable thing? (*He goes out.*)

CHARLEY:   Jesus!

*Charley stares after him a moment and follows. All light blacks out. Suddenly raucous music is heard, and a red glow rises behind the screen at right. Stanley, a young waiter, appears, carrying a table, followed by Happy, who is carrying two chairs.*

STANLEY (*putting the table down*):   That's all right, Mr. Loman, I can handle it myself. (*He turns and takes the chairs from Happy and places them at the table.*)

HAPPY (*glancing around*):   Oh, this is better.

STANLEY:   Sure, in the front there you're in the middle of all kinds of noise. Whenever you got a party, Mr. Loman, you just tell me and I'll put you back here. Y'know, there's a lotta people they don't like it private, because when they go out they like to see a lotta action around them because they're sick and tired to stay in the house by theirself. But I know you, you ain't from Hackensack. You know what I mean?

HAPPY (*sitting down*):   So how's it coming, Stanley?

STANLEY:   Ah, it's a dog life. I only wish during the war they'd a took me in the Army. I coulda been dead by now.

HAPPY:   My brother's back, Stanley.

STANLEY:   Oh, he come back, heh? From the Far West.

HAPPY:   Yeah, big cattle man, my brother, so treat him right. And my father's coming too.

STANLEY: Oh, your father too!

HAPPY: You got a couple of nice lobsters?

STANLEY: Hundred per cent, big.

HAPPY: I want them with the claws.

STANLEY: Don't worry, I don't give you no mice. (*Happy laughs.*) How about some wine? It'll put a head on the meal.

HAPPY: No. You remember, Stanley, that recipe I brought you from overseas? With the champagne in it?

STANLEY: Oh, yeah, sure. I still got it tacked up yet in the kitchen. But that'll have to cost a buck apiece anyways.

HAPPY: That's all right.

STANLEY: What'd you, hit a number or somethin'?

HAPPY: No, it's a little celebration. My brother is—I think he pulled off a big deal today. I think we're going into business together.

STANLEY: Great! That's the best for you. Because a family business, you know what I mean?—that's the best.

HAPPY: That's what I think.

STANLEY: 'Cause what's the difference? Somebody steals? It's in the family. Know what I mean? (*Sotto voce.*) Like this bartender here. The boss is goin' crazy what kinda leak he's got in the cash register. You put it in but it don't come out.

HAPPY (*raising his head*): Sh!

STANLEY: What?

HAPPY: You notice I wasn't lookin' right or left, was I?

STANLEY: No.

HAPPY: And my eyes are closed.

STANLEY: So what's the . . . ?

HAPPY: Strudel's comin'.

STANLEY (*catching on, looks around*): Ah, no, there's no . . .

*He breaks off as a furred, lavishly dressed Girl enters and sits at the next table. Both follow her with their eyes.*

STANLEY: Geez, how'd ya know?

HAPPY: I got radar or something. (*Staring directly at her profile.*) Oooooooo . . . Stanley.

STANLEY: I think that's for you, Mr. Loman.

HAPPY: Look at that mouth. Oh, God. And the binoculars.

STANLEY: Geez, you got a life, Mr. Loman.

HAPPY: Wait on her.

STANLEY (*going to the Girl's table*): Would you like a menu, ma'am?

GIRL: I'm expecting someone, but I'd like a . . .

HAPPY: Why don't you bring her—excuse me, miss, do you mind? I sell champagne, and I'd like you to try my brand. Bring her a champagne, Stanley.

GIRL: That's awfully nice of you.

HAPPY: Don't mention it. It's all company money. (*He laughs.*)

GIRL: That's a charming product to be selling, isn't it?

HAPPY: Oh, gets to be like everything else. Selling is selling, y'know.

GIRL: I suppose.

HAPPY: You don't happen to sell, do you?

GIRL: No, I don't sell.

HAPPY: Would you object to a compliment from a stranger? You ought to be on a magazine cover.

GIRL (*looking at him a little archly*): I have been.

*Stanley comes in with a glass of champagne.*

HAPPY: What'd I say before, Stanley? You see? She's a cover girl.

STANLEY: Oh, I could see, I could see.

HAPPY (*to the Girl*): What magazine?

GIRL: Oh, a lot of them. (*She takes the drink.*) Thank you.

HAPPY: You know what they say in France, don't you? "Champagne is the drink of the complexion"—Hya, Biff!

*Biff has entered and sits with Happy.*

BIFF: Hello, kid. Sorry I'm late.

HAPPY: I just got here. Uh, Miss . . . ?

GIRL: Forsythe.

HAPPY: Miss Forsythe, this is my brother.

BIFF: Is Dad here?

HAPPY: His name is Biff. You might've heard of him. Great football player.

GIRL: Really? What team?

HAPPY: Are you familiar with football?

GIRL: No, I'm afraid I'm not.

HAPPY: Biff is quarterback with the New York Giants.

GIRL: Well, that is nice, isn't it? (*She drinks.*)

HAPPY: Good health.

GIRL: I'm happy to meet you.

HAPPY: That's my name. Hap. It's really Harold, but at West Point they called me Happy.

GIRL (*now really impressed*): Oh, I see. How do you do? (*She turns her profile.*)

BIFF: Isn't Dad coming?

HAPPY: You want her?

BIFF: Oh, I could never make that.

HAPPY: I remember the time that idea would never come into your head. Where's the old confidence, Biff?

BIFF: I just saw Oliver . . .

HAPPY: Wait a minute. I've got to see that old confidence again. Do you want her? She's on call.

BIFF: Oh, no. (*He turns to look at the Girl.*)

HAPPY: I'm telling you. Watch this. (*Turning to the Girl.*) Honey? (*She turns to him.*) Are you busy?

GIRL: Well, I am . . . but I could make a phone call.

HAPPY: Do that, will you, honey? And see if you can get a friend. We'll be here for a while. Biff is one of the greatest football players in the country.

GIRL (*standing up*): Well, I'm certainly happy to meet you.

HAPPY: Come back soon.

GIRL: I'll try.

HAPPY: Don't try, honey, try hard.

*The Girl exits. Stanley follows, shaking his head in bewildered admiration.*

HAPPY: Isn't that a shame now? A beautiful girl like that? That's why I can't get married. There's not a good woman in a thousand. New York is loaded with them, kid!

BIFF: Hap, look . . .

HAPPY: I told you she was on call!

BIFF (*strangely unnerved*): Cut it out, will ya? I want to say something to you.

HAPPY: Did you see Oliver?

BIFF: I saw him all right. Now look, I want to tell Dad a couple of things and I want you to help me.

HAPPY: What? Is he going to back you?

BIFF: Are you crazy? You're out of your goddam head, you know that?

HAPPY: Why? What happened?

BIFF (*breathlessly*): I did a terrible thing today, Hap. It's been the strangest day I ever went through. I'm all numb, I swear.

HAPPY: You mean he wouldn't see you?

BIFF: Well, I waited six hours for him, see? All day. Kept sending my name in. Even tried to date his secretary so she'd get me to him, but no soap.

HAPPY: Because you're not showin' the old confidence, Biff. He remembered you, didn't he?

BIFF (*stopping Happy with a gesture*): Finally, about five o'clock, he comes out. Didn't remember who I was or anything. I felt like such an idiot, Hap.

HAPPY: Did you tell him my Florida idea?

BIFF: He walked away. I saw him for one minute. I got so mad I could've torn the walls down! How the hell did I ever get the idea I was a salesman there? I even believed myself that I'd been a salesman for him! And then he gave me one look and—I realized what a ridiculous lie my whole life has been! We've been talking in a dream for fifteen years. I was a shipping clerk.

HAPPY: What'd you do?

BIFF (*with great tension and wonder*): Well, he left, see. And the secretary went out. I was all alone in the waiting room. I don't know what came over me, Hap. The next thing I know I'm in his office—paneled walls, everything. I can't explain it. I—Hap. I took his fountain pen.

HAPPY: Geez, did he catch you?

BIFF: I ran out. I ran down all eleven flights. I ran and ran and ran.

HAPPY: That was an awful dumb—what'd you do that for?

BIFF (*agonized*): I don't know, I just—wanted to take something, I don't know. You gotta help me, Hap. I'm gonna tell Pop.

HAPPY: You crazy? What for?

BIFF: Hap, he's got to understand that I'm not the man somebody lends that kind of money to. He thinks I've been spiting him all these years and it's eating him up.

HAPPY: That's just it. You tell him something nice.

BIFF: I can't.

HAPPY: Say you got a lunch date with Oliver tomorrow.

BIFF: So what do I do tomorrow?

HAPPY: You leave the house tomorrow and come back at night and say Oliver is thinking it over. And he thinks it over for a couple of weeks, and gradually it fades away and nobody's the worse.

BIFF: But it'll go on forever!

HAPPY: Dad is never so happy as when he's looking forward to something!

*Willy enters.*

HAPPY: Hello, scout!

WILLY: Gee, I haven't been here in years!

*Stanley has followed Willy in and sets a chair for him. Stanley starts off but Happy stops him.*

HAPPY: Stanley!

*Stanley stands by, waiting for an order.*

BIFF (*going to Willy with guilt, as to an invalid*): Sit down, Pop. You want a drink?

WILLY: Sure, I don't mind.

BIFF: Let's get a load on.

WILLY: You look worried.

BIFF: N-no. (*To Stanley.*) Scotch all around. Make it doubles.

STANLEY: Doubles, right. (*He goes.*)

WILLY: You had a couple already, didn't you?

BIFF: Just a couple, yeah.

WILLY: Well, what happened, boy? (*Nodding affirmatively, with a smile.*) Everything go all right?

BIFF (*takes a breath, then reaches out and grasps Willy's hand*): Pal . . . (*He is smiling bravely, and Willy is smiling too.*) I had an experience today.

HAPPY: Terrific, Pop.

WILLY: That so? What happened?

BIFF (*high, slightly alcoholic, above the earth*): I'm going to tell you everything from first to last. It's been a strange day. (*Silence. He looks around, composes himself as best he can, but his breath keeps breaking the rhythm of his voice.*) I had to wait quite a while for him, and . . .

WILLY: Oliver?

BIFF: Yeah, Oliver. All day, as a matter of cold fact. And a lot of—instances—facts, Pop, facts about my life came back to me. Who was it, Pop? Who ever said I was a salesman with Oliver?

WILLY: Well, you were.

BIFF: No, Dad, I was a shipping clerk.

WILLY: But you were practically . . .

BIFF (*with determination*): Dad, I don't know who said it first, but I was never a salesman for Bill Oliver.

WILLY: What're you talking about?

BIFF: Let's hold on to the facts tonight, Pop. We're not going to get anywhere bullin' around. I was a shipping clerk.

WILLY (*angrily*): All right, now listen to me . . .

BIFF: Why don't you let me finish?

WILLY: I'm not interested in stories about the past or any crap of that kind because the woods are burning, boys, you understand? There's a big blaze going on all around. I was fired today.

BIFF (*shocked*): How could you be?

WILLY: I was fired, and I'm looking for a little good news to tell your mother, because the woman has waited and the woman has suffered. The gist of it is that I haven't got a story left in my head, Biff. So don't give me a lecture about facts and aspects. I am not interested. Now what've you got to say to me?

*Stanley enters with three drinks. They wait until he leaves.*

WILLY: Did you see Oliver?

BIFF: Jesus, Dad!

WILLY: You mean you didn't go up there?

HAPPY: Sure he went up there.

BIFF: I did. I—saw him. How could they fire you?

WILLY (*on the edge of his chair*): What kind of a welcome did he give you?

BIFF: He won't even let you work on commission?

WILLY: I'm out! (*Driving.*) So tell me, he gave you a warm welcome?

HAPPY: Sure, Pop, sure!

BIFF (*driven*): Well, it was kind of . . .

WILLY: I was wondering if he'd remember you. (*To Happy.*) Imagine, man doesn't see him for ten, twelve years and gives him that kind of a welcome!

HAPPY: Damn right!

BIFF (*trying to return to the offensive*): Pop, look . . .

WILLY: You know why he remembered you, don't you? Because you impressed him in those days.

BIFF: Let's talk quietly and get this down to the facts, huh?

WILLY (*as though Biff had been interrupting*): Well, what happened? It's great news, Biff. Did he take you into his office or'd you talk in the waiting room?

BIFF: Well, he came in, see, and . . .

WILLY (*with a big smile*): What'd he say? Betcha he threw his arm around you.

BIFF: Well, he kinda . . .

WILLY: He's a fine man. (*To Happy.*) Very hard man to see, y'know.

HAPPY (*agreeing*): Oh, I know.

WILLY (*to Biff*): Is that where you had the drinks?

BIFF: Yeah, he gave me a couple of—no, no!

HAPPY (*cutting in*):   He told him my Florida idea.

WILLY:   Don't interrupt. (*To Biff.*) How'd he react to the Florida idea?

BIFF:   Dad, will you give me a minute to explain?

WILLY:   I've been waiting for you to explain since I sat down here! What happened? He took you into his office and what?

BIFF:   Well—I talked. And—and he listened, see.

WILLY:   Famous for the way he listens, y'know. What was his answer?

BIFF:   His answer was—(*He breaks off, suddenly angry.*) Dad, you're not letting me tell you what I want to tell you!

WILLY (*accusing, angered*):   You didn't see him, did you?

BIFF:   I did see him!

WILLY:   What'd you insult him or something? You insulted him, didn't you?

BIFF:   Listen, will you let me out of it, will you just let me out of it!

HAPPY:   What the hell!

WILLY:   Tell me what happened!

BIFF (*to Happy*):   I can't talk to him!

*A single trumpet note jars the ear. The light of green leaves stains the house, which holds the air of night and a dream. Young Bernard enters and knocks on the door of the house.*

YOUNG BERNARD (*frantically*):   Mrs. Loman, Mrs. Loman!

HAPPY:   Tell him what happened!

BIFF (*to Happy.*):   Shut up and leave me alone!

WILLY:   No, no! You had to go and flunk math!

BIFF:   What math? What're you talking about?

YOUNG BERNARD:   Mrs. Loman, Mrs. Loman!

*Linda appears in the house, as of old.*

WILLY (*wildly*):   Math, math, math!

BIFF:   Take it easy, Pop!

YOUNG BERNARD:   Mrs. Loman!

WILLY (*furiously*):   If you hadn't flunked you'd've been set by now!

BIFF:   Now, look, I'm gonna tell you what happened, and you're going to listen to me.

YOUNG BERNARD:   Mrs. Loman!

BIFF:   I waited six hours . . .

HAPPY:   What the hell are you saying?

BIFF:   I kept sending in my name but he wouldn't see me. So finally he . . . (*He continues unheard as light fades low on the restaurant.*)

YOUNG BERNARD:   Biff flunked math!

LINDA: No!

YOUNG BERNARD: Birnbaum flunked him! They won't graduate him!

LINDA: But they have to. He's gotta go to the university. Where is he? Biff! Biff!

YOUNG BERNARD: No, he left. He went to Grand Central.

LINDA: Grand—You mean he went to Boston!

YOUNG BERNARD: Is Uncle Willy in Boston?

LINDA: Oh, maybe Willy can talk to the teacher. Oh, the poor, poor boy!

*Light on house area snaps out.*

BIFF (*at the table, now audible, holding up a gold fountain pen*): . . . so I'm washed up with Oliver, you understand? Are you listening to me?

WILLY (*at a loss*): Yeah, sure. If you hadn't flunked . . .

BIFF: Flunked what? What're you talking about?

WILLY: Don't blame everything on me! I didn't flunk math—you did! What pen?

HAPPY: That was awful dumb, Biff, a pen like that is worth—

WILLY (*seeing the pen for the first time*): You took Oliver's pen?

BIFF (*weakening*): Dad, I just explained it to you.

WILLY: You stole Bill Oliver's fountain pen!

BIFF: I didn't exactly steal it! That's just what I've been explaining to you!

HAPPY: He had it in his hand and just then Oliver walked in, so he got nervous and stuck it in his pocket!

WILLY: My God, Biff!

BIFF: I never intended to do it, Dad!

OPERATOR'S VOICE: Standish Arms, good evening!

WILLY (*shouting*): I'm not in my room!

BIFF (*frightened*): Dad, what's the matter? (*He and Happy stand up.*)

OPERATOR: Ringing Mr. Loman for you!

WILLY: I'm not there, stop it!

BIFF (*horrified, gets down on one knee before Willy*): Dad, I'll make good, I'll make good. (*Willy tries to get to his feet. Biff holds him down.*) Sit down now.

WILLY: No, you're no good, you're no good for anything.

BIFF: I am, Dad, I'll find something else, you understand? Now don't worry about anything. (*He holds up Willy's face.*) Talk to me, Dad.

OPERATOR: Mr. Loman does not answer. Shall I page him?

WILLY (*attempting to stand, as though to rush and silence the Operator*): No, no, no!

HAPPY: He'll strike something, Pop.

WILLY: No, no . . .

BIFF (*desperately, standing over Willy*): Pop, listen! Listen to me! I'm telling you something good. Oliver talked to his partner about the Florida idea. You listening? He—he talked to his partner, and he came to me . . . I'm going to be all right, you hear? Dad, listen to me, he said it was just a question of the amount!

WILLY: Then you . . . got it?

HAPPY: He's gonna be terrific, Pop!

WILLY (*trying to stand*): Then you got it, haven't you? You got it! You got it!

BIFF (*agonized, holds Willy down*): No, no. Look, Pop. I'm supposed to have lunch with them tomorrow. I'm just telling you this so you'll know that I can still make an impression, Pop. And I'll make good somewhere, but I can't go tomorrow, see.

WILLY: Why not? You simply . . .

BIFF: But the pen, Pop!

WILLY: You give it to him and tell him it was an oversight!

HAPPY: Sure, have lunch tomorrow!

BIFF: I can't say that . . .

WILLY: You were doing a crossword puzzle and accidentally used his pen!

BIFF: Listen, kid, I took those balls years ago, now I walk in with his fountain pen? That clinches it, don't you see? I can't face him like that! I'll try elsewhere.

PAGE'S VOICE: Paging Mr. Loman!

WILLY: Don't you want to be anything?

BIFF: Pop, how can I go back?

WILLY: You don't want to be anything, is that what's behind it?

BIFF (*now angry at Willy for not crediting his sympathy*): Don't take it that way! You think it was easy walking into that office after what I'd done to him? A team of horses couldn't have dragged me back to Bill Oliver!

WILLY: Then why'd you go?

BIFF: Why did I go? Why did I go! Look at you! Look at what's become of you!

*Off left, The Woman laughs.*

WILLY: Biff, you're going to go to that lunch tomorrow, or . . .

BIFF: I can't go. I've got no appointment!

HAPPY: Biff, for . . . !

WILLY: Are you spiting me?

BIFF: Don't take it that way! Goddammit!

WILLY (*strikes Biff and falters away from the table*): You rotten little louse! Are you spiting me?

THE WOMAN: Someone's at the door, Willy!

BIFF: I'm no good, can't you see what I am?

HAPPY (*separating them*): Hey, you're in a restaurant! Now cut it out, both of you! (*The girls enter.*) Hello, girls, sit down.

*The Woman laughs, off left.*

MISS FORSYTHE: I guess we might as well. This is Letta.

THE WOMAN: Willy, are you going to wake up?

BIFF (*ignoring Willy*): How're ya, miss, sit down. What do you drink?

MISS FORSYTHE: Letta might not be able to stay long.

LETTA: I gotta get up very early tomorrow. I got jury duty. I'm so excited! Were you fellows ever on a jury?

BIFF: No, but I been in front of them! (*The girls laugh.*) This is my father.

LETTA: Isn't he cute? Sit down with us, Pop.

HAPPY: Sit him down, Biff!

BIFF (*going to him*): Come on, slugger, drink us under the table. To hell with it! Come on, sit down, pal.

*On Biff's last insistence, Willy is about to sit.*

THE WOMAN (*now urgently*): Willy, are you going to answer the door!

*The Woman's call pulls Willy back. He starts right, befuddled.*

BIFF: Hey, where are you going?

WILLY: Open the door.

BIFF: The door?

WILLY: The washroom . . . the door . . . where's the door?

BIFF (*leading Willy to the left*): Just go straight down.

*Willy moves left.*

THE WOMAN: Willy, Willy, are you going to get up, get up, get up, get up?

*Willy exits left.*

LETTA: I think it's sweet you bring your daddy along.

MISS FORSYTHE: Oh, he isn't really your father!

BIFF (*at left, turning to her resentfully*): Miss Forsythe, you've just seen a prince walk by. A fine, troubled prince. A hardworking, unappreciated prince. A pal, you understand? A good companion. Always for his boys.

LETTA: That's so sweet.

HAPPY: Well, girls, what's the program? We're wasting time. Come on, Biff. Gather round. Where would you like to go?

BIFF: Why don't you do something for him?

HAPPY: Me!

BIFF: Don't you give a damn for him, Hap?

HAPPY: What're you talking about? I'm the one who . . .

BIFF: I sense it, you don't give a good goddam about him. (*He takes the rolled-up hose from his pocket and puts it on the table in front of Happy.*) Look what I found in the cellar, for Christ's sake. How can you bear to let it go on?

HAPPY: Me? Who goes away? Who runs off and . . .

BIFF: Yeah, but he doesn't mean anything to you. You could help him—I can't! Don't you understand what I'm talking about? He's going to kill himself, don't you know that?

HAPPY: Don't know it! Me!

BIFF: Hap, help him! Jesus . . . help him . . . Help me, help me, I can't bear to look at his face! (*Ready to weep, he hurries out, up right.*)

HAPPY (*starting after him*): Where are you going?

MISS FORSYTHE: What's he so mad about?

HAPPY: Come on, girls, we'll catch up with him.

MISS FORSYTHE (*as Happy pushes her out*): Say, I don't like that temper of his!

HAPPY: He's just a little overstrung, he'll be all right!

WILLY (*off left, as The Woman laughs*): Don't answer! Don't answer!

LETTA: Don't you want to tell your father . . .

HAPPY: No, that's not my father. He's just a guy. Come on, we'll catch Biff, and, honey, we're going to paint this town! Stanley, where's the check! Hey, Stanley!

*They exit. Stanley looks toward left.*

STANLEY (*calling to Happy indignantly*):   Mr. Loman! Mr. Loman!

*Stanley picks up a chair and follows them off. Knocking is heard off left. The Woman enters, laughing. Willy follows her. She is in a black slip; he is buttoning his shirt. Raw, sensuous music accompanies their speech:*

WILLY:   Will you stop laughing? Will you stop?

THE WOMAN:   Aren't you going to answer the door? He'll wake the whole hotel.

WILLY:   I'm not expecting anybody.

THE WOMAN:   Whyn't you have another drink, honey, and stop being so damn self-centered?

WILLY:   I'm so lonely.

THE WOMAN:   You know you ruined me, Willy? From now on, whenever you come to the office, I'll see that you go right through to the buyers. No waiting at my desk anymore, Willy. You ruined me.

WILLY:   That's nice of you to say that.

THE WOMAN:   Gee, you are self-centered! Why so sad? You are the saddest, self-centeredest soul I ever did see-saw. (*She laughs. He kisses her.*) Come on inside, drummer boy. It's silly to be dressing in the middle of the night. (*As knocking is heard.*) Aren't you going to answer the door?

WILLY:   They're knocking on the wrong door.

THE WOMAN:   But I felt the knocking. And he heard us talking in here. Maybe the hotel's on fire!

WILLY (*his terror rising*):   It's a mistake.

THE WOMAN:   Then tell him to go away!

WILLY:   There's nobody there.

THE WOMAN:   It's getting on my nerves, Willy. There's somebody standing out there and it's getting on my nerves!

WILLY (*pushing her away from him*):   All right, stay in the bathroom here, and don't come out. I think there's a law in Massachusetts about it, so don't come out. It may be that new room clerk. He looked very mean. So don't come out. It's a mistake, there's no fire.

*The knocking is heard again. He takes a few steps away from her, and she vanishes into the wing. The light follows him, and now he is facing Young Biff, who carries a suitcase. Biff steps toward him. The music is gone.*

BIFF: Why didn't you answer?

WILLY: Biff! What are you doing in Boston?

BIFF: Why didn't you answer? I've been knocking for five minutes, I called you on the phone . . .

WILLY: I just heard you. I was in the bathroom and had the door shut. Did anything happen home?

BIFF: Dad—I let you down.

WILLY: What do you mean?

BIFF: Dad . . .

WILLY: Biffo, what's this about? (*Putting his arm around Biff.*) Come on, let's go downstairs and get you a malted.

BIFF: Dad, I flunked math.

WILLY: Not for the term?

BIFF: The term. I haven't got enough credits to graduate.

WILLY: You mean to say Bernard wouldn't give you the answers?

BIFF: He did, he tried, but I only got a sixty-one.

WILLY: And they wouldn't give you four points?

BIFF: Birnbaum refused absolutely. I begged him, Pop, but he won't give me those points. You gotta talk to him before they close the school. Because if he saw the kind of man you are, and you just talked to him in your way, I'm sure he'd come through for me. The class came right before practice, see, and I didn't go enough. Would you talk to him? He'd like you, Pop. You know the way you could talk.

WILLY: You're on. We'll drive right back.

BIFF: Oh, Dad, good work! I'm sure he'll change it for you!

WILLY: Go downstairs and tell the clerk I'm checkin' out. Go right down.

BIFF: Yes, sir! See, the reason he hates me, Pop—one day he was late for class so I got up at the blackboard and imitated him. I crossed my eyes and talked with a lithp.

WILLY (*laughing*): You did? The kids like it?

BIFF: They nearly died laughing!

WILLY: Yeah? What'd you do?

BIFF: The thquare root of thixthy twee is . . . (*Willy bursts out laughing; Biff joins.*) And in the middle of it he walked in!

*Willy laughs and The Woman joins in offstage.*

WILLY (*without hesitation*): Hurry downstairs and . . .

BIFF: Somebody in there?

WILLY: No, that was next door.

*The Woman laughs offstage.*

BIFF: Somebody got in your bathroom!
WILLY: No, it's the next room, there's a party . . .
THE WOMAN (*enters, laughing; she lisps this*): Can I come in? There's something in the bathtub, Willy, and it's moving!

*Willy looks at Biff; who is staring open-mouthed and horrified at The Woman.*

WILLY: Ah—you better go back to your room. They must be finished painting by now. They're painting her room so I let her take a shower here. Go back, go back . . . (He pushes her.)
THE WOMAN (*resisting*): But I've got to get dressed, Willy, I can't . . .

WILLY: Get out of here! Go back, go back . . . (*Suddenly striving for the ordinary.*) This is Miss Francis, Biff, she's a buyer. They're painting her room. Go back, Miss Francis, go back . . .
THE WOMAN: But my clothes, I can't go out naked in the hall!
WILLY (*pushing her offstage*): Get outa here! Go back, go back!

*Biff slowly sits down on his suitcase as the argument continues offstage.*

THE WOMAN: Where's my stockings? You promised me stockings, Willy!
WILLY: I have no stockings here!
THE WOMAN: You had two boxes of size nine sheers for me, and I want them!
WILLY: Here, for God's sake, will you get outa here!
THE WOMAN (*enters holding a box of stockings*): I just hope there's nobody in the hall. That's all I hope. (*To Biff.*) Are you football or baseball?
BIFF: Football.
THE WOMAN (*angry, humiliated*): That's me too. G'night. (*She snatches her clothes from Willy, and walks out.*)
WILLY (*after a pause*): Well, better get going. I want to get to the school first thing in the morning. Get my suits out of the closet. I'll get my valise. (*Biff doesn't move.*) What's the matter! (*Biff remains motionless, tears falling.*) She's a buyer. Buys for J. H. Simmons.

She lives down the hall—they're painting. You don't imagine—(*He breaks off. After a pause.*) Now listen, pal, she's just a buyer. She sells merchandise in her room and they have to keep it looking just so . . . (*Pause. Assuming command.*) All right, get my suits. (*Biff doesn't move.*) Now stop crying and do as I say. I gave you an order. Biff, I gave you an order! Is that what you do when I give you an order? How dare you cry! (*Putting his arm around Biff.*) Now look, Biff, when you grow up you'll understand about these things. You mustn't—you mustn't overemphasize a thing like this. I'll see Birnbaum first thing in the morning.

BIFF: Never mind.

WILLY (*getting down beside Biff*):   Never mind! He's going to give you those points. I'll see to it.

BIFF: He wouldn't listen to you.

WILLY: He certainly will listen to me. You need those points for the U. of Virginia.

BIFF: I'm not going there.

WILLY: Heh? If I can't get him to change that mark you'll make it up in summer school. You've got all summer to . . .

BIFF (*his weeping breaking from him*): Dad . . .

WILLY (*infected by it*): Oh, my boy . . .

BIFF: Dad . . .

WILLY: She's nothing to me, Biff. I was lonely, I was terribly lonely.

BIFF: You—you gave her Mama's stockings! (*His tears break through and he rises to go.*)

WILLY (*grabbing for Biff*):   I gave you an order!

BIFF: Don't touch me, you—liar!

WILLY: Apologize for that!

BIFF: You fake! You phony little fake! You fake! (*Overcome, he turns quickly and weeping fully goes out with his suitcase. Willy is left on the floor on his knees.*)

WILLY: I gave you an order! Biff, come back here or I'll beat you! Come back here! I'll whip you!

*Stanley comes quickly in from the right and stands in front of Willy.*

WILLY (*shouts at Stanley*):   I gave you an order . . .

STANLEY: Hey, let's pick it up, pick it up, Mr. Loman. (*He helps Willy to his feet.*) Your boys left with the chippies. They said they'll see you home.

*A second waiter watches some distance away.*

WILLY: But we were supposed to have dinner together.

*Music is heard, Willy's theme.*

STANLEY: Can you make it?

WILLY: I'll—sure, I can make it. (*Suddenly concerned about his clothes.*) Do I—I look all right?

STANLEY: Sure, you look all right. (*He flicks a speck off Willy's lapel.*)

WILLY: Here—here's a dollar.

STANLEY: Oh, your son paid me. It's all right.

WILLY (*putting it in Stanley's hand*): No, take it. You're a good boy.

STANLEY: Oh, no, you don't have to . . .

WILLY: Here—here's some more, I don't need it any more. (*After a slight pause.*) Tell me—is there a seed store in the neighborhood?

STANLEY: Seeds? You mean like to plant?

*As Willy turns, Stanley slips the money back into his jacket pocket.*

WILLY: Yes. Carrots, peas . . .

STANLEY: Well, there's hardware stores on Sixth Avenue, but it may be too late now.

WILLY (*anxiously*): Oh, I'd better hurry. I've got to get some seeds. (*He starts off to the right.*) I've got to get some seeds, right away. Nothing's planted. I don't have a thing in the ground.

*Willy hurries out as the light goes down. Stanley moves over to the right after him, watches him off. The other waiter has been staring at Willy.*

STANLEY (*to the waiter*): Well, whatta you looking at?

*The waiter picks up the chairs and moves off right. Stanley takes the table and follows him. The light fades on this area. There is a long pause, the sound of the flute coming over. The light gradually rises on the kitchen, which is empty. Happy appears at the door of the house, followed by Biff. Happy is carrying a large bunch of long-stemmed roses. He enters the kitchen, looks around for Linda. Not seeing her, he turns to Biff, who is just outside the house door, and makes a gesture with his hands, indicating "Not here, I guess." He looks into the living room and freezes. Inside, Linda, unseen, is seated, Willy's coat on her lap. She rises ominously and quietly and moves toward Happy, who backs up into the kitchen, afraid.*

HAPPY:  Hey, what're you doing up? (*Linda says nothing but moves toward him implacably.*) Where's Pop? (*He keeps backing to the right, and now Linda is in full view in the doorway to the living room.*) Is he sleeping?

LINDA:  Where were you?

HAPPY (*trying to laugh it off*):  We met two girls, Mom, very fine types. Here, we brought you some flowers. (*Offering them to her.*) Put them in your room, Ma.

*She knocks them to the floor at Biff's feet. He has now come inside and closed the door behind him. She stares at Biff, silent.*

HAPPY:  Now what'd you do that for? Mom, I want you to have some flowers . . .

LINDA (*cutting Happy off, violently to Biff*):  Don't you care whether he lives or dies?

HAPPY (*going to the stairs*):  Come upstairs, Biff.

BIFF (*with a flare of disgust, to Happy*):  Go away from me! (*To Linda.*) What do you mean, lives or dies? Nobody's dying around here, pal.

LINDA:  Get out of my sight! Get out of here!

BIFF:  I wanna see the boss.

LINDA:  You're not going near him!

BIFF:  Where is he? (*He moves into the living room and Linda follows.*)

LINDA (*shouting after Biff.*):  You invite him for dinner. He looks forward to it all day—(*Biff appears in his parents' bedroom, looks around, and exits*)—and then you desert him there. There's no stranger you'd do that to!

HAPPY:  Why? He had a swell time with us. Listen, when I—(*Linda comes back into the kitchen*)—desert him I hope I don't outlive the day!

LINDA:  Get out of here!

HAPPY:  Now look, Mom . . .

LINDA:  Did you have to go to women tonight? You and your lousy rotten whores!

*Biff re-enters the kitchen.*

HAPPY: Mom, all we did was follow Biff around trying to cheer him up! (*To Biff.*) Boy, what a night you gave me!

LINDA: Get out of here, both of you, and don't come back! I don't want you tormenting him any more. Go on now, get your things together! (*To Biff.*) You can sleep in his apartment. (*She starts to pick up the flowers and stops herself.*) Pick up this stuff, I'm not your maid any more. Pick it up, you bum, you!

*Happy turns his back to her in refusal. Biff slowly moves over and gets down on his knees, picking up the flowers.*

LINDA: You're a pair of animals! Not one, not another living soul would have had the cruelty to walk out on that man in a restaurant!

BIFF (*not looking at her*): Is that what he said?

LINDA: He didn't have to say anything. He was so humiliated he nearly limped when he came in.

HAPPY: But, Mom, he had a great time with us . . .

BIFF (*cutting him off violently*): Shut up!

*Without another word, Happy goes upstairs.*

LINDA: You! You didn't even go in to see if he was all right!

BIFF (*still on the floor in front of Linda, the flowers in his hand; with self-loathing*): No. Didn't. Didn't do a damned thing. How do you like that, heh? Left him babbling in a toilet.

LINDA: You louse. You . . .

BIFF: Now you hit it on the nose! (*He gets up, throws the flowers in the wastebasket.*) The scum of the earth, and you're looking at him!

LINDA: Get out of here!

BIFF: I gotta talk to the boss, Mom. Where is he?

LINDA: You're not going near him. Get out of this house!

BIFF (*with absolute assurance, determination*): No. We're gonna have an abrupt conversation, him and me.

LINDA: You're not talking to him.

*Hammering is heard from outside the house, off right. Biff turns toward the noise.*

LINDA (*suddenly pleading*): Will you please leave him alone?

BIFF: What's he doing out there?

LINDA: He's planting the garden!

BIFF (*quietly*):   Now? Oh, my God!

*Biff moves outside, Linda following. The light dies down on
them and comes up on the center of the apron as Willy walks
into it. He is carrying a flashlight, a hoe, and a handful of
seed packets. He raps the top of the hoe sharply to fix it
firmly, and then moves to the left, measuring off the distance
with his foot. He holds the flashlight to look at the seed packets, reading off the instructions. He is in the blue of night.*

WILLY:   Carrots . . . quarter-inch apart. Rows . . . one-foot rows.
(*He measures it off.*) One foot. (*He puts down a package and measures off.*) Beets. (*He puts down another package and measures
again.*) Lettuce. (*He reads the package, puts it down.*) One foot—
(*He breaks off as Ben appears at the right and moves slowly down
to him.*) What a proposition, ts, ts. Terrific, terrific. 'Cause she's
suffered, Ben, the woman has suffered. You understand me? A man
can't go out the way he came in, Ben, a man has got to add up to
something. You can't, you can't—(*Ben moves toward him as
though to interrupt.*) You gotta consider now. Don't answer so
quick. Remember, it's a guaranteed twenty-thousand-dollar proposition. Now look, Ben, I want you to go through the ins and outs
of this thing with me. I've got nobody to talk to, Ben, and the
woman has suffered, you hear me?
BEN (*standing still, considering*):   What's the proposition?
WILLY:   It's twenty thousand dollars on the barrelhead. Guaranteed,
gilt-edged, you understand?
BEN:   You don't want to make a fool of yourself. They might not
honor the policy.
WILLY:   How can they dare refuse? Didn't I work like a coolie to meet
every premium on the nose? And now they don't pay off? Impossible!
BEN:   It's called a cowardly thing, William.
WILLY:   Why? Does it take more guts to stand here the rest of my life
ringing up a zero?
BEN (*yielding*):   That's a point, William. (*He moves, thinking, turns.*)
And twenty thousand—that is something one can feel with the
hand, it is there.
WILLY (*now assured, with rising power*):   Oh, Ben, that's the whole
beauty of it! I see it like a diamond, shining in the dark, hard and
rough, that I can pick up and touch in my hand. Not like—like an

appointment! This would not be another damned-fool appointment, Ben, and it changes all the aspects. Because he thinks I'm nothing, see, and so he spites me. But the funeral . . . (*Straightening up.*) Ben, that funeral will be massive! They'll come from Maine, Massachusetts, Vermont, New Hampshire! All the old-timers with the strange license plates—that boy will be thunderstruck, Ben, because he never realized—I am known! Rhode Island, New York, New Jersey—I am known, Ben, and he'll see it with his eyes once and for all. He'll see what I am, Ben! He's in for a shock, that boy!

BEN (*coming down to the edge of the garden*): He'll call you a coward.

WILLY (*suddenly fearful*): No, that would be terrible.

BEN: Yes. And a damned fool.

WILLY: No, no, he mustn't, I won't have that! (*He is broken and desperate.*)

BEN: He'll hate you, William.

*The gay music of the Boys is heard.*

WILLY: Oh, Ben, how do we get back to all the great times? Used to be so full of light, and comradeship, the sleigh-riding in winter, and the ruddiness on his cheeks. And always some kind of good news coming up, always something nice coming up ahead. And never even let me carry the valises in the house, and simonizing, simonizing that little red car! Why, why can't I give him something and not have him hate me?

BEN: Let me think about it. (*He glances at his watch.*) I still have a little time. Remarkable proposition, but you've got to be sure you're not making a fool of yourself.

*Ben drifts off upstage and goes out of sight. Biff comes down from the left.*

WILLY (*suddenly conscious of Biff, turns and looks up at him, then begins picking up the packages of seeds in confusion*): Where the hell is that seed? (*Indignantly.*) You can't see nothing out here! They boxed in the whole goddam neighborhood!

BIFF: There are people all around here. Don't you realize that?

WILLY: I'm busy. Don't bother me.

BIFF (*taking the hoe from Willy*): I'm saying good-by to you, Pop. (*Willy looks at him, silent, unable to move.*) I'm not coming back any more.

WILLY:   You're not going to see Oliver tomorrow?

BIFF:   I've got no appointment, Dad.

WILLY:   He put his arm around you, and you've got no appointment?

BIFF:   Pop, get this now, will you? Everytime I've left it's been a—fight that sent me out of here. Today I realized something about myself and I tried to explain it to you and I—I think I'm just not smart enough to make any sense out of it for you. To hell with whose fault it is or anything like that. (*He takes Willy's arm.*) Let's just wrap it up, heh? Come on in, we'll tell Mom. (*He gently tries to pull Willy to left.*)

WILLY (*frozen, immobile, with guilt in his voice*):   No, I don't want to see her.

BIFF:   Come on! (*He pulls again, and Willy tries to pull away.*)

WILLY (*highly nervous*):   No, no, I don't want to see her.

BIFF (*tries to look into Willy's face, as if to find the answer there*):   Why don't you want to see her?

WILLY (*more harshly now*):   Don't bother me, will you?

BIFF:   What do you mean, you don't want to see her? You don't want them calling you yellow, do you? This isn't your fault; it's me, I'm a bum. Now come inside! (*Willy strains to get away.*) Did you hear what I said to you?

*Willy pulls away and quickly goes by himself into the house. Biff follows.*

LINDA (*to Willy*):   Did you plant, dear?

BIFF (*at the door, to Linda*):   All right, we had it out. I'm going and I'm not writing any more.

LINDA (*going to Willy in the kitchen*):   I think that's the best way, dear. 'Cause there's no use drawing it out, you'll just never get along.

*Willy doesn't respond.*

BIFF:   People ask where I am and what I'm doing, you don't know, and you don't care. That way it'll be off your mind and you can start brightening up again. All right? That clears it, doesn't it? (*Willy is silent, and Biff goes to him.*) You gonna wish me luck, scout? (*He extends his hand.*) What do you say?

LINDA:   Shake his hand, Willy.

WILLY (*turning to her, seething with hurt*):   There's no necessity—to mention the pen at all, y'know.

BIFF (*gently*):   I've got no appointment, Dad.
WILLY (*erupting fiercely*):   He put his arm around . . . ?
BIFF:   Dad, you're never going to see what I am, so what's the use of arguing? If I strike oil I'll send you a check. Meantime forget I'm alive.
WILLY (*to Linda*):   Spite, see?
BIFF:   Shake hands, Dad.
WILLY:   Not my hand.
BIFF:   I was hoping not to go this way.
WILLY:   Well, this is the way you're going. Good-by.

*Biff looks at him a moment, then turns sharply and goes to the stairs.*

WILLY (*stops him with*):   May you rot in hell if you leave this house!
BIFF (*turning*):   Exactly what is it that you want from me?
WILLY:   I want you to know, on the train, in the mountains, in the valleys, wherever you go, that you cut down your life for spite!
BIFF:   No, no.
WILLY:   Spite, spite, is the word of your undoing! And when you're down and out, remember what did it. When you're rotting somewhere beside the railroad tracks, remember, and don't you dare blame it on me!
BIFF:   I'm not blaming it on you!
WILLY:   I won't take the rap for this, you hear?

*Happy comes down the stairs and stands on the bottom step, watching.*

BIFF:   That's just what I'm telling you!
WILLY (*sinking into a chair at a table, with full accusation*):   You're trying to put a knife in me—don't think I don't know what you're doing!
BIFF:   All right, phony! Then let's lay it on the line. (*He whips the rubber tube out of his pocket and puts it on the table.*)
HAPPY:   You crazy . . .
LINDA:   Biff! (*She moves to grab the hose, but Biff holds it down with his hand.*)
BIFF:   Leave it there! Don't move it!
WILLY (*not looking at it*):   What is that?
BIFF:   You know goddam well what that is.
WILLY (*caged, wanting to escape*):   I never saw that.

BIFF:   You saw it. The mice didn't bring it into the cellar! What is this supposed to do, make a hero out of you? This supposed to make me sorry for you?

WILLY:   Never heard of it.

BIFF:   There'll be no pity for you, you hear it? No pity!

WILLY (*to Linda*):   You hear the spite!

BIFF:   No, you're going to hear the truth—what you are and what I am!

LINDA:   Stop it!

WILLY:   Spite!

HAPPY (*coming down toward Biff*):   You cut it now!

BIFF (*to Happy*):   The man don't know who we are! The man is gonna know! (*To Willy.*) We never told the truth for ten minutes in this house!

HAPPY:   We always told the truth!

BIFF (*turning on him*):   You big blow, are you the assistant buyer? You're one of the two assistants to the assistant, aren't you?

HAPPY:   Well, I'm practically . . .

BIFF:   You're practically full of it! We all are! and I'm through with it. (*To Willy.*) Now hear this, Willy, this is me.

WILLY:   I know you!

BIFF:   You know why I had no address for three months? I stole a suit in Kansas City and I was in jail. (*To Linda, who is sobbing.*) Stop crying. I'm through with it.

*Linda turns away from them, her hands covering her face.*

WILLY:   I suppose that's my fault!

BIFF:   I stole myself out of every good job since high school!

WILLY:   And whose fault is that?

BIFF:   And I never got anywhere because you blew me so full of hot air I could never stand taking orders from anybody! That's whose fault it is!

WILLY:   I hear that!

LINDA:   Don't, Biff!

BIFF:   It's goddam time you heard that! I had to be boss big shot in two weeks, and I'm through with it!

WILLY:   Then hang yourself! For spite, hang yourself!

BIFF:   No! Nobody's hanging himself, Willy! I ran down eleven flights with a pen in my hand today. And suddenly I stopped, you hear me? And in the middle of that office building, do you hear this? I stopped in the middle of that building and I saw—the sky. I saw the things that I love in this world. The work and the food and time to sit and smoke. And I looked at the pen and said to myself, what the hell am I grabbing this for? Why am I trying to become what I don't want to be? What am I doing in an office, making a contemptuous, begging fool of myself, when all I want is out there, waiting for me the minute I say I know who I am! Why can't I say that, Willy? (*He tries to make Willy face him, but Willy pulls away and moves to the left.*)

WILLY (*with hatred, threateningly*): The door of your life is wide open!

BIFF: Pop! I'm a dime a dozen, and so are you!

WILLY (*turning on him now in an uncontrolled outburst*): I am not a dime a dozen! I am Willy Loman, and you are Biff Loman!

*Biff starts for Willy, but is blocked by Happy. In his fury, Biff seems on the verge of attacking his father.*

BIFF: I am not a leader of men, Willy, and neither are you. You were never anything but a hard-working drummer who landed in the ash can like all the rest of them! I'm one dollar an hour, Willy! I tried seven states and couldn't raise it. A buck an hour! Do you gather my meaning? I'm not bringing home any prizes any more, and you're going to stop waiting for me to bring them home!

WILLY (*directly to Biff*): You vengeful, spiteful mutt!

*Biff breaks from Happy. Willy, in fright, starts up the stairs. Biff grabs him.*

BIFF (*at the peak of his fury*): Pop! I'm nothing! I'm nothing, Pop. Can't you understand that? There's no spite in it any more. I'm just what I am, that's all.

*Biff's fury has spent itself and he breaks down, sobbing, holding on to Willy, who dumbly fumbles for Biff's face.*

WILLY (*astonished*): What're you doing? What're you doing? (*To Linda.*) Why is he crying?

BIFF (*crying, broken*): Will you let me go, for Christ's sake? Will you take that phony dream and burn it before something happens? (*Struggling to contain himself, he pulls away and moves to the stairs.*) I'll go in the morning. Put him—put him to bed. (*Exhausted, Biff moves up the stairs to his room.*)

WILLY (*after a long pause, astonished, elevated*):   Isn't that—isn't that remarkable? Biff—he likes me!

LINDA:   He loves you, Willy!

HAPPY (*deeply moved*):   Always did, Pop.

WILLY:   Oh, Biff! (*Staring wildly.*) He cried! Cried to me. (*He is choking with his love, and now cries out his promise.*) That boy—that boy is going to be magnificent!

*Ben appears in the light just outside the kitchen.*

BEN:   Yes, outstanding, with twenty thousand behind him.

LINDA (*sensing the racing of his mind, fearfully, carefully*):   Now come to bed, Willy. It's all settled now.

WILLY (*finding it difficult not to rush out of the house*):   Yes, we'll sleep. Come on. Go to sleep, Hap.

BEN:   And it does take a great kind of a man to crack the jungle.

*In accents of dread, Ben's idyllic music starts up.*

HAPPY (*his arm around Linda*):   I'm getting married, Pop, don't forget it. I'm changing everything. I'm gonna run that department before the year is up. You'll see, Mom. (*He kisses her.*)

BEN:   The jungle is dark but full of diamonds, Willy.

*Willy turns, moves, listening to Ben.*

LINDA:   Be good. You're both good boys, just act that way, that's all.

HAPPY:   'Night, Pop. (*He goes upstairs.*)

LINDA (*to Willy*):   Come, dear.

BEN (*with greater force*):   One must go in to fetch a diamond out.

WILLY (*to Linda, as he moves slowly along the edge of the kitchen, toward the door*):   I just want to get settled down, Linda. Let me sit alone for a little.

LINDA (*almost uttering her fear*):   I want you upstairs.

WILLY (*taking her in his arms*):   In a few minutes, Linda. I couldn't sleep right now. Go on, you look awful tired. (*He kisses her.*)

BEN:   Not like an appointment at all. A diamond is rough and hard to the touch.

WILLY:   Go on now. I'll be right up.

LINDA:   I think this is the only way, Willy.

WILLY:   Sure, it's the best thing.

BEN:   Best thing!

WILLY:   The only way. Everything is gonna be—go on, kid, get to bed. You look so tired.

LINDA: Come right up.
WILLY: Two minutes.

*Linda goes into the living room, then reappears in her bed-room. Willy moves just outside the kitchen door.*

WILLY: Loves me. (*Wonderingly.*) Always loved me. Isn't that a re-markable thing? Ben, he'll worship me for it!
BEN (*with promise*): It's dark there, but full of diamonds.
WILLY: Can you imagine that magnificence with twenty thousand dollars in his pocket?
LINDA (*calling from her room*): Willy! Come up!
WILLY (*calling into the kitchen*): Yes! Yes. Coming! It's very smart, you realize that, don't you, sweetheart? Even Ben sees it. I gotta go, baby. 'By! 'By! (*Going over to Ben, almost dancing.*) Imagine? When the mail comes he'll be ahead of Bernard again!
BEN: A perfect proposition all around.
WILLY: Did you see how he cried to me? Oh, if I could kiss him, Ben!
BEN: Time, William, time!
WILLY: Oh, Ben, I always knew one way or another we were gonna make it, Biff and I.
BEN (*looking at his watch*): The boat. We'll be late. (*He moves slowly off into the darkness.*)
WILLY (*elegiacally, turning to the house*): Now when you kick off, boy, I want a seventy-yard boot, and get right down the field under the ball, and when you hit, hit low and hit hard, because it's im-portant, boy. (*He swings around and faces the audience.*) There's all kinds of important people in the stands, and the first thing you know . . . (*Suddenly realizing he is alone.*) Ben! Ben, where do I . . . ? (*He makes a sudden movement of search.*) Ben, how do I . . . ?
LINDA (*calling*): Willy, you coming up?
WILLY (*uttering a gasp of fear, whirling about as if to quiet her*): Sh! (*He turns around as if to find his way; sounds, faces, voices, seem to be swarming in upon him and he flicks at them, crying.*) Sh! Sh! (*Suddenly music, faint and high, stops him. It rises in intensity, al-most to an unbearable scream. He goes up and down on his toes, and rushes off around the house.*) Shhh!
LINDA: Willy?

*There is no answer. Linda waits. Biff gets up off his bed. He is still in his clothes. Happy sits up. Biff stands listening.*

LINDA (*with real fear*): Willy, answer me! Willy!

*There is the sound of a car starting and moving away at full speed.*

LINDA: No!
BIFF (*rushing down the stairs*): Pop!

*As the car speeds off the music crashes down in a frenzy of sound, which becomes the soft pulsation of a single cello string. Biff slowly returns to his bedroom. He and Happy gravely don their jackets. Linda slowly walks out of her room. The music has developed into a dead march. The leaves of day are appearing over everything. Charley and Bernard, somberly dressed, appear and knock on the kitchen door. Biff and Happy slowly descend the stairs to the kitchen as Charley and Bernard enter. All stop a moment when Linda, in clothes of mourning, bearing a little bunch of roses, comes through the draped doorway into the kitchen. She goes to Charley and takes his arm. Now all move toward the audience, through the wall-line of the kitchen. At the limit of the apron, Linda lays down the flowers, kneels, and sits back on her heels. All stare down at the grave.*

## REQUIEM

CHARLEY: It's getting dark, Linda.

*Linda doesn't react. She stares at the grave.*

BIFF: How about it, Mom? Better get some rest, heh? They'll be closing the gate soon.

*Linda makes no move. Pause.*

HAPPY (*deeply angered*): He had no right to do that. There was no necessity for it. We would've helped him.
CHARLEY (*grunting*): Hmmm.
BIFF: Come along, Mom.
LINDA: Why didn't anybody come?
CHARLEY: It was a very nice funeral.
LINDA: But where are all the people he knew? Maybe they blame him.
CHARLEY: Naa. It's a rough world, Linda. They wouldn't blame him.

LINDA: I can't understand it. At this time especially. First time in thirty-five years we were just about free and clear. He only needed a little salary. He was even finished with the dentist.

CHARLEY: No man only needs a little salary.

LINDA: I can't understand it.

BIFF: There were a lot of nice days. When he'd come home from a trip; or on Sundays, making the stoop; finishing the cellar; putting on the new porch; when he built the extra bathroom; and put up the garage. You know something, Charley, there's more of him in that front stoop than in all the sales he ever made.

CHARLEY: Yeah. He was a happy man with a batch of cement.

LINDA: He was so wonderful with his hands.

BIFF: He had the wrong dreams. All, all, wrong.

HAPPY (*almost ready to fight Biff*): Don't say that!

BIFF: He never knew who he was.

CHARLEY (*stopping Happy's movement and reply; to Biff*): Nobody dast blame this man. You don't understand: Willy was a salesman. And for a salesman, there is no rock bottom to the life. He don't put a bolt to a nut, he don't tell you the law or give you medicine. He's a man way out there in the blue, riding on a smile and a shoeshine. And when they start not smiling back—that's an earthquake. And then you get yourself a couple of spots on your hat, and you're finished. Nobody dast blame this man. A salesman is got to dream, boy. It comes with the territory.

BIFF: Charley, the man didn't know who he was.

HAPPY (*infuriated*): Don't say that!

BIFF: Why don't you come with me, Happy?

HAPPY: I'm not licked that easily. I'm staying right in this city, and I'm gonna beat this racket! (*He looks at Biff, his chin set.*) The Loman Brothers!

BIFF: I know who I am, kid.

HAPPY: All right, boy. I'm gonna show you and everybody else that Willy Loman did not die in vain. He had a good dream. It's the only dream you can have—to come out number-one man. He fought it out here, and this is where I'm gonna win it for him.

BIFF (*with a hopeless glance at Happy, bends toward his mother*): Let's go, Mom.

LINDA: I'll be with you in a minute. Go on, Charley. (*He hesitates.*) I want to, just for a minute. I never had a chance to say good-by.

*Charley moves away, followed by Happy. Biff remains a slight distance up and left of Linda. She sits there, summoning herself. The flute begins, not far away, playing behind her speech.*

LINDA: Forgive me, dear. I can't cry. I don't know what it is, but I can't cry. I don't understand it. Why did you ever do that? Help me, Willy, I can't cry. It seems to me that you're just on another trip. I keep expecting you. Willy, dear, I can't cry. Why did you do it? I search and search and I search, and I can't understand it, Willy. I made the last payment on the house today. Today, dear. And there'll be nobody home. (*A sob rises in her throat.*) We're free and clear. (*Sobbing mournfully, released.*) We're free. (*Biff comes slowly toward her.*) We're free . . . We're free . . .

*Biff lifts her to her feet and moves out up right with her in his arms. Linda sobs quietly. Bernard and Charley come together and follow them, followed by Happy. Only the music of the flute is left on the darkening stage as over the house the hard towers of the apartment buildings rise into sharp focus and the curtain falls.*

—1949

# Edward Albee (b. 1928)

*Edward Albee began his career as the author of one-act plays that were performed off-Broadway and in Europe.* The Zoo Story *was first produced in Berlin on a double bill with another one-act play by Samuel Beckett, and Albee was immediately recognized as one of the earliest American playwrights associated with the theatre of the absurd. Albee first came to the attention of mainstream audiences with the 1962 Broadway production of the full-length* Who's Afraid of Virginia Woolf?, *which was later made into a successful film by Mike Nichols, starring Elizabeth Taylor and Richard Burton. Since then, Albee's work has been frequently performed, and three plays—* A Delicate Balance *(1966),* Seascape *(1975), and* Three Tall Women *(1994)—have won Pulitzer Prizes. In 1996, Albee was a Kennedy Center Honoree and was awarded a National Medal of the Arts. Now in his 70s, Albee continues teaching at the University of Houston's Edward Albee New Playwrights Workshop and has recently won a Tony Award for best play for* The Goat, or Who Is Sylvia? *(2002).* Who's Afraid of Virginia Woolf *was successfully revived on Broadway in 2005, starring Kathleen Turner.*

# The Sandbox

## CHARACTERS

The Young Man, 25, *a good looking, well-built boy in a bathing suit*
Mommy, 55, *a well-dressed, imposing woman*
Daddy, 60, *a small man; gray, thin*
Grandma, 86, *a tiny, wizened woman with bright eyes*
The Musician, *no particular age, but young would be nice*

Note: When, in the course of the play, Mommy and Daddy call each other by these names, there should be no suggestion of regionalism. These names are of empty affection and point up the pre-senility and vacuity of their children.

Scene: A bare stage, with only the following: Near the footlights, far stage-right, two simple chairs set side by side, facing the audience; near the footlights, far stage-left, a chair facing stage-right with a music stand before it; farther back, and stage-center, slightly elevated and raked, a large child's sandbox with a toy pail and shovel; the background is the sky, which alters from brightest day to deepest night.

At the beginning, it is brightest day, the Young Man is alone on stage, to the rear of the sandbox, and to one side. He is doing calisthenics; he *does calisthenics until quite at the very end of the play. These calisthenics, employing the arms only, should suggest the beating and fluttering of wings. The Young Man is, after all, the Angel of Death.*

*Mommy and Daddy enter from the stage-left, Mommy first.*

**MOMMY** *(motioning to Daddy):*   Well, here we are; this is the beach.

**DADDY** *(whining):*   I'm cold.

**MOMMY** *(dismissing him with a little laugh):*   Don't be silly; it's as warm as toast. Look at that nice young man over there: *he* doesn't think it's cold. *(Waves to the Young Man.)* Hello.

**YOUNG MAN** *(with an endearing smile):*   Hi!

**MOMMY** *(looking about):*   This will do perfectly . . . don't you think so, Daddy? There's sand there . . . and the water beyond. What do you think, Daddy?

**DADDY** *(vaguely):*   Whatever you say, Mommy.

**MOMMY** *(with the same little laugh):*   Well, of course . . . whatever I say. Then, it's settled, is it?

**DADDY** *(shrugs):*   She's your mother, not mine.

**MOMMY:**   I know she's my mother. What do you take me for? *(A pause.)* All right, now; let's get on with it. *(She shouts into the wings, stage-left.)* You! Out there! You can come in now.

*The Musician enters, seats himself in the chair, stage-left, places music on the music stand, is ready to play. Mommy nods approvingly.*

**MOMMY:**   Very nice; very nice. Are you ready, Daddy? Let's go get Grandma.

**DADDY:**   Whatever you say, Mommy.

**MOMMY** *(leading the way out, stage-left):*   Of course, whatever I say. *(To the Musician.)* You can begin now.

*The Musician begins playing; Mommy and Daddy exit; the Musician, all the while playing nods to the Young Man.*

**YOUNG MAN** *(with the same endearing smile):*   Hi!

*After a moment, Mommy and Daddy re-enter, carrying Grandma. She is borne in by their hands under her armpits; she is quite rigid; her legs are drawn up; her feet do not touch the ground; the expression on her ancient face is that of puzzlement and fear.*

**DADDY:**   Where do we put her?

MOMMY *(the same little laugh):* Wherever I say, of course. Let me see . . . well . . . all right, over there . . . in the sandbox. *(Pause.)* Well, what are you waiting for Daddy? . . . The sandbox!

*Together they carry Grandma over to the sandbox and more or less dump her in.*

GRANDMA *(righting herself to a sitting position; her voice a cross between a baby's laugh and cry):* Ahhhhhh! Graaaaa!

DADDY *(dusting himself):* What do we do now?

MOMMY *(to the Musician):* You can stop now. *(The Musician stops.)* *(Back to Daddy.)* What do you mean, what do we do now? We go over there and sit down, of course. *(To the Young Man.)* Hello there.

YOUNG MAN *(again smiling):* Hi!

*Mommy and Daddy move to the chairs, stage-right, and sit down. A pause.*

GRANDMA *(same as before):* Ahhhhhh! Ahhaaaaaa! Graaaaaa!

DADDY: Do you think . . . do you think she's . . . comfortable?

MOMMY *(impatiently):* How would I know?

DADDY *(pause):* What do we do now?

MOMMY *(as if remembering):* We . . . wait. We . . . sit here . . . and we wait . . . that's what we do.

DADDY *(after a pause):* Shall we talk to each other?

MOMMY *(with that little laugh; picking something off her dress):* Well, *you* can talk, if you want to . . . if you can think of anything to *say* . . . if you can think of anything *new.*

DADDY *(thinks):* No . . . I suppose not.

MOMMY *(with a triumphant laugh):* Of course not!

GRANDMA *(banging the toy shovel against the pail):* Haaaaaa! Ah-haaaaaa!

MOMMY *(out over the audience):* Be quiet, Grandma . . . just be quiet, and wait.

*Grandma throws a shovelful of sand at Mommy.*

MOMMY *(still out over the audience):* She's throwing sand at me! You stop that, Grandma; you stop throwing sand at Mommy! *(To Daddy.)* She's throwing sand at me.

*Daddy looks around at Grandma, who screams at him.*

GRANDMA: GRAAAAAA!

MOMMY: Don't look at her. Just . . . sit here . . . be very still . . . and wait. *(To the Musician.)* You . . . uh . . . you go ahead and do whatever it is you do.

*The Musician plays. Mommy and Daddy are fixed, staring out beyond the audience. Grandma looks at them, looks at the Musician, looks at the sandbox, throws down the shovel.*

GRANDMA: Ah-haaaaaa! Graaaaaa! *(Looks for reaction; gets none.)* Now . . . *(directly to the audience.)* Honestly! What a way to treat an old woman! Drag her out of the house . . . stick her in a car . . . bring her out here from the city . . . dump her in a pile of sand . . . and leave her here to set. I'm eighty-six years old! I was married when I was seventeen. To a farmer. He died when I was thirty. *(To the Musician.)* Will you stop that, please?

*The Musician stops playing.*

I'm a feeble old woman . . . how do you expect anybody to hear me over that peep! peep! peep! *(To herself.)* There's no respect around here. *(To the Young Man.)* There's no respect around here!

YOUNG MAN *(same smile):* Hi!

GRANDMA *(after a pause, a mild double-take, continues, to the audience):* My husband died when I was thirty *(indicates Mommy)*, and I had to raise that big cow over there all by my lonesome. You can imagine what *that* was like. Lordy! *(To the Young Man.)* Where'd they get *you?*

YOUNG MAN: Oh . . . I've been around for a while.

GRANDMA: I'll bet you have! Heh, heh, heh. Will you look at you!

YOUNG MAN *(flexing his muscles):* Isn't that something? *(Continues his calisthenics.)*

GRANDMA: Boy, oh boy; I'll say. Pretty good.

YOUNG MAN *(sweetly):* I'll say.

GRANDMA: Where ya from?

YOUNG MAN: Southern California.

GRANDMA *(nodding):* Figgers, figgers. What's your name, honey?

YOUNG MAN: I don't know . . .

GRANDMA *(to the audience):* Bright, too!

YOUNG MAN: I mean . . . I mean, they haven't given me one yet . . . the studio . . .

GRANDMA: *(giving him the once-over).* You don't say . . . you don't say. Well . . . uh, I've got to talk some more . . . don't you go 'way.

YOUNG MAN: Oh, no.

GRANDMA *(turning her attention back to the audience):* Fine; fine.

*(Then, once more, back to the Young Man.)* You're . . . you're an actor, hunh?

**YOUNG MAN** *(beaming):*   Yes. I am.

**GRANDMA** *(to the audience again; shrugs):*   I'm smart that way. *Anyhow,* I had to raise . . . that over there all by my lonesome; and what's next to her there . . . that's what she married. Rich? I tell you . . . money, money, money. They took me off the *farm* . . . which was real decent of them . . . and they moved me into the big town house with *them* . . . fixed a nice place for me under the stove . . . gave me an army blanket . . . and my own dish . . . my very own dish! So, what have I got to complain about? Nothing, of course, I'm not complaining. *(She looks up at the sky, shouts to someone offstage.)* Shouldn't it be getting dark now, dear?

*The lights dim; night comes on. The Musician begins to play; it becomes deepest night. There are spots on all the players, including the Young Man, who is, of course, continuing his calisthenics.*

**DADDY** *(stirring):*   It's nighttime.

**MOMMY:**   Shhhh. Be still . . . wait.

**DADDY** *(whining):*   It's so hot.

**MOMMY:**   Shhhhhh. Be still . . . wait.

**GRANDMA** *(to herself):*   That's better. Night. *(To the Musician.)* Honey, do you play all through this part?

*The Musician nods.*

Well, keep it nice and soft; that's a good boy.

*The Musician nods again; plays softly.*

That's nice.

*There is an off-stage rumble.*

**DADDY** *(starting):*   What was that?

**MOMMY** *(beginning to weep):*   It was nothing.

**DADDY:**   It was . . . it was . . . thunder . . . or a wave breaking . . . or something.

**MOMMY:** *(whispering, through her tears):*   It was an off-stage rumble . . . and you know what *that* means . . .

**DADDY:**   I forget. . . .

**MOMMY** *(barely able to talk):*   It means the time has come for poor Grandma . . . and I can't bear it!

DADDY: *(vacantly):* I . . . I suppose you've got to be brave.
GRANDMA *(mocking):* That's right, kid; be brave. You'll bear up; you'll get over it.

*(Another off-stage rumble . . . louder.)*

MOMMY: Ohhhhhhhhhh . . . poor Grandma . . . poor Grandma. . . .
GRANDMA *(to Mommy):* I'm fine! I'm all right! It hasn't happened yet!

*A violent off-stage rumble. All the lights go out, save the spot on the Young Man; the Musician stops playing.*

MOMMY: Ohhhhhhhhhh. . . . Ohhhhhhhhhh. . . .

*Silence.*

GRANDMA: Don't put the lights up yet . . . I'm not ready; I'm not quite ready. *(Silence.)* All right, dear . . . I'm about done.

*The lights come up again, to brightest day; the Musician begins to play. Grandma is discovered, still in the sandbox, lying on her side, propped up on an elbow, half covered, busily shoveling sand over herself.*

GRANDMA *(muttering):* I don't know how I'm supposed to do anything with this goddam toy shovel. . . .
DADDY: Mommy! It's daylight!
MOMMY *(brightly):* So it is! Well! Our long night is over. We must put away our tears, take off our mourning . . . and face the future. It's our duty.
GRANDMA *(still shoveling; mimicking):* . . . take off our mourning . . . face the future. . . . Lordy!

*Mommy and Daddy rise, stretch. Mommy waves to the young man.*

YOUNG MAN *(with that smile):* Hi!

*Grandma plays dead. (!) Mommy and Daddy go over to look at her; she is a little more than half buried in the sand; the toy shovel is in her hands, which are crossed on her breast.*

MOMMY *(before the sandbox; shaking her head):* Lovely! It's . . . it's hard to be sad . . . she looks . . . so happy. *(With pride and conviction.)* It pays to do things well. *(To the Musician.)* All right, you can stop now, if you want to. I mean, stay around for a swim, or something; it's all right with us. *(She sighs heavily.)* Well, Daddy . . . off we go.

**DADDY:** Brave Mommy!

**MOMMY:** Brave Daddy!

*They exit, stage-left.*

**GRANDMA** *(after they leave; lying quite still):* It pays to do things well. . . . Boy, oh boy! *(She tries to sit up)* . . . well, kids . . . *(but she finds she can't)* . . . I . . . I can't get up, I . . . I can't move. . . .

*The Young Man stops his calisthenics, nods to the Musician, walks over to Grandma, kneels down by the sandbox.*

**GRANDMA:** I . . . can't move. . . .

**YOUNG MAN:** Shhhhh . . . be very still. . . .

**GRANDMA:** I . . . I can't move. . . .

**YOUNG MAN:** Uh . . . ma'am; I . . . I have a line here.

**GRANDMA:** Oh, I'm sorry, sweetie; you go right ahead.

**YOUNG MAN:** I am . . . uh . . .

**GRANDMA:** Take your time, dear.

**YOUNG MAN** *(prepares; delivers the line like a real amateur):* I am the Angel of Death. I am . . . uh . . . I am come for you.

**GRANDMA:** What . . . wha . . . *(Then, with resignation.)* . . . ohhhh . . . ohhhh, I see.

*The Young Man bends over, kisses Grandma gently on the forehead.*

**GRANDMA** *(her eyes closed, her hands folded on her breast again, the shovel between her hands, a sweet smile on her face):* Well . . . that was very nice, dear . . .

**YOUNG MAN** *(still kneeling):* Shhhhhh . . . be still. . . .

**GRANDMA:** What I mean was . . . you did that very well, dear. . . .

**YOUNG MAN** *(blushing):* . . . oh . . .

**GRANDMA:** No; I mean it. You've got that . . . you've got a quality.

**YOUNG MAN** *(with his endearing smile):* Oh . . . thank you; thank you very much . . . ma'am.

**GRANDMA** *(slowly; softly—as the Young Man puts his hands on top of Grandma's):* You're . . . you're welcome . . . dear.

*Tableau. The Musician continues to play as the curtain slowly comes down.*

CURTAIN

# Athol Fugard (b. 1932)

*Athol Fugard was born in Middelburg, Cape Province, South Africa, and was educated at the University of Cape Town. Growing up during the period of South African apartheid, Fugard both resisted and participated in the segregationist policies of the government, even insisting, at one point, that the family servants call him Master Harold (his given first name) and, in a moment of anger, spitting on one with whom he had been especially close. As he later said to an interviewer, "I think at a fairly early age I became suspicious of what the system was trying to do to me. . . . I became conscious of what attitudes it was trying to implant in me and what prejudices it was trying to pass on to me." Fugard founded the first important black theatrical company in South Africa, and he gained early prominence in his native country by his exploration of racial issues. While Fugard does not consider himself a political writer, his depictions of the interplay of black and white lives made him a controversial figure as a critic of apartheid. "Master Harold". . . and the boys is clearly an autobiographical work, for Fugard's father was a wounded war veteran, and his mother helped to support the family by running a tea room. After leaving college to travel to the Far East as a crew member of a tramp steamer, Fugard at first attempted to write novels but soon turned to the theater. Fugard began to produce his plays in the mid-1950s, and the New York production of* The Blood Knot *in 1964 established his American reputation.* "Master Harold" . . . and the boys *was first produced in New Haven, Connecticut, in 1982 and soon enjoyed a successful Broadway run. Since the end of the apartheid era, Fugard has continued to write plays and autobiographical memoirs. He has often been mentioned as a possible recipient of the Nobel Prize.*

# "Master Harold" . . . and the boys

## CHARACTERS

Hally
Sam
Willie

*The St. George's Park Tea Room on a wet and windy Port Elizabeth afternoon.*

*Tables and chairs have been cleared and are stacked on one side except for one which stands apart with a single chair. On this table a knife, fork, spoon and side plate in anticipation of a simple meal, together with a pile of comic books.*

*Other elements: a serving counter with a few stale cakes under glass and a not very impressive display of sweets, cigarettes and cool drinks, etc.; a few cardboard advertising handouts—Cadbury's Chocolate, Coca-Cola—and a blackboard on which an untrained hand has chalked up the prices of Tea, Coffee, Scones, Milkshakes—all flavors—and Cool Drinks; a few sad ferns in pots; a telephone; an old-style jukebox.*

*There is an entrance on one side and an exit into a kitchen on the other.*

*Leaning on the solitary table, his head cupped in one hand as he pages through one of the comic books, is Sam. A black man in his mid-forties. He wears the white coat of a waiter. Behind him on his knees, mopping down the floor with a bucket of water and a rag, is Willie. Also black and about the same age as Sam. He has his sleeves and trousers rolled up.*

*The year: 1950*

WILLIE (*Singing as he works*):
"She was scandalizin' my name,
She took my money
She called me honey
But she was scandalizin' my name.
Called it love but was playin' a game . . ."

(*He gets up and moves the bucket. Stands thinking for a moment, then, raising his arms to hold an imaginary partner, he launches into an intricate ballroom dance step. Although a mildly comic figure, he reveals a reasonable degree of accomplishment*)

Hey, Sam.

(*Sam, absorbed in the comic book, does not respond*)

Hey, Boet Sam!

(*Sam looks up*)

I'm getting it. The quickstep. Look now and tell me. (*He repeats the step*) Well?
SAM (*Encouragingly*): Show me again.
WILLIE: Okay, count for me.
SAM: Ready?

WILLIE: Ready.

SAM: Five, six, seven, eight . . . (*Willie starts to dance*) A-n-d one two three four . . . and one two three four . . . (*Ad libbing as Willie dances*) Your shoulders, Willie . . . your shoulders! Don't look down! Look happy, Willie! Relax, Willie!

WILLIE (*Desperate but still dancing*): I am relax.

SAM: No, you're not.

WILLIE (*He falters*): Ag no man, Sam! Mustn't talk. You make me make mistakes.

SAM: But you're too stiff.

WILLIE: Yesterday I'm not straight . . . today I'm too stiff!

SAM: Well, you are. You asked me and I'm telling you.

WILLIE: Where?

SAM: Everywhere. Try to glide through it.

WILLIE: Glide?

SAM: Ja, make it smooth. And give it more style. It must look like you're enjoying yourself.

WILLIE (*Emphatically*): I wasn't.

SAM: Exactly.

WILLIE: How can I enjoy myself? Not straight, too stiff and now it's also glide, give it more style, make it smooth. . . . Haai! Is hard to remember all those things, Boet Sam.

SAM: That's your trouble. You're trying too hard.

WILLIE: I try hard because it *is* hard.

SAM: But don't let me see it. The secret is to make it look easy. Ballroom must look happy, Willie, not like hard work. It must . . . Ja! . . . it must look like romance.

WILLIE: Now another one! What's romance?

SAM: Love story with happy ending. A handsome man in tails, and in his arms, smiling at him, a beautiful lady in evening dress!

WILLIE: Fred Astaire, Ginger Rogers.

SAM: You got it. Tapdance or ballroom, it's the same. Romance. In two weeks' time when the judges look at you and Hilda, they must see a man and a woman who are dancing their way to a happy ending. What I saw was you holding her like you were frightened she was going to run away.

WILLIE: Ja! Because that is what she wants to do! I got no romance left for Hilda anymore, Boet Sam.

SAM: Then pretend. When you put your arms around Hilda, imagine she is Ginger Rogers.

WILLIE: With no teeth? You try.

SAM: Well, just remember, there's only two weeks left.

WILLIE: I know, I know! (*To the jukebox*) I do it better with music. You got sixpence for Sarah Vaughan?

SAM: That's a slow foxtrot. You're practicing the quick-step.

WILLIE: I'll practice slow foxtrot.

SAM (*Shaking his head*): It's your turn to put money in the jukebox.

WILLIE: I only got bus fare to go home. (*He returns disconsolately to his work*) Love story and happy ending! She's doing it all right, Boet Sam, but is not me she's giving happy endings. Fuckin' whore! Three nights now she doesn't come practice. I wind up gramophone, I get record ready and I sit and wait. What happens? Nothing. Ten o'clock I start dancing with my pillow. You try and practice romance by yourself, Boet Sam. Struesgod, she doesn't come tonight I take back my dress and ballroom shoes and I find me new partner. Size twenty-six. Shoes size seven. And now she's also making trouble for me with the baby again. Reports me to Child Wellfed, that I'm not giving her money. She lies! Every week I am giving her money for milk. And how do I know is my baby? Only his hair looks like me. She's fucking around all the time I turn my back. Hilda Samuels is a bitch! (*Pause*) Hey, Sam!

SAM: Ja.

WILLIE: You listening?

SAM: Ja.

WILLIE: So what you say?

SAM: About Hilda?

WILLIE: Ja.

SAM: When did you last give her a hiding?

WILLIE (*Reluctantly*): Sunday night.

SAM: And today is Thursday.

WILLIE (*He knows what's coming*): Okay.

SAM: Hiding on Sunday night, then Monday, Tuesday and Wednesday she doesn't come to practice . . . and you are asking me why?

WILLIE: I said okay, Boet Sam!

SAM: You hit her too much. One day she's going to leave you for good.

WILLIE: So? She makes me the hell-in too much.

SAM (*Emphasizing his point*): *Too* much and *too* hard. You had the same trouble with Eunice.

WILLIE: Because she also make the hell-in, Boet Sam. She never got the steps right. Even the waltz.

SAM: Beating her up every time she makes a mistake in the waltz?

(*Shaking his head*) No, Willie! That takes the pleasure out of ballroom dancing.

WILLIE: Hilda is not too bad with the waltz, Boet Sam. Is the quickstep where the trouble starts.

SAM (*Teasing him gently*): How's your pillow with the quickstep?

WILLIE (*Ignoring the tease*): Good! And why? Because it got no legs. That's her trouble. She can't move them quick enough, Boet Sam. I start the record and before halfway Count Basie is already winning. Only time we catch up with him is when gramophone runs down.

(*Sam laughs*)

Haaikona, Boet Sam, is not funny.

SAM (*Snapping his fingers*): I got it! Give her a handicap.

WILLIE: What's that?

SAM: Give her a ten-second start and then let Count Basie go. Then I put my money on her. Hot favorite in the Ballroom Stakes: Hilda Samuels ridden by Willie Malopo.

WILLIE (*Turning away*): I'm not talking to you no more.

SAM (*Relenting*): Sorry, Willie . . .

WILLIE: It's finish between us.

SAM: Okay, okay . . . I'll stop.

WILLIE: You can also fuck off.

SAM: Willie, listen! I want to help you!

WILLIE: No more jokes?

SAM: I promise.

WILLIE: Okay. Help me.

SAM (*His turn to hold an imaginary partner*): Look and learn. Feet together. Back straight. Body relaxed. Right hand placed gently in the small of her back and wait for the music. Don't start worrying about making mistakes or the judges or the other competitors. It's just you, Hilda and the music, and you're going to have a good time. What Count Basie do you play?

WILLIE: "You the cream in my coffee, you the salt in my stew."

SAM: Right. Give it to me in strict tempo.

WILLIE: Ready?

SAM: Ready.

WILLIE: A-n-d . . . (*Singing*)
"You the cream in my coffee.
You the salt in my stew.
You will always be my
    necessity.

I'd be lost without
  you. . . ." (*etc.*)

(*Sam launches into the quickstep. He is obviously a much more accomplished dancer than Willie. Hally enters. A seventeen-year-old white boy. Wet raincoat and school case. He stops and watches Sam. The demonstration comes to an end with a flourish. Applause from Hally and Willie*)

HALLY:   Bravo! No question about it. First place goes to Mr. Sam Semela.

WILLIE (*In total agreement*):   You was gliding with style, Boet Sam.

HALLY (*Cheerfully*):   How's it, chaps?

SAM:   Okay, Hally.

WILLIE (*Springing to attention like a soldier and saluting*):   At your service, Master Harold!

HALLY:   Not long to the big event, hey!

SAM:   Two weeks.

HALLY:   You nervous?

SAM:   No.

HALLY:   Think you stand a chance?

SAM:   Let's just say I'm ready to go out there and dance.

HALLY:   It looked like it. What about you, Willie?

(*Willie groans*)

What's the matter?

SAM:   He's got leg trouble.

HALLY (*Innocently*):   Oh, sorry to hear that, Willie.

WILLIE:   Boet Sam! You promised. (*Willie returns to his work*)

(*Hally deposits his school case and takes off his raincoat. His clothes are a little neglected and untidy: black blazer with school badge, gray flannel trousers in need of an ironing, khaki shirt and tie, black shoes. Sam has fetched a towel for Hally to dry his hair*)

HALLY:   God, what a lousy bloody day. It's coming down cats and dogs out there. Bad for business, chaps . . . (*Conspiratorial whisper*) . . . but it also means we're in for a nice quiet afternoon.

SAM:   You can speak loud. Your Mom's not here.

HALLY:   Out shopping?

SAM:   No. The hospital.

HALLY:   But it's Thursday. There's no visiting on Thursday afternoons. Is my Dad okay?

SAM: Sounds like it. In fact, I think he's going home.

HALLY (*Stopped short by Sam's remark*): What do you mean?

SAM: The hospital phoned.

HALLY: To say what?

SAM: I don't know. I just heard your Mom talking.

HALLY: So what makes you say he's going home?

SAM: It sounded as if they were telling her to come and fetch him.

(*Hally thinks about what Sam has said for a few seconds*)

HALLY: When did she leave?

SAM: About an hour ago. She said she would phone you. Want to eat?

(*Hally doesn't respond*)

Hally, want your lunch?

HALLY: I suppose so. (*His mood has changed*) What's on the menu?
. . . as if I don't know.

SAM: Soup, followed by meat pie and gravy.

HALLY: Today's?

SAM: No.

HALLY: And the soup?

SAM: Nourishing pea soup.

HALLY: Just the soup. (*The pile of comic books on the table*) And these?

SAM: For your Dad. Mr. Kempston brought them.

HALLY: You haven't been reading them, have you?

SAM: Just looking.

HALLY (*Examining the comics*): *Jungle Jim . . . Batman and Robin . . . Tarzan . . .* God, what rubbish! Mental pollution. Take them away.

(*Sam exits waltzing into the kitchen. Hally turns to Willie*)

HALLY: Did you hear my Mom talking on the telephone, Willie?

WILLIE: No, Master Hally. I was at the back.

HALLY: And she didn't say anything to you before she left?

WILLIE: She said I must clean the floors.

HALLY: I mean about my Dad.

WILLIE: She didn't say nothing to me about him, Master Hally.

HALLY (*With conviction*): No! It can't be. They said he needed at least another three weeks of treatment. Sam's definitely made a mistake. (*Rummages through his school case, finds a book and settles down at the table to read*) So, Willie!

WILLIE: Yes, Master Hally! Schooling okay today?

HALLY:   Yes, okay.... (*He thinks about it*) ... No, not really. Ag, what's the difference? I don't care. And Sam says you've got problems.
WILLIE:   Big problems.
HALLY:   Which leg is sore?

(*Willie groans*)

Both legs.
WILLIE:   There is nothing wrong with my legs. Sam is just making jokes.
HALLY:   So then you *will* be in the competition.
WILLIE:   Only if I can find me a partner.
HALLY:   But what about Hilda?
SAM (*Returning with a bowl of soup*):   She's the one who's got trouble with her legs.
HALLY:   What sort of trouble, Willie?
SAM:   From the way he describes it, I think the lady has gone a bit lame.
HALLY:   Good God! Have you taken her to see a doctor?
SAM:   I think a vet would be better.
HALLY:   What do you mean?
SAM:   What do you call it again when a racehorse goes very fast?
HALLY:   Gallop?
SAM:   That's it!
WILLIE:   Boet Sam!
HALLY:   "A gallop down the homestretch to the winning post." But what's that got to do with Hilda?
SAM:   Count Basie always gets there first.

(*Willie lets fly with his slop rag. It misses Sam and hits Hally*)

HALLY (*Furious*):   For Christ's sake, Willie! What the hell do you think you're doing!
WILLIE:   Sorry, Master Hally, but it's him....
HALLY:   Act your bloody age! (*Hurls the rag back at Willie*) Cut out the nonsense now and get on with your work. And you too, Sam. Stop fooling around.

(*Sam moves away*)

No. Hang on. I haven't finished! Tell me exactly what my Mom said.
SAM:   I have. "When Hally comes, tell him I've gone to the hospital and I'll phone him."

HALLY: She didn't say anything about taking my Dad home?

SAM: No. It's just that when she was talking on the phone . . .

HALLY (*Interrupting him*): No, Sam. They can't be discharging him. She would have said so if they were. In any case, we saw him last night and he wasn't in good shape at all. Staff nurse even said there was talk about taking more X-rays. And now suddenly today he's better? If anything, it sounds more like a bad turn to me . . . which I sincerely hope it isn't. Hang on . . . how long ago did you say she left?

SAM: Just before two . . . (*His wrist watch*) . . . hour and a half.

HALLY: I know how to settle it. (*Behind the counter to the telephone. Talking as he dials*) Let's give her ten minutes to get to the hospital, ten minutes to load him up, another ten, at the most, to get home and another ten to get him inside. Forty minutes. They should have been home for at least half an hour already. (*Pause—he waits with the receiver to his ear*) No reply, chaps. And you know why? Because she's at his bedside in hospital helping him pull through a bad turn. You definitely heard wrong.

SAM: Okay.

(*As far as Hally is concerned, the matter is settled. He returns to his table, sits down and divides his attention between the book and his soup. Sam is at his school case and picks up a textbook*)

*Modern Graded Mathematics for Standards Nine and Ten.* (*Opens it at random and laughs at something he sees*) Who is this supposed to be?

HALLY: Old fart-face Prentice.

SAM: Teacher?

HALLY: Thinks he is. And believe me, that is not a bad likeness.

SAM: Has he seen it?

HALLY: Yes.

SAM: What did he say?

HALLY: Tried to be clever, as usual. Said I was no Leonardo da Vinci and that bad art had to be punished. So, six of the best, and his are bloody good.

SAM: On your bum?

HALLY: Where else? The days when I got them on my hands are gone forever, Sam.

SAM: With your trousers down!

HALLY: No. He's not quite that barbaric.

SAM: That's the way they do it in jail.

HALLY (*Flicker of morbid interest*): Really?

SAM: Ja. When the magistrate sentences you to "strokes with a light cane."

HALLY: Go on.

SAM: They make you lie down on a bench. One policeman pulls down your trousers and holds your ankles, another one pulls your shirt over your head and holds your arms . . .

HALLY: Thank you! That's enough.

SAM: . . . and the one that gives you the strokes talks to you gently and for a long time between each one. (*He laughs*)

HALLY: I've heard enough, Sam! Jesus! It's a bloody awful world when you come to think of it. People can be real bastards.

SAM: That's the way it is, Hally.

HALLY: It doesn't *have* to be that way. There is something called progress, you know. We don't exactly burn people at the stake anymore.

SAM: Like Joan of Arc.

HALLY: Correct. If she was captured today, she'd be given a fair trial.

SAM: And then the death sentence.

HALLY (*A world-weary sigh*): I know, I know! I oscillate between hope and despair for this world as well, Sam. But things will change, you wait and see. One day somebody is going to get up and give history a kick up the backside and get it going again.

SAM: Like who?

HALLY (*After thought*): They're called social reformers. Every age, Sam, has got its social reformer. My history book is full of them.

SAM: So where's ours?

HALLY: Good question. And I hate to say it, but the answer is: I don't know. Maybe he hasn't even been born yet. Or is still only a babe in arms at his mother's breast. God, what a thought.

SAM: So we just go on waiting.

HALLY: Ja, looks like it. (*Back to his soup and the book*)

SAM (*Reading from the textbook*): "Introduction: In some mathematical problems only the magnitude . . ." (*He mispronounces the word "magnitude"*)

HALLY (*Correcting him without looking up*): Magnitude.

SAM: What's it mean?

HALLY: How big it is. The size of the thing.

SAM (*Reading*): ". . . magnitude of the quantities is of importance. In other problems we need to know whether these quantities are negative or positive. For example, whether there is a debit or credit bank balance . . ."

HALLY: Whether you're broke or not.

SAM: ". . . whether the temperature is above or below Zero . . ."

HALLY: Naught degrees. Cheerful state of affairs! No cash and you're freezing to death. Mathematics won't get you out of that one.

SAM: "All these quantities are called . . ." (*Spelling the word*) . . . s-c-a-l . . .

HALLY: Scalars.

SAM: Scalars! (*Shaking his head with a laugh*) You understand all that?

HALLY (*Turning a page*): No. And I don't intend to try.

SAM: So what happens when the exams come?

HALLY: Failing a maths exam isn't the end of the world, Sam. How many times have I told you that examination results don't measure intelligence?

SAM: I would say about as many times as you've failed one of them.

HALLY (*Mirthlessly*): Ha, ha, ha.

SAM (*Simultaneously*): Ha, ha, ha.

HALLY: Just remember Winston Churchill didn't do particularly well at school.

SAM: You've also told me that one many times.

HALLY: Well, it just so happens to be the truth.

SAM (*Enjoying the word*): Magnitude! Magnitude! Show me how to use it.

HALLY (*After thought*): An intrepid social reformer will not be daunted by the magnitude of the task he has undertaken.

SAM (*Impressed*): Couple of jaw-breakers in there!

HALLY: I gave you three for the price of one. Intrepid, daunted and magnitude. I did that once in an exam. Put five of the words I had to explain in one sentence. It was half a page long.

SAM: Well, I'll put my money on you in the English exam.

HALLY: Piece of cake. Eighty percent without even trying.

SAM (*Another textbook from Hally's case*): And history?

HALLY: So-so. I'll scrape through. In the fifties if I'm lucky.

SAM: You didn't do too badly last year.

HALLY: Because we had World War One. That at least had some action. You try to find that in the South African Parliamentary system.

SAM (*Reading from the history textbook*): "Napoleon and the principle of equality." Hey! This sounds interesting. "After concluding peace with Britain in 1802, Napoleon used a brief period of calm to in-sti-tute . . ."

HALLY:   Introduce.

SAM:   ". . . many reforms. Napoleon regarded all people as equal before the law and wanted them to have equal opportunities for advancement. All ves-ti-ges of the feu-dal system with its oppression of the poor were abolished." Vestiges, feudal system and abolished. I'm all right on oppression.

HALLY:   I'm thinking. He swept away . . . abolished . . . the last remains . . . vestiges . . . of the bad old days . . . feudal system.

SAM:   Ha! There's the social reformer we're waiting for. He sounds like a man of some magnitude.

HALLY:   I'm not so sure about that. It's a damn good title for a book, though. A man of magnitude!

SAM:   He sounds pretty big to me, Hally.

HALLY:   Don't confuse historical significance with greatness. But maybe I'm being a bit prejudiced. Have a look in there and you'll see he's two chapters long. And hell! . . . has he only got dates, Sam, all of which you've got to remember! This campaign and that campaign, and then, because of all the fighting, the next thing is we get Peace Treaties all over the place. And what's the end of the story? Battle of Waterloo, which he loses. Wasn't worth it. No, I don't know about him as a man of magnitude.

SAM:   Then who would you say was?

HALLY:   To answer that, we need a definition of greatness, and I suppose that would be somebody who . . . somebody who benefited all mankind.

SAM:   Right. But like who?

HALLY (*He speaks with total conviction*):   Charles Darwin. Remember him? That big book from the library. *The Origin of the Species.*

SAM   Him?

HALLY:   Yes. For his Theory of Evolution.

SAM:   You didn't finish it.

HALLY:   I ran out of time. I didn't finish it because my two weeks was up. But I'm going to take it out again after I've digested what I read. It's safe. I've hidden it away in the Theology section. Nobody ever goes in there. And anyway who are you to talk? You hardly even looked at it.

SAM:   I tried. I looked at the chapters in the beginning and I saw one called "The Struggle for an Existence." Ah ha, I thought. At last! But what did I get? Something called the mistiltoe which needs the apple tree and there's too many seeds and all are going to die except one . . . ! No, Hally.

HALLY (*Intellectually outraged*):   What do you mean, No! The poor man had to start somewhere. For God's sake, Sam, he revolutionized science. Now we know.

SAM:   What?

HALLY:   Where we come from and what it all means.

SAM:   And that's a benefit to mankind? Anyway, I still don't believe it.

HALLY:   God, you're impossible. I showed it to you in black and white.

SAM:   Doesn't mean I got to believe it.

HALLY:   It's the likes of you that kept the Inquisition in business. It's called bigotry. Anyway, that's my man of magnitude. Charles Darwin! Who's yours?

SAM (*Without hesitation*):   Abraham Lincoln.

HALLY:   I might have guessed as much. Don't get sentimental, Sam. You've never been a slave, you know. And anyway we freed your ancestors here in South Africa long before the Americans. But if you want to thank somebody on their behalf, do it to Mr. William Wilberforce. Come on. Try again. I want a real genius. (*Now enjoying himself, and so is Sam. Hally goes behind the counter and helps himself to a chocolate*)

SAM:   William Shakespeare.

HALLY (*No enthusiasm*):   Oh. So you're also one of them, are you? You're basing that opinion on only one play, you know. You've only read my *Julius Caesar* and even I don't understand half of what they're talking about. They should do what they did with the old Bible: bring the language up to date.

SAM:   That's all you've got. It's also the only one *you've* read.

HALLY:   I know. I admit it. That's why I suggest we reserve our judgment until we've checked up on a few others. I've got a feeling, though, that by the end of this year one is going to be enough for me, and I can give you the names of twenty-nine other chaps in the Standard Nine class of the Port Elizabeth Technical College who feel the same. But if you want him, you can have him. My turn now. (*Pacing*) This is a damned good exercise, you know! It started off looking like a simple question and here it's got us really probing into the intellectual heritage of our civilization.

SAM:   So who is it going to be?

HALLY:   My next man . . . and he gets the title on two scores: social reform and literary genius . . . is Leo Nikolaevich Tolstoy.

SAM:   That Russian.

HALLY:   Correct. Remember the picture of him I showed you?

SAM:   With the long beard.

HALLY (*Trying to look like Tolstoy*):   And those burning, visionary eyes. My God, the face of a social prophet if ever I saw one! And remember my words when I showed it to you? Here's a *man*, Sam!

SAM:   Those were words, Hally.

HALLY:   Not many intellectuals are prepared to shovel manure with the peasants and then go home and write a "little book" called *War and Peace*. Incidentally, Sam, he was somebody else who, to quote, ". . . did not distinguish himself scholastically."

SAM:   Meaning?

HALLY:   He was also no good at school.

SAM:   Like you and Winston Churchill.

HALLY (*Mirthlessly*):   Ha, ha, ha.

SAM (*Simultaneously*):   Ha, ha, ha.

HALLY:   Don't get clever, Sam. That man freed his serfs of his own free will.

SAM:   No argument. He was a somebody, all right. I accept him.

HALLY:   I'm sure Count Tolstoy will be very pleased to hear that. Your turn. Shoot. (*Another chocolate from behind the counter*) I'm waiting, Sam.

SAM:   I've got him.

HALLY:   Good. Submit your candidate for examination.

SAM:   Jesus.

HALLY (*Stopped dead in his tracks*):   Who?

SAM:   Jesus Christ.

HALLY:   Oh, come on, Sam!

SAM:   The Messiah.

HALLY:   Ja, but still . . . No, Sam. Don't let's get started on religion. We'll just spend the whole afternoon arguing again. Suppose I turn around and say Mohammed?

SAM:   All right.

HALLY:   You can't have them both on the same list!

SAM:   Why not? You like Mohammed, I like Jesus.

HALLY:   I *don't* like Mohammed. I never have. I was merely being hypothetical. As far as I'm concerned, the Koran is as bad as the Bible. No. Religion is out! I'm not going to waste my time again arguing with you about the existence of God. You know perfectly well I'm an atheist . . . and I've got homework to do.

SAM:   Okay, I take him back.

HALLY:   You've got time for one more name.

SAM (*After thought*): I've got one I know we'll agree on. A simple straightforward great Man of Magnitude . . . and no arguments. And *he* really *did* benefit all mankind.

HALLY: I wonder. After your last contribution I'm beginning to doubt whether anything in the way of an intellectual agreement is possible between the two of us. Who is he?

SAM: Guess.

HALLY: Socrates? Alexandre Dumas? Karl Marx? Dostoevsky? Nietzsche?

(*Sam shakes his head after each name*)

Give me a clue.

SAM: The letter P is important . . .

HALLY: Plato!

SAM: . . . and his name begins with an F.

HALLY: I've got it. Freud and Psychology.

SAM: No. I didn't understand him.

HALLY: That makes two of us.

SAM: Think of mouldy apricot jam.

HALLY (*After a delighted laugh*): Penicillin and Sir Alexander Fleming! And the title of the book: *The Microbe Hunters*. (*Delighted*) Splendid, Sam! Splendid. For once we are in total agreement. The major breakthrough in medical science in the Twentieth Century. If it wasn't for him, we might have lost the Second World War. It's deeply gratifying, Sam, to know that I haven't been wasting my time in talking to you. (*Strutting around proudly*) Tolstoy may have educated his peasants, but I've educated you.

SAM: Standard Four to Standard Nine.

HALLY: Have we been at it as long as that?

SAM: Yep. And my first lesson was geography.

HALLY (*Intrigued*): Really? I don't remember.

SAM: My room there at the back of the old Jubilee Boarding House. I had just started working for your Mom. Little boy in short trousers walks in one afternoon and asks me seriously: "Sam, do you want to see South Africa?" Hey man! Sure I wanted to see South Africa!

HALLY: Was that me?

SAM: . . . So the next thing I'm looking at a map you had just done for homework. It was your first one and you were very proud of yourself.

HALLY: Go on.

**SAM:** Then came my first lesson. "Repeat after me, Sam: Gold in the Transvaal, mealies in the Free State, sugar in Natal and grapes in the Cape." I still know it!

**HALLY:** Well, I'll be buggered. So that's how it all started.

**SAM:** And your next map was one with all the rivers and the mountains they came from. The Orange, the Vaal, the Limpopo, the Zambezi . . .

**HALLY:** You've got a phenomenal memory!

**SAM:** You should be grateful. That is why you started passing your exams. You tried to be better than me.

(*They laugh together. Willie is attracted by the laughter and joins them*)

**HALLY:** The old Jubilee Boarding House. Sixteen rooms with board and lodging, rent in advance and one week's notice. I haven't thought about it for donkey's years . . . and I don't think that's an accident. God, was I glad when we sold it and moved out. Those years are not remembered as the happiest ones of an unhappy childhood.

**WILLIE** (*Knocking on the table and trying to imitate a woman's voice*): "Hally, are you there?"

**HALLY:** Who's that supposed to be?

**WILLIE:** "What you doing in there, Hally? Come out at once!"

**HALLY** (*To Sam*): What's he talking about?

**SAM:** Don't you remember?

**WILLIE:** "Sam, Willie . . . is he in there with you boys?"

**SAM:** Hiding away in our room when your mother was looking for you.

**HALLY** (*Another good laugh*): Of course! I used to crawl and hide under your bed! But finish the story, Willie. Then what used to happen? You chaps would give the game away by telling her I was in there with you. So much for friendship.

**SAM:** We couldn't lie to her. She knew.

**HALLY:** Which meant I got another rowing for hanging around the "servants' quarters." I think I spent more time in there with you chaps than anywhere else in that dump. And do you blame me? Nothing but bloody misery wherever you went. Somebody was always complaining about the food, or my mother was having a fight with Micky Nash because she'd caught her with a petty officer in her room. Maud Meiring was another one. Remember those two? They were prostitutes, you know. Soldiers and sailors from the troopships. Bottom fell out of the business when the war ended. God, the flotsam and jetsam that life washed up on our shores! No joking, if it wasn't for your room, I would have been the first certified ten-year-old in medical history. Ja, the memories are coming back now. Walking home from school and thinking: "What can I do this afternoon?" Try out a few ideas, but sooner or later I'd end up in there with you fellows. I bet you I could still find my way to your room with my eyes closed. (*He does exactly that*). Down the corridor . . . telephone on the right, which my Mom keeps locked because somebody is using it on the sly and not paying . . . past the kitchen and unappetizing cooking smells . . . around the corner into the backyard, hold my breath again because there are more smells coming when I pass your lavatory, then into that little passageway, first door on the right and into your room. How's that?

SAM: Good. But, as usual, you forgot to knock.

HALLY: Like that time I barged in and caught you and Cynthia . . . at it. Remember? God, was I embarrassed! I didn't know what was going on at first.

SAM: Ja, that taught you a lesson.

HALLY: And about a lot more than knocking on doors, I'll have you know, and I don't mean geography either. Hell, Sam, couldn't you have waited until it was dark?

SAM: No.

HALLY: Was it that urgent?

SAM: Yes, and if you don't believe me, wait until your time comes.

HALLY: No, thank you. I am not interested in girls. (*Back to his memories . . . Using a few chairs he recreates the room as he lists the items*) A gray little room with a cold cement floor. Your bed against that wall . . . and I now know why the mattress sags so much! . . . Willie's bed . . . it's propped up on bricks because one leg is broken . . . that wobbly little table with the washbasin and jug of water . . . Yes! . . . stuck to the wall above it are some pin-up pictures from magazines. Joe Louis . . .

WILLIE: Brown Bomber. World Title. (*Boxing pose*) Three rounds and knockout.

HALLY: Against who?

SAM: Max Schmeling.

HALLY: Correct. I can also remember Fred Astaire and Ginger Rogers, and Rita Hayworth in a bathing costume which always made me hot and bothered when I looked at it. Under Willie's bed is an old suitcase with all his clothes in a mess, which is why I never hide there. Your things are neat and tidy in a trunk next to your bed, and on it there is a picture of you and Cynthia in your ballroom clothes, your first silver cup for third place in a competition and an old radio which doesn't work anymore. Have I left out anything?

SAM: No.

HALLY: Right, so much for the stage directions. Now the characters. (*Sam and Willie move to their appropriate positions in the bedroom*) Willie is in bed, under his blankets with his clothes on, complaining nonstop about something, but we can't make out a word of what he's saying because he's got his head under the blankets as well. You're on your bed trimming your toenails with a knife—not a very edifying sight—and as for me . . . What am I doing?

SAM: You're sitting on the floor giving Willie a lecture about being a good loser while you get the checker board and pieces ready for a game. Then you go to Willie's bed, pull off the blankets and make him play with you first because you know you're going to win, and that gives you the second game with me.

HALLY: And you certainly were a bad loser, Willie!

WILLIE: Haai!

HALLY: Wasn't he, Sam? And so slow! A game with you almost took the whole afternoon. Thank God I gave up trying to teach you how to play chess.

WILLIE: You and Sam cheated.

HALLY: I never saw Sam cheat, and mine were mostly the mistakes of youth.

WILLIE: Then how is it you two was always winning?

HALLY: Have you ever considered the possibility, Willie, that it was because we were better than you?

WILLIE: Every time better?

HALLY: Not every time. There were occasions when we deliberately let you win a game so that you would stop sulking and go on playing with us. Sam used to wink at me when you weren't looking to show me it was time to let you win.

WILLIE: So then you two didn't play fair.

HALLY: It was for your benefit, Mr. Malopo, which is more than being fair. It was an act of self-sacrifice. (*To Sam*) But you know what my best memory is, don't you?

SAM: No.

HALLY: Come on, guess. If your memory is so good, you must remember it as well.

SAM: We got up to a lot of tricks in there, Hally.

HALLY: This one was special, Sam.

SAM: I'm listening.

HALLY: It started off looking like another of those useless nothing-to-do afternoons. I'd already been down to Main Street looking for adventure, but nothing had happened. I didn't feel like climbing trees in the Donkin Park or pretending I was a private eye and following a stranger . . . so as usual: See what's cooking in Sam's room. This time it was you on the floor. You had two thin pieces of wood and you were smoothing them down with a knife. It didn't look particularly interesting, but when I asked you what you were doing, you just said, "Wait and see, Hally. Wait . . . and see" . . . in that secret sort of way of yours, so I knew there was a surprise coming. You teased me, you bugger, by being deliberately slow and not answering my questions!

*(Sam laughs)*

And whistling while you worked away! God, it was infuriating! I could have brained you! It was only when you tied them together in a cross and put that down on the brown paper that I realized what you were doing. "Sam is making a kite?" And when I asked you and you said "Yes" . . . ! *(Shaking his head with disbelief)* The sheer audacity of it took my breath away. I mean, seriously, what the hell does a black man know about flying a kite? I'll be honest with you, Sam, I had no hopes for it. If you think I was excited and happy, you got another guess coming. In fact, I was shit-scared that we were going to make fools of ourselves. When we left the boarding house to go up onto the hill, I was praying quietly that there wouldn't be any other kids around to laugh at us.

SAM *(Enjoying the memory as much as Hally)*: Ja, I could see that.

HALLY: I made it obvious, did I?

SAM: Ja. You refused to carry it.

HALLY: Do you blame me? Can you remember what the poor thing looked like? Tomato-box wood and brown paper! Flour and water for glue! Two of my mother's old stockings for a tail, and then all those bits and pieces of string you made me tie together so that we could fly it! Hell, no, that was now only asking for a miracle to happen.

SAM: Then the big argument when I told you to hold the string and run with it when I let go.

HALLY: I was prepared to run, all right, but straight back to the boarding house.

SAM (*Knowing what's coming*):   So what happened?

HALLY:   Come on, Sam, you remember as well as I do.

SAM:   I want to hear it from you.

(*Hally pauses. He wants to be as accurate as possible*)

HALLY:   You went a little distance from me down the hill, you held it up ready to let it go. . . . "This is it," I thought. "Like everything else in my life, here comes another fiasco." Then you shouted, "Go, Hally!" and I started to run. (*Another pause*) I don't know how to describe it, Sam. Ja! The miracle happened! I was running, waiting for it to crash to the ground, but instead suddenly there was something alive behind me at the end of the string, tugging at it as if it wanted to be free. I looked back . . . (*Shakes his head*) . . . I still can't believe my eyes. It was flying! Looping around and trying to climb even higher into the sky. You shouted to me to let it have more string. I did, until there was none left and I was just holding that piece of wood we had tied it to. You came up and joined me. You were laughing.

SAM:   So were you. And shouting, "It works, Sam! We've done it!"

HALLY:   And we had! I was so proud of us! It was the most splendid thing I had ever seen. I wished there were hundreds of kids around to watch us. The part that scared me, though, was when you showed me how to make it dive down to the ground and then just when it was on the point of crashing, swoop up again!

SAM:   You didn't want to try yourself.

HALLY:   Of course not! I would have been suicidal if anything had happened to it. Watching you do it made me nervous enough. I was quite happy just to see it up there with its tail fluttering behind it. You left me after that, didn't you? You explained how to get it down, we tied it to the bench so that I could sit and watch it, and you went away. I wanted you to stay, you know. I was a little scared of having to look after it by myself.

SAM (*Quietly*):   I had work to do, Hally.

HALLY:   It was sort of sad bringing it down, Sam. And it looked sad again when it was lying there on the ground. Like something that had lost its soul. Just tomato-box wood, brown paper and two of my mother's old stockings! But, hell, I'll never forget that first moment when I saw it up there. I had a stiff neck the next day from looking up so much.

(*Sam laughs. Hally turns to him with a question he never thought of asking before*)

Why did you make that kite, Sam?

SAM (*Evenly*):   I can't remember.

HALLY:   Truly?

SAM:   Too long ago, Hally.

HALLY:   Ja, I suppose it was. It's time for another one, you know.

SAM:   Why do you say that?

HALLY:   Because it feels like that. Wouldn't be a good day to fly it, though.

SAM:   No. You can't fly kites on rainy days.

HALLY (*He studies Sam. Their memories have made him conscious of the man's presence in his life*):   How old are you, Sam?

SAM:   Two score and five.

HALLY:   Strange, isn't it?

SAM:   What?

HALLY:   Me and you.

SAM:   What's strange about it?

HALLY:   Little white boy in short trousers and a black man old enough to be his father flying a kite. It's not every day you see that.

SAM:   But why strange? Because the one is white and the other black?

HALLY:   I don't know. Would have been just as strange, I suppose, if it had been me and my Dad . . . cripple man and a little boy! Nope! There's no chance of me flying a kite without it being strange. (*Simple statement of fact—no self-pity*) There's a nice little short story there. "The Kite-Flyers." But we'd have to find a twist in the ending.

SAM:   Twist?

HALLY:   Yes. Something unexpected. The way it ended with us was too straightforward . . . me on the bench and you going back to work. There's no drama in that.

WILLIE:   And me?

HALLY:   You?

WILLIE:   Yes me.

HALLY:   You want to get into the story as well, do you? I got it! Change the title: "Afternoons in Sam's Room" . . . expand it and tell all the stories. It's on its way to being a novel. Our days in the old Jubilee. Sad in a way that they're over. I almost wish we were still in that little room.

SAM:   We're still together.

HALLY:   That's true. It's just that life felt the right size in there . . . not too big and not too small. Wasn't so hard to work up a bit of courage. It's got so bloody complicated since then.

(*The telephone rings. Sam answers it*)

**SAM:** St. George's Park Tea Room . . . Hello, Madam . . . Yes, Madam, he's here. . . . Hally, it's your mother.

**HALLY:** Where is she phoning from?

**SAM:** Sounds like the hospital. It's a public telephone.

**HALLY** (*Relieved*): You see! I told you. (*The telephone*) Hello, Mom . . . Yes . . . Yes no fine. Everything's under control here. How's things with poor old Dad? . . . Has he had a bad turn? . . . What? . . . Oh, God! . . . Yes, Sam told me, but I was sure he'd made a mistake. But what's this all about, Mom? He didn't look at all good last night. How can he get better so quickly? . . . Then very obviously you must say no. Be firm with him. You're the boss. . . . You know what it's going to be like if he comes home. . . . Well then, don't blame me when I fail my exams at the end of the year. . . . Yes! How am I expected to be fresh for school when I spend half the night massaging his gammy leg? . . . So am I! . . . So tell him a white lie. Say Dr. Colley wants more X-rays of his stump. Or bribe him. We'll sneak in double tots of brandy in future. . . . What? . . . Order him to get back into bed at once! If he's going to behave like a child, treat him like one. . . . All right, Mom! I was just trying to . . . I'm sorry. . . . I said I'm sorry. . . . Quick, give me your number. I'll phone you back. (*He hangs up and waits a few seconds*) Here we go again! (*He dials*) I'm sorry, Mom. . . . Okay . . . But now listen to me carefully. All it needs is for you to put your foot down. Don't take no for an answer. . . . Did you hear me? And whatever you do, don't discuss it with him. . . . Because I'm frightened you'll give in to him. . . . Yes, Sam gave me lunch. . . . I ate all of it! . . . No, Mom not a soul. It's still raining here. . . . Right, I'll tell them. I'll just do some homework and then lock up. . . . But remember now, Mom. Don't listen to anything he says. And phone me back and let me know what happens. . . . Okay. Bye, Mom. (*He hangs up. The men are staring at him*) My Mom says that when you're finished with the floors you must do the windows. (*Pause*) Don't misunderstand me, chaps. All I want is for him to get better. And if he was, I'd be the first person to say: "Bring him home." But he's not, and we can't give him the medical care and attention he needs at home. That's what hospitals are there for. (*Brusquely*) So don't just stand there! Get on with it!

(*Sam clears Hally's table*)

You heard right. My Dad wants to go home.

SAM: Is he better?

HALLY (*Sharply*): No! How the hell can he be better when last night he was groaning with pain? This is not an age of miracles!

SAM: Then he should stay in hospital.

HALLY (*Seething with irritation and frustration*): Tell me something I don't know, Sam. What the hell do you think I was saying to my Mom? All I can say is fuck-it-all.

SAM: I'm sure he'll listen to your Mom.

HALLY: You don't know what she's up against. He's already packed his shaving kit and pajamas and is sitting on his bed with his crutches, dressed and ready to go. I know him when he gets in that mood. If she tries to reason with him, we've had it. She's no match for him when it comes to a battle of words. He'll tie her up in knots. (*Trying to hide his true feelings*)

SAM: I suppose it gets lonely for him in there.

HALLY: With all the patients and nurses around? Regular visits from the Salvation Army? Balls! It's ten times worse for him at home. I'm at school and my mother is here in the business all day.

SAM: He's at least got you at night.

HALLY (*Before he can stop himself*): And we've got him! Please! I don't want to talk about it anymore. (*Unpacks his school case, slamming down books on the table*) Life is just a plain bloody mess, that's all. And people are fools.

SAM: Come on, Hally.

HALLY: Yes, they are! They bloody well deserve what they get.

SAM: Then don't complain.

HALLY: Don't try to be clever, Sam. It doesn't suit you. Anybody who thinks there's nothing wrong with this world needs to have his head examined. Just when things are going along all right, without fail someone or something will come along and spoil everything. Somebody should write that down as a fundamental law of the Universe. The principle of perpetual disappointment. If there is a God who created this world, he should scrap it and try again.

SAM: All right, Hally, all right. What you got for homework?

HALLY: Bullshit, as usual. (*Opens an exercise book and reads*) "Write five hundred words describing an annual event of cultural or historical significance."

SAM: That should be easy enough for you.

HALLY: And also plain bloody boring. You know what he wants, don't you? One of their useless old ceremonies. The commemoration of the landing of the 1820 Settlers, or if it's going to be culture, Carols by Candlelight every Christmas.

SAM: It's an impressive sight. Make a good description, Hally. All those candles glowing in the dark and the people singing hymns.

HALLY: And it's called religious hysteria. (*Intense irritation*) Please, Sam! Just leave me alone and let me get on with it. I'm not in the mood for games this afternoon. And remember my Mom's orders . . . you're to help Willie with the windows. Come on now, I don't want any more nonsense in here.

SAM: Okay, Hally, okay.

(*Hally settles down to his homework; determined preparations . . . pen, ruler, exercise book, dictionary, another cake . . . all of which will lead to nothing*)

(*Sam waltzes over to Willie and starts to replace tables and chairs. He practices a ballroom step while doing so. Willie watches. When Sam is finished, Willie tries*)

Good! But just a little bit quicker on the turn and only move in to her after she's crossed over. What about this one?

(*Another step. When Sam is finished, Willie again has a go*)

Much better. See what happens when you just relax and enjoy yourself? Remember that in two weeks' time and you'll be all right.

WILLIE: But I haven't got partner, Boet Sam.

SAM: Maybe Hilda will turn up tonight.

WILLIE: No, Boet Sam. (*Reluctantly*) I gave her a good hiding.

SAM: You mean a bad one.

WILLIE: Good bad one.

SAM: Then you mustn't complain either. Now you pay the price for losing your temper.

WILLIE: I also pay two pounds ten shilling entrance fee.

SAM: They'll refund you if you withdraw now.

WILLIE (*Appalled*): You mean, don't dance?

SAM: Yes.

WILLIE: No! I wait too long and I practice too hard. If I find me new partner, you think I can be ready in two weeks? I ask Madam for my leave now and we practice every day.

SAM: Quickstep non-stop for two weeks. World record, Willie, but you'll be mad at the end.

WILLIE: No jokes, Boet Sam.

SAM:  I'm not joking.

WILLIE:  So then what?

SAM:  Find Hilda. Say you're sorry and promise you won't beat her again.

WILLIE:  No.

SAM:  Then withdraw. Try again next year.

WILLIE:  No.

SAM:  Then I give up.

WILLIE:  Haaikona, Boet Sam, you can't.

SAM:  What do you mean, I can't? I'm telling you: I give up.

WILLIE (*Adamant*):  No! (*Accusingly*) It was you who start me ballroom dancing.

SAM:  So?

WILLIE:  Before that I use to be happy. And is you and Miriam who bring me to Hilda and say here's partner for you.

SAM:  What are you saying, Willie?

WILLIE:  You!

SAM:  But me what? To blame?

WILLIE:  Yes.

SAM:  Willie . . . ? (*Bursts into laughter*)

WILLIE:  And now all you do is make jokes at me. You wait. When Miriam leaves you is my turn to laugh. Ha! Ha! Ha!

SAM (*He can't take Willie seriously any longer*):  She can leave me tonight! I know what to do. (*Bowing before an imaginary partner*) May I have the pleasure? (*He dances and sings*)
"Just a fellow with his pillow . . .
Dancin' like a willow . . .
In an autumn breeze . . ."

WILLIE:  There you go again!

(*Sam goes on dancing and singing*)

Boet Sam!

SAM:  There's the answer to your problem! Judges' announcement in two weeks' time: "Ladies and gentlemen, the winner in the open section . . . Mr. Willie Malopo and his pillow!"

(*This is too much for a now really angry Willie. He goes for Sam, but the latter is too quick for him and puts Hally's table between the two of them*)

HALLY (*Exploding*):  For Christ's sake, you two!

WILLIE (*Still trying to get at Sam*):  I donner you, Sam! Struesgod!

**SAM** (*Still laughing*): Sorry, Willie . . . Sorry . . .

**HALLY:** Sam! Willie! (*Grabs his ruler and gives Willie a vicious whack on the bum*) How the hell am I supposed to concentrate with the two of you behaving like bloody children!

**WILLIE:** Hit him too!

**HALLY:** Shut up, Willie.

**WILLIE:** He started jokes again.

**HALLY:** Get back to your work. You too, Sam. (*His ruler*) Do you want another one, Willie?

(*Sam and Willie return to their work. Hally uses the opportunity to escape from his unsuccessful attempt at homework. He struts around like a little despot, ruler in hand, giving vent to his anger and frustration*)

Suppose a customer had walked in then? Or the Park Superintendent. And seen the two of you behaving like a pair of hooligans. That would have been the end of my mother's license, you know. And your jobs! Well, this is the end of it. From now on there will be no more of your ballroom nonsense in here. This is a business establishment, not a bloody New Brighton dancing school. I've been far too lenient with the two of you. (*Behind the counter for a green cool drink and a dollop of ice cream. He keeps up his tirade as he prepares it*) But what really makes me bitter is that I allow you chaps a little freedom in here when business is bad and what do you do with it? The foxtrot! Specially you, Sam. There's more to life than trotting around a dance floor and I thought at least you knew it.

**SAM:** It's a harmless pleasure, Hally. It doesn't hurt anybody.

**HALLY:** It's also a rather simple one, you know.

**SAM:** You reckon so? Have you ever tried?

**HALLY:** Of course not.

**SAM:** Why don't you? Now.

**HALLY:** What do you mean? Me dance?

**SAM:** Yes. I'll show you a simple step—the waltz—then you try it.

**HALLY:** What will that prove?

**SAM:** That it might not be as easy as you think.

**HALLY:** I didn't say it was easy. I said it was simple—like in simple-minded, meaning mentally retarded. You can't exactly say it challenges the intellect.

**SAM:** It does other things.

**HALLY:** Such as?

SAM:   Make people happy.

HALLY (*The glass in his hand*):   So do American cream sodas with ice cream. For God's sake, Sam, you're not asking me to take ballroom dancing serious, are you?

SAM:   Yes.

HALLY (*Sigh of defeat*):   Oh, well, so much for trying to give you a decent education. I've obviously achieved nothing.

SAM:   You still haven't told me what's wrong with admiring something that's beautiful and then trying to do it yourself.

HALLY:   Nothing. But we happen to be talking about a foxtrot, not a thing of beauty.

SAM:   But that is just what I'm saying. If you were to see two champions doing, two masters of the art . . . !

HALLY:   Oh, God, I give up. So now it's also art!

SAM:   Ja.

HALLY:   There's a limit, Sam. Don't confuse art and entertainment.

SAM:   So then what is art?

HALLY:   You want a definition?

SAM:   Ja.

HALLY (*He realizes he has got to be careful. He gives the matter a lot of thought before answering*):   Philosophers have been trying to do that for centuries. What is Art? What is Life? But basically I suppose it's . . . the giving of meaning to matter.

SAM:   Nothing to do with beautiful?

HALLY:   It goes beyond that. It's the giving of form to the formless.

SAM:   Ja, well, maybe it's not art, then. But I still say it's beautiful.

HALLY:   I'm sure the word you mean to use is entertaining.

SAM (*Adamant*):   No. Beautiful. And if you want proof, come along to the Centenary Hall in New Brighton in two weeks' time.

(*The mention of the Centenary Hall draws Willie over to them*)

HALLY:   What for? I've seen the two of you prancing around in here often enough.

SAM (*He laughs*):   This isn't the real thing, Hally. We're just playing around in here.

HALLY:   So? I can use my imagination.

SAM:   And what do you get?

HALLY:   A lot of people dancing around and having a so-called good time.

SAM:   That all?

HALLY:   Well, basically it is that, surely.

SAM: No, it isn't. Your imagination hasn't helped you at all. There's a lot more to it than that. We're getting ready for the championships, Hally, not just another dance. There's going to be a lot of people, all right, and they're going to have a good time, but they'll only be spectators, sitting around and watching. It's just the competitors out there on the dance floor. Party decorations and fancy lights all around the walls! The ladies in beautiful evening dresses!

HALLY: My mother's got one of those, Sam, and, quite frankly, it's an embarrassment every time she wears it.

SAM (*Undeterred*): Your imagination left out the excitement.

(*Hally scoffs*)

Oh, yes. The finalists are not going to be out there just to have a good time. One of those couples will be the 1950 Eastern Province Champions. And your imagination left out the music.

WILLIE: Mr. Elijah Gladman Guzana and his Orchestral Jazzonions.

SAM: The sound of the big band, Hally. Trombone, trumpet, tenor and alto sax. And then, finally, your imagination also left out the climax of the evening when the dancing is finished, the judges have stopped whispering among themselves and the Master of Ceremonies collects their scorecards and goes up onto the stage to announce the winners.

HALLY: All right. So you make it sound like a bit of a do. It's an occasion. Satisfied?

SAM (*Victory*): So you admit that!

HALLY: Emotionally yes, intellectually no.

SAM: Well, I don't know what you mean by that, all I'm telling you is that it is going to be *the* event of the year in New Brighton. It's been sold out for two weeks already. There's only standing room left. We've got competitors coming from Kingwilliamstown, East London, Port Alfred.

(*Hally starts pacing thoughtfully*)

HALLY: Tell me a bit more.

SAM: I thought you weren't interested . . . intellectually.

HALLY (*Mysteriously*): I've got my reasons.

SAM: What do you want to know?

HALLY: It takes place every year?

SAM: Yes. But only every third year in New Brighton. It's East London's turn to have the championships next year.

HALLY: Which, I suppose, makes it an even more significant event.

**SAM:** Ah ha! We're getting somewhere. Our "occasion" is now a "significant event."

**HALLY:** I wonder.

**SAM:** What?

**HALLY:** I wonder if I would get away with it.

**SAM:** But what?

**HALLY** (*To the table and his exercise book*): "Write five hundred words describing an annual event of cultural or historical significance." Would I be stretching poetic license a little too far if I called your ballroom championships a cultural event?

**SAM:** You mean . . . ?

**HALLY:** You think we could get five hundred words out of it, Sam?

**SAM:** Victor Sylvester has written a whole book on ballroom dancing.

**WILLIE:** You going to write about it, Master Hally?

**HALLY:** Yes, gentlemen, that is precisely what I am considering doing. Old Doc Bromely—he's my English teacher—is going to argue with me, of course. He doesn't like natives. But I'll point out to him that in strict anthropological terms the culture of a primitive black society includes its dancing and singing. To put my thesis in a nutshell: The war-dance has been replaced by the waltz. But it still amounts to the same thing: the release of primitive emotions through movement. Shall we give it a go?

**SAM:** I'm ready.

**WILLIE:** Me also.

**HALLY:** Ha! This will teach the old bugger a lesson. (*Decision taken*) Right. Let's get ourselves organized. (*This means another cake on the table. He sits*) I think you've given me enough general atmosphere, Sam, but to build the tension and suspense I need facts. (*Pencil poised*)

**WILLIE:** Give him facts, Boet Sam.

**HALLY:** What you called the climax . . . how many finalists?

**SAM:** Six couples.

**HALLY** (*Making notes*): Go on. Give me the picture.

**SAM:** Spectators seated right around the hall. (*Willie becomes a spectator*)

**HALLY:** . . . and it's a full house.

**SAM:** At one end, on the stage, Gladman and his Orchestral Jazzonions. At the other end is a long table with the three judges. The six finalists go onto the dance floor and take up their positions. When they are ready and the spectators have settled down, the

Master of Ceremonies goes to the microphone. To start with, he makes some jokes to get the people laughing . . .

HALLY: Good touch! (*As he writes*) ". . . creating a relaxed atmosphere which will change to one of tension and drama as the climax is approached."

SAM (*Onto a chair to act out the M.C.*): "Ladies and gentlemen, we come now to the great moment you have all been waiting for this evening. . . . The finals of the 1950 Eastern Province Open Ballroom Dancing Championships. But first let me introduce the finalists! Mr. and Mrs. Welcome Tchabalala from Kingwilliamstown . . ."

WILLIE (*He applauds after every name*): Is when the people clap their hands and whistle and make a lot of noise, Master Hally.

SAM: "Mr. Mulligan Njikelane and Miss Nomhle Nkonyeni of Grahamstown; Mr. and Mrs. Norman Nchinga from Port Alfred; Mr. Fats Bokolane and Miss Dina Plaatjies from East London; Mr. Sipho Dugu and Mrs. Mable Magada from Peddie; and from New Brighton our very own Mr. Willie Malopo and Miss Hilda Samuels."

(*Willie can't believe his ears. He abandons his role as spectator and scrambles into position as a finalist*)

WILLIE: Relaxed and ready to romance!

SAM: The applause dies down. When everybody is silent, Gladman lifts up his sax, nods at the Orchestral Jazzonions . . .

WILLIE: Play the jukebox please, Boet Sam!

SAM: I also only got bus fare, Willie.

HALLY: Hold it, everybody. (*Heads for the cash register behind the counter*) How much is in the till, Sam?

SAM: Three shillings. Hally . . . your Mom counted it before she left.

(*Hally hesitates*)

HALLY: Sorry, Willie. You know how she carried on the last time I did it. We'll just have to pool our combined imaginations and hope for the best. (*Returns to the table*) Back to work. How are the points scored, Sam?

SAM: Maximum of ten points each for individual style, deportment, rhythm and general appearance.

WILLIE: Must I start?

HALLY: Hold it for a second, Willie. And penalties?

SAM: For what?

HALLY: For doing something wrong. Say you stumble or bump into somebody . . . do they take off any points?

SAM (*Aghast*): Hally . . . !

HALLY: When you're dancing. If you and your partner collide into another couple.

(*Hally can get no further. Sam has collapsed with laughter. He explains to Willie*)

SAM: If me and Miriam bump into you and Hilda . . .

(*Willie joins him in another good laugh*)

Hally, Hally . . . !

HALLY (*Perplexed*): Why? What did I say?

SAM: There's no collisions out there, Hally. Nobody trips or stumbles or bumps into anybody else. That's what that moment is all about. To be one of those finalists on that dance floor is like . . . like being in a dream about a world in which accidents don't happen.

HALLY (*Genuinely moved by Sam's image*): Jesus, Sam! That's beautiful!

WILLIE (*Can endure waiting no longer*): I'm starting! (*Willie dances while Sam talks*)

SAM: Of course it is. That's what I've been trying to say to you all afternoon. And it's beautiful because that is what we want life to be like. But instead, like you said, Hally, we're bumping into each other all the time. Look at the three of us this afternoon: I've bumped into Willie, the two of us have bumped into you, you've bumped into your mother, she bumping into your Dad. . . . None of us knows the steps and there's no music playing. And it doesn't stop with us. The whole world is doing it all the time. Open a newspaper and what do you read? America has bumped into Russia, England is bumping into India, rich man bumps into poor man. Those are big collisions, Hally. They make for a lot of bruises. People get hurt in all that bumping, and we're sick and tired of it now. It's been going on for too long. Are we never going to get it right? . . . Learn to dance life like champions instead of always being just a bunch of beginners at it?

HALLY (*Deep and sincere admiration of the man*): You've got a vision, Sam!

SAM: Not just me. What I'm saying to you is that everybody's got it. That's why there's only standing room left for the Centenary Hall in two weeks' time. For as long as the music lasts, we are going to see six couples get it right, the way we want life to be.

HALLY: But is that the best we can do, Sam . . . watch six finalists dreaming about the way it should be?

SAM: I don't know. But it starts with that. Without the dream we won't know what we're going for. And anyway I reckon there are a few people who have got past just dreaming about it and are trying for something real. Remember that thing we read once in the paper about the Mahatma Gandhi? Going without food to stop those riots in India?

HALLY: You're right. He certainly was trying to teach people to get the steps right.

SAM: And the Pope.

HALLY: Yes, he's another one. Our old General Smuts as well, you know. He's also out there dancing. You know, Sam, when you come to think of it, that's what the United Nations boils down to . . . a dancing school for politicians!

SAM: And let's hope they learn.

HALLY (*A little surge of hope*): You're right. We mustn't despair. Maybe there's some hope for mankind after all. Keep it up, Willie. (*Back to his table with determination*) This is a lot bigger than I thought. So what have we got? Yes, our title: "A World Without Collisions."

SAM: That sounds good! "A World Without Collisions."

HALLY: Subtitle: "Global Politics on the Dance Floor." No. A bit too heavy, hey? What about "Ballroom Dancing as a Political Vision"?

(*The telephone rings. Sam answers it*)

SAM: St. George's Park Tea Room . . . Yes, Madam . . . Hally, it's your Mom.

HALLY (*Back to reality*): Oh, God, yes! I'd forgotten all about that. Shit! Remember my words, Sam? Just when you're enjoying yourself, someone or something will come along and wreck everything.

SAM: You haven't heard what she's got to say yet.

HALLY: Public telephone?

SAM: No.

HALLY: Does she sound happy or unhappy?

SAM: I couldn't tell. (*Pause*) She's waiting, Hally.

HALLY (*To the telephone*): Hello, Mom . . . No, everything is okay here. Just doing my homework. . . . What's your news? . . . You've what? . . . (*Pause. He takes the receiver away from his ear for a few seconds. In the course of Hally's telephone conversation, Sam and Willie discretely position the stacked tables and chairs. Hally places the receiver back to his ear)* Yes, I'm still here. Oh, well, I give up now. Why did you do it, Mom? . . . Well, I just hope you know what you've let us in for. . . . *(Loudly)* I said I hope you know what you've let us in for! It's the end of the peace and quiet we've been having. *(Softly)* Where is he? *(Normal voice)* He can't hear us from in there. But for God's sake, Mom, what happened? I told you to be firm with him. . . . Then you and the nurses should have held him down, taken his crutches away. . . . I know only too well he's my father! . . . I'm not being disrespectful, but I'm sick and tired of emptying stinking chamberpots full of phlegm and piss. . . . Yes, I do! When you're not there, he asks *me* to do it. . . . If you really want to know the truth, that's why I've got no appetite for my food. . . . Yes! There's a lot of things you don't know about. For your information, I still haven't got that science textbook I need. And you know why? He borrowed the money you gave me for it. . . . Because I didn't want to start another fight between you two. . . . He says that every time. . . . All right, Mom! *(Viciously)* Then just remember to start hiding your bag away again, because he'll be at your purse before long for money for booze. And when he's well enough to come down here, you better keep an eye on the till as well, because that is also going to develop a leak. . . . Then don't complain to me when he starts his old tricks. . . . Yes, you do. I get it from you on one side and from him on the other, and it makes life hell for me. I'm not going to be the peacemaker anymore. I'm warning you now: when the two of you start fighting again, I'm leaving home. . . . Mom, if you start crying, I'm going to put down the receiver. . . . Okay . . . *(Lowering his voice to a vicious whisper)* Okay, Mom. I heard you. *(Desperate)* No. . . . Because I don't want to. I'll see him when I get home! Mom! . . . *(Pause. When he speaks again, his tone changes completely. It is not simply pretense. We sense a genuine emotional conflict)* Welcome home, chum! . . . What's that? . . . Don't be silly, Dad. You being home is just about the best news in the world. . . . I bet you are. Bloody depressing there with everybody going on about their ailments, hey! . . . How you feeling? . . . Good . . . Here as well, pal. Coming down cats and dogs. . . . That's right. Just the day for a kip and a toss in your old Uncle Ned. . . . Everything's just hunky-dory on my side, Dad. . . . Well, to start with, there's a nice pile of comics for you on the counter. . . . Yes, old Kemple brought them in. *Batman and Robin, Submariner* . . . just your cup of tea . . . I will. . . . Yes, we'll spin a few yarns tonight. . . . Okay, chum, see you in a little while. . . . No, I promise. I'll come straight home. . . .

(*Pause—his mother comes back on the phone*) Mom? Okay. I'll lock up now. . . . What? . . . Oh, the brandy . . . Yes, I'll remember! . . . I'll put it in my suitcase now, for God's sake. I know well enough what will happen if he doesn't get it. . . . (*Places a bottle of brandy on the counter*) I *was* kind to him, Mom. I didn't say anything nasty! . . . All right. Bye. (*End of telephone conversation. A desolate Hally doesn't move. A strained silence*)

SAM (*Quietly*):   That sounded like a bad bump, Hally.

HALLY (*Having a hard time controlling his emotions. He speaks carefully*):   Mind your own business, Sam.

SAM:   Sorry. I wasn't trying to interfere. Shall we carry on? Hally? (*He indicates the exercise book. No response from Hally*)

WILLIE (*Also trying*):   Tell him about when they give out the cups, Boet Sam.

SAM:   Ja! That's another big moment. The presentation of the cups after the winners have been announced. You've got to put that in.

(*Still no response from Hally*)

WILLIE:   A big silver one, Master Hally, called floating trophy for the champions.

SAM:   We always invite some big-shot personality to hand them over. Guest of honor this year is going to be His Holiness Bishop Jabulani of the All African Free Zionist Church.

(*Hally gets up abruptly, goes to his table and tears up the page he was writing on*)

HALLY:   So much for a bloody world without collisions.

SAM:   Too bad. It was on its way to being a good composition.

HALLY:   Let's stop bullshitting ourselves, Sam.

SAM:   Have we been doing that?

HALLY:   Yes! That's what all our talk about a decent world has been . . . just so much bullshit.

SAM:   We did say it was still only a dream.

HALLY:   And a bloody useless one at that. Life's a fuck-up and it's never going to change.

SAM:   Ja, maybe that's true.

HALLY:   There's no maybe about it. It's a blunt and brutal fact. All we've done this afternoon is waste our time.

SAM:   Not if we'd got your homework done.

HALLY:   I don't give a shit about my homework, so, for Christ's sake, just shut up about it. (*Slamming books viciously into his school case*) Hurry up now and finish your work. I want to lock up and get out of here. (*Pause*) And then go where? Home-sweet-fucking-home. Jesus, I hate that word.

(*Hally goes to the counter to put the brandy bottle and comics in his school case. After a moment's hesitation, he smashes the bottle of brandy. He abandons all further attempts to hide his feelings. Sam and Willie work away as unobtrusively as possible*)

Do you want to know what is really wrong with your lovely little dream, Sam? It's not just that we are all bad dancers. That does happen to be perfectly true, but there's more to it than just that. You left out the cripples.

SAM:  Hally!

HALLY (*Now totally reckless*):  Ja! Can't leave them out, Sam. That's why we always end up on our backsides on the dance floor. They're also out there dancing . . . like a bunch of broken spiders trying to do the quick-step! (*An ugly attempt at laughter*) When you come to think of it, it's a bloody comical sight. I mean, it's bad enough on two legs . . . but one and a pair of crutches! Hell, no, Sam. That's guaranteed to turn that dance floor into a shambles. Why you shaking your head? Picture it, man. For once this afternoon let's use our imaginations sensibly.

SAM:  Be careful, Hally.

HALLY:  Of what? The truth? I seem to be the only one around here who is prepared to face it. We've had the pretty dream, it's time now to wake up and have a good long look at the way things really are. Nobody knows the steps, there's no music, the cripples are also out there tripping up everybody and trying to get into the act, and it's all called the All-Comers-How-to-Make-a-Fuckup-of-Life Championships. (*Another ugly laugh*) Hang on, Sam! The best bit is still coming. Do you know what the winner's trophy is? A beautiful big chamber-pot with roses on the side, and it's full to the brim with piss. And guess who I think is going to be this year's winner.

SAM (*Almost shouting*):  Stop now!

HALLY (*Suddenly appalled by how far he has gone*):  Why?

SAM:  Hally? It's your father you're talking about.

HALLY:  So?

SAM:  Do you know what you've been saying?

(*Hally can't answer. He is rigid with shame. Sam speaks to him sternly*)

No, Hally, you mustn't do it. Take back those words and ask for forgiveness! It's a terrible sin for a son to mock his father with jokes like that. You'll be punished if you carry on. Your father is your father, even if he is a . . . cripple man.

WILLIE: Yes, Master Hally. Is true what Sam say.

SAM: I understand how you are feeling, Hally, but even so . . .

HALLY: No, you don't!

SAM: I think I do.

HALLY: And I'm telling you you don't. Nobody does. (*Speaking carefully as his shame turns to rage at Sam*) It's your turn to be careful, Sam. Very careful! You're treading on dangerous ground. Leave me and my father alone.

SAM: I'm not the one who's been saying things about him.

HALLY: What goes on between me and my Dad is none of your business!

SAM: Then don't tell me about it. If that's all you've got to say about him, I don't want to hear.

(*For a moment Hally is at loss for a response*)

HALLY: Just get on with your bloody work and shut up.

SAM: Swearing at me won't help you.

HALLY: Yes, it does! Mind your own fucking business and shut up!

SAM: Okay. If that's the way you want it, I'll stop trying.

(*He turns away. This infuriates Hally even more*)

HALLY: Good. Because what you've been trying to do is meddle in something you know nothing about. All that concerns you in here, Sam, is to try and do what you get paid for—keep the place clean and serve the customers. In plain words, just get on with your job. My mother is right. She's always warning me about allowing you to get too familiar. Well, this time you've gone too far. It's going to stop right now.

(*No response from Sam*)

You're only a servant in here, and don't forget it.

(*Still no response. Hally is trying hard to get one*)

And as far as my father is concerned, all you need to remember is that he is your boss.

SAM (*Needled at last*): No, he isn't. I get paid by your mother.

HALLY: Don't argue with me, Sam!

SAM: Then don't say he's my boss.

HALLY: He's a white man and that's good enough for you.

SAM: I'll try to forget you said that.

HALLY: Don't! Because you won't be doing me a favor if you do. I'm telling you to remember it.

(*A pause. Sam pulls himself together and makes one last effort*)

SAM: Hally, Hally . . . ! Come on now. Let's stop before it's too late. You're right. We *are* on dangerous ground. If we're not careful, somebody is going to get hurt.

HALLY: It won't be me.

SAM: Don't be so sure.

HALLY: I don't know what you're talking about, Sam.

SAM: Yes, you do.

HALLY (*Furious*): Jesus, I wish you would stop trying to tell me what I do and what I don't know.

(*Sam gives up. He turns to Willie*)

SAM: Let's finish up.

HALLY: Don't turn your back on me! I haven't finished talking.

(*He grabs Sam by the arm and tries to make him turn around. Sam reacts with a flash of anger*)

SAM: Don't do that, Hally! (*Facing the boy*) All right, I'm listening. Well? What do you want to say to me?

HALLY (*Pause as Hally looks for something to say*): To begin with, why don't you also start calling me Master Harold, like Willie.

SAM: Do you mean that?

HALLY: Why the hell do you think I said it?

SAM: And if I don't?

HALLY: You might just lose your job.

SAM (*Quietly and very carefully*): If you make me say it once, I'll never call you anything else again.

HALLY: So? (*The boy confronts the man*) Is that meant to be a threat?

SAM: Just telling you what will happen if you make me do that. You must decide what it means to you.

HALLY: Well, I have. It's good news. Because that is exactly what Master Harold wants from now on. Think of it as a little lesson in respect, Sam, that's long overdue, and I hope you remember it as well as you do your geography. I can tell you now that somebody who will be glad to hear I've finally given it to you will be my Dad. Yes! He agrees with my Mom. He's always going on about it as well. "You must teach the boys to show you more respect, my son."

SAM: So now you can stop complaining about going home. Everybody is going to be happy tonight.

HALLY: That's perfectly correct. You see, you mustn't get the wrong idea about me and my Dad, Sam. We also have our good times together. Some bloody good laughs. He's got a marvelous sense of humor. Want to know what our favorite joke is? He gives out a big groan, you see, and says: "It's not fair, is it, Hally?" Then I have to ask: "What, chum?" And then he says: "A nigger's arse" . . . and we both have a good laugh.

(*The men stare at him with disbelief*)

What's the matter, Willie? Don't you catch the joke? You always were a bit slow on the uptake. It's what is called a pun. You see, fair means both light in color and to be just and decent. (*He turns to Sam*) I thought *you* would catch it, Sam.

SAM: Oh ja, I catch it all right.

HALLY: But it doesn't appeal to your sense of humor.

SAM: Do you really laugh?

HALLY: Of course.

SAM: To please him? Make him feel good?

HALLY: No, for heaven's sake! I laugh because I think it's a bloody good joke.

SAM: You're really trying hard to be ugly, aren't you? And why drag poor old Willie into it? He's done nothing to you except show you the respect you want so badly. That's also not being fair, you know . . . and *I* mean just or decent.

WILLIE: It's all right, Sam. Leave it now.

SAM: It's me you're after. You should just have said "Sam's arse" . . . because that's the one you're trying to kick. Anyway, how do you know it's not fair? You've never seen it. Do you want to? (*He drops his trousers and underpants and presents his backside for Hally's inspection*) Have a good look. A real Basuto arse . . . which is about as nigger as they can come. Satisfied? (*Trousers up*) Now you can make your Dad even happier when you go home tonight. Tell him I showed you my arse and he is quite right. It's not fair. And if it will give him an even better laugh next time, I'll also let *him* have a look. Come, Willie, let's finish up and go.

(*Sam and Willie start to tidy up the tea room. Hally doesn't move. He waits for a moment when Sam passes him*)

HALLY (*Quietly*):   Sam . . .

(*Sam stops and looks expectantly at the boy. Hally spits in his face. A long and heartfelt groan from Willie. For a few seconds Sam doesn't move*)

SAM (*Taking out a handkerchief and wiping his face*):   It's all right, Willie.

(*To Hally*)

Ja, well, you've done it . . . Master Harold. Yes, I'll start calling you that from now on. It won't be difficult anymore. You've hurt yourself, Master Harold. I saw it coming. I warned you, but you wouldn't listen. You've just hurt yourself *bad*. And you're a coward, Master Harold. The face you should be spitting in is your father's . . . but you used mine, because you think you're safe inside your fair skin . . . and this time I don't mean just or decent. (*Pause, then moving violently towards Hally*) Should I hit him, Willie?

WILLIE (*Stopping Sam*):   No, Boet Sam.

SAM (*Violently*):   Why not?

WILLIE:   It won't help, Boet Sam.

SAM:   I don't want to help! I want to hurt him.

WILLIE:   You also hurt yourself.

SAM:   And if he had done it to you, Willie?

WILLIE:   Me? Spit at me like I was a dog? (*A thought that had not occurred to him before. He looks at Hally*) Ja. Then I want to hit him. I want to hit him hard!

(*A dangerous few seconds as the men stand staring at the boy. Willie turns away, shaking his head*)

But maybe all I do is go cry at the back. He's little boy, Boet Sam. Little *white* boy. Long trousers now, but he's still little boy.

SAM (*His violence ebbing away into defeat as quickly as it flooded*):   You're right. So go on, then: groan again, Willie. You do it better than me. (*To Hally*) You don't know all of what you've just done . . . Master Harold. It's not just that you've made me feel dirtier than I've ever been in my life . . . I mean, how do I wash off yours and your father's filth? . . . I've also failed. A long time ago I promised myself I was going to try and do something, but you've just shown me . . . Master Harold . . . that I've failed. (*Pause*) I've also got a memory of a little white boy when he was still wearing short trousers and a black man, but they're not flying a kite. It was the old Jubilee days, after dinner one night. I was in my room. You came in and just stood against the wall, looking down at the ground, and only after I'd asked you what you wanted, what was wrong, I don't know how many times, did you speak and even then so softly I almost didn't hear you. "Sam, please help me to go and fetch my Dad." Remember? He was dead drunk on the floor of the Central Hotel Bar. They'd phoned for your Mom, but you were the only one at home. And do you remember how we did it? You went in first by yourself to ask permission for me to go into the bar. Then I loaded him onto my back like a baby and carried him back to the boarding house with you following behind carrying his crutches. (*Shaking his head as he remembers*) A crowded Main Street with all the people watching a little white boy following his drunk father on a nigger's back! I felt for that little boy . . . Master Harold. I felt for him. After that we still had to clean him up, remember? He'd messed in his trousers, so we had to clean him up and get him into bed.

HALLY (*Great pain*):   I love him, Sam.

SAM:   I know you do. That's why I tried to stop you from saying these things about him. It would have been so simple if you could have just despised him for being a weak man. But he's your father. You love him and you're ashamed of him. You're ashamed of so much! . . . And now that's going to include yourself. That was the promise I made to myself: to try and stop that happening. (*Pause*) After we got him to bed you came back with me to my room and sat in a corner and carried on just looking down at the ground. And for days after that! You hadn't done anything wrong, but you went around as if you owed the world an apology for being alive. I didn't like seeing that! That's not the way a boy grows up to be a man!. . . But the one person who should have been teaching you what that means was the cause of your shame. If you really want to know, that's why I made you that kite. I wanted you to look up, be proud of something, of yourself . . . (*Bitter smile at the memory*) . . . and you certainly were that when I left you with it up there on the hill. Oh, ja . . . something else! . . . If you ever do write it as a short story, there *was* a twist in our ending. I couldn't sit down there and stay with you. It was a "Whites Only" bench. You were too young, too excited to notice then. But not anymore. If you're not careful . . . Master Harold . . . you're going to be sitting up there by yourself for a long time to come, and there won't be a kite in the sky. (*Sam has got nothing more to say. He exits into the kitchen, taking off his waiter's jacket*)

WILLIE: Is bad. Is all all bad in here now.

HALLY (*Books into his school case, raincoat on*): Willie . . . (*It is difficult to speak*) Will you lock up for me and look after the keys?

WILLIE: Okay.

(*Sam returns. Hally goes behind the counter and collects the few coins in the cash register. As he starts to leave . . .*)

SAM: Don't forget the comic books.

(*Hally returns to the counter and puts them in his case. He starts to leave again*)

SAM (*To the retreating back of the boy*): Stop . . . Hally . . .

(*Hally stops, but doesn't turn to face him*)

Hally . . . I've got no right to tell you what being a man means if I don't behave like one myself, and I'm not doing so well at that this afternoon. Should we try again, Hally?

HALLY: Try what?

SAM: Fly another kite, I suppose. It worked once, and this time I need it as much as you do.

HALLY: It's still raining, Sam. You can't fly kites on rainy days, remember.

SAM: So what do we do? Hope for better weather tomorrow?

HALLY (*Helpless gesture*): I don't know. I don't know anything anymore.

SAM: You sure of that, Hally? Because it would be pretty hopeless if that was true. It would mean nothing has been learnt in here this afternoon, and there was a hell of a lot of teaching going on . . . one way or the other. But anyway, I don't believe you. I reckon there's one thing you know. You don't *have* to sit up there by yourself. You know what that bench means now, and you can leave it any time you choose. All you've got to do is stand up and walk away from it.

(*Hally leaves. Willie goes up quietly to Sam*)

WILLIE: Is okay, Boet Sam. You see. Is . . . (*He can't find any better words*) . . . is going to be okay tomorrow. (*Changing his tone*) Hey, Boet Sam! (*He is trying hard*) You right. I think about it and you right. Tonight I find Hilda and say sorry. And make promise I won't beat her no more. You hear me, Boet Sam?

SAM:   I hear you, Willie.

WILLIE:   And when we practice I relax and romance with her from beginning to end. Non-stop! You watch! Two weeks' time: "First
prize for promising newcomers: Mr. Willie Malopo and Miss Hilda
Samuels." (*Sudden impulse*) To hell with it! I walk home. (*He goes
to the jukebox, puts in a coin and selects a record. The machine
comes to life in the gray twilight, blushing its way through a spec-
trum of soft, romantic colors*) How did you say it, Boet Sam? Let's
dream. (*Willie sways with the music and gestures for Sam to
dance*)

(*Sarah Vaughan sings*)

"Little man you're crying,
I know why you're blue,
Someone took your kiddy car away;
Better go to sleep now,
Little man you've had a busy day." (*etc. etc.*)

You lead. I follow.

(*The men dance together*)

"Johnny won your marbles,
Tell you what we'll do;
Dad will get you new ones
    right away;
Better go to sleep now,
Little man you've had a
    busy day."

—1982

# *August Wilson*   (b. 1945)

August Wilson, *whose birth name was Frederick August Kittel, was born in Pittsburgh's predominantly African-American Hill District, the setting of many of his plays. The child of a mixed-race marriage, he grew up fatherless and credits his real education in life and, incidentally, in language to the older men in his neighborhood, whose distinctive voices echo memorably in his plays. A school dropout at fifteen after a teacher unjustly accused him of plagiarism, he joined in the Black Power movement of the 1960s, eventually founding the Black Horizon on the Hill, an African-American theater company. Wilson admits to having had little confidence in his own ability to write dialogue during his early career, and his first publications were poems. A move to St. Paul, Minnesota, led to work with the Minneapolis Playwrights' Center. After his return to Pittsburgh he wrote* Jitney *and* Fullerton Street, *which were staged by regional theaters. His career hit full stride with the successful debut of* Ma Rainey's Black Bottom *(1984), which was first produced at the Yale Repertory Theater and later moved to Broadway.* Joe Turner's Come and Gone *(1986) was his next success, and* Fences *(1987) and* The Piano Lesson *(1990) both won Pulitzer Prizes and other major awards, establishing Wilson as the most prominent African-American dramatist. In most of Wilson's plays a historical theme is prominent, as Wilson attempts to piece together the circumstances that led African Americans to northern cities, depicting how they remain united and sometimes divided by a common cultural heritage that transcends even the ties of friendship and family. But to these social concerns Wilson brings a long training in the theatre and a poet's love of language. As he said to an interviewer in 1991, "[Poetry] is the bedrock of my playwriting. . . . The idea of metaphor is a very large idea in my plays and something that I find lacking in most contemporary plays. I think I write the kinds of plays that I do because I have twenty-six years of writing poetry underneath all of that."* Two Trains Running *(1992),* Seven Guitars *(1995), and* King Hedley II *(2001) are recent plays.*

# Fences

for Lloyd Richards,
who adds to whatever he touches.

When the sins of our fathers visit us
We do not have to play host.
We can banish them with forgiveness
As God, in His Largeness and Laws.

—*August Wilson*

## LIST OF CHARACTERS

Troy Maxson
Jim Bono, *Troy's friend*
Rose, *Troy's wife*
Lyons, *Troy's oldest son by previous marriage*
Gabriel, *Troy's brother*
Cory, *Troy and Rose's son*
Raynell, *Troy's daughter*

Setting: *The setting is the yard which fronts the only entrance to the Maxson household, an ancient two-story brick house set back off a small alley in a big-city neighborhood. The entrance to the house is gained by two or three steps leading to a wooden porch badly in need of paint.*

*A relatively recent addition to the house and running its full width, the porch lacks congruence. It is a sturdy porch with a flat roof. One or two chairs of dubious value sit at one end where the kitchen window opens onto the porch. An old-fashioned icebox stands silent guard at the opposite end.*

*The yard is a small dirt yard, partially fenced, except for the last scene, with a wooden saw horse, a pile of lumber, and other fence-building equipment set off to the side. Opposite is a tree from which hangs a ball made of rags. A baseball bat leans against the tree. Two oil drums serve as garbage receptacles and sit near the house at right to complete the setting.*

The Play: *Near the turn of the century, the destitute of Europe sprang on the city with tenacious claws and an honest and solid dream. The city devoured them. They swelled its belly until it burst into a thousand furnaces and sewing machines, a thousand butcher shops and bakers' ovens, a thousand churches and hospitals and funeral parlors and money-lenders. The city grew. It nourished itself and offered each man a partnership limited only by his talent, his guile, and his willingness and capacity for hard work. For the immigrants of Europe, a dream dared and won true.*

*The descendants of African slaves were offered no such welcome or participation. They came from places called the Carolinas and the Virginias, Georgia, Alabama, Mississippi, and Tennessee. They came strong, eager, searching. The city rejected them and they fled and settled along the riverbanks and under bridges in shallow, ramshackle houses made of sticks and tarpaper. They collected rags and wood. They sold the use of their muscles and their bodies. They cleaned houses and washed clothes, they shined shoes, and in quiet desperation and vengeful pride, they stole, and lived in pursuit of their own dream. That they could breathe free, finally, and stand to meet life with the force of dignity and whatever eloquence the heart could call upon.*

*By 1957, the hard-won victories of the European immigrants had solidified the industrial might of America. War had been confronted and won with new energies that used loyalty and patriotism as its fuel. Life was rich, full, and flourishing. The Milwaukee Braves won the World Series, and the hot winds of change that would make the sixties a turbulent, racing, dangerous, and provocative decade had not yet begun to blow full.*

## ACT 1

### SCENE 1

*It is 1957. Troy and Bono enter the yard, engaged in conversation. Troy is fifty-three years old, a large man with thick, heavy hands; it is this largeness that he strives to fill out and make an accommodation with. Together with his blackness, his largeness informs his sensibilities and the choices he has made in his life.*

*Of the two men, Bono is obviously the follower. His commitment to their friendship of thirty-odd years is rooted in his admiration of Troy's honesty, capacity for hard work, and his strength, which Bono seeks to emulate.*

*It is Friday night, payday, and the one night of the week the two men engage in a ritual of talk and drink. Troy is usually the most talkative and at times he can be crude and almost vulgar, though he is capable of rising to profound heights of expression. The men carry lunch buckets and wear or carry burlap aprons and are dressed in clothes suitable to their jobs as garbage collectors.*

BONO: Troy, you ought to stop that lying!

TROY: I ain't lying! The nigger had a watermelon this big. (*He indicates with his hands.*) Talking about . . . "What watermelon, Mr. Rand?" I liked to fell out! "What watermelon, Mr. Rand?" . . . And it sitting there big as life.

BONO: What did Mr. Rand say?

TROY: Ain't said nothing. Figure if the nigger too dumb to know he carrying a watermelon, he wasn't gonna get much sense out of him.

Trying to hide that great big old watermelon under his coat. Afraid to let the white man see him carry it home.

BONO: I'm like you . . . I ain't got no time for them kind of people.

TROY: Now what he look like getting mad cause he see the man from the union talking to Mr. Rand?

BONO: He come to me talking about . . . "Maxson gonna get us fired." I told him to get away from me with that. He walked away from me calling you a troublemaker. What Mr. Rand say?

TROY: Ain't said nothing. He told me to go down the Commissioner's office next Friday. They called me down there to see them.

BONO: Well, as long as you got your complaint filed, they can't fire you. That's what one of them white fellows tell me.

TROY: I ain't worried about them firing me. They gonna fire me cause I asked a question? That's all I did. I went to Mr. Rand and asked him, "Why? Why you got the white mens driving and the colored lifting?" Told him, "what's the matter, don't I count? You think only white fellows got sense enough to drive a truck. That ain't no paper job! Hell, anybody can drive a truck. How come you got all whites driving and the colored lifting?" He told me "take it to the union." Well, hell, that's what I done! Now they wanna come up with this pack of lies.

BONO: I told Brownie if the man come and ask him any questions . . . just tell the truth! It ain't nothing but something they done trumped up on you cause you filed a complaint on them.

TROY: Brownie don't understand nothing. All I want them to do is change the job description. Give everybody a chance to drive the truck. Brownie can't see that. He ain't got that much sense.

BONO: How you figure he be making out with that gal be up at Taylor's all the time . . . that Alberta gal?

TROY: Same as you and me. Getting just as much as we is. Which is to say nothing.

BONO: It is, huh? I figure you doing a little better than me . . . and I ain't saying what I'm doing.

TROY: Aw, nigger, look here . . . I know you. If you had got anywhere near that gal, twenty minutes later you be looking to tell somebody. And the first one you gonna tell . . . that you gonna want to brag to . . . is me.

BONO: I ain't saying that. I see where you be eyeing her.

TROY: I eye all the women. I don't miss nothing. Don't never let nobody tell you Troy Maxson don't eye the women.

BONO: You been doing more than eyeing her. You done bought her a drink or two.

TROY: Hell yeah, I bought her a drink! What that mean? I bought you one, too. What that mean cause I buy her a drink? I'm just being polite.

BONO: It's all right to buy her one drink. That's what you call being polite. But when you wanna be buying two or three . . . that's what you call eyeing her.

TROY: Look here, as long as you known me . . . you ever known me to chase after women?

BONO: Hell yeah! Long as I done known you. You forgetting I knew you when.

TROY: Naw, I'm talking about since I been married to Rose?

BONO: Oh, not since you been married to Rose. Now, that's the truth, there. I can say that.

TROY: All right then! Case closed.

BONO: I see you be walking up around Alberta's house. You supposed to be at Taylors' and you be walking up around there.

TROY: What you watching where I'm walking for? I ain't watching after you.

BONO: I seen you walking around there more than once.

TROY: Hell, you liable to see me walking anywhere! That don't mean nothing cause you see me walking around there.

BONO: Where she come from anyway? She just kinda showed up one day.

TROY: Tallahassee. You can look at her and tell she one of them Florida gals. They got some big healthy women down there. Grow them right up out the ground. Got a little bit of Indian in her. Most of them niggers down in Florida got some Indian in them.

BONO: I don't know about that Indian part. But she damn sure big and healthy. Woman wear some big stockings. Got them great big old legs and hips as wide as the Mississippi River.

TROY: Legs don't mean nothing. You don't do nothing but push them out of the way. But them hips cushion the ride!

BONO: Troy, you ain't got no sense.

TROY: It's the truth! Like you riding on Goodyears!

*Rose enters from the house. She is ten years younger than Troy, her devotion to him stems from her recognition of the possibilities of her life without him: a succession of abusive men and their babies, a life of partying and running the streets, the Church, or aloneness with its attendant pain and frustration. She recognizes Troy's spirit as a fine and illuminating one and she either ignores or forgives his faults, only some of which she recognizes. Though she doesn't drink, her presence is an integral part of the Friday night rituals. She alternates between the porch and the kitchen, where supper preparations are under way.*

ROSE: What you all out here getting into?

TROY: What you worried about what we getting into for? This is men talk, woman.

ROSE: What I care what you all talking about? Bono, you gonna stay for supper?

BONO: No, I thank you, Rose. But Lucille say she cooking up a pot of pigfeet.

TROY: Pigfeet! Hell, I'm going home with you! Might even stay the night if you got some pigfeet. You got something in there to top them pigfeet, Rose?

ROSE: I'm cooking up some chicken. I got some chicken and collard greens.

TROY: Well, go on back in the house and let me and Bono finish what we was talking about. This is men talk. I got some talk for you later. You know what kind of talk I mean. You go on and powder it up.

ROSE: Troy Maxson, don't you start that now!

TROY (*puts his arm around her*): Aw, woman . . . come here. Look here, Bono . . . when I met this woman . . . I got out that place, say, "Hitch up my pony, saddle up my mare . . . there's a woman out there for me somewhere. I looked here. Looked there. Saw Rose and latched on to her." I latched on to her and told her—I'm gonna tell you the truth—I told her, "Baby, I don't wanna marry, I just wanna be your man." Rose told me . . . tell him what you told me, Rose.

ROSE: I told him if he wasn't the marrying kind, then move out the way so the marrying kind could find me.

TROY: That's what she told me. "Nigger, you in my way. You blocking the view! Move out the way so I can find me a husband." I thought it over two or three days. Come back—

ROSE: Ain't no two or three days nothing. You was back the same night.

TROY: Come back, told her . . . "Okay, baby . . . but I'm gonna buy me a banty rooster and put him out there in the backyard . . . and when he see a stranger come, he'll flap his wings and crow. . . ." Look here, Bono, I could watch the front door by myself . . . it was that back door I was worried about.

ROSE: Troy, you ought not talk like that. Troy ain't doing nothing but telling a lie.

TROY: Only thing is . . . when we first got married . . . forget the rooster . . . we ain't had no yard!

BONO: I hear you tell it. Me and Lucille was staying down there on Logan Street. Had two rooms with the outhouse in the back. I ain't mind the outhouse none. But when that goddamn wind blow through there in the winter . . . that's what I'm talking about! To this day I wonder why in the hell I ever stayed down there for six long years. But see, I didn't know I could do no better. I thought only white folks had inside toilets and things.

ROSE: There's a lot of people don't know they can do no better than they doing now. That's just something you got to learn. A lot of folks still shop at Bella's.

TROY: Ain't nothing wrong with shopping at Bella's. She got fresh food.

ROSE: I ain't said nothing about if she got fresh food. I'm talking about what she charge. She charge ten cents more than the A&P.

TROY: The A&P ain't never done nothing for me. I spends my money where I'm treated right. I go down to Bella, say, "I need a loaf of bread, I'll pay you Friday." She give it to me. What sense that make when I got money to go and spend it somewhere else and ignore the person who done right by me? That ain't in the Bible.

ROSE: We ain't talking about what's in the Bible. What sense it make to shop there when she overcharge?

TROY: You shop where you want to. I'll do my shopping where the people been good to me.

ROSE: Well, I don't think it's right for her to overcharge. That's all I was saying.

BONO: Look here . . . I got to get on. Lucille going be raising all kind of hell.

TROY: Where you going, nigger? We ain't finished this pint. Come here, finish this pint.

BONO: Well, hell, I am . . . if you ever turn the bottle loose.

TROY (*hands him the bottle*): The only thing I say about the A&P is I'm glad Cory got that job down there. Help him take care of his school clothes and things. Gabe done moved out and things getting tight around here. He got that job. . . . He can start to look out for himself.

ROSE: Cory done went and got recruited by a college football team.

TROY: I told that boy about that football stuff. The white man ain't gonna let him get nowhere with that football. I told him when he first come to me with it. Now you come telling me he done went and got more tied up in it. He ought to go and get recruited in how to fix cars or something where he can make a living.

ROSE: He ain't talking about making no living playing football. It's just something the boys in school do. They gonna send a recruiter by to talk to you. He'll tell you he ain't talking about making no living playing football. It's a honor to be recruited.

TROY: It ain't gonna get him nowhere. Bono'll tell you that.

BONO: If he be like you in the sports . . . he's gonna be all right. Ain't but two men ever played baseball as good as you. That's Babe Ruth and Josh Gibson.[1] Them's the only two men ever hit more home runs than you.

TROY: What it ever get me? Ain't got a pot to piss in or a window to throw it out of.

ROSE: Times have changed since you was playing baseball, Troy. That was before the war. Times have changed a lot since then.

TROY: How in hell they done changed?

ROSE: They got lots of colored boys playing ball now. Baseball and football.

BONO: You right about that, Rose. Times have changed, Troy. You just come along too early.

TROY: There ought not never have been no time called too early! Now you take that fellow . . . what's that fellow they had playing right field for the Yankees back then? You know who I'm talking about, Bono. Used to play right field for the Yankees.

ROSE: Selkirk?

TROY: Selkirk! That's it! Man batting .269, understand? .269. What kind of sense that make? I was hitting .432 with thirty-seven home runs! Man batting .269 and playing right field for the Yankees! I saw Josh Gibson's daughter yesterday. She walking around with raggedy shoes on her feet. Now I bet you Selkirk's daughter ain't walking around with raggedy shoes on the feet! I bet you that!

ROSE: They got a lot of colored baseball players now. Jackie Robinson[2] was the first. Folks had to wait for Jackie Robinson.

TROY: I done seen a hundred niggers play baseball better than Jackie Robinson. Hell, I know some teams Jackie Robinson couldn't even make! What you talking about Jackie Robinson. Jackie Robinson

---

[1] African-American ballplayer (1911–1947).
[2] Robinson (1919–1972) became the first African-American to play baseball in the major leagues, starring for the Brooklyn Dodgers.

wasn't nobody. I'm talking about if you could play ball then they ought to have let you play. Don't care what color you were. Come telling me I come along too early. If you could play . . . then they ought to have let you play.

*Troy takes a long drink from the bottle.*

ROSE: You gonna drink yourself to death. You don't need to be drinking like that.

TROY: Death ain't nothing. I done seen him. Done wrassled with him. You can't tell me nothing about death. Death ain't nothing but a fastball on the outside corner. And you know what I'll do to that! Lookee here, Bono . . . am I lying? You get one of them fastballs, about waist high, over the outside corner of the plate where you can get the meat of the bat on it . . . and good god! You can kiss it goodbye. Now, am I lying?

BONO: Naw, you telling the truth there. I seen you do it.

TROY: If I'm lying . . . that 450 feet worth of lying! (*Pause.*) That's all death is to me. A fastball on the outside corner.

ROSE: I don't know why you want to get on talking about death.

TROY: Ain't nothing wrong with talking about death. That's part of life. Everybody gonna die. You gonna die, I'm gonna die. Bono's gonna die. Hell, we all gonna die.

ROSE: But you ain't got to talk about it. I don't like to talk about it.

TROY: You the one brought it up. Me and Bono was talking about baseball . . . you tell me I'm gonna drink myself to death. Ain't that right, Bono? You know I don't drink this but one night out of the week. That's Friday night. I'm gonna drink just enough to where I can handle it. Then I cuts it loose. I leave it alone. So don't you worry about me drinking myself to death. 'Cause I ain't worried about Death. I done seen him. I done wrestled with him.

Look here, Bono . . . I looked up one day and Death was marching straight at me. Like Soldiers on Parade! The Army of Death was marching straight at me. The middle of July, 1941. It got real cold just like it be winter. It seem like Death himself reached out and touched me on the shoulder. He touch me just like I touch you. I got cold as ice and Death standing there grinning at me.

ROSE:   Troy, why don't you hush that talk.

TROY:   I say . . . what you want, Mr. Death? You be wanting me? You done brought your army to be getting me? I looked him dead in the eye. I wasn't fearing nothing. I was ready to tangle. Just like I'm ready to tangle now. The Bible say be ever vigilant. That's why I don't get but so drunk. I got to keep watch.

ROSE:   Troy was right down there in Mercy Hospital. You remember he had pneumonia? Laying there with a fever talking plumb out of his head.

TROY:   Death standing there staring at me . . . carrying that sickle in his hand. Finally he say, "You want bound over for another year?" See, just like that . . . "You want bound over for another year?" I told him, "Bound over hell! Let's settle this now!"

It seem like he kinda fell back when I said that, and all the cold went out of me. I reached down and grabbed that sickle and threw it just as far as I could throw it . . . and me and him commenced to wrestling.

We wrestled for three days and three nights. I can't say where I found the strength from. Everytime it seemed like he was gonna get the best of me, I'd reach way down deep inside myself and find the strength to do him one better.

ROSE:   Everytime Troy tell that story he find different ways to tell it. Different things to make up about it.

TROY:   I ain't making up nothing. I'm telling you the facts of what happened. I wrestled with Death for three days and three nights and I'm standing here to tell you about it. (*Pause.*) All right. At the end of the third night we done weakened each other to where we can't hardly move. Death stood up, throwed on his robe . . . had him a white robe with a hood on it. He throwed on that robe and went off to look for his sickle. Say, "I'll be back." Just like that. "I'll be back." I told him, say, "Yeah, but . . . you gonna have to find me!" I wasn't no fool. I wasn't going looking for him. Death ain't nothing to play with. And I know he's gonna get me. I know I got to join his army . . . his camp followers. But as long as I keep my strength and see him coming . . . as long as I keep up my vigilance . . . he's gonna have to fight to get me. I ain't going easy.

BONO:   Well, look here, since you got to keep up your vigilance . . . let me have the bottle.

TROY: Aw hell, I shouldn't have told you that part. I should have left out that part.

ROSE: Troy be talking that stuff and half the time don't even know what he be talking about.

TROY: Bono know me better than that.

BONO: That's right. I know you. I know you got some Uncle Remus[3] in your blood. You got more stories than the devil got sinners.

TROY: Aw hell, I done seen him too! Done talked with the devil.

ROSE: Troy, don't nobody wanna be hearing all that stuff.

*Lyons enters the yard from the street. Thirty-four years old, Troy's son by a previous marriage, he sports a neatly trimmed goatee, sport coat, white shirt, tieless and buttoned at the collar. Though he fancies himself a musician, he is more caught up in the rituals and "idea" of being a musician than in the actual practice of the music. He has come to borrow money from Troy, and while he knows he will be successful, he is uncertain as to what extent his lifestyle will be held up to scrutiny and ridicule.*

LYONS: Hey, Pop.

TROY: What you come "Hey, Popping" me for?

LYONS: How you doing, Rose? (*He kisses her.*) Mr. Bono. How you doing?

BONO: Hey, Lyons . . . how you been?

TROY: He must have been doing all right. I ain't seen him around here last week.

ROSE: Troy, leave your boy alone. He come by to see you and you wanna start all that nonsense.

TROY: I ain't bothering Lyons. (*Offers him the bottle.*) Here . . . get you a drink. We got an understanding. I know why he come by to see me and he know I know.

LYONS: Come on, Pop . . . I just stopped by to say hi . . . see how you was doing.

TROY: You ain't stopped by yesterday.

ROSE: You gonna stay for supper, Lyons? I got some chicken cooking in the oven.

LYONS: No, Rose . . . thanks. I was just in the neighborhood and thought I'd stop by for a minute.

[3]Narrator of dialect/written tales in a book by Joel Chandler Harris.

TROY: You was in the neighborhood all right, nigger. You telling the truth there. You was in the neighborhood cause it's my payday.

LYONS: Well, hell, since you mentioned it . . . let me have ten dollars.

TROY: I'll be damned! I'll die and go to hell and play blackjack with the devil before I give you ten dollars.

BONO: That's what I wanna know about . . . that devil you done seen.

LYONS: What . . . Pop done seen the devil? You too much, Pops.

TROY: Yeah, I done seen him. Talked to him too!

ROSE: You ain't seen no devil. I done told you that man ain't had nothing to do with the devil. Anything you can't understand, you want to call it the devil.

TROY: Look here, Bono . . . I went down to see Hertzberger about some furniture. Got three rooms for two-ninety-eight. That what it say on the radio. "Three rooms . . . two-ninety-eight." Even made up a little song about it. Go down there . . . man tell me I can't get no credit. I'm working every day and can't get no credit. What to do? I got an empty house with some raggedy furniture in it. Cory ain't got no bed. He's sleeping on a pile of rags on the floor. Working every day and can't get no credit. Come back here—Rose'll tell you—madder than hell. Sit down . . . try to figure what I'm gonna do. Come a knock on the door. Ain't been living here but three days. Who know I'm here? Open the door . . . devil standing there bigger than life. White fellow . . . white fellow . . . got on good clothes and everything. Standing there with a clipboard in his hand. I ain't had to say nothing. First words come out of his mouth was . . . "I understand you need some furniture and can't get no credit." I liked to fell over. He say, "I'll give you all the credit you want, but you got to pay the interest on it." I told him, "Give me three rooms worth and charge whatever you want." Next day a truck pulled up here and two men unloaded them three rooms. Man what drove the truck give me a book. Say send ten dollars, first of every month to the address in the book and every thing will be all right. Say if I miss a payment the devil was coming back and it'll be hell to pay. That was fifteen years ago. To this day . . . the first of the month I send my ten dollars, Rose'll tell you.

ROSE: Troy lying.

TROY: I ain't never seen that man since. Now you tell me who else that could have been but the devil? I ain't sold my soul or nothing like that, you understand. Naw, I wouldn't have truck with the devil about nothing like that. I got my furniture and pays my ten dollars the first of the month just like clockwork.

BONO: How long you say you been paying this ten dollars a month?

TROY: Fifteen years!

BONO: Hell, ain't you finished paying for it yet? How much the man done charged you?

TROY: Ah hell, I done paid for it. I done paid for it ten times over! The fact is I'm scared to stop paying it.

ROSE: Troy lying. We got that furniture from Mr. Glickman. He ain't paying no ten dollars a month to nobody.

TROY: Aw hell, woman. Bono know I ain't that big a fool.

LYONS: I was just getting ready to say . . . I know where there's a bridge for sale.

TROY: Look here, I'll tell you this . . . it don't matter to me if he was the devil. It don't matter if the devil give credit. Somebody has got to give it.

ROSE: It ought to matter. You going around talking about having truck with the devil . . . God's the one you gonna have to answer to. He's the one gonna be at the Judgment.

LYONS: Yeah, well, look here, Pop . . . Let me have that ten dollars. I'll give it back to you. Bonnie got a job working at the hospital.

TROY: What I tell you, Bono? The only time I see this nigger is when he wants something. That's the only time I see him.

LYONS: Come on, Pop, Mr. Bono don't want to hear all that. Let me have the ten dollars. I told you Bonnie working.

TROY: What that mean to me? "Bonnie working." I don't care if she working. Go ask her for the ten dollars if she working. Talking about "Bonnie working." Why ain't you working?

LYONS: Aw, Pop, you know I can't find no decent job. Where am I gonna get a job at? You know I can't get no job.

TROY: I told you I know some people down there. I can get you on the rubbish if you want to work. I told you that the last time you came by here asking me for something.

LYONS: Naw, Pop . . . thanks. That ain't for me. I don't wanna be carrying nobody's rubbish. I don't wanna be punching nobody's time clock.

TROY: What's the matter, you too good to carry people's rubbish? Where you think that ten dollars you talking about come from? I'm just supposed to haul people's rubbish and give my money to you cause you too lazy to work. You too lazy to work and wanna know why you ain't got what I got.

ROSE: What hospital Bonnie working at? Mercy?

LYONS: She's down at Passavant working in the laundry.

TROY: I ain't got nothing as it is. I give you that ten dollars and I got to eat beans the rest of the week. Naw . . . you ain't getting no ten dollars here.

LYONS: You ain't got to be eating no beans. I don't know why you wanna say that.

TROY: I ain't got no extra money. Gabe done moved over to Miss Pearl's paying her the rent and things done got tight around here. I can't afford to be giving you every payday.

LYONS: I ain't asked you to give me nothing. I asked you to loan me ten dollars. I know you got ten dollars.

TROY: Yeah, I got it. You know why I got it? Cause I don't throw my money away out there in the streets. You living the fast life . . . wanna be a musician . . . running around in them clubs and things . . . then, you learn to take care of yourself. You ain't gonna find me going and asking nobody for nothing. I done spent too many years without.

LYONS: You and me is two different people, Pop.

TROY: I done learned my mistake and learned to do what's right by it. You still trying to get something for nothing. Life don't owe you nothing. You owe it to yourself. Ask Bono. He'll tell you I'm right.

LYONS: You got your way of dealing with the world . . . I got mine. The only thing that matters to me is the music.

TROY: Yeah, I can see that! It don't matter how you gonna eat . . . where your next dollar is coming from. You telling the truth there.

LYONS: I know I got to eat. But I got to live too. I need something that gonna help me to get out of the bed in the morning. Make me feel like I belong in the world. I don't bother nobody. I just stay with the music cause that's the only way I can find to live in the world. Otherwise there ain't no telling what I might do. Now I don't come criticizing you and how you live. I just come by to ask you for ten dollars. I don't wanna hear all that about how I live.

TROY: Boy, your mamma did a hell of a job raising you.

LYONS: You can't change me, Pop. I'm thirty-four years old. If you wanted to change me, you should have been there when I was growing up. I come by to see you . . . ask for ten dollars and you want to talk about how I was raised. You don't know nothing about how I was raised.

ROSE: Let the boy have ten dollars, Troy.

TROY (*to Lyons*): What the hell you looking at me for? I ain't got no ten dollars. You know what I do with my money. (*To Rose.*) Give him ten dollars if you want him to have it.

ROSE: I will. Just as soon as you turn it loose.

TROY (*handing Rose the money*): There it is. Seventy-six dollars and forty-two cents. You see this, Bono? Now, I ain't gonna get but six of that back.

ROSE: You ought to stop telling that lie. Here, Lyons. (*She hands him the money.*)

LYONS: Thanks, Rose. Look . . . I got to run . . . I'll see you later.

TROY: Wait a minute. You gonna say, "thanks, Rose" and ain't gonna look to see where she got that ten dollars from? See how they do me, Bono?

LYONS: I know she got it from you, Pop. Thanks. I'll give it back to you.

TROY: There he go telling another lie. Time I see that ten dollars . . . he'll be owing me thirty more.

LYONS: See you, Mr. Bono.

BONO: Take care, Lyons!

LYONS: Thanks, Pop. I'll see you again.

*Lyons exits the yard.*

TROY: I don't know why he don't go and get him a decent job and take care of that woman he got.

BONO: He'll be all right, Troy. The boy is still young.

TROY: The *boy* is thirty-four years old.

ROSE: Let's not get off into all that.

BONO: Look here . . . I got to be going. I got to be getting on. Lucille gonna be waiting.

TROY (*puts his arm around Rose*): See this woman, Bono? I love this woman. I love this woman so much it hurts. I love her so much . . . I done run out of ways of loving her. So I got to go back to basics. Don't you come by my house Monday morning talking about time to go to work . . .'cause I'm still gonna be stroking!

ROSE: Troy! Stop it now!

BONO: I ain't paying him no mind, Rose. That ain't nothing but gin-talk. Go on, Troy. I'll see you Monday.

TROY: Don't you come by my house, nigger! I done told you what I'm gonna be doing.

*The lights go down to black.*

## Scene 2

*The lights come up on Rose hanging up clothes. She hums and sings softly to herself. It is the following morning.*

ROSE (*sings*):

Jesus, be a fence all around me every day

Jesus, I want you to protect me as I travel on my way.

Jesus, be a fence all around me every day.

*Troy enters from the house.*

Jesus, I want you to protect me

As I travel on my way.

(*To Troy.*) 'Morning. You ready for breakfast? I can fix it soon as I finish hanging up these clothes?

TROY: I got the coffee on. That'll be all right. I'll just drink some of that this morning.

ROSE: That 651 hit yesterday. That's the second time this month. Miss Pearl hit for a dollar . . . seem like those that need the least always get lucky. Poor folks can't get nothing.

TROY: Them numbers don't know nobody. I don't know why you fool with them. You and Lyons both.

ROSE: It's something to do.

TROY: You ain't doing nothing but throwing your money away.

ROSE: Troy, you know I don't play foolishly. I just play a nickel here and a nickel there.

TROY: That's two nickels you done thrown away.

ROSE: Now I hit sometimes . . . that makes up for it. It always comes in handy when I do hit. I don't hear you complaining then.

TROY: I ain't complaining now. I just say it's foolish. Trying to guess out of six hundred ways which way the number gonna come. If I had all the money niggers, these Negroes, throw away on numbers for one week—just one week—I'd be a rich man.

ROSE: Well, you wishing and calling it foolish ain't gonna stop folks from playing numbers. That's one thing for sure. Besides . . . some good things come from playing numbers. Look where Pope done bought him that restaurant off of numbers.

TROY: I can't stand niggers like that. Man ain't had two dimes to rub together. He walking around with his shoes all run over bumming money for cigarettes. All right. Got lucky there and hit the numbers . . .

ROSE: Troy, I know all about it.

TROY: Had good sense, I'll say that for him. He ain't throwed his money away. I seen niggers hit the numbers and go through two thousand dollars in four days. Man bought him that restaurant down there . . . fixed it up real nice . . . and then didn't want nobody to come in it! A Negro go in there and can't get no kind of service. I seen a white fellow come in there and order a bowl of stew. Pope picked all the meat out of the pot for him. Man ain't had nothing but a bowl of meat! Negro come behind him and ain't got nothing but the potatoes and carrots. Talking about what numbers do for people, you picked a wrong example. Ain't done nothing but make a worser fool out of him than he was before.

ROSE: Troy, you ought to stop worrying about what happened at work yesterday.

TROY: I ain't worried. Just told me to be down there at the Commissioner's office on Friday. Everybody think they gonna fire me. I ain't worried about them firing me. You ain't got to worry about that. (*Pause.*) Where's Cory? Cory in the house? (*Calls.*) Cory?

ROSE: He gone out.

TROY: Out, huh? He gone out 'cause he know I want him to help me with this fence. I know how he is. That boy scared of work.

*Gabriel enters. He comes halfway down the alley and, hearing Troy's voice, stops.*

TROY (*continues*): He ain't done a lick of work in his life.

ROSE: He had to go to football practice. Coach wanted them to get in a little extra practice before the season start.

TROY: I got his practice . . . running out of here before he get his chores done.

ROSE: Troy, what is wrong with you this morning? Don't nothing set right with you. Go on back in there and go to bed . . . get up on the other side.

TROY: Why something got to be wrong with me? I ain't said nothing wrong with me.

ROSE: You got something to say about everything. First it's the numbers . . . then it's the way the man runs his restaurant . . . then you done got on Cory. What's it gonna be next? Take a look up there and see if the weather suits you . . . or is it gonna be how you gonna put up the fence with the clothes hanging in the yard.

TROY: You hit the nail on the head then.

ROSE:   I know you like I know the back of my hand. Go on in there and get you some coffee . . . see if that straighten you up. 'Cause you ain't right this morning.

*Troy starts into the house and sees Gabriel. Gabriel starts singing. Troy's brother, he is seven years younger than Troy. Injured in World War II, he has a metal plate in his head. He carries an old trumpet tied around his waist and believes with every fiber of his being that he is the Archangel Gabriel. He carries a chipped basket with an assortment of discarded fruits and vegetables he has picked up in the strip district and which he attempts to sell.*

GABRIEL (*singing*):
　　Yes, ma'am I got plums
　　You ask me how I sell them
　　Oh ten cents apiece
　　Three for a quarter
　　Come and buy now
　　'Cause I'm here today
　　And tomorrow I'll be gone

*Gabriel enters.*

　　Hey, Rose!
ROSE:   How you doing Gabe?
GABRIEL:   There's Troy . . . Hey, Troy!
TROY:   Hey, Gabe.

*Exit into kitchen.*

ROSE (*to Gabriel*):   What you got there?
GABRIEL:   You know what I got, Rose. I got fruits and vegetables.
ROSE (*looking in basket*):   Where's all these plums you talking about?
GABRIEL:   I ain't got no plums today, Rose. I was just singing that. Have some tomorrow. Put me in a big order for plums. Have enough plums tomorrow for St. Peter and everybody.

*Troy reenters from kitchen, crosses to steps.*

　　(*To Rose.*) Troy's mad at me.
TROY:   I ain't mad at you. What I got to be mad at you about? You ain't done nothing to me.

GABRIEL: I just moved over to Miss Pearl's to keep out from in your way. I ain't mean no harm by it.

TROY: Who said anything about that? I ain't said anything about that.

GABRIEL: You ain't mad at me, is you?

TROY: Naw . . . I ain't mad at you, Gabe. If I was mad at you I'd tell you about it.

GABRIEL: Got me two rooms. In the basement. Got my own door too. Wanna see my key? (*He holds up a key.*) That's my own key! My two rooms!

TROY: Well, that's good, Gabe. You got your own key . . . that's good.

ROSE: You hungry, Gabe? I was just fixing to cook Troy his breakfast.

GABRIEL: I'll take some biscuits. You got some biscuits? Did you know when I was in heaven . . . every morning me and St. Peter would sit down by the gate and eat some big fat biscuits? Oh, yeah! We had us a good time. We'd sit there and eat us them biscuits and then St. Peter would go off to sleep and tell me to wake him up when it's time to open the gates for the judgment.

ROSE: Well, come on . . . I'll make up a batch of biscuits.

*Rose exits into the house.*

GABRIEL: Troy . . . St. Peter got your name in the book. I seen it. It say . . . Troy Maxson. I say . . . I know him! He got the same name like what I got. That's my brother!

TROY: How many times you gonna tell me that, Gabe?

GABRIEL: Ain't got my name in the book. Don't have to have my name. I done died and went to heaven. He got your name though. One morning St. Peter was looking at his book . . . marking it up for the judgment . . . and he let me see your name. Got it in there under M. Got Rose's name . . . I ain't seen it like I seen yours . . . but I know it's in there. He got a great big book. Got everybody's name what was ever been born. That's what he told me. But I seen your name. Seen it with my own eyes.

TROY: Go on in the house there. Rose going to fix you something to eat.

GABRIEL: Oh, I ain't hungry. I done had breakfast with Aunt Jemimah. She come by and cooked me up a whole mess of flapjacks. Remember how we used to eat them flapjacks?

TROY: Go on in the house and get you something to eat now.

GABRIEL: I got to sell my plums. I done sold some tomatoes. Got me two quarters. Wanna see? (*He shows Troy his quarters.*) I'm gonna save them and buy me a new horn so St. Peter can hear me when it's time to open the gates. (*Gabriel stops suddenly. Listens.*) Hear that? That's the hellhounds. I got to chase them out of here. Go on get out of here! Get out!

*Gabriel exits singing.*

Better get ready for the judgment
Better get ready for the judgment
My Lord is coming down

*Rose enters from the house.*

TROY: He's gone off somewhere.

GABRIEL (*offstage*):
Better get ready for the judgment
Better get ready for the judgment morning
Better get ready for the judgment
My God is coming down

ROSE: He ain't eating right. Miss Pearl say she can't get him to eat nothing.

TROY: What you want me to do about it, Rose? I done did everything I can for the man. I can't make him get well. Man got half his head blown away . . . what you expect?

ROSE: Seem like something ought to be done to help him.

TROY: Man don't bother nobody. He just mixed up from that metal plate he got in his head. Ain't no sense for him to go back into the hospital.

ROSE: Least he be eating right. They can help him take care of himself.

TROY: Don't nobody wanna be locked up, Rose. What you wanna lock him up for? Man go over there and fight the war . . . messin' around with them Japs, get half his head blow off . . . and they give him a lousy three thousand dollars. And I had to swoop down on that.

ROSE: Is you fixing to go into that again?

TROY: That's the only way I got a roof over my head . . . cause of that metal plate.

ROSE: Ain't no sense you blaming yourself for nothing. Gabe wasn't in no condition to manage that money. You done what was right by him. Can't nobody say you ain't done what was right by him. Look how long you took care of him . . . till he wanted to have his own place and moved over there with Miss Pearl.

TROY: That ain't what I'm saying, woman! I'm just stating the facts. If my brother didn't have that metal plate in his head . . . I wouldn't have a pot to piss in or a window to throw it out of. And I'm fifty-three years old. Now see if you can understand that!

*Troy gets up from the porch and starts to exit the yard.*

ROSE: Where you going off to? You been running out of here every Saturday for weeks. I thought you was gonna work on this fence?

TROY: I'm gonna walk down to Taylor's. Listen to the ball game. I'll be back in a bit. I'll work on it when I get back.

*He exits the yard. The lights go to black.*

## SCENE 3

*The lights come up on the yard. It is four hours later. Rose is taking down the clothes from the line. Cory enters carrying his football equipment.*

ROSE: Your daddy like to had a fit with you running out of here this morning without doing your chores.

CORY: I told you I had to go to practice.

ROSE: He say you were supposed to help him with this fence.

CORY: He been saying that the last four or five Saturdays, and then he don't never do nothing, but go down to Taylors'. Did you tell him about the recruiter?

ROSE: Yeah, I told him.

CORY: What he say?

ROSE: He ain't said nothing too much. You get in there and get started on your chores before he gets back. Go on and scrub down them steps before he gets back here hollering and carrying on.

CORY: I'm hungry. What you got to eat, Mama?

ROSE: Go on and get started on your chores. I got some meat loaf in there. Go on and make you a sandwich . . . and don't leave no mess in there.

*Cory exits into the house. Rose continues to take down the clothes. Troy enters the yard and sneaks up and grabs her from behind.*

Troy! Go on, now. You liked to scared me to death. What was the score of the game? Lucille had me on the phone and I couldn't keep up with it.

TROY: What I care about the game? Come here, woman. (*He tries to kiss her.*)

ROSE:  I thought you went down Taylors' to listen to the game. Go on, Troy! You supposed to be putting up this fence.

TROY *(attempting to kiss her again)*:  I'll put it up when I finish with what is at hand.

ROSE:  Go on, Troy. I ain't studying you.

TROY *(chasing after her)*:  I'm studying you . . . fixing to do my homework!

ROSE:  Troy, you better leave me alone.

TROY:  Where's Cory? That boy brought his butt home yet?

ROSE:  He's in the house doing his chores.

TROY *(calling)*:  Cory! Get your butt out here, boy!

*Rose exits into the house with the laundry. Troy goes over to the pile of wood, picks up a board, and starts sawing. Cory enters from the house.*

TROY:  You just now coming in here from leaving this morning?

CORY:  Yeah, I had to go to football practice.

TROY:  Yeah, what?

CORY:  Yessir.

TROY:  I ain't but two seconds off you noway. The garbage sitting in there overflowing . . . you ain't done none of your chores . . . and you come in here talking about "Yeah."

CORY:  I was just getting ready to do my chores now, Pop . . .

TROY:  Your first chore is to help me with this fence on Saturday. Everything else come after that. Now get that saw and cut them boards.

*Cory takes the saw and begins cutting the boards. Troy continues working. There is a long pause.*

CORY:  Hey, Pop . . . why don't you buy a TV?

TROY:  What I want with a TV? What I want one of them for?

CORY:  Everybody got one. Earl, Ba Bra . . . Jesse!

TROY:  I ain't asked you who had one. I say what I want with one?

CORY:  So you can watch it. They got lots of things on TV. Baseball games and everything. We could watch the World Series.

TROY:  Yeah . . . and how much this TV cost?

CORY:  I don't know. They got them on sale for around two hundred dollars.

TROY:  Two hundred dollars, huh?

CORY:  That ain't that much, Pop.

TROY: Naw, it's just two hundred dollars. See that roof you got over your head at night? Let me tell you something about that roof. It's been over ten years since that roof was last tarred. See now . . . the snow come this winter and sit up there on that roof like it is . . . and it's gonna seep inside. It's just gonna be a little bit . . . ain't gonna hardly notice it. Then the next thing you know, it's gonna be leaking all over the house. Then the wood rot from all that water and you gonna need a whole new roof. Now, how much you think it cost to get that roof tarred?

CORY: I don't know.

TROY: Two hundred and sixty-four dollars . . . cash money. While you thinking about a TV, I got to be thinking about the roof . . . and whatever else go wrong here. Now if you had two hundred dollars, what would you do . . . fix the roof or buy a TV?

CORY: I'd buy a TV. Then when the roof started to leak . . . when it needed fixing . . . I'd fix it.

TROY: Where you gonna get the money from? You done spent it for a TV. You gonna sit up and watch the water run all over your brand new TV.

CORY: Aw, Pop. You got money. I know you do.

TROY: Where I got it at, huh?

CORY: You got it in the bank.

TROY: You wanna see my bankbook? You wanna see that seventy-three dollars and twenty-two cents I got sitting up in there?

CORY: You ain't got to pay for it all at one time. You can put a down payment on it and carry it on home with you.

TROY: Not me. I ain't gonna owe nobody nothing if I can help it. Miss a payment and they come and snatch it right out of your house. Then what you got? Now, soon as I get two hundred dollars clear, then I'll buy a TV. Right now, as soon as I get two hundred and sixty-four dollars, I'm gonna have this roof tarred.

CORY: Aw . . . Pop!

TROY: You go on and get you two hundred dollars and buy one if ya want it. I got better things to do with my money.

CORY: I can't get no two hundred dollars. I ain't never seen two hundred dollars.

TROY: I'll tell you what . . . you get you a hundred dollars and I'll put the other hundred with it.

CORY: All right, I'm gonna show you.

TROY: You gonna show me how you can cut them boards right now.

*Cory begins to cut the boards. There is a long pause.*

CORY: The Pirates won today. That makes five in a row.

TROY: I ain't thinking about the Pirates. Got an all-white team. Got that boy . . . that Puerto Rican boy . . . Clemente. Don't even half-play him. That boy could be something if they give him a chance. Play him one day and sit him on the bench the next.

CORY: He gets a lot of chances to play.

TROY: I'm talking about playing regular. Playing every day so you can get your timing. That's what I'm talking about.

CORY: They got some white guys on the team that don't play every day. You can't play everybody at the same time.

TROY: If they got a white fellow sitting on the bench . . . you can bet your last dollar he can't play! The colored guy got to be twice as good before he get on the team. That's why I don't want you to get all tied up in them sports. Man on the team and what it get him? They got colored on the team and don't use them. Same as not having them. All them teams the same.

CORY: The Braves got Hank Aaron and Wes Covington. Hank Aaron hit two home runs today. That makes forty-three.

TROY: Hank Aaron ain't nobody. That what you supposed to do. That's how you supposed to play the game. Ain't nothing to it. It's just a matter of timing . . . getting the right follow-through. Hell, I can hit forty-three home runs right now!

CORY: Not off no major-league pitching, you couldn't.

TROY: We had better pitching in the Negro leagues. I hit seven home runs off of Satchel Paige.[4] You can't get no better than that!

CORY: Sandy Koufax. He's leading the league in strikeouts.

TROY: I ain't thinking of no Sandy Koufax.

CORY: You got Warren Spahn and Lew Burdette. I bet you couldn't hit no home runs off of Warren Spahn.

TROY: I'm through with it now. You go on and cut them boards. *(Pause.)* Your mama tell me you done got recruited by a college football team? Is that right?

CORY: Yeah. Coach Zellman say the recruiter gonna be coming by to talk to you. Get you to sign the permission papers.

TROY: I thought you supposed to be working down there at the A&P. Ain't you suppose to be working down there after school?

---

[4]Paige (1906–1982) was a pitcher in the Negro leagues and later played briefly in the majors.

CORY: Mr. Stawicki say he gonna hold my job for me until after the football season. Say starting next week I can work weekends.

TROY: I thought we had an understanding about this football stuff? You suppose to keep up with your chores and hold that job down at the A&P. Ain't been around here all day on a Saturday. Ain't none of your chores done . . . and now you telling me you done quit your job.

CORY: I'm going to be working weekends.

TROY: You damn right you are! And ain't no need for nobody coming around here to talk to me about signing nothing.

CORY: Hey, Pop . . . you can't do that. He's coming all the way from North Carolina.

TROY: I don't care where he coming from. The white man ain't gonna let you get nowhere with that football noway. You go on and get your book-learning so you can work yourself up in that A&P or learn how to fix cars or build houses or something, get you a trade. That way you have something can't nobody take away from you. You go on and learn how to put your hands to some good use. Besides hauling people's garbage.

CORY: I get good grades, Pop. That's why the recruiter wants to talk with you. You got to keep up your grades to get recruited. This way I'll be going to college. I'll get a chance . . .

TROY: First you gonna get your butt down there to the A&P and get your job back.

CORY: Mr. Stawicki done already hired somebody else 'cause I told him I was playing football.

TROY: You a bigger fool than I thought . . . to let somebody take away your job so you can play some football. Where you gonna get your money to take out your girlfriend and whatnot? What kind of foolishness is that to let somebody take away your job?

CORY: I'm still gonna be working weekends.

TROY: Naw . . . naw. You getting your butt out of here and finding you another job.

CORY: Come on, Pop! I got to practice. I can't work after school and play football too. The team needs me. That's what Coach Zellman say . . .

TROY: I don't care what nobody else say. I'm the boss . . . you understand? I'm the boss around here. I do the only saying what counts.

CORY: Come on, Pop!

TROY: I asked you . . . did you understand?

CORY: Yeah . . .

TROY: What?!

CORY: Yessir.

TROY: You go on down there to that A&P and see if you can get your job back. If you can't do both . . . then you quit the football team. You've got to take the crookeds with the straights.

CORY: Yessir. (*Pause.*) Can I ask you a question?

TROY: What the hell you wanna ask me? Mr. Stawicki the one you got the questions for.

CORY: How come you ain't never liked me?

TROY: Liked you? Who the hell say I got to like you? What law is there say I got to like you? Wanna stand up in my face and ask a damn foolass question like that. Talking about liking somebody. Come here, boy, when I talk to you.

*Cory comes over to where Troy is working. He stands slouched over and Troy shoves him on his shoulder.*

Straighten up, goddammit! I asked you a question . . . what law is there say I got to like you?

CORY: None.

TROY: Well, all right then! Don't you eat every day? (*Pause.*) Answer me when I talk to you! Don't you eat every day?

CORY: Yeah.

TROY: Nigger, as long as you in my house, you put that sir on the end of it when you talk to me.

CORY: Yes . . . sir.

TROY: You eat every day.

CORY: Yessir!

TROY: Got a roof over your head.

CORY: Yessir!

TROY: Got clothes on your back.

CORY: Yessir.

TROY: Why you think that is?

CORY: Cause of you.

TROY: Ah, hell I know it's cause of me . . . but why do you think that is?

CORY (*hesitant*): Cause you like me.

TROY: Like you? I go out of here every morning . . . bust my butt
. . . putting up with them crackers every day . . . cause I like you?
You are the biggest fool I ever saw. (*Pause.*) It's my job. It's my responsibility! You understand that? A man got to take care of his
family. You live in my house . . . sleep you behind on my bed-
clothes . . . fill you belly up with my food . . . cause you my son.
You my flesh and blood. Not cause I like you! Cause it's my duty to
take care of you. I owe a responsibility to you! Let's get this
straight right here . . . before it go along any further . . . I ain't
got to like you. Mr. Rand don't give me my money come payday
cause he likes me. He gives me cause he owe me. I done give you
everything I had to give you. I gave you your life! Me and your
mama worked that out between us. And liking your black ass was-
n't part of the bargain. Don't you try and go through life worrying
about if somebody like you or not. You best be making sure they
doing right by you. You understand what I'm saying boy?

CORY: Yessir.

TROY: Then get the hell out of my face, and get on down to that
A&P.

*Rose has been standing behind the screen door for much of
the scene. She enters as Cory exits.*

ROSE: Why don't you let the boy go ahead and play football, Troy?
Ain't no harm in that. He's just trying to be like you with the sports.

TROY: I don't want him to be like me! I want him to move as far away
from my life as he can get. You the only decent thing that ever happened to me. I wish him that. But I don't wish him a thing else from
my life. I decided seventeen years ago that boy wasn't getting involved in no sports. Not after what they did to me in the sports.

ROSE: Troy, why don't you admit you was too old to play in the major leagues? For once . . . why don't you admit that?

TROY: What do you mean too old? Don't come telling me I was too
old. I just wasn't the right color. Hell, I'm fifty-three years old and
can do better than Selkirk's .269 right now!

ROSE: How's was you gonna play ball when you were over forty?
Sometimes I can't get no sense out of you.

TROY: I got good sense, woman. I got sense enough not to let my boy
get hurt over playing no sports. You been mothering that boy too
much. Worried about if people like him.

ROSE: Everything that boy do . . . he do for you. He wants you to say "Good job, son." That's all.

TROY: Rose, I ain't got time for that. He's alive. He's healthy. He's got to make his own way. I made mine. Ain't nobody gonna hold his hand when he get out there in that world.

ROSE: Times have changed from when you was young, Troy. People change. The world's changing around you and you can't even see it.

TROY (*slow, methodical*): Woman . . . I do the best I can do. I come in here every Friday. I carry a sack of potatoes and a bucket of lard. You all line up at the door with your hands out. I give you the lint from my pockets. I give you my sweat and my blood. I ain't got no tears. I done spent them. We go upstairs in that room at night . . . and I fall down on you and try to blast a hole into forever. I get up Monday morning . . . find my lunch on the table. I go out. Make my way. Find my strength to carry me through to the next Friday. (*Pause.*) That's all I got, Rose. That's all I got to give. I can't give nothing else.

*Troy exits into the house. The lights go down to black.*

## Scene 4

*It is Friday. Two weeks later. Cory starts out of the house with his football equipment. The phone rings.*

CORY (*calling*): I got it! (*He answers the phone and stands in the screen door talking.*) Hello? Hey, Jesse. Naw . . . I was just getting ready to leave now.

ROSE (*calling*): Cory!

CORY: I told you, man, them spikes is all tore up. You can use them if you want, but they ain't no good. Earl got some spikes.

ROSE (*calling*): Cory!

CORY (*calling to Rose*): Mam? I'm talking to Jesse. (*Into phone.*) When she say that? (*Pause.*) Aw, you lying, man. I'm gonna tell her you said that.

ROSE (*calling*): Cory, don't you go nowhere!

CORY: I got to go to the game, Ma! (*Into the phone.*) Yeah, hey, look, I'll talk to you later. Yeah, I'll meet you over Earl's house. Later. Bye, Ma.

*Cory exits the house and starts out the yard.*

ROSE:   Cory, where you going off to? You got that stuff all pulled out and thrown all over your room.

CORY *(in the yard)*:   I was looking for my spikes. Jesse wanted to borrow my spikes.

ROSE:   Get up there and get that cleaned up before your daddy get back in here.

CORY:   I got to go to the game! I'll clean it up *when I get back.*

*Cory exits.*

ROSE:   That's all he need to do is see that room all messed up.

*Rose exits into the house. Troy and Bono enter the yard. Troy is dressed in clothes other than his work clothes.*

BONO:   He told him the same thing he told you. Take it to the union.

TROY:   Brownie ain't got that much sense. Man wasn't thinking about nothing. He wait until I confront them on it . . . then he wanna come crying seniority. *(Calls.)* Hey, Rose!

BONO:   I wish I could have seen Mr. Rand's face when he told you.

TROY:   He couldn't get it out of his mouth! Liked to bit his tongue! When they called me down there to the Commissioner's office . . . he thought they was gonna fire me. Like everybody else.

BONO:   I didn't think they was gonna fire you. I thought they was gonna put you on the warning paper.

TROY:   Hey, Rose! *(To Bono.)* Yeah, Mr. Rand like to bit his tongue.

*Troy breaks the seal on the bottle, takes a drink, and hands it to Bono.*

BONO:   I see you run right down to Taylors' and told that Alberta gal.

TROY *(calling)*:   Hey Rose! *(To Bono.)* I told everybody. Hey, Rose! I went down there to cash my check.

ROSE *(entering from the house)*:   Hush all that hollering, man! I know you out here. What they say down there at the Commissioner's office?

TROY:   You supposed to come when I call you, woman. Bono'll tell you that. *(To Bono.)* Don't Lucille come when you call her?

ROSE:   Man, hush your mouth. I ain't no dog . . . talk about "come when you call me."

TROY *(puts his arm around Rose)*:   You hear this, Bono? I had me an old dog used to get uppity like that. You say, "C'mere, Blue!" . . .

and he just lay there and look at you. End up getting a stick and chasing him away trying to make him come.

ROSE: I ain't studying you and your dog. I remember you used to sing that old song.

TROY (*he sings*):
Hear it ring! Hear it ring! I had a dog his name was Blue.

ROSE: Don't nobody wanna hear you sing that old song.

TROY (*sings*):
You know Blue was mighty true.

ROSE: Used to have Cory running around here singing that song.

BONO: Hell, I remember that song myself.

TROY (*sings*):
You know Blue was a good old dog.
Blue treed a possum in a hollow log.
That was my daddy's song. My daddy made up that song.

ROSE: I don't care who made it up. Don't nobody wanna hear you sing it.

TROY (*makes a song like calling a dog*): Come here, woman.

ROSE: You come in here carrying on, I reckon they ain't fired you. What they say down there at the Commissioner's office?

TROY: Look here, Rose . . . Mr. Rand called me into his office today when I got back from talking to them people down there . . . it come from up top . . . he called me in and told me they was making me a driver.

ROSE: Troy, you kidding!

TROY: No I ain't. Ask Bono.

ROSE: Well, that's great, Troy. Now you don't have to hassle them people no more.

*Lyons enters from the street.*

TROY: Aw hell, I wasn't looking to see you today. I thought you was in jail. Got it all over the front page of the *Courier* about them raiding Sefus's place . . . where you be hanging out with all them thugs.

LYONS: Hey, Pop . . . that ain't got nothing to do with me. I don't go down there gambling. I go down there to sit in with the band. I ain't got nothing to do with the gambling part. They got some good music down there.

TROY: They got some rogues . . . is what they got.

LYONS: How you been, Mr. Bono? Hi, Rose.

BONO: I see where you playing down at the Crawford Grill tonight.

ROSE: How come you ain't brought Bonnie like I told you? You should have brought Bonnie with you, she ain't been over in a month of Sundays.

LYONS: I was just in the neighborhood . . . thought I'd stop by.

TROY: Here he come . . .

BONO: Your daddy got a promotion on the rubbish. He's gonna be the first colored driver. Ain't got to do nothing but sit up there and read the paper like them white fellows.

LYONS: Hey, Pop . . . if you knew how to read you'd be all right.

BONO: Naw . . . naw . . . you mean if the nigger knew how to drive he'd be all right. Been fighting with them people about driving and ain't even got a license. Mr. Rand know you ain't got no driver's license?

TROY: Driving ain't nothing. All you do is point the truck where you want it to go. Driving ain't nothing.

BONO: Do Mr. Rand know you ain't got no driver's license? That's what I'm talking about. I ain't asked if driving was easy. I asked if Mr. Rand know you ain't got no driver's license.

TROY: He ain't got to know. The man ain't got to know my business. Time he find out, I have two or three driver's licenses.

LYONS (*going into his pocket*): Say, look here, Pop . . .

TROY: I knew it was coming. Didn't I tell you, Bono? I know what kind of "Look here, Pop" that was. The nigger fixing to ask me for some money. It's Friday night. It's my payday. All them rogues down there on the avenue . . . the ones that ain't in jail . . . and Lyons is hopping in his shoes to get down there with them.

LYONS: See, Pop . . . if you give somebody else a chance to talk sometimes, you'd see that I was fixing to pay you back your ten dollars like I told you. Here . . . I told you I'd pay you when Bonnie got paid.

TROY: Naw . . . you go ahead and keep that ten dollars. Put it in the bank. The next time you feel like you wanna come by here and ask me for something . . . you go on down there and get that.

LYONS: Here's your ten dollars, Pop. I told you I don't want you to give me nothing. I just wanted to borrow ten dollars.

TROY: Naw . . . you go on and keep that for the next time you want to ask me.

LYONS: Come on, Pop . . . here go your ten dollars.

ROSE: Why don't you go on and let the boy pay you back, Troy?

LYONS: Here you go, Rose. If you don't take it I'm gonna have to hear about it for the next six months. (*He hands her the money.*)

ROSE: You can hand yours over here too, Troy.

TROY: You see this, Bono. You see how they do me.

BONO: Yeah, Lucille do me the same way.

*Gabriel is heard singing off stage. He enters.*

GABRIEL: Better get ready for the Judgment! Better get ready for . . . Hey!. . . Hey!. . . There's Troy's boy!

LYONS: How are you doing, Uncle Gabe?

GABRIEL: Lyons . . . The King of the Jungle! Rose . . . hey, Rose. Got a flower for you. (*He takes a rose from his pocket.*) Picked it myself. That's the same rose like you is!

ROSE: That's right nice of you, Gabe.

LYONS: What you been doing, Uncle Gabe?

GABRIEL: Oh, I been chasing hellhounds and waiting on the time to tell St. Peter to open the gates.

LYONS: You been chasing hellhounds, huh? Well . . . you doing the right thing, Uncle Gabe. Somebody got to chase them.

GABRIEL: Oh, yeah . . . I know it. The devil's strong. The devil ain't no pushover. Hellhounds snipping at everybody's heels. But I got my trumpet waiting on the judgment time.

LYONS: Waiting on the Battle of Armageddon, huh?

GABRIEL: Ain't gonna be too much of a battle when God get to waving that Judgment sword. But the people's gonna have a hell of a time trying to get into heaven if them gates ain't open.

LYONS (*putting his arm around Gabriel*): You hear this, Pop. Uncle Gabe, you all right!

GABRIEL (*laughing with Lyons*): Lyons! King of the Jungle.

ROSE: You gonna stay for supper, Gabe? Want me to fix you a plate?

GABRIEL: I'll take a sandwich, Rose. Don't want no plate. Just wanna eat with my hands. I'll take a sandwich.

ROSE: How about you, Lyons? You staying? Got some short ribs cooking.

LYONS: Naw, I won't eat nothing till after we finished playing. (*Pause.*) You ought to come down and listen to me play, Pop.

TROY: I don't like that Chinese music. All that noise.

ROSE: Go on in the house and wash up, Gabe . . . I'll fix you a sandwich.

GABRIEL (*to Lyons, as he exits*): Troy's mad at me.

LYONS: What you mad at Uncle Gabe for, Pop?

ROSE: He thinks Troy's mad at him cause he moved over to Miss Pearl's.

TROY: I ain't mad at the man. He can live where he want to live at.

LYONS: What he move over there for? Miss Pearl don't like nobody.

ROSE: She don't mind him none. She treats him real nice. She just don't allow all that singing.

TROY: She don't mind that rent he be paying . . . that's what she don't mind.

ROSE: Troy, I ain't going through that with you no more. He's over there cause he want to have his own place. He can come and go as he please.

TROY: Hell, he could come and go as he please here. I wasn't stopping him. I ain't put no rules on him.

ROSE: It ain't the same thing, Troy. And you know it.

*Gabriel comes to the door.*

Now, that's the last I wanna hear about that. I don't wanna hear nothing else about Gabe and Miss Pearl. And next week . . .

GABRIEL: I'm ready for my sandwich, Rose.

ROSE: And next week . . . when that recruiter come from that school . . . I want you to sign that paper and go on and let Cory play football. Then that'll be the last I have to hear about that.

TROY (*to Rose as she exits into the house*): I ain't thinking about Cory nothing.

LYONS: What . . . Cory got recruited? What school he going to?

TROY: That boy walking around here smelling his piss . . . thinking he's grown. Thinking he's gonna do what he want, irrespective of what I say. Look here, Bono . . . I left the Commissioner's office and went down to the A&P . . . that boy ain't working down there. He lying to me. Telling me he got his job back . . . telling me he working weekends . . . telling me he working after school . . . Mr. Stawicki tell me he ain't working down there at all!

LYONS: Cory just growing up. He's just busting at the seams trying to fill out your shoes.

TROY: I don't care what he's doing. When he get to the point where he wanna disobey me . . . then it's time for him to move on. Bono'll tell you that. I bet he ain't never disobeyed his daddy without paying the consequences.

BONO: I ain't never had a chance. My daddy came on through . . . but I ain't never knew him to see him . . . or what he had on his mind or where he went. Just moving on through. Searching out the New Land. That's what the old folks used to call it. See a fellow moving around from place to place . . . woman to woman . . . called it searching out the New Land. I can't say if he ever found it.

I come along, didn't want no kids. Didn't know if I was gonna be in one place long enough to fix on them right as their daddy. I figured I was going searching too. As it turned out I been hooked up with Lucille near about as long as your daddy been with Rose. Going on sixteen years.

TROY: Sometimes I wish I hadn't known my daddy. He ain't cared nothing about no kids. A kid to him wasn't nothing. All he wanted was for you to learn how to walk so he could start you to working. When it come time for eating . . . he ate first. If there was anything left over, that's what you got. Man would sit down and eat two chickens and give you the wing.

LYONS: You ought to stop that, Pop. Everybody feed their kids. No matter how hard times is . . . everybody care about their kids. Make sure they have something to eat.

TROY: The only thing my daddy cared about was getting them bales of cotton in to Mr. Lubin. That's the only thing that mattered to him. Sometimes I used to wonder why he was living. Wonder why the devil hadn't come and got him. "Get them bales of cotton in to Mr. Lubin" and find out he owe him money . . .

LYONS: He should have just went on and left when he saw he couldn't get nowhere. That's what I would have done.

TROY: How he gonna leave with eleven kids? And where he gonna go? He ain't knew how to do nothing but farm. No, he was trapped and I think he knew it. But I'll say this for him . . . he felt a responsibility toward us. Maybe he ain't treated us the way I felt he should have . . . but without that responsibility he could have walked off and left us . . . made his own way.

BONO: A lot of them did. Back in those days what you talking about . . . they walk out their front door and just take on down one road or another and keep on walking.

LYONS: There you go! That's what I'm talking about.

BONO: Just keep on walking till you come to something else. Ain't you never heard of nobody having the walking blues? Well, that's what you call it when you just take off like that.

TROY: My daddy ain't had them walking blues! What you talking about? He stayed right there with his family. But he was just as evil as he could be. My mama couldn't stand him. Couldn't stand that evilness. She run off when I was about eight. She sneaked off one night after he had gone to sleep. Told me she was coming back for me. I ain't never seen her no more. All his women run off and left him. He wasn't good for nobody.

When my turn come to head out, I was fourteen and got to sniffing around Joe Canewell's daughter. Had us an old mule we called Greyboy. My daddy sent me out to do some plowing and I tied up Greyboy and went to fooling around with Joe Canewell's daughter. We done found us a nice little spot, got real cozy with each other. She about thirteen and we done figured we was grown anyway . . . so we down there enjoying ourselves . . . ain't thinking about nothing. We didn't know Greyboy had got loose and wandered back to the house and my daddy was looking for me. We down there by the creek enjoying ourselves when my daddy come up on us. Surprised us. He had them leather straps off the mule and commenced to whupping me like there was no tomorrow. I jumped up, mad and embarrassed. I was scared of my daddy. When he commenced to whupping on me . . . quite naturally I run to get out of the way. (*Pause.*) Now I thought he was mad cause I ain't done my work. But I see where he was chasing me off so he could have the gal for himself. When I see what the matter of it was, I lost all fear of my daddy. Right there is where I become a man . . . at fourteen years of age. (*Pause.*) Now it was my turn to run him off. I picked up them same reins that he had used on me. I picked up them reins and commenced to whupping on him. The gal jumped up and run off . . . and when my daddy turned to face me, I could see why the devil had never come to get him . . . cause he was the devil himself. I don't know what happened. When I woke up, I was laying right there by the creek, and Blue . . . this old dog we had . . . was licking my face. I thought I was blind. I couldn't see nothing. Both my eyes were swollen shut. I laid there and cried. I didn't know what I was gonna do. The only thing I knew was the time had come for me to leave my daddy's house. And right there the world suddenly got big. And it was a long time before I could cut it down to where I could handle it.

Part of that cutting down was when I got to the place where I could feel him kicking in my blood and knew that the only thing that separated us was the matter of a few years.

*Gabriel enters from the house with a sandwich.*

LYONS: What you got there, Uncle Gabe?

GABRIEL: Got me a ham sandwich. Rose gave me a ham sandwich.

TROY: I don't know what happened to him. I done lost touch with everybody except Gabriel. But I hope he's dead. I hope he found some peace.

LYONS: That's a heavy story, Pop. I didn't know you left home when you was fourteen.

TROY: And didn't know nothing. The only part of the world I knew was the forty-two acres of Mr. Lubin's land. That's all I knew about life.

LYONS: Fourteen's kinda young to be out on your own. (*Phone rings.*) I don't even think I was ready to be out on my own at fourteen. I don't know what I would have done.

TROY: I got up from the creek and walked on down to Mobile. I was through with farming. Figured I could do better in the city. So I walked the two hundred miles to Mobile.

LYONS: Wait a minute . . . you ain't walked no two hundred miles, Pop. Ain't nobody gonna walk no two hundred miles. You talking about some walking there.

BONO: That's the only way you got anywhere back in them days.

LYONS: Shhh. Damn if I wouldn't have hitched a ride with somebody!

TROY: Who you gonna hitch it with? They ain't had no cars and things like they got now. We talking about 1918.

ROSE (*entering*): What you all out here getting into?

TROY (*to Rose*): I'm telling Lyons how good he got it. He don't know nothing about this I'm talking.

ROSE: Lyons, that was Bonnie on the phone. She say you supposed to pick her up.

LYONS: Yeah, okay, Rose.

TROY: I walked on down to Mobile and hitched up with some of them fellows that was heading this way. Got up here and found out . . . not only couldn't you get a job . . . you couldn't find no place to live. I thought I was in freedom. Shhh. Colored folks living down there on the riverbanks in whatever kind of shelter they could find for themselves. Right down there under the Brady Street Bridge. Living in shacks made of sticks and tarpaper. Messed around there and went from bad to worse. Started stealing. First it was food. Then I figured, hell, if I steal money I can buy me some food. Buy me some shoes too! One thing led to another. Met your mama. I was young and anxious to be a man. Met your mama and had you. What I do that for? Now I got to worry about feeding you and her. Got to steal three times as much. Went out one day looking for somebody to rob . . . that's what I was, a robber. I'll tell you the truth. I'm ashamed of it today. But it's the truth. Went to rob this fellow . . . pulled out my knife . . . and he pulled out a gun. Shot me in the chest. I felt just like somebody had taken a hot branding iron and laid it on me. When he shot me I jumped at him with my knife. They told me I killed him and they put me in the penitentiary and locked me up for fifteen years. That's where I met Bono. That's where I learned how to play baseball. Got out that place and your mama had taken you and went on to make life without me. Fifteen years was a long time for her to wait. But that fifteen years cured me of that robbing stuff. Rose'll tell you. She asked me when I met her if I had gotten all that foolishness out of my system. And I told her, "Baby, it's you and baseball all what count with me." You hear me, Bono? I meant it too. She say, "Which one comes first?" I told her, "Baby, ain't no doubt it's baseball . . . but you stick and get old with me and we'll both outlive this baseball." Am I right, Rose? And it's true.

ROSE: Man, hush your mouth. You ain't said no such thing. Talking about, "Baby you know you'll always be number one with me." That's what you was talking.

TROY: You hear that, Bono. That's why I love her.

BONO: Rose'll keep you straight. You get off the track, she'll straighten you up.

ROSE: Lyons, you better get on up and get Bonnie. She waiting on you.

LYONS (*gets up to go*): Hey, Pop, why don't you come on down to the Grill and hear me play?

TROY: I ain't going down there. I'm too old to be sitting around in them clubs.

BONO: You got to be good to play down at the Grill.

LYONS: Come on, Pop . . .

TROY: I got to get up in the morning.

LYONS: You ain't got to stay long.

TROY: Naw, I'm gonna get my supper and go on to bed.

LYONS: Well, I got to go. I'll see you again.

TROY: Don't you come around my house on my payday.

ROSE: Pick up the phone and let somebody know you coming. And bring Bonnie with you. You know I'm always glad to see her.

LYONS: Yeah, I'll do that, Rose. You take care now. See you, Pop. See you, Mr. Bono. See you, Uncle Gabe.

GABRIEL: Lyons! King of the Jungle!

*Lyons exits.*

TROY: Is supper ready, woman? Me and you got some business to take care of. I'm gonna tear it up too.

ROSE: Troy, I done told you now!

TROY (*puts his arm around Bono*): Aw hell, woman . . . this is Bono. Bono like family. I done known this nigger since . . . how long I done know you?

BONO: It's been a long time.

TROY: I done know this nigger since Skippy was a pup. Me and him done been through some times.

BONO: You sure right about that.

TROY: Hell, I done know him longer than I known you. And we still standing shoulder to shoulder. Hey, look here, Bono . . . a man can't ask for no more than that. (*Drinks to him.*) I love you, nigger.

BONO: Hell, I love you too . . . I got to get home see my woman. You got yours in hand. I got to get mine.

*Bono starts to exit as Cory enters the yard, dressed in his football uniform. He gives Troy a hard, uncompromising look.*

CORY: What you do that for, Pop?

*He throws his helmet down in the direction of Troy.*

ROSE: What's the matter? Cory . . . what's the matter?

CORY: Papa done went up to the school and told Coach Zellman I can't play football no more. Wouldn't even let me play the game. Told him to tell the recruiter not to come.

ROSE: Troy . . .

TROY: What you Troying me for. Yeah, I did it. And the boy know why I did it.

CORY: Why you wanna do that to me? That was the one chance I had.

ROSE: Ain't nothing wrong with Cory playing football, Troy.

TROY: The boy lied to me. I told the nigger if he wanna play football . . . to keep up his chores and hold down that job at the A&P. That was the conditions. Stopped down there to see Mr. Stawicki . . .

CORY: I can't work after school during the football season, Pop! I tried to tell you that Mr. Stawicki's holding my job for me. You don't never want to listen to nobody. And then you wanna go and do this to me!

TROY: I ain't done nothing to you. You done it to yourself.

CORY: Just cause you didn't have a chance! You just scared I'm gonna be better than you, that's all.

TROY: Come here.

ROSE: Troy . . .

*Cory reluctantly crosses over to Troy.*

TROY: All right! See. You done made a mistake.

CORY: I didn't even do nothing!

TROY: I'm gonna tell you what your mistake was. See . . . you swung at the ball and didn't hit it. That's strike one. See, you in the batter's box now. You swung and you missed. That's strike one. Don't you strike out!

*Lights fade to black.*

## Act 2

### Scene 1

*The following morning. Cory is at the tree hitting the ball with the bat. He tries to mimic Troy, but his swing is awkward, less sure. Rose enters from the house.*

ROSE: Cory, I want you to help me with this cupboard.

CORY: I ain't quitting the team. I don't care what Poppa say.

ROSE: I'll talk to him when he gets back. He had to go see about your Uncle Gabe. The police done arrested him. Say he was disturbing the peace. He'll be back directly. Come on in here and help me clean out the top of this cupboard.

*Cory exits into the house. Rose sees Troy and Bono coming down the alley.*

Troy, . . . what they say down there?

TROY: Ain't said nothing. I give them fifty dollars and they let him go. I'll talk to you about it. Where's Cory?

ROSE: He's in there helping me clean out these cupboards.

TROY: Tell him to get his butt out here.

*Troy and Bono go over to the pile of wood. Bono picks up the saw and begins sawing.*

TROY (*to Bono*): All they want is the money. That makes six or seven times I done went down there and got him. See me coming they stick out their hands.

BONO: Yeah. I know what you mean. That's all they care about . . . that money. They don't care about what's right. (*Pause.*) Nigger, why you got to go and get some hard wood? You ain't doing nothing but building a little old fence. Get you some soft pine wood. That's all you need.

TROY: I know what I'm doing. This is outside wood. You put pine wood inside the house. Pine wood is inside wood. This here is outside wood. Now you tell me where the fence is gonna be?

BONO: You don't need this wood. You can put it up with pine wood and it'll stand as long as you gonna be here looking at it.

TROY: How you know how long I'm gonna be here, nigger? Hell, I might just live forever. Live longer than old man Horsely.

BONO: That's what Magee used to say.

TROY: Magee's damn fool. Now you tell me who you ever heard of gonna pull their own teeth with a pair of rusty pliers.

BONO: The old folks . . . my granddaddy used to pull his teeth with pliers. They ain't had no dentists for the colored folks back then.

TROY: Get clean pliers! You understand? Clean pliers! Sterilize them! Besides we ain't living back then. All Magee had to do was walk over to Doc Goldblum's.

BONO: I see where you and that Tallahassee gal . . . that Alberta . . . I see where you all done got tight.

TROY: What you mean "got tight"?

BONO: I see where you be laughing and joking with her all the time.

TROY: I laughs and jokes with all of them, Bono. You know me.

BONO: That ain't the kind of laughing and joking I'm talking about.

*Cory enters from the house.*

CORY: How you doing. Mr. Bono?

TROY: Cory? Get that saw from Bono and cut some wood. He talking about the wood's too hard to cut. Stand back there, Jim, and let that young boy show you how it's done.

BONO: He's sure welcome to it.

*Cory takes the saw and begins to cut the wood.*

Whew-e-e! Look at that. Big old strong boy. Look like Joe Louis. Hell, must be getting old the way I'm watching that boy whip through that wood.

CORY: I don't see why Mama want a fence around the yard noways.

TROY: Damn if I know either. What the hell she keeping out with it? She ain't got nothing nobody want.

BONO: Some people build fences to keep people out . . . and other people build fences to keep people in. Rose wants to hold on to you all. She loves you.

TROY: Hell, nigger, I don't need nobody to tell me my wife loves me. Cory . . . go on in the house and see if you can find that other saw.

CORY: Where's it at?

TROY: I said find it! Look for it till you find it!

*Cory exits into the house.*

What's that supposed to mean? Wanna keep us in?

BONO: Troy . . . I done known you seem like damn near my whole life. You and Rose both. I done know both of you all for a long time. I remember when you met Rose. When you was hitting them baseball out the park. A lot of them old gals was after you then. You had the pick of the litter. When you picked Rose, I was happy for you. That was the first time I knew you had any sense. I said . . . My man Troy knows what he's doing . . . I'm gonna follow this nigger . . . he might take me somewhere. I been following you too. I done learned a whole heap of things about life watching you. I done learned how to tell where the shit lies. How to tell it from the alfalfa. You done learned me a lot of things. You showed me how to not make the same mistakes . . . to take life as it comes along and keep putting one foot in front of the other. (*Pause.*) Rose a good woman, Troy.

TROY: Hell, nigger, I know she a good woman. I been married to her for eighteen years. What you got on your mind, Bono?

BONO: I just say she a good woman. Just like I say anything. I ain't got to have nothing on my mind.

TROY: You just gonna say she a good woman and leave it hanging out there like that? Why you telling me she a good woman?

BONO: She loves you, Troy. Rose loves you.

TROY: You saying I don't measure up. That's what you trying to say. I don't measure up cause I'm seeing this other gal. I know what you trying to say.

BONO: I know what Rose means to you, Troy. I'm just trying to say I don't want to see you mess up.

TROY: Yeah, I appreciate that, Bono. If you was messing around on Lucille I'd be telling you the same thing.

BONO: Well, that's all I got to say. I just say that because I love you both.

TROY: Hell, you know me . . . I wasn't out there looking for nothing. You can't find a better woman than Rose. I know that. But seems like this woman just stuck onto me where I can't shake her loose. I done wrestled with it, tried to throw her off me . . . but she just stuck on tighter. Now she's stuck on for good.

BONO: You's in control . . . that's what you tell me all the time. You responsible for what you do.

TROY: I ain't ducking the responsibility of it. As long as it sets right in my heart . . . then I'm okay. Cause that's all I listen to. It'll tell me right from wrong every time. And I ain't talking about doing Rose no bad turn. I love Rose. She done carried me a long ways and I love and respect her for that.

BONO: I know you do. That's why I don't want to see you hurt her. But what you gonna do when she find out? What you got then? If you try and juggle both of them . . . sooner or later you gonna drop one of them. That's common sense.

TROY: Yeah, I hear what you saying, Bono. I been trying to figure a way to work it out.

BONO: Work it out right, Troy. I don't want to be getting all up between you and Rose's business . . . but work it so it come out right.

TROY: Ah hell, I get all up between you and Lucille's business. When you gonna get that woman that refrigerator she been wanting? Don't tell me you ain't got no money now. I know who your banker is. Mellon don't need that money bad as Lucille want that refrigerator. I'll tell you that.

BONO: Tell you what I'll do . . . when you finish building this fence for Rose . . . I'll buy Lucille that refrigerator.

TROY: You done stuck your foot in your mouth now!

*Troy grabs up a board and begins to saw. Bono starts to walk out the yard.*

Hey, nigger . . . where you going?

BONO: I'm going home. I know you don't expect me to help you now. I'm protecting my money. I wanna see you put that fence up by yourself. That's what I want to see. You'll be here another six months without me.

TROY: Nigger, you ain't right.

BONO: When it comes to my money . . . I'm right as fireworks on the Fourth of July.

TROY: All right, we gonna see now. You better get out your bankbook.

*Bono exits, and Troy continues to work. Rose enters from the house.*

ROSE: What they say down there? What's happening with Gabe?

TROY: I went down there and got him out. Cost me fifty dollars. Say he was disturbing the peace. Judge set up a hearing for him in three weeks. Say to show cause why he shouldn't be recommitted.

ROSE: What was he doing that cause them to arrest him?

TROY: Some kids was teasing him and he run them off home. Say he was howling and carrying on. Some folks seen him and called the police. That's all it was.

ROSE: Well, what's you say? What'd you tell the judge?

TROY: Told him I'd look after him. It didn't make no sense to recommit the man. He stuck out his big greasy palm and told me to give him fifty dollars and take him on home.

ROSE: Where's he at now? Where'd he go off to?

TROY: He's gone about his business. He don't need nobody to hold his hand.

ROSE: Well, I don't know. Seem like that would be the best place for him if they did put him into the hospital. I know what you're gonna say. But that's what I think would be best.

TROY: The man done had his life ruined fighting for what? And they wanna take and lock him up. Let him be free. He don't bother nobody.

ROSE: Well, everybody got their own way of looking at it I guess. Come on and get your lunch. I got a bowl of lima beans and some cornbread in the oven. Come and get something to eat. Ain't no sense you fretting over Gabe.

*Rose turns to go into the house.*

TROY: Rose . . . got something to tell you.

ROSE: Well, come on . . . wait till I get this food on the table.

TROY: Rose!

*She stops and turns around.*

I don't know how to say this. (*Pause.*) I can't explain it none. It just sort of grows on you till it gets out of hand. It starts out like a little bush . . . and the next thing you know it's a whole forest.

ROSE: Troy . . . what is you talking about?

TROY: I'm talking, woman, let me talk. I'm trying to find a way to tell you . . . I'm gonna be a daddy. I'm gonna be somebody's daddy.

ROSE: Troy . . . you're not telling me this? You're gonna be . . . what?

TROY: Rose . . . now . . . see . . .

ROSE: You telling me you gonna be somebody's daddy? You telling your *wife* this?

*Gabriel enters from the street. He carries a rose in his hand.*

GABRIEL: Hey, Troy! Hey, Rose!

ROSE: I have to wait eighteen years to hear something like this.

GABRIEL: Hey, Rose . . . I got a flower for you. (*He hands it to her.*) That's a rose. Same rose like you is.

ROSE: Thanks, Gabe.

GABRIEL: Troy, you ain't mad at me is you? Them bad mens come and put me away. You ain't mad at me is you?

TROY: Naw, Gabe, I ain't mad at you.

ROSE: Eighteen years and you wanna come with this.

GABRIEL (*takes a quarter out of his pocket*): See what I got? Got a brand new quarter.

TROY: Rose . . . it's just . . .

ROSE: Ain't nothing you can say, Troy. Ain't no way of explaining that.

GABRIEL: Fellow that give me this quarter had a whole mess of them. I'm gonna keep this quarter till it stop shining.

ROSE: Gabe, go on in the house there. I got some watermelon in the Frigidaire. Go on and get you a piece.

GABRIEL: Say, Rose . . . you know I was chasing hellhounds and them bad mens come and get me and take me away. Troy helped me. He come down there and told them they better let me go before he beat them up. Yeah, he did!

ROSE: You go on and get you a piece of watermelon, Gabe. Them bad mens is gone now.

GABRIEL:   Okay, Rose . . . gonna get me some watermelon. The kind with the stripes on it.

*Gabriel exits into the house.*

ROSE:   Why, Troy? Why? After all these years to come dragging this in to me now. It don't make no sense at your age. I could have expected this ten or fifteen years ago, but not now.

TROY:   Age ain't got nothing to do with it, Rose.

ROSE:   I done tried to be everything a wife should be. Everything a wife could be. Been married eighteen years and I got to live to see the day you tell me you been seeing another woman and done fathered a child by her. And you know I ain't never wanted no half nothing in my family. My whole family is half. Everybody got different fathers and mothers . . . my two sisters and my brother. Can't hardly tell who's who. Can't never sit down and talk about Papa and Mama. It's your papa and your mama and my papa and my mama . . .

TROY:   Rose . . . stop it now.

ROSE:   I ain't never wanted that for none of my children. And now you wanna drag your behind in here and tell me something like this.

TROY:   You ought to know. It's time for you to know.

ROSE:   Well, I don't want to know, goddamn it!

TROY:   I can't just make it go away. It's done now. I can't wish the circumstance of the thing away.

ROSE:   And you don't want to either. Maybe you want to wish me and my boy away. Maybe that's what you want? Well, you can't wish us away. I've got eighteen years of my life invested in you. You ought to have stayed upstairs in my bed where you belong.

TROY:   Rose . . . now listen to me . . . we can get a handle on this thing. We can talk this out . . . come to an understanding.

ROSE:   All of a sudden it's "we." Where was "we" at when you was down there rolling around with some godforsaken woman? "We" should have come to an understanding before you started making a damn fool of yourself. You're a day late and a dollar short when it comes to an understanding with me.

TROY:   It's just . . . She gives me a different idea . . . a different understanding about myself. I can step out of this house and get away from the pressures and problems . . . be a different man. I ain't got to wonder how I'm gonna pay the bills or get the roof fixed. I can just be a part of myself that I ain't never been.

ROSE: What I want to know . . . is do you plan to continue seeing her. That's all you can say to me.

TROY: I can sit up in her house and laugh. Do you understand what I'm saying. I can laugh out loud . . . and it feels good. It reaches all the way down to the bottom of my shoes. (*Pause.*) Rose, I can't give that up.

ROSE: Maybe you ought to go on and stay down there with her . . . if she's a better woman than me.

TROY: It ain't about nobody being a better woman or nothing. Rose, you ain't the blame. A man couldn't ask for no woman to be a better wife than you've been. I'm responsible for it. I done locked myself into a pattern trying to take care of you all that I forgot about myself.

ROSE: What the hell was I there for? That was my job, not somebody else's.

TROY: Rose, I done tried all my life to live decent . . . to live a clean . . . hard . . . useful life. I tried to be a good husband to you. In every way I knew how. Maybe I come into the world backwards, I don't know. But . . . you born with two strikes on you before you come to the plate. You got to guard it closely . . . always looking for the curve ball on the inside corner. You can't afford to let none get past you. You can't afford a call strike. If you going down . . . you going down swinging. Everything lined up against you. What you gonna do. I fooled them, Rose. I bunted. When I found you and Cory and a halfway decent job . . . I was safe. Couldn't nothing touch me. I wasn't gonna strike out no more. I wasn't going back to the penitentiary. I wasn't gonna lay in the streets with a bottle of wine. I was safe. I had me a family. A job. I wasn't gonna get that last strike. I was on first looking for one of them boys to knock me in. To get me home.

ROSE: You should have stayed in my bed, Troy.

TROY: Then when I saw that gal . . . she firmed up my backbone. And I got to thinking that if I tried . . . I just might be able to steal second. Do you understand after eighteen years I wanted to steal second.

ROSE: You should have held me tight. You should have grabbed me and held on.

TROY: I stood on first base for eighteen years and I thought . . . well, goddamn it . . . go on for it!

ROSE: We're not talking about baseball! We're talking about you going off to lay in bed with another woman . . . and then bring it home to me. That's what we're talking about. We ain't talking about no baseball.

TROY: Rose, you're not listening to me. I'm trying the best I can to explain it to you. It's not easy for me to admit that I been standing in the same place for eighteen years.

ROSE: I been standing with you! I been right here with you, Troy. I got a life too. I gave eighteen years of my life to stand in the same spot with you. Don't you think I ever wanted other things? Don't you think I had dreams and hopes? What about my life? What about me. Don't you think it ever crossed my mind to want to know other men? That I wanted to lay up somewhere and forget about my responsibilities? That I wanted someone to make me laugh so I could feel good? You not the only one who's got wants and needs. But I held on to you, Troy. I took all my feelings, my wants and needs, my dreams . . . and I buried them inside you. I planted a seed and watched and prayed over it. I planted myself inside you and waited to bloom. And it didn't take me no eighteen years to find out the soil was hard and rocky and it wasn't never gonna bloom.

But I held on to you, Troy. I held you tighter. You was my husband. I owed you everything I had. Every part of me I could find to give you. And upstairs in that room . . . with the darkness falling in on me . . . I gave everything I had to try and erase the doubt that you wasn't the finest man in the world. And wherever you was going . . . I wanted to be there with you. Cause you was my husband. Cause that's the only way I was gonna survive as your wife. You always talking about what you give . . . and what you don't have to give. But you take too. You take . . . and don't even know nobody's giving!

*Rose turns to exit into the house; Troy grabs her arm.*

TROY: You say I take and don't give!

ROSE: Troy! You're hurting me!

TROY: You say I take and don't give!

ROSE: Troy . . . you're hurting my arm! Let go!

TROY: I done give you everything I got. Don't you tell that lie on me.

ROSE: Troy!

TROY: Don't you tell that lie on me!

*Cory enters from the house.*

**CORY:**  Mama!

**ROSE:**  Troy. You're hurting me.

**TROY:**  Don't you tell me about no taking and giving.

*Cory comes up behind Troy and grabs him. Troy, surprised, is thrown off balance just as Cory throws a glancing blow that catches him on the chest and knocks him down. Troy is stunned, as is Cory.*

**ROSE:**  Troy. Troy. No!

*Troy gets to his feet and starts at Cory.*

Troy . . . no. Please! Troy!

*Rose pulls on Troy to hold him back. Troy stops himself.*

**TROY** (*to Cory*):  All right. That's strike two. You stay away from around me, boy. Don't you strike out. You living with a full count. Don't you strike out.

*Troy exits out the yard as the lights go down.*

## Scene 2

*It is six months later, early afternoon. Troy enters from the house and starts to exit the yard. Rose enters from the house.*

**ROSE:**  Troy, I want to talk to you.

**TROY:**  All of a sudden, after all this time, you want to talk to me, huh? You ain't wanted to talk to me for months. You ain't wanted to talk to me last night. You ain't wanted no part of me then. What you wanna talk to me about now?

**ROSE:**  Tomorrow's Friday.

**TROY:**  I know what day tomorrow is. You think I don't know tomorrow's Friday? My whole life I ain't done nothing but look to see Friday coming and you got to tell me it's Friday.

**ROSE:**  I want to know if you're coming home.

**TROY:**  I always come home, Rose. You know that. There ain't never been a night I ain't come home.

**ROSE:**  That ain't what I mean . . . and you know it. I want to know if you're coming straight home after work.

**TROY:**  I figure I'd cash my check . . . hang out at Taylors' with the boys . . . maybe play a game of checkers . . .

ROSE: Troy, I can't live like this. I won't live like this. You livin' on borrowed time with me. It's been going on six months now you ain't been coming home.

TROY: I be here every night. Every night of the year. That's 365 days.

ROSE: I want you to come home tomorrow after work.

TROY: Rose . . . I don't mess up my pay. You know that now. I take my pay and I give it to you. I don't have no money but what you give me back. I just want to have a little time to myself . . . a little time to enjoy life.

ROSE: What about me? When's my time to enjoy life?

TROY: I don't know what to tell you, Rose. I'm doing the best I can.

ROSE: You ain't been home from work but time enough to change your clothes and run out . . . and you wanna call that the best you can do?

TROY: I'm going over to the hospital to see Alberta. She went into the hospital this afternoon. Look like she might have the baby early. I won't be gone long.

ROSE: Well, you ought to know. They went over to Miss Pearl's and got Gabe today. She said you told them to go ahead and lock him up.

TROY: I ain't said no such thing. Whoever told you that is telling a lie. Pearl ain't doing nothing but telling a big fat lie.

ROSE: She ain't had to tell me. I read it on the papers.

TROY: I ain't told them nothing of the kind.

ROSE: I saw it right there on the papers.

TROY: What it say, huh?

ROSE: It said you told them to take him.

TROY: Then they screwed that up, just the way they screw up everything. I ain't worried about what they got on the paper.

ROSE: Say the government send part of his check to the hospital and the other part to you.

TROY: I ain't got nothing to do with that if that's the way it works. I ain't made up the rules about how it work.

ROSE: You did Gabe just like you did Cory. You wouldn't sign the paper for Cory . . . but you signed for Gabe. You signed that paper.

*The telephone is heard ringing inside the house.*

TROY: I told you I ain't signed nothing, woman! The only thing I signed was the release form. Hell, I can't read, I don't know what they had on that paper! I ain't signed nothing about sending Gabe away.

ROSE: I said send him to the hospital . . . you said let him be free
. . . now you done went down there and signed him to the hospital for half his money. You went back on yourself, Troy. You gonna have to answer for that.

TROY: See now . . . you been over there talking to Miss Pearl. She done got mad cause she ain't getting Gabe's rent money. That's all it is. She's liable to say anything.

ROSE: Troy, I seen where you signed the paper.

TROY: You ain't seen nothing I signed. What she doing got papers on my brother anyway? Miss Pearl telling a big fat lie. And I'm gonna tell her about it too! You ain't seen nothing I signed. Say . . . you ain't seen nothing I signed.

*Rose exits into the house to answer the telephone. Presently she returns.*

ROSE: Troy . . . that was the hospital. Alberta had the baby.

TROY: What she have? What is it?

ROSE: It's a girl.

TROY: I better get on down to the hospital to see her.

ROSE: Troy . . .

TROY: Rose . . . I got to go see her now. That's only right . . . what's the matter . . . the baby's all right, ain't it?

ROSE: Alberta died having the baby.

TROY: Died . . . you say she's dead? Alberta's dead?

ROSE: They said they done all they could. They couldn't do nothing for her.

TROY: The baby? How's the baby?

ROSE: They say it's healthy. I wonder who's gonna bury her.

TROY: She had family, Rose. She wasn't living in the world by herself.

ROSE: I know she wasn't living in the world by herself.

TROY: Next thing you gonna want to know if she had any insurance.

ROSE: Troy, you ain't got to talk like that.

TROY: That's the first thing that jumped out your mouth. "Who's gonna bury her?" Like I'm fixing to take on that task for myself.

ROSE: I am your wife. Don't push me away.

TROY: I ain't pushing nobody away. Just give me some space. That's all. Just give me some room to breathe.

*Rose exits into the house. Troy walks about the yard.*

TROY (*with a quiet rage that threatens to consume him*):   All right . . . Mr. Death. See now . . . I'm gonna tell you what I'm gonna do. I'm gonna take and build me a fence around this yard. See? I'm gonna build me a fence around what belongs to me. And then I want you to stay on the other side. See? You stay over there until you're ready for me. Then you come on. Bring your army. Bring your sickle. Bring your wrestling clothes. I ain't gonna fall down on my vigilance this time. You ain't gonna sneak up on me no more. When you ready for me . . . when the top of your list say Troy Maxson . . . that's when you come around here. You come up and knock on the front door. Ain't nobody else got nothing to do with this. This is between you and me. Man to man. You stay on the other side of that fence until you ready for me. Then you come up and knock on the front door. Anytime you want. I'll be ready for you.

*The lights go down to black.*

SCENE 3

*The lights come up on the porch. It is late evening three days later. Rose sits listening to the ball game waiting for Troy. The final out of the game is made and Rose switches off the radio. Troy enters the yard carrying an infant wrapped in blankets. He stands back from the house and calls.*

*Rose enters and stands on the porch. There is a long, awkward silence, the weight of which grows heavier with each passing second.*

TROY:   Rose . . . I'm standing here with my daughter in my arms. She ain't but a wee bittie little old thing. She don't know nothing about grownups' business. She innocent . . . and she ain't got no mama.

ROSE:   What you telling me for, Troy?

*She turns and exits into the house.*

TROY:   Well . . . I guess we'll just sit out here on the porch.

*He sits down on the porch. There is an awkward indelicateness about the way he handles the baby. His largeness engulfs and seems to swallow it. He speaks loud enough for Rose to hear.*

A man's got to do what's right for him. I ain't sorry for nothing I done. It felt right in my heart. (*To the baby.*) What you smiling at? Your daddy's a big man. Got these great big old hands. But sometimes he's scared. And right now your daddy's scared cause we sitting out here and ain't got no home. Oh, I been homeless before. I ain't had no little baby with me. But I been homeless. You just be out on the road by your lonesome and you see one of them trains coming and you just kinda go like this . . .

*He sings as a lullaby.*

Please, Mr. Engineer let a man ride the line
Please, Mr. Engineer let a man ride the line
I ain't got no ticket please let me ride the blinds.

*Rose enters from the house. Troy, hearing her steps behind him, stands and faces her.*

She's my daughter, Rose. My own flesh and blood. I can't deny her no more than I can deny them boys. (*Pause.*) You and them boys is my family. You and them and this child is all I got in the world. So I guess what I'm saying is . . . I'd appreciate it if you'd help me take care of her.

ROSE: Okay, Troy . . . you're right. I'll take care of your baby for you . . . cause . . . like you say . . . she's innocent . . . and you can't visit the sins of the father upon the child. A motherless child has got a hard time. (*She takes the baby from him.*) From right now . . . this child got a mother. But you a womanless man.

*Rose turns and exits into the house with the baby. Lights go down to black.*

SCENE 4

*It is two months later. Lyons enters the street. He knocks on the door and calls.*

LYONS:   Hey, Rose! (*Pause.*) Rose!

ROSE (*from inside the house*):   Stop that yelling. You gonna wake up Raynell. I just got her to sleep.

LYONS:   I just stopped by to pay Papa this twenty dollars I owe him. Where's Papa at?

ROSE:   He should be here in a minute. I'm getting ready to go down to the church. Sit down and wait on him.

LYONS:   I got to go pick up Bonnie over her mother's house.

ROSE:   Well, sit it down there on the table. He'll get it.

LYONS (*enters the house and sets the money on the table*):   Tell Papa I said thanks. I'll see you again.

ROSE:   All right, Lyons. We'll see you.

*Lyons starts to exit as Cory enters.*

CORY:   Hey, Lyons.

LYONS:   What's happening, Cory? Say man, I'm sorry I missed your graduation. You know I had a gig and couldn't get away. Otherwise, I would have been there, man. So what you doing?

CORY:   I'm trying to find a job.

LYONS:   Yeah I know how that go, man. It's rough out here. Jobs are scarce.

CORY:   Yeah, I know.

LYONS:   Look here, I got to run. Talk to Papa . . . he know some people. He'll be able to help get you a job. Talk to him . . . see what he say.

CORY:   Yeah . . . all right, Lyons.

LYONS:   You take care. I'll talk to you soon. We'll find some time to talk.

*Lyons exits the yard. Cory wanders over to the tree, picks up the bat, and assumes a batting stance. He studies an imaginary pitcher and swings. Dissatisfied with the result, he tries again. Troy enters. They eye each other for a beat. Cory puts the bat down and exits the yard. Troy starts into the house as Rose exits with Raynell. She is carrying a cake.*

TROY:   I'm coming in and everybody's going out.

ROSE:   I'm taking this cake down to the church for the bake sale. Lyons was by to see you. He stopped by to pay you your twenty dollars. It's laying in there on the table.

TROY (*going into his pocket*):   Well . . . here go this money.
ROSE:   Put it in there on the table, Troy. I'll get it.
TROY:   What time you coming back?
ROSE:   Ain't no use in you studying me. It don't matter what time I come back.
TROY:   I just asked you a question, woman. What's the matter . . . can't I ask you a question?
ROSE:   Troy, I don't want to go into it. Your dinner's in there on the stove. All you got to do is heat it up. And don't you be eating the rest of them cakes in there. I'm coming back for them. We having a bake sale at the church tomorrow.

*Rose exits the yard. Troy sits down on the steps, takes a pint bottle from his pocket, opens it, and drinks. He begins to sing.*

TROY:
Hear it ring! Hear it ring!
Had an old dog his name was Blue
You know Blue was mighty true
You know Blue as a good old dog
Blue trees a possum in a hollow log
You know from that he was a good old dog.

*Bono enters the yard.*

BONO:   Hey, Troy.
TROY:   Hey, what's happening, Bono?
BONO:   I just thought I'd stop by to see you.
TROY:   What you stop by and see me for? You ain't stopped by in a month of Sundays. Hell, I must owe you money or something.
BONO:   Since you got your promotion I can't keep up with you. Used to see you every day. Now I don't even know what route you working.
TROY:   They keep switching me around. Got me out in Greentree now . . . hauling white folks' garbage.
BONO:   Greentree, huh? You lucky, at least you ain't got to be lifting them barrels. Damn if they ain't getting heavier. I'm gonna put in my two years and call it quits.
TROY:   I'm thinking about retiring myself.
BONO:   You got it easy. You can drive for another five years.

TROY: It ain't the same, Bono. It ain't like working the back of the truck. Ain't got nobody to talk to . . . feel like you working by yourself. Naw, I'm thinking about retiring. How's Lucille?

BONO: She all right. Her arthritis get to acting up on her sometime. Saw Rose on my way in. She going down to the church, huh?

TROY: Yeah, she took up going down there. All them preachers looking for somebody to fatten their pockets. (*Pause.*) Got some gin here.

BONO: Naw, thanks. I just stopped by to say hello.

TROY: Hell, nigger . . . you can take a drink. I ain't never known you to say no to a drink. You ain't got to work tomorrow.

BONO: I just stopped by. I'm fixing to go over to Skinner's. We got us a domino game going over his house every Friday.

TROY: Nigger, you can't play no dominoes. I used to whup you four games out of five.

BONO: Well, that learned me. I'm getting better.

TROY: Yeah? Well, that's all right.

BONO: Look here . . . I got to be getting on. Stop by sometime, huh?

TROY: Yeah, I'll do that, Bono. Lucille told Rose you bought her a new refrigerator.

BONO: Yeah, Rose told Lucille you had finally built your fence . . . so I figured we'd call it even.

TROY: I knew you would.

BONO: Yeah . . . okay. I'll be talking to you.

TROY: Yeah, take care, Bono. Good to see you. I'm gonna stop over.

BONO: Yeah. Okay, Troy.

*Bono exits. Troy drinks from the bottle.*

TROY:

Old Blue died and I dig his grave
Let him down with a golden chain
Every night when I hear old Blue bark
I know Blue treed a possum in Noah's Ark.
Hear it ring! Hear it ring!

*Cory enters the yard. They eye each other for a beat. Troy is sitting in the middle of the steps. Cory walks over.*

CORY: I got to get by.

TROY: Say what? What's you say?

CORY: You in my way. I got to get by.

TROY: You got to get by where? This is my house. Bought and paid for. In full. Took me fifteen years. And if you wanna go in my house and I'm sitting on the steps . . . you say excuse me. Like your mama taught you.

CORY: Come on, Pop . . . I got to get by.

*Cory starts to maneuver his way past Troy. Troy grabs his leg and shoves him back.*

TROY: You just gonna walk over top of me?

CORY: I live here too!

TROY (*advancing toward him*): You just gonna walk over top of me in my own house?

CORY: I ain't scared of you.

TROY: I ain't asked if you was scared of me. I asked you if you was fixing to walk over top of me in my own house? That's the question. You ain't gonna say excuse me? You just gonna walk over top of me?

CORY: If you wanna put it like that.

TROY: How else am I gonna put it?

CORY: I was walking by you to go into the house cause you sitting on the steps drunk, singing to yourself. You can put it like that.

TROY: Without saying excuse me???

*Cory doesn't respond.*

I asked you a question. Without saying excuse me???

CORY: I ain't got to say excuse me to you. You don't count around here no more.

TROY: Oh, I see . . . I don't count around here no more. You ain't got to say excuse me to your daddy. All of a sudden you done got so grown that your daddy don't count around here no more . . . Around here in his own house and yard that he done paid for with the sweat of his brow. You done got so grown to where you gonna take over. You gonna take over my house. Is that right? You gonna wear my pants. You gonna go in there and stretch out on my bed. You ain't got to say excuse me cause I don't count around here no more. Is that right?

CORY: That's right. You always talking this dumb stuff. Now, why don't you just get out my way?

TROY: I guess you got someplace to sleep and something to put in your belly. You got that, huh? You got that? That's what you need. You got that, huh?

CORY: You don't know what I got. You ain't got to worry about what I got.

TROY: You right! You one hundred percent right! I done spent the last seventeen years worrying about what you got. Now it's your turn, see? I'll tell you what to do. You grown . . . we done established that. You a man. Now, let's see you act like one. Turn your behind around and walk out this yard. And when you get out there in the alley . . . you can forget about this house. See? Cause this is my house. You go on and be a man and get your own house. You can forget about this. Cause this is mine. You go on and get yours cause I'm through with doing for you.

CORY: You talking about what you did for me . . . what'd you ever give me?

TROY: Them feet and bones! That pumping heart, nigger! I give you more than anybody else is ever gonna give you.

CORY: You ain't never gave me nothing! You ain't never done nothing but hold me back. Afraid I was gonna be better than you. All you ever did was try and make me scared of you. I used to tremble every time you called my name. Every time I heard your footsteps in the house. Wondering all the time . . . what's Papa gonna say if I do this?. . . What's he gonna say if I do that?. . . What's Papa gonna say if I turn on the radio? And Mama, too . . . she tries . . . but she's scared of you.

TROY: You leave your mama out of this. She ain't got nothing to do with this.

CORY: I don't know how she stand you . . . after what you did to her.

TROY: I told you to leave your mama out of this!

*He advances toward Cory.*

CORY: What you gonna do . . . give me a whupping? You can't whup me no more. You're too old. You just an old man.

TROY (*shoves him on his shoulder*): Nigger! That's what you are. You just another nigger on the street to me!

CORY: You crazy! You know that?

TROY: Go on now! You got the devil in you. Get on away from me!

CORY: You just a crazy old man . . . talking about I got the devil in me.

TROY: Yeah, I'm crazy! If you don't get on the other side of that yard . . . I'm gonna show you how crazy I am! Go on . . . get the hell out of my yard.

CORY: It ain't your yard. You took Uncle Gabe's money he got from the army to buy this house and then you put him out.

TROY (*advances on Cory*): Get your black ass out of my yard!

*Troy's advance backs Cory up against the tree. Cory grabs up the bat.*

CORY: I ain't going nowhere! Come on . . . put me out! I ain't scared of you.

TROY: That's my bat!

CORY: Come on!

TROY: Put my bat down!

CORY: Come on, put me out.

*Cory swings at Troy, who backs across the yard.*

What's the matter? You so bad . . . put me out!

*Troy advances toward Cory.*

CORY (*backing up*): Come on! Come on!

TROY: You're gonna have to use it! You wanna draw that bat back on me . . . you're gonna have to use it.

CORY: Come on!. . . Come on!

*Cory swings the bat at Troy a second time. He misses. Troy continues to advance toward him.*

TROY: You're gonna have to kill me! You wanna draw that bat back on me. You're gonna have to kill me.

*Cory, backed up against the tree, can go no farther. Troy taunts him. He sticks out his head and offers him a target.*

Come on! Come on!

*Cory is unable to swing the bat. Troy grabs it.*

TROY: Then I'll show you.

*Cory and Troy struggle over the bat. The struggle is fierce and fully engaged. Troy ultimately is the stronger and takes the bat from Cory and stands over him ready to swing. He stops himself.*

Go on and get away from around my house.

*Cory, stung by his defeat, picks himself up, walks slowly out of the yard and up the alley.*

CORY: Tell Mama I'll be back for my things.
TROY: They'll be on the other side of that fence.

*Cory exits.*

TROY: I can't taste nothing. Helluljah! I can't taste nothing no more. (*Troy assumes a batting posture and begins to taunt Death, the fastball on the outside corner.*) Come on! It's between you and me now! Come on! Anytime you want! Come on! I be ready for you . . . but I ain't gonna be easy.

*The lights go down on the scene.*

SCENE 5

*The time is 1965. The lights come up in the yard. It is the morning of Troy's funeral. A funeral plaque with a light hangs beside the door. There is a small garden plot off to the side. There is noise and activity in the house as Rose, Lyons, and Bono have gathered. The door opens and Raynell, seven years old, enters dressed in a flannel nightgown. She crosses to the garden and pokes around with a stick. Rose calls from the house.*

ROSE: Raynell!
RAYNELL: Mam?
ROSE: What you doing out there?
RAYNELL: Nothing.

*Rose comes to the door.*

ROSE: Girl, get in here and get dressed. What you doing?

RAYNELL:   Seeing if my garden growed.

ROSE:   I told you it ain't gonna grow overnight. You got to wait.

RAYNELL:   It don't look like it never gonna grow. Dag!

ROSE:   I told you a watched pot never boils. Get in here and get dressed.

RAYNELL:   This ain't even no pot, Mama.

ROSE:   You just have to give it a chance. It'll grow. Now you come on and do what I told you. We got to be getting ready. This ain't no morning to be playing around. You hear me?

RAYNELL:   Yes, mam.

*Rose exits into the house. Raynell continues to poke at her garden with a stick. Cory enters. He is dressed in a Marine corporal's uniform, and carries a duffelbag. His posture is that of a military man, and his speech has a clipped sternness.*

CORY (*to Raynell*):   Hi. (*Pause.*) I bet your name is Raynell.

RAYNELL:   Uh huh.

CORY:   Is your mama home?

*Raynell runs up on the porch and calls through the screen door.*

RAYNELL:   Mama . . . there's some man out here. Mama?

*Rose comes to the door.*

ROSE:   Cory? Lord have mercy! Look here, you all!

*Rose and Cory embrace in a tearful reunion as Bono and Lyons enter from the house dressed in funeral clothes.*

BONO:   Aw, looka here . . .

ROSE:   Done got all grown up!

CORY:   Don't cry, Mama. What you crying about?

ROSE:   I'm just so glad you made it.

CORY:   Hey Lyons. How you doing, Mr. Bono.

*Lyons goes to embrace Cory.*

LYONS:   Look at you, man. Look at you. Don't he look good, Rose. Got them Corporal stripes.

ROSE:   What took you so long?

CORY:   You know how the Marines are, Mama. They got to get all their paperwork straight before they let you do anything.

ROSE: Well, I'm sure glad you made it. They let Lyons come. Your Uncle Gabe's still in the hospital. They don't know if they gonna let him out or not. I just talked to them a little while ago.

LYONS: A Corporal in the United States Marines.

BONO: Your daddy knew you had it in you. He used to tell me all the time.

LYONS: Don't he look good, Mr. Bono?

BONO: Yeah, he remind me of Troy when I first met him. (*Pause.*) Say, Rose, Lucille's down at the church with the choir. I'm gonna go down and get the pallbearers lined up. I'll be back to get you all.

ROSE: Thanks, Jim.

CORY: See you, Mr. Bono.

LYONS (*with his arm around Raynell*): Cory . . . look at Raynell. Ain't she precious? She gonna break a whole lot of hearts.

ROSE: Raynell, come and say hello to your brother. This is your brother, Cory. You remember Cory.

RAYNELL: No, Mam.

CORY: She don't remember me, Mama.

ROSE: Well, we talk about you. She heard us talk about you. (*To Raynell.*) This is your brother, Cory. Come on and say hello.

RAYNELL: Hi.

CORY: Hi. So you're Raynell. Mama told me a lot about you.

ROSE: You all come on into the house and let me fix you some breakfast. Keep up your strength.

CORY: I ain't hungry, Mama.

LYONS: You can fix me something, Rose. I'll be in there in a minute.

ROSE: Cory, you sure you don't want nothing? I know they ain't feeding you right.

CORY: No, Mama . . . thanks. I don't feel like eating. I'll get something later.

ROSE: Raynell . . . get on upstairs and get that dress on like I told you.

*Rose and Raynell exit into the house.*

LYONS: So . . . I hear you thinking about getting married.

CORY: Yeah, I done found the right one, Lyons. It's about time.

LYONS: Me and Bonnie been split up about four years now. About the time Papa retired. I guess she just got tired of all them changes I was putting her through. (*Pause.*) I always knew you was gonna make something out yourself. Your head was always in the right direction. So . . . you gonna stay in . . . make it a career . . . put in your twenty years?

CORY: I don't know. I got six already, I think that's enough.

LYONS: Stick with Uncle Sam and retire early. Ain't nothing out here. I guess Rose told you what happened with me. They got me down the workhouse. I thought I was being slick cashing other people's checks.

CORY: How much time you doing?

LYONS: They give me three years. I got that beat now. I ain't got but nine more months. It ain't so bad. You learn to deal with it like anything else. You got to take the crookeds with the straights. That's what Papa used to say. He used to say that when he struck out. I seen him strike out three times in a row . . . and the next time up he hit the ball over the grandstand. Right out there in Homestead Field. He wasn't satisfied hitting in the seats . . . he want to hit it over everything! After the game he had two hundred people standing around waiting to shake his hand. You got to take the crookeds with the straights. Yeah, Papa was something else.

CORY: You still playing?

LYONS: Cory . . . you know I'm gonna do that. There's some fellows down there we got us a band . . . we gonna try and stay together when we get out . . . but yeah, I'm still playing. It still helps me to get out of bed in the morning. As long as it do that I'm gonna be right there playing and trying to make some sense out of it.

ROSE (*calling*): Lyons, I got these eggs in the pan.

LYONS: Let me go on and get these eggs, man. Get ready to go bury Papa. (*Pause.*) How you doing? You doing all right?

*Cory nods. Lyons touches him on the shoulder and they share a moment of silent grief. Lyons exits into the house. Cory wanders about the yard. Raynell enters.*

RAYNELL: Hi.

CORY: Hi.

RAYNELL: Did you used to sleep in my room?

CORY: Yeah . . . that used to be my room.

RAYNELL: That's what Papa call it. "Cory's room." It got your football in the closet.

*Rose comes to the door.*

ROSE: Raynell, get in there and get them good shoes on.

RAYNELL: Mama, can't I wear these? Them other one hurt my feet.

ROSE: Well, they just gonna have to hurt your feet for a while. You ain't said they hurt your feet when you went down to the store and got them.

RAYNELL: They didn't hurt then. My feet done got bigger.

ROSE: Don't you give me no backtalk now. You get in there and get them shoes on.

*Raynell exits into the house.*

Ain't too much changed. He still got that piece of rag tied to that tree. He was out here swinging that bat. I was just ready to go back in the house. He swung that bat and then he just fell over. Seem like he swung it and stood there with this grin on his face . . . and then he just fell over. They carried him on down to the hospital, but I knew there wasn't no need . . . why don't you come on in the house?

CORY: Mama . . . I got something to tell you. I don't know how to tell you this . . . but I've got to tell you . . . I'm not going to Papa's funeral.

ROSE: Boy, hush your mouth. That's your daddy you talking about. I don't want hear that kind of talk this morning. I done raised you to come to this? You standing there all healthy and grown talking about you ain't going to your daddy's funeral?

CORY: Mama . . . listen . . .

ROSE: I don't want to hear it, Cory. You just get that thought out of your head.

CORY: I can't drag Papa with me everywhere I go. I've got to say no to him. One time in my life I've got to say no.

ROSE: Don't nobody have to listen to nothing like that. I know you and your daddy ain't seen eye to eye, but I ain't got to listen to that kind of talk this morning. Whatever was between you and your daddy . . . the time has come to put it aside. Just take it and set it over there on the shelf and forget about it. Disrespecting your daddy ain't gonna make you a man, Cory. You got to find a way to come to that on your own. Not going to your daddy's funeral ain't gonna make you a man.

CORY: The whole time I was growing up . . . living in his house . . . Papa was like a shadow that followed you everywhere. It weighed on you and sunk into your flesh. It would wrap around you and lay there until you couldn't tell which one was you anymore. That shadow digging in your flesh. Trying to crawl in. Trying to live through you. Everywhere I looked, Troy Maxson was staring back at me . . . hiding under the bed . . . in the closet. I'm just saying I've got to find a way to get rid of that shadow, Mama.

ROSE: You just like him. You got him in you good.

CORY: Don't tell me that, Mama.

ROSE: You Troy Maxson all over again.

CORY: I don't want to be Troy Maxson. I want to be me.

ROSE: You can't be nobody but who you are, Cory. That shadow wasn't nothing but you growing into yourself. You either got to grow into it or cut it down to fit you. But that's all you got to make life with. That's all you got to measure yourself against that world out there. Your daddy wanted you to be everything he wasn't . . . and at the same time he tried to make you into everything he was. I don't know if he was right or wrong . . . but I do know he meant to do more good than he meant to do harm. He wasn't always right. Sometimes when he touched he bruised. And sometimes when he took me in his arms he cut.

When I first met your daddy I thought . . . Here is a man I can lay down with and make a baby. That's the first thing I thought when I seen him. I was thirty years old and had done seen my share of men. But when he walked up to me and said, "I can dance a waltz that'll make you dizzy," I thought, Rose Lee, here is a man that you can open yourself up to and be filled to bursting. Here is a man that can fill all them empty spaces you been tipping around the edges of. One of them empty spaces was being somebody's mother.

I married your daddy and settled down to cooking his supper and keeping clean sheets on the bed. When your daddy walked through the house he was so big he filled it up. That was my first mistake. Not to make him leave some room for me. For my part in the matter. But at that time I wanted that. I wanted a house that I could sing in. And that's what your daddy gave me. I didn't know to keep up his strength I had to give up little pieces of mine. I did that. I took on his life as mine and mixed up the pieces so that you couldn't hardly tell which was which anymore. It was my choice. It was my life and I didn't have to live it like that. But that's what life offered me in the way of being a woman and I took it. I grabbed hold of it with both hands.

By the time Raynell came into the house, me and your daddy had done lost touch with one another. I didn't want to make my blessing off of nobody's misfortune . . . but I took on to Raynell like she was all them babies I had wanted and never had.

*The phone rings.*

Like I'd been blessed to relive a part of my life. And if the Lord see
fit to keep up my strength . . . I'm gonna do her just like your
daddy did you . . . I'm gonna give her the best of what's in me.

RAYNELL (*entering, still with her old shoes*): Mama . . . Reverend
Tollivier on the phone.

*Rose exits into the house.*

RAYNELL: Hi.
CORY: Hi.
RAYNELL: You in the Army or the Marines?
CORY: Marines.
RAYNELL: Papa said it was the Army. Did you know Blue?
CORY: Blue? Who's Blue?
RAYNELL: Papa's dog what he sing about all the time.
CORY (*singing*):
Hear it ring! Hear it ring!
I had a dog his name was Blue
You know Blue was mighty true
You know Blue was a good old dog
Blue treed a possum in a hollow log
You know from that he was a good old dog.
Hear it ring! Hear it ring!

*Raynell joins in singing.*

CORY AND RAYNELL:
Blue treed a possum out on a limb
Blue looked at me and I looked at him
Grabbed that possum and put him in a sack
Blue stayed there till I came back
Old Blue's feets was big and round
Never allowed a possum to touch the ground.

Old Blue died and I dug his grave
I dug his grave with a silver spade
Let him down with a golden chain
And every night I call his name
Go on Blue, you good dog you
Go on Blue, you good dog you.

RAYNELL:
> Blue laid down and died like a man
> Blue laid down and died . . .

BOTH:
> Blue laid down and died like a man
> Now he's treeing possums in the Promised Land
> I'm gonna tell you this to let you know
> Blue's gone where the good dogs go
> When I hear old Blue bark
> When I hear old Blue bark
> Blue treed a possum in Noah's Ark
> Blue treed a possum in Noah's Ark.

*Rose comes to the screen door.*

ROSE: Cory, we gonna be ready to go in a minute.

CORY (*to Raynell*): You go on in the house and change them shoes like Mama told you so we can go to Papa's funeral.

RAYNELL: Okay, I'll be back.

*Raynell exits into the house. Cory gets up and crosses over to the tree. Rose stands in the screen door watching him. Gabriel enters from the alley.*

GABRIEL (*calling*): Hey, Rose!

ROSE: Gabe?

GABRIEL: I'm here, Rose. Hey Rose, I'm here!

*Rose enters from the house.*

ROSE: Lord . . . Look here, Lyons!

LYONS: See, I told you, Rose . . . I told you they'd let him come.

CORY: How you doing, Uncle Gabe?

LYONS: How you doing, Uncle Gabe?

GABRIEL: Hey, Rose. It's time. It's time to tell St. Peter to open the gates. Troy, you ready? You ready, Troy. I'm gonna tell St. Peter to open the gates. You get ready now.

*Gabriel, with great fanfare, braces himself to blow. The trumpet is without a mouthpiece. He puts the end of it into his mouth and blows with great force, like a man who has been waiting some twenty-odd years for this single moment. No sound comes out of the trumpet. He braces himself and blows again with the same result. A third time he blows. There is a weight of impossible description that falls away and leaves him bare and exposed to a frightful realization. It is a trauma that a sane and normal mind would be unable to withstand. He begins to dance. A slow, strange dance, eerie and life-giving. A dance of atavistic signature and ritual. Lyons attempts to embrace him. Gabriel pushes Lyons away. He begins to howl in what is an attempt at song, or perhaps a song turning back into itself in an attempt at speech. He finishes his dance and the gates of heaven stand open as wide as God's closet.*

That's the way that go!

BLACKOUT

—1987

# David Ives (b. 1950)

David Ives grew up on Chicago's South Side, the son of working-class parents, writing his first play at the age of nine: "But then I realized you had to have a copy of the script for each person in the play, so that was the end of it." Impressed by theatrical productions he saw in his teens, Ives entered Northwestern University and after graduation attended Yale Drama School. After several attempts to become a "serious writer" he decided to "aspire to silliness on a daily basis" and began creating the short comic plays on which his reputation rests. An evening of six one-act comedies, All in the Timing, had a successful off-Broadway production in 1994, running over two years. In 1996 it was the most performed contemporary play in the nation, and Sure Thing, its signature piece, remains popular, especially with student drama groups. A second collection of one acts, Mere Mortals, had a successful run at Primary Stages in 1997, and a third collection, Lives of Saints, was produced in 1999. A number of his collections, including All in the Timing (1995), Time Flies (2001) and Polish Joke and Other Plays (2004) have been published. Ives's comedic skills range from a hilarious parody of David Mamet's plays (presented at an event honoring Mamet) to his witty revision of a legendary character in the full-length Don Juan in Chicago (1995). His short plays, in many cases, hinge on brilliant theatrical conceits; in Mayflies, a boy mayfly and girl mayfly must meet, court, and consummate their relationship before their one day of adult life ends. Sure Thing, a piece that plays witty tricks with time, resembles a scene in the Bill Murray film Groundhog Day, the script of which was written some years after Ives's play. Recently Ives has published a children's novel and has been working on stage adaptations of the Disney film The Little Mermaid and Batman: The Musical. In an article titled "Why I Shouldn't Write Plays," Ives notes, among other reasons, "All reviews should carry a Surgeon General's warning. The good ones turn your head, the bad ones break your heart."

# Sure Thing

## CHARACTERS

Betty
Bill

Scene: A café.

Betty, a woman in her late twenties, is reading at a café table. An empty chair is opposite her. Bill, same age, enters.

BILL:   Excuse me. Is this chair taken?
BETTY:   Excuse me?
BILL:   Is this taken?
BETTY:   Yes it is.
BILL:   Oh. Sorry.
BETTY:   Sure thing.

(*A bell rings softly.*)

BILL:   Excuse me. Is this chair taken?
BETTY:   Excuse me?
BILL:   Is this taken?
BETTY:   No, but I'm expecting somebody in a minute.
BILL:   Oh. Thanks anyway.
BETTY:   Sure thing.

(*A bell rings softly.*)

BILL:   Excuse me. Is this chair taken?
BETTY:   No, but I'm expecting somebody very shortly.
BILL:   Would you mind if I sit here till he or she or it comes?
BETTY (*glances at her watch*):   They do seem to be pretty late. . . .
BILL:   You never know who you might be turning down.
BETTY:   Sorry. Nice try, though.
BILL:   Sure thing.

(*Bell.*)

Is this seat taken?
BETTY:   No it's not.
BILL:   Would you mind if I sit here?
BETTY:   Yes I would.
BILL:   Oh.

(*Bell.*)

Is this chair taken?
BETTY:   No it's not.
BILL:   Would you mind if I sit here?
BETTY:   No. Go ahead.
BILL:   Thanks. (*He sits. She continues reading.*) Everyplace else seems
   to be taken.
BETTY:   Mm-hm.
BILL:   Great place.

BETTY: Mm-hm.
BILL: What's the book?
BETTY: I just wanted to read in quiet, if you don't mind.
BILL: No. Sure thing.

(*Bell.*)

BILL: Everyplace else seems to be taken.
BETTY: Mm-hm.
BILL: Great place for reading.
BETTY: Yes, I like it.
BILL: What's the book?
BETTY: *The Sound and the Fury.*
BILL: Oh. Hemingway.

(*Bell.*)

What's the book?
BETTY: *The Sound and the Fury.*
BILL: Oh. Faulkner.
BETTY: Have you read it?
BILL: Not . . . actually. I've sure read *about* it, though. It's supposed
to be great.
BETTY: It is great.
BILL: I hear it's great. (*Small pause.*) Waiter?

(*Bell.*)

What's the book?
BETTY: *The Sound and the Fury.*
BILL: Oh. Faulkner.
BETTY: Have you read it?
BILL: I'm a Mets fan, myself.

(*Bell.*)

BETTY: Have you read it?
BILL: Yeah, I read it in college.
BETTY: Where was college?
BILL: I went to Oral Roberts University.

(*Bell.*)

BETTY: Where was college?
BILL: I was lying. I never really went to college. I just like to party.

(*Bell.*)

BETTY: Where was college?

BILL: Harvard.

BETTY: Do you like Faulkner?

BILL: I love Faulkner. I spent a whole winter reading him once.

BETTY: I've just started.

BILL: I was so excited after ten pages that I went out and bought everything else he wrote. One of the greatest reading experiences of my life. I mean, all that incredible psychological understanding. Page after page of gorgeous prose. His profound grasp of the mystery of time and human existence. The smells of the earth . . . What do you think?

BETTY: I think it's pretty boring.

(*Bell.*)

BILL: What's the book?

BETTY: *The Sound and the Fury.*

BILL: Oh! Faulkner!

BETTY: Do you like Faulkner?

BILL: I love Faulkner.

BETTY: He's incredible.

BILL: I spent a whole winter reading him once.

BETTY: I was so excited after ten pages that I went out and bought everything else he wrote.

BILL: All that incredible psychological understanding.

BETTY: And the prose is so gorgeous.

BILL: And the way he's grasped the mystery of time—

BETTY: —and human existence. I can't believe I've waited this long to read him.

BILL: You never know. You might not have liked him before.

BETTY: That's true.

BILL: You might not have been ready for him. You have to hit these things at the right moment or it's no good.

BETTY: That's happened to me.

BILL: It's all in the timing. (*Small pause.*) My name's Bill, by the way.

BETTY: I'm Betty.

BILL: Hi.

BETTY: Hi. (*Small pause.*)

BILL: Yes I thought reading Faulkner was . . . a great experience.

BETTY: Yes. (*Small pause.*)

BILL: *The Sound and the Fury* . . . (*Another small pause.*)

BETTY:  Well. Onwards and upwards. (*She goes back to her book.*)
BILL:  Waiter—?

(*Bell.*)

You have to hit these things at the right moment or it's no good.
BETTY:  That's happened to me.
BILL:  It's all in the timing. My name's Bill, by the way.
BETTY:  I'm Betty.
BILL:  Hi.
BETTY:  Hi.
BILL:  Do you come in here a lot?
BETTY:  Actually I'm just in town for two days from Pakistan.
BILL:  Oh. Pakistan.

(*Bell.*)

My name's Bill, by the way.
BETTY:  I'm Betty.
BILL:  Hi.
BETTY:  Hi.
BILL:  Do you come in here a lot?
BETTY:  Every once in a while. Do you?
BILL:  Not so much anymore. Not as much as I used to. Before my nervous breakdown.

(*Bell.*)

Do you come in here a lot?
BETTY:  Why are you asking?
BILL:  Just interested.
BETTY:  Are you really interested, or do you just want to pick me up?
BILL:  No, I'm really interested.
BETTY:  Why would you be interested in whether I come in here a lot?
BILL:  I'm just . . . getting acquainted.
BETTY:  Maybe you're only interested for the sake of making small talk long enough to ask me back to your place to listen to some music, or because you've just rented this great tape for your VCR, or because you've got some terrific unknown Django Reinhardt record, only all you really want to do is fuck—which you won't do very well—after which you'll go into the bathroom and pee very loudly, then pad into the kitchen and get yourself a beer from the refrigerator without asking me whether I'd like anything, and then you'll proceed to lie back down beside me and confess that you've

got a girlfriend named Stephanie who's away at medical school in Belgium for a year, and that you've been involved with her—*off and on*—in what you'll call a very "intricate" relationship, for the past *seven YEARS*. None of which *interests* me, mister!

**BILL:** Okay.

(*Bell.*)

Do you come in here a lot?

**BETTY:** Every other day, I think.

**BILL:** I come in here quite a lot and I don't remember seeing you.

**BETTY:** I guess we must be on different schedules.

**BILL:** Missed connections.

**BETTY:** Yes. Different time zones.

**BILL:** Amazing how you can live right next door to somebody in this town and never even know it.

**BETTY:** I know.

**BILL:** City life.

**BETTY:** It's crazy.

**BILL:** We probably pass each other in the street every day. Right in front of this place, probably.

**BETTY:** Yep.

**BILL** (*looks around*): Well the waiters here sure seem to be in some different time zone. I can't seem to locate one anywhere. . . . Waiter! (*He looks back.*) So what do you—(*He sees that she's gone back to her book.*)

**BETTY:** I beg pardon?

**BILL:** Nothing. Sorry.

(*Bell.*)

**BETTY:** I guess we must be on different schedules.

**BILL:** Missed connections.

**BETTY:** Yes. Different time zones.

**BILL:** Amazing how you can live right next door to somebody in this town and never even know it.

**BETTY:** I know.

**BILL:** City life.

**BETTY:** It's crazy.

**BILL:** You weren't waiting for somebody when I came in, were you?

**BETTY:** Actually I was.

**BILL:** Oh. Boyfriend?

**BETTY:** Sort of.

BILL:   What's a sort-of boyfriend?
BETTY:   My husband.
BILL:   Ah-ha.

(*Bell.*)

You weren't waiting for somebody when I came in, were you?
BETTY:   Actually I was.
BILL:   Oh. Boyfriend?
BETTY:   Sort of.
BILL:   What's a sort-of boyfriend?
BETTY:   We were meeting here to break up.
BILL:   Mm-hm . . .

(*Bell.*)

What's a sort-of boyfriend?
BETTY:   My lover. Here she comes right now!

(*Bell.*)

BILL:   You weren't waiting for somebody when I came in, were you?
BETTY:   No, just reading.
BILL:   Sort of a sad occupation for a Friday night, isn't it? Reading here, all by yourself?
BETTY:   Do you think so?
BILL:   Well sure. I mean, what's a good-looking woman like you doing out alone on a Friday night?
BETTY:   Trying to keep away from lines like that.
BILL:   No, listen—

(*Bell.*)

You weren't waiting for somebody when I came in, were you?
BETTY:   No, just reading.
BILL:   Sort of a sad occupation for a Friday night, isn't it? Reading here all by yourself?
BETTY:   I guess it is, in a way.
BILL:   What's a good-looking woman like you doing out alone on a Friday night anyway? No offense, but . . .
BETTY:   I'm out alone on a Friday night for the first time in a very long time.
BILL:   Oh.
BETTY:   You see, I just recently ended a relationship.
BILL:   Oh.

BETTY: Of rather long standing.

BILL: I'm sorry. (*Small pause.*) Well listen, since reading by yourself *is* such a sad occupation for a Friday night, would you like to go elsewhere?

BETTY: No . . .

BILL: Do something else?

BETTY: No thanks.

BILL: I was headed out to the movies in a while anyway.

BETTY: I don't think so.

BILL: Big chance to let Faulkner catch his breath. All those long sentences get him pretty tired.

BETTY: Thanks anyway.

BILL: Okay.

BETTY: I appreciate the invitation.

BILL: Sure thing.

(*Bell.*)

You weren't waiting for somebody when I came in, were you?

BETTY: No, just reading.

BILL: Sort of a sad occupation for a Friday night, isn't it? Reading here all by yourself?

BETTY: I guess I was trying to think of it as existentially romantic. You know—cappuccino, great literature, rainy night . . .

BILL: That only works in Paris. We *could* hop the late plane to Paris. Get on a Concorde. Find a café . . .

BETTY: I'm a little short on plane fare tonight.

BILL: Darn it, so am I.

BETTY: To tell you the truth, I was headed to the movies after I finished this section. Would you like to come along? Since you can't locate a waiter?

BILL: That's a very nice offer, but . . .

BETTY: Uh-huh. Girlfriend?

BILL: Two, actually. One of them's pregnant, and Stephanie—

(*Bell.*)

BETTY: Girlfriend?

BILL: No, I don't have a girlfriend. Not if you mean the castrating bitch I dumped last night.

(*Bell.*)

BETTY: Girlfriend?

BILL: Sort of. Sort of.

BETTY: What's a sort-of girlfriend?

BILL: My mother.

(*Bell.*)

I just ended a relationship, actually.

BETTY: Oh.

BILL: Of rather long standing.

BETTY: I'm sorry to hear it.

BILL: This is my first night out alone in a long time. I feel a little bit at sea, to tell you the truth.

BETTY: So you didn't stop to talk because you're a Moonie, or you have some weird political affiliation—?

BILL: Nope. Straight-down-the-ticket Republican.

(*Bell.*)

Straight-down-the-ticket Democrat.

(*Bell.*)

Can I tell you something about politics?

(*Bell.*)

I like to think of myself as a citizen of the universe.

(*Bell.*)

I'm unaffiliated.

BETTY: That's a relief. So am I.

BILL: I vote my beliefs.

BETTY: Labels are not important.

BILL: Labels are not important, exactly. Take me, for example. I mean, what does it matter if I had a two-point at—

(*Bell.*)

three-point at—

(*Bell.*)

four-point at college? Or if I did come from Pittsburgh—

(*Bell.*)

Cleveland—

(*Bell.*)

Westchester County?

BETTY: Sure.

BILL: I believe that a man is what he is.

(*Bell.*)

A person is what he is.

(*Bell.*)

A person is . . . what they are.

BETTY: I think so too.

BILL: So what if I admire Trotsky?

(*Bell.*)

So what if I once had a total-body liposuction?

(*Bell.*)

So what if I don't have a penis?

(*Bell.*)

So what if I spent a year in the Peace Corps? I was acting on my convictions.

BETTY: Sure.

BILL: You just can't hang a sign on a person.

BETTY: Absolutely. I'll bet you're a Scorpio.

(*Many bells ring.*)

Listen, I was headed to the movies after I finished this section. Would you like to come along?

BILL: That sounds like fun. What's playing?

BETTY: A couple of the really early Woody Allen movies.

BILL: Oh.

BETTY: You don't like Woody Allen?

BILL: Sure. I like Woody Allen.

BETTY: But you're not crazy about Woody Allen.

BILL: Those early ones kind of get on my nerves.

BETTY: Uh-huh.

(*Bell.*)

BILL: Y'know I was headed to the—

BETTY (*simultaneously*):   I was thinking about—
BILL:   I'm sorry.
BETTY:   No, go ahead.
BILL:   I was going to say that I was headed to the movies in a little while, and . . .
BETTY:   So was I.
BILL:   The Woody Allen festival?
BETTY:   Just up the street.
BILL:   Do you like the early ones?
BETTY:   I think anybody who doesn't ought to be run off the planet.
BILL:   How many times have you seen *Bananas?*
BETTY:   Eight times.
BILL:   Twelve. So are you still interested? (*Long pause.*)
BETTY:   Do you like Entenmann's crumb cake . . . ?
BILL:   Last night I went out at two in the morning to get one. Did you have an Etch-a-Sketch as a child?
BETTY:   Yes! And do you like Brussels sprouts? (*Pause.*)
BILL:   No, I think they're disgusting.
BETTY:   They *are* disgusting!
BILL:   Do you still believe in marriage in spite of current sentiments against it?
BETTY:   Yes.
BILL:   And children?
BETTY:   Three of them.
BILL:   Two girls and a boy.
BETTY:   Harvard, Vassar, and Brown.
BILL:   And will you love me?
BETTY:   Yes.
BILL:   And cherish me forever?
BETTY:   Yes.
BILL:   Do you still want to go to the movies?
BETTY:   Sure thing.
BILL AND BETTY (*together*):   *Waiter!*

BLACKOUT

—1988

## Paula Vogel (b. 1951)

*Paula Vogel was born in Washington, D. C., and studied drama at the Catholic University of America and Cornell University. After working for fifteen years in regional theatre, she had her first major success with* The Baltimore Waltz *(1992), a play that drew on her experiences caring for her brother during his battle with AIDS. Vogel said to the* Washington Post, *"I wrote this play in my head while in the hospital, waiting for the doctors." In 1998,* How I Learned to Drive *appeared off-Broadway, and Vogel won the Pulitzer Prize for drama. Vogel has said that Vladimir Nabokov's novel* Lolita *provided the original impetus for the play, and, like Nabokov, Vogel has attracted controversy for her complex, often comical approach to the subject of pedophilia. As Vogel said in a PBS interview, "I also feel that having watched a kind of climate of victimization occur, having watched younger women and younger men that I teach, I sometimes feel that being in that kind of mind set of victimization causes almost as much trauma as the original abuse."* How I Learned to Drive *and another successful play,* The Mineola Twins, *have been published in a single volume,* The Mammary Plays.

# How I Learned to Drive

## CHARACTERS

Li'l Bit *A woman who ages forty-something to eleven years old. (See Notes on the New York Production.)*
Peck *Attractive man in his forties. Despite a few problems, he should be played by an actor one might cast in the role of Atticus in* To Kill a Mockingbird.
The Greek Chorus *If possible, these three members should be able to sing three-part harmony.*

> Male Greek Chorus *Plays Grandfather, Waiter, High School Boys. Thirties–forties. (See Notes on the New York Production.)*

> Female Greek Chorus *Plays Mother, Aunt Mary, High School Girls. Thirty–fifty. (See Notes on the New York Production.)*

> Teenage Greek Chorus *Plays Grandmother, high school girls and the voice of eleven-year-old Li'l Bit. Note on the casting of this actor: I would strongly recommend casting a young woman who*

*is "of legal age," that is, twenty-one to twenty-five years old who can look as close to eleven as possible. The contrast with the other cast members will help. If the actor is too young, the audience may feel uncomfortable. (See Notes on the New York Production.)*

## PRODUCTION NOTES

I urge directors to use the Greek Chorus in staging as environment and, well, part of the family—with the exception of the Teenage Greek Chorus member who, after the last time she appears onstage, should perhaps disappear.

**As For Music:** Please have fun. I wrote sections of the play listening to music like Roy Orbison's "Dream Baby" and The Mamas and the Papa's "Dedicated to the One I Love." The vaudeville sections go well to the Tijuana Brass or any music that sounds like a *Laugh-In* soundtrack. Other sixties music is rife with pedophilish (?) reference: the "You're Sixteen" genre hits; The Beach Boys' "Little Surfer Girl"; Gary Puckett and the Union Gap's "This Girl Is a Woman Now"; "Come Back When You Grow Up," etc.

And whenever possible, please feel free to punctuate the action with traffic signs: "No Passing," "Slow Children," "Dangerous Curves," "One Way," and the visual signs for children, deer crossings, hills, school buses, etc. (See Notes on the New York Production.)

This script uses the notion of slides and projections, which were not used in the New York production of the play.

**On Titles:** Throughout the script there are bold-faced titles. In production these should be spoken in a neutral voice (the type of voice that driver education films employ). In the New York production these titles were assigned to various members of the Greek Chorus and were done live.

## NOTES ON THE NEW YORK PRODUCTION

The role of Li'l Bit was originally written as a character who is forty-something. When we cast Mary-Louise Parker in the role of Li'l Bit, we cast the Greek Chorus members with younger actors as the Female Greek and the Male Greek, and cast the Teenage Greek with an older (that is, mid-twenties) actor as well. There is a great deal of flexibility in age. Directors should change the age in the last monologue for Li'l Bit ("And before you know it, I'll be thirty-five. . . .") to reflect the actor's age who is playing Li'l Bit.

*As the house lights dim, a Voice announces*

**Safety first—You and Driver Education.**

*Then the sound of a key turning the ignition of a car. Li'l Bit steps into a spotlight on the stage; "well-endowed," she is a softer-looking woman in the present time than she was at seventeen.*

LI'L BIT:     Sometimes to tell a secret, you first have to teach a lesson. We're going to start our lesson tonight on an early, warm summer evening.

In a parking lot overlooking the Beltsville Agricultural Farms in suburban Maryland.

Less than a mile away, the crumbling concrete of U.S. One wends its way past one-room revival churches, the porno drive-in, and boarded up motels with For Sale signs tumbling down.

Like I said, it's a warm summer evening.

Here on the land the Department of Agriculture owns, the smell of sleeping farm animal is thick on the air. The smells of clover and hay mix in with the smells of the leather dash-board. You can still imagine how Maryland used to be, before the malls took over. This countryside was once dotted with farmhouses—from their porches you could have witnessed the Civil War raging in the front fields.

Oh yes. There's a moon over Maryland tonight, that spills into the car where I sit beside a man old enough to be—did I mention how still the night is? Damp soil and tranquil air. It's the kind of night that makes a middle-aged man with a mortgage feel like a country boy again.

It's 1969. And I am very old, very cynical of the world, and I know it all. In short, I am seventeen years old, parking off a dark lane with a married man on an early summer night.

*(Lights up on two chairs facing front—or a Buick Riviera, if you will. Waiting patiently, with a smile on his face, Peck sits sniffing the night air. Li'l Bit climbs in beside him, seventeen years old and tense. Throughout the following, the two sit facing directly front. They do not touch. Their bodies remain passive. Only their facial expressions emote.)*

PECK:     Ummm. I love the smell of your hair.
LI'L BIT:     Uh-huh.
PECK:     Oh, Lord. Ummmm. *(Beat)* A man could die happy like this.

LI'L BIT: Well, *don't.*

PECK: What shampoo is this?

LI'L BIT: Herbal Essence.

PECK: Herbal Essence. I'm gonna buy me some. Herbal Essence. And when I'm all alone in the house, I'm going to get into the bathtub, and uncap the bottle and—

LI'L BIT: —Be good.

PECK: What?

LI'L BIT: Stop being . . . bad.

PECK: What did you think I was going to say? What do you think I'm going to do with the shampoo?

LI'L BIT: I don't want to know. I don't want to hear it.

PECK: I'm going to wash my hair. That's all.

LI'L BIT: Oh.

PECK: What did you think I was going to do?

LI'L BIT: Nothing. . . . I don't know. Something . . . nasty.

PECK: With shampoo? Lord, gal—your mind!

LI'L BIT: And whose fault is it?

PECK: Not mine. I've got the mind of a boy scout.

LI'L BIT: Right. A horny boy scout.

PECK: Boy scouts are always horny. What do you think the first Merit Badge is for?

LI'L BIT: There. You're going to be nasty again.

PECK: Oh, no. I'm good. Very good.

LI'L BIT: It's getting late.

PECK: Don't change the subject. I was talking about how good I am. *(Beat)* Are you ever gonna let me show you how good I am?

LI'L BIT: Don't go over the line now.

PECK: I won't. I'm not gonna do anything you don't want me to do.

LI'L BIT: That's right.

PECK: And I've been good all week.

LI'L BIT: You have?

PECK: Yes. All week. Not a single drink.

LI'L BIT: Good boy.

PECK: Do I get a reward? For not drinking?

LI'L BIT: A small one. It's getting late.

PECK: Just let me undo you. I'll do you back up.

LI'L BIT: All right. But be quick about it. *(Peck pantomimes undoing Li'l Bit's brassiere with one hand)* You know, that's amazing. The way you can undo the hooks through my blouse with one hand.

PECK: Years of practice.

LI'L BIT: You would make an incredible brain surgeon with that dexterity.

PECK: I'll bet Clyde—what's the name of the boy taking you to the prom?

LI'L BIT: Claude Souders.

PECK: Claude Souders. I'll bet it takes him two hands, lights on, and you helping him on to get to first base.

LI'L BIT: Maybe.

*(Beat.)*

PECK: Can I . . . kiss them? Please?

LI'L BIT: I don't know.

PECK: Don't make a grown man beg.

LI'L BIT: Just one kiss.

PECK: I'm going to lift your blouse.

LI'L BIT: It's a little cold.

*(Peck laughs gently.)*

PECK: That's not why you're shivering. *(They sit, perfectly still, for a long moment of silence. Peck makes gentle, concentric circles with his thumbs in the air in front of him)* How does that feel?

*(Li'l Bit closes her eyes, carefully keeps her voice calm:)*

LI'L BIT: It's . . . okay.

*(Sacred music, organ music or a boy's choir swells beneath the following.)*

PECK: I tell you, you can keep all the cathedrals of Europe. Just give me a second with these—these celestial orbs—

*(Peck bows his head as if praying. But he is kissing her nipple. Li'l Bit, eyes still closed, rears back her head on the leather Buick car seat.)*

LI'L BIT: Uncle Peck—we've got to go. I've got graduation rehearsal at school tomorrow morning. And you should get on home to Aunt Mary—

PECK: —All right, Li'l Bit.

LI'L BIT: —*Don't* call me that no more. *(Calmer)* Any more. I'm a big girl now, Uncle Peck. As you know.

*(Li'l Bit pantomimes refastening her bra behind her back.)*

PECK: That you are. Going on eighteen. Kittens will turn into cats.

*(Sighs)* I live all week long for these few minutes with you—you know that?

LI'L BIT: I'll drive.

*(A Voice cuts in with:)*

**Idling in the Neutral Gear.**

*(Sound of car revving cuts off the sacred music; Li'l Bit, now an adult, rises out of the car and comes to us.)*

LI'L BIT: In most families, relatives get names like "Junior," or "Brother," or "Bubba." In my family, if we call someone "Big Papa," it's not because he's tall. In my family, folks tend to get nicknamed for their genitalia. Uncle Peck, for example. My mama's adage was "the titless wonder," and my cousin Bobby got branded for life as "B.B."

*(In unison with Greek Chorus:)*

| LI'L BIT: For blue balls. | GREEK CHORUS: For blue balls. |
| --- | --- |

FEMALE GREEK CHORUS *(As Mother):* And of course, we were so excited to have a baby girl that when the nurse brought you in and said, "It's a girl! It's a baby girl!" I just had to see for myself. So we whipped your diapers down and parted your chubby little legs—and right between your legs there was—

*(Peck has come over during the above and chimes along:)*

| PECK: Just a little bit. | GREEK CHORUS: Just a little bit. |
| --- | --- |

FEMALE GREEK CHORUS *(As Mother):* And when you were born, you were so tiny that you fit in Uncle Peck's outstretched hand.

*(Peck stretches his hand out.)*

PECK: Now that's fact. I held you, one day old, right in this hand.

*(A traffic signal is projected of a bicycle in a circle with a diagonal red slash.)*

LI'L BIT: Even with my family background, I was sixteen or so before I realized that pedophilia did not mean people who loved to bicycle. . . .

*(A Voice intrudes:)*

**Driving in First Gear.**

LI'L BIT:   1969. A typical family dinner.

FEMALE GREEK CHORUS *(As Mother):*   Look, Grandma. Li'l Bit's getting to be as big in the bust as you are.

LI'L BIT:   Mother! Could we please change the subject?

TEENAGE GREEK CHORUS *(As Grandmother):*   Well, I hope you are buying her some decent bras. I never had a decent bra, growing up in the Depression, and now my shoulders are just crippled—crippled from the weight hanging on my shoulders—the dents from my bra straps are big enough to put your finger in. —Here, let me show you—

*(As Grandmother starts to open her blouse:)*

LI'L BIT:   Grandma! Please don't undress at the dinner table.

PECK:   I thought the entertainment came *after* the dinner.

LI'L BIT *(To the audience):*   This is how it always starts. My grandfather, Big Papa, will chime in next with—

MALE GREEK CHORUS *(As Grandfather):*   Yup. If Li'l Bit gets any bigger, we're gonna haveta buy her a wheelbarrow to carry in front of her—

LI'L BIT:   —Damn it—

PECK:   —How about those Redskins on Sunday, Big Papa?

LI'L BIT *(To the audience):*   The only sport Big Papa followed was chasing Grandma around the house—

MALE GREEK CHORUS *(As Grandfather):*   Or we could write to Kate Smith. Ask her for somma her used brassieres she don't want anymore—she could maybe give to Li'l Bit here—

LI'L BIT:   —I can't stand it. I can't.

PECK:   Now, honey, that's just their way—

FEMALE GREEK CHORUS *(As Mother):*   I tell you, Grandma, Li'l Bit's at that age. She's so sensitive, you can't say boo—

LI'L BIT:   I'd like some privacy, that's all. Okay? Some goddamn privacy—

PECK:   —Well, at least she didn't use the savior's name—

LI'L BIT *(To the audience):*   And Big Papa wouldn't let a dead dog lie. No sirree.

MALE GREEK CHORUS *(As Grandfather):*   Well, she'd better stop being so sensitive. 'Cause five minutes before Li'l Bit turns the corner, her tits turn first—

LI'L BIT *(Starting to rise from the table):*   —That's it. That's it.

PECK:   Li'l Bit, you can't let him get to you. Then he wins.

LI'L BIT:   I hate him. *Hate* him.

PECK:   That's fine. But hate him and eat a good dinner at the same time.

*(Li'l Bit calms down and sits with perfect dignity.)*

LI'L BIT:   The gumbo is really good, Grandma.

MALE GREEK CHORUS *(As Grandfather):*   A'course, Li'l Bit's got a big surprise coming for her when she goes to that fancy college this fall—

PECK:   Big Papa—let it go.

MALE GREEK CHORUS *(As Grandfather):*   What does she need a college degree for? She's got all the credentials she'll need on her chest—

LI'L BIT:   —Maybe I want to learn things. Read. Rise above my cracker background—

PECK:   —Whoa, now, Li'l Bit—

MALE GREEK CHORUS *(As Grandfather):*   What kind of things do you want to read?

LI'L BIT:   There's a whole semester course, for example, on Shakespeare—

*(Greek Chorus, as Grandfather, laughs until he weeps.)*

MALE GREEK CHORUS *(As Grandfather):*   Shakespeare. That's a good one. Shakespeare is really going to help you in life.

PECK:   I think it's wonderful. And on scholarship!

MALE GREEK CHORUS *(As Grandfather):*   How is Shakespeare going to help her lie on her back in the dark?

*(Li'l Bit is on her feet.)*

LI'L BIT:   You're getting old, Big Papa. You are going to die—very very soon. Maybe even *tonight*. And when you get to heaven, God's going to be a beautiful black woman in a long white robe. She's gonna look at your chart and say: Uh-oh. Fornication. Dog-ugly mean with blood relatives. Oh. Uh-oh. Voted for George Wallace. Well, one last chance: If you can name the play, all will be forgiven. And then she'll quote: "The quality of mercy is not strained." Your answer? Oh, too bad—*Merchant of Venice*: Act IV, Scene iii. And then she'll send your ass to fry in hell with all the other crackers. Excuse me, please.

*(To the audience)* And as I left the house, I would always hear Big Papa say:

**MALE GREEK CHORUS** *(As Grandfather):* Lucy, your daughter's got a mouth on her. Well, no sense in wasting good gumbo. Pass me her plate, Mama.

**LI'L BIT:** And Aunt Mary would come up to Uncle Peck:

**FEMALE GREEK CHORUS** *(As Aunt Mary):* Peck, go after her, will you? You're the only one she'll listen to when she gets like this.

**PECK:** She just needs to cool off.

**FEMALE GREEK CHORUS** *(As Aunt Mary):* Please, honey—Grandma's been on her feet cooking all day.

**PECK:** All right.

**LI'L BIT:** And as he left the room, Aunt Mary would say:

**FEMALE GREEK CHORUS** *(As Aunt Mary):* Peck's so good with them when they get to be this age.

*(Li'l Bit has stormed to another part of the stage, her back turned, weeping with a teenage fury. Peck, cautiously, as if stalking a deer, comes to her. She turns away even more. He waits a bit.)*

**PECK:** I don't suppose you're talking to family. *(No response)* Does it help that I'm in-law?

**LI'L BIT:** Don't you dare make fun of this.

**PECK:** I'm not. There's nothing funny about this. *(Beat)* Although I'll bet when Big Papa is about to meet his maker, he'll remember *The Merchant of Venice.*

**LI'L BIT:** I've got to get away from here.

**PECK:** You're going away. Soon. Here, take this.

*(Peck hands her his folded handkerchief. Li'l Bit uses it, noisily. Hands it back. Without her seeing, he reverently puts it back.)*

**LI'L BIT:** I hate this family.

**PECK:** Your grandfather's ignorant. And you're right—he's going to die soon. But he's family. Family is . . . family.

**LI'L BIT:** Grown-ups are always saying that. Family.

**PECK:** Well, when you get a little older, you'll see what we're saying.

**LI'L BIT:** Uh-huh. So family is another acquired taste, like French kissing?

**PECK:** Come again?

**LI'L BIT:** You know, at first it really grosses you out, but in time you grow to like it?

**PECK:** Girl, you are . . . a handful.

**LI'L BIT:** Uncle Peck—you have the keys to your car?
**PECK:** Where do you want to go?
**LI'L BIT:** Just up the road.
**PECK:** I'll come with you.
**LI'L BIT:** No—please? I just need to . . . to drive for a little bit. Alone.

*(Peck tosses her the keys.)*

**PECK:** When can I see you alone again?
**LI'L BIT:** Tonight.

*(Li'l Bit crosses to center stage while the lights dim around her. A Voice directs:)*

**Shifting Forward from First to Second Gear.**

**LI'L BIT:** There were a lot of rumors about why I got kicked out of that fancy school in 1970. Some say I got caught with a man in my room. Some say as a kid on scholarship I fooled around with a rich man's daughter.

*(Li'l Bit smiles innocently at the audience)* I'm not talking.

But the real truth was I had a constant companion in my dorm room—who was less than discrete. Canadian V.O. A fifth a day.

1970. A Nixon recession. I slept on the floors of friends who were out of work themselves. Took factory work when I could find it. A string of dead-end day jobs that didn't last very long.

What I did, most nights, was cruise the Beltway and the back roads of Maryland, where there was still country, past the battle-fields and farm houses. Racing in a 1965 Mustang—and as long as I had gasoline for my car and whiskey for me, the nights would pass. Fully tanked, I would speed past the churches and the trees on the bend, thinking just one notch of the steering wheel would be all it would take, and yet some . . . reflex took over. My hands on the wheel in the nine and three o'clock position—I never so much as got a ticket. He taught me well.

*(A Voice announces:)*

**You and the Reverse Gear.**

**LI'L BIT:** Back up. 1968. On the Eastern Shore. A celebration dinner.

*(Li'l Bit joins Peck at a table in a restaurant.)*

**PECK:** Feeling better, missy?

LI'L BIT: The bathroom's really amazing here, Uncle Peck! They have these little soaps—instead of borax or something—and they're in the shape of shells.

PECK: I'll have to take a trip to the gentleman's room just to see.

LI'L BIT: How did you know about this place?

PECK: This inn is famous on the Eastern Shore—it's been open since the seventeenth century. And I know how you like history . . .

*(Li'l Bit is shy and pleased.)*

LI'L BIT: It's great.

PECK: And you've just done your first, legal, long-distance drive. You must be hungry.

LI'L BIT: I'm starved.

PECK: I would suggest a dozen oysters to start, and the crab imperial . . . *(Li'l Bit is genuinely agog)* You might be interested to know the town history. When the British sailed up this very river in the dead of night—see outside where I'm pointing?—they were going to bombard the heck out of this town. But the town fathers were ready for them. They crept up all the trees with lanterns so that the British would think they saw the town lights and they aimed their cannons too high. And that's why the inn is still here for business today.

LI'L BIT: That's a great story.

PECK *(Casually):* Would you like to start with a cocktail?

LI'L BIT: You're not . . . you're not going to start drinking, are you, Uncle Peck?

PECK: Not me. I told you, as long as you're with me, I'll never drink. I asked you if *you'd* like a cocktail before dinner. It's nice to have a little something with the oysters.

LI'L BIT: But . . . I'm not . . . legal. We could get arrested. Uncle Peck, they'll never believe I'm twenty-one!

PECK: So? Today we celebrate your driver's license—on the first try. This establishment reminds me a lot of places back home.

LI'L BIT: What does that mean?

PECK: In South Carolina, like here on the Eastern Shore, they're . . . *(Searches for the right euphemism)* . . . "European." Not so puritanical. And very understanding if gentlemen wish to escort very attractive young ladies who might want a before-dinner cocktail. If you want one, I'll order one.

LI'L BIT: Well—sure. Just . . . one.

*(The Female Greek Chorus appears in a spot.)*

FEMALE GREEK CHORUS *(As Mother):* A Mother's Guide to Social Drinking: A lady never gets sloppy—she may, however, get tipsy and a little gay.

Never drink on an empty stomach. Avail yourself of the bread basket and generous portions of butter. *Slather* the butter on your bread.

Sip your drink, slowly, let the beverage linger in your mouth—interspersed with interesting, fascinating conversation. Sip, never . . . slurp or gulp. Your glass should always be three-quarters full when his glass is empty.

Stay away from *ladies'* drinks: drinks like pink ladies, slow gin fizzes, daiquiris, gold cadillacs, Long Island iced teas, margaritas, piña coladas, mai tais, planters punch, white Russians, black Russians, red Russians, melon balls, blue balls, hummingbirds, hemorrhages and hurricanes. In short, avoid anything with sugar, or anything with an umbrella. Get your vitamin C from *fruit.* Don't order anything with Voodoo or Vixen in the title or sexual positions in the name like Dead Man Screw or the Missionary. *(She sort of titters)* Believe me, they are lethal. . . . I think you were conceived after one of those.

Drink, instead, like a man: straight up or on the rocks, with plenty of water in between.

Oh, yes. And never mix your drinks. Stay with one all night long, like the man you came in with: bourbon, gin, or tequila till dawn, damn the torpedoes, full speed ahead!

*(As the Female Greek Chorus retreats, the Male Greek Chorus approaches the table as a Waiter.)*

MALE GREEK CHORUS *(As Waiter):* I hope you all are having a pleasant evening. Is there something I can bring you, sir, before you order?

*(Li'l Bit waits in anxious fear. Carefully, Uncle Peck says with command:)*

PECK: I'll have a plain iced tea. The lady would like a drink, I believe.

*(The Male Greek Chorus does a double take; there is a moment when Uncle Peck and he are in silent communication.)*

MALE GREEK CHORUS *(As Waiter):* Very good. What would the . . . lady like?

LI'L BIT: *(A bit flushed):* Is there . . . is there any sugar in a martini?

PECK: None that I know of.

LI'L BIT: That's what I'd like then—a dry martini. And could we maybe have some bread?

PECK: A drink fit for a woman of the world. —Please bring the lady a dry martini, be generous with the olives, straight up.

*(The Male Greek Chorus anticipates a large tip.)*

MALE GREEK CHORUS *(As Waiter)*: Right away. Very good, sir.

*(The Male Greek Chorus returns with an empty martini glass which he puts in front of Li'l Bit.)*

PECK: Your glass is empty. Another martini, madam?

LI'L BIT: Yes, thank you.

*(Peck signals the Male Greek Chorus, who nods)*

So why did you leave South Carolina, Uncle Peck?

PECK: I was stationed in D.C. after the war, and decided to stay. Go North, Young Man, someone might have said.

LI'L BIT: What did you do in the service anyway?

PECK: *(Suddenly taciturn)*: I . . . I did just this and that. Nothing heroic or spectacular.

LI'L BIT: But did you see fighting? Or go to Europe?

PECK: I served in the Pacific Theater. It's really nothing interesting to talk about.

LI'L BIT: It is to me. *(The Waiter has brought another empty glass)* Oh, goody. I love the color of the swizzle sticks. What were we talking about?

PECK: Swizzle sticks.

LI'L BIT: Do you ever think of going back?

PECK: To the Marines?

LI'L BIT: No—to South Carolina.

PECK: Well, we do go back. To visit.

LI'L BIT: No, I mean to live.

PECK: Not very likely. I think it's better if my mother doesn't have a daily reminder of her disappointment.

LI'L BIT: Are these floorboards slanted?

PECK: Yes, the floor is very slanted. I think this is the original floor.

LI'L BIT: Oh, good.

*(The Female Greek Chorus as Mother enters swaying a little, a little past tipsy.)*

**FEMALE GREEK CHORUS** *(As Mother):* Don't leave your drink unattended when you visit the ladies' room. There is such a thing as white slavery; the modus operandi is to spike an unsuspecting young girl's drink with a "mickey" when she's left the room to powder her nose.

But if you feel you have had more than your sufficiency in liquor, do go to the ladies' room—often. Pop your head out of doors for a refreshing breath of the night air. If you must, wet your face and head with tap water. Don't be afraid to dunk your head if necessary. A wet woman is still less conspicuous than a drunk woman.

*(The Female Greek Chorus stumbles a little; conspiratorially)*

When in the course of human events it becomes necessary, go to a corner stall and insert the index and middle finger down the throat almost to the epiglottis. Divulge your stomach contents by such persuasion, and then wait a few moments before rejoining your beau waiting for you at your table.

Oh, no. Don't be shy or embarrassed. In the very best of establishments, there's always one or two debutantes crouched in the corner stalls, their beaded purses tossed willy-nilly, sounding like cats in heat, heaving up the contents of their stomachs.

*(The Female Greek Chorus begins to wander off)* I wonder what it is they do in the men's rooms . . .

**LI'L BIT:** So why is your mother disappointed in you, Uncle Peck?

**PECK:** Every mother in Horry Country has Great Expectations.

**LI'L BIT:** —Could I have another mar-ti-ni, please?

**PECK:** I think this is your last one.

*(Peck signals the Waiter. The Waiter looks at Li'l Bit and shakes his head no. Peck raises his eyebrow, raises his finger to indicate one more, and then rubs his fingers together. It looks like a secret code. The Waiter sighs, shakes his head sadly, and brings over another empty martini glass. He glares at Peck.)*

**LI'L BIT:** The name of the country where you grew up is "Horry?" *(Li'l Bit, plastered, begins to laugh. Then she stops)* I think your mother should be proud of you.

*(Peck signals for the check.)*

**PECK:** Well, missy, she wanted me to do—to *be* everything my father was not. She wanted me to amount to something.

**LI'L BIT:**  But you have! You've amounted a lot. . . .

**PECK:**  I'm just a very ordinary man.

*(The Waiter has brought the check and waits. Peck draws out a large bill and hands it to the Waiter. Li'l Bit is in the soppy stage.)*

**LI'L BIT:**  I'll bet your mother loves you, Uncle Peck.

*(Peck freezes a bit. To Male Greek Chorus as Waiter:)*

**PECK:**  Thank you. The service was exceptional. Please keep the change.

**MALE GREEK CHORUS** *(As Waiter, in a tone that could freeze):*  Thank you, sir. Will you be needing any help?

**PECK:**  I think we can manage, thank you.

*(Just then, the Female Greek Chorus as Mother lurches on stage; the Male Greek Chorus as Waiter escorts her off as she delivers:)*

**FEMALE GREEK CHORUS** *(As Mother):*  Thanks to judicious planning and several trips to the ladies' loo, your mother once out-drank an entire regiment of British officers on a good-will visit to Washington! Every last man of them! Milquetoasts! How'd they ever kick Hitler's cahones, huh? No match for an American lady—I could drink every man in here under the table.

*(She delivers one last crucial hint before she is gently "bounced")*

As a last resort, when going out for an evening on the town, be sure to wear a skin-tight girdle—so tight that only a surgical knife or acetylene torch can get it off you—so that if you do pass out in the arms of your escort, he'll end up with rubber burns on his fingers before he can steal your virtue—

*(A Voice punctures the interlude with:)*

**Vehicle Failure.**
**Even with careful maintenance and preventive operation of your automobile, it is all too common for us to experience an unexpected breakdown. If you are driving at any speed when a breakdown occurs, you must slow down and guide the automobile to the side of the road.**

*(Peck is slowly propping up Li'l Bit as they work their way to his car in the parking lot of the inn.)*

PECK: How are you doing, missy?

LI'L BIT: It's so far to the car, Uncle Peck. Like the lanterns in the trees the British fired on . . .

*(Li'l Bit stumbles. Peck swoops her up in his arms.)*

PECK: Okay. I think we're going to take a more direct route. *(Li'l Bit closes her eyes)* Dizzy? *(She nods her head)* Don't look at the ground. Almost there—do you feel sick to your stomach? *(Li'l Bit nods. They reach the "car." Peck gently deposits her on the front seat)* Just settle here a little while until things stop spinning. *(Li'l Bit opens her eyes)*

LI'L BIT: What are we doing?

PECK: We're just going to sit here until your tummy settles down.

LI'L BIT: It's such nice upholst'ry—

PECK: Think you can go for a ride, now?

LI'L BIT: Where are you taking me?

PECK: Home.

LI'L BIT: You're not taking me—upstairs? There's no room at the inn? *(Li'l Bit giggles)*

PECK: Do you want to go upstairs? *(Li'l Bit doesn't answer)* Or home?

LI'L BIT: —This isn't right, Uncle Peck.

PECK: What isn't right?

LI'L BIT: What we're doing. It's wrong. It's very wrong.

PECK: What are we doing? *(Li'l Bit does not answer)* We're just going out to dinner.

LI'L BIT: You know. It's not nice to Aunt Mary.

PECK: You let me be the judge of what's nice and not nice to my wife.

*(Beat.)*

LI'L BIT: Now you're mad.

PECK: I'm not mad. It's just that I thought you . . . understood me, Li'l Bit. I think you're the only one who does.

LI'L BIT: Someone will get hurt.

PECK: Have I forced you to do anything?

*(There is a long pause as Li'l Bit tries to get sober enough to think this through.)*

LI'L BIT: . . . I guess not.

PECK: We are just enjoying each other's company. I've told you, nothing is going to happen between us until you want it to. Do you know that?

LI'L BIT: Yes.

PECK: Nothing is going to happen until you want it to. *(A second more, with Peck staring ahead at the river while seated at the wheel of his car. Then, softly:)* Do you want something to happen?

*(Peck reaches over and strokes her face, very gently. Li'l Bit softens, reaches for him, and buries her head in his neck. Then she kisses him. Then she moves away, dizzy again.)*

LI'L BIT: . . . I don't know.

*(Peck smiles; this has been good news for him—it hasn't been a "no.")*

PECK: Then I'll wait. I'm a very patient man. I've been waiting for a long time. I don't mind waiting.

LI'L BIT: Someone is going to get hurt.

PECK: No one is going to get hurt. *(Li'l Bit closes her eyes)* Are you feeling sick?

LI'L BIT: Sleepy.

*(Carefully, Peck props Li'l Bit up on the seat.)*

PECK: Stay here a second.

LI'L BIT: Where're you going?

PECK: I'm getting something from the back seat.

LI'L BIT *(Scared; too loud)*: What? What are you going to do?

*(Peck reappears in the front seat with a lap rug.)*

PECK: Shhhh. *(Peck covers Li'l Bit. She calms down)* There. Think you can sleep?

*(Li'l Bit nods. She slides over to rest on his shoulder. With a look of happiness, Peck turns the ignition key. Beat. Peck leaves Li'l Bit sleeping in the car and strolls down to the audience. Wagner's Flying Dutchman comes up faintly.*

*A Voice interjects:)*

**Idling in the Neutral Gear.**

TEENAGE GREEK CHORUS: Uncle Peck Teaches Cousin Bobby How to Fish.

PECK: I get back once or twice a year—supposedly to visit Mama and the family, but the real truth is to fish. I miss this the most of all.

There's a smell in the Low Country—where the swamp and fresh inlet join the saltwater—a scent of sand and cypress, that I haven't found anywhere yet.

I don't say this very often up North because it will just play into the stereotype everyone has, but I will tell you: I didn't wear shoes in the summertime until I was sixteen. It's unnatural down here to pen up your feet in leather. Go ahead—take 'em off. Let yourself breathe—it really will make you feel better.

We're going to aim for some pompano today—and I have to tell you, they're a very shy, mercurial fish. Takes patience, and psychology. You have to believe it doesn't matter if you catch one or not.

Sky's pretty spectacular—there's some beer in the cooler next to the crab salad I packed, so help yourself if you get hungry. Are you hungry? Thirsty? Holler if you are.

Okay. You don't want to lean over the bridge like that—pompano feed in shallow water, and you don't want to get too close—they're frisky and shy little things—wait, check your line. Yep, something's been munching while we were talking.

Okay, look: We take the sand flea and you take the hook like this—right through his little sand flea rump. Sand fleas should always keep their backs to the wall. Okay. Cast it in, like I showed you. That's great! I can taste that pompano now, sautéed with some pecans and butter, a little bourbon—now—let it lie on the bottom—now, reel, jerk, reel, jerk—

Look—look at your line. There's something calling, all right.

Okay, tip the rod up—not too sharp—hook it—all right, now easy, reel and then rest—let it play. And reel—play it out, that's right—really good! I can't believe it! It's a pompano. —Good work! Way to go! You are an official fisherman now. Pompano are hard to catch. We are going to have a delicious little—

What? Well, I don't know how much pain a fish feels—you can't think of that. Oh, no, don't cry, come on now, it's just a fish—the other guys are going to see you. —No, no, you're just real sensitive, and I think that's wonderful at your age—look, do you want me to cut it free? You do?

Okay, hand me those pliers—look—I'm cutting the hook—okay? And we're just going to drop it in—no I'm not mad. It's just for fun, okay? There—it's going to swim back to its lady friend and tell her what a terrible day it had and she's going to stroke him with her fins until he feels better, and then they'll do something alone together that will make them both feel good and sleepy. . . .

*(Peck bends down, very earnest)* I don't want you to feel ashamed about crying. I'm not going to tell anyone, okay? I can keep secrets. You know, men cry all the time. They just don't tell anybody, and they don't let anybody catch them. There's nothing you could do that would make me feel ashamed of you. Do you know that? Okay. *(Peck straightens up, smiles)*

Do you want to pack up and call it a day? I tell you what—I think I can still remember—there's a really neat tree house where I used to stay for days. I think it's still here—it was the last time I looked. But it's a secret place—you can't tell anybody we've gone there—least of all your mom or your sisters. —This is something special just between you and me. Sound good? We'll climb up there and have a beer and some crab salad—okay, B.B.? Bobby? Robert . . .

*(Li'l Bit sits at a kitchen table with the two Female Greek Chorus members.)*

LI'L BIT *(To the audience):*   Three women, three generations, sit at the kitchen table.

**On Men, Sex, and Women: Part I:**

FEMALE GREEK CHORUS *(As Mother):*   Men only want one thing.

LI'L BIT *(Wide-eyed):*   But what? What is it they want?

FEMALE GREEK CHORUS *(As Mother):*   And once they have it, they lose all interest. So Don't Give It to Them.

TEENAGE GREEK CHORUS *(As Grandmother):*   I never had the luxury of the rhythm method. Your grandfather is just a big bull. A big bull. Every morning, every evening.

FEMALE GREEK CHORUS *(As Mother, whispers to Li'l Bit):*   And he used to come home for lunch every day.

LI'L BIT:   My god, Grandma!

TEENAGE GREEK CHORUS *(As Grandmother):*   Your grandfather only cares that I do two things: have the table set and the bed turned down.

FEMALE GREEK CHORUS *(As Mother):*   And in all that time, Mother, you never have experienced—?

LI'L BIT *(To the audience):*   —Now my grandmother believed in all the sacraments of the church, to the day she died. She believed in Santa Claus and the Easter Bunny until she was fifteen. But she didn't believe in—

TEENAGE GREEK CHORUS *(As Grandmother):*   —Orgasm! That's just something you and Mary have made up! I don't believe you.

**FEMALE GREEK CHORUS** *(As Mother):* Mother, it happens to women all the time—

**TEENAGE GREEK CHORUS** *(As Grandmother):* —Oh, now you're going to tell me about the G force!

**LI'L BIT:** No, Grandma, I think that's astronauts—

**FEMALE GREEK CHORUS** *(As Mother):* Well, Mama, after all, you were a child bride when Big Papa came and got you—you were a married woman and you still believed in Santa Claus.

**TEENAGE GREEK CHORUS** *(As Grandmother):* It was legal, what Daddy and I did! I was fourteen and in those days, fourteen was a grown-up woman—

*(Big Papa shuffles in the kitchen for a cookie.)*

**MALE GREEK CHORUS** *(As Grandfather):* —Oh, now we're off on Grandma and the Rape of the Sa-bean Women!

**TEENAGE GREEK CHORUS** *(As Grandmother):* Well, you were the one in such a big hurry—

**MALE GREEK CHORUS** *(As Grandfather to Li'l Bit):* —I picked your grandmother out of that herd of sisters just like a lion chooses the gazelle—the plump, slow, flaky gazelle dawdling at the edge of the herd—your sisters were too smart and too fast and too scrawny—

**LI'L BIT** *(To the audience):* —The family story is that when Big Papa came for Grandma, my Aunt Lily was waiting for him with a broom—and she beat him over the head all the way down the stairs as he was carrying out Grandma's hope chest—

**MALE GREEK CHORUS** *(As Grandfather):* —And they were *mean.* 'Specially Lily.

**FEMALE GREEK CHORUS** *(As Mother):* Well, you were robbing the baby of the family!

**TEENAGE GREEK CHORUS** *(As Grandmother):* I still keep a broom handy in the kitchen! And I know how to use it! So get your hand out of the cookie jar and don't you spoil your appetite for dinner—out of the kitchen!

*(Male Greek Chorus as Grandfather leaves chuckling with a cookie.)*

**FEMALE GREEK CHORUS** *(As Mother):* Just one thing a married woman needs to know how to use—the rolling pin or the broom. I prefer a heavy, cast-iron fry pan—they're great on a man's head, no matter how thick the skull is.

TEENAGE GREEK CHORUS *(As Grandmother):* Yes, sir, your father is ruled by only two bosses! Mr. Gut and Mr. Peter! And sometimes, first thing in the morning, Mr. Sphincter Muscle!

FEMALE GREEK CHORUS *(As Mother):* It's true. Men are like children. Just like little boys.

TEENAGE GREEK CHORUS *(As Grandmother):* Men are bulls! Big bulls!

*(The Greek Chorus is getting aroused.)*

FEMALE GREEK CHORUS *(As Mother):* They'd still be crouched on their haunches over a fire in a cave if we hadn't cleaned them up!

TEENAGE GREEK CHORUS *(As Grandmother, flushed):* Coming in smelling of sweat—

FEMALE GREEK CHORUS *(As Mother):* —Looking at those naughty pictures like boys in a dime store with a dollar in their pockets!

TEENAGE GREEK CHORUS *(As Grandmother, raucous):* No matter to them what they smell like! They've got to have it, right then, on the spot, right there! Nasty!—

FEMALE GREEK CHORUS *(As Mother):* —Vulgar!

TEENAGE GREEK CHORUS *(As Grandmother):* Primitive!—

FEMALE GREEK CHORUS *(As Mother):* —Hot!—

LI'L BIT: And just about then, Big Papa would shuffle in with—

MALE GREEK CHORUS *(As Grandfather):* —What are you all cackling about in here?

TEENAGE GREEK CHORUS *(As Grandmother):* Stay out of the kitchen! This is just for girls!

*(As Grandfather leaves:)*

MALE GREEK CHORUS *(As Grandfather):* Lucy, you'd better not be filling Mama's head with sex! Every time you and Mary come over and start in about sex, when I ask a simple question like, "What time is dinner going to be ready?," Mama snaps my head off!

TEENAGE GREEK CHORUS *(As Grandmother):* Dinner will be ready when I'm good and ready! Stay out of this kitchen!

*(Li'l Bit steps out. A Voice directs:)*

**When Making a Left Turn, You Must Downshift While Going Forward.**

LI'L BIT: 1979. A long bus trip to Upstate New York. I settled in to read, when a young man sat beside me.

MALE GREEK CHORUS *(As Young Man; voice cracking):* "What are you reading?"

LI'L BIT: He asked. His voice broke into that miserable equivalent of vocal acne, not quite falsetto and not tenor, either. I glanced a side view. He was appealing in an odd way, huge ears at a defiant angle springing forward at ninety degrees. He must have been shaving, because his face, with a peach sheen, was speckled with nicks and styptic. "I have a class tomorrow," I told him.

MALE GREEK CHORUS *(As Young Man):* "You're taking a class?"

LI'L BIT: "I'm teaching a class." He concentrated on lowering his voice.

MALE GREEK CHORUS *(As Young Man):* "I'm a senior. Walt Whitman High."

LI'L BIT: The light was fading outside, so perhaps he was—with a very high voice.

I felt his "interest" quicken. Five steps ahead of the hopes in his head, I slowed down, waited, pretended surprise, acted at listening, all the while knowing we would get off the bus, he would just then seem to think to ask me to dinner, he would chivalrously insist on walking me home, he would continue to converse in the street until I would casually invite him up to my room—and—I was only into the second moment of conversation and I could see the whole evening before me.

And dramaturgically speaking, after the faltering and slightly comical "first act," there was the very briefest of intermissions, and an extremely capable and forceful and *sustained* second act. And after the second act climax and a gentle denouement—before the post-play discussion—I lay on my back in the dark and I thought about you, Uncle Peck. Oh. Oh—this is the allure. Being older. Being the first. Being the translator, the teacher, the epicure, the already jaded. This is how the giver gets taken.

*(Li'l Bit changes her tone)* On Men, Sex, and Women: Part II:

*(Li'l Bit steps back into the scene as a fifteen year old, gawky and quiet, as the gazelle at the edge of the herd.)*

TEENAGE GREEK CHORUS *(As Grandmother, to Li'l Bit):* You're being mighty quiet, missy. Cat Got Your Tongue?

LI'L BIT: I'm just listening. Just thinking.

TEENAGE GREEK CHORUS *(As Grandmother):* Oh, yes, Little Miss Radar Ears? Soaking it all in? Little Miss Sponge? Penny for your thoughts?

*(Li'l Bit hesitates to ask but she really wants to know.)*

FEMALE GREEK CHORUS *(As Mother):* Now, see, she's getting upset—you're scaring her.

TEENAGE GREEK CHORUS *(As Grandmother):* Good! Let her be good and scared! It hurts! You bleed like a stuck pig! And you lay there and say, "Why, O Lord, have you forsaken me?!"

LI'L BIT: It's not fair! Why does everything have to hurt for girls? Why is there always blood?

FEMALE GREEK CHORUS *(As Mother):* It's not a lot of blood—and it feels wonderful after the pain subsides . . .

TEENAGE GREEK CHORUS *(As Grandmother):* You're encouraging her to just go out and find out with the first drugstore joe who buys her a milk shake!

FEMALE GREEK CHORUS *(As Mother):* Don't be scared. It won't hurt you—if the man you go to bed with really loves you. It's important that he loves you.

TEENAGE GREEK CHORUS *(As Grandmother):* —Why don't you just go out and rent a motel room for her, Lucy?

FEMALE GREEK CHORUS *(As Mother):* I believe in telling my daughter the truth! We have a very close relationship! I want her to be able to ask me anything—I'm not scaring her with stories about Eve's sin and snakes crawling on their bellies for eternity and women bearing children in mortal pain—

TEENAGE GREEK CHORUS *(As Grandmother):* —If she stops and thinks before she takes her knickers off, maybe someone in this family will finish high school!

*(Li'l Bit knows what is about to happen and starts to retreat from the scene at this point.)*

FEMALE GREEK CHORUS *(As Mother):* Mother! If you and Daddy had helped me—I wouldn't have had to marry that—that no-good-son-of-a—

TEENAGE GREEK CHORUS *(As Grandmother):* —He was good enough for you on a full moon! I hold you responsible!

FEMALE GREEK CHORUS *(As Mother):* —You could have helped me! You could have told me something about the facts of life!

TEENAGE GREEK CHORUS *(As Grandmother):* —I told you what my mother told me! A girl with her skirt up can outrun a man with his pants down!

*(The Male Greek Chorus enters the fray; L'il Bit edges further downstage.)*

FEMALE GREEK CHORUS *(As Mother)*: And when I turned to you for a little help, all I got afterwards was—
MALE GREEK CHORUS *(As Grandfather)*: You Made Your Bed; Now Lie On It!

*(The Greek Chorus freezes, mouths open, argumentatively.)*

LI'L BIT *(To the audience)*: Oh, please! I still can't bear to listen to it, after all these years—
(The Male Greek Chorus "unfreezes," but out of his open mouth, as if to his surprise, comes a base refrain from a Motown song.)
MALE GREEK CHORUS: "Do-Bee-Do-Wah!"

*(The Female Greek Chorus member is also surprised; but she, too, unfreezes.)*

FEMALE GREEK CHORUS: "Shoo-doo-be-doo-be-doo; shoo-doo-be-doo-be-doo."

*(The Male and Female Greek Chorus members continue with their harmony, until the Teenage member of the Chorus starts in with Motown lyrics such as "Dedicated to the One I Love," or "In the Still of the Night," or "Hold Me"—any Sam Cooke will do. The three modulate down into three part harmony, softly, until they are submerged by the actual recording playing over the radio in the car in which Uncle Peck sits in the driver's seat, waiting. Li'l Bit sits in the passenger's seat.)*

LI'L BIT: Ahh. That's better.

*(Uncle Peck reaches over and turns the volume down; to Li'l Bit:)*

PECK: How can you hear yourself think?

*(Li'l Bit does not answer. A Voice insinuates itself in the pause:)*

Before You Drive.
Always check under your car for obstructions—broken bottles, fallen tree branches, and the bodies of small children. Each year hundreds of children are crushed beneath the wheels of unwary

drivers in their own driveways. Children depend on *you* to watch them.

*(Pause. The Voice continues:)*

**You and the Reverse Gear.**

*(In the following section, it would be nice to have slides of erotic photographs of women and cars: women posed over the hood; women draped along the sideboards; women with water hoses spraying the car; and the actress playing Li'l Bit with a Bel Air or any 1950s car one can find for the finale.)*

LI'L BIT:   1967. In a parking lot of the Beltsville Agricultural Farms. The Initiation into a Boy's First Love.

PECK *(With a soft look on his face):*   Of course, my favorite car will always be the '56 Bel Air Sports Coupe. Chevy sold more '55s, but the '56!—a V-8 with Corvette option, 225 horsepower; went from zero to sixty miles per hour in 8.9 seconds.

LI'L BIT *(To the audience):*   Long after a mother's tits, but before a woman's breasts:

PECK:   Super-Turbo-Fire! What a Power Pack—mechanical lifters, twin four-barrel carbs, lightweight valves, dual exhausts—

LI'L BIT *(To the audience):*   After the milk but before the beer:

PECK:   A specific intake manifold, higher-lift camshaft, and the tightest squeeze Chevy had ever made—

LI'L BIT *(To the audience):*   Long after he's squeezed down the birth canal but before he's pushed his way back in: The boy falls in love with the thing that bears his weight with speed.

PECK:   I want you to know your automobile inside and out. —Are you there? Li'l Bit?

*(Slides end here.)*

LI'L BIT:   —What?

PECK:   You're drifting. I need you to concentrate.

LI'L BIT:   Sorry.

PECK:   Okay. Get into the driver's seat. *(Li'l Bit does)* Okay. Now. Show me what you're going to do before you start the car.

*(Li'l Bit sits, with her hands in her lap. She starts to giggle.)*

LI'L BIT:   I don't know, Uncle Peck.

PECK:   Now, come on. What's the first thing you're going to adjust?

LI'L BIT:   My bra strap?—

PECK:   —Li'l Bit. What's the most important thing to have control of on the inside of the car?

LI'L BIT:   That's easy. The radio. I tune the radio from Mama's old fart tunes to—

*(Li'l Bit turns the radio up so we can hear a 1960s tune. With surprising firmness, Peck commands:)*

LI'L BIT:   —Radio off. Right now. *(Li'l Bit turns the radio off)* When you are driving your car, with your license, you can fiddle with the stations all you want. But when you are driving with a learner's permit in my car, I want all your attention to be on the road.

LI'L BIT:   Yes, sir.

PECK:   Okay. Now the seat—forward and up. *(Li'l Bit pushes it forward)* Do you want a cushion?

LI'L BIT:   No—I'm good.

PECK:   You should be able to reach all the switches and controls. Your feet should be able to push the accelerator, brake and clutch all the way down. Can you do that?

LI'L BIT:   Yes.

PECK:   Okay, the side mirrors. You want to be able to see just a bit of the right side of the car in the right mirror—can you?

LI'L BIT:   Turn it out more.

PECK:   Okay. How's that?

LI'L BIT:   A little more. . . . Okay, that's good.

PECK:   Now the left—again, you want to be able to see behind you— but the left lane—adjust it until you feel comfortable. *(Li'l Bit does so)* Next. I want you to check the rearview mirror. Angle it so you have a clear vision of the back. *(Li'l Bit does so)* Okay. Lock your door. Make sure all the doors are locked.

LI'L BIT: *(Making a joke of it):*   But then I'm locked in with you.

PECK:   Don't fool.

LI'L BIT:   All right. We're locked in.

PECK:   We'll deal with the air vents and defroster later. I'm teaching you on a manual—once you learn manual, you can drive anything. I want you to be able to drive any car, any machine. Manual gives you *control*. In ice, if your brakes fail, if you need more power— okay? It's a little harder at first, but then it becomes like breathing. Now. Put your hands on the wheel. I never want to see you driving with one hand. Always two hands. *(Li'l Bit hesitates)* What? What is it now?

LI'L BIT: If I put my hands on the wheel—how do I defend myself?

PECK *(Softly):* Now listen. Listen up close. We're not going to fool around with this. This is serious business. I will never touch you when you are driving a car. Understand?

LI'L BIT: Okay.

PECK: Hands on the nine o'clock and three o'clock position gives you maximum control and turn.

*(Peck goes silent for a while. Li'l Bit waits for more instruction)*

Okay. Just relax and listen to me, Li'l Bit, okay? I want you to lift your hands for a second and look at them. *(Li'l Bit feels a bit silly, but does it)*

Those are your two hands. When you are driving, your life is in your own two hands. Understand? *(Li'l Bit nods)*

I don't have any sons. You're the nearest to a son I'll ever have—and I want to give you something. Something that really matters to me.

There's something about driving—when you're in control of the car, just you and the machine and the road—that nobody can take from you. A power. I feel more myself in my car than anywhere else. And that's what I want to give to you.

There's a lot of assholes out there. Crazy men, arrogant idiots, drunks, angry kids, geezers who are blind—and you have to be ready for them. I want to teach you to drive like a man.

LI'L BIT: What does that mean?

PECK: Men are taught to drive with confidence—with aggression. The road belongs to them. They drive defensively—always looking out for the other guy. Women tend to be polite—to hesitate. And that can be fatal.

You're going to learn to think what the other guy is going to do before he does it. If there's an accident, and ten cars pile up, and people get killed, you're the one who's gonna steer through it, put your foot on the gas if you have to, and be the only one to walk away. I don't know how long you or I are going to live, but we're for damned sure not going to die in a car.

So if you're going to drive with me, I want you to take this very seriously.

LI'L BIT: I will, Uncle Peck. I want you to teach me to drive.

PECK: Good. You're going to pass your test on the first try. Perfect score. Before the next four weeks are over, you're going to know this baby inside and out. Treat her with respect.

LI'L BIT: Why is it a "she?"

PECK: Good question. It doesn't have to be a "she"—but when you close your eyes and think of someone who responds to your touch—someone who performs just for you and gives you what you ask for—I guess I always see a "she." You can call her what you like.

LI'L BIT *(To the audience):* I closed my eyes—and decided not to change the gender.

*(A Voice:)*

**Defensive driving involves defending yourself from hazardous and sudden changes in your automotive environment. By thinking ahead, the defensive driver can adjust to weather, road conditions and road kill. Good defensive driving involves mental and physical preparation. Are you prepared?**

*(Another Voice chimes in:)*

**You and the Reverse Gear.**

LI'L BIT: 1966. The Anthropology of the Female Body in Ninth Grade—Or A Walk Down Mammary Lane.

*(Throughout the following, there is occasional rhythmic beeping, like a transmitter signalling. Li'l Bit is aware of it, but can't figure out where it is coming from. No one else seems to hear it.)*

MALE GREEK CHORUS: In the hallway of Francis Scott Key Middle School.

*(A bell rings; the Greek Chorus is changing classes and meets in the hall, conspiratorially.)*

TEENAGE GREEK CHORUS: She's coming!

*(Li'l Bit enters the scene; the Male Greek Chorus member has a sudden, violent sneezing and lethal allergy attack.)*

FEMALE GREEK CHORUS: Jerome? Jerome? Are you all right?

MALE GREEK CHORUS: I—don't—know. I can't breathe—get Li'l Bit—

TEENAGE GREEK CHORUS:   —He needs oxygen! —
FEMALE GREEK CHORUS:   —Can you help us here?
LI'L BIT:   What's wrong? Do you want me to get the school nurse—

*(The Male Greek Chorus member wheezes, grabs his throat and sniffs at Li'l Bit's chest, which is beeping away.)*

MALE GREEK CHORUS:   No—it's okay—I only get this way when I'm around an allergy trigger—
LI'L BIT:   Golly. What are you allergic to?
MALE GREEK CHORUS *(With a sudden grab of her breast)*:   Foam rubber.

*(The Greek Chorus members break up with hilarity; Jerome leaps away from Li'l Bit's kicking rage with agility; as he retreats:)*

LI'L BIT:   Jerome! Creep! Cretin! Cro-Magnon!
TEENAGE GREEK CHORUS:   Rage is not attractive in a girl.
FEMALE GREEK CHORUS:   Really. Get a Sense of Humor.

*(A Voice echoes:)*

**Good defensive driving involves mental and physical preparation. Were You Prepared?**

FEMALE GREEK CHORUS:   Gym Class: In the showers.

*(The sudden sound of water; the Female Greek Chorus members and Li'l Bit, while fully clothed, drape towels across their fronts, miming nudity. They stand, hesitate, at an imaginary shower's edge.)*

LI'L BIT:   Water looks hot.
FEMALE GREEK CHORUS:   Yesss. . . .

*(Female Greek Chorus members are not going to make the first move. One dips a tentative toe under the water, clutching the towel around her.)*

LI'L BIT:   Well, I guess we'd better shower and get out of here.
FEMALE GREEK CHORUS:   Yep. You go ahead. I'm still cooling off.
LI'L BIT:   Okay. —Sally? Are you gonna shower?
TEENAGE GREEK CHORUS:   After you—

*(Li'l Bit takes a deep breath for courage, drops the towel and plunges in: The two Female Greek Chorus members look at*

*Li'l Bit in the all together, laugh, gasp and high-five each other.)*

TEENAGE GREEK CHORUS: Oh my god! Can you believe—
FEMALE GREEK CHORUS: Told you! It's not foam rubber! I win! Jerome owes me fifty cents!

*(A Voice editorializes:)*

**Were You Prepared?**

*(Li'l Bit tries to cover up; she is exposed, as suddenly 1960s Motown fills the room and we segue into:)*

FEMALE GREEK CHORUS: The Sock Hop.

*(Li'l Bit stands up against the wall with her female class-mates. Teenage Greek Chorus is mesmerized by the music and just sways alone, lip-synching the lyrics.)*

LI'L BIT: I don't know. Maybe it's just me—but—do you ever feel like you're just a walking Mary Jane joke?
FEMALE GREEK CHORUS: I don't know what you mean.
LI'L BIT: You haven't heard the Mary Jane jokes? *(Female Greek Chorus member shakes her head no)* Okay. "Little Mary Jane is walking through the woods, when all of a sudden this man who was hiding behind a tree *jumps* out, rips open Mary Jane's blouse, and plunges his hands on her breasts. And Little Mary Jane just laughed and laughed because she knew her money was in her shoes."

*(Li'l Bit laughs; the Female Greek Chorus does not.)*

FEMALE GREEK CHORUS: You're weird.

*(In another space, in a strange light, Uncle Peck stands and stares at Li'l Bit's body. He is setting up a tripod, but he just stands, appreciative, watching her.)*

LI'L BIT: Well, don't you ever feel . . . self-conscious? Like you're be-ing looked at all the time?
FEMALE GREEK CHORUS: That's not a problem for me. —Oh— look—Greg's coming over to ask you to dance.

*(Teenage Greek Chorus becomes attentive, flustered. Male Greek Chorus member, as Greg, bends slightly as a very short young man, whose head is at Li'l Bit's chest level. Ardent,*

*sincere and socially inept, Greg will become a successful gynecologist.)*

TEENAGE GREEK CHORUS *(Softly):* Hi, Greg.

*(Greg does not hear. He is intent on only one thing.)*

MALE GREEK CHORUS *(As Greg, to Li'l Bit):* Good Evening. Would you care to dance?

LI'L BIT *(Gently):* Thank you very much, Greg—but I'm going to sit this one out.

MALE GREEK CHORUS *(As Greg):* Oh. Okay. I'll try my luck later.

*(He disappears.)*

TEENAGE GREEK CHORUS: Oohhh.

*(Li'l Bit relaxes. Then she tenses, aware of Peck's gaze.)*

TEENAGE GREEK CHORUS: Take pity on him. Someone should.

LI'L BIT: But he's so short.

TEENAGE GREEK CHORUS: He can't help it.

LI'L BIT: But his head comes up to *(Li'l Bit gestures)* here. And I think he asks me on the fast dances so he can watch me—you know—jiggle.

FEMALE GREEK CHORUS: I wish I had your problems.

*(The tune changes; Greg is across the room in a flash.)*

MALE GREEK CHORUS *(As Greg):* Evening again. May I ask you for the honor of a spin on the floor?

LI'L BIT: I'm . . . very complimented, Greg. But I . . . I just don't do fast dances.

MALE GREEK CHORUS *(As Greg):* Oh. No problem. That's okay.

*(He disappears. Teenage Greek Chorus watches him go.)*

TEENAGE GREEK CHORUS: That is just so—sad.

*(Li'l Bit becomes aware of Peck waiting.)*

FEMALE GREEK CHORUS: You know, you should take it as a compliment that the guys want to watch you jiggle. They're guys. That's what they're supposed to do.

LI'L BIT: I guess you're right. But sometimes I feel like these alien life forces, these two mounds of flesh have grafted themselves onto my chest, and they're using me until they can "propagate" and take over the world and they'll just keep growing, with a mind of their own until I collapse under their weight and they suck all the nourishment out of my body and I finally just waste away while they get bigger and bigger and— *(Li'l Bit's classmates are just staring at her in disbelief)*

FEMALE GREEK CHORUS:  —You are the strangest girl I have ever met.

*(Li'l Bit's trying to joke but feels on the verge of tears.)*

LI'L BIT:  Or maybe someone's implanted radio transmitters in my chest at a frequency I can't hear, that girls can't detect, but they're sending out these signals to men who get mesmerized, like sirens, calling them to dash themselves on these "rocks"—

*(Just then, the music segues into a slow dance, perhaps a Beach Boys tune like "Little Surfer," but over the music there's a rhythmic, hypnotic beeping transmitted, which both Greg and Peck hear. Li'l Bit hears it too, and in horror she stares at her chest. She, too, is almost hypnotized. In a trance, Greg responds to the signals and is called to her side—actually, her front. Like a zombie, he stands in front of her, his eyes planted on her two orbs.)*

MALE GREEK CHORUS *(As Greg):*  This one's a slow dance. I hope your dance card isn't . . . filled?

*(Li'l Bit is aware of Peck; but the signals are calling her to him. The signals are no longer transmitters, but an electromagnetic force, pulling Li'l Bit to his side, where he again waits for her to join him. She must get away from the dance floor.)*

LI'L BIT:  Greg—you really are a nice boy. But I don't like to dance.

MALE GREEK CHORUS *(As Greg):*  That's okay. We don't have to move or anything. I could just hold you and we could just sway a little—

LI'L BIT:  —No! I'm sorry—but I think I have to leave; I hear someone calling me—

*(Li'l Bit starts across the dance floor, leaving Greg behind. The beeping stops. The lights change, although the music does not. As Li'l Bit talks to the audience, she continues to change and prepare for the coming session. She should be*

*wearing a tight tank top or a sheer blouse and very tight pants. To the audience:)*

In every man's home some small room, some zone in his house, is set aside. It might be the attic, or the study, or a den. And there's an invisible sign as if from the old treehouse: Girls Keep Out.

Here, away from female eyes, lace doilies and crochet, he keeps his manly toys: the Vargas pinups, the tackle. A scent of tobacco and WD-40. *(She inhales deeply)* A dash of his Bay Rum. Ahhh . . . *(Li'l Bit savors it for just a moment more)*

Here he keeps his secrets: a violin or saxophone, drum set or darkroom, and the stacks of *Playboy*. *(In a whisper)* Here, in my aunt's home, it was the basement. Uncle Peck's turf.

*(A Voice commands:)*

**You and the Reverse Gear.**
LI'L BIT:   1965. The Photo Shoot.

*(Li'l Bit steps into the scene as a nervous but curious thirteen year old. Music, from the previous scene, continues to play, changing into something like Roy Orbison later—something seductive with a beat. Peck fiddles, all business, with his camera. As in the driving lesson, he is all competency and concentration. Li'l Bit stands awkwardly. He looks through the Leica camera on the tripod, adjusts the back lighting, etc.)*

PECK:   Are you cold? The lights should heat up some in a few minutes—
LI'L BIT:   —Aunt Mary is?
PECK:   At the National Theatre matinee. With your mother. We have time.
LI'L BIT:   But—what if—
PECK:   —And so what if they return? I told them you and I were going to be working with my camera. They won't come down. *(Li'l Bit is quiet, apprehensive)* —Look, are you sure you want to do this?
LI'L BIT:   I said I'd do it. But—
PECK:   —I know. You've drawn the line.
LI'L BIT *(Reassured):*   That's right. No frontal nudity.
PECK:   Good heavens, girl, where did you pick that up?
LI'L BIT *(Defensive):*   I read.

*(Peck tries not to laugh.)*

PECK: And I read *Playboy* for the interviews. Okay. Let's try some different music.

*(Peck goes to an expensive reel-to-reel and forwards. Something like "Sweet Dreams" begins to play.)*

LI'L BIT: I didn't know you listened to this.

PECK: I'm not dead, you know. I try to keep up. Do you like this song? *(Li'l Bit nods with pleasure)* Good. Now listen—at professional photo shoots, they always play music for the models. Okay? I want you to just enjoy the music. Listen to it with your body, and just—respond.

LI'L BIT: Respond to the music with my . . . body?

PECK: Right. Almost like dancing. Here—let's get you on the stool, first. *(Peck comes over and helps her up)*

LI'L BIT: But nothing showing—

*(Peck firmly, with his large capable hands, brushes back her hair, angles her face. Li'l Bit turns to him like a plant to the sun.)*

PECK: Nothing showing. Just a peek.

*(He holds her by the shoulder, looking at her critically. Then he unbuttons her blouse to the midpoint, and runs his hands over the flesh of her exposed sternum, arranging the fabric, just touching her. Deliberately, calmly. Asexually. Li'l Bit quiets, sits perfectly still, and closes her eyes)*

Okay?

LI'L BIT: Yes.

*(Peck goes back to his camera.)*

PECK: I'm going to keep talking to you. Listen without responding to what I'm saying; you want to listen to the music. Sway, move just your torso or your head—I've got to check the light meter.

LI'L BIT: But—you'll be watching.

PECK: No—I'm not here—just my voice. Pretend you're in your room all alone on a Friday night with your mirror—and the music feels good—just move for me, Li'l Bit—

*(Li'l Bit closes her eyes. At first self-conscious; then she gets more into the music and begins to sway. We hear the camera*

*start to whir. Throughout the shoot, there can be a slide montage of actual shots of the actor playing Li'l Bit—interspersed with other models à la* Playboy, Calvin Klein *and Victoriana/Lewis Carroll's Alice Liddell)*

That's it. That looks great. Okay. Just keep doing that. Lift your head up a bit more, good, good, just keep moving, that a girl— you're a very beautiful young woman. Do you know that? *(Li'l Bit looks up, blushes. Peck shoots the camera. The audience should see this shot on the screen)*

LI'L BIT:   No. I don't know that.

PECK:   Listen to the music. *(Li'l Bit closes her eyes again)* Well you are. For a thirteen year old, you have a body a twenty-year-old woman would die for.

LI'L BIT:   The boys in school don't think so.

PECK:   The boys in school are little Neanderthals in short pants. You're ten years ahead of them in maturity; it's gonna take a while for them to catch up.

*(Peck clicks another shot; we see a faint smile on Li'l Bit on the screen)*

Girls turn into women long before boys turn into men.

LI'L BIT:   Why is that?

PECK:   I don't know, Li'l Bit. But it's a blessing for men. *(Li'l Bit turns silent)* Keep moving. Try arching your back on the stool, hands behind you, and throw your head back. *(The slide shows a* Playboy *model in this pose)* Oohh, great. That one was great. Turn your head away, same position. *(Whir)* Beautiful.

*(Li'l Bit looks at him a bit defiantly.)*

LI'L BIT:   I think Aunt Mary is beautiful.

*(Peck stands still.)*

PECK:   My wife is a very beautiful woman. Her beauty doesn't cancel yours out. *(More casually; he returns to the camera)* All the women in your family are beautiful. In fact, I think all women are. You're not listening to the music. *(Peck shoots some more film in silence)* All right, turn your head to the left. Good. Now take the back of your right hand and put in on your right cheek—your elbow angled up—now slowly, slowly, stroke your cheek, draw back your

hair with the back of your hand. *(Another classic* Playboy *or Vargas)* Good. One hand above and behind your head; stretch your body; smile. *(Another pose)*
    Li'l Bit. I want you to think of something that makes you laugh—
LI'L BIT: I can't think of anything.
PECK: Okay. Think of Big Papa chasing Grandma around the living room. *(Li'l Bit lifts her head and laughs. Click. We should see this shot)* Good. Both hands behind your head. Great! Hold that. *(From behind his camera)* You're doing great work. If we keep this up, in five years we'll have a really professional portfolio.

*(Li'l Bit stops.)*

LI'L BIT: What do you mean in five years?
PECK: You can't submit work to *Playboy* until you're eighteen.—

*(Peck continues to shoot; he knows he's made a mistake.)*

LI'L BIT: —Wait a minute. You're joking, aren't you, Uncle Peck?
PECK: Heck, no. You can't get into *Playboy* unless you're the very best. And you are the very best.
LI'L BIT: I would never do that!

*(Peck stops shooting. He turns off the music.)*

PECK: Why? There's nothing wrong with Playboy—it's a very classy maga—
LI'L BIT *(More upset):* But I thought you said I should go to college!
PECK: Wait—Li'l Bit—it's nothing like that. Very respectable women model for *Playboy*—actresses with major careers—women in college—there's an Ivy League issue every—
LI'L BIT: —I'm never doing anything like that! You'd show other people these—other *men*—these—what I'm doing. —Why would you do that?! Any *boy* around here could just pick up, just go into The Stop & Go and *buy*— Why would you ever want to—to share—
PECK: —Whoa, whoa. Just stop a second and listen to me. Li'l Bit. Listen. There's nothing wrong in what we're doing. I'm very proud of you. I think you have a wonderful body and an even more wonderful mind. And of course I want other people to *appreciate* it. It's not anything shameful.
LI'L BIT *(Hurt):* But this is something—that I'm only doing for you. This is something—that you said was just between us.
PECK: It is. And if that's how you feel, five years from now, it will re-

main that way. Okay? I know you're not going to do anything you don't feel like doing.

*(He walks back to the camera)* Do you want to stop now? I've got just a few more shots on this roll—

**LI'L BIT:** I don't want anyone seeing this.

**PECK:** I swear to you. No one will. I'll treasure this—that you're doing this only for me.

*(Li'l Bit, still shaken, sits on the stool. She closes her eyes)* Li'l Bit? Open your eyes and look at me. *(Li'l Bit shakes her head no)* Come on. Just open your eyes, honey.

**LI'L BIT:** If I look at you—if I look at the camera: You're gonna know what I'm thinking. You'll see right through me—

**PECK:** —No, I won't. I want you to look at me. All right, then. I just want you to listen. Li'l Bit. *(She waits)* I love you. *(Li'l Bit opens her eyes; she is startled. Peck captures the shot. On the screen we see right though her. Peck says softly)* Do you know that? *(Li'l Bit nods her head yes)* I have loved you every day since the day you were born.

**LI'L BIT:** Yes.

*(Li'l Bit and Peck just look at each other. Beat. Beneath the shot of herself on the screen, Li'l Bit, still looking at her uncle, begins to unbutton her blouse.*

*A neutral Voice cuts off the above scene with:)*

Implied Consent.
As an individual operating a motor vehicle in the state of Maryland, you must abide by "Implied Consent." If you do not consent to take the blood alcohol content test, there may be severe penalties: a suspension of license, a fine, community service and a possible jail sentence.

*(The Voice shifts tone:)*

Idling in the Neutral Gear.

**MALE GREEK CHORUS** *(Announcing):* Aunt Mary on behalf of her husband.

*(Female Greek Chorus checks her appearance, and with dignity comes to the front of the stage and sits down to talk to the audience.)*

**FEMALE GREEK CHORUS** *(As Aunt Mary):* My husband was such a good man—is. Is such a good man. Every night, he does the dishes. The second he comes home, he's taking out the garbage, or doing yard work, lifting the heavy things I can't. Everyone in the neighborhood borrows Peck—it's true—women with husbands of their own, men who just don't have Peck's abilities—there's always a knock on our door for a jump start on cold mornings, when anyone needs a ride, or help shoveling the sidewalk—I look out, and there Peck is, without a coat, pitching in.

I know I'm lucky. The man works from dawn to dusk. And the overtime he does every year—my poor sister. She sits every Christmas when I come to dinner with a new stole, or diamonds, or with the tickets to Bermuda.

I know he has troubles. And we don't talk about them. I wonder, sometimes, what happened to him during the war. The men who fought World War II didn't have "rap sessions" to talk about their feelings. Men in his generation were expected to be quiet about it and get on with their lives. And sometimes I can feel him just fighting the trouble—whatever has burrowed deeper than the scar tissue—and we don't talk about it. I know he's having a bad spell because he comes looking for me in the house, and just hangs around me until it passes. And I keep my banter light—I discuss a new recipe, or sales, or gossip—because I think domesticity can be a balm for men when they're lost. We sit in the house and listen to the peace of the clock ticking in his well-ordered living room, until it passes.

*(Sharply)* I'm not a fool. I know what's going on. I wish you could feel how hard Peck fights against it—he's swimming against the tide, and what he needs is to see me on the shore, believing in him, knowing he won't go under, he won't give up—

And I want to say this about my niece. She's a sly one, that one is. She knows exactly what she's doing; she's twisted Peck around her little finger and thinks it's all a big secret. Yet another one who's borrowing my husband until it doesn't suit her anymore.

Well. I'm counting the days until she goes away to school. And she manipulates someone else. And then he'll come back again, and sit in the kitchen while I bake, or beside me on the sofa when I sew in the evenings. I'm a very patient woman. But I'd like my husband back.

I am counting the days.

*(A Voice repeats:)*

**You and the Reverse Gear.**

MALE GREEK CHORUS: Li'l Bit's Thirteenth Christmas. Uncle Peck Does the Dishes. Christmas 1964.

*(Peck stands in a dress shirt and tie, nice pants, with an apron. He is washing dishes. He's in a mood we haven't seen. Quiet, brooding. Li'l Bit watches him a moment before seeking him out.)*

LI'L BIT: Uncle Peck? *(He does not answer. He continues to work on the pots)* I didn't know where you'd gone to. *(He nods. She takes this as a sign to come in)* Don't you want to sit with us for a while?
PECK: No. I'd rather do the dishes.

*(Pause. Li'l Bit watches him.)*

LI'L BIT: You're the only man I know who does dishes. *(Peck says nothing)* I think it's really nice.
PECK: My wife has been on her feet all day. So's your grandmother and your mother.
LI'L BIT: I know. *(Beat)* Do you want some help?
PECK: No. *(He softens a bit towards her)* You can help by just talking to me.
LI'L BIT: Big Papa never does the dishes. I think it's nice.
PECK: I think men should be nice to women. Women are always working for us. There's nothing particularly manly in wolfing down food and then sitting around in a stupor while the women clean up.
LI'L BIT: That looks like a really neat camera that Aunt Mary got you.
PECK: It is. It's a very nice one.

*(Pause, as Peck works on the dishes and some demon that Li'l Bit intuits.)*

LI'L BIT: Did Big Papa hurt your feelings?
PECK *(Tired):* What? Oh, no—it doesn't hurt me. Family is family. I'd rather have him picking on me than—I don't pay him any mind, Li'l Bit.
LI'L BIT: Are you angry with us?
PECK: No, Li'l Bit. I'm not angry.

*(Another pause.)*

LI'L BIT: We missed you at Thanksgiving. . . . I did. I missed you.

PECK: Well, there were . . . "things" going on. I didn't want to spoil anyone's Thanksgiving.

LI'L BIT: Uncle Peck? *(Very carefully)* Please don't drink anymore tonight.

PECK: I'm not . . . overdoing it.

LI'L BIT: I know. *(Beat)* Why do you drink so much?

*(Peck stops and thinks, carefully.)*

PECK: Well, Li'l Bit—let me explain it this way. There are some people who have a . . . a "fire" in the belly. I think they go to work on Wall Street or they run for office. And then there are people who have a "fire" in their heads—and they become writers or scientists or historians. *(He smiles a little at her)* You. You've got a "fire" in the head. And then there are people like me.

LI'L BIT: Where do you have . . . a fire?

PECK: I have a fire in my heart. And sometimes the drinking helps.

LI'L BIT: There's got to be other things that can help.

PECK: I suppose there are.

LI'L BIT: Does it help—to talk to me?

PECK: Yes. It does. *(Quiet)* I don't get to see you very much.

LI'L BIT: I know. *(Li'l Bit thinks)* You could talk to me more.

PECK: Oh?

LI'L BIT: I could make a deal with you, Uncle Peck.

PECK: I'm listening.

LI'L BIT: We could meet and talk—once a week. You could just store up whatever's bothering you during the week—and then we could talk.

PECK: Would you like that?

LI'L BIT: As long as you don't drink. I'd meet you somewhere for lunch or for a walk—on the weekends—as long as you stop drinking. And we could talk about whatever you want.

PECK: You would do that for me?

LI'L BIT: I don't think I'd want Mom to know. Or Aunt Mary. I wouldn't want them to think—

PECK: —No. It would just be us talking.

LI'L BIT: I'll tell Mom I'm going to a girlfriend's. To study. Mom doesn't get home until six, so you can call me after school and tell me where to meet you.

PECK: You get home at four?

**LI'L BIT:** We can meet once a week. But only in public. You've got to let me—draw the line. And once it's drawn, you mustn't cross it.

**PECK:** Understood.

**LI'L BIT:** Would that help?

*(Peck is very moved.)*

**PECK:** Yes. Very much.

**LI'L BIT:** I'm going to join the others in the living room now. *(Li'l Bit turns to go)*

**PECK:** Merry Christmas, Li'l Bit.

*(Li'l Bit bestows a very warm smile on him.)*

**LI'L BIT:** Merry Christmas, Uncle Peck.

*(A Voice dictates:)*

**Shifting Forward from Second to Third Gear.**

*(The Male and Female Greek Chorus members come forward.)*

**MALE GREEK CHORUS:** 1969. Days and Gifts: A Countdown:

**FEMALE GREEK CHORUS:** A note. "September 3, 1969. Li'l Bit: You've only been away two days and it feels like months. Hope your dorm room is cozy. I'm sending you this tape cassette—it's a new model—so you'll have some music in your room. Also that music you're reading about for class—*Carmina Burana*. Hope you enjoy. Only ninety days to go!—Peck."

**MALE GREEK CHORUS:** September 22. A bouquet of roses. A note: "Miss you like crazy. Sixty-nine days . . ."

**TEENAGE GREEK CHORUS:** September 25. A box of chocolates. A card: "Don't worry about the weight gain. You still look great. Got a post office box—write to me there. Sixty-six days.—Love, your candy man."

**MALE GREEK CHORUS:** October 16. A note: "Am trying to get through the Jane Austin you're reading—*Emma*—here's a book in return: *Liaisons Dangereuses*. Hope you're saving time for me." Scrawled in the margin the number: "47."

**FEMALE GREEK CHORUS:** November 16. "Sixteen days to go!—Hope you like the perfume.—Having a hard time reaching you on the dorm phone. You must be in the library a lot. Won't you think about me getting you your own phone so we can talk?"

**TEENAGE GREEK CHORUS:** November 18. "Li'l Bit—got a package returned to the P.O. Box. Have you changed dorms? Call me at work or write to the P.O. Am still on the wagon. Waiting to see you. Only two weeks more!"

MALE GREEK CHORUS: November 23. A letter. "Li'l Bit. So disappointed you couldn't come home for the turkey. Sending you some money for a nice dinner out—nine days and counting!"

GREEK CHORUS *(In unison):* November 25th. A letter:

LI'L BIT: "Dear Uncle Peck: I am sending this to you at work. Don't come up next weekend for my birthday. I will not be here—"

*(A Voice directs:)*

**Shifting Forward from Third to Fourth Gear.**

MALE GREEK CHORUS: December 10, 1969. A hotel room. Philadelphia. There is no moon tonight.

*(Peck sits on the side of the bed while Li'l Bit paces. He can't believe she's in his room, but there's a desperate edge to his happiness. Li'l Bit is furious, edgy. There is a bottle of champagne in an ice bucket in a very nice hotel room.)*

PECK: Why don't you sit?

LI'L BIT: I don't want to.—What's the champagne for?

PECK: I thought we might toast your birthday—

LI'L BIT: —I am so pissed off at you, Uncle Peck.

PECK: Why?

LI'L BIT: I mean, are you crazy?

PECK: What did I do?

LI'L BIT: You scared the holy crap out of me—sending me that stuff in the mail—

PECK: —They were gifts! I just wanted to give you some little perks your first semester—

LI'L BIT: —Well, what the hell were those numbers all about! Forty-four days to go—only two more weeks.—And then just numbers—69—68—67—like some serial killer!

PECK: Li'l Bit! Whoa! This is me you're talking to—I was just trying to pick up your spirits, trying to celebrate your birthday.

LI'L BIT: My *eighteenth* birthday. I'm not a child, Uncle Peck. You were counting down to my eighteenth birthday.

PECK: So?

LI'L BIT: So? So statutory rape is not in effect when a young woman turns eighteen. And you and I both know it.

*(Peck is walking on ice.)*

PECK: I think you misunderstand.

LI'L BIT: I think I understand all too well. I know what you want to do five steps ahead of you doing it. Defensive Driving 101.

PECK: Then why did you suggest we meet here instead of the restaurant?

LI'L BIT: I don't want to have this conversation in public.

PECK: Fine. Fine. We have a lot to talk about.

LI'L BIT: Yeah. We do.

*(Li'l Bit doesn't want to do what she has to do)* Could I . . . have some of that champagne?

PECK: Of course, madam! *(Peck makes a big show of it)* Let me do the honors. I wasn't sure which you might prefer—Taittingers or Veuve Clicquot—so I thought we'd start out with an old standard—Perrier Jouet. *(The bottle is popped)*
     Quick—Li'l Bit—your glass! *(Uncle Peck fills Li'l Bit's glass. He puts the bottle back in the ice and goes for a can of ginger ale)* Let me get some of this ginger ale—my bubbly—and toast you.

*(He turns and sees that Li'l Bit has not waited for him.)*

LI'L BIT: Oh—sorry, Uncle Peck. Let me have another. *(Peck fills her glass and reaches for his ginger ale; she stops him)* Uncle Peck—maybe you should join me in the champagne.

PECK: You want me to—drink?

LI'L BIT: It's not polite to let a lady drink alone.

PECK: Well, missy, if you insist. . . . *(Peck hesitates)* — Just one. It's been a while. *(Peck fills another flute for himself)* There. I'd like to propose a toast to you and your birthday! *(Peck sips it tentatively)* I'm not used to this anymore.

LI'L BIT: You don't have anywhere to go tonight, do you?

*(Peck hopes this is a good sign.)*

PECK: I'm all yours. —God, it's good to see you! I've gotten so used to . . . to . . . talking to you in my head. I'm used to seeing you every week—there's so much—I don't quite know where to begin. How's school, Li'l Bit?

LI'L BIT: I—it's hard. Uncle Peck. Harder than I thought it would be. I'm in the middle of exams and papers and—I don't know.

PECK: You'll pull through. You always do.

LI'L BIT: Maybe. I . . . might be flunking out.

PECK: You always think the worse, Li'l Bit, but when the going gets tough—*(Li'l Bit shrugs and pours herself another glass)* —Hey, honey, go easy on that stuff, okay?

LI'L BIT: Is it very expensive?

PECK: Only the best for you. But the cost doesn't matter—champagne should be "sipped." *(Li'l Bit is quiet)* Look—if you're in trouble in school—you can always come back home for a while.

LI'L BIT: No—*(Li'l Bit tries not to be so harsh)* —Thanks, Uncle Peck, but I'll figure some way out of this.

PECK: You're supposed to get in scrapes, your first year away from home.

LI'L BIT: Right. How's Aunt Mary?

PECK: She's fine. *(Pause)* Well—how about the new car?

LI'L BIT: It's real nice. What is it, again?

PECK: It's a Cadillac El Dorado.

LI'L BIT: Oh. Well, I'm real happy for you, Uncle Peck.

PECK: I got it for you.

LI'L BIT: What?

PECK: I always wanted to get a Cadillac—but I thought, Peck, wait until Li'l Bit's old enough—and thought maybe you'd like to drive it, too.

LI'L BIT *(Confused):* Why would I want to drive your car?

PECK: Just because it's the best—I want you to have the best.

*(They are running out of "gas"; small talk.)*

LI'L BIT: Listen, Uncle Peck, I don't know how to begin this, but—

PECK: I have been thinking of how to say this in my head, over and over—

PECK: Sorry.

LI'L BIT: You first.

PECK: Well, your going away—has just made me realize how much I miss you. Talking to you and being alone with you. I've really come to depend on you, Li'l Bit. And it's been so hard to get in touch with you lately—the distance and—and you're never in when I call—I guess you've been living in the library—

LI'L BIT: —No—the problem is, I haven't been in the library—

PECK: —Well, it doesn't matter—I hope you've been missing me as much.

LI'L BIT: Uncle Peck—I've been thinking a lot about this—and I came here tonight to tell you that—I'm not doing very well. I'm getting very confused—I can't concentrate on my work—and now that I'm away—I've been going over and over it in my mind—and I don't want us to "see" each other anymore. Other than with the rest of the family.

PECK *(Quiet):*  Are you seeing other men?

LI'L BIT *(Getting agitated):*  I—no, that's not the reason—I—well, yes, I am seeing other—listen, it's not really anybody's business!

PECK:  Are you in love with anyone else?

LI'L BIT:  That's not what this is about.

PECK:  Li'l Bit—you're scared. Your mother and your grandparents have filled your head with all kinds of nonsense about men—I hear them working on you all the time—and you're scared. It won't hurt you—if the man you go to bed with really loves you. *(Li'l Bit is scared. She starts to tremble)* And I have loved you since the day I held you in my hand. And I think everyone's just gotten you frightened to death about something that is just like breathing—

LI'L BIT:  Oh, my god—*(She takes a breath)* I can't see you anymore, Uncle Peck.

*(Peck downs the rest of his champagne.)*

PECK:  Li'l Bit. Listen. Listen. Open your eyes and look at me. Come on. Just open your eyes, honey. *(Li'l Bit, eyes squeezed shut, refuses)* All right then. I just want you to listen. Li'l Bit—I'm going to ask you just this once. Of your own free will. Just lie down on the bed with me—our clothes on—just lie down with me, a man and a woman . . . and let's . . . hold one another. Nothing else. Before you say anything else. I want the chance to . . . hold you. Because sometimes the body knows things that the mind isn't listening to . . . and after I've held you, then I want you to tell me what you feel.

LI'L BIT:  You'll just . . . hold me?

PECK:  Yes. And then you can tell me what you're feeling.

*(Li'l Bit—half wanting to run, half wanting to get it over with, half wanting to be held by him:)*

LI'L BIT:  Yes. All right. Just hold. Nothing else.

*(Peck lies down on the bed and holds his arms out to her. Li'l Bit lies beside him, putting her head on his chest. He looks as*

*if he's trying to soak her into his pores by osmosis. He strokes her hair, and she lies very still. The Male Greek Chorus member and the Female Greek Chorus member as Aunt Mary come into the room.)*

MALE GREEK CHORUS:   Recipe for a Southern Boy:
FEMALE GREEK CHORUS *(As Aunt Mary):*   A drawl of molasses in the way he speaks.
MALE GREEK CHORUS:   A gumbo of red and brown mixed in the cream of his skin.

*(While Peck lies, his eyes closed, Li'l Bit rises in the bed and responds to her aunt.)*

LI'L BIT:   Warm brown eyes—
FEMALE GREEK CHORUS *(As Aunt Mary):*   Bedroom eyes—
MALE GREEK CHORUS:   A dash of Southern Baptist Fire and Brimstone—
LI'L BIT:   A curl of Elvis on his forehead—
FEMALE GREEK CHORUS *(As Aunt Mary):*   A splash of Bay Rum—
MALE GREEK CHORUS:   A closely shaven beard that he razors just for you—
FEMALE GREEK CHORUS *(As Aunt Mary):*   Large hands—rough hands—
LI'L BIT:   Warm hands—
MALE GREEK CHORUS:   The steel of the military in his walk —
LI'L BIT:   The slouch of the fishing skiff in his walk —
MALE GREEK CHORUS:   Neatly pressed khakis—
FEMALE GREEK CHORUS *(As Aunt Mary):*   And under the wide leather of the belt —
LI'L BIT:   Sweat of cypress and sand —
MALE GREEK CHORUS:   Neatly pressed khakis—
LI'L BIT:   His heart beating Dixie—
FEMALE GREEK CHORUS *(As Aunt Mary):*   The whisper of the zipper—you could reach out with your hand and—
LI'L BIT:   His mouth—
FEMALE GREEK CHORUS *(As Aunt Mary):*   You could just reach out and—
LI'L BIT:   Hold him in your hand—
FEMALE GREEK CHORUS *(As Aunt Mary):*   And his mouth—

*(Li'l Bit rises above her uncle and looks at his mouth; she starts to lower herself to kiss him—and wrenches herself free.*

*She gets up from the bed.)*

**LI'L BIT:** —I've got to get back.

**PECK:** Wait—Li'l Bit. Did you . . . feel nothing?

**LI'L BIT** *(Lying):* No. Nothing.

**PECK:** Do you—do you think of me?

*(The Greek Chorus whispers:)*

**FEMALE GREEK CHORUS:** Khakis —

**MALE GREEK CHORUS:** Bay Rum —

**FEMALE GREEK CHORUS:** The whisper of the—

**LI'L BIT:** —No.

*(Peck, in a rush, trembling, gets something out of his pocket.)*

**PECK:** I'm forty-five. That's not old for a man. And I haven't been able to do anything else but think of you. I can't concentrate on my work—Li'l Bit. You've got to—I want you to think about what I am about to ask you.

**LI'L BIT:** I'm listening.

*(Peck opens a small ring box.)*

**PECK:** I want you to be my wife.

**LI'L BIT:** This isn't happening.

**PECK:** I'll tell Mary I want a divorce. We're not blood-related. It would be legal—

**LI'L BIT:** —What have you been thinking! You are married to my aunt, Uncle Peck. She's my family. You have—you have gone way over the line. Family is family.

*(Quickly, Li'l Bit flies through the room, gets her coat) I'm leaving. Now. I am not seeing you. Again.*

*(Peck lies down on the bed for a moment, trying to absorb the terrible news. For a moment, he almost curls into a fetal position)*

I'm not coming home for Christmas. You should go home to Aunt Mary. Go home now, Uncle Peck.

*(Peck gets control, and sits, rigid)*

Uncle Peck?—I'm sorry but I have to go.

*(Pause)*

Are you all right.

*(With a discipline that comes from being told that boys don't cry, Peck stands upright.)*

PECK: I'm fine. I just think—I need a real drink.

*(The Male Greek Chorus has become a bartender. At a small counter, he is lining up shots for Peck. As Li'l Bit narrates, we see Peck sitting, carefully and calmly downing shot glasses.)*

LI'L BIT *(To the audience):* I never saw him again. I stayed away from Christmas and Thanksgiving for years after.

It took my uncle seven years to drink himself to death. First he lost his job, then his wife, and finally his driver's license. He retreated to his house, and had his bottles delivered.

*(Peck stands, and puts his hands in front of him—almost like Superman flying)*

One night he tried to go downstairs to the basement—and he flew down the steep basement stairs. My aunt came by weekly to put food on the porch, and she noticed the mail and the papers stacked up, uncollected.

They found him at the bottom of the stairs. Just steps away from his dark room.

Now that I'm old enough, there are some questions I would have liked to have asked him. Who did it to you, Uncle Peck? How old were you? Were you eleven?

*(Peck moves to the driver's seat of the car and waits)*

Sometimes I think of my uncle as a kind of Flying Dutchman. In the opera, the Dutchman is doomed to wander the sea; but every seven years he can come ashore, and if he finds a maiden who will love him of her own free will—he will be released.

And I see Uncle Peck in my mind, in his Chevy '56, a spirit driving up and down the back roads of Carolina—looking for a young girl who, of her own free will, will love him. Release him.

*(A Voice states:)*

**You and the Reverse Gear.**

LI'L BIT: The summer of 1962. On Men, Sex, and Women: Part III:

*(Li'l Bit steps, as an eleven year old, into:)*

**FEMALE GREEK CHORUS** *(As Mother):* It is out of the question. End of Discussion.

**LI'L BIT:** But why?

**FEMALE GREEK CHORUS** *(As Mother):* Li'l Bit—we are not discussing this. I said no.

**LI'L BIT:** But I could spend an extra week at the beach! You're not telling me why!

**FEMALE GREEK CHORUS** *(As Mother):* Your uncle pays entirely too much attention to you.

**LI'L BIT:** He listens to me when I talk. And—and he talks to me. He teaches me about things. Mama—he knows an awful lot.

**FEMALE GREEK CHORUS** *(As Mother):* He's a small town hick who's learned how to mix drinks from Hugh Hefner.

**LI'L BIT:** Who's Hugh Hefner?

*(Beat.)*

**FEMALE GREEK CHORUS** *(As Mother):* I am not letting an eleven-year-old girl spend seven hours alone in the car with a man. . . . I don't like the way your uncle looks at you.

**LI'L BIT:** For god's sake, mother! Just because you've gone through a bad time with my father—you think every man is evil!

**FEMALE GREEK CHORUS** *(As Mother):* Oh no, Li'l Bit—not all men. . . . We . . . we just haven't been very lucky with the men in our family.

**LI'L BIT:** Just because you lost your husband—I still deserve a chance at having a father! Someone! A man who will look out for me! Don't I get a chance?

**FEMALE GREEK CHORUS** *(As Mother):* I will feel terrible if something happens.

**LI'L BIT:** Mother! It's in your head! Nothing will happen! I can take care of myself. And I can certainly handle Uncle Peck.

**FEMALE GREEK CHORUS** *(As Mother):* All right. But I'm warning you—if anything happens, I hold you responsible.

*(Li'l Bit moves out of this scene and toward the car.)*

**LI'L BIT:** 1962. On the Back Roads of Carolina: The First Driving Lesson.

*(The Teenage Greek Chorus member stands apart on stage. She will speak all of Li'l Bit's lines. Li'l Bit sits beside Peck in the front seat. She looks at him closely, remembering.)*

PECK: Li'l Bit? Are you getting tired?

TEENAGE GREEK CHORUS: A little.

PECK: It's a long drive. But we're making really good time. We can take the back road from here and see . . . a little scenery. Say—I've got an idea— *(Peck checks his rearview mirror)*

TEENAGE GREEK CHORUS: Are we stopping, Uncle Peck?

PECK: There's no traffic here. Do you want to drive?

TEENAGE GREEK CHORUS: I can't drive.

PECK: It's easy. I'll show you how. I started driving when I was your age. Don't you want to?—

TEENAGE GREEK CHORUS: —But it's against the law at my age!

PECK: And that's why you can't tell anyone I'm letting you do this—

TEENAGE GREEK CHORUS: —But—I can't reach the pedals.

PECK: You can sit in my lap and steer. I'll push the pedals for you. Did your father ever let you drive his car?

TEENAGE GREEK CHORUS: No way.

PECK: Want to try?

TEENAGE GREEK CHORUS: Okay. *(Li'l Bit moves into Peck's lap. She leans against him, closing her eyes)*

PECK: You're just a little thing, aren't you? Okay—now think of the wheel as a big clock—I want you to put your right hand on the clock where three o'clock would be; and your left hand on the nine—

*(Li'l Bit puts one hand to Peck's face, to stroke him. Then, she takes the wheel.)*

TEENAGE GREEK CHORUS: Am I doing it right?

PECK: That's right. Now, whatever you do, don't let go of the wheel. You tell me whether to go faster or slower—

TEENAGE GREEK CHORUS: Not so fast, Uncle Peck!

PECK: Li'l Bit—I need you to watch the road—

*(Peck puts his hands on Li'l Bit's breasts. She relaxes against him, silent, accepting his touch.)*

TEENAGE GREEK CHORUS: Uncle Peck—what are you doing?

PECK: Keep driving. *(He slips his hands under her blouse)*

TEENAGE GREEK CHORUS: Uncle Peck—please don't do this—

PECK: —Just a moment longer . . . *(Peck tenses against Li'l Bit)*

TEENAGE GREEK CHORUS *(Trying not to cry):* This isn't happening.

*(Peck tenses more, sharply. He buries his face in Li'l Bit's neck, and moans softly. The Teenage Greek Chorus exits, and Li'l Bit steps out of the car. Peck, too, disappears.*

*A Voice reflects:)*

**Driving in Today's World.**

LI'L BIT: That day was the last day I lived in my body. I retreated above the neck, and I've lived inside the "fire" in my head ever since.

And now that seems like a long, long time ago. When we were both very young.

And before you know it, I'll be thirty-five. That's getting up there for a woman. And I find myself believing in things that a younger self vowed never to believe in. Things like family and forgiveness.

I know I'm lucky. Although I still have never known what it feels like to jog or dance. Any thing that . . . "jiggles." I do like to watch people on the dance floor, or out on the running paths, just jiggling away. And I say—good for them. *(Li'l Bit moves to the car with pleasure)*

The nearest sensation I feel—of flight in the body—I guess I feel when I'm driving. On a day like today. It's five A.M. The radio says it's going to be clear and crisp. I've got five hundred miles of highway ahead of me—and some back roads too. I filled the tank last night, and had the oil checked. Checked the tires, too. You've got to treat her . . . with respect.

First thing I do is: Check under the car. To see if any two year olds or household cats have crawled beneath, and strategically placed their skulls behind my back tires. *(Li'l Bit crouches)*

Nope. Then I get in the car. *(Li'l Bit does so)*

I lock the doors. And turn the key. Then I adjust the most important control on the dashboard—the radio— *(Li'l Bit turns the radio on: We hear all of the Greek Chorus overlapping, and static:)*

FEMALE GREEK CHORUS *(Overlapping):* —"You were so tiny you fit in his hand—"

MALE GREEK CHORUS *(Overlapping):* —"How is Shakespeare gonna help her lie on her back in the —"

TEENAGE GREEK CHORUS *(Overlapping):* —"Am I doing it right?"

*(Li'l Bit fine-tunes the radio station. A song like "Dedicated*

*to the One I Love"* or Orbison's *"Sweet Dreams" comes on,
and cuts off the Greek Chorus.)*

LI'L BIT: Ahh . . . *(Beat)* I adjust my seat. Fasten my seat belt. Then I
check the right side mirror—check the left side. *(She does)* Finally, I
adjust the rearview mirror. *(As Li'l Bit adjusts the rearview mirror,
a faint light strikes the spirit of Uncle Peck, who is sitting in the
back seat of the car. She sees him in the mirror. She smiles at him,
and he nods at her. They are happy to be going for a long drive together. Li'l Bit slips the car into first gear; to the audience:)* And
then—I floor it. *(Sound of a car taking off. Blackout)*

END OF PLAY

## Catherine Celesia Allen

*Cathy Celesia Allen has written seven full-length plays and numerous one-acts. She won a 1993 Beverly Hills Theatre Guild Award for* The Essence of Being.

# Anything for You

Anything for You *was originally produced at the Circle Repertory Lab in New York City, June 1993. Scott Segall directed the following cast:*

*Lynette* Johanna Day
*Gail* Jo Twiss

**CHARACTERS**
*Lynette:* thirtyish, stylish
*Gail:* same age, a bit more conservative
Time: the present
Place: an urban café

*At Rise: Lynette sits alone at a table for two, staring into her drink. Gail approaches the table, a bit harried. She kisses the preoccupied Lynette on the cheek, sits.*

GAIL: Sorry I'm late. I was just about to walk out when this rap artist of ours plops himself in the outer office, announces he's not leaving until somebody acknowledges his artistic crisis. This is a kid, nineteen years old mind you, who has a house in the Hamptons and a hot tub for every day of the week, and he's having an artistic crisis. That needs acknowledgment. *(She picks up a menu.)* Have you ordered yet? *(perusing the menu)* So I have to sit there for twenty minutes trying to sound sincere when I tell him "It's not so bad, Roger. Money doesn't compromise your art. It just makes it more affordable." When what I really wanted to say was, This is the legal department. We work here. You're feeling screwed up or dysfunctional, go to artistic, bother them. So anyway . . . the squab looks good. What do you think?

*(Gail continues to study the menu. Lynette leans forward in her chair.)*

LYNETTE:   I need to have an affair.
GAIL:   Hmm? did you say something?
LYNETTE:   I said, Gail, that I need to have an affair.
GAIL *(looking up):*   You don't mean that.
LYNETTE:   Yes I do.
GAIL:   An affair?
LYNETTE:   Yes.
GAIL:   You?
LYNETTE:   Uh-huh.
GAIL:   But you and Richard—
LYNETTE:   I know.
GAIL:   Then I don't understand.
LYNETTE:   Neither do I.
GAIL:   So basically you're sitting here telling me for no good reason that you want to—
LYNETTE:   Not want. Need. Capital N. The big guns.
GAIL:   Why?
LYNETTE:   I don't know. An overwhelming biological necessity for alternate body types. I don't know.
GAIL:   I don't think this is the place we should be discussing this.
LYNETTE:   This is exactly the place. You are exactly the person. Gail. If I don't sleep with someone other than my husband very soon, I won't be responsible for myself.
GAIL:   Lynette.
LYNETTE:   Time bomb. Tick tick tick.
GAIL:   Don't you think you're being a little overdramatic?
LYNETTE:   No. Tick.
GAIL:   Have you met someone?
LYNETTE:   No. Although when you get right down to it, everybody's a candidate.
GAIL:   You're kidding, right? All right, joke's over, very funny, ha ha, you're kidding.
LYNETTE:   Gail, you don't know what it's like. I can't work. I can't sleep. All I know is I want a hot roll in the hay. That's the extent of my cognizant abilities.
GAIL:   I think you should try to show a little control.
LYNETTE:   Yesterday I looked at a clock. I forgot how to tell time.
GAIL:   What are you drinking?

LYNETTE:  I'm losing my mind.

GAIL:  You certainly are. Richard—

LYNETTE:  Is sweet and kind and good, I know. He adapts, no matter how crazy I am. "You're right honey, I'll be more careful, I'll try not to let my heels touch the floor in that irritating manner anymore." I could tell him I want to chuck it all for a sugar cane farm in Borneo and he'd be researching farming techniques and plane fares within the hour.

GAIL:  So it seems to me you have nothing to complain about.

LYNETTE:  I'm not complaining. But God, if I don't find someone to sear me to the bones I am going to explode. Little pieces of me flying out my office window and over New York, settling on some old ladies in the park. Explode.

GAIL:  I don't know what to say. You've put me in a difficult position. I love Richard.

LYNETTE:  I do too.

GAIL:  He and George are best friends.

LYNETTE:  Like brothers.

GAIL:  And you're my best friend—

LYNETTE *(expectantly):*  Yes?

GAIL:  Yes what?

LYNETTE:  I'm your best friend.

GAIL:  Yes.

LYNETTE:  You'd do anything for me.

GAIL:  Of course I would, you know that. What are you driving at?

LYNETTE:  Sleep with me.

GAIL:  What?!

LYNETTE:  Sleep with me, Gail. Make love to me until I beg you to stop.

GAIL:  You can't be serious.

LYNETTE:  I couldn't live with myself if I did it with another man, not to mention what it would do to Richard if he found out. But you—

GAIL:  Are astonished.

LYNETTE:  You're a woman, Gail. It wouldn't be cheating. It would be experimenting.

GAIL:  You're out of your mind.

LYNETTE:  Will you do it?

GAIL:  Of course not.

LYNETTE:  Why not?

GAIL:  In the first place, no offense, but I'm not physically attracted to you.

LYNETTE: Liar.

GAIL: What did you call me?

LYNETTE: You're lying. You've wanted me from the day we met.

GAIL: Oh, now I agree with you, Lynette, you have gone over the deep end.

LYNETTE: You stare at me. You watch my mouth when I speak. When we kiss hello you let your nose linger in my hair a little bit longer than necessary and you breathe in.

GAIL: I can't really have this conversation anymore, okay? Can we order? *(pause)* I think you should see a doctor.

LYNETTE: You're angry.

GAIL: I'm not, I'm flabbergasted. To think that after all these years of what I thought was a close friendship you would suddenly come up with this insane notion that I—that we—I'm married, Lynette.

LYNETTE: I know.

GAIL: And I love George. Not to mention I'm one hundred percent heterosexual.

LYNETTE: I'm going out of my mind.

GAIL: I wish I could help you. I really do.

LYNETTE: You love me.

GAIL: Of course I do. But that doesn't mean I desire you in a sexual manner.

LYNETTE: What about New Year's Eve?

GAIL *(after a pause):* What about it?

LYNETTE: New Year's Eve, two years ago. The four of us spent it together. I drank too many peach margaritas.

GAIL: I remember.

LYNETTE: I got sick. Richard ended up carrying me into the bathroom and you stayed to help.

GAIL: You were so sick. Richard was so angry.

LYNETTE: I thought I'd never stop throwing up. When I finally did, I laid down on the bathroom floor, closed my eyes, and you kissed me. On the mouth.

GAIL: I didn't.

LYNETTE: You did. For a good long time.

GAIL: You must have dreamt it, Lynette, I think I would remember—

LYNETTE: I remember thinking, "how soft her mouth is." You held my lower lip for an extra second. Then you let go and the air hissed out of me like a balloon.

GAIL: I did not kiss you, Lynette. I mean, I may have given you a peck on the cheek because I felt sorry for you, but beyond that, you are mistaken.

LYNETTE: I felt your tongue.

GAIL: Lynette! *(She looks around, lowers her voice.)* This is really inappropriate.

LYNETTE: Why are you so against this? You have me, I have my fling—everybody wins.

GAIL: Except Richard, and George.

LYNETTE: We don't tell them. This is a secret between friends. Inviolable.

GAIL: It's not that simple.

LYNETTE: Why not?

GAIL: Lynette, look—do you want me to fix you up with someone? There are a lot of lesbians in the music business.

LYNETTE: I want you.

GAIL: No you don't.

LYNETTE: I do. You're my friend, I can trust you, there's no danger of falling in love. I was going to say you're honest but you can't even admit to kissing me when we both know—

GAIL: All right, all right, I kissed you, I kissed you! I'd had a little to drink myself that night— *(to an unseen patron)* Can I help you?

LYNETTE: You were stone cold sober. The antibiotics, remember?

GAIL *(helplessly):* You looked so pretty. Lying there with your hair spread out over the mat. So vulnerable and so . . . beautiful, actually.

LYNETTE: Sleep with me, Gail.

GAIL: I can't.

LYNETTE: Why not?

GAIL: Because I'm in love with you.

LYNETTE: What?

GAIL: I'm in love with you, Lynette. You think I go around kissing drunken smelly women on the mouth because it's a thing of mine?

LYNETTE: But I thought—

GAIL: That my heart couldn't possibly leap every time I see you? That I don't feel profound jealousy when you and Richard reach for each other like any other happily married couple? That my feelings can't be real?

LYNETTE: No, I mean . . .

GAIL: What, Lynette? What did you think?

LYNETTE: I don't know. A harmless crush. Like schoolgirls.

GAIL: Not exactly.

LYNETTE: No. *(pause)* So where does this leave us?

GAIL: I don't know.

LYNETTE *(after a pause):* Maybe I do drink too much.

GAIL: Maybe.

LYNETTE: I have a problem.

GAIL: Yes.

LYNETTE: And you have a problem.

GAIL: Yes.

LYNETTE: What do you think we should do?

GAIL: I think we should order.

*(They return to looking at their menus.)*

END

—1993

# Acknowledgments

# *Index of Critical Terms*

# Additional Titles of Interest

Note to Instructors: Any of these Penguin-Putnam, Inc., titles can be packaged with this book at a special discount. Contact your local Allyn & Bacon/Longman sales representative for details on how to create a Penguin-Putnam, Inc., Value Package.

Albee, *The Three Tall Women*
Allison, *Bastard Out of Carolina*
Alvarez, *How the García Girls Lost the Accent*
Austen, *Persuasion*
Austen, *Pride & Prejudice*
Bellow, *The Adventures of Augie March*
Boyle, *Tortilla Curtain*
Cather, *My Antonia*
Cather, *O Pioneers!*
Chopin, *The Awakening*
Conrad, *Nostromo*
DeVantes, *Don Quixote*
DeLillo, *White Noise*
Desal, *Journey to Ithaca*
Douglass, *Narrative of the Life of Frederick Douglass*
Golding, *Lord of the Flies*
Hawthorne, *The Scarlet Letter*
Homer, *Iliad*
Horner, *Odyssey*
Huang, *Madame Butterfly*
Hulme, *Bone People*
Jen, *Typical American*
Karr, *The Liar's Club*
Kerouac, *On The Road*
Kesey, *One Flew Over the Cuckoo's Nest*
King, *Misery*
Larson, *Passing*
Lavin, *In a Cafe*
Marquez, *Love in the time of Cholera*
McBride, *The Color of Water*
Miller, *Death of a Salesman*
Molière, *Tartuffe and Other Plays*
Morrison, *Beloved*

Morrison, *The Bluest Eye*
Morrison, *Sula*
Naylor, *Women of Brewster Place*
Orwell, *1984*
Postman, *Amusing Ourselves to Death*
Rayben, *My First White Friend*
Rose, *Lives on the Boundary*
Rose, *Possible Lives: The Promise of Public*
Rushdie, *Midnight's Children*
Shakespeare, *Four Great Comedies*
Shakespeare, *Four Great Tragedies*
Shakespeare, *Hamlet*
Shakespeare, *Four Histories*
Shakespeare, *King Lear*
Shakespeare, *Macbeth*
Shakespeare, *Othello*
Shakespeare, *Twelfth Night*
Shelley, *Frankenstein*
Silko, *Ceremony*
Solzhenitsyn, *One Day in the Life of Ivan Denisovich*
Sophocles, *The Three Theban Plays*
Spence, *The Death of a Woman Wang*
Steinbeck, *Grapes of Wrath*
Steinbeck, *The Pearl*
Stevenson, *Dr. Jekyll & Mr. Hyde*
Swift, *Gulliver's Travels*
Twain, *Adventures of Huckleberry Finn*
Wilde, *The Importance of Being Earnest*
Wilson, *Joe Turner's Come and Gone*
Wilson, *Fences*
Woolf, *Jacob's Room*